Computer Vision and Image Analysis

Computer Vision and Image Analysis, focuses on techniques and methods for image analysis and their use in the development of computer vison applications. The field is advancing at an ever increasing pace, with applications ranging from medical diagnostics to space exploration. The diversity of applications is one of the driving forces that make it such an exciting field to be involved in for the 21st century. This book presents a unique engineering approach to the practice of computer vision and image analysis, which starts by presenting a global model to help gain an understanding of the overall process, followed by a breakdown and explanation of each individual topic. Topics are presented as they become necessary for understanding the practical imaging model under study, which provides the reader with the motivation to learn about and use the tools and methods being explored.

The book includes chapters on image systems and software, image analysis, edge, line and shape detection, image segmentation, feature extraction and pattern classification. Numerous examples, including over 500 color images are used to illustrate the concepts discussed. Readers can explore their own application development with any programming language, including C/C ++, MATLAB®, Python, and R, and software is provided for both the Windows/C/C ++ and MATLAB environment.

The book can be used by the academic community in teaching and research, with over 700 PowerPoint Slides and a complete Solutions Manual to the over 150 included problems. It can also be used for self-study by those involved with developing computer vision applications, whether they are engineers, scientists, or artists. The new edition has been extensively updated and includes numerous problems and programming exercises that will help the reader and student develop their skills.

Computer Vision and Image Analysis

Digital Image Processing and Analysis

Fourth Edition

Scott E Umbaugh

CRC Press
Taylor & Francis Group
Boca Raton London New York

CRC Press is an imprint of the
Taylor & Francis Group, an **informa** business

Fourth edition published 2023
by CRC Press
6000 Broken Sound Parkway NW, Suite 300, Boca Raton, FL 33487-2742

and by CRC Press
4 Park Square, Milton Park, Abingdon, Oxon, OX14 4RN

CRC Press is an imprint of Taylor & Francis Group, LLC

© 2023 Scott E Umbaugh

Third edition published by CRC press 2018

ISBN: 9781032071299 (hbk)
ISBN: 9781032117089 (pbk)
ISBN: 9781003221135 (ebk)
ISBN: 9781032384450 (eBook+)

DOI: 10.1201/9781003221135

Typeset in Palatino
by codeMantra

To Robin and David

and

In loving memory of

Richard Eugene Umbaugh and Elnora Mae Umbaugh

Contents

Preface

Digital image processing and analysis is a field that continues to experience rapid growth, with applications ranging from areas such as space exploration to the entertainment industry. The diversity of applications is one of the driving forces that make it such an exciting field to be involved in for the 21st century. *Digital image processing* can be defined as the acquisition and processing of visual information by computer. This book presents a unique approach to the practice of digital image processing, and it will be of interest to those who want to learn about and use computer imaging techniques.

Digital image processing can be divided into two primary application areas, human vision and computer vision, with image analysis tying these two together. *Computer Vision and Image Analysis*, focuses on the tools needed for development of computer vision applications. The culminating chapter provides the reader with examples of using the tools discussed throughout the book necessary for developing computer vision applications. The automatic identification of land types in satellite images, robotic control of a mars rover and the automatic classification of abnormalities in medical images are all examples of computer vision applications. Human vision applications involve manipulation of image data for viewing by people. Examples include the development of better compression algorithms, special effects imaging for motion pictures and the restoration of satellite images distorted by atmospheric disturbance. eResources (PowerPoint slides, software documentation, Solutions manuals, and quizzes) are also available on the Routledge website: www.routledge.com\9781032071299

Why Write a New Edition of This Book?

The primary reasons for a new edition of the book are (1) to create two separate volumes corresponding to each application area, (2) to include new material for the CVIPtools MATLAB Toolbox GUI, (3) to update the book for this rapidly changing field and (4) to add more examples and images. The reason to separate the textbook, *Digital Image Processing and Analysis*, into two volumes for the new edition is that we will have separate texts for computer vision and human-based vision applications. In my computer vison and image processing (CVIP) courses here at SIUE, they are divided accordingly. Our department at SIUE has programs in both electrical engineering and computer engineering, and it has a primary area in CVIP. However, quite often in Computer Science or Industrial Engineering programs, that may only be interested in the computer vision material, and for some electrical engineering programs, they may be primarily interested in the digital image processing for human vision–based applications. With separate volumes, we have created textbooks that can be completely covered in either type of course, with no need to jump around in the textbook. Additionally, without the need to be comprehensive to the entire CVIP area in one book, we can focus on each specific area exclusively, thereby enabling a more focused and comprehensive approach to the material.

After many requests from CVIPtools users regarding the MATLAB version, we decided it is a good idea to expand the MATLAB version to include a graphical user interface (GUI), similar to the one in the standard Windows CVIPtools. Although there are a number of imaging tools currently available for use with MATLAB, we believe that there are important aspects of the CVIPtools libraries that are unique. The comprehensive nature of the libraries and the fact that they have been in use by the imaging community for over 25 years are important considerations which guided us in the decision to create the CVIP MATLAB Toolbox and its new GUI.

As with previous editions of the book, an engineering approach to digital image processing is taken, and computer vision and image analysis are brought together into a unified framework that provides a useful paradigm for the development of computer vision applications. Additionally, the theoretical foundation is presented as needed in order to fully understand the material. Although theoretical-based textbooks are available, they do not really take what I consider an engineering approach. I still feel that there is a need for an application-oriented book that brings computer vision and analysis together in a unified framework, and this book fills that gap.

As with the most recent edition, color is used throughout and more materials have been added regarding the processing of color images. I also reorganized, updated, expanded and added more materials that make it more useful as an applications-oriented textbook. I added more exercises, expanded the chapter on computer vision development tools and moved it earlier in the book – it is now Chapter 2 and was Chapter 11 in the previous edition. The creation of a GUI for the new CVIP MATLAB Toolbox will provide an additional platform for imaging exploration and development, which is of particular interest to engineers.

The CVIP MATLAB Toolbox is a major new part of the continuing development of the comprehensive CVIPtools environment. In conjunction with the previous development tools, the Computer Vision and Image Processing Algorithm Test and Analysis Tool (CVIP-ATAT) and the CVIP Feature Extraction and Pattern Classification Tool (CVIP-FEPC), we now realize a much more powerful development environment. The new Windows version of CVIPtools, which has been integrated even more throughout the book, in conjunction with the new development tools, creates a valuable environment for learning about imaging as well as providing a set of reusable tools for applications development.

Who Will Use This Book?

Computer Vision and Image Analysis is intended for use by the academic community in teaching and research, as well as working professionals performing research and development in the commercial sectors. This includes all areas of computer vision and image analysis, and presents a computer vision system as a deployed image analysis system. It will be useful to academics and practicing engineers, consultants and programmers, as well as those in the graphics fields, medical imaging professionals, multimedia specialists and others. The book can be used for self-study and is of interest to anyone involved with developing computer vision applications, whether they are engineers, geographers, biologists, oceanographers or astronomers. At the university, it can be used as a text in standard computer vision senior-level or graduate course, or it may be used at any level in an applications-oriented course. One essential component that is missing from standard theoretical textbooks is a conceptual presentation of the material, which is fundamental to gaining a solid understanding of these complex topics. Additionally, this book provides the theory necessary to understand the foundations of computer vision, as well as that which is needed for new algorithm development.

The prerequisites for the book are an interest in the field, a basic background in computers and a basic math background provided in an undergraduate science or engineering program. Knowledge of the C family of programming languages, including C, C++ and C#, and/or MATLAB experience will be necessary for those intending to develop algorithms at the application level. The book is written so that readers without a complete engineering background can learn to *use* the tools and achieve a conceptual understanding of the material.

Approach

To help motivate the reader, I have taken an approach to learning that presents topics as needed. This approach starts by presenting a global model to help gain an understanding of the overall process, followed by a breakdown and explanation of each individual topic. Instead of presenting techniques or mathematical tools when they fit into a nice, neat *theoretical* framework, topics are presented as they become necessary for understanding the practical imaging model under study. This approach provides the reader with the motivation to learn about and use the tools and topics, because they see an immediate need for them. For example, the mathematical process of convolution is introduced when it is needed for an image zoom algorithm, and morphological operations are introduced when morphological filtering operations are needed after image segmentation. This approach also makes the book more useful as a reference, or for those who may not work through the book sequentially, but will reference a specific section as the need arises.

Organization of the Book

The book is divided into eight primary chapters. The first chapter is an introductory chapter and overview of digital image processing and analysis; it discusses terms and describes application areas with examples. Chapter 1 also provides a description of imaging systems, both hardware and software, and material regarding image acquisition and representation. Chapter 2 includes material about the CVIPtools software development environment, both C/C++ and MATLAB, to ease the reader into programming at an early stage. Chapter 3 leads the reader through the various stages of image analysis, culminating in a simple binary computer vision application example. Chapter 4 discusses edge, line, boundary and shape detection. Chapter 5 provides an overview of image segmentation methods, with representative examples of each algorithm type, and shows how morphological filtering is used as segmentation postprocessing to clarify object shapes. Chapter 5 also discusses how segmentation and morphological filters are applied to computer vision system development. Chapter 6 includes feature selection, feature extraction and feature analysis. To complete the tools needed for image analysis, and our view of computer vision as deployed image analysis systems, Chapter 7 covers algorithm development and pattern classification methods. The final chapter, Chapter 8, has more detailed examples of application development, including the Feature Extraction and Pattern Classification (FEPC) and Algorithm Test and Analysis Tool (ATAT) development tools, as well as new edited conference papers describing computer vision applications developed with CVIPtools. The reader who wants to develop applications within a CVIP-development environment will find what is needed here. Also note that complete documentation for the software is available on the publisher's web site for the book: www.routledge.com/9781032071299 as "Online Docs".

Using the Book in Your Courses

The book is intended for use in computer vision, robot vision, machine vision or image analysis courses at the senior or beginning graduate level. To use *Computer Vision and Image Analysis* in a one semester course, I suggest covering Chapters 1 through 6 and selected pattern classification topics of interest from Chapter 7. If time allows, application development tools and examples in Chapter 8 can be explored. At our university, I have a follow-on graduate-only course that is project oriented where I use Chapter 8 as introductory material and supplement it with journal papers and application exploration.

The programming material in Chapter 2 can be used depending on the desire of the instructor – the skeleton program, CVIPlab, can be used either with C/C++ or in the MATLAB environment, or both. I encourage all who use the book to explore the programming exercises because they provide a valuable tool to learn about computer vision applications. There are also many tutorial exercises using the CVIP environment included with each chapter, which provide hands-on experience and allow the user to gain insight into the various algorithms and parameters. Detailed syllabi for the courses at Southern Illinois University Edwardsville can be seen at my home page: www.siue.edu/~sumbaug.

The CVIPtools Software Development Environment

The software development environment includes an extensive set of standard C libraries, a skeleton program for using the C libraries called *CVIPlab*, a dynamically linked library (cviptools.dll) based on the common object module (COM) interface, a GUI-based program for the exploration of computer imaging called *CVIPtools*, two algorithm development and batch processing tools *CVIP-ATAT* and *CVIP-FEPC*, and the new *CVIP MATLAB Toolbox*. The CVIPlab program and all the standard libraries are all ANSI-C compatible. The new version of CVIPtools has been developed exclusively for the Windows operating system, but various UNIX versions are available at the web site (http://cviptools.siue.edu/). The CVIPtools software, the libraries, the CVIPlab program, CVIP-ATAT, CVIP-FEPC, the CVIP MATLAB Toolbox and GUI, and images used in the textbook are available on the web site (cviptools.siue.edu).

The CVIPtools software has been used in projects funded by the National Institutes of Health, the United States Department of Defense and numerous corporations in the commercial sector. CVIPtools has been used in the medical, aerospace, printing and manufacturing fields in applications such as the development of a helicopter simulation, automated classification of lumber, skin tumor evaluation and analysis, embedded image processing for print technology, the automatic classification of defects in microdisplay chips and the analysis of veterinary thermographic images for disease evaluation. Since it is a university-sponsored project, it is continually being upgraded and expanded, and the updates are available from the web site. This software allows the reader to learn about imaging topics in an interactive and exploratory manner, and to develop their own programming expertise with the

CVIPlab program and the associated laboratory exercises. With the addition of the new GUI for the CVIP Toolbox for MATLAB, the users can explore the functions in a manner similar to using the Windows GUI. The CVIPlab program and the CVIP MATLAB Toolbox both allow the user access to any of the already-defined CVIPtools functions, ranging from general purpose input/output and matrix functions to more advanced transform functions and complex imaging algorithms; some of these functions are state-of-the-art algorithms since CVIPtools is continually being enhanced at the Computer Vision and Image Processing Laboratory at Southern Illinois University Edwardsville (SIUE).

MATLAB® is a registered trademark of The MathWorks, Inc. For product information, please contact:

The MathWorks, Inc.
3 Apple Hill Drive
Natick, MA 01760-2098 USA
Tel: 508-647-7000
Fax: 508-647-7001
E-mail: info@mathworks.com
Web: www.mathworks.com

Acknowledgments

I thank Southern Illinois University Edwardsville, specifically the School of Engineering and the Electrical and Computer Engineering Department, for their support of this endeavor. I also thank all the students who have taken my imaging courses and provided valuable feedback regarding the learning and teaching of computer vision and image analysis.

The initial version of the CVIPtools software was developed primarily by myself and a few graduate students: Gregory Hance, Arve Kjoelen, Kun Luo, Mark Zuke and Yansheng Wei; without their hard work and dedication, the foundation that was built upon for the subsequent versions would not be solid. The next major Windows version of CVIPtools was developed primarily by myself and Iris Cheng, Xiaohe Chen, Dejun Zhang and Huashi Ding. Additional students who contributed were Husain Kagalwalla and Sushma Gouravaram.

The next version of CVIPtools was initially developed by Patrick Solt and Evan Bian. The work was completed by Patrick Solt, Jhansi Akkineni, Mouinika Mamidi, Pelin Guvenc, Serkan Kefel and Hari Krishna Akkineni. Jhansi Akkineni served as project coordinator, and her efforts deserve special recognition. Her dedication to the project and the help she provided to others working on the project were substantial. Iris Cheng, who was the primary contributor on the original Windows version of CVIPtools, also deserves special recognition for her continued support as a consultant on the project. CVIPtools development continued with Hari Siva Kumar Reddy Bhogala, followed by Sai Chaitanya Gorantla. The current version of CVIPtools was created by Rohini Dahal, Gita Pant, John M. Hilbing (Jack) and Charles Stacey. All the graduate students who worked on the CVIPtools project deserve my special recognition and thanks.

The Computer Vision and Image Processing Algorithm Test and Analysis Tool, CVIP-ATAT, underwent many changes during its development. The initial version was provided by Sid Smith and Jeremy Wood. Geer Shaung and Evan Bian provided substantial new development for this tool, which helped to make it more practical for its use with CVIPtools. Further development was completed, tested and utilized in projects by Pelin Guvenc. Hari Siva Kumar Reddy Bhogala worked on the improvement of CVIP-ATAT and Ravneet Kaur performed testing for the previous version. The CVIP-ATAT was worked on extensively by Charles Stacey, who has provided wonderful improvements and updated methods for the software.

The Computer Vision and Image Processing Feature Extraction and Pattern Classification Tool, CVIP-FEPC, was created and developed by Patrick Solt, and its development was partially funded by the Long Island Veterinary Specialists. Additional work was performed for the improvement and enhancement of CVIP-FEPC by Kumari Heema Poudel. Following that, Rohini Dahal took over programming development with Norsang Lama providing extensive testing to create the first robust version of CVIP-FEPC. The current version has undergone enhancements, primarily implemented by Charles Stacey. All the hard work and dedication of my graduate students is greatly appreciated.

The MATLAB CVIP Toolbox was initially developed by the porting of CVIPtools C functions to *mex* (MATLAB executable) files by Krishna Regmi, whose great effort laid the foundation and provided valuable insight into our future development. The *mex* file development for the project was continued by Deependra Mishra. After encountering numerous complications with various versions of compilers and operating systems, we decided to continue development of the CVIP Toolbox using m-files. Mehrdad Alvandipour and Norsang Lama teamed up with Deependra to complete the first version consisting primarily of m-files. Lakshmi Gorantla continued development and testing before the release of version 2.5. Their long hours and perseverance during development is greatly appreciated. This first version of the MATLAB CVIP Toolbox has gotten extensive use and has been a benefit to those who are using CVIPtools and want to perform development in the MATLAB environment. For the new version of the MATLAB Toolbox, we added a GUI and a number of functions. Julian Buritica was instrumental with the GUI development, with the work continued by Hridoy Biswas and Al Mahmud. This version of the CVIP Toolbox for MATLAB will be released in conjunction with this new book edition.

In small but important parts of CVIPtools, public domain software was used, and kudos to those who provided it: Jef Pokanzer's pbmplus, Sam Leffler's TIFF library, Paul Heckbert's Graphics Gems, the Independent JPEG Group's software, Yuval Fisher's fractal code and the Texas Agricultural Experiment Station's code for the original texture features.

I'd like to thank those who contributed photographs and images: Howard Ash, Mark Zuke, Mike Wilson, Tony Berke, George Dean, Sara Sawyer, Sue Eder, Jeff Zuke, Bill White, the National Oceanic and Atmospheric Administration, NASA and MIT. H. Kipsang Choge, Charles Stacey and Hridoy Biswas deserve credit for helping out with some of the figures, and I thank them for this work. Thanks also to David, Robin, Michael, Jeanie, Jeff, Mom, Greg, Glicer, Gaby, Dad, Pat, Angi, Tyler, Connor, Kayla, Aaron, Ava, Kenley, Kaiden, Chris, Ryder, Chad, Jamie, Noah, Rohini, Gita, Hridoy, Charles, Iris and Alice for letting me use their smiling faces in some of the figures.

I also want to extend my gratitude to my graduate students and others who helped with the review of various sections of the book. This primarily includes Julian Buritica, Charles Stacey, Hridoy Biswas and Al Mahmud, as well as the numerous students who have used my books to learn about imaging in the courses I teach and those taught world-wide. I also want to thank all the other authors and coauthors of the papers used in Chapter 8.

I also thank the publisher, Nora Konopka at CRC Press/Taylor & Francis Group, for having the vision, sagacity and good taste in publishing the fourth edition of the book. Nora has been very supportive throughout the project and very helpful in making sure that everything was put together the way I wanted. The entire staff at the CRC Press, especially Prachi Mishra, Glenon Butler and Swapnil Joshi, have been very helpful in getting and keeping the project rolling, and special thanks go to them. Their encouragement and enthusiasm is much appreciated; they all have done a wonderful job managing project details as we approach production. Thanks also go to Gayathri Tamilselvan and the production staff who survived my many requests regarding the book layout, but still managed to get it done in a timely manner.

Finally, I thank my family for all their contributions; without them, this book would not have been possible. I thank my mom who instilled in me a love of learning and a sense of wonder about the world around me; my dad, who taught me how to think like an engineer and the importance of self-discipline and hard work. I want to thank my brothers, Greg and Jeff, for being there during those formative years. And I am especially grateful to Jeanie, Robin, David and Michael, who lived through the ordeal and endured the many long hours I put into the new edition of this book.

Author

Dr. Scott E Umbaugh is a University Distinguished Research Professor of Electrical and Computer Engineering and Graduate Program director for the Department of Electrical and Computer Engineering at Southern Illinois University Edwardsville (SIUE). He is also the director of the Computer Vision and Image Processing (CVIP) Laboratory at SIUE. He has been teaching computer vision and image processing, as well as computer and electrical engineering design, for over 30 years. His professional interests include computer vision and image processing education, research and development of both human and computer vision applications, and engineering design education.

Prior to his academic career, Dr. Umbaugh worked as a computer design engineer and project manager in the avionics and telephony industries. He has been a computer imaging consultant since 1986 and has provided consulting services for the aerospace, medical and manufacturing industries with projects ranging from automatic identification of defects in microdisplay chips to analysis of thermographic images for clinical diagnosis of brain disease. He has performed research and development for projects funded by the National Institutes of Health, the National Science Foundation and the U.S. Department of Defense.

Dr. Umbaugh is the author or co-author of numerous technical papers, two edited books and multiple editions of his textbooks on computer vision and image processing. His books are used at academic and research organizations throughout the world. He has served on editorial boards and as a reviewer for a variety of IEEE journals, and has evaluated research monographs and textbooks in the imaging field.

Dr. Umbaugh received his B.S.E. degree with honors from Southern Illinois University Edwardsville in 1982, M.S.E.E. in 1987 and Ph.D. in 1990 from the Missouri University of Science and Technology, where he was a Chancellor's Fellow. He is a life senior member of the Institute of Electrical and Electronic Engineers (IEEE) and a member of Sigma Xi and the International Society for Optical Engineering (SPIE). Dr. Umbaugh is also the primary developer of the CVIPtools software package and the associated CVIP MATLAB Toolbox.

1

Digital Image Processing and Analysis

1.1 Introduction

Digital image processing is a field that continues to grow, with new applications being developed at an ever-increasing pace. It is a fascinating and exciting area to be involved in today with application areas ranging from medicine to the entertainment industry to the space program. The internet, with its ease of use via web browsers, combined with the advances in computer power and network bandwidth has brought the world into our offices and into our homes. One of the most interesting aspects of this information revolution is the ability to send and receive complex data that transcends ordinary written text. Visual information, transmitted in the form of digital images, has become a major method of communication for the 21st century. With the advent of modern mobile phones, this information is available anywhere and anytime, with uses limited only by the imagination.

Digital image processing can be defined as the acquisition and processing of visual information by computer. The importance of digital image processing is derived from the fact that our primary sense is our visual sense. Our vision system allows us to gather information without the need for physical interaction; it enables us to analyze many types of information directly from pictures or video. It provides us with the ability to navigate about our environment, and the human visual system is the most sophisticated, advanced neural system in the human body. Most of the scientific discoveries and advancements have relied on the visual system for their development – from the discovery of fire to the design of a smart phone.

The information that can be conveyed in images has been known throughout the centuries to be extraordinary – one picture *is* worth a thousand words. Fortunately, this is the case because the computer representation of an image requires the equivalent of many thousands of words of data, and without a corresponding amount of information, the medium would be prohibitively inefficient. The massive amount of data required for images is a primary reason for the development of many subareas within the field of image processing, such as image segmentation and image compression. Another important aspect of computer imaging involves the ultimate "receiver" of the visual information – in some cases the human visual system and in others the computer itself.

This distinction allows us to separate digital image processing into two primary application areas: (1) computer vision applications and (2) human vision applications, with image analysis being a key component in the development and deployment of both (Figure 1.1-1). In *computer vision* applications, the processed (output) images

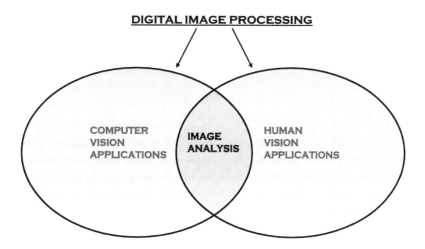

FIGURE 1.1-1
Digital image processing can be separated into computer vision and human vision applications, with image analysis being essential to both.

DOI: 10.1201/9781003221135-1

are for use by a computer, while in *human vision* applications, the output images are for human consumption. The human visual system and the computer as a vision system have varying limitations and strengths, and the image processing specialist needs to be aware of the functionality of these two very different systems. The human vision system is limited to visible wavelengths of light, which cover only a small portion of the electromagnetic (EM) spectrum. The computer is capable of dealing with the entire EM spectrum, ranging from gamma rays to radio waves, and it can process other imaging modalities such as ultrasound and magnetic resonance imaging (MRI).

Historically, the field of digital image processing grew from electrical engineering as an extension of the signal processing branch, while the computer science discipline was largely responsible for developments in computer vision applications. At some universities, these two are still separate and distinct, but the commonalities and the perceived needs have brought the two together. Here, we will simply refer to digital image processing as the general field while allowing for separate application areas in computer and human vision. As shown in Figure 1.1-1, image analysis applies to both applications' areas.

Image analysis involves the examination of the image data to facilitate solving an imaging problem. Image analysis methods comprise the major components of a computer vision system, where the system is to analyze images and have a computer act on the results. In one sense, a computer vision application is simply a *deployed* image analysis system. In the development of a human vision image processing application, many images must be examined and tested so image analysis is necessary during the *development* of the system.

This book focuses on computer vision and image analysis. Chapters 1 and 2 introduce the basic concepts, and will provide the necessary background for those who are new to the field, and an overview of software tools that have been developed for use with the book. This includes a discussion of image acquisition, imaging systems and image representation. Chapters 3–7 cover a system model for the image analysis process and then describe each major part of this model in separate chapters. Each of these chapters concludes with a *key points* section, followed by references and suggestions for further reading, and a series of exercises to help the learning process. The exercises include definitions, discussions, problems, advanced problems and computer exercises using the CVIPtools software and programming exercises. Chapter 8 concludes the book with a discussion of application development with an overview of the more advanced tools in the development environment, the Algorithm Test and Analysis Tool and the Feature Pattern and Classification Tool.

For the programming exercises, the reader has multiple options. The new CVIP MATLAB Toolbox is available to MATLAB users, and the CVIPlab prototype program can be used by C, C++ or C# programmers. The programming environment provided with the CVIPtools software is a comprehensive environment for computer vision and image processing education and application development. Chapter 8 describes the development tools in more detail, including examples, and provides applications that were developed with the CVIPtools environment. For downloading, installing and updating CVIPtools, and a description of the CVIPtools software organization, see the web site: cviptools.siue.edu. Note that more information is available on the publisher's web site, including function quick reference lists, application papers and useful image processing resources.

1.2 Image Analysis and Computer Vision Overview

Image analysis involves investigation of the image data for a specific application. Typically, we have a set of images and want to look beyond the raw image data to evaluate the images at a higher level and gain insight for the application to determine how they can be used to extract the information we need. The image analysis process requires the use of tools such as image segmentation, image transforms, feature extraction and pattern classification. *Image segmentation* is often one of the first steps in finding higher-level objects from the raw image data. *Feature extraction and analysis* is the process of acquiring higher-level image information, such as shape or color information, and it may require the use of *image transforms* to find spatial frequency information. *Pattern classification* is the act of taking this higher-level information and identifying objects within the image.

Image analysis methods comprise the major components of a computer vision system. Computer vision may be best understood by considering different types of applications. Many of these applications involve tasks that are either tedious for people to perform, require work in a hostile environment, require a high rate of processing, or require access and use of a large database of information. Computer vision systems are used in many and various types of environments – from manufacturing plants to hospital surgical suites to the surface of Mars. For example, in manufacturing systems, computer vision is often used for quality control. There, the computer vision system will scan manufactured items for defects and provide control signals to a robotic manipulator to automatically remove defective parts. To develop an application of this nature, an image database consisting of sample images is first created. Next, image analysis is applied to develop the necessary algorithms to solve the problem. One interesting example of this type of system involves the automated inspection of microdisplay chips.

Microdisplay chips are used in digital cameras, projection systems, televisions, heads-up-displays and any application that requires a small imaging device. Prior to the design of this computer vision system, these chips were inspected manually – a process that is slow and prone to error. Once the market demand for these chips accelerated, the manual inspection process was not practical. In Figure 1.2-1, we see the microdisplay chip inspection system along with two sample images. The original images were captured at 3:1 magnification, which means each picture element in the microdisplay chip corresponds to a 3×3 array in the image. The system automatically finds various types of defects in the chips, such as the pixel defects and the faint display defects shown here.

An active area of computer vison research today involves applications for facial recognition. This is desired for many reasons, including recognizing terrorist suspects in airport crowds or pictures of your long-lost cousin in a stack of photos. The first step in facial recognition is to find faces in an image. An algorithm to select subimages within an image that are likely to contain faces was developed using convolutional neural networks (see Chapters 5 and 7), and a resulting output image is shown in Figure 1.2-2a. In this image, the subimages that contain faces have been marked with boxes. In addition to facial recognition, Figure 1.2-2b shows results from an algorithm developed to identify chairs and computer monitors.

Another interesting computer vision application that required image analysis for algorithm development involved the automatic counting and grading of lumber. Before this system was implemented, this task was done manually, which was a boring task, had an unacceptable error rate and was inefficient. This application was challenging due to the variation in the lumber stack, such as gaps in between boards, variation in the wood color, cracks in the boards or holes in the boards. Figure 1.2-3 shows an example of the system in operation, with a sample input image, processed image and system output. The processed image is used by high-level software to count and grade the lumber in stack. With the system in place, the lumberyard can minimize errors, increase efficiency and provide their workers with more rewarding tasks.

Image analysis is used in the development of many computer vision applications for the medical community, with the only certainty being that the variety of applications will continue to grow. Current examples of medical systems being developed include systems to automatically diagnose skin lesions, systems to aid neurosurgeons during brain surgery and systems to automatically perform clinical tests. Systems that automate the diagnostic process are being developed for various reasons, including pre-screening to determine appropriate subsequent tests or analysis, as tools by medical professionals where specialists are unavailable, or to act as consultants to the primary care givers, and they may serve their most useful purpose in the training of medical professionals. These types of systems may be experimental, and some are still in the research stages, but more and more of them are being integrated into medical practice. Computer vision systems that are being used in the surgical suite have already been used to improve the surgeon's ability to "see" what is happening in the body during surgery, and consequently, improve the quality of medical care. Systems are also currently being used for tissue and cell analysis; for example, to automate applications that require the identification and counting of certain types of cells (see Figure 1.2-4). Computer vision is being used more and more in medical applications, but it will still be some time before we see computers playing doctor like the holographic doctor in the *Star Trek* series.

The field of law enforcement and security is an active area for image analysis research and development, with applications ranging from automatic identification of fingerprints to DNA analysis. Security systems to identify people by retinal scans, facial scans and the veins in the hand have been developed. Reflected ultraviolet (UV) imaging systems are being used to find latent fingerprints, shoeprints, body fluids and bite marks that are not visible to the human visual system. Infrared (IR) imaging to count bugs has been used at Disney World to help keep their greenery green. Currently, cars are equipped with systems to automatically avoid accidents, and systems are under development and being tested to fully automate our transportation systems to make travel safer. The United States space program and the Defense department, with their needs for robots with visual capabilities, are actively involved in image analysis research and development. Applications range from autonomous vehicles to target tracking and identification. Satellites orbiting the earth collect massive amounts of image data every day, and these images are automatically scanned to aid in making maps, predicting the weather and helping us to understand the changes taking place on our home planet.

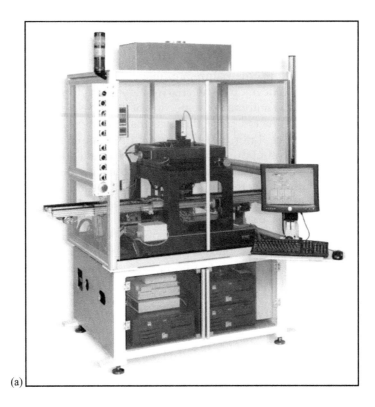

(a)

Input images   **Pixel defect detection**   **After blob analysis**

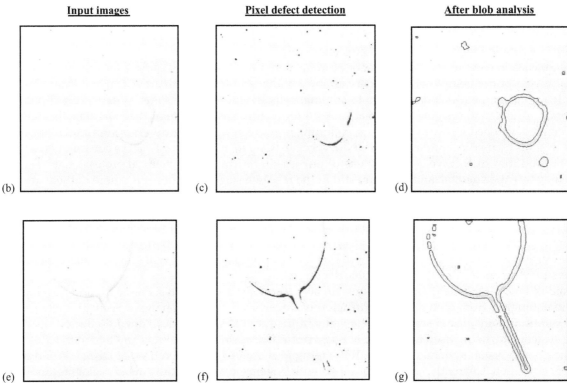

(b)   (c)   (d)

(e)   (f)   (g)

FIGURE 1.2-1
Microdisplay chip inspection. (a) Computer vision system for microdisplay chip inspection, (b) microdisplay chip *image1* at 3:1 magnification, (c) *Image1* after pixel defect detection, (d) *Image1* after blob analysis to find faint defects, (e) microdisplay chip *Image2* at 3:1 magnification, (f) *Image2* after pixel defect detection and (g) *Image2* after blob analysis to find faint defects (photo courtesy of Mike Wilson and Iris Cheng, Westar Display Technologies, Inc.)

(a)

(b)

FIGURE 1.2-2
Face and object recognition. (a) Image after being processed by a computer vision algorithm to find and identify faces. (b) Image processed to identify chairs and monitors.

(a)

(b)
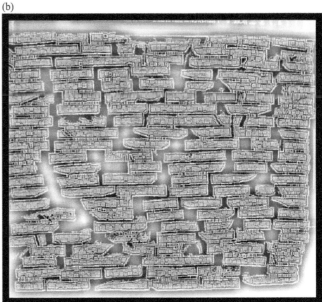

(c)
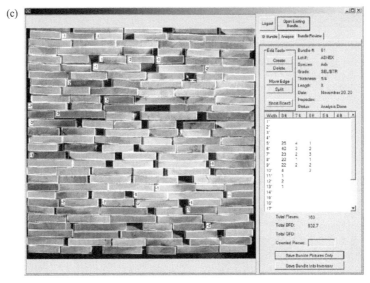

FIGURE 1.2-3
Lumber grading. (a) Image captured by the computer vision system for lumber counting grading, (b) intermediate image after processing, (c) example of system output after software analysis. (Photo courtesy of Tony Berke, River City Software.)

1.3   Digital Imaging Systems

Digital image processing systems come in many different configurations, depending on the application. As technology advances, these systems get smaller, faster and more sophisticated. Here, we will focus on the primary aspects of a generic imaging system. We will look at how images are sensed and transformed into computer files, and how these computer files are used to represent image information.

Computer imaging systems are comprised of two primary component types: hardware and software. The hardware components, as seen in Figure 1.3-1, can be divided into the image acquisition subsystem, the computer itself and the display and storage devices. The computer system may contain special-purpose imaging hardware, as well as computer vision and image processing software. The software allows us to manipulate the image and perform

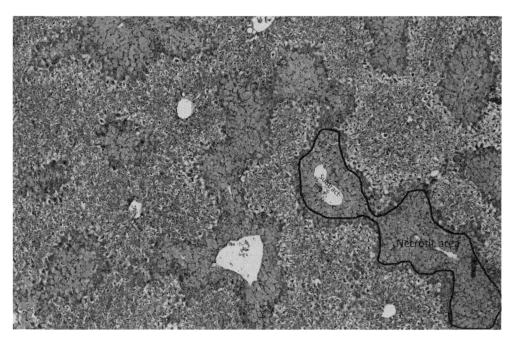

FIGURE 1.2-4
Necrotic liver tissue classification. An image that was used to develop a computer vision algorithm to automatically segment and classify necrotic (dead) liver tissue from surrounding tissue. The research investigated the toxicity of an acetaminophen overdose, the leading cause of acute liver failure in the United States, with the goal of identifying novel therapeutic targets. The small gray areas are blood vessels and its area should be subtracted from the necrotic area. (Image courtesy of David Umbaugh and the University of Kansas Medical Center.)

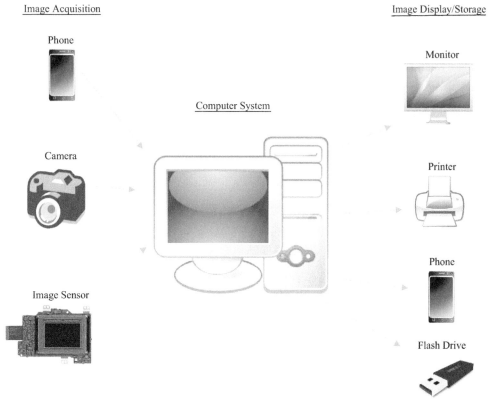

FIGURE 1.3-1
Digital image processing system hardware.

any desired analysis or processing on the image data. Additionally, we may also use software to control the image acquisition and storage process.

The computer system may be a general-purpose computer with an imaging device connected. Images may be acquired by the computer via a standalone camera or phone camera, or they can be input from any image sensing device or downloaded from the internet. The primary device for capturing live images is the camera, which can use either a digital or analog format. Digital cameras store image data in a format similar to that used directly by the computer, while analog cameras output a continuous video signal which must be modified to create an image suitable for computer processing. Although digital cameras are the newer format, analog cameras are still used in many applications due to the large installed base, well-established standards and inexpensive, easily available parts.

A standard analog video camera requires a frame grabber, or image digitizer, to interface with the computer. The *frame grabber* is a special-purpose piece of hardware that accepts a standard analog video signal and outputs an image in the form that a computer can understand – a digital image. Analog video standards vary throughout the world; RS-170A, RS-330 and RS-343A are the monochrome video standards in the North America and Japan. RS-343A is used for high-resolution video with 675–1,023 lines per frame. CCIR is the monochrome standard used primarily in Europe. The three color video standards are NTSC, PAL and SECAM. NTSC is used in North America, Japan and parts of South America, while PAL is used in parts of Africa, Asia and Northern Europe. SECAM is used in parts of Africa, Asia, Eastern Europe, Russia and France. NTSC is 525 lines, 30 frames (60 fields) per second, 2:1 interlaced standard. PAL and SECAM are 625 lines, 25 frames (50 fields) per second, 2:1 interlaced standards.

The process of transforming a standard analog video signal into a digital image is called digitization. This transformation is necessary because the standard video signal is in analog (continuous) form, and the computer requires a digitized or sampled version of that continuous signal. A typical video signal contains frames of video information, where each *frame* corresponds to a full screen of visual information. Each frame may then be divided into *fields*, and each field consists of alternating lines of video information. In Figure 1.3-2a, we see the typical image on a display device, where the solid lines represent one field of information and the dotted lines represent the other field. These two fields make up one frame of visual information. This two fields per frame model is referred to as *interlaced* video. Some types of video signals, called *progressive scan* or *non-interlaced* video, have only one field per frame. Non-interlaced video is typically used in computer monitors.

In Figure 1.3-2b, we see the electrical signal that corresponds to one line of video information. Note the *horizontal synch pulse* between each line of information, and this synchronization pulse tells the display hardware to start a new line. After one frame has been displayed, a longer synchronization pulse, called the *vertical synch pulse*, tells the display hardware to start a new field or frame.

The analog video signal is converted to a digital image by sampling the continuous signal at a fixed rate. In Figure 1.3-3, we see one line of a video signal being sampled (digitized) by instantaneously measuring the voltage of the signal at fixed intervals in time. The value of the voltage at each instant is converted into a number that is stored, corresponding to the brightness of the image at that point. Note that the image brightness at a point

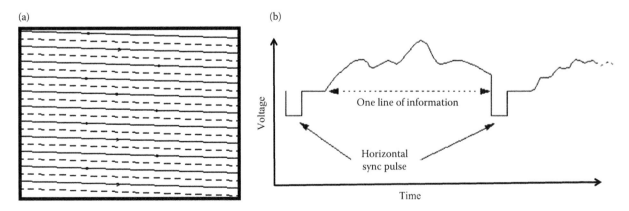

FIGURE 1.3-2
The video signal. (a) One frame, two fields. Each field is obtained by taking very other line. One field is represented by solid lines and the other by dotted lines. (b) The analog video signal. One line of information is one row of image data, and the horizontal synch pulse is the control signal for the hardware to designate the end of a line.

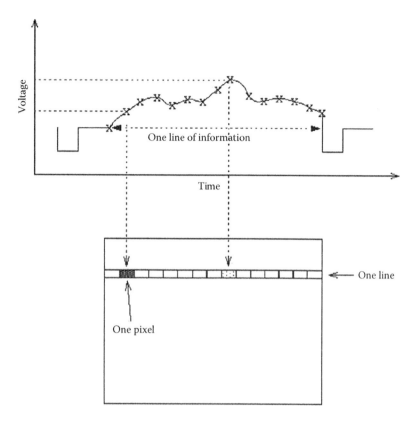

FIGURE 1.3-3
Digitizing (sampling) an analog video signal. The sampled voltage corresponds to the brightness of the image at that point.

depends on both the intrinsic properties of the object *and* the lighting conditions in the scene. Once this process has been completed for an entire frame of video information, we have "grabbed" a frame, and the computer can store it and process it as a digital image. Although analog video has been phased out for most broadcast applications, the frame rate provides a common foundation.

Today, digital television (DTV) standards for transmission of video signals are most common, and they support a wide variety of formats with varying resolution and interlacing defined. The US government required the change to the digital broadcast format in 2009, and worldwide, the standards were changed soon thereafter – as examples, Japan and Canada in 2010, United Kingdom in 2012, and China in 2015. In general terms, DTV can be divided into two main categories: standard-definition television (SDTV) and high-definition television (HDTV). The SDTV formats are similar to the previously defined analog NTSC, SECAM and PAL in terms of resolution and interlacing.

The current standards for HDTV use several different formats. These include a resolution of 1280 columns by 720 rows (lines), in progressive scan mode (non-interlaced), referred to as *720p*, 1920 columns by 1080 rows for *1080p*, or 1920 × 1080 in interlaced mode, called *1080i*. While the SDTV uses a 4:3 aspect ratio, the HDTV standards specify a 16:9 aspect ratio. The *aspect ratio* is the width to height ratio of the display device, as shown in Figure 1.3-4. The aspect ratio of 35 mm film cameras is 3:2, and standard digital cameras typically use 3:2 or 4:3.

The newest standard for video signals is *ultra high definition* (UHD). The UHD standard uses an aspect ratio of 16:9, the same aspect ratio as HDTV. However, the UHD standard specifies a higher resolution than HDTV. The UHD standards currently defined include *2160p or 4K*, which is a progressive scan of 3840 columns by 2160 rows, and *4320p or 8K*, a progressive scan of 7680 pixels columns by 4320 rows. Although very few television stations are broadcasting UHD, the *2160p* level of resolution is supported by blu-ray video players and the *4320p* is equivalent to images shown at commercial movie theaters. For most in-home television viewing, consumers will not be able to discern the difference between HD and UHD due to the typical distance that people use for watching television – the extra resolution is only noticeable up very close to the screen.

A digital camera can be interfaced with the computer via USB (Universal Serial Bus), Camera Link or Gigabit Ethernet (IEEE 802.3). Specifications for these are shown in Table 1-1. Although digital cameras are becoming more prevalent, analog cameras still have a share of the market, especially when cost is a factor.

(a)   (b)

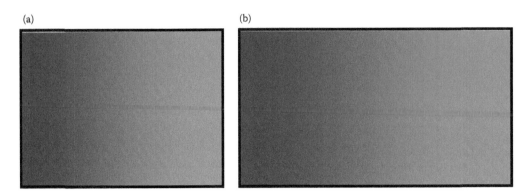

FIGURE 1.3-4
Aspect ratio. The *aspect ratio* is the ratio of the image or display width to the image or display height. The aspect ratio is (a) 4:3 for standard-definition television (SDTV) and (b) 16:9 for high-definition television (HDTV) and ultra high definition (UHD).

TABLE 1.1

Camera Interface Specifications

	10/40/100 Gigabit Ethernet	USB 3.0/3.1/3.2	USB 4.0	Camera Link
Type of standard	Public	Public	Public	Commercial
Connection type	Point-to-point or Local Area Network (LAN)	Master-slave, shared bus	Master-slave, shared bus	Point-to-point
Maximum bandwidth for images	10/40/100 Gigabit/ sec (Gbs)	5, 10, 20 Gbs	40 Gbs	2 to 16 Gbs
Distance	100 m, no limit with switches or fiber	5, 3, 1, 30m with switches	5, 3, 1, 30 m with switches	10 ms
PC interface	Network	PCI card	PCI card	PCI frame grabber
Wireless support	Yes	No	No	No
Max # of devices	Unlimited	63	127	1

After the image data is in digital form, whether from a digitized analog signal or directly from a digital camera, the image can now be accessed as a two-dimensional array of data, where each data point is referred to as a *pixel* (picture element). For digital images, we will use the following notation:

$$I(r, c) = \text{the brightness of the image at the point } (r, c) \tag{1.3-1}$$

where
r is the row and c is the column

- *Note that this notation, I(r, c), is used for consistency with how matrices are defined in many programming languages, such as "C".*
- *Imaging software tools (Photoshop, CVIPtools), some other textbooks and resolution standards use I(x, y) with column first and row second.*
- *Look carefully at which coordinate is the row and which is the column.*
- *Another potential point of confusion is that, in most programming languages, the upper left corner of the image has coordinates (0,0), but in MATLAB the upper left corner starts at (1,1).*

Digital image processing involves taking the digital image, *I(r, c)*, and performing various imaging operations, often by applying computer vision and image processing software, to modify the image data. The different levels and various types of processing can be illustrated by the *hierarchical image pyramid*, as seen in Figure 1.3-5. In this figure, the image operations are on the left and the corresponding image representation is on the right. As we traverse this pyramid from the bottom up, we get increasingly higher levels of information representation and smaller numbers of items. At the

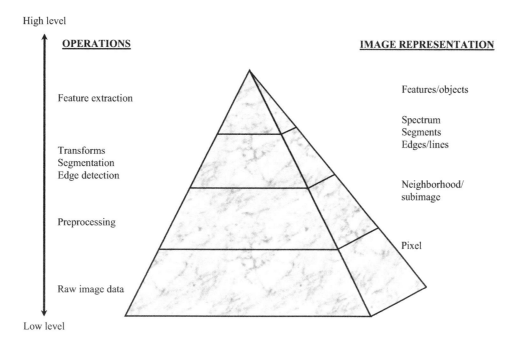

FIGURE 1.3-5
The hierarchical image pyramid. At the lowest level is the raw image data, the pixel brightness values $I(r, c)$. As the image is processed by various operations, and we ascend the pyramid, the image is represented by less data and fewer objects. These are referred to as higher-level representations of the image. At the highest level are the objects as the human visual system sees them.

very lowest level, we deal with the very large number of individual pixels, where we may perform some low-level preprocessing. The next level up is the *neighborhood*, which typically consists of a single pixel and the surrounding pixels, and we may continue to perform some preprocessing operations at this level. As we ascend the pyramid, we get higher and higher-level representations of the image, and consequently, a reduction in the amount of data. At the highest level are the objects as the human visual system sees them and often the desired output for a computer vision system. All of the types of operations and image representations in Figure 1.3-5 will be explored in the following chapters.

1.4   Image Formation and Sensing

Digital images are formed by energy interacting with a device that responds in a way that can be measured. These measurements are taken at various points across a two-dimensional grid in the world in order to create the digital image. These measuring devices are called *sensors*, and many different types are in use. Sensors may respond to various parts of the EM spectrum, acoustical (sound) energy, electron beams, lasers or any other signal that can be measured.

The EM spectrum consists of visible light, IR, UV, X-rays, microwaves, radio waves and gamma waves (see Figure 1.4-1). EM radiation consists of alternating (sinusoidal) electric and magnetic fields that are perpendicular to each other as well as to the direction of propagation. These waves all travel at the speed of light in free space, approximately $3 \cdot 10^8$ m/s, and they are classified by their frequency or wavelength. Figure 1.4-1 shows various spectral bands and their associated names, wavelengths, frequencies and energy. Various bands in the EM spectrum are named for historical reasons related to their discovery or to their application.

In addition to the wave model, EM radiation can be modeled as a stream of massless particles called *photons*, where a photon corresponds to the minimum amount of energy, the quantum, which can be measured in the EM signal. The energy of a photon is measured in electron volts, a very small unit, which is the kinetic (motion) energy that an electron acquires in being accelerated through an electronic potential of one volt. In Figure 1.4-1, we see that as frequency decreases, the energy contained in a photon decreases. Radio waves have the smallest frequencies

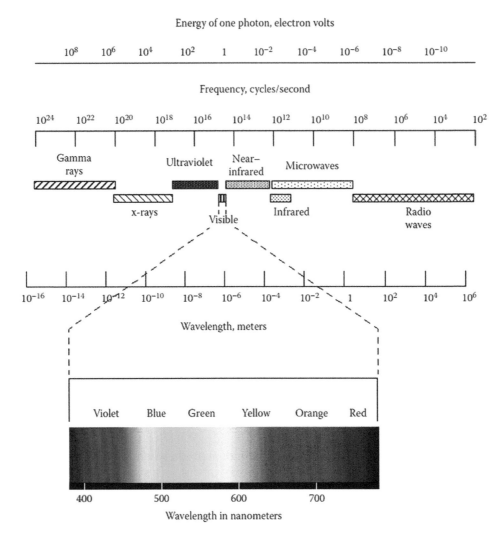

FIGURE 1.4-1
The electromagnetic spectrum. Higher frequencies have higher energy and are more dangerous. Note that the visible spectrum is only a small part of the entire EM spectrum.

so we believe that it is safe to be immersed in them (they're everywhere!), whereas gamma rays have the highest energy which makes them very dangerous to biological systems.

Sensors may also respond to acoustical energy as in ultrasound images. In some cases, images are created to produce *range* images, which do not correspond to what we typically think of as images, but are measures of distance to objects, and they may be created by radar (*r*adio *d*etection *a*nd *r*anging), sound energy or lasers. In this section, and in this book, visible light images are the primary focus; however, we will briefly discuss other types of images. After an image is acquired, it can be analyzed or processed using all the tools discussed in this book, regardless of the type of acquisition process.

We will consider two key components of image formation:

- Where will the image point appear?
- What value will be assigned to that point?

The first question can be answered by investigating basic properties of lenses and the physics of light, the science of *optics*, and the second will require a look into sensor and electronic technology.

1.4.1 Visible Light Imaging

The basic model for visible light imaging is shown in Figure 1.4-2. Here, the light source emits light that is reflected from the object and focused by the lens onto the image sensor. The sensor responds to the light energy by converting it into electrical energy which is then measured. This measurement is proportional to the incident energy, and it determines the brightness of the image at that point. The appearance of an object in an image is highly dependent on the way in which it reflects light; this is called the *reflectance function* of the object and is related to what we see as color and texture. The color determines which wavelengths of light are absorbed and which are reflected, and the texture determines the angle at which the light is reflected. In Figure 1.4-3, objects of very different reflectance functions are shown.

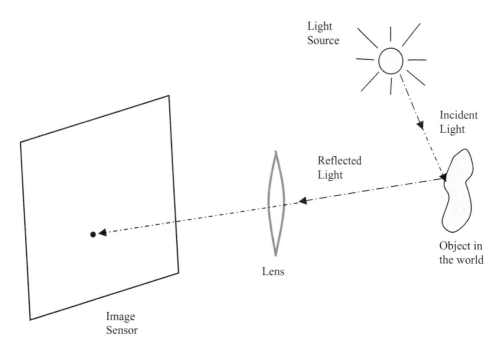

FIGURE 1.4-2
Model for visible light imaging. The light source emits light that is reflected from the object and focused by the lens onto the image sensor.

(a)   (b)

FIGURE 1.4-3
The reflectance function. Here, we see that the way in which an object reflects the incident light, the reflectance function, has a major effect on its appearance in the resulting image. The reflectance function is an intrinsic property of the object, and it relates to both color and texture. (a) Monochrome image showing brightness only, the color determines how much light is reflected and the surface texture determines the angle at which the light is reflected. (b) Color image, the color determines which wavelengths are absorbed and which are reflected.

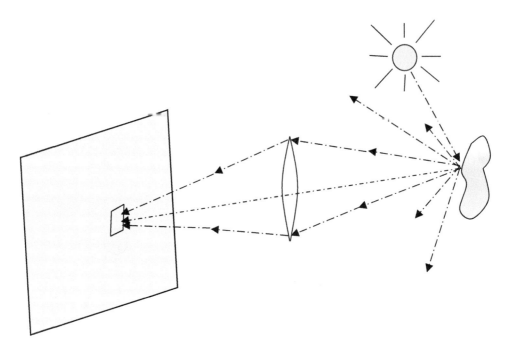

FIGURE 1.4-4
Irradiance and radiance. Irradiance is the measured light falling on the image plane. It is measured in power per unit area. Radiance is the power reflected or emitted per unit area into a directional cone having a unit of solid angle. Note that all the reflected light is not captured by the lens.

In imaging, two terms are necessary to define brightness. What is measured is called *irradiance*, while the light reflected from an object is referred to as *radiance*. Figure 1.4-4 illustrates the difference between these two terms. Irradiance is the amount of light falling on a surface, such as an image sensor, while radiance is the amount of light emitted from a surface into a solid unit angle. So, the units used for these two measures are different:

$$\text{irrradiance} \rightarrow \frac{\text{Power}}{\text{Area}}$$

$$\text{radiance} \rightarrow \frac{\text{Power}}{(\text{Area})(\text{Solid Angle})}$$
(1.4-1)

The irradiance is the brightness of an image at a point and is proportional to the scene radiance.

A lens is necessary to focus light in a real imaging system. In Figure 1.4-5, we see the relationship between points in the world and points in the image. The relationship of distance of the object in the world and the image plane is defined by the lens equation:

$$\frac{1}{a} + \frac{1}{b} = \frac{1}{f}$$
(1.4-2)

where f is the *focal length* of the lens and is an intrinsic property of the lens, and a and b are the two distances in question. In this figure, three rays of light are shown; note that the one through the center of the lens goes straight through to the image plane, and if the system is in focus, the other rays will meet at that point. If the object is moved closer to the lens, the single point will become a blur circle; the diameter of the circle is given by the *blur equation*:

$$c = \frac{d}{b'}|b' - b|$$
(1.4-3)

where c is the circle diameter, d is the diameter of the lens and a' and b' are the distances shown in Figure 1.4-6. This equation can be derived by the property of similar triangles.

A real object typically does not appear in a single plane, so some blurring will occur. The question is – What are the conditions that will allow an object to be focused sufficiently well? This will be determined by the spatial

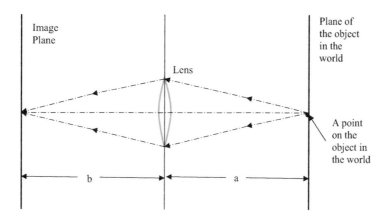

FIGURE 1.4-5

Relationship between points in the world and points in the image. A lens will focus an image of an object only at a specific distance given by the lens equation: $\dfrac{1}{a} + \dfrac{1}{b} = \dfrac{1}{f}$, where f is the *focal length* of the lens and is an intrinsic property of the lens, and a and b are the two distances shown.

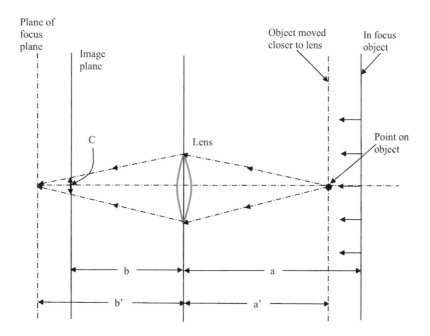

FIGURE 1.4-6

The blur circle from a poorly focused lens. As the object is moved closer to the lens, it gets blurry. Application of the lens equation shows the object is actually focused behind the image plane. The blur equation defines the amount of blur. Specifically, it gives the diameter of a blur circle, corresponding to a point in the original in focus image.

resolution of the imaging device. If the blur circles are equal to or smaller than the device resolution, the object will be focused sufficiently well. The range of distances over which objects are focused sufficiently well is called the *depth of field*. With many imaging devices, a diaphragm can be adjusted to allow some control over the depth of field (also called depth of focus). If the diaphragm is closed somewhat, not only does it let less light in but it also changes the effective diameter, $D_{\text{effective}}$, of the lens. The *f-number (or f-stop)* is defined as the ratio of the focal length to the lens diameter, and as the f-number increases, the depth of field increases:

$$f - \text{number} = \frac{f}{D_{\text{effective}}}$$

(1.4-4)

Another important parameter of an imaging device is the field of view (FOV). The *field of view* is the amount of the scene that the imaging device actually "sees"; that is, the angle of the cone of directions from which the device will create the image. Note that the FOV depends not only on the focal length of the lens but also on the size of the imaging sensor. Figure 1.4-7 shows that the FOV can be defined as follows:

$$\text{FOV} = 2\varphi, \text{ where } \varphi = \tan^{-1}\left(\frac{d/2}{f}\right) \tag{1.4-5}$$

with d being the diagonal size of the image sensor and f being the focal length of the lens. Thus, for a fixed-size image sensor, a wider field of view requires a lens with a shorter focal length. A lens with a very short focal length compared to image sensor size is called a wide-angle lens. The three basic types of lenses are the following: (1) wide-angle – short focal length, FOV greater than 45°; (2) normal – medium focal length, FOV 25° – 45°; and (3) telephoto – long focal length, FOV less than 25°.

Real lenses do not typically consist of a single lens, but there are multiple lenses aligned together. This is primarily due to the fact that a single lens will have various types of distortions, called aberrations. The effect of these aberrations can be mitigated by aligning multiple lenses of varying types and sizes to create a compound lens. One of the negative effects of a compound lens is the vignetting effect. This effect, shown in Figure 1.4-8, causes the

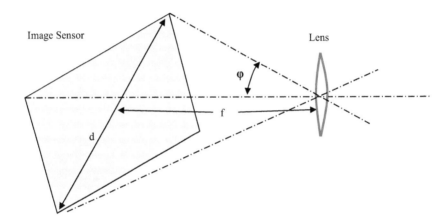

FIGURE 1.4-7
Field of View (FOV). The FOV for an imaging system depends on both the focal length of lens, f, and the size of image sensor,

d. For a fixed-size image sensor, a wider field of view requires a lens with a shorter focal length. FOV = 2φ, where $\varphi = \tan^{-1}\left(\frac{d/2}{f}\right)$

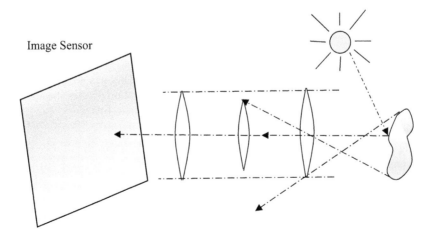

FIGURE 1.4-8
The vignetting effect. A compound lens causes less light on the edges of the image to get through to the image sensor. This has the effect of decreasing brightness as we move away from the center of the image.

amount of energy that actually makes it through the lens to the image plane to decrease as we move farther away from the center of the image. This effect can be avoided by using only the center portion of the lens. It is interesting to note that the human visual system is not sensitive to these types of slow spatial brightness variations.

We have briefly considered where the image objects will appear; next, we will consider how the brightness of the image is measured. How will we sense the object and turn it into an image? How will we measure the energy? As mentioned before, sensors are used to convert the light energy into electrical energy; this is done by using a material that emits electrons when bombarded with photons. In Figure 1.4-9, generic imaging sensors are shown. Single imaging sensors are typically arranged in lines or in two-dimensional arrays. The line sensor is typically used in imaging applications that require a single line scan at a time, such as in manufacturing applications. With a line scanner, speed and resolution can be increased, while cost is minimized. The array sensor is the primary type used in digital cameras, and the sensing element is typically a charge-coupled device (CCD) or a complementary

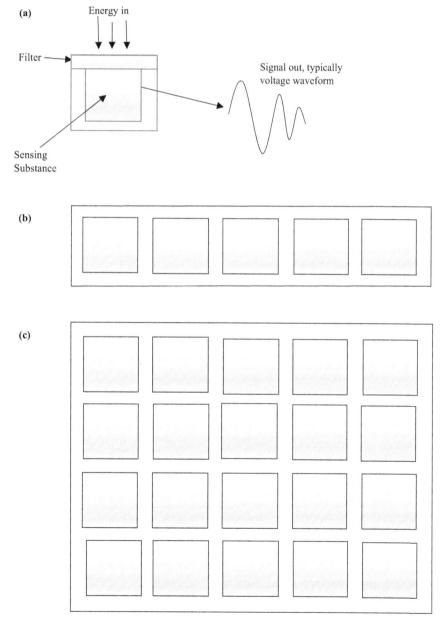

FIGURE 1.4-9
Generic imaging sensors. (a) Single imaging sensor, the filter is used to allow the sensor to respond to specific wavelengths of light, (b) linear or line sensor and (c) two-dimensional or array sensor.

metal-oxide-semiconductor (CMOS) device. An image sensor may have a filter so that it will respond only to specific wavelengths of light corresponding to colors such as red, green or blue.

These devices are packaged in arrays of up to about 10k×8k elements (80 megapixels), and they continue to get larger as technology advances. Currently, the CMOS image sensors are faster, cheaper and require less power than the CCDs, but the image quality is not quite as good as CCDs. This makes the CMOS sensors attractive for mass market applications where cost is a factor, low power is desired and lower-quality images are acceptable, such as with inexpensive cell phones and toys. However, the quality of CMOS sensors is improving, so they are being used more in industrial and scientific applications that have more stringent requirements.

When light energy (photonic energy) impinges upon the sensor, the sensing substance will output electrons to form electrical energy. We can approximate the number of electrons liberated in a sensor with the following *sensor equation*:

$$N = \delta A \delta t \int b(\lambda)q(\lambda)d\lambda \qquad (1.4\text{-}6)$$

where N is the approximate number of electrons liberated, δA is the area, δt is the time interval, $q(\lambda)$ is the quantum efficiency and $b(\lambda)$ is the incident photon flux, and the integration takes place over the wavelengths of interest. The *quantum efficiency* of the material is the ratio of the electron flux produced to the incident photon flux; in other words, it is the amount of incoming light energy that is converted to electrical energy. Older tube technology devices had a quantum efficiency of about 5%, and modern solid-state devices may vary from about 60% to 95% efficiency, depending on the wavelength.

Equation (1.4-6) shows that light energy is measured over a finite area, δA, and a finite time interval, δt; thus, these measurements cannot be performed instantaneously. This is because the devices measuring the signal are not sensitive enough to count only a few electrons, and even if they did, the signal would be overwhelmed by random noise which exists in electronic systems. One bonus of these requirements is that some of the noise will be averaged out by measuring across a time interval and a fixed area.

The two primary sources of noise in a typical CCD camera are dark current and photon noise. *Dark current* consists of thermally induced electrons generated by temperature (heat) and not by impinging photons. It is particularly problematic in low-light and long-exposure applications, which is the reason for nitrogen cooling in many scientific applications requiring extremely precise measurements. *Photon noise* refers to the random nature of photonic emission specified by the quantum properties of light energy, and it is related to the square root of the signal strength.

1.4.2 Imaging Outside the Visible Range of the EM Spectrum

Imaging with gamma rays is performed by measuring the rays as they are emitted from the object. In nuclear medicine using positron emission tomography (PET), a patient is injected with a radioactive isotope, and as it decays, gamma rays are detected and measured. X-rays are used in medical diagnostics by using film that responds to X-ray energy. The X-rays are passed through the patient and recorded on the film. X-rays are also used in computerized tomography (CT), where a ring of detectors encircles the patient and is rotated to obtain two-dimensional "slices" which can be assembled into a three-dimensional image. Fluorescence microscopy works by using dyes that emit visible light when UV light is beamed upon it. Examples of X-ray and UV images are shown in Figure 1.4-10.

UV imaging is used in industrial applications, law enforcement, microscopy and astronomy. Reflected UV imaging is used in forensics to find evidence that is invisible to the human visual system. For example, fingerprints, body fluids, bite marks and even shoe prints on waxed floors have been found. Since these systems use UV illumination, the background elements in the image are suppressed, which is an advantage for these types of applications. These systems use short UV, below 300 nm wavelengths, and have the added benefit of not requiring powders or chemicals on non-porous surfaces.

IR imaging can be used in any application with the need for temperature information, such as medical applications, satellite imaging, weather analysis, firefighting or fault analysis in industrial systems. IR images are often used in satellite imaging (remote sensing), since features of interest, for example, moisture content and mineral mapping, are found in the IR spectral bands (Figure 1.4-11). IR imaging is also used in law enforcement and fire detection, primarily in the middle and long wave ranges. IR images can be divided into four primary spectral ranges – near IR, 780 nm–1.3 μm; middle wave IR, 3–5 μm; long wave IR, 7–14 μm; and very long wave IR, 30 μm and above. Recent advances in technology have dramatically reduced size, power consumption and cost of these IR units thereby making these devices much more widely available, more practical and more cost effective.

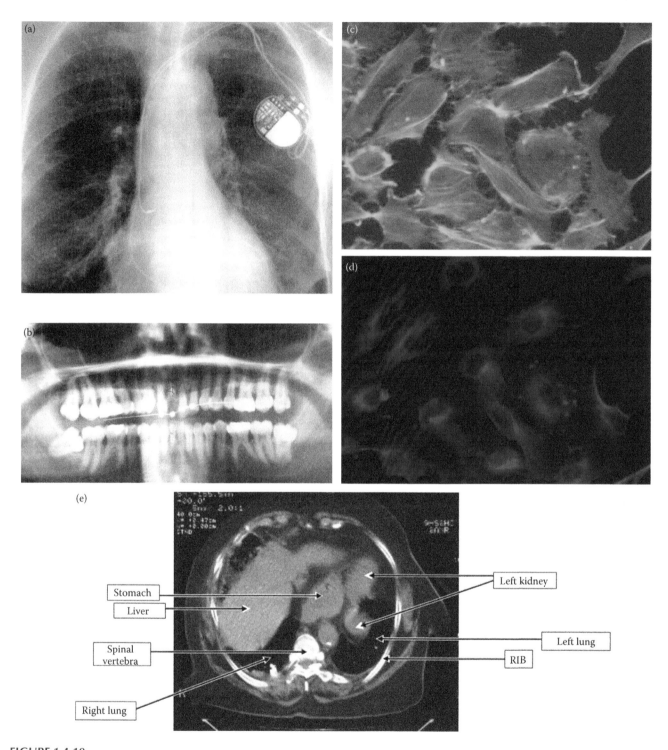

FIGURE 1.4-10

X-ray and UV images. (a) X-ray of a chest with an implanted electronic device to assist the heart. (Image courtesy of George Dean.) (b) Dental X-ray. (c) and (d) Fluorescence microscopy images of cells, generated by emitting visible light when illuminated by ultraviolet (UV) light. (Cell images courtesy of Sara Sawyer, SIUE.) (e) One "slice" of a computerized tomography (CT) image of a patient's abdomen, multiple 2-D image "slices" are taken at various angles and are then assembled to create a 3-D image. (Image courtesy of George Dean.)

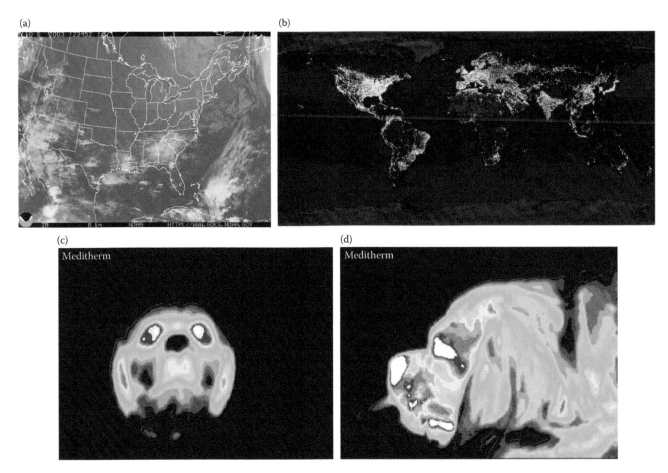

FIGURE 1.4-11
Infrared images. (a) Infrared satellite image showing water vapor. (b) Infrared satellite imagery in the near infrared band. (Images courtesy of National Oceanic and Atmospheric Administration (NOAA).) (c) and (d) Thermographic images being used in research to determine their efficacy in diagnosing brain diseases in canines. (Images courtesy of Long Island Veterinary Specialists.)

A recent area for application research is the use of IR imaging for diagnostic purposes in both animals and humans; this type of imaging is called *thermographic imaging*. It is believed that the temperature variation and thermographic patterns in living creatures can be useful in the diagnosis of various pathologies (diseases). Figure 1.4-11c and d shows thermographic images which are currently being used to determine their efficacy in diagnosing the Chiari malformation, a brain disease, in canines.

Multispectral images, which include IR bands, are often used in weather analysis (Figure 1.4-12a). Microwave images are used most often in radar applications, where the primary requirement is the capability to acquire information even through clouds or other obstacles, regardless of lighting conditions. In the radio band of the EM spectrum, applications are primarily in astronomy and medicine. In astronomy, radio waves can be detected and measured in a manner similar to collecting visible light information, except that the sensor responds to radio wave energy.

In medicine, MRI works by sending radio waves through a patient in short pulses in the presence of a powerful magnetic field. The body responds to these pulses by emitting radio waves, which are measured to create an image of any part of the patient's body (Figure 1.4-12b). MRI systems use a special antenna (receiver coil) to detect these interactions between radio-frequency EM and atomic nuclei in the patient's body. The superconducting magnets used in MRI systems can generate fields with magnitudes from 0.1 to 3.0 Tesla (1,000 to 30,000 Gauss). By comparison, the magnetic field of the Earth is 0.00005 Tesla (0.5 Gauss). MRI systems have excellent contrast resolution, which means they are much better at showing subtle differences among the soft tissues and organs of the body that are not easily viewed on conventional X-ray or CT films.

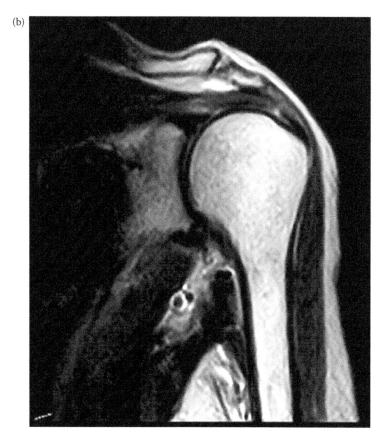

FIGURE 1.4-12
Multispectral and radio wave images. (a) Multispectral Geostationary Operational Environmental Satellite (GOES) image of North America, showing a large tropical storm off Baja California, a frontal system over the Midwest and tropical storm Diana off the east coast of Florida. (Courtesy of NOAA.) (b) Magnetic resonance image (MRI) of a patient's shoulder, MRI images are created using radio waves, this is a single 2-D "slice", multiple images are taken at different angles and assembled to create a 3-D image. (Image Courtesy of George Dean.)

1.4.3   Acoustic Imaging

Acoustic imaging operates by sending out pulses of sonic energy (sound) at various frequencies and then measuring the reflected waves. The time it takes for the reflected signal to appear contains distance information, and the amount of energy reflected contains information about the object's density and material. The measured information is then used to create a two- or three-dimensional image. Acoustic imaging is used in biological systems, for example, bats use it to "see", and in man made systems such as the sonar used in submarines.

The frequency of the acoustic signals depends on the application and the medium in which the signal is transmitted. Geological applications, for example, oil and mineral exploration, typically use low-frequency sounds – around hundreds of hertz. Ultrasonic, or high-frequency sound, imaging is often used in manufacturing and in medicine. One common use in medicine is to follow the development of the unborn baby inside the womb. Here, at frequencies ranging from 1 to 5 megahertz, the health and gender of the baby can be determined (see Figure 1.4-13). Because

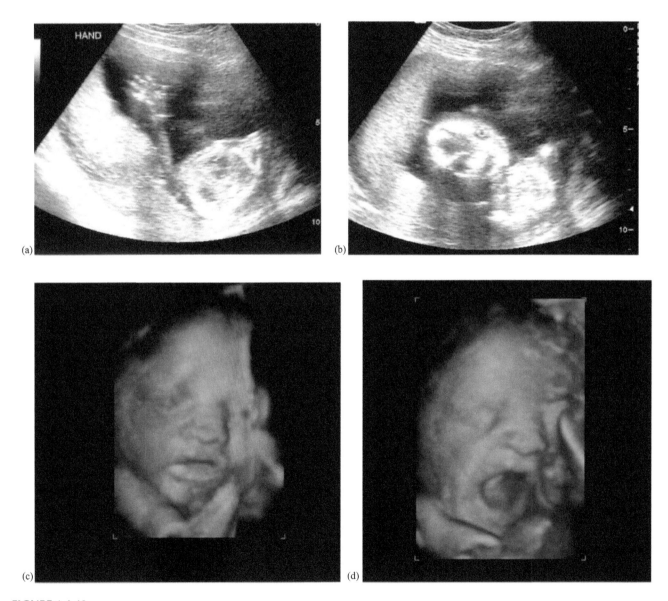

FIGURE 1.4-13
Ultrasound images. (a) Standard ultrasound image of a baby showing the head, arm and body, (b) standard ultrasound image showing face and eyes, (c) newer 3-D ultrasound image showing baby face and arm and (d) 3-D ultrasound of baby yawning. (Images courtesy of Kayla and Aaron Szczeblewski.)

ultrasonic imaging allows us to "see" inside opaque objects, it is also commonly used in manufacturing to detect defects in materials.

1.4.4 Electron Imaging

Electron microscopes are used in applications which require extremely high magnification. Standard light microscopes can magnify up to two thousand times, but electron microscopes can magnify up to ten *million* times. These microscopes function by producing a focused beam of electrons, which is used to image a specimen similar to the way a light beam is used in a standard microscope. These microscopes come in two types: transmission electron microscope (TEM) and scanning electron microscope (SEM). TEMs typically can magnify up to an order of magnitude greater than SEMs.

A TEM works by transmitting a beam of electrons through the specimen and then projecting the results onto a screen for viewing. A SEM, as the name implies, scans the electronic beam across the specimen and detects various signals generated by the electrons interacting with the specimen and uses these to produce an image. A TEM requires extremely thin specimens, around 100 nm, which is a limitation not found with a SEM. The SEM can scan objects many centimeters in size, and along with a greater depth of field, it allows for generation of three-dimensional images of scanned objects. Figure 1.4-14 shows a SEM and sample images.

1.4.5 Laser Imaging

Lasers (*l*ight *a*mplification by *s*timulated *e*mission of *r*adiation) are specialized light sources that produce a narrow light beam in the visible, IR or UV range of the EM spectrum. In standard light sources, such as light bulbs, the atoms do not cooperate as they emit photons; they behave in a random or chaotic manner which produces *incoherent* light. Lasers are designed so that all the atoms cooperate (all the waves are in phase), which produces a *coherent* light source that is highly intense and monochromatic (one color). Thus, lasers, first developed in the 1960s, provide a method of controlling visible light energy in a manner similar to that in which radio waves and microwaves can be controlled.

Lasers are often used to create *range* images (also called *depth maps*) which contain information about the distance of a point in the world to the image sensor. One of the methods for this involves using structured lighting, which can be generated with a laser and two rotating mirrors. Special lenses of cylindrical shape can also be used to create a plane of light so that only one rotating mirror is needed. These techniques will not work for objects which are highly reflective, unless the sensor happens to be in the direction of the surface normal (perpendicular), since the light will not be reflected back to the sensor.

Another approach is to measure time-of-flight, that is, how long does it take a transmitted signal to be return? As in radar imaging, a transmitter and a receiver are required, and the time it takes for a signal to be sent, reflected and received is measured. Various types of signals are used, including pulses, amplitude-modulated (AM) phase shift and frequency-modulated (FM) beat signals.

1.4.6 Computer-Generated Images

Images are not always generated by sensing real-world objects; for example, computers can be used to create images for a myriad of applications. These include computer-generated models for engineering, medicine and education, computer graphics for movies, art and games, and many other applications. In engineering, computer-generated models are used in design and drafting, while in medicine, they are used for surgical planning and training. Three-dimensional computer-generated simulations are also created for training pilots in both military and commercial aviation. The quality of computer-generated images has improved dramatically in the past several years as a result of advancements in technology and applied research in computer graphics. Computer graphics images are shown in Figure 1.4-15a and b.

Images are also created by computers as a result of applying image processing methods to images of real-world objects. For example, the output of an edge detection operation (Figure 1.4-15c), a Fourier transform spectrum (Figure 1.4-15d), pseudocolor applied to an X-ray image (Figure 1.4-15e) or an error image from a compression scheme (Figure 1.4-15f) can all be thought of as computer-generated images which use the original real-world image as a model. Any image that has been remapped for display is, in a sense, a computer-generated image since the image as viewed is not really the data itself but a representation of the underlying image data.

FIGURE 1.4-14

Electron microscope images. (a) Scanning electron microscope (SEM). SEM image of a (b) mosquito (c) logic gate in a microchip, (d) strawberry (e) brittlestar and (f) hollyhock pollen. (Photos courtesy of Sue Eder, Southern Illinois University Edwardsville.)

(a)

(b)

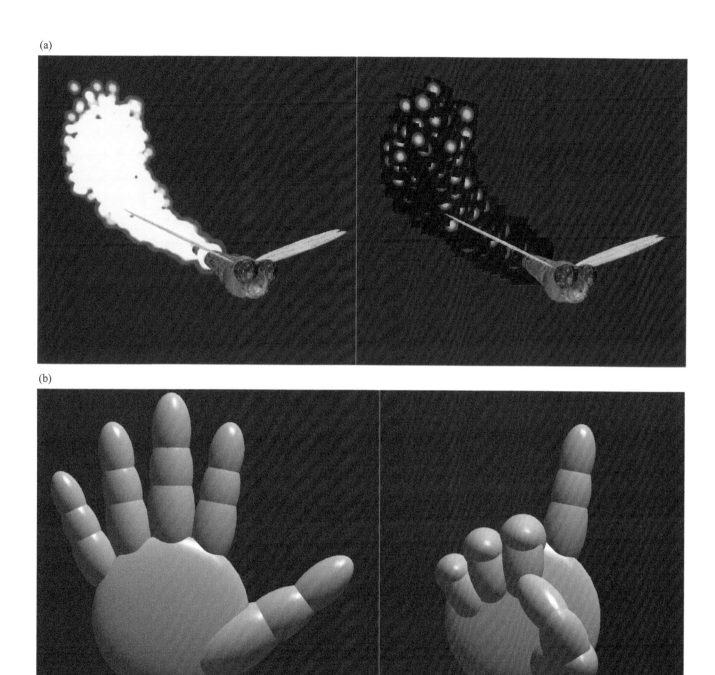

FIGURE 1.4-15

Computer-generated images. (a) Graphics image of an insect that employs a particle system to simulate a plume of fire, the right image shows the individual particles are texture-mapped squares. (b) Graphics image of a simple 3-D hand where each section of the hand is a sphere, the right image shows the hand after rotating the joints to produce a specific gesture.

(Continued)

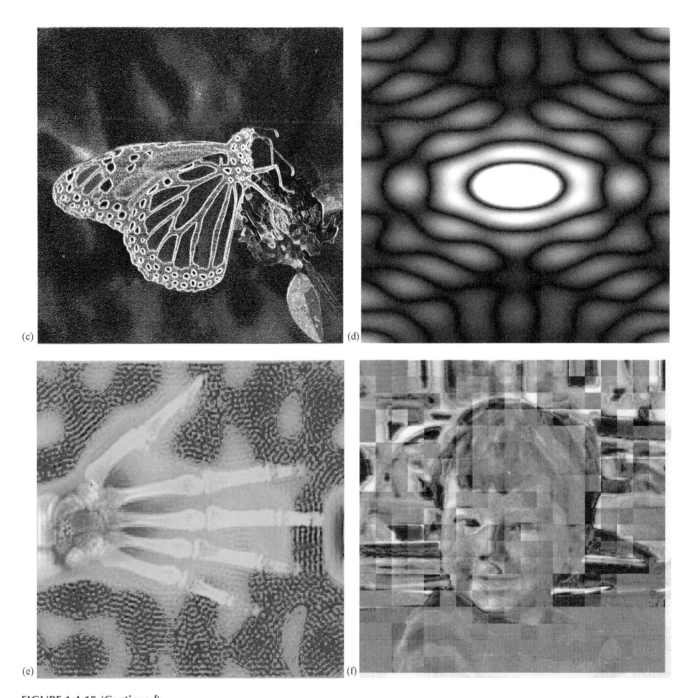

FIGURE 1.4-15 (*Continued*)
(c) An image of a butterfly processed by edge detection (see Chapter 4). (d) Fourier transform spectrum image of an ellipse. (e) X-ray image of a hand processed by frequency domain pseudocolor. (f) Error image from an image compressed with block truncation coding. (Graphics images courtesy of William White, Southern Illinois University Edwardsville; original butterfly photo courtesy of Mark Zuke.)

1.5 Image Representation

Imaging sensors receive an input image as a collection of spatially distributed light energy; this form is called an *optical image*. Optical images are what we see – cameras capture them, monitors display them and we act on them. These optical images can be represented as video information in the form of analog electrical signals, and they are sampled to generate the digital image $I(r, c)$.

The digital image, $I(r, c)$, is represented as a two-dimensional array of data, where each pixel value corresponds to the brightness of the image at the point (r, c). In linear algebra terms, a two-dimensional array like our image model, $I(r, c)$, is referred to as a *matrix*, and one row or column is called a *vector*. This image model is for monochrome ("one color"), or gray-scale, image data, but there are other types of image data that require extensions or modifications to this model. Typically, these are multiband images, such as color and multispectral, and they can be modeled by a different $I(r, c)$ function corresponding to each separate band of brightness information. The image types we will consider are (1) binary, (2) gray-scale, (3) color and (4) multispectral.

1.5.1 Binary Images

Binary images are the simplest type of images, and they can take on two values, typically black and white or "0" and "1". A binary image is referred to as a 1-bit-per-pixel image, because it takes only 1 binary digit to represent each pixel. These types of images are most frequently used in computer vision applications where the only information required for the task is general shape, or outline, information. Examples include positioning a robotic gripper to grasp an object, checking a manufactured object for shape deformations, transmission of facsimile (FAX) images or in optical character recognition (OCR).

Binary images are often created from gray-scale images via a threshold operation, where every pixel above the threshold value is turned white ("1") and those below the threshold are turned black ("0"). Although in this process much information is lost, the resulting image file is much smaller making it easier to store and transmit. In Figure 1.5-1, we see examples of binary images. Figure 1.5-1a is a page of text, which might be used in an OCR application; Figure 1.5-1b is created by performing a threshold operation on a monochrome image; and in Figure 1.5-1c are the results of an edge detection operation (see Section 4.2).

1.5.2 Gray-Scale Images

Gray-scale images are referred to as monochrome ("one color") images. They contain brightness information only, but not color information. The number of bits used for each pixel determines the number of different brightness levels available. The typical image contains 8-bit-per-pixel data, which allows for 256 different brightness (gray) levels, values of 0–255. This representation provides more than adequate brightness resolution, in terms of the human visual system's requirements, and provides a "noise margin" by allowing for approximately twice as many gray levels as required. This noise margin is useful in real-world applications due to many different types of noise, or false information in the signal, that is inherent in real systems. Additionally, the 8-bit representation is typical due to the fact that the *byte*, which corresponds to 8 bits of data, is the standard small unit in the world of digital computers. Figure 1.5-2 shows typical monochrome, gray-scale, or gray-level, images.

In applications requiring higher brightness resolution, such as medical imaging or astronomy, 12- or 16-bit-per-pixel representations are used. These extra brightness levels only become useful when the image is "blown up" or zoomed, that is, a small section of the image is made much larger. In this case, small details may be discernable that would be missing without this additional brightness resolution. Of course, to be useful, this also requires a higher level of spatial resolution, which means more samples for the same area and more pixels. Beyond these levels of brightness resolution, the light energy is typically divided into different bands, where each *band* refers to a specific subsection of the visible image spectrum. In these cases, the image may be referenced in terms of pixels-per-band or total number of bits per pixel.

1.5.3 Color Images

Color images can be modeled as three-band monochrome image data, where each band of data corresponds to a different color. The actual information stored in the digital image data is the brightness information in each spectral band. When the image is displayed, the corresponding brightness information is displayed on the screen by

(a)   (b)

```
wht2d(3)                    C Library Functions                    wht2d(3)

NAME
     wht2d - performs Walsh or Hadamard transform

SYNOPSIS
     #include <stdio.h>
     #include <stdlib.h>
     #include <math.h>
     #include "CVIPtools.h"
     #include "CVIPimage.h"
     #include "CVIPdef.h"

     IMAGE *wht2d(IMAGE *in_IMAGE, int ibit, int block_size)

     <in_IMAGE> - pointer to an IMAGE structure
     <ibit> - 0=inverse Walsh transform, 1=Walsh transform
              2=inverse Hadamard transform, 3=Hadamard transform
     <block_size> - block size (4,8,16,...largest_dimension/2)

PATH
     $CVIPHOME/TRANSFORMS/wht2d.c

DESCRIPTION
     This function performs a fast Hadamard-ordered Walsh-
     Hadamard Transform on an image. The result is then reor-
     dered for display in sequence order. The routine works on
     any image with dimensions that are powers of 2. Optional
     zero-padding may be performed if input image has different
     dimensions.
```

(c)

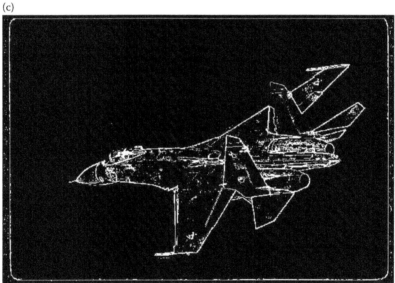

FIGURE 1.5-1
Binary images. (a) Binary text, (b) image created by a threshold operation (c) edge detection and threshold operation.

picture elements that emit light energy corresponding to that particular color. Typical color images are represented as red, green and blue or RGB images. Using the 8-bit monochrome standard as a model, the corresponding color image has 24-bit per pixel – 8 bits for each of the three color bands: red, green and blue. Figure 1.5-3a shows the three individual color bands of a typical RGB color image. Figure 1.5-3b shows the image bands combined to create the color image, and Figure 1.5-3c illustrates that, in addition to referring to a row or column of an image as a vector, a single pixel's red, green and blue values are referred to as a *color pixel vector* – (R, G, B). Note that in commercial software, the spectral *bands* of an RGB color image are often referred as color *channels*.

For many applications, RGB color information is transformed into a mathematical space that decouples the brightness information from the color information; this transformation is referred as a *color model*, a *color transform* or mapping into another *color space*. These color transforms can be accessed in CVIPtools via *Utilities→Convert→Color Space*. After application of a color transform, the image information consists of a one-dimensional brightness, or luminance, space and a two-dimensional color space. Now, the two-dimensional color space does not contain any brightness information, but typically contains information regarding the relative

(a)   (b)

FIGURE 1.5-2
Monochrome, gray-scale or gray-level images. (a and b) These images are typically 8-bit per pixel for a total of 256 brightness values (0–255). In some applications requiring higher brightness resolution, such as medical imaging or astronomy, 12- or 16-bit-per-pixel representations are used.

amounts of different colors. An additional benefit of modeling the color information in this manner is that it creates a more people-oriented way of describing the colors.

For example, the Hue/Saturation/Lightness (HSL) color transform allows for a description of colors in terms that is more readily understandable (see Figure 1.5-4). The *lightness*, also referred to as *intensity* or *value*, is the brightness of the color, and the *hue* is what is normally thought of as "color", for example, green, blue or orange. The *saturation* is a measure of the amount of white in the color; for example, pink is red with more white, so it is less saturated than a pure red. Most people can relate to this method of describing color, for example, "a deep, bright orange" has a large intensity ("bright"), a hue of "orange" and a high value of saturation ("deep"). We can picture this color in our minds, but if the color is defined in terms of its RGB components, $R = 245$, $G = 110$ and $B = 20$, most people have no idea how this color appears. Since the HSL color space was developed based on heuristics relating to human perception, various methods are available to transform RGB pixel values into the HSL color space. Most of these are algorithmic in nature and are geometric approximations to mapping the RGB color cube into some HSL-type color space (see Figure 1.5-5). Equations for mapping RGB to *HSL* are given below. These equations assume that the red, green and blue values are normalized to lie between 0 and 1. The normalization is often done by dividing the red, green and blue values by their sum, but other normalization methods are possible, for example, dividing by the maximum of (R, G, B). The max and min values in the equations below are, respectively, the largest and smallest of the red, green and blue normalized values:

$$\text{Hue} = \begin{cases} 0 & \text{if max} = \text{min} \\ 60° \times \dfrac{g-b}{\text{max}-\text{min}} + 360° & \text{if max} = r \\ 60° \times \dfrac{b-r}{\text{max}-\text{min}} + 120° & \text{if max} = g \\ 60° \times \dfrac{r-g}{\text{max}-\text{min}} + 240° & \text{if max} = b \end{cases} \qquad (1.5\text{-}1)$$

FIGURE 1.5-3
Color image representation. (a) A typical color image can be thought of as three separate images: $I_R(r, c)$, $I_G(r, c)$ and $I_B(r)$, one for each of the red, green and blue color bands. (b) the three color bands combined into a single color image. (c) A color pixel vector consists of the red, green and blue pixel values (R, G, B) at one given row/column pixel coordinate (r, c). (Original image courtesy of Scott R. Smith.)

$$\text{Lightness} = L = \frac{1}{2}\left(\text{max} + \text{min}\right) \tag{1.5-2}$$

$$\text{Saturation} = \begin{cases} 0 & \text{if max} = \text{min} \\ \dfrac{\text{max} - \text{min}}{\text{max} + \text{min}} = \dfrac{\text{max} - \text{min}}{2L} & \text{if } L \leq 1/2 \\ \dfrac{\text{max} - \text{min}}{2 - \left(\text{max} + \text{min}\right)} = \dfrac{\text{max} - \text{min}}{2 - 2L} & \text{if } L > 1/2 \end{cases} \tag{1.5-3}$$

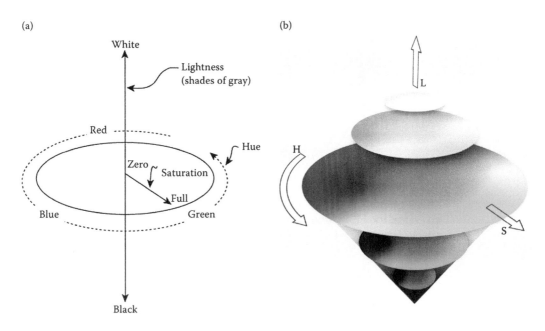

FIGURE 1.5-4
HSL color space. (a) Schematic representation of the HSL color space and (b) color representation of the HSL color space.

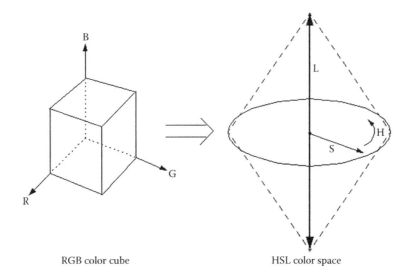

FIGURE 1.5-5
RGB to HSL mapping.

Note that if the maximum and minimum RGB values are equal, then the concepts of hue and saturation are not meaningful because the "color" is gray – it is essentially a monochrome pixel, so hue and saturation are set equal to 0. In other cases, the value of hue is usually found modulo 360° to lie between 0° and 360° (or 0 and 2π radians). However, in typical image formats, these values are remapped to the 8-bit range of 0–255. For HSV color spaces, the equation for *hue* is the same as in HSL conversion, *saturation* is similar, but the *value* parameter, *V*, equation is given by the maximum of the red, green and blue values.

Another similar color transform is the HSI, hue, saturation and intensity, color space. Equations for mapping RGB to HSI are given below:

$$H = \begin{cases} \theta & \text{if } B \le G \\ 360 - \theta & \text{if } B > G \end{cases} \tag{1.5-4}$$

where

$$\theta = \cos^{-1}\left\{\frac{\frac{1}{2}[(R-G)+(R-B)]}{[(R-G)^2+(R-B)(G-B)]^{1/2}}\right\}$$

$$S = 1 - \frac{3}{(R+G+B)}[\min(R,G,B)] \tag{1.5-5}$$

$$I = \frac{(R+G+B)}{3} \tag{1.5-6}$$

These equations assume that the *R, G* and *B* values are normalized to lie between 0 and 1, and θ is measured in degrees from the red axis. Converting the HSI values back into the RGB coordinates requires consideration of three different sectors in the color space, namely Red-Green (RG), Green-Blue (GB) and Blue-Red sectors. The following equations apply:

RG Sector ($0° \leq H < 120°$)

$$R = I\left[1 + \frac{S\cos(H)}{\cos(60°-H)}\right] \tag{1.5-7}$$

$$G = 3I - (R+B) \quad \left(\text{note: find } R \text{ and } B \text{ first}\right) \tag{1.5-8}$$

$$B = I(1-S) \tag{1.5-9}$$

GB Sector ($120° < H < 240°$)

$$R = I(1-S) \tag{1.5-10}$$

$$G = I\left[1 + \frac{S\cos(H-120°)}{\cos(180°-H)}\right] \tag{1.5-11}$$

$$B = 3I - (R+G) \tag{1.5-12}$$

BR Sector($240° \leq H \leq 360°$)

$$R = 3I - (G+B) \quad \left(\text{note: find } G \text{ and } B \text{ first}\right) \tag{1.5-13}$$

$$G = I(1-S) \tag{1.5-14}$$

$$B = I\left[1 + \frac{S\cos(H-240°)}{\cos(300°-H)}\right] \tag{1.5-15}$$

A color transform can be based on a geometrical coordinate mapping, such as the spherical or cylindrical transforms. With the spherical transform, the RGB color space will be mapped to a one-dimensional brightness space and a two-dimensional color space. The spherical coordinate transform (SCT) has been successfully used in a color segmentation algorithm described in Chapter 5. The equations mapping the RGB to SCT components are as follows:

$$L = \sqrt{R^2 + G^2 + B^2}$$

$$\angle A = \cos^{-1}\left[\frac{B}{L}\right] \tag{1.5-16}$$

$$\angle B = \cos^{-1}\left[\frac{R}{L\sin(\angle A)}\right]$$

where L is the length of the RGB vector, angle A is the angle from the blue axis to the RG-plane and angle B is the angle between the R and G axes. Here, L contains the brightness information and the two angles contain the color information (see Figure 1.5-6).

The cylindrical coordinate transform (CCT) is different than most color mappings because it does not completely decouple brightness from color information. With this transform, the z-axis can be aligned along the R, G or B axis; the choice will be application dependent. The cylindrical coordinates are found as follows, assuming the z-axis aligned along the blue axis:

$$z = B$$

$$d = \sqrt{R^2 + G^2} \tag{1.5-17}$$

$$\theta = \tan^{-1}\left(\frac{G}{R}\right)$$

The CCT may be useful in applications where one of the RGB colors is of primary importance, since it can be mapped directly to the z component, and where the ratio of the other two is significant. Here, the brightness information is now contained in the d and z coordinates, while the color information is still distributed across all three components, but in a different manner than with the original RGB data. This is illustrated in Figure 1.5-7, where we can see that θ is related to hue in the RG-plane and d is related to the saturation in the RG-plane.

One problem associated with the color spaces previously described is that they are not perceptually uniform. This means that two different colors in one part of the color space will not exhibit the same degree of perceptual difference as two colors in another part of the color space, even though they are the same "distance" apart

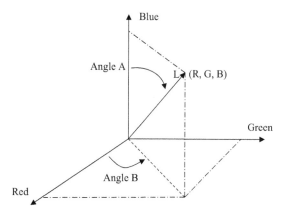

FIGURE 1.5-6
Spherical coordinate transform (SCT). The SCT separates the red, green and blue information into a 2-D color space defined by the angles A and B, and a 1-D brightness space defined by L, the (R,G,B) vector length.

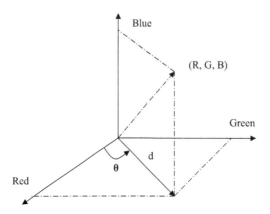

FIGURE 1.5-7
Cylindrical coordinates transform.

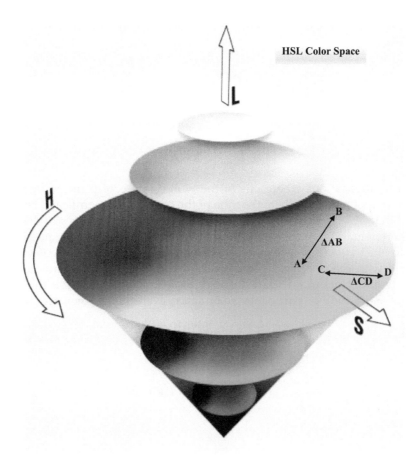

FIGURE 1.5-8
Color perception. Color A may be green, and color B may be orange. Colors C and D may be slightly different shades of green, but ΔCD = ΔAB. In this case, we have two pairs of colors with the same "color difference", but the perceptual difference is much greater for one pair than the other.

(see Figure 1.5-8). Therefore, a distance metric cannot be defined to determine how close, or far apart, two colors are in terms of human perception. In image processing applications, a perceptually uniform color space is very useful.

For example, in the identification of objects by color information, we need some method to compare the object's color to a database of the colors of the available objects. Or in the development of a new image compression algorithm, we need a way to determine if one color can be mapped to another without losing significant information.

The science of color and how the human visual system perceives color has been studied extensively by an international body, the *Commission Internationale de l'eclairage* (CIE or International Commission on Illumination). The CIE has defined internationally recognized color standards. One of the basic concepts developed by the CIE involves chromaticity coordinates. For our RGB color space, *chromaticity coordinates* are defined as follows:

$$r = \frac{R}{R+G+B}$$

$$g = \frac{G}{R+G+B} \tag{1.5-18}$$

$$b = \frac{B}{R+G+B}$$

These equations basically normalize the individual color components to the sum of the three, which is one way to represent the brightness information. This decouples the brightness information from the coordinates, and the CIE uses chromaticity coordinates as the basis of the color transforms they define. These include the standard CIE XYZ color space and the perceptually uniform $L^*u^*v^*$, $L^*a^*b^*$ color spaces. The science of color and human perception is a fascinating topic and can be explored in greater depth with the references.

Another important international committee for developing standards of interest to those involved in image processing is the International Telecommunications Union Radio (ITU-R, previously CCIR). This committee has specified the standard for digital video known as ITU-R 601. This standard is based on one *luminance* signal (Y) and two color difference signals (C_R and C_B). Given a 24-bit RGB signal, we can find Y, C_R and C_B values as follows:

$$Y = 0.299R + 0.587G + 0.114B$$

$$C_B = 0.564(B-Y) + 128 = -0.1687R - 0.3313G + 0.5B + 128 \tag{1.5-19}$$

$$C_R = 0.713(R-Y) + 128 = 0.5R - 0.4187G - 0.0813B + 128$$

The 128 offset factor is included here to maintain the data range of [0–255] for 8-bit per color band data. This transform is used in many color image compression algorithms, such as MPEG and JPEG, implemented in both hardware and software. This transform is also called YUV encoding and is defined as follows:

$$Y = 0.299R + 0.587G + 0.114B$$

$$U = 0.493(B-Y) \tag{1.5-20}$$

$$V = 0.877(R-Y)$$

Note that the 128 offset value for U and V can be added to these equations, if desired.

All the previous color transforms are based on an additive color model such as RGB, modeled as adding red, green or blue light to a black background. For color printing, a subtractive color model is used. Here, the model subtracts cyan, magenta or yellow (CMY) from white, such as printing on white paper illuminated by white light. The model for white light is that it consists of red, green and blue. The CMY conversion from RGB is defined as follows – these equations assume that the *RGB* values are normalized to the range of 0–1:

$$C = 1 - R$$

$$M = 1 - G \tag{1.5-21}$$

$$Y = 1 - B$$

Cyan absorbs red light, magenta absorbs green and yellow absorbs blue. Thus, to print a normalized RGB triple that appears green, (0, 1, 0), CMY (1, 0, 1) are used. For this example, the cyan will absorb the red light and the yellow absorbs the blue light, leaving only the green light to be reflected and seen. Also, to print black, all three (CMY) inks are printed, and all the components of white light, RGB, will be absorbed. In practice, this produces a poor looking black, so black ink is added to the printing process leading to a four-color printing system, called CMYK.

The final color transform introduced here is the principal components transform. This mathematical transform allows us to apply statistical methods to put as much of the three-dimensional color information as possible into only one band. This process decorrelates the RGB data components. The *principal components transform* (PCT) works by examining all the RGB vectors within an image and finding the linear transform that aligns the coordinate axes so that most of the information is along one axis, the principal axis. Often, we can get 90% or more of the information into one band. The PCT is used in image segmentation (see Chapter 5) and for image compression.

1.5.4   Multispectral and Multiband Images

Multispectral images typically contain information outside the normal human perceptual range, as discussed in Section 1.4.2. They may include IR, UV, X-ray, microwave, and other bands in the EM spectrum. Multiband images may also include information from laser or acoustic signals. These are not images in the usual sense, since the information represented is not directly visible by the human visual system. However, the information is often represented in visual form by mapping the different spectral bands to RGB components. If more than three bands of information are in the multispectral/multiband image, the dimensionality is reduced for display by applying a PCT (see Chapter 5).

Sources for these types of images include satellite systems, underwater sonar systems, various types of airborne radar, IR imaging systems and medical diagnostic imaging systems. The number of bands into which the data is divided is strictly a function of the sensitivity of the imaging sensors used to capture the images. For example, even the visible spectrum can be divided into many more than three bands; three are used because this mimics the human visual system. The Landsat satellites currently in orbit collect image information in seven to eleven spectral bands; typically, three are in the visible spectrum and one or more in the IR region, and some have sensors that operate in the microwave range. Special-purpose satellites have sensors that collect image information in 30 or more bands. For example, the NASA/Jet Propulsion Laboratory Airborne Visible/Infrared Imaging Spectrometer (AVRIS) collects information in 224 spectral bands covering the wavelength region from 0.4 to 2.5 µm (400–2500 nm). As the quantity of data that needs to be transmitted, stored and processed increases, the importance of topics such as image segmentation and compression becomes more and more apparent.

1.5.5   Digital Image File Formats

Why do we need so many different types of image file formats? The short answer is that there are many different types of images and applications with varying requirements. A more complete answer also considers market share, proprietary information and a lack of coordination within the imaging industry. However, there have been standard file formats developed, and the ones presented here are widely available. Many other image types can be readily converted to one of the types presented here by easily available image conversion software.

A field related to computer vision is that of computer graphics. *Computer graphics* is a specialized field within the computer science realm which refers to the creation or reproduction of visual data through the use of the computer. This includes the creation of computer images for display or print, and the process of generating and manipulating any images (real or artificial) for output to a monitor, printer, camera or any other device that will provide an image. Computer graphics can be considered a part of image processing, insofar as many of the same tools the graphics artist uses may be used by the image processing specialist.

In computer graphics, types of image data are divided into two primary categories: bitmap and vector. *Bitmap images*, or *raster images*, can be represented by our image model, $I(r, c)$, where the pixel data and the corresponding brightness values are stored in a specified file format. *Vector images* refer to methods of representing lines, curves and shapes by storing only the key points. These *key points* are sufficient to define the shapes, and the process of turning these into an image is called *rendering*. Once the image has been rendered, it can be thought of as being in bitmap format, where each pixel has specific values associated with it.

Most of the types of file formats discussed are bitmap images, although some are compressed, so the $I(r, c)$ values are not directly available until the file is decompressed. In general, these types of images contain both header information and the pixel data itself. The *image file header* is a set of parameters normally found at the start of the file and must contain information regarding (1) the number of rows, height, (2) the number of columns, width, (3) the number of color or spectral bands, (4) the number of bits per pixel (bpp) and (5) the file type. Additionally, with some of the more complex file formats, the header may contain information about the type of compression used and any other necessary parameters to create the image, $I(r, c)$.

The simplest file formats are the BIN and the PNM file formats. The BIN format is simply the raw image data, $I(r, c)$. This file contains no header information, so the user must know the necessary parameters – size, number of bands and bits per pixel – to use the file as an image. The PNM formats are widely distributed and file conversion utilities are freely available (pbmplus and Netpbm), but used primarily in UNIX systems. They basically contain raw image data with the simplest header possible. The PPM format includes PBM (binary), PGM (gray-scale), PPM (color) and PNM (handles any of the previous types). The headers for these image file formats contain a "magic number" that identifies the file type, the image width and height, the number of bands and the maximum brightness value – determines the required number of bits per pixel for each band.

The Microsoft Windows bitmap (BMP) format is commonly used today in Windows-based machines. Most imaging and graphics programs in this environment support the BMP format. This file format is fairly simple, with basic headers followed by the raw image data. The most commonly used format is JPEG (Joint Photographic Experts Group), which is ubiquitous throughout the imaging industry. This file format is capable of high degrees of image compression, so it is typically used to reduce bandwidth requirements for transmission on the internet or storage requirements on your smart phone. JPEG files come in two main varieties, the original JPEG and the newer JPEG2000. The JPEG2000 file format provides higher compression ratios, while still maintaining high quality images, but is not used often due to its higher decompression time.

Two image file formats commonly used on many different computer platforms, as well as on the internet, are the TIFF (Tagged Image File Format) and GIF (Graphics Interchange Format) file formats. GIF files are limited to a maximum of 8-bit per pixel, and they allow for a type of compression called LZW (Lempel-Ziv-Welch). The 8-bit-per-pixel limitation does not mean it does not support color images, it simply means that no more than 256 colors (2^8) are allowed in an image. This is typically implemented by means of a look-up table (LUT), where the 256 colors are stored in a table and one byte (8 bits) is used as an index (address) into that table for each pixel (see Figure 1.5-9).

8-bit Index	Red	Green	Blue
0	R_0	G_0	B_0
1	R_1	G_1	B_1
2	R_2	G_2	B_2
⋮	⋮	⋮	⋮
254	R_{254}	G_{254}	B_{254}
255	R_{255}	G_{255}	B_{255}

FIGURE 1.5-9
Look-up table (LUT). One byte is stored for each color pixel in $I(r, c)$. When displayed, this 8-bit value is used as an index into the LUT, and the corresponding RGB values are displayed for that pixel.

The concept of LUT-based images is also referred to palette-based images. The GIF image header is 13 bytes long, and it contains the basic information required.

The TIFF file format is more sophisticated than GIF, and it has many more options and capabilities. TIFF files allow a maximum of 24 bits per pixel, and they support five types of compression, including RLE (run length encoding), LZW and JPEG. The TIFF header is of variable size and is arranged in a hierarchical manner. The TIFF format is one of the most comprehensive formats available and is designed to allow the user to customize it for specific applications.

Two formats that were initially computer specific, but became commonly used throughout the industry, are the Sun Raster and the SGI (Silicon Graphics, Inc.) file formats. As the Windows operating system has become more prevalent in the imaging industry, these two file formats are being used less often. The SGI format handles up to 16 million colors and supports RLE compression. The Sun Raster format is defined to allow for any number of bits per pixel, and it also supports RLE compression.

PNG, portable network graphics, is a file format that supports LUT-type images (1, 2, 4, 8-bit) like GIF, as well as full 24-bit color like TIFF. It provides direct support for color correction, which theoretically allows an image to look the same on different computer systems – although in practice this is quite difficult to achieve. The PICT format is unique to Apple computers, which are widely used in many imaging applications. However, Apple has switched to using the PDF (Portable Document Format) for images, so the PICT format is currently defunct and will only be found in legacy applications.

Encapsulated PostScript (EPS) is a graphics file format for vector images that has been commonly used in desktop publishing. EPS was designed to be directly supported by many printers (in the hardware itself), making it easy for data interchange across hardware and software platforms. Currently, the PDF or portable document format is used more commonly in publishing and also has the capability for use across multiple hardware and software platforms.

The final image file type discussed here is the VIP (Visualization in Image Processing) and the VIPM (VIP for MATLAB) format, developed specifically for the CVIPtools software. When performing image processing tasks, temporary images are often created that use floating point representations that are beyond the standard 8-bit-per-pixel capabilities of most display devices. The process of representing this type of data as an image is referred to as *data visualization*, and it can be achieved by remapping the data to the 8-bit range of 0–255. *Remapping* is the process of taking the original data and defining an equation to translate the original data to the output data range, typically 0–255 for 8-bit display. The two most commonly used methods in image processing are linear and logarithmic mapping. In Figure 1.5-10, we see a graphical representation and example of how this process is performed.

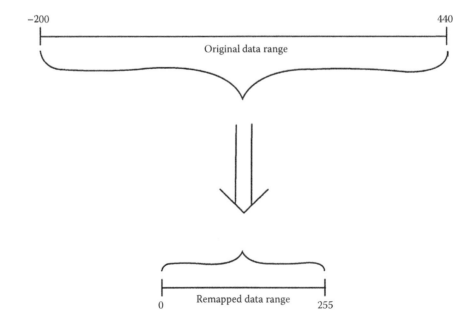

FIGURE 1.5-10
Remapping for display. When the data range for the pixel values in an image exceeds the bounds of a standard 8-bit (per band) image, it must be remapped for display. Typically, this is done with a linear remapping process. Note that data precision will be lost.

In this example, the original data ranges from –200 to 440. An equation is found that will map the lowest value (–200) to 0 and the highest value (440) to 255, while all the intermediate values are remapped to values within this range (0–255). This process may result in a loss of information.

The VIP/VIPM file format is required to support many non-standard image data formats. This format was defined to allow disk file support for the image data structure used within the CVIPtools software. It allows any data type, including floating point and complex numbers, any image size, any number of bands and contains a history data structure designed for keeping image-specific parameters.

1.6 Key Points

Digital image processing: the acquisition and processing of visual information by computer. It can be divided into two main application areas: (1) computer vision and (2) human vision, with image analysis being a key component of both.

Computer vision applications: imaging applications where the output images are for computer use.

Human vision applications: imaging applications where the output images are for human consumption.

Image analysis: the examination of image data to solve an imaging problem.

Image segmentation: used to find higher-level objects from raw image data.

Feature extraction: acquiring higher-level information, such as shape or texture of objects.

Image transforms: may be used in feature extraction to find spatial frequency information.

Pattern classification: used for identifying objects in an image.

CVIPtools: a comprehensive computer vision and image processing (CVIP) software package to allow for the exploration of image processing and analysis functions, including algorithm development for applications.

Digital Imaging Systems

Two primary components: hardware and software.

> **Hardware**: image acquisition, computer, display, printing and storage.

> **Software**: allows for image manipulation, processing and analysis.

Digital camera interface: USB, Camera Link or Gigabit Ethernet.

Frame grabber: special-purpose hardware that converts an analog video signal into a digital image.

RS-170A/RS-330/RS-343A: monochrome analog video standards used in North America.

NTSC: color analog video standard used in North America.

CCIR or PAL: color analog video standards used in northern Europe, Africa and Asia.

SECAM: color analog video standard used in Asia, Africa, Eastern Europe, France and Russia, a CCIR equivalent.

Frame: one screen of video information.

Field: alternating lines of video information creating one-half of a frame in interlaced video.

Interlaced video: two fields per frame video, used in television and video cameras.

Non-interlaced video: one field per frame video, also called *progressive scan.*

Horizontal synch pulse: control signal in the video signal that occurs between each line of video information.

Vertical synch pulse: control signal in the video signal that occurs between each field or frame of video information.

Digital television (DTV): two main categories: standard-definition television (SDTV) and high-definition television (HDTV).

HDTV standard formats: *720p* operates in progressive scan mode is 1,280 columns by 720 rows (lines); *1,080p*, progressive scan 1,920 columns by 1,080 rows; 1,080i is 1,920×1,080 in interlaced mode.

Ultra High Definition (UHD): *2,160p or 4K,* progressive scan is 3,840 pixels columns by 2,160 rows; *4,320p or 8K,* progressive scan is 7,680 pixels columns by 4,320 rows.

Aspect ratio: width to height ratio of the display device (Figure 1.3-4). SDTV uses a 4:3 aspect ratio, HDTV and UHD standards specify a 16:9 aspect ratio. Aspect ratio of 35 mm film cameras is 3:2, and standard digital cameras typically use 3:2 or 4:3.

$I(r, c)$. a two-dimensional array of data, the digital image function, a matrix where the brightness of the image at the point (r, c) is given, with r being row and c being column.

Image brightness: depends on both lighting conditions and the intrinsic object properties.

Hierarchical image pyramid: describes the various levels for processing of images (see Figure 1.3-5).

Image Formation and Sensing

Sensor: a device to measure a signal which can be converted into a digital image.

Electromagnetic (EM) spectrum: electromagnetic signals which, at various wavelengths, consist of gamma rays, X-rays, ultraviolet light, visible light, infrared, microwaves and radio waves, and they can be measured by sensors to produce images (see Figure 1.4-1).

Photon: massless particles which correspond to the minimum amount of energy, the quantum, can be measured in the EM signal.

Range image: created by radar, sonar or lasers to produce an image which depicts distance as brightness.

Image formation: two key components: (1) where will the image point appear, the row and column coordinates, and (2) what value will be assigned to that point, the brightness value.

Optics: the physics of light and the study of lenses, required to determine where an image point appears.

Reflectance function: defines how an object reflects light.

Irradiance: the amount of light energy falling on a surface, measured by a sensor to create an image.

Radiance: the amount of light energy emitted or reflected from an object into a solid unit angle.

Lens: necessary to focus light in an imaging system.

Focal length: designated as f in the lens equation, it is a fixed, intrinsic property of a lens and it is the distance from the lens that an object at infinity is focused.

Lens equation: $\dfrac{1}{a} + \dfrac{1}{b} = \dfrac{1}{f}$ (see Figure 1.4-5) Equation (1.4-2).

Blur equation: $c = \dfrac{d}{b'} |b - b'|$ (see Figure 1.4-6) Equation (1.4-3).

Depth of field: range of distances over which an object is focused sufficiently well.

Field of view (FOV): angle of the cone of directions from which the device will create the image.

Lens types – normal: FOV: 25°–45°; telephoto: FOV < 25°; and wide-angle: FOV > 45°.

Charge-coupled device (CCD): sensor used in digital cameras for imaging.

Complementary metal-oxide-semiconductor (CMOS) device: sensor used for imaging; image quality not as good as CCD, but cheaper and requires less power.

Quantum efficiency [$q(\lambda)$]: the ratio of the electron flux produced to the incident photon flux.

Sensor equation: $N = \delta A \delta t \int b(\lambda) q(\lambda) d\lambda$ Equation (1.4-6).

Dark current: thermally induced electrons, not from impinging photons, problem in low-light applications, nitrogen cooling in applications requiring extremely precise measurements.

Photon noise: random nature of photonic emission specified by the quantum properties of light energy, related to the square root of the signal.

Imaging outside of visible EM spectrum: used in medicine, astronomy, microscopy, satellite imaging, military, law enforcement and industrial applications.

Thermographic imaging: infrared (IR) imaging can be used in any application with the need for temperature information, such as medical applications, satellite imaging, weather analysis, firefighting or fault analysis in industrial systems.

Acoustic imaging: measures reflected sound waves, applications in medicine, military, geology and manufacturing.

Electron imaging: using a focused beam of electrons to magnify up to about ten million times.

Laser imaging: used to create range images.

Image Representation

Optical image: a collection of spatially distributed light energy to be measured by an image sensor to generate $I(r, c)$.

Binary image: a simple image type that can take on two values, typically black and white or "0" and "1".

Gray-scale image: monochrome or "one color" image that contains only brightness information, but no color information, and it is a one band image.

Color image: modeled as a three-band monochrome image; the three bands are typically red, green and blue or RGB. Red, green and blue spectral *bands* are often called color *channels* in commercial software.

Color pixel vector: a single pixel's values for a color image, (R, G, B).

Color transform/color model: a mathematical method or algorithm to map RGB data into another color space, typically to decouple brightness and color information.

   HSL (Hue/Saturation/Lightness): a color transform that describes colors in terms that we can easily relate to the human visual system's perception, where *hue* is the "color", for example, red or yellow, *saturation* is the amount of white in the color and *lightness* is the brightness.

   HSV (Hue/Saturation/Value): similar to HSL, but *Value* is the maximum of (R, G, B).

   HSI (Hue/Saturation/Intensity): similar to HSL, but *Intensity* is the average of (R, G, B).

   SCT (spherical coordinate transform): maps the color information into two angles and the brightness into the color vector length.

   CCT (cylindrical coordinate transform): does not completely decouple color and brightness, unlike most color transforms, definition tends to be application specific.

   Chromaticity coordinates: normalize RGB values to the sum of all three.

   CIE L*u*v*/CIE L*a*b*: perceptually uniform color spaces defined by the Commission Internationale de l'eclairage (CIE or International Commission on Illumination), the international standards group for color science.

   YUV/YC_BC_R: linear transforms of RGB data used in compression algorithms, Y is the luminance and the other two are color difference signals.

   CMY (Cyan, Magenta, Yellow)/CMYK: color transforms based on a subtractive model, used for color printing; K is added as a separate ink for black.

   PCT (principal components transform): decorrelates RGB data by finding a linear transform using statistical methods to align the coordinate axes along the path of maximal variance in the data (see Figure 5.3-5)

Multispectral/Multiband image: images of many bands containing information outside of the visible spectrum.

Digital Image File Formats

Bitmap images: images we can represent by our model, $I(r, c)$, also called raster images.

Vector images: artificially generated images by storing only mathematical descriptions of geometric shapes using *key points.*

Rendering: the process of turning a vector image into a bitmap image.

Image file header: a set of parameters normally found at the start of the image file and must contain information regarding (1) the number of rows (height), (2) the number of columns (width), (3) the number of bands, (4) the number of bits per pixel (bpp) and (5) the file type; additional information may be included.

Image file formats: BIN, PPM, PBM, PGM, BMP, JPEG, JPEG2000, TIFF, GIF, RAS, SGI, PNG, PICT, PDF, EPS, VIP, VIPM.

LUT: look-up table, used for storing RGB values for 8-bit color images.

1.7 References and Further Reading

Additional resources for computer vision include Szeliski (2022), Davies (2018), Forsyth and Ponce (2011), Shapiro/Stockman (2001), Granland and Knutsson (1995), Jain, Kasturi and Schnuck (1995), Haralick and Shapiro (1992), Horn (1986) and Ballard and Brown (1982). Comprehensive image processing texts include Gonzalez and Woods (2018), Trussell and Vrhel (2008), Pratt (2007), Bracewell (2004), Castleman (1996), Jain (1989) and Rosenfeld and Kak (1982).

Other books that bring computer vision and image processing together include Bhuyan (2019), Sonka, Hlavac and Boyle (2014), Schalkoff (1989), Granlund and Knutsson (1995) and Banks (1991). Books for practical algorithm implementation (including code) are Parker (2010), Burger and Burge (2008), Seul, Sammon and O'Gorman (2008), Baxes (1994) and Myler and Weeks (1993). Russ (2015) provides a good handbook for the image processing specialist. Some of the applications discussed can be found in the trade magazines *Biophotonics International, Design News, Photonics Spectra* and the *Journal of Forensic Identification*.

More information can be found on imaging in various EM spectral bands and on image acquisition devices in Nixon and Aguado (2020), Gonzalez and Woods (2018), Sinha (2012), Shapiro and Stockman (2001) and Sanchez and Canton (1999). Laser-based range images are discussed in more detail in Russ (2015) and Forsyth and Ponce (2011), and Gonzalez and Woods (2018) contain information regarding electron imaging. For further study of satellite imaging, see Weng (2012), Sanchez and Canton (1999), and for more information on UV and IR imaging in law enforcement, see Russ (2016) and Kummer (2003). More on lenses and optics can be found in Sinha (2012), Forsyth and Ponce (2011), Horn (1986) and Jain, Kasturi and Schunck (1995). More information on input and output devices for imaging can be found in Davies (2018), Trussell and Vrhel (2008) and Burdick (1997). For more on image sensors, types of noise and sampling, see Sinha (2012) and Szeliski (2022).

For further study of digital video processing, see Tekalp (2015), Orzessek and Sommer (1998) and Sid-Ahmed (1995). Tekalp (2015) has much information on motion estimation methods not available in other texts. For details on video standards and hardware, see Poynton (2012) and Jack (2001). For further study regarding color, see Szeliski (2022), Lee (2009), Jain (2009), Giorgianni and Madden (2009), Trussell and Vrhel (2008), Pratt (2007), Malacara (2001), Wyszecki and Stiles (1982) and Durrett (1987). For more information on JPEG2000, see Taubman and Marcellin (2002). For further study on computer-generated images, see Blundell (2008), Watt and Policarpo (1998), Foley, van Dam, Feiner, and Hughes (1995) and Hill (1990).

For other sources of software, see Gonzalez, Woods, and Eddins (2020), Parker (2010, Burger and Burge (2008), Seul, Sammon, and O'Gorman (2008), Myler and Weeks (1993), Baxes (1994) and Sid-Ahmed (1995). Also, the CVIPtools homepage (*cviptools.siue.edu*) has useful Internet links. Two sources for information on image and graphics file formats, which include code, are Burdick (1997) and Murray and VanRyper (1994).

Ballard, D.H., Brown, C.M., *Computer Vision*, Upper Saddle River, NJ: Prentice Hall, 1982.

Banks, S., *Signal Processing, Image Processing and Pattern Recognition*, Cambridge: Prentice Hall International (UK) Ltd., 1991.

Baxes, G.A., *Digital Image Processing: Principles and Applications*, New York: Wiley, 1994.

Bhuyan, M.K., *Computer Vision and Image Processing: Fundamentals and Applications*, Boca Raton, FL: CRC Press, 2019.

Blundell, B., *An Introduction to Computer Graphics and Creative 3-D Environments*, New York: Springer, 2008.

Bracewell, R.N., *Fourier Analysis and Imaging*, New York: Springer, 2004.

Burdick, H.E., *Digital Imaging: Theory and Applications*, New York: McGraw-Hill, 1997.

Burger, W., Burge, M.J., *Digital Image Processing: An Algorithmic Introduction Using Java*, New York: Springer, 2008.

Castleman, K.R., *Digital Image Processing*, Upper Saddle River, NJ: Prentice Hall, 1996.

Davies, E.R., *Computer Vision*, 5th edition, Waltham, MA: Academic Press, 2018.

Durrett, H.J., editor, *Color and the Computer*, San Diego, CA: Academic Press, 1987.

Foley, J.D., van Dam, A., Feiner, S.K., Hughes, J.F., *Computer Graphics: Principles and Practice in C*, Reading, MA: Addison Wesley, 1995.

Forsyth, D.A., Ponce, J., *Computer Vision*, Upper Saddle River, NJ: Pearson, 2011.

Giorgianni, E.J., Madden, T.E., *Digital Color Management: Encoding Solutions*, Hoboken, NJ: Wiley, 2009.

Gonzalez, R.C., Woods, R.E., *Digital Image Processing*, 4th Edition, New York: Pearson, 2018.

Gonzalez, R.C., Woods, R.E., Eddins, S.L., *Digital Image Processing Using MATLAB*, 3rd Edition, Knoxville, TN: Gatesmark, 2020.

Granlund, G., Knutsson, H., *Signal Processing for Computer Vision*, Boston, MA: Kluwer Academic Publishers, 1995.

Haralick, R.M., Shapiro, L.G., *Computer and Robot Vision*, Reading, MA: Addison-Wesley, 1992.

Hill, F.S., *Computer Graphics*, New York: Macmillan, 1990.

Horn, B.K.P., *Robot Vision*, Cambridge, MA: The MIT Press, 1986.

Jack, K., *Video Demystified: A Handbook for the Digital Engineer*, 3rd Edition, San Diego, CA: HighText Interactive, 1996.

Jain, A.K., *Fundamentals of Digital Image Processing*, Englewood Cliffs, NJ: Prentice Hall, 1989.

Jain, R., Kasturi, R., Schnuck, B.G., *Machine Vision*, New York: McGraw Hill, 1995.

Kummer, S., "The eye of the law", *OE Magazine*, pp. 22–25, October 2003.

Lee, H., *Introduction to Color Imaging Science*, Cambridge: Cambridge University Press, 2009.

Malacara, D., *Color Vision and Colorimetry: Theory and Applications*, Bellingham, WA: SPIE Press, 2001.

Myler, H.R., Weeks, A.R., *Computer Imaging Recipes in C*, Englewood Cliffs, NJ: Prentice Hall, 1993.

Murray, J.D., VanRyper, W., *Encyclopedia of Graphics File Formats*, Sebastopol, CA: O'Reilly and Associates, 1994.

Nixon, M., Aguado, A., *Feature Extraction and Image Processing for Computer Vision*, 4th Edition, Cambridge, MA: Academic Press, 2020.

Orzessek, M., Sommer, P., *ATM and MPEG-2: Integrating Digital Video into Broadband Networks*, Upper Saddle River, NJ: Prentice Hall PTR, 1998.

Parker, J.R., *Algorithms for Image Processing and Computer Vision*, New York: Wiley, 2010.

Poynton, C., *Digital Video and HDTV Algorithms and Interfaces*, 2nd Edition, Burlington, MA: Morgan Kahfmann, 2012.

Pratt, W.K., *Digital Image Processing*, New York: Wiley, 2007.

Rosenfeld, A., Kak, A.C., *Digital Picture Processing*, San Diego, CA: Academic Press, 1982.

Russ, J.C., *Forensic Uses of Digital Imaging*, 2nd Edition, Boca Raton, FL: CRC Press, 2016.

Russ, J.C., Neal, F.B., *The Image Processing Handbook*, 7th Edition, Boca Raton, FL: CRC Press, 2015.

Sanchez, J., Canton, M.P., *Space Image Processing*, Boca Raton, FL: CRC Press, 1999.

Schalkoff, R.J., *Digital Image Processing and Computer Vision*, New York: Wiley, 1989.

Seul, M., O'Gorman, L., Sammon, M.J., O'Gorman, L., *Practical Algorithms for Image Analysis with CD-ROM*, Cambridge, UK: Cambridge University Press, 2008.

Shapiro, L., Stockman, G., *Computer Vision*, Upper Saddle River, NJ: Prentice Hall, 2001.

Sid-Ahmed, M.A. *Image Processing: Theory, Algorithms, and Architectures*, Englewood Cliffs, NJ: Prentice Hall, 1995.

Sinha, P.K., *Image Acquisition and Preprocessing for Machine Vision Systems*, Bellingham, WA: SPIE Press, 2012.

Sonka, M., Hlavac, V., Boyle, R., *Image Processing, Analysis and Machine Vision*, 4th Edition, Boston, MA: Cengage Learning, 2014.

Szeliski, R., *Computer Vision: Algorithms and Applications*, 2nd Edition, Switzerland AG Springer, 2022.

Taubman, D., Marcellin, M., *JPEG2000: Image Compression Fundamentals, Standards and Practice*, Boston, MA: Kluwer Academic Publishers 2002.

Tekalp, A.M., *Digital Video Processing*, 2nd Edition, Englewood Cliffs, NJ: Prentice Hall, 2015.

Trussell, H.J, Vrhel, M.J., *Fundamentals of Digital Imaging*, Cambridge: Cambridge University Press, 2008.

Watt, A., Policarpo, F., *The Computer Image*, New York: Addison-Wesley, 1998.

Weng, Q., *An Introduction to Contemporary Remote Sensing*, New York: McGraw-Hill Education, 2012.

Wyszecki, G., and Stiles, W. S., *Color Science: Concepts and Methods, Quantitative Data and Formulae*, 2nd Edition, New York: Wiley, 1982.

1.8 Exercises

Problems

1. Define and discuss how digital image processing, image analysis, computer vision applications and human vision applications are related.

2. Discuss two computer vision applications.

3. List and describe the tools used in image analysis.

4. What are the two types of components in an image processing system?

5. Name three types of video camera interfaces.

6. Describe how a frame grabber works.

7. What is a sensor? How are they used in imaging systems?

8. What is a range image? How are they created?

9. What is a reflectance function? How does it relate our description of object characteristics?

10. Describe the difference between radiance and irradiance.

11. What is a photon? What does CCD stand for? What is quantum efficiency?

12. Show that the focal length of a lens can be defined by the distance from the lens at which an object at infinity is focused.

13. Find the number of electrons liberated in a sensor if:

    irradiation $= 600\lambda$ photons/(second)nm^2

    quantum efficiency of device $= 0.95$

    area $= 20\,$nm^2

    time period $= 10$ ms

    the photon flux is bandlimited to visible wavelengths
       Is this a solid-state device? Explain.

14. A video frame is scanned in 1/30 of a second using interlaced scanning. If we have 480 lines of interest and 640 pixels per line, at what rate must we perform the analog to digital conversion? (ignore synch pulse time)

15. Which band in the electromagnetic spectrum has the most energy? Which has the least energy? What significance does this have on human life?

16. Name some applications for UV and IR imaging.

17. How does acoustic imaging work? What is it used for?

18. How does an electron microscope differ from a standard light microscope?

19. What are two methods for lasers to create depth maps?

20. What is an optical image? How are they used to create digital images?

21. What is the difference between a "real" image and a computer-generated image?

22. Discuss advantages and disadvantages of binary, gray-scale, color and multispectral images.

23. Why transform a standard color image consisting of RGB data into another color space? Describe the HSL color space.

24. What does it mean that a color space is not perceptually uniform? Name a color space that is perceptually uniform.

25. Find the inverse equations for the SCT and the CCT.

26. Describe the difference between a bitmap and a vector image.

27. Name the elements required in an image file header.

28. Name the image file type used by CVIPtools. Why not use a standard file type, such as TIFF or GIF? Why do we sometimes remap image data?

29. Run the CVIPtools software and load a color image. Experiment. Have fun.

Supplementary Problems

1. Draw a picture and write the equations that shows the blur equation which is given by

$$c = \frac{d}{b'}\,|b' - b|$$

2. (a) Show that the f-number of a lens can be increased by placing a variable size aperture in front of the lens and (b) show that the image brightness will be inversely proportional to the f-number squared. Hint: Consider how light energy is measured related to the surface area of the sensor.

3.

   a. Find the approximate number of electrons liberated in a sensor if:

      irradiation $= \lambda/(5\lambda + 8)^2$ photons/(second)nm^2

      quantum efficiency of device $= 0.8$

      area $= 1{,}000\,$nm^2

      time period $= 10\,$s

      the photon flux is bandlimited to visible wavelengths

   b. Is this a solid-state device? Explain.

4. An imaging system has a lens with a diameter of 50 mm and a focal length of 10 mm. The system is set up so that objects at a distance of 3.0 m are correctly focused. Quantitatively and qualitatively describe how an object at 2.0 m appears in the image. Assume that the imaging device is a CCD with round pixel elements that have a 0.1 mm diameter.

5. Consider the imaging situation in the figure. Find *a* and *b* so that a 50 mm focal length lens will correctly focus the object onto the image plane.

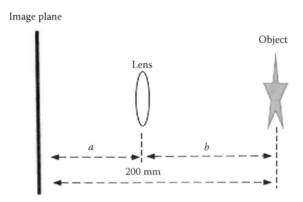

6. Given an image with a data range of −333 to 577, at what gray level will the CVIPtools viewer display the following values: (a) −333, (b) 577 and (c) 455?

7. An imaging system has a lens with a diameter of 100 mm and a focal length of 10 mm. The system is set up so that objects at a distance of 4.0 m are correctly focused. Quantitatively and qualitatively describe how an object at 3.0 m appears in the image. Assume that the imaging device is a CCD with round pixel elements that have a 0.075 mm diameter.

2

Computer Vision Development Tools

2.1 Introduction and Overview

The CVIPtools (Computer Vision and Image Processing tools) software was developed at Southern Illinois University Edwardsville, and it contains functions to perform the operations that are discussed in this book. These were originally written in ANSI-compatible C code and divided into libraries based on function category. For the current version of CVIPtools, a wrapper based on the Common Object Module (COM) interface was added to each function, and these COM functions are all contained in a dynamically linked library (dll) for use under the Windows operating system. A graphical user interface (GUI) was created for algorithm development and exploratory learning. Additionally, two development utility tools have been integrated into the CVIPtools environment. The newest addition to the CVIPtools environment is the MATLAB CVIP Toolbox, which allows for exploration and application development by MATLAB users. The CVIPtools software can be accessed at *cviptools.siue.edu*. The only requirement for the CVIPtools software, version 5.x, is a Windows operating system. To use the MATLAB CVIP Toolbox, MATLAB is needed. Note that version 3.9 of CVIPtools is available for UNIX operating systems, including FreeBSD and Linux. The libraries, and the CVIPlab program which is used for all the programming exercises, are also available for all platforms.

The philosophy underlying the development of the GUI-based CVIPtools is to allow the non-programmer to have access to a wide variety of computer vision and image processing operations (not just the "standard" ones) and to provide a platform for the exploration of these operations by allowing the user to vary all the parameters and observe the results in almost real time. In addition, through the use of the CVIPlab program and the MATLAB CVIP Toolbox, with the associated programming exercises and tutorials, those with programming skills develop their own imaging applications with a minimum of coding.

The CVIPtools software will perform image processing operations from simple image editing to complex analysis and computer vision application development. One of the primary advantages of the software is that it is continually under development in a university environment; so, as algorithms are developed, they are made available for exploration and research. Another advantage is that it is being developed for educational purposes, not simply end-user results, so the focus is on *learning* about computer vision and image processing. Because it is designed specifically for research and education and the user has access to the many different parameters for the different algorithms, it is not constrained by what the market has deemed "works best". In some cases, the algorithms may not work very well (for commercial applications), but have educational and research value. Some of these same algorithms that "do not work very well" may be useful to researchers for specific applications or may become part of a larger processing algorithm that does work well.

2.2 CVIPtools Windows GUI

When CVIPtools is first invoked, the main window appears as shown in Figure 2.2-1a. The main window contains the image queue, the image viewing area, the toolbar, the status bar and access to all the windows and operations. The *image queue* is on the left of the main window and contains the names of all the images loaded, as well as any images that are created by CVIPtools. The image queue was implemented to facilitate fast processing – output images are automatically put into the queue and are not written to disk files unless the user explicitly saves them. Note that there is a checkbox at the top of the image queue labeled *Lock Input*. If it is checked, it will retain (lock) the current image as input for each successive operation. This is useful when comparing various operations on the same image. When applying a sequence of operations to an image, it may be desirable to have

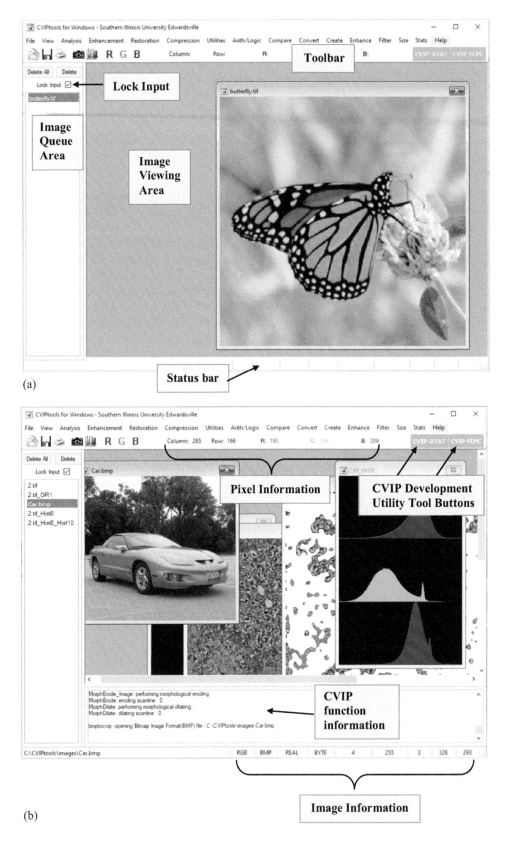

FIGURE 2.2-1
CVIPtools main window. (a) The main CVIPtools window when the program is invoked and an image is opened (loaded). (b) Main window with multiple images in the queue and the *View* option *CVIP Function Information* at the bottom.

each sequential function operate on the output image, which happens when the *Lock Input* box is unchecked. Above the *Lock Input* checkbox are buttons to delete selected images or all the images in the queue. The user can select images to be deleted using standard Windows keys – the *Ctrl* key to select specific images or the *Shift* key to select blocks of images.

Across the top of the window are the standard *File* and *View* selections and the primary window selections for analysis and processing – *Analysis, Enhancement, Restoration, Compression, Utilities* and *Help*. Directly under these, we see the toolbar which contains icons for opening, saving, printing and capturing image files as well as frequently used functions such as histogram display and RGB band extraction. To the right of these icons, the column, row, red, green and blue values are displayed for the current pixel position and values, and buttons to select the development tools, *CVIP-ATAT* and *CVIP-FEPC* (see Figure 2.2-1b and Chapter 8). The status bar at the bottom contains image specific information as determined by the image viewer. When an operation is performed, the image viewer automatically displays the output image and its corresponding information on the status bar.

The items on the *View* menu provide useful options. Here, the user can select the *Toolbar, Image Queue, CVIP Function Information* and/or the *Status Bar* to appear (or not) on the main window. Removing any or all of these will free up screen space, if desired. Additionally, the user can grab the border of the *image queue* or the *CVIP function information* with the mouse and move them to minimize their size in the main CVIPtools window. The *CVIP Function Information* appears in a text window at the bottom of the main window, as shown in Figure 2.2-1b. This window displays information that is text output from the lower level functions and is often useful to gain insight into the inner workings of a specific function. Examples of information displayed include convolution mask coefficients, type of data conversion, type of remapping, compression ratios of output images and the number of clusters found for a segmentation algorithm.

2.2.1 Image Viewer

To load an image into CVIPtools, you simply *open* it using the standard file open icon of a file folder opening in the upper left of the main window. When this is done, the image is read into memory and its name will appear in the image queue, and the image will be displayed in the main window. Additionally, image information will appear in the status bar at the bottom of the main window (see Figure 2.2-1b). This information includes color format, image (file) format, data format, data type, data range (minimum and maximum), number of bands and image width and height. The user can select multiple images to be loaded into the image queue by using standard Windows keys – the *Ctrl* key to select specific images or the *Shift* key to select blocks of images.

When an image is loaded, it becomes the active image and the active image can be changed by either clicking on the name in the queue or clicking on the image itself. When selected, the image is brought to the front, and as the mouse is moved around the image, the row and column coordinates, and the gray or color pixel values, will appear in the toolbar at the top of the main window. The active image can then be processed by selecting functions and clicking *Apply* on any of the processing windows.

The image viewer allows the user to perform standard image geometry operations, such as resizing, rotating, flipping, as well as image enhancement via histogram equalization. It is important to note that *these operations affect only the image that is displayed, not the image in the CVIPtools image queue*. They are for viewing convenience only, and any changes to the image itself (in the queue) can be accomplished by use of the standard CVIPtools windows. Even if the image is resized within the viewer, the row and column coordinates displayed will still correspond to the original image. Therefore, the image can be enlarged to ease the selection of small image features or the image can be shrunk to minimize screen use. The keyboard and mouse can be used to perform the operations listed in Table 2-1. In addition to the keyboard commands, the user can stretch the image by grabbing the edge or corner of the image with the left mouse button and dragging it.

The CVIPtools image viewer allows the user to select a specific portion of an image (a region of interest or ROI) by drawing a box with a press of the *Shift* key and drag of the left mouse button. This information is automatically passed back to the CVIPtools GUI for use in, for example, the image crop function. A new select box can be created on an image and it automatically destroys the first select box on that image, or the middle mouse button can be used to remove the drawn box. Once a select box has been drawn, it retains its position throughout any image geometry operations. The viewer can also be used to draw borders of any shape on images by pressing the *Control* key and using the left mouse button, and the middle mouse button will remove it. Drawn borders are useful to extract features about specific objects or to provide more control for an image crop function. Other functions are listed in Table 2-1. Note that each image can have its own ROI selected.

TABLE 2-1

CVIPtools Image Viewer Keyboard and Mouse Commands

DRAW, MARK, SELECT	Shift key – drag left mouse button	Select rectangular area of image used in crop
	Control key – drag left mouse button	Select irregular shaped area of image used in *Utilities→Create→Border Mask* and *Border Image* and *crop*
	Control key – click left mouse button	Select *Original Image* for *Analysis→Features*
	Control-A	Select entire image for copy/paste
	Control-C	If image has area currently selected, copy area to clipboard – this is used for copying images into documents Else, if image has current mesh (from *Restoration→Geometric Transforms*), copy mesh to clipboard
	Control-V	If mesh (from *Restoration→Geometric Transforms)* is available on clipboard, paste mesh to image
	Alt key – click left mouse button	Mark mesh points for *Restoration→Geometric Transforms* for *Enter a new mesh file*; select *Segmented Image* for *Analysis→Features*; select *Second Image* for the *Utility→Arith/Logic* operations; select Green band image for *Utility→Create→Assemble Bands*
	Shift key – click left mouse button	Select Blue band image for *Utility→Create→Assemble Bands*
	Alt key – click left mouse button drag	After a mesh is entered in *Restoration→Geometric Transforms*, this will allow the user to move mesh points
	Right mouse button on image	Mesh display select box (followed by left button to select) Copy/paste current mesh
	Middle mouse button on image	Removes drawn boxes and borders
ROTATE	t	Turn 90° clockwise
	T	Turn 90° counterclockwise
FLIP	h, H	Horizontal flip
	v, V	Vertical flip
OTHERS	N	Change back to original image, including size
	n	Change back to original image, without changing size
	q, Q	Quit – removes image from display but leaves in queue (clicking on **X** in the upper right corner will remove the image from queue)
	e, E	Histogram equalization
	Right mouse button in image viewing area (workspace)	Brings up *Utilities* menu

2.2.2 Analysis Window

When *Analysis* is first selected from the main window, the drop-down menu appears as shown in Figure 2.2-2a. Upon selection of one of the menu items, the *Analysis* window appears with the tab corresponding to the menu item selected (Figure 2.2-2b). At any time, the user can select another category of image analysis operations: *Geometry, Edge/Line Detection, Segmentation, Transforms, Features* and *Pattern Classification*. When the user makes a selection by clicking one of the file tabs with the left mouse button, the CVIPtools functions available under that selection will appear.

Most of the functions can be selected by the round buttons on the left of the window. These are called *radio, or option, buttons* – only one can be active at a time. Once the operation has been selected, the necessary input parameters can be typed in the text boxes or selected with the mouse using the arrows. Note that the text boxes will initially contain default values, which allow for immediate use of an operation by simply selecting it via the option button on the left and clicking on the *Apply* button (assuming an image has been selected). Any parameters that are not used with a particular function will be grayed out or disappear from the screen whenever that particular function is selected. The individual tabs and functions will be discussed in more detail in Chapters 3–7.

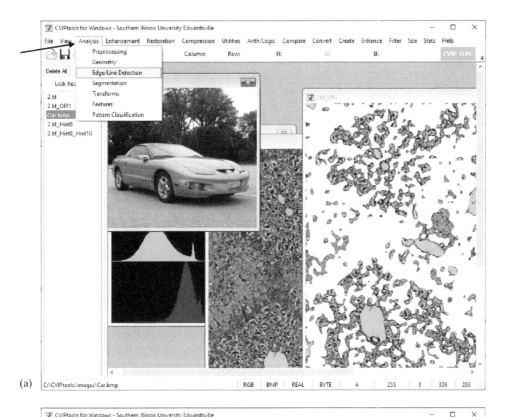

(a)

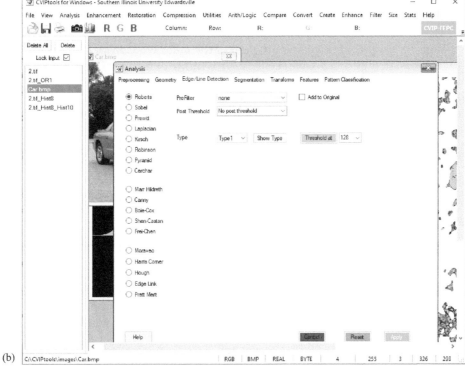

(b)

FIGURE 2.2-2
CVIPtools Analysis window. (a) The drop-down menu for the Analysis window. (b) The Analysis window with the Edge/Line Detection tab being selected.

In addition to the *Apply* button at the bottom of the window, there are buttons for *Help, Cancel* and *Reset*. The *Help* button will bring up the *Help* window (see Section 2.2.4). Use of the *Cancel* button or the ▣ in the upper right corner will remove the window from the screen and automatically reset all the parameters in all the tabs in the window to their default values. The *Reset* button will leave the window on the screen, but reset all the parameters in the current tab to the default values. These buttons and their functionality are also standard in the Enhancement, Restoration, Compression and Utilities windows.

2.2.3   Utilities Window

The *Utilities* window works differently than the previously discussed windows. This is because it contains functions that are commonly used regardless of the type of processing being performed. It can be accessed with two methods, depending on the user's preferences. The first method is to right click the mouse anywhere in the image viewing area. When this is done, a two-level menu will pop up as shown in Figure 2.2-3a. This menu contains various categories of commonly used utilities: *Arith/Logic, Compare, Convert, Create, Enhance, Filter, Size* and *Stats*. Alternately, the user can select *Utilities* at the top of the main window, and the previously mentioned menu items will appear across the top of the main window as shown in Figure 2.2-3b. Selecting the *Utilities* button again will toggle the menu items on/off across the top of the main window.

After using either method to invoke *Utilities*, the user selects a menu item, and the necessary information appears in the *Utilities* window for that particular function (see an example in Figure 2.2-3c). By limiting screen usage in this manner, the *Utilities* window is easily accessible when other primary windows are in use. The general philosophy guiding the design of the Utilities GUI is to maximize utility and usage, while minimizing the use of screen space. In some cases, for example, with *Utilities→Enhancement*, only the most commonly used functions will appear in the *Utilities* window, and the choices for the various parameters may be limited. This allows *Utilities* to be used easily and quickly, and if the user needs more, the main *Enhancement* window can be selected.

2.2.4   Help Window

The CVIPtools *Help* window can be accessed from the top of the main window or with the button in the lower left of any of the other windows. In Figure 2.2-4, we see the *Help* window which contains information about CVIPtools development, how to use the CVIPtools functions and documentation for the libraries, C and the COM functions. The *Help* pages for the libraries include a list of all the functions in the library as well as the location of the files. The documentation for the C functions includes a complete description and examples of their use in CVIPlab. Documentation for the COM functions contains the function prototypes, parameter definitions and a description. The *Help* window also contains help for using the CVIPtools functions from the GUI, and it has links to CVIPtools-related websites. The *Help* window has an index of all the documents it contains and allows for keyword searches to assist the user in finding what they need.

2.2.5   Development Tools

The GUI-based CVIPtools has two built-in development tools. The computer vision and image processing algorithm test and analysis tool, *CVIP-ATAT*, was created to perform many permutations of a computer vision algorithm, by changing processes and parameters automatically, and perform the experiments on sets of multiple images. The computer vision and image processing feature extraction and pattern classification tool, *CVIP-FEPC*, was created to explore feature extraction and pattern classification and allow for batch processing with large image sets. The tools are accessed via the CVIPtools toolbar as shown in Figure 2.2-1b. The primary windows for these tools are seen in Figure 2.2-5. More on using these tools for application development is in Chapter 8.

The CVIPlab program allows C and C++ programmers access to all the functions through the use of C libraries. Alternately, the CVIPtools dynamically linked library, or *dll*, and the associated COM functions can be used by C# programmers. The newest addition to the CVIPtools environment is the MATLAB CVIP Toolbox. This allows MATLAB users access to the library functions. The MATLAB CVIP Toolbox has its own Help documentation that includes examples for use of all of the available functions. Sample MATLAB Help pages are shown in Figure 2.2-6.

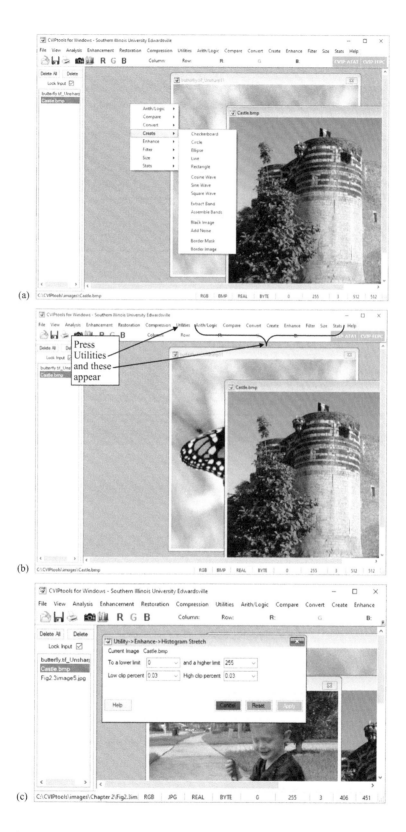

FIGURE 2.2-3

CVIPtools utilities. The utility functions can be accessed with two methods. (a) The two-level menu for *Utilities* will pop up with a right mouse click in the image viewing area or (b) click on *Utilities* at the top of the main window and the primary menu for *Utilities* will appear across the top and will toggle each time the *Utilities* button is selected. (c) An example Utilities window selection.

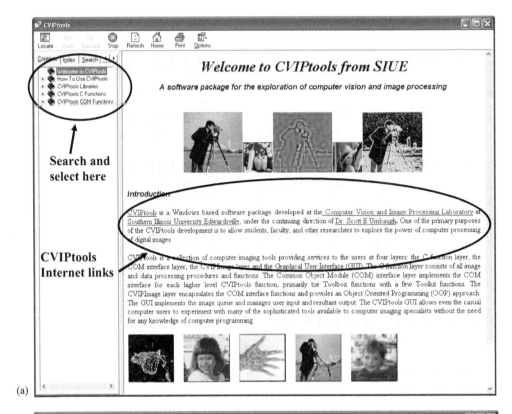

(a)

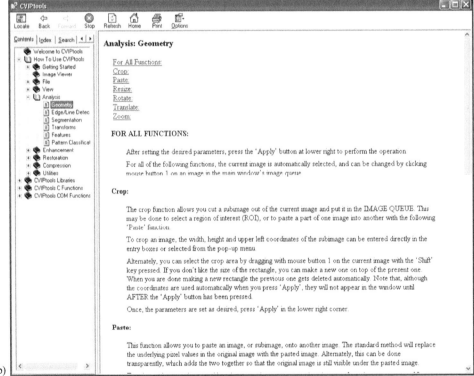

(b)

FIGURE 2.2-4

The CVIPtools Help window. The Help window contains information about using CVIPtools and contains documentation for the libraries and C functions, and includes CVIPtools-related Internet links. It has an index of all the documents it contains and allows for keyword searches to assist the user in finding what they need. (a) The Help window as it appears when first selected, (b) Help window showing an example of a page under *How to Use CVIPtools*

(Continued)

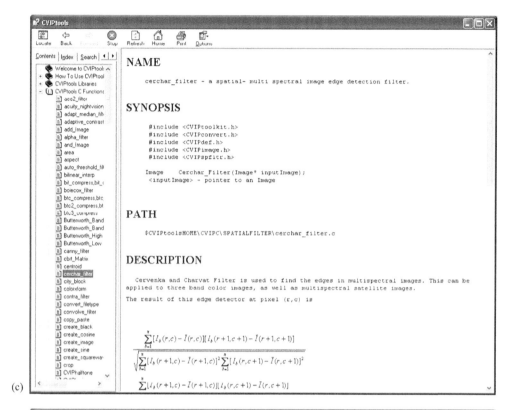

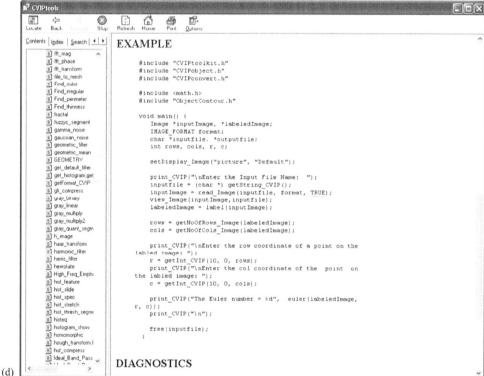

FIGURE 2.2-4 (*Continued*)
(c) Help window showing an example of C function documentation, and (d) if the user scrolls down a C function Help page, an example of usage in a CVIPlab program is included.

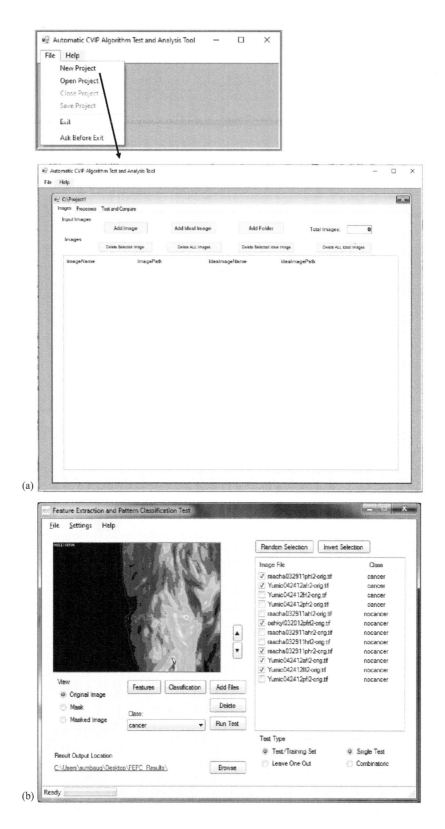

FIGURE 2.2-5
CVIPtools development utilities main windows. (a) Computer vision and image processing algorithm test and analysis tool, *CVIP-ATAT*, showing the main window after a project is opened. (b) Computer vision and image processing feature extraction and pattern classification tool, *CVIP-FEPC*, showing the main window with images loaded.

(a)

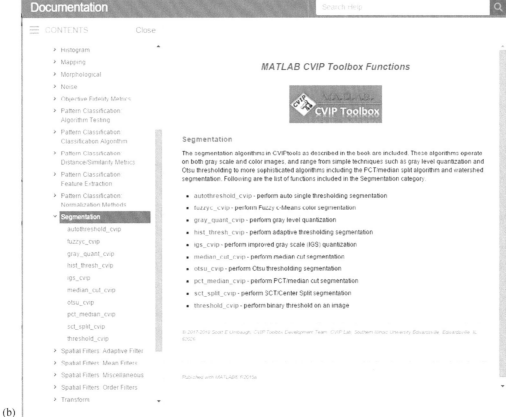

(b)

FIGURE 2.2-6
The CVIP MATLAB Help window. The CVIP Help window for the Toolbox contains information about the available functions along with examples.

(Continued)

(c)

FIGURE 2.2-6 (*Continued*)
(c) Help window showing detailed information for a function, image subtraction. By scrolling down the function page, an example will show input and output images, so that the user can verify proper usage.

2.3   CVIPlab for C/C++ Programming

The CVIPlab C program was originally created to allow for experimentation with the CVIPtools C functions outside of the CVIPtools environment. It is essentially a prototype program containing a sample CVIP function and a simple menu-driven user interface. By following the format of the prototype function, using the library function prototypes contained in the *Help* pages (with CVIPtools), the user can implement any algorithms developed in the CVIPtools environment in their own stand-alone program. Additionally, the user can incorporate any of their own C or C++ functions into this program. Any compiler can be used by the experienced programmer.

In addition to the CVIPtools libraries, the CVIPlab C program requires these three files: *CVIPlab.c, threshold_lab.c* and *CVIPlab.h*. The *CVIPlab.c* file contains the main CVIPlab program, the *threshold_lab.c* file contains a sample function and the *CVIPlab.h* is a header file for function declarations. *CVIPlab.c* also contains a list of header files to include, function declarations and three functions: *main_cviplab, input* and *threshold_Setup*. The *main_cviplab* function is declared as a *void*, indicating a function with no return value, and it contains code for the menu-driven user interface for CVIPlab. The *input* function illustrates how to read an image file into a CVIPtools image structure and display the resulting image. A pointer to the populated CVIPtools image structure is returned to the calling function. The *threshold_Setup* function accepts a pointer to a CVIPtools image structure as input, gets the threshold value from the user and then passes these parameters to the *threshold_lab* function. A pointer to the resultant CVIPtools image structure is returned to the calling function. The actual processing, in this case performing a threshold operation on an image, is done by the *threshold_lab* function which is contained in the file *threshold_lab.c*. By studying these functions, the reader can see how to access and process image files using CVIPtools library functions. The CVIPlab.c program is commented to describe the details more completely and is included here:

```c
/* ================================================================================
 *
 *   Computer Vision and Image Processing Lab - Dr. Scott Umbaugh SIUE
 *
 *
 * ================================================================================
 *
 *                 File Name: CVIPlab.c
 *               Description: This is the skeleton program for the Computer Vision
 *                            and Image Processing Labs
 *       Initial Coding Date: April 23, 1996
 *          Last update Date: March 23, 2021
 *              .NET version: September 21, 2006
 *               Portability: Standard (ANSI) C
 *                 Credit(s): Scott Umbaugh, Zhen Li, Kun Luo, Dejun Zhang,
 *                            Wenjun (Evan) Bian, Rohini Dahal, Norsang Lama
 *                            Southern Illinois University Edwardsville
 *   Copyright (C) 1996, 2006, 2021 Scott Umbaugh and SIUE
 *
 *   Permission to use, copy, modify, and distribute this software and its
 *   documentation for any non-commercial purpose and without fee is hereby
 *   granted, provided that the above copyright notice appear in all copies
 *   and that both that copyright notice and this permission notice appear
 *   in supporting documentation.  This software is provided "as is"
 *   without express or implied warranty.
 *
 *********************************************************************************/
/*
** include header files
*/
#include "CVIPtoolkit.h"
#include "CVIPconvert.h"
#include "CVIPdef.h"
#include "CVIPimage.h"
#include "CVIPlab.h"
//#include "CVIPview.h"
#define CASE_MAX 20
/* Put the command here, as VIDEO_APP, to run your image acquisition application program */
#define VIDEO_APP "explorer.exe"
/*
** function declarations
*/
Image *threshold_Setup(Image *inputImage);
Image *input();
/*
** start main funct
*/
void main_cviplab() {
        IMAGE_FORMAT  format;       /* the input image format */
        Image    *cvipImage;        /* pointer to the CVIP Image structure */
        Image    *cvipImage1;       /* pointer to the CVIP Image structure */
        char     *outputfile;       /* output file name */
        int      choice;
        CVIP_BOOLEAN  done=CVIP_NO;
        print_CVIP("\n\n\n\n****************************************");
        print_CVIP("***************************  ");
        print_CVIP("\n*\t\t Computer Vision and Image Processing Lab\t  *");
```

```
        print_CVIP("\n*\t\t\t <Your Name Here> \t\t   *");
        print_CVIP("\n*****************************************");
        print_CVIP("*************************\n\n\n");
        while (!done) {
                print_CVIP("\t\t0.\tExit \n");
                print_CVIP("\t\t1.\tGrab and Snap an Image  \n");
                print_CVIP("\t\t2.\tThreshold Operation\n");
                print_CVIP("\n\nCVIPlab>>");
                /*
                ** obtain an integer between 0 and CASE_MAX from the user
                */
                choice=getInt_CVIP(10, 0, CASE_MAX);
                switch (choice) {
                case 0:
                        done=CVIP_YES;
                        break;
                case 1:
                        if (ShellExecute(NULL, "Open", VIDEO_APP, NULL, NULL, SW_SHOW) <= 32)
                                print_CVIP("Error while running Video Program");
                        break;
                case 2:
                        /*Get the input image */
                        cvipImage=input();
                        if (cvipImage == NULL)
                        {
                                error_CVIP("main", "could not read input image");
                                break;
                        }
                        /* calls the threshold function */
                        cvipImage=threshold_Setup(cvipImage);
                        if (!cvipImage)
                        {
                                error_CVIP("main", "threshold fails");
                                break;
                        }
                        /*
                        ** display the resultant image
                        */

                        view_Image(cvipImage, "threshold");
                        delete_Image(cvipImage);
                        break;
                default:
                        print_CVIP("Sorry ! You Entered a wrong choice ");
                        break;
                }
        }
}
/*
** end of the function main
*/
/*
** The following function reads in the image file specified by the user,
** stores the data and other image info. in a CVIPtools Image structure,
** and displays the image.
*/
Image* input() {
        char            *inputfile;
        Image           *cvipImage;
```

```
                /*
                ** get the name of the file and stores it in the string 'inputfile '
                */
                print_CVIP("\n\t\tEnter the Input File Name:   ");
                inputfile=getString_CVIP();
                /*
                ** creates the CVIPtools Image structure from the input file
                */
                cvipImage=read_Image(inputfile, 1);
                if (cvipImage == NULL) {
                        error_CVIP("init_Image", "could not read image file");
                        free(inputfile);
                        return NULL;
                }
                /*
                ** display the source image
                */
                view_Image(cvipImage, inputfile);
                /*
                **IMPORTANT: free the dynamic allocated memory when it is not needed
                */
                free(inputfile);
                return cvipImage;
}
/*
** The following setup function asks the threshold value from the user. After
** it gets the threshold value, it will call the threshold_Image() function.
*/
Image *threshold_Setup(Image *inputImage) {
        unsigned int threshval;        /* Threshold value */
        /*** Gets a value between 0 and 255 for threshold */
        print_CVIP("\n\t\tEnter the threshold value:   ");
        threshval=getInt_CVIP(10, 0, 255);
        return threshold_lab(inputImage, threshval);
}
```

The following is the threshold function contained in the *threshold_lab.c* file. Note that it is a good idea in the programming exercises to append all of your file and function names with something, such as _lab or your initials, to avoid compilation or linker naming conflicts.

```
/*****************************************************************************************/
*  ========================================================================
*
*    Computer Vision and Image Processing Lab - Dr. Scott Umbaugh SIUE
*
*
*  ========================================================================
*
*             File Name: threshold_lab.c
*           Description: it contains the function to threshold BYTE images
*   Initial Coding Date: April 23, 1996
*           Last update: March 23, 2017
*           Portability: Standard (ANSI) C
*            Credit(s): Zhen Li & Kun Luo
*                        Southern Illinois University at Edwardsville
*
```

```
** Copyright (c) 1996, 2017, SIUE - Scott Umbaugh, Kun Luo, Yansheng Wei
*******************************************************************************/
/*
** include header files
*/
#include "CVIPtoolkit.h"
#include "CVIPconvert.h"
#include "CVIPdef.h"
#include "CVIPimage.h"
#include "CVIPlab.h"
/*
** The following function will compare the actual gray level of the input image
** with the threshold limit. If the gray-level value is greater than the
** threshold limit then the gray level is set to 255 (WHITE_LAB) else to
** 0 (BLACK_LAB). Note that the '_LAB' or '_lab' is appended to names used
** in CVIPlab to avoid naming conflicts with existing constant and function
** (e.g. threshold_lab) names.
*/
#define     WHITE_LAB    255
#define     BLACK_LAB    0

Image *threshold_lab(Image *inputImage, unsigned int threshval) {
      byte          **image;      /* 2-d matrix data pointer */
      unsigned int  r,            /* row index */
                    c,            /* column index */
                    bands;        /* band index */
      unsigned int  no_of_rows,   /* number of rows in image */
                    no_of_cols,   /* number of columns in image */
                    no_of_bands;  /* number of image bands */
      /*
      ** Gets the number of image bands (planes)
      */
      no_of_bands=getNoOfBands_Image(inputImage);
      /*
      ** Gets the number of rows in the input image
      */
      no_of_rows=getNoOfRows_Image(inputImage);
      /*
      ** Gets the number of columns in the input image
      */
      no_of_cols=getNoOfCols_Image(inputImage);
      /*
      ** Compares the pixel value at the location (r,c)
      ** with the threshold value. If it is greater than
      ** the threshold value it writes 255 at the location
      ** else it writes 0. Note that this assumes the input
      ** image is of data type BYTE.
      */
      for (bands=0; bands<no_of_bands; bands++) {
            /*
            ** reference each band of image data in 2-d matrix form;
            ** which is used for reading and writing the pixel values
            */
            image=getData_Image(inputImage, bands);
            for (r=0; r<no_of_rows; r++) {
                  for (c=0; c<no_of_cols; c++) {
                        if (image[r][c] >(byte) threshval)
                              image[r][c]=WHITE_LAB;
```

```
                             else
                                    image[r][c]=BLACK_LAB;
                            }
                    }
            }
        return inputImage;
}
/*
** end of function threshold_lab
*/
```

To use CVIPlab in the programing exercises with the existing file organization and program format using any compiler, do the following:

1. Create a file similar to threshold_lab.c for the *new_function.* The easiest method is to select the threshold.c file and perform a *Save As* the new_function.c. Next, edit the header to change the file name, description, modify the date, add your name and change the old comments and the function name. The last step is to modify the code inside the band, row and column *for* loop to perform the new function (see Figure 2.3-1).

2. Add the new function to the CVIPlab menu as shown in Figure 2.3-2a. Next, add a case statement for the function as shown in Figure 2.3-2b. The case statement code for case 2 can be copied and used by modifying *threshold_Setup* to *new_function_Setup.*

3. Add the *new_function_Setup* to CVIPlab.c, similar to *threshold_Setup.*

4. Add the function prototype to the CVIPlab.h header file:

```
extern Image *new_function(new_function parameters...)
```

2.3.1   Toolkit, Toolbox Libraries and Memory Management in C/C++

All of the functions in the CVIPtools program are accessible to those programming with CVIPlab. The functions are arranged in a hierarchical grouping of libraries, with the Toolkit Libraries at the lowest level and the Toolbox Libraries at the next level. This hierarchical grouping is devised such that each successive level can use the building blocks (functions) available to it from the previous level(s). The developer can create their own application libraries by using the lower level libraries, as illustrated in Figure 2.3-3.

The *Toolkit Libraries* contain low level functions, such as input/output functions, matrix manipulation functions and memory management functions. The *Toolbox Libraries* are the primary libraries for use in application development; they contain the functions that are available from the GUI in CVIPtools, such as the many analysis, enhancement, restoration, compression and utility functions. At the highest level, the *Application Libraries* are the libraries generated by those using the CVIPlab environment to develop application software.

In general, many functions return pointers to CVIPtools Image structures (IMAGE and Image are both valid designations). If the return value is NULL, an error has occurred. The general philosophy regarding memory management is that *whoever has control is responsible.* This means that any parameters passed to a function will be either used for return data or freed. It also means that if a programmer wants to retain a data structure, they should pass a *copy* of it to any CVIPtools function. By clearly following this simple rule, memory leaks can be avoided. For details of the operation of a specific function, see the *Help* pages in the CVIPtools.

2.3.2   Image Data and File Structures

Details of the image data structures used in CVIPtools and CVIPlab are contained in this section. The CVIPlab programmer who is using the CVIPtools library functions typically does not need to understand all the details for using them. The library functions provide the user with a higher level interface so that they can focus on learning

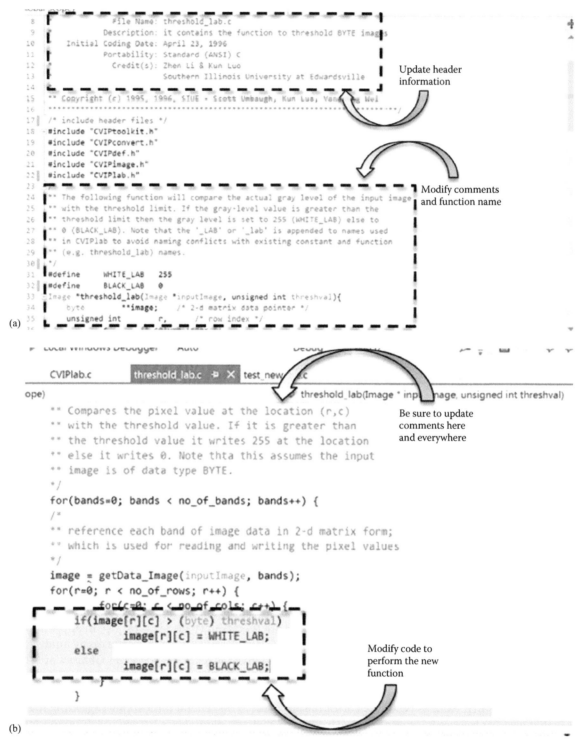

FIGURE 2.3-1
Create your new function by using the threshold function as a prototype. (a) Edit the header to change the file name, description, modify the date, add your name and change the old comments and the function name. (b) The last step is to modify the code inside the band, row and column *for* loop to perform the new function.

about computer vision and image processing. However, a basic understanding of the underlying data structures is necessary and useful for understanding problems that arise during development.

The data and file structures of interest are those that are required to process images. In traditional structured programming, a system can be modeled as a hierarchical set of functional modules, where the modules at one

```
void main_cviplab(){
    IMAGE_FORMAT  format;       /* the input image format */
    Image      *cvipImage;   /* pointer to the CVIP Image structure */
    Image      *cvipImage1;  /* pointer to the CVIP Image structure */
    char       *outputfile;  /* output file name */
    int        choice;
    CVIP_BOOLEAN  done = CVIP_NO;

    print_CVIP("test new function, return value is %d\n", test_function(5));

    print_CVIP("\n\n\n\n********************************************");
    print_CVIP("***************************** ");
    print_CVIP("\n*\t\t Computer Vision and Image Processing Lab\t *"):
    print_CVIP("\n*\t\t\t <Your Name Here> \t *");
    print_CVIP("\n********************************************");
    print_CVIP("*************************\n\n\n")

    while(!done) {
        print_CVIP("\t\t0.\tExit \n");
        print_CVIP("\t\t1.\tGrab and Snap an Image  \n");
        print_CVIP("\t\t2.\tThreshold Operation \n")
        print_CVIP("\t\t3.\tNew Function \n")
        print_CVIP("\n\nCVIPlab>");

        /*
        ** obtain an integer between 0 and CASE_MAX from the user
        */
        choice = getInt_CVIP(10, 0, CASE_MAX);
```

(a)

Add here

```
    case 2:
        /*Get the input image */
        cvipImage = input();
        if(cvipImage == NULL)
        {
            error_CVIP("main", "could not read input image");
            break;
        }
        /* calls the threshold function */
        cvipImage = threshold_Setup(cvipImage);
        if (!cvipImage)
        {
            error_CVIP("main", "threshold fails");
            break;
        }
        /* display the resultant image */
        view_Image(cvipImage,"threshold");
        delete_Image (cvipImage);
        break;
    case 3:
        /*Get the input image */
        cvipImage = input();
        if(cvipImage == NULL)
        {
            error_CVIP("main", "could not read input image");
            break;
        }
        /* calls the threshold function */
        int x = test_function(8);
```

(b)

Copy here

FIGURE 2.3-2
Add the case statement for the new function to CVIPlab. (a) Add your new function to the menu. (b) Simply copy the statement from Case 2, and change the function name and update the comment.

level are built of lower level modules. Similarly, the information used in CVIPlab, which consists primarily of image data, uses this hierarchical model. In this case, we have a five-tiered model with the pixel data at the bottom, the vector data structure at the next level, the matrix data structure at the next level, image data structures next, and finally, the image files at the top level. Figure 2.3-4a shows a triangle to illustrate this model, since it is

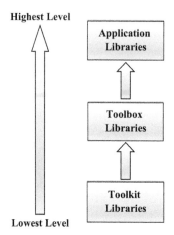

Highest Level

Application
Libraries

Toolbox
Libraries

Toolkit
Libraries

Lowest Level

FIGURE 2.3-3
CVIPtools C libraries. The libraries are arranged in a hierarchical manner. At the lowest level are the Toolkit libraries (see the Online Docs for function list), which contain basic data manipulation and memory management functions that are not normally used by the CVIPlab programmer. The Toolbox functions (see the Online Docs for function list) are higher level libraries which call the Toolkit functions and are meant for ease of use by the CVIPlab programmer. At the highest level are libraries created by the application developer.

naturally larger at the lower levels – it takes many pixels to make up a vector, many vectors to make an image and so on.

In Figure 2.3-4b, we see that a vector can be used to represent one row or column of an image, and the 2-D image data itself can be modeled by a matrix. The image data structure (Figure 2.3-4c) consists of a header that contains information about the type of image, followed by a matrix for each band of image data values. When the image data structure is written to a disk file, it is translated into the specified file format (for example, BMP, JPG or TIFF). CVIPtools has its own image file format, the Visualization in Image Processing (VIP) format, and it also supports many other standard image file formats. Since many standard image file formats assume 8-bit data, the VIP format is required for floating point data, complex data, as well as CVIPtools specific information such as CVIPtools compression file formats.

The vector data structure can be defined by declaring an array in C of a given type or by assigning a pointer and allocating a contiguous block of memory for the vector. A *pointer* is simply the address of the memory location where the data resides. In Figure 2.3-5, we see an illustration of a vector; the pointer to the vector is actually the address of the first element in the vector. For images, each element of the vector represents one pixel value, and the entire vector represents one row or column. The *Vector* library contains these functions.

The matrix structure is at the level above vectors. A matrix can be viewed as a one-dimensional vector, with M multiplied by N elements that has been mapped into a matrix with M rows and N columns. This is illustrated in Figure 2.3-6, where we see how a one-dimensional array can be mapped to a two-dimensional matrix via a pointer map. The matrix data structure is defined as follows:

```
typedef enum {CVIP_BYTE, CVIP_SHORT, CVIP_INTEGER, CVIP_FLOAT, CVIP_DOUBLE} CVIP_TYPE;
typedef enum {REAL, COMPLEX} FORMAT;
typedef struct {
   CVIP_TYPE data_type;
   FORMAT data_format;
   unsigned int rows;
   unsigned int cols;
   void **rptr;                /*real data pointer*/
   void **iptr;                /*imaginary data pointer*/
} Matrix;
```

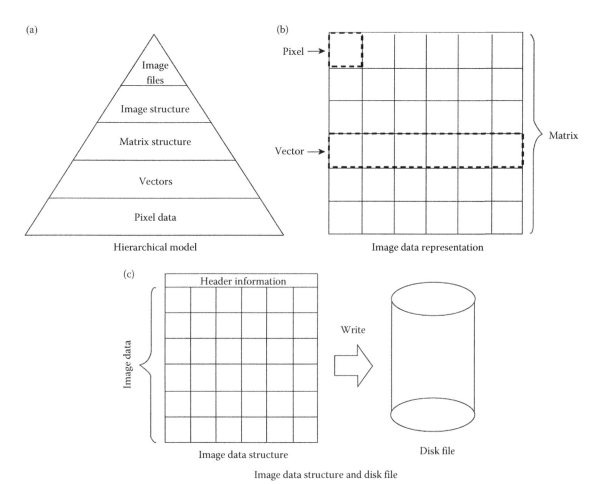

FIGURE 2.3-4
Image data and file structures. (a) The hierarchical model for data structures in the CVIPlab programming environment where higher level structures build on lower level structures. (b) Data in the image itself corresponding to the module level. (c) Image data structure includes header information describing the image data format which is dependent on the file type, such as *bmp*, *jpg*, or the CVIPtools format *vip*.

Address	A	A+1	A+2	A+3	...	A+N−2	A+N−1
datum	255	128	38	234		69	10

FIGURE 2.3-5
Vector representation. The pointer to the vector is the address of the first element in the vector.

The *data_type* field defines the type of data, such as BYTE or FLOAT, which is stored in the matrix. The *data_format* field describes whether the matrix elements are real or complex. The next two fields, *rows* and *cols*, contain the number of rows and columns in the matrix, and the last two, ***rptr* and ***iptr*, are two-dimensional pointers to the matrix elements – if the data_format is REAL, then the imaginary pointer is a null pointer. The *Matrix* library contains these functions, and the associated memory allocation and deallocation functions are called *new_Matrix* and *delete_Matrix*, respectively. The data type for the real and imaginary pointers is passed as a parameter to the function that creates and allocates memory for a matrix, the *new_Matrix* function. Once the matrix has been set up with *new_Matrix*, the data is accessed as a two-dimensional array by assigning a pointer with the *getData_Matrix* function; note that care must be taken to cast it to the appropriate data type.

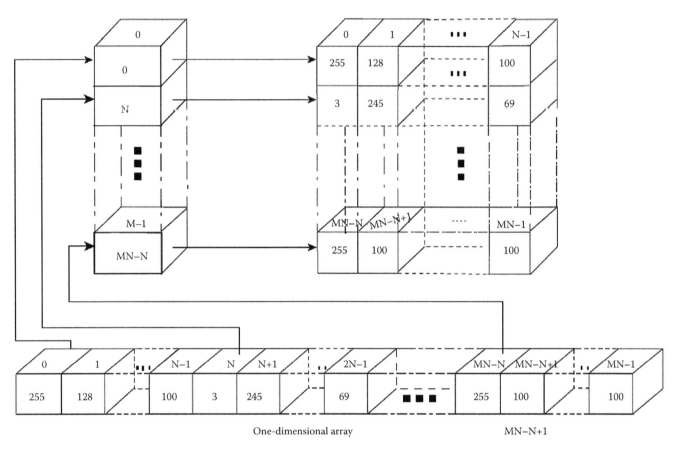

FIGURE 2.3-6

Matrices and pointers. A matrix can be viewed as a one-dimensional vector, with M multiplied by N elements that has been mapped into a matrix with M rows and N columns. Here, we see a one-dimensional array that can be mapped to a two-dimensional matrix via a pointer map.

The image structure is the primary data structure used for processing of digital images. It is at the level above the matrix data structure, since it consists of a matrix and additional information. The image data structure is defined as follows:

```
typedef enum {BINARY, GRAY_SCALE, RGB, HSL, HSV, SCT, CCT, LUV, LAB, XYZ} COLOR_FORMAT;
typedef enum {PBM, PGM, PPM, EPS, TIF, GIF, RAS, ITX,IRIS, CCC, BIN, VIP, GLR, BTC, BRC,
HUF, ZVL, ARITH, BTC2, BTC3, DPC, ZON, ZON2, SAFVR, JPG, WVQ, FRA, VQ, XVQ, TRCM, PS,
BMP, JP2, PNG} IMAGE_FORMAT;
typedef enum {Btc, Btc2, Btc3, Dpcm, Zvl, Glr, Brc, Huf, Zon, Zon2, Jpg, Wvq, Fra, Vq,
Xvq, Trcm, TOP} CMPR_FORMAT;
typedef struct {
   IMAGE_FORMAT image_format;
   COLOR_FORMAT color_space;
   int bands;
   Matrix **image_ptr;
   HISTORY story;
} IMAGE;
```

The first field, *image_format*, contains the file type of the original image. When the image is read into CVIPtools, this information is retained for use during a *save* operation if the user does not specify the desired file type. Note, however, that the image format does not necessarily tell us anything about the actual data in the image structure, especially

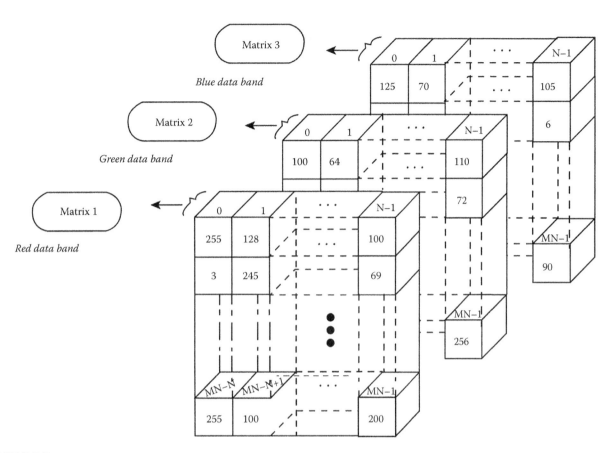

FIGURE 2.3-7
Image data. Multiband image data is represented in the image data structure as shown here. In addition, the image structure contains header information.

after it has been processed. The second field, *color_space*, determines if the image is binary (two-valued), gray-scale (typically 8-bit) or color (typically three-plane, 24-bit, RGB). If it is a color image, then this field is updated when a color space conversion is performed. The third field, *bands*, contains the number of bands in the image; for example, a color image has three bands and a gray-scale image has one band. The next field, ***image_ptr*, is a pointer to an array of pointers to matrix data structures, where each matrix contains one band of pixel data (see Figure 2.3-7). The last field is for history information and is used by the CVIPtools software to keep track of certain functions, such as transforms, that have been applied to an image.

The history field in the image structure, *story*, is a pointer to a history data structure. The history data structure consists of packets of history information, where each *packet* contains information from a particular function. The history data structure is defined as follows:

```
typedef struct packet PACKET;
   struct packet {
      CVIP_TYPE *dtype;
      unsigned int dsize;
      void **dptr;
   };
typedef struct history *HISTORY;
   struct history {
      PROGRAMS ftag;
      PACKET *packetP;
      HISTORY next;
   };
```

Functions relating to the history are in the *Image* library, also see the header file *CVIPhistory.h*.

At the highest level is the image file. The image file can be any of the types previously described as supported by CVIPtools. If the file type is an 8-bit per pixel image file, which is typical, then it may need to be remapped after processing. For example, if the range of the data is too large for 8-bits, if the data is in floating point format or if it contains negative numbers, then the data in the image structure must be remapped before it can be written in 8-bit format. This is done automatically by the *write_Image* function, if required. However, in some cases, this may not be what is desired – we may want to retain the data as it is in the image data structure. To do this, the image must be saved in the CVIPtools image file format, the VIP format. The VIP file format allows the image data structure to be written to disk and consists of an image header and the image data structure. The VIP structure is as follows:

```
VIP                   - 3 bytes (the ASCII letters "ViP")
COMPRESS              - 1 byte, ON or OFF, depending on whether the data is compressed)
IMAGE_FORMAT          - 1 byte, (defined in image data structure)
COLOR_FORMAT          - 1 byte, (e.g. BINARY, GRAYSCALE, RGB, LUV)
CVIP_TYPE             - 1 byte, data type, (e.g. CVIP_SHORT, CVIP_BYTE)
NO_OF_BANDS           - 1 byte, (1 for graylevel, 3 for color, other numbers allowed too)
NO_OF_COLS            - 2 bytes,
NO_OF_ROWS            - 2 bytes,
FORMAT                - 1 byte (REAL or COMPLEX)
SIZEOF HISTORY        - 4 bytes, (Size of history information, in bytes)
HISTORY               - variable size (history information)
RAW DATA              - variable size
```

If the file is a CVIPtools compressed image file, the first field in the RAW DATA corresponds to the type of compression that was performed (such as *btc* and *vq*). Note that if the actual data stored in a VIP image file is examined, the number of bytes stored may vary from the above. This is due to the fact that we use the standard XDR (External Data Representation) functions to write the VIP files. By using these functions, we assure file portability across computer platforms, but it results in most data types smaller than 32 bits (4 bytes) being written to the file in a standard 32-bit format. For example, in the Windows operating system, the actual number of bytes stored in the image file is as follows:

```
VIP                   - 3 bytes (the ASCII letters "ViP")
COMPRESS              - 4 bytes, ON or OFF, depending on whether the data is compressed)
IMAGE_FORMAT          - 4 bytes, (defined in image data structure)
COLOR_FORMAT          - 4 bytes, (e.g. BINARY, GRAYSCALE, RGB, LUV)
CVIP_TYPE             - 4 bytes, data type, (e.g. CVIP_SHORT, CVIP_BYTE)
NO_OF_BANDS           - 4 bytes, (1 for graylevel, 3 for color, other numbers allowed too)
NO_OF_COLS            - 4 bytes,
NO_OF_ROWS            - 4 bytes,
FORMAT                - 4 bytes (REAL or COMPLEX)
SIZEOF HISTORY        - 4 bytes, (Size of history information, in bytes)
HISTORY               - variable size (history information)
RAW DATA              - variable size
```

To use the VIP image file format, simply use the *read_Image* and *write_Image* functions contained in the *Conversion* library. These file read/write functions are in the *Conversion* library since a large portion of their functionality is to convert file types to and from the CVIPtools image data structure. These read/write functions will read/write any of the image file formats supported by CVIPtools, and require the programmer to deal with only one data structure, the image data structure.

2.4 The MATLAB CVIP Toolbox

The MATLAB CVIP Toolbox was developed to allow CVIPtools and CVIPlab users access to the library functions within the MATLAB environment. The CVIP Toolbox is organized into categories based on the type of operation the function performs. The general naming convention for the functions in the Toolbox is to take the C function name and append "_cvip"; this will avoid naming conflicts and help CVIPtools users access the functions. In some cases, the names may be slightly modified for clarity. The MATLAB versions of the functions have the same or improved functionality as the original CVIPtools functions. For details of the operation of a specific function, see the *Help* pages. For a complete function list, see the Online Docs.

2.4.1 Help Files

The basic help for the CVIP Toolbox functions is available from the command line as follows:

```
> help function_name
```

This method will provide a standard description of the function, including the input parameters and options. In addition, we have provided more complete Help files which can be invoked in various ways. The keyword "doc" can be typed into the command window at the command prompt, F1 can be selected on the keyboard, or Help or "?" from the toolbar can be selected. After the Help window is invoked, the user can select the Supplemental Software link in the lower left, and the CVIP Help window will appear as in Figure 2.4-1. The CVIP Help contains individual help pages for each function which are organized by categories as described. In Figure 2.4-2, we see a sample function page. The function page contains all the information needed to use the function, including the syntax, the parameters required, a description, an example of its use and the expected output.

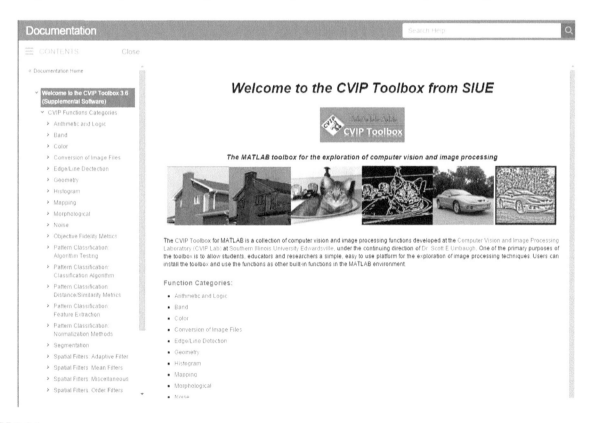

FIGURE 2.4-1
MATLAB CVIP Toolbox Help. To invoke Help: enter "doc" at the command prompt, use F1 on the keyboard, or select "Help" or "?". This will bring up the Help window where the user selects Supplemental Help in the lower left corner to invoke the CVIP Toolbox Help window as shown.

(a)

(b)

FIGURE 2.4-2
CVIP Toolbox Help. (a) Example category page, Segmentation (b) example function page. The function page has all the information needed to use the function, as well as an example of its use.

2.4.2 M-Files

For rapid prototyping, it is often useful to use MATLAB's development environment to experiment with algorithms in the Command Window through the use of the interpreted programming language. After the application developer has finalized the algorithm of interest, it can be compiled and converted to C or C++ with an add-on compiler. Compiled code can be as much as ten times faster than the interpreted version, but this depends on how the MATLAB code is written. For example, if the original code is optimized by proper vectorization, there may not be any increase in execution time for the compiled version. Note that MATLAB was developed as a <u>Mat</u>rix <u>Lab</u>oratory, so it is optimized to process vectors and matrices.

An M-file is a file that can be interpreted and executed in the Command Window, and it can be developed with the built-in editor or any other editor of your choice, but the file should be saved with a ".m" extension. The user can use create *scripts*, which consist of a series of MATLAB commands, but take no input parameters and do not return any output. After a script has been created as an M-file, it can be executed by simply typing its name on the command line. Alternately, M-files can be used to create *functions* that take input *parameters* (arguments) and produce one or more *outputs*. The CVIP Toolbox was created by writing the CVIPtools C functions as M-files and then put together into a toolbox. To make the functions executable, the filename of M-file and the function name must be the same. When a new M-file is created with the same name as an existing M-file, MATLAB will select the one that appears first in the path order and execute it. To avoid the conflict of usage of functions, "_cvip" is appended to the name of functions in the CVIP Toolbox. An additional feature of M-files is that *help* information can be included in the header of the file itself.

2.4.3 CVIPtools for MATLAB GUI

The CVIPtools for MATLAB GUI is based on the original Windows GUI as described in Section 2.2. Figure 2.4-3 shows the CVIPtools MATLAB GUI after an image file is opened and the Analysis→Geometry tab is selected. Here, we see the similarity with the same selections across the top for each of the windows and their associated tabs, and under those are the icons to open, print and save files. Alongside the file icons, we also see the histogram icon which looks like a bookshelf and the RGB icons to display individual color bands. We also have the same layout within each tab, with radio-buttons on the left to select the function, parameters to the right of that, and the color-coded *Cancel*, *Reset* and *Apply* buttons on the lower right.

Operations are performed by opening an image or selecting an image if the images are already loaded by clicking on the image tab, selecting the function with the radio-button on the left side, setting the parameters as desired and then clicking on the green *Apply* button. After the operation is performed, the output image will appear in another tab. One of the unique properties of the MATLAB GUI is that the user can grab and drag any of the tabs with the mouse and change the screen layout as desired.

2.4.4 CVIPlab for MATLAB

We have created a *CVIPlab.m* script for use with our CVIP Toolbox. The CVIPlab is meant to be used by students in developing their programs and exercises as well as for those working on research and performing algorithm development. It is essentially a skeleton program provided to get the user started with MATLAB and CVIP applications. It provides a simple user interface and a framework to organize your functions, while showing examples of commonly used methods for image processing applications.

To use the CVIPlab for MATLAB, three files are necessary: the *CVIPlab.m* script, and two function files, *input_image.m* and *threshold.m*. *CVIPlab.m* provides the skeleton program and a basic text-based user interface, *input_image.m* is a utility function for reading (opening) image files and *threshold.m* is an example of a simple CVIP function which can be used as a model for writing new functions in the programming exercises. Here is the code for the *CVIPlab.m* script file, with complete comments throughout:

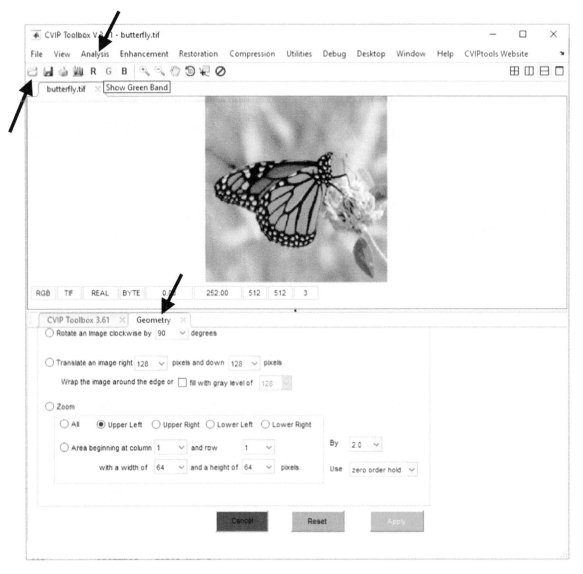

FIGURE 2.4-3
MATLAB CVIPtools GUI is shown after the butterfly image has been opened or loaded and the *Analysis→Geometry* tab has been selected. The functionality is similar to the Windows GUI, but the layout is flexible and the tabs on the screen can be rearranged by grabbing the tab with the mouse and dragging it to the desired location.

```
% *  ========================================================================
% *
% *   Computer Vision and Image Processing Lab - Dr. Scott Umbaugh SIUE
% *
% *  ========================================================================
% *
% *             File Name: CVIPlab.m
% *           Description: This is the skeleton program for the Computer Vision
% *                        and Image Processing Labs
% *   Initial Coding Date: Jan 15, 2017
% *      Last Update Date: March 9, 2017
% *            Credit(s): Norsang Lama, Scott E Umbaugh
% *                        Southern Illinois University Edwardsville
% *
```

```matlab
% *   Copyright (C) 2017 Scott E Umbaugh and SIUE
% *
% *   Permission to use, copy, modify, and distribute this software and its
% *   documentation for any non-commercial purpose and without fee is hereby
% *   granted, provided that the above copyright notice appear in all copies
% *   and that both that copyright notice and this permission notice appear
% *   in supporting documentation.  This software is provided "as is"
% *   without express or implied warranty.
% *
% ***************************************************************************************/

    clc; %clear command window
    close all;  %close all the figure windows
    exitLab = false;   %flag to exit program or continue on, flag is OFF

    %Create user interface (UI), print the string in command window
    fprintf('\n***************************************');
    fprintf('***************************  ');
    fprintf('\n*\t\t\t Computer Vision and Image Processing Lab\t\t\t  *');
    fprintf('\n*\t\t\t\t\t\t <Your Name Here> \t\t\t\t\t\t  *');
    fprintf('\n***************************************');
    fprintf('***********************\n');

    while ~exitLab  %continue until user selects the Exit option.
        fprintf('\n\t0.\tExit ');
        fprintf('\n\t1.\tThreshold Operation \n\n\t');

        % obtain an integer between 0 and CASE_MAX from the user
        choice = input('Enter your choice: ');        %input from user

        %switch case for multiple operations
        switch choice

            %   0. Exit
            case 0
                exitLab = true;  %turn exit program flag ON to exit program

            %   1. Threshold Operation
            case 1
                % Get the input image from user
                cvipImage = input_image();  %call input_image function
%check if input image entered, otherwise escape the remaining statements
                if isempty(cvipImage), continue;
                end
                figure;  %creates new figure window
%divide figure window into two sub-regions, and select first sub-region to plot
                subplot(1,2,1);
                datacursormode on; %allows viewer to see pixel values
                imshow(cvipImage); %display input image in first sub-region
                title('Input Image'); %show title of input image in figure window

                % calls the threshold function
                [outputImage, time_taken] = threshold_lab(cvipImage);
fprintf('The execution time was %f sec.\n\n', time_taken); %display execution time of
threshold operation

                % display the resultant image
                subplot(1,2,2); %select second sub-region to plot
                imshow(outputImage); %display output image in second sub-region
```

```
            title('Thresholded Image'); %output image title in figure window

         % Other cases
         Otherwise
%display warning for incorrect choice in command window
             fprintf('Sorry ! You Entered a wrong choice\n');
      end %end of switch


   end %end of while
```

The second file, *input_image.m,* contains a function that opens a dialog box which allows the user to select an image to be loaded (opened). It is an example M-file which implements a simple function. The first line contains the keyword *function,* which means this file implements a function, and it is not simply a script, so it can take inputs and return outputs. Following this are lines of text which comprise the command line *help* information for the function. This function illustrates the input of standard monochrome or color images, or indexed images that require a separate colormap, such as some TIFF image files. The program listing for the *input_image.m* file:

```
function cvipImage = input_image()
%INPUT_IMAGE Input an image file using file selection dialog box.
%The function reads an image selected by user via file selection dialog
%box, and returns it as a RGB image. If the input image is an indexed
%image, it will be converted to RGB image using ind2rgb() function.
%Furthermore, if user cancels the file selection, the function will return
%an empty matrix.
%-------------------------------------------------------------------------
%
%              Credit(s): Norsang Lama, Scott E Umbaugh
%                         Southern Illinois University Edwardsville
%              Date : 1-15-2017
%
%    Copyright (C) 2017 Scott Umbaugh and SIUE
%
%              _____


   %open file selection dialog box to input image
   [filename, pathname] = uigetfile({'*.*', 'All Files (*.*)';...
       '*.tif','TIFF (*.tif)'; '*.bmp','BMP (*.bmp)';...
       '*.jpg', 'JPEG/JPEG2000 (*.jpg)'; '*.png','PNG (*.png)';...
       '*.pbm ; *.ppm;*.pgm; *.pnm',...
       'PBM/PPM/PGM/PNM (*.pbm,*.ppm,*.pgm, *.pnm)';...
       '*.gif','GIF (*.gif)'}, ...
       'Select an input image file', 'MultiSelect','off');
        %multiple file selection option is OFF, single file only

   %check if user has successfully made the file selection
   if ~isequal(filename,0)
       % read the selected image from given path
       [cvipImage,map]=imread([pathname filename]);

       %check image is either indexed image or rgb image
       %indexed image consists of a data matrix and a colormap matrix
       %rgb image consists of a data matrix only
       if ~isempty(map) %indexed image if map is not empty
```

```
            cvipImage = ind2rgb(cvipImage,map);%convert indexed image to rgb image
        end

    else
        warning('Image file not selected!!!');  %warn user if cancelled
        cvipImage=[];                %return empty matrix if selection cancelled
    end

end %end of input_image function
```

The code for the third and final file, *threshold.m*, is an example of a simple CVIP function, a threshold function. Note that in this file, we provide two versions of the threshold function: (1) Using the standard programing loop(s) to cycle through an image and (2) a vectorized version of the code, which is discussed in more detail in the next section. In addition to the output image that is returned, the function returns the time it takes so that the user can compare the loop-based and vectorized methods. The first line contains the keyword *function*, which means this file implements a function and it is not simply a script, so it can take inputs and return outputs. Following this are lines of text which comprise the command line *help* information for the function. The program listing for the *threshold_lab.m* file:

```
function [ outputImage, time_taken] = threshold_lab( inputImage)
%THRESHOLD_LAB Image thresholding.
%The function performs the multiband thresholding of an input image.
%The user can select either Loop-based method or Vectorization method to
%perform the threshold operation. Vectorization method involves vectorized
%code, which looks like a mathematical expressions and is easier to
%understand. Also, it runs much faster than the non-vectorized code, i.e.
%loop-based code.
%The threshold function will compare the actual gray level of the input
%image with the threshold value. If the gray-level value is greater than
%the threshold value, then the gray level is set to WHITE, else to BLACK.
%This function assumes inputImage as of either 'double' or 'uint8' class.
%The output arguments are a thresholded image, and the execution time of
%threshold operation.
%-------------------------------------------------------------------------
%
%            Credit(s): Norsang Lama, Scott E Umbaugh
%                       Southern Illinois University Edwardsville
%               Date : 1-15-2017
%
%   Copyright (C) 2017 Scott Umbaugh and SIUE
%
%   _____

MAX = 255; %Set maximum pixel value as 255

%Assuming the data type of input image as either 'double' or 'uint8'
if isa(inputImage,'double')  %check if datatype of image is double
    WHITE_LAB = 1.0;    BLACK_LAB = 0.0; %imread puts double data1 range 0 to 1.
elseif isa(inputImage,'uint8') %check if datatype of image is uint8
    WHITE_LAB = 255;    BLACK_LAB = 0; %uint8, data matrix's range 0 to 255.
end

while true %continues on until the successful threshold operation
```

```
%Analyze the performance of Loop-based method vs. vectorization method
fprintf('\n\t\t1. Loop-based method');
fprintf('\n\t\t2. Vectorization method');
fprintf('\n\n\t\tPlease enter your choice:');
option = input(' ');  %request user input, input argument is a space character
fprintf('\t\t');
%check if user input is numeric, and equal to either 1 or 2
if ~isnumeric(option ) || option ~= 1 && option ~=2
    warning('Incorrect choice!')  %display warning message for incorrect choice
      continue;   %avoid remaining statements, repeat the loop
end

%  ask user to input threshold value (0 to 255)
fprintf('\n\t\tPlease enter a threshold value (0 - 255):');
%request user input, input argument is a space character
threshval = input(' ');
% convert threshold value in the range [0,1] if input image double type
if ~(WHITE_LAB == MAX)
    threshval = threshval/MAX;
end

fprintf('\t\t');
if (~isnumeric(threshval)) || (threshval<BLACK_LAB) || (threshval>WHITE_LAB) %check
if entered value is numeric and within a range of 0-255.
    warning('Entered value is not numeric or not within the range of 0-255!');
    continue;   %avoid remaining statements, repeat the loop
end

outputImage = inputImage; %set output image equal to input image

switch option    %switch option for two methods

    % loop-based method
    case 1
        tic;   %start stopwatch timer
        [row,col,band] = size(inputImage); % get #rows, #cols, #bands
        for b=1:band  %first for-loop to run for each band
            for r=1:row %second for-loop to run for each row
                for c=1:col %third for-loop to run for each column
                    if inputImage(r,c,b)>threshval %compare current pixel
                                                    %value with threshold
                        outputImage(r,c,b) = WHITE_LAB;
                                                %set current pixel as
                                                %WHITE if greater
                    else
                        outputImage(r,c,b) = BLACK_LAB;
                                                %else set current
                                                %pixel as BLACK
                    end %end of if
                end %end of third for-loop
            end %end of second for-loop
        end %end of first for-loop
        time_taken = toc; %stop timer, assign execution time to 'time_taken'
        return;  %return control to invoking function

    % vectorization method
    case 2
        tic; %start stopwatch timer
```

```
                outputImage(outputImage>threshval)=WHITE_LAB; %compare each pixel to
                                        %threshold, if greater set WHITE
                outputImage(outputImage<=threshval)=BLACK_LAB; %compare each pixel to
                                        %threshold,less or equal set BLACK
            time_taken = toc; %stop timer, assign execution time to 'time_taken'
            return;    %return control to invoking function
      end %end of switch

  end %end of while

  end %end of function
```

The input and threshold functions can be used as models for development of your own functions in the programming exercises and in project development.

2.4.5 Vectorization

MATLAB scripts in the form of M-files represent an interpreted language and so have no need for compilation and linking, such as our CVIPlab for C programming requires. This has the advantage of rapid prototyping, but the disadvantage of potentially running slowly. MATLAB is optimized to operate on vectors and matrices (remember MATLAB is short for <u>Mat</u>rix <u>Lab</u>oratory), so even a script can be written to run fast if the code is written to take advantage of this property. To do this, the code must be written using the concept of *vectorization*, which means writing the code to maximize the use of array operations. This means we avoid the use of *for loops* on scalar elements in an array (such as an image), if we can use array operations directly. Due to the importance of this, we have provided two examples of our model function, in the *threshold.m* file, and we will illustrate the difference.

An example of using *for loop* programing structure on scalar elements is shown in the first example of the threshold functions as follows:

```
% loop-based method
      case 1
          tic;   %start stopwatch timer
          [row,col,band]=size(inputImage); %get image info
          for b=1:band   %band for-loop
              for r=1:row %row for-loop
                  for c=1:col %column for-loop
                      if inputImage(r,c,b)>threshval
                          outputImage(r,c,b)=WHITE_LAB;
                      else
                          outputImage(r,c,b)=BLACK_LAB;
                      end %end of if
                  end %end of column for-loop
              end %end of row for-loop
          end %end of band for-loop
          time_taken=toc; %stop timer, assign execution time to 'time_taken'
          return;  %return control to invoking function
```

Here, we also show how to time a function using *tic* to start a stopwatch timer and *toc* to stop the timer and assign it to a variable, in this case *time_taken*. This type of loop structure can be used to process multiband images. However, it is much more efficient to vectorize the code by taking advantage of array operations available. Any function that performs the same operation on all the pixels in the image lends itself to vectorization. Implementation of the threshold operation with array operations or vectorization of the code is shown here:

```
% vectorization method, note: output image was initialized to equal input image
      case 2
            tic; %start stopwatch timer
            outputImage(outputImage>threshval)=WHITE_LAB;
            outputImage(outputImage<=threshval)=BLACK_LAB;
            time_taken=toc; %stop timer, assign execution time to 'time_taken'
            return;    %return control to invoking function
```

A comparison of executing the loop-based method and the vectorized code will be performed in the introductory laboratory exercise at the end of the chapter.

2.4.6 Using CVIPlab for MATLAB

To use CVIPlab, run MATLAB and open the folder where the CVIPlab files reside. The CVIPlab can be executed by typing "CVIPlab" at a command prompt or by selecting the file in the editor and clicking on the Run button. Upon execution of CVIPlab, the command window will appear as shown in Figure 2.4-4. The skeleton program provides a simple text-based user interface for the student or developer. Functions can be easily added and customized allowing the user to focus on the CVIP development.

After an image is loaded into CVIPlab, a figure window is created as shown in Figure 2.4-5. Initially, the input image is displayed on the left side of the window, as a result of this code in CVIPlab:

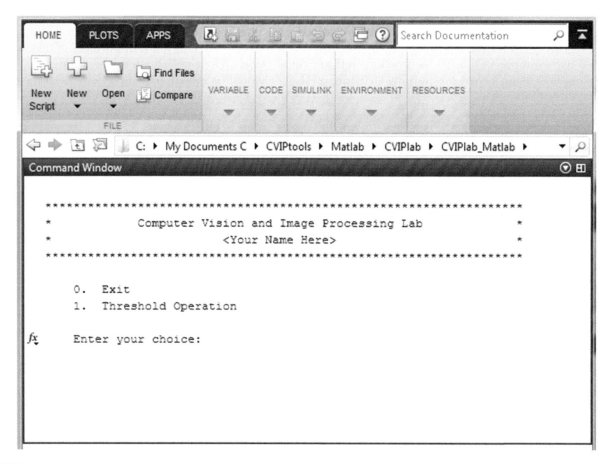

FIGURE 2.4-4
CVIPlab command window. When the CVIPlab is invoked, a command window will appear as shown. The skeleton program provides a simple text-based user interface for the student or developer. Functions can be easily added and customized allowing the user to focus on the CVIP development.

FIGURE 2.4-5
The CVIPlab figure display window. After an image is loaded into CVIPlab, it is displayed on the left side of the figure window that is created. After the function is executed, the output image is displayed on the right side of the window. MATLAB has many built-in functions for image manipulation within this window, such as displaying the pixel values and image geometry operations.

```
figure;  %creates new figure window
subplot(1,2,1); %divide figure window into two sub-regions,select first sub-region
datacursormode on; %allows viewer to see pixel values
imshow(cvipImage); %display input image in first sub-region
title('Input Image'); %show title of input image in figure window
```

After the function is executed, the output image is shown on the right side of the CVIPlab display window (MATLAB figure), as a result of the following code in CVIPlab:

```
subplot(1,2,2); %select second sub-region to plot
imshow(outputImage); %display output image in second sub-region
title('Thresholded Image'); %output image title in figure window
```

The CVIPlab display window is shown in Figure 2.4-5. MATLAB has many built-in functions for image manipulation within this window, such as displaying the pixel values and image geometry operations.

To verify gains attained by vectorization compared to loop-based code, we performed the threshold operation with both methods. The results are shown in Figure 2.4-6 where we see that, even for the most basic operation such as an image threshold, the vectorization provides a speed increase of more than a factor of 4. It took close to 0.9 seconds for the loop-based code and only about 0.2 seconds for the vectorized code. With a more complex operation, the difference can be orders of magnitude, and if batch processing a large set of images for algorithm development, the time savings can be very significant.

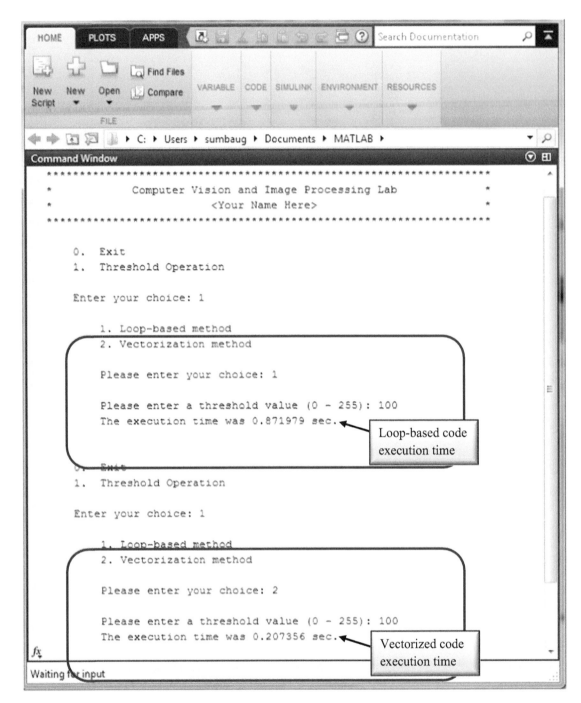

FIGURE 2.4-6
Executing the threshold function in CVIPlab: comparison of loop-based code to vectorized code. Even for a simple threshold function, the loop-based code takes more than four times as long as the vectorized code.

2.4.7 Adding a Function

To add a function to CVIPlab in MATLAB, first open the *CVIPlab.m* file in the editor. This can be done by selecting the file itself or by typing "edit CVIPlab.m" in a command window prompt. If this is the first new function you are adding to CVIPlab, update the file header and insert your name into the user interface text as shown in Figure 2.4-7. Next, add your function name to the text-based user interface with an *fprintf()* statement as shown in Figure 2.4-8. Now we can insert the new *case* to the *switch* statement for the new function using the threshold function case statement as a prototype.

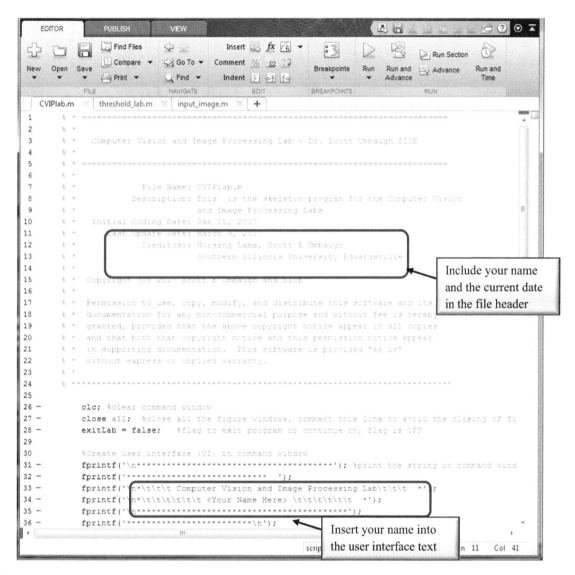

FIGURE 2.4-7
Initial edits for CVIPlab. First update the header with your name and the current date, then insert your name into the user interface text.

The next step is to create the new function, and here, we can use the threshold function M-file as a prototype and modify it accordingly. As the *threshold_lab.m* file contains code in both the loop-based and the vector-based implementation, the developer can select the desired prototype and copy it into the file for the new function. Be sure to thoroughly comment your code, so that anyone examining the code can understand it easily.

2.4.8   A Sample Batch Processing M-File

Research and development for CVIP applications often requires running experiments to process large groups of images. Examples include developing and testing computer vision algorithms for facial recognition, medical image diagnosis or robotic control. In applications development, whether for human vision or computer vision applications, the need to process large sets of different groups of images leads to the creation of tools to automate the process. This is the underlying philosophy of CVIPtools, and in particular, the associated utilities CVIP-ATAT and CVIP-FEPC.

To facilitate this process in MATLAB, a utility for batch processing of images was created. The utility was written as an M-file script, and it allows for batch processing of a user selected set of images with a fixed sequence of

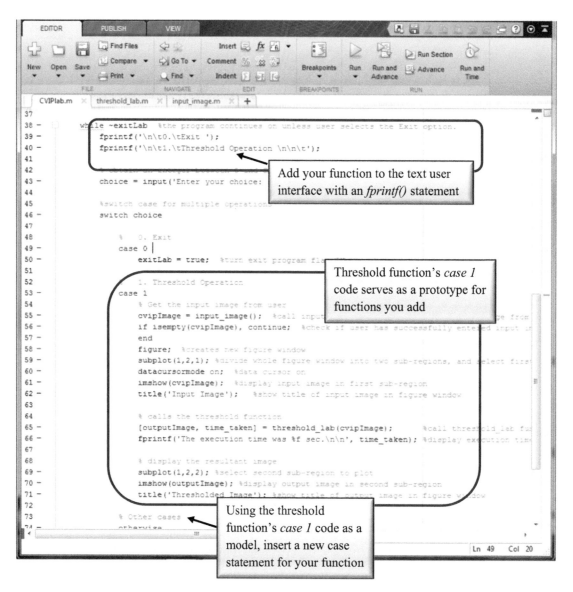

FIGURE 2.4-8
Modifications to the CVIPlab.m file for adding a function to CVIPlab. Insert your function name into the text user interface. Next, using the threshold case statement as a model, insert a new case statement after the comment "Other cases".

operations and then writes the output images to a user-specified directory. A sample version of the batch processing file, *batch_cvip.m*, is included with the CVIP Toolbox distribution, which illustrates its use with a few sample functions. To run your own algorithm on a set of images, simply replace the sample functions with the sequence of functions needed to implement your algorithm.

The M-file script for this sample function, *batch_cvip.m*, is shown here:

```
% batch_cvip: This script is for performing a sequence of image processing
% operations in batch mode. It reads multiple images as selected by the user and
% performs a sequence of operations on the set of input images. The output images
% are then stored in the folder specified by the user.

clc;
clear;
```

```
[filename, pathname] = uigetfile({'*.*', 'All Files (*.*)';...
        '*.tif','TIFF (*.tif)'; '*.bmp','BMP (*.bmp)';...
        '*.jpg', 'JPEG/JPEG2000 (*.jpg)'; '*.png','PNG (*.png)';...
        '*.pbm ; *.ppm;*.pgm; *.pnm',...
        'PBM/PPM/PGM/PNM (*.pbm,*.ppm,*.pgm, *.pnm)';...
        '*.gif','GIF (*.gif)'}, ...
        'Select an input image file', 'MultiSelect','on');% prompts user to select
                                                % the input files
 if ~isa(filename,'cell')
    filename = cellstr(filename); % converts filename to cell structure
end
folder_name = uigetdir; % prompts user to select folder to save output images
for i = 1:size(filename,2) % iterate through all input image files
    imageName = char(filename(i)); % read the name of input image
    im = imread([pathname imageName]); % load the particular image for operation

%_____REPLACE THESE SAMPLE FUNCTIONS WITH YOUR ALGORITHM_____

    a=rgb2lab_cvip(im); % converts rgb image to L*a*b* color space
    b=luminance_cvip(a); % performs luminance operation
    c=not_cvip(b); % performs NOT operation

%_____

    [~,name,ext] = fileparts(filename{i}); % separate the filename and extension
    FinalImageName = strcat(name,'_',int2str(i),ext); % create new output filename
    imwrite(a,[folder_name '\' FinalImageName]); % write image to disk
    disp(i); % display the image number in process
end
```

2.4.9 VIPM File Format

The <u>V</u>isualization in <u>I</u>mage <u>P</u>rocessing for <u>MATLAB</u> image file format, *vipm*, was created to handle any data types or formats, including complex data (similar to the *vip* format in CVIPtools). This allows us to save image spectra or any processed images without losing information. This capability is useful during research and development where we may want to examine images at each stage of an algorithm to help guide the development process.

To facilitate use of the *vipm* file format, the functions *vipmread_cvip* and *vipmwrite_cvip* are available. Details and examples of the use of these functions can be found in the Help pages. The file format is described in Table 2-2. When the file is opened for reading, various fields are stored in the order as listed in the table. The size of the pixel data varies and depends on the number of rows, number of columns, number of bands, data type and data format (real or complex). The pixel data is stored by band (not pixel vector); so, a typical color image has the red band first, then green, then the blue band. Additionally, to take advantage of vectorization, the pixel data is ordered by column (not row). If the data is complex, the real image data is stored first for all the bands, followed by the imaginary data for all bands. To access the pixel data, the offset from the beginning of file (BOF) to both the real and imaginary data is provided. Note that a *history* structure is included in the defined format for custom and future use. The parameter options for pertinent data fields are shown in Table 2-3.

TABLE 2-2

VIPM File Format

Name	Description	Type/Length	Size	Value	Remarks
byte_order	Byte ordering	char/2	2 bytes	le or be	le: little-endian be: big-endian ascii character string
vip_version	Version of VIP image	char/4	4 bytes	vipm	ascii character string
file_mod_date	Latest file modification date	double/1	8 bytes	Serial date number	
cmpr_format	Compression method	uint8/1	1 bytes	0–18	See Table 2-3.
image_format	Original image format	uint8/1	1 bytes	0–33	See Table 2-3
color_format	Color space type	uint8/1	1 bytes	0–9	See Table 2-3
cvip_type	Data type of the image data	uint8/1	1 bytes	0–4	See Table 2-3
no_of_bands	Number of bands	uint8/1	1 bytes		
no_of_cols	Image width or number of columns	uint16/1	2 bytes		
no_of_rows	Image height or number of rows	uint16/1	2 bytes		
data_format	Data format of image data	uint8/1	1 bytes	0 or 1	0: real 1: complex
history_info	History information	struct/1	7 bytes	History status (1 byte, uint8), Size of history (2 bytes, uint16), History pointer offset (4 bytes, uint32)	
real_pixdata_offset	Offset from beginning of file to real image data	uint32/1	4 bytes		
imag_pixdata_offset	Offset from beginning of file to imaginary image data, if complex	uint32/1	4 bytes		
Pixel data pointed to by the offset values (above)	The raw pixel values	cvip_type	Varies	The pixel data is ordered by band; red, then green, etc. It is stored by columns (not row). Use offsets to index to pixel data	

TABLE 2-3

Parameter Options for *VIPM* File Format

Name	Parameter Options
cvip_type	cvip_byte, cvip_short, cvip_long, cvip_float, cvip_double
data_format	real, complex
color_format	binary, gray_scale, rgb, hsl, hsv, sct, cct, luv, lab, xyz
image_format	pbm, pgm, ppm, eps, tif, gif, ras, itx, iris, ccc, bin, vip, glr, btc, brc, huf, zvl, arith, btc2, btc3, dpc, zon, zon2, safvr, jpg, wvq, fra, vq, xvq, trcm, ps, bmp, jp2, png
cmpr_format	none, btc, btc2, btc3, dpcm, zvl, glr, brc, huf, zon, zon2, jpg, wvq, fra, vq, xvq, trcm, top, jp2

2.5 References and Further Reading

Details for using Visual Studio with CVIPlab can be found in the Online Docs at www.routledge.com/9781032071299. In addition to the information on the Help pages with the software, complete function lists for the C, COM and MATLAB functions are in the Online Docs zip file. For a good introduction to general MATLAB use and programming for engineers, as well as a good basic reference with examples, see Hahn and Valentine (2013). The basics of computer imaging with MATLAB are included in Solomon and Breckon (2011), along with simple examples relating to enhancement, frequency domain processing, segmentation, feature extraction and classification. The Theodoridis et al. (2010) book is a supplement to their Pattern Recognition text and its focus is in this area. It is a brief book, but has many MATLAB examples and exercises.

To learn more about medical image processing in the MATLAB environment, Birkfellner (2014) provides a very useful introduction. The classic Gonzalez image processing textbook has a companion MATLAB text (Gonzalez, Woods, & Eddins, 2020). It has a number of examples, tutorials and is based on using the MATLAB Image Processing (IP) Toolbox. The new Gonzalez image processing text includes MATLAB projects and examples (Gonzalez and Woods 2018). Another book with tutorials based on the MATLAB IP Toolbox, examples and image processing basics is Marques (2011). For robotics applications, which include computer and pattern recognition, see Corke (2013); although not an introductory book, it contains numerous examples and images. In addition to these books, much information is available on the internet, including tutorials on the MATLAB web site and many users groups. For the C programmers, the classic book written by the creators of the language is still one of the best (Kernighan & Ritchie, 1988).

Birkfellner, W., *Applied Medical Image Processing: A Basic Course*, 2nd Edition, Boca Raton, FL: CRC Press, Taylor and Francis Group, 2014.
Corke, P., *Robotics, Vision and Control: Fundamental Algorithms in MATLAB*, New York: Springer, 2013.
Gonzalez, R.C., Woods, R.E., Eddins, S.L., *Digital Image Processing Using MATLAB*, 3rd Edition, Knoxville, TN: Gatesmark, 2020.
Gonzalez, R.C., Woods, R.E., *Digital Image Processing*, 4th Edition, Hoboken, NJ: Pearson Education, 2018.
Hahn, B. Valentine, D.T., *Essential MATLAB for Engineers and Scientists*, 5th Edition, Cambridge, MA: Academic Press, 2013.
Kernighan, B.W., Ritchie, D.M, *The C Programming Language*, 2nd Edition, Upper Saddle River, NJ: Prentice Hall, 1988.
Marques, O., *Practical Image and Video Processing MATLAB*, Piscataway, NJ: IEEE Press/Wiley, 2011.
Solomon, C., Breckon, T., *Fundamentals of Digital Image Processing: Practical Approach with Examples in MATLAB*, West Sussex: Wiley-Blackwell, 2011.
Theodoridis, S., Pikrakis, A., Koutroumbas, K., Cavouras, D., *Introduction to Pattern Recognition: A MATLAB Approach*, Burlington, MA: Elsevier, Academic Press, 2010.

2.6   Introductory Programming Exercises

Introduction to CVIPlab and C Libraries

1. Refer to Section 2.3 to become familiar with the CVIPlab C functions.

2. Build the CVIPlab project. This will compile CVIPlab.c and threshold_lab.c functions and link them with any necessary library functions.

3. Run CVIPlab, select menu choice 2, threshold, and experiment with various threshold values.

4. Edit the CVIPlab.c program to include your name in the header. Study the CVIPlab.c file and understand how this program is organized and how the threshold function works. In particular, learn how images are read, written and manipulated.

5. Modify your CVIPlab to save the output image after it is displayed. The image is saved with the *write_Image* function. The prototype for the *write_Image* function is:

```
write_Image(Image *cvip_Image, char *filename, CVIP_BOOLEAN, retain_image, CVIP_BOOLEAN
set_up, IMAGE_FORMAT new_format, CVIP_BOOLEAN showmessages)
      <cvip_Image> - pointer to valid CVIP Image structure
      <filename> - pointer to a character string containing the file name
      <retain_image> - retain image after writing?
      <set_up> - run setup?
      <new_format> - enumerated constant specifying the format of the file to be written
      <showmessages> - shall I be verbose?
```

The CVIP_BOOLEAN parameters are 0 or 1, for NO or YES, and the file format is one from the following list:

```
typedef enum {PBM, PGM, PPM, EPS, TIF, GIF, RAS, ITX, IRIS, CCC, BIN, VIP, GLR, BTC,
BRC, HUF, ZVL, ARITH, BTC2, BTC3, DPC, ZON, ZON2, SAFVR, JPG, WVQ, FRA, VQ, XVQ, TRCM,
PS, BMP, JP2, PNG} IMAGE_FORMAT;
```

More details and an example for using *write_Image,* or any CVIPtools C function, can be found in the Help pages in CVIPtools. After incorporating *write_Image* into CVIPlab, build the CVIPlab project, run the program and save the output from at least 3 different threshold values.

6. Run the GUI-based CVIPtools program. Open the original image and the output images from CVIPlab with the file open icon near the top left of the main window. Select *Utilities,* then select the *Convert/Binary Threshold* option and perform the same threshold operations that were done in CVIPlab. Next, compare CVIPtools results to your CVIPlab results to verify correctness. Use the *Utilities→Compare* option to compare the images. Are they the same? Why or why not? At the end of this exercise, you should understand the CVIPlab environment and be able to write your own functions by using the threshold function as a prototype.

Introduction to the CVIP Toolbox for MATLAB

1. Refer to Section 2.4 and review the MATLAB Help pages for the CVIP Toolbox functions to become familiar with the CVIP Toolbox.

2. Run the CVIPlab to load an image, threshold the image and display the output image.

3. Compare the time for the loop-based method and vectorization method. Which method is faster? Why? How does the time change if a larger image is used?

4. Edit the CVIPlab.m program to include your name in the header. Study the CVIPlab.m, input_image.m and threshold_lab.m files and understand how CVIPlab is organized and how the threshold function works. In particular, learn how images are read, manipulated and displayed.

5. Modify your CVIPlab to save the output image after it is displayed. The image is saved with the *imwrite* function. The basic method of using this function is:

```
> imwrite(A, FILENAME, FMT)
```

This will write (save) the image A to the file specified by FILENAME in the format specified by FMT. More information for imwrite, or any MATLAB function, can be found by typing:

```
> help imwrite
```

After incorporating *imwrite* into CVIPlab, run the program and save the output from at least three different threshold values.

6. Run the GUI-based CVIPtools program. Open the original image and the output images from CVIPlab with the file open icon near the top left of the main window. Select *Utilities,* then select the *Convert/Binary Threshold* option and perform the same threshold operations that were done in CVIPlab. Next, compare CVIPtools results to your CVIPlab results to verify correctness. Use the *Utilities→Compare* option to compare the images. Are they the same? Why or why not? At the end of this exercise, you should understand the CVIPlab environment and be able to write your own functions by using the threshold function as a prototype.

Color Space Conversion

1. Write a function to perform color space conversion. Include forward and inverse transforms for HIS, SCT and CCT. This can be done in MATLAB or in C with the CVIPlab program.

2. Compare your results to those obtained with CVIPtools using *Utilities→Convert→Color Space.* Are the results the same? Why or why not?

3. Research the CIE color spaces and implement the $L^*u^*v^*$ and $L^*a^*b^*$ color conversion functions.

4. Compare your results to those obtained with CVIPtools using *Utilities→Convert→Color Space.* Are the results the same? Why or why not?

Image Viewer

1. Write your own image viewer to use in MATLAB or CVIPlab. Model it on the CVIPtools viewer.

2. Integrate the viewer with the image processing functions so that the user can vary parameters in real time and the image will be updated accordingly.

Graphical User Interface

1. Implement a GUI for the CVIPlab program with the CVIP threshold function.

2. Allow the user to vary parameters of the function via the GUI and have the image results displayed in (almost) real time. For example, use sliders to vary the threshold parameter.

3. Add three more functions of your choice to the GUI and make the parameters interactive.

2.7 Computer Vision and Image Analysis Projects

These projects can be approached in two ways: the reader can cover the pertinent topics before attempting to develop a project or the reader can start project development and refer to the appropriate material as needed. The best projects are the ones that are created by you. We live in a visual world surrounded by images: Images in our lives, images on television, images on the internet and images in our minds. Look around and see how to apply what you learn to the world as you see it. Select an area of interest to explore and capture or find the images needed. Here, we provide procedures for project development, as well as example topics. Do not limit project ideas to these, but rather use them as a starting point and motivation for a project of your own. The following process can be followed to streamline project development:

1. Use CVIPtools to explore algorithm development, using primarily the *Analysis* window for these types of projects. Use the image analysis process as described in Chapter 3 and outlined as follows.

   a. First, apply any necessary or desired preprocessing.

   b. Experiment with the *Edge/Line Detection* (Chapter 4), *Segmentation* (Chapter 5) and *Transforms* (Fourier Transform: Chapter 6) windows to investigate spatial and spectral properties of the images.

   c. Apply filtering techniques to the resulting images. Morphological filters are used for segmented images, and transform filters are used for the transformed images. Examine the results, keeping in the mind the application.

   d. After determining a suitable algorithm to separate the image into objects of interest, use the *Features* window to perform feature extraction (Chapter 6). Spectral features can be selected based on results from examining spectral information. Create separate training and test sets, if desired.

   e. Use the *Pattern Classification* window (Chapter 7) to determine the success for your test set. If the results are satisfactory, proceed to the next step or else go back to algorithm development starting with (a) above.

2. Code the algorithm developed into the CVIPlab program using either C/C++ or MATLAB and the associated functions. Information for use of the functions, including examples, can be found in the Help files.

3. Test the algorithm(s) on real images input from an imaging device or on a test set of images.

4. Analyze the results and present them visually in graphs or charts. If averages are used, be sure to include information about variation, such as standard deviations.

Example Project Topics

1. Implement a program for the recognition of geometric shapes, for example, circles, squares, rectangles and triangles. Make it robust so that it can determine if a shape is unknown. Images can be created with CVIPtools, but they should be blurred and noise added to them for realism. Alternately, the images can be captured with your image acquisition system by drawing the shapes or by capturing images of real objects.

2. Experiment with the classification of tools, for example, screwdrivers, wrenches and hammers. Find features that will differentiate the classes of tools. Design a method for system calibration and then identify various sizes of nuts and bolts, as well as number of threads per inch.

3. Implement a program to identify different types of currencies – coins or bills. Experiment with extracting regions of interest (ROI) that you think will best classify the various items selected for your project. Experiment with various histogram, texture and spectral features. Make it robust so that it cannot be fooled by counterfeits.

4. Design a program to read bar codes. Experiment with different types of codes. Experiment with different methods to bring images into the system. In general, scanners will be easier to work with than cameras – verify this.

5. Implement a program to perform character recognition. Start with a subset, such as numbers 0–9, and then expand using what you have learned. Experiment with different fonts, printers and lighting conditions.

6. Imagine we are designing a robotic system to put dishes in the dishwasher after a meal. Collect an image database of cups, glasses, bowls, plates, forks, knives and spoons. Develop an algorithm to identify the objects.

7. Take pictures of your fellow students. Develop an algorithm to identify them. This could be done via facial recognition, iris (eye) recognition or other suitable features based on your image set.

8. Acquire medical images from the web for a specific pathology (disease) along with normal images. These types of images may include X-rays, MRI or PET scans. Develop an algorithm to differentiate the diseased images from the normal images.

9. Capture images with various colored objects in a scene. Experiment with different color spaces to find an algorithm to identify the objects.

10. Capture images with different textures in a scene. Experiment with different features to find an algorithm to identify the objects. Write functions for your own texture features that are not included in the CVIPtools libraries.

3

Image Analysis and Computer Vision

3.1 Introduction

Digital image analysis is a key factor in solving any imaging problem. Acquisition of a sample image database and examination of these images for the application is the first step in the development of an imaging solution. *Image analysis* involves detailed investigation of the image data to determine exactly the information required to develop the computer vision system. The solution to the problem may require the use of existing hardware and software or may require the development of new algorithms and system designs. The image analysis process helps to define the requirements for the system being developed. This analysis is typically part of a larger process, is iterative in nature and allows us to answer application-specific questions such as: How much spatial and brightness resolution is needed? Will the existing methods solve the problem? Is color or multispectral information needed? Do we need to transform the image data into the frequency domain? Do we need to segment the image to find object information? What are the important features in the images? Is the hardware fast enough for the application?

3.1.1 Overview

Image analysis is primarily a data reduction process. A single image contains on the order of many megabytes of data, so a large image database may contain vast amounts of data. Often much of this information is not necessary to solve a specific imaging problem, so a primary part of the image analysis task is to determine exactly what information is necessary. With many applications, the feasibility of system development is determined by the results from the preliminary image analysis. Image analysis is used in the development of both computer vision and human vision imaging applications.

For computer vision applications, the end product is typically the extraction of high-level information for computer analysis, manipulation or control. This high-level information may include shape parameters to control a robotic manipulator, terrain analysis to enable a vehicle to navigate on mars, or color and texture features to aid in the diagnosis of a skin lesion. Image analysis is central to the computer vision process and is often uniquely associated with computer vision; *a computer vision system is essentially a deployed image analysis system.*

3.1.2 System Model

The *image analysis process*, illustrated in Figure 3.1-1, can be broken down into three primary stages: (1) preprocessing, (2) data reduction and (3) feature analysis. Preprocessing is used to remove noise and eliminate irrelevant, visually unnecessary information. *Noise* is unwanted information that can result from the image acquisition process. Other preprocessing steps might include gray level or spatial quantization – reducing the number of bits per pixel or the image size, or finding regions of interest for further processing. The second stage, data reduction, involves either reducing the data in the spatial domain and/or transforming it into another domain called the frequency domain (Figure 3.1-2) and then extracting features for the analysis process. In the third stage, feature analysis, the features extracted by the data reduction process are examined and evaluated for their use in the application.

A more detailed diagram of this process is shown in Figure 3.1-3. After preprocessing, segmentation can be performed in the spatial domain (Chapter 5) or the image can be converted into the frequency domain via a Fourier transform (Chapter 6). Note the dotted line between segmentation and the transform block; this is for extracting spectral features on segmented parts of the image. After either of these processes, the image may undergo filtering. The filtering process further reduces the data, and it is followed by the extraction of features required for image analysis. After the analysis block, a feedback loop provides for an application-specific review of the analysis results. This approach often leads to an iterative process that is not complete until satisfactory results are achieved. The application feedback loop is a key aspect of the entire process.

DOI: 10.1201/9781003221135-3

FIGURE 3.1-1
Image analysis. To analyze the image, useful higher level information must be extracted from the raw pixel data.

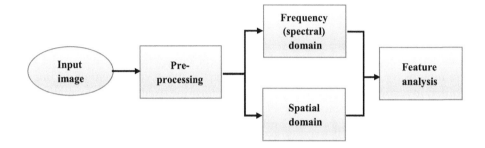

FIGURE 3.1-2
Image analysis domains. The image data can be analyzed in either or both the spatial doman, which is the raw pixel data $I(r, c)$, or can be transformed into another mathematical space called the frequency domain.

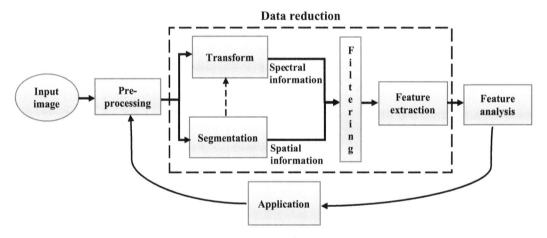

FIGURE 3.1-3
Image analysis details of data reduction. A detailed diagram of the data reduction process is shown. To obtain spectral (frequency) information, a transform is applied, followed by filtering and feature extraction. In the spatial domain, we perform a segmentation process to reduce the amount of data spatially, then filter and extract features. To complete the block diagram for image analysis, an application feedback loop has been added. This is a critical part of the analysis process as it is used to solve a computer vision problem. It also creates a process that is iterative in nature; as each time the results are fed back through the application, improvements can be made to the developed solution.

3.2 Preprocessing

The preprocessing algorithms, techniques and operators are used to perform initial processing that makes the primary data reduction and analysis task easier. They include operations related to extracting regions of interest, performing basic mathematical operations on images, simple enhancement of specific image features, color space transforms (see Chapters 1 and 5) and data reduction in both resolution and brightness. Preprocessing is a stage where the requirements are typically obvious and simple, such as the removal of artifacts from images or the elimination of image information that is not required for the application. For example, in one application, we needed to eliminate borders from the images that resulted from taking the pictures by looking out a window; in another, we had to mask out rulers that were present in skin tumor slides. Another example of a preprocessing step involves a

(a)   (b)

(c)   (d)

FIGURE 3.2-1
Preprocessing examples. (a) An image needing border removal, (b) the image after the border is removed, (c) an image where only shape information is necessary in order to control a robotic gripper and (d) the image after unnecessary information removal which leaves only the object shape.

robotic gripper that needs to pick and place an object; for this, a gray level image is reduced to a binary (two-valued) image, which contains all the information necessary to discern the object's outline. For applications involving color, a color space transform may be desired. Two of these examples can be seen in Figure 3.2-1.

3.2.1 Region of Interest Geometry

Investigation of a specific area within the image, called a region of interest (ROI), is often required in image analysis. To do this, we need operations that modify the spatial coordinates of the image and these are categorized as image geometry operations. The image geometry operations discussed here include crop, zoom, enlarge, shrink, translate and rotate.

The image *crop* process is the process of selecting a portion of the image, a sub-image, and cutting it away from the rest of the image – that's how the border was removed in Figure 3.2-1b. Once a sub-image is cropped from the original image, we can *zoom* in on it by enlarging it. Image enlargement is useful in a variety of applications since it can help visual analysis of object detail. For example, some imaging applications require that two input images be in tight geometrical alignment prior to their combination; this process is called image registration. Improper alignment of images can produce distortion at object boundaries. Enlargement of the images eases the task of manual alignment. Another example is with satellite images, where the resolution is very high and we are looking for specific objects within the larger image. The image zoom process can be used to scan throughout the image, selecting only areas most likely to contain the objects of interest.

The zoom process can be performed in numerous ways, but typically a zero-order hold or a first-order hold is used. A zero-order hold is performed by repeating previous pixel values, thus creating a blocky effect. To increase the image size with a first-order hold, linear interpolation is performed between adjacent pixels. A comparison of the images resulting from these two methods is shown in Figure 3.2-2.

(a)

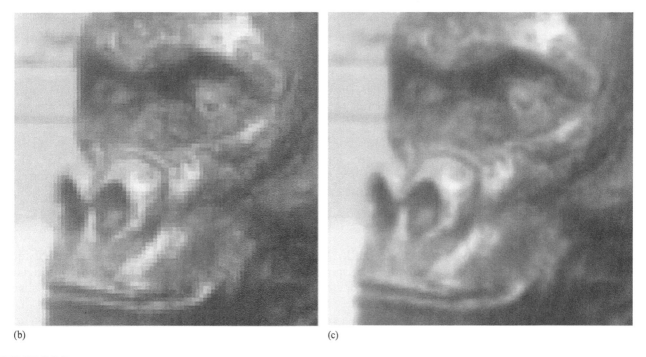

(b)   (c)

FIGURE 3.2-2
Zooming methods. (a) Original image. The ape's face will be zoomed by a factor of five. (b) Image enlarged by zero-order hold, notice the blocky effect. (c) Image enlarged by first-order hold, note the smoother effect.

Although the implementation of the zero-order hold is straightforward, the first-order hold is more complicated. The easiest way to do this is to find the average value between two pixels and use that as the pixel value between those two; this can be done for the rows first, as follows:

ORIGINAL IMAGE ARRAY   IMAGE WITH ROWS EXPANDED

$$
\begin{bmatrix}
8 & 4 & 8 \\
4 & 8 & 4 \\
8 & 2 & 8
\end{bmatrix}
\qquad
\begin{bmatrix}
8 & 6 & 4 & 6 & 8 \\
4 & 6 & 8 & 6 & 4 \\
8 & 5 & 2 & 5 & 8
\end{bmatrix}
$$

The first two pixels in the first row are averaged, $(8 + 4)/2 = 6$, and this number is inserted in between those two pixels. This is done for every pixel pair in each row. Next, take that result and expand the columns in the same way, as follows:

IMAGE WITH ROWS AND COLUMNS EXPANDED

$$
\begin{bmatrix}
8 & 6 & 4 & 6 & 8 \\
6 & 6 & 6 & 6 & 6 \\
4 & 6 & 8 & 6 & 4 \\
6 & 5.5 & 5 & 5.5 & 6 \\
8 & 5 & 2 & 5 & 8
\end{bmatrix}
$$

This method will allow us to enlarge an $N \times N$ sized image to a size of $(2N-1) \times (2N-1)$, and it can be repeated as desired. This method is called *bilinear interpolation* as it uses linear interpolation in two directions.

Another method that achieves a similar result requires a mathematical process called convolution. With this method of image enlargement, a two-step process is required: (1) extend the image by adding rows and columns of zeros between the existing rows and columns and (2) perform the convolution. The image is extended as follows:

ORIGINAL IMAGE ARRAY   IMAGE EXTENDED WITH ZERO

$$
\begin{bmatrix}
3 & 5 & 7 \\
2 & 7 & 6 \\
3 & 4 & 9
\end{bmatrix}
\qquad
\begin{bmatrix}
0 & 0 & 0 & 0 & 0 & 0 & 0 \\
0 & 3 & 0 & 5 & 0 & 7 & 0 \\
0 & 0 & 0 & 0 & 0 & 0 & 0 \\
0 & 2 & 0 & 7 & 0 & 6 & 0 \\
0 & 0 & 0 & 0 & 0 & 0 & 0 \\
0 & 3 & 0 & 4 & 0 & 9 & 0 \\
0 & 0 & 0 & 0 & 0 & 0 & 0
\end{bmatrix}
$$

Next, we use what is called a convolution mask which is slid across the extended image and a simple arithmetic operation is performed at each pixel location.

CONVOLUTION MASK FOR FIRST-ORDER HOLD

$$
\begin{bmatrix}
\tfrac{1}{4} & \tfrac{1}{2} & \tfrac{1}{4} \\
\tfrac{1}{2} & 1 & \tfrac{1}{2} \\
\tfrac{1}{4} & \tfrac{1}{2} & \tfrac{1}{4}
\end{bmatrix}
$$

The *convolution process* requires us to overlay the mask on the image, multiply the coincident values and sum all these results. This is equivalent to finding the *vector inner product* of the mask with the underlying sub-image.

For example, if we put the mask over the upper left corner of the image, we obtain (from right to left and top to bottom):

$$\tfrac{1}{4}\,(0)+\tfrac{1}{2}\,(0)+\tfrac{1}{4}\,(0)+\tfrac{1}{2}\,(0)+1\,(3)+\tfrac{1}{2}\,(0)+\tfrac{1}{4}\,(0)+\tfrac{1}{2}\,(0)+\tfrac{1}{4}\,(0)=3,$$

Note that the existing image values do not change. The next step is to slide the mask over by one pixel and repeat the process, as follows:

$$\tfrac{1}{4}\,(0)+\tfrac{1}{2}\,(0)+\tfrac{1}{4}\,(0)+\tfrac{1}{2}\,(3)+1\,(0)+\tfrac{1}{2}\,(5)+\tfrac{1}{4}\,(0)+\tfrac{1}{2}\,(0)+\tfrac{1}{4}\,(0)=4,$$

Note this is the average of the two existing neighbors. This process continues until we get to the end of the row, each time placing the result of the operation in the location corresponding to center of the mask. Once the end of the row is reached, the mask is moved down one row and the process is repeated row by row until this procedure has been performed on the entire image; the process of sliding, multiplying and summing is called convolution (see Figure 3.2-3). Note that the output image must be put in a separate image array, called a buffer, so that the existing values are not overwritten during the convolution process. If we designate the convolution mask as $M(r, c)$ and the image as $I(r, c)$, the convolution equation is given by:

$$\sum_{x=-\infty}^{+\infty}\sum_{y=-\infty}^{+\infty} I(r-x, c-y)M(x,y) \qquad\qquad (3.2\text{-}1)$$

For theoretical reasons beyond the scope of this discussion, this equation assumes that the image and mask are extended with zeros infinitely in all directions and that the origin of the mask is at its center. Also, for theoretical reasons, the previous description of convolution assumes that the convolution mask is symmetric; meaning if it is flipped about its center, it will remain the same. If it is not symmetric, it must be flipped before the procedure given can be followed. For computer imaging applications, these convolution masks are typically symmetric.

At this point, a good question would be: Why use this convolution method when it requires so many more calculations than the basic averaging-of-neighbors method? The answer is that many imaging systems can perform convolution in hardware, which is generally very fast, typically much faster than applying a faster algorithm in software. Not only can first-order hold be performed via convolution but zero-order hold can also be achieved by extending the image with zeros and using the following convolution mask:

ZERO-ORDER HOLD CONVOLUTION MASK

$$\begin{bmatrix} 1 & 1 \\ 1 & 1 \end{bmatrix}$$

Note that for this mask, the result will be put in the pixel location corresponding to the lower right corner, since there is no center pixel.

The above methods will only allow enlargement of an image by a factor of $(2N-1)$, but what if enlargement by a different factor is needed? To do this, a more general method is applied that takes two adjacent values and linearly interpolates more than one value between them. This *linear interpolation* technique is equivalent to finding the line that connects the two values in the brightness space and sampling it faster to get more samples, thus artificially increasing the resolution. This is done by defining an enlargement number K, then following this process: (1) subtract the two adjacent values, (2) divide the result by K, (3) add that result to the smaller value and keep adding the result from (2) in a running total until all $(K-1)$ intermediate pixel locations are filled.

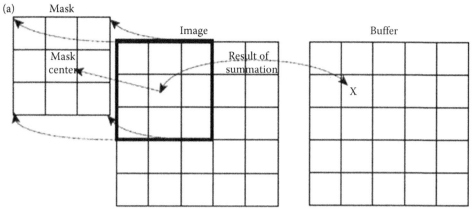

Overlay the convolution mask in the upper left corner of the image.
Multiply coincident terms, sum, put result into the image buffer
at the location that corresponds to the mask's current center,
which is $(r, c) = (1, 1)$.

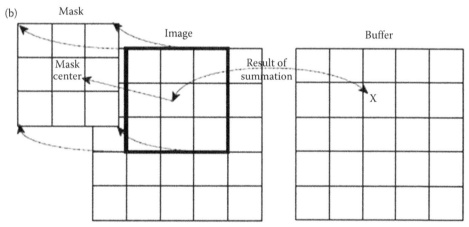

Move the mask one pixel to the right, multiply coincident terms,
sum and place the new result into the buffer at the location that
corresponds to the new center location of the convolution mask,
now at $(r, c) = (1, 2)$. Continue to the end of the row.

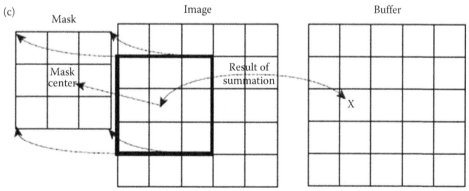

Move the mask down one row and repeat the process until the mask is
convolved with the entire image. Note that we "lose" the outer row(s)
and column(s).

FIGURE 3.2-3
The convolution process.

EXAMPLE 3.2.1

We want to enlarge an image to about three times its original size and have two adjacent pixel values 125 and 140.

1. Find the difference between the two values, $140-125=15$.
2. Enlargement desired is $K=3$, so we get $15/3=5$.
3. Next determine how many intermediate pixel values we need: $K-1=3-1=2$. The two pixel values between 125 and 140 are:

$$125+5=130 \text{ and } 125+2*5=135.$$

This is done for every pair of adjacent pixels, first along the rows and then along the columns. This will allow enlargement of the image to a size of $K(N-1)+1$, where K is an integer and $N \times N$ is the image size. Typically, N is large and K is small, so this is approximately equal to KN.

Image enlargement methods that use more complex mathematical models are also available. These more sophisticated methods fit curves and surfaces to the existing points and then sample these surfaces to obtain more points. In general, these complex techniques do not provide substantially better visual results than the basic methods presented here. They are most useful if the model is developed for a specific application, where the application drives the model development; they can be explored in the references.

The process opposite to enlarging an image is shrinking it. This is not typically done to examine an ROI more closely, but to reduce the amount of data that needs to be processed. Shrinking is explored more in Section 3.2.4.

Two other operations of interest for the ROI image geometry are translation and rotation. These processes may be performed for many application-specific reasons, for example, to align an image with a known template in a pattern matching process or to make certain image details easier to see. The translation process can be done with the following equations:

$$r' = r + r_0$$

$$c' = c + c_0 \tag{3.2-2}$$

where r' and c' are the new coordinates, r and c are the original coordinates and r_0 and c_0 are the distances to move or translate the image.

The rotation process requires the use of these equations:

$$\hat{r} = r(\cos\theta) + c(\sin\theta)$$

$$\hat{c} = -r(\sin\theta) + c(\cos\theta) \tag{3.2-3}$$

where $\hat{r}$ and $\hat{c}$ are the new coordinates, r and c are the original coordinates and θ is the angle to rotate the image. θ is defined in a clockwise direction from the horizontal axis at the image origin in the upper left corner.

The rotation and translation process can be combined into one set of equations:

$$\hat{r}' = (r + r_0)(\cos\theta) + (c + c_0)(\sin\theta)$$

$$\hat{c}' = -(r + r_0)(\sin\theta) + (c + c_0)(\cos\theta) \tag{3.2-4}$$

where $\hat{r}'$ and $\hat{c}'$ are the new coordinates, and r, c, r_0, c_0 and θ are defined as above.

There are some practical difficulties with the direct application of these equations. When translating, what is done with the "left-over" space? If we move everything one row down, what do we put in the top row? There are two basic options: fill the top row with a constant value, typically black (0) or white (255), or wrap around by shifting the bottom row to the top, as shown in Figure 3.2-4. Rotation also creates some practical difficulties. As Figure 3.2-5a illustrates, the image may be rotated off the "screen" (image plane). Although this can be fixed by a translation back to the center (Figure 3.2-5b and c), leftover space appears in the corners. This space can be filled with a constant or we can extract the central, rectangular portion of the image and enlarge it to the original image size.

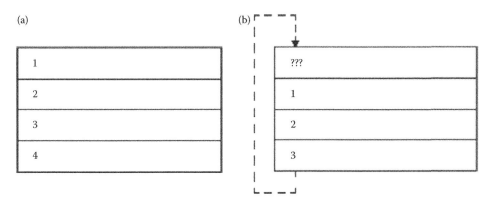

FIGURE 3.2-4
Image translation. It involves movement within the image by modifying the row and column coordinates. (a) A four row image before translation down by one row, $r_0=1$. (b) After translation, the row that was translated out of the image space is either inserted into the blank space (wrap-around) or discarded and the empty space is filled with a constant.

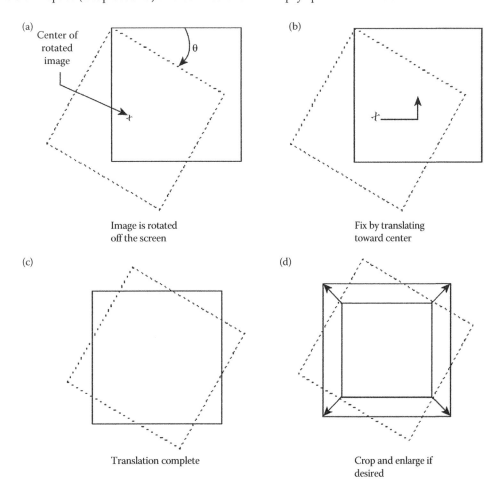

FIGURE 3.2-5
Image rotation.

3.2.2 Arithmetic and Logic Operations

Arithmetic and logic operations are often applied as preprocessing steps in image analysis in order to combine images in various ways. Addition, subtraction, division and multiplication comprise the arithmetic operations, while AND, OR and NOT make up the logic operations. These operations are performed on two images, except the NOT logic operation which requires only one image, and are done on a pixel by pixel basis.

To apply the arithmetic operations to two images, we simply operate on corresponding pixel values. For example, to add images I_1 and I_2 to create I_3:

EXAMPLE 3.2.2

$$I_1(r,\,c) + I_2(r,c) = I_3(r,\,c)$$

$$I_1 = \begin{bmatrix} 3 & 4 & 7 \\ 3 & 4 & 5 \\ 2 & 4 & 6 \end{bmatrix} \quad I_2 = \begin{bmatrix} 6 & 6 & 6 \\ 4 & 2 & 6 \\ 3 & 5 & 5 \end{bmatrix} \quad I_3 = \begin{bmatrix} 3+6 & 4+6 & 7+6 \\ 3+4 & 4+2 & 5+6 \\ 2+3 & 4+5 & 6+5 \end{bmatrix} = \begin{bmatrix} 9 & 10 & 13 \\ 7 & 6 & 11 \\ 5 & 9 & 11 \end{bmatrix}$$

Addition is used to combine the information in two images. Applications include the development of noise removal algorithms for modeling additive noise, as part of image sharpening algorithms, and for special effects, such as image morphing, in motion pictures (Figure 3.2-6). Note that true *image morphing* also requires the use of geometric transforms to align the two images. Image morphing is also usually a time-based operation, so that a proportionally increasing amount of the second image is added to the first image over time.

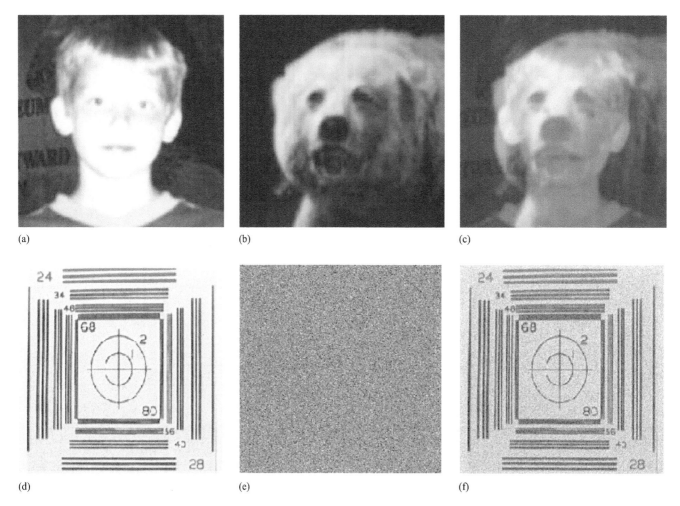

(a)   (b)   (c)

(d)   (e)   (f)

FIGURE 3.2-6
Image addition examples. This example shows one step in the *image morphing* process, where an increasing percentage of the one image is slowly added to another image and a geometric transformation is usually required to align the images. (a) First original, (b) second original, and (c) addition of 50% of (a) and 100% of (b). The next example shows adding noise to an image which is often useful for developing noise removal algorithms. (d) Original image, (e) Gaussian noise, variance=400, mean=0, and (f) addition of images (d) and (e).

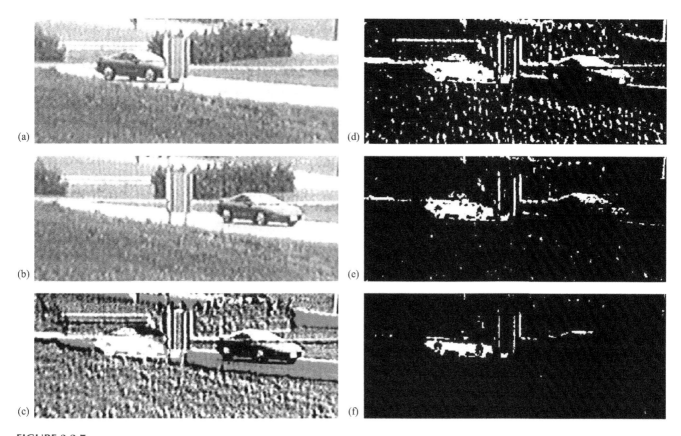

FIGURE 3.2-7
Image subtraction. (a) Original scene, (b) same scene later, (c) enhanced version of *scene a* image subtracted from *scene b*, (d) the subtracted image with a threshold of 150, (e) the subtracted image with a threshold of 175 and (f) the subtracted image with a threshold of 200. Theoretically, only image elements that have moved should show up in the resultant image. However, artifacts may appear due to imperfect alignment between images or environmental conditions such as wind blowing. Note also that because the car is approximately the same gray level as the grass, parts of the new car location disappear in the subtracted image.

Subtraction of two images is often used to detect motion. Consider the case where nothing has changed in a scene; the image resulting from subtraction of two sequential images is filled with zeros – a black image. If something has moved in the scene, subtraction produces a non-zero result at the location of movement, enabling detection of both the motion and the direction. If the time between image acquisitions is known, the moving object's speed can also be calculated. Figure 3.2-7 illustrates the use of subtraction for motion detection. Here, we can learn two things: (1) we must threshold the result and (2) the process is imperfect and will require some further processing.

Another term for image subtraction is *background subtraction*, since we are really simply removing the parts that are unchanged, the background. Although the process is the same as in motion detection, it is thought of differently. In comparing complex images, it may be difficult to see small changes. By subtracting out common background image information, the differences are more easily detectable. Medical imaging often uses this type of operation to allow the medical professional to more readily see changes which are helpful in the diagnosis. The technique is also used in law enforcement and military applications; for example, to find an individual in a crowd or to detect changes in a military installation. The complexity of the image analysis is greatly reduced when working with an image enhanced through this process.

Multiplication and division are used to adjust the brightness of an image. This is done on a pixel by pixel basis, and the options are to multiply or divide an image by a constant value or by another image. Multiplication of the pixel values by a value greater than one will brighten the image (or division by a value less than 1), and division by a factor greater than one will darken the image (or multiplication by a value less than 1). Brightness adjustment by a constant is often used as a preprocessing step in image enhancement and is shown in Figure 3.2-8.

Applying multiplication or division to two images can be done to model a multiplicative noise process or to combine two images in unique ways for special effects. In Figure 3.2-9, the results of multiplying two images together

(a)

(b)

(c)

FIGURE 3.2-8
Image division. (a) Original image, (b) image divided by a value less than 1 to brighten and (c) image divided by a value greater than 1 to darken.

are shown. The first set of images superimposes an X-ray of a hand onto another image and the second set shows how multiplication can be used to add texture to a computer-generated image. In both cases, the output image has been remapped to byte data range (0–255) for display purposes. Note that multiplication and division of images can also be used for image filtering in the spectral domain.

The logic operations AND, OR and NOT form a complete set, meaning that any other logic operation (XOR, NOR, NAND) can be created by a combination of these basic operations. They operate in a bit-wise fashion on pixel data.

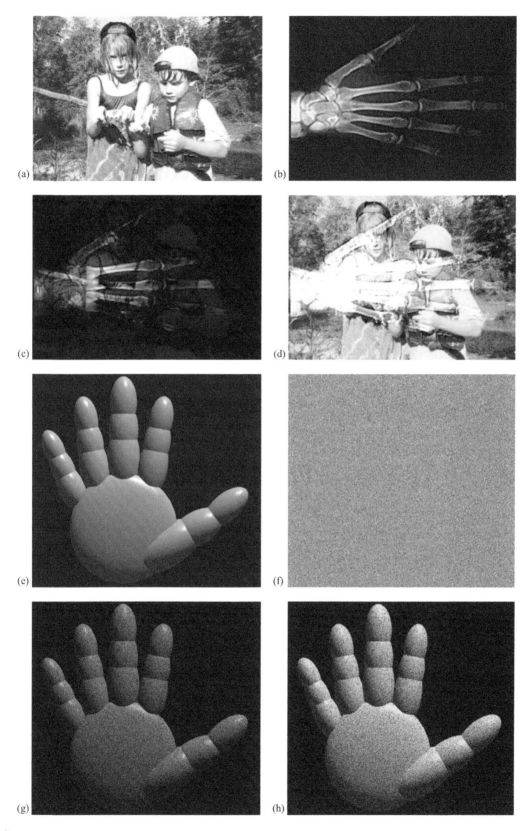

FIGURE 3.2-9
Image multiplication. (a) Original image, (b) X-ray image of a hand, (c) images (a) and (b) multiplied together which superimposes the hand onto the original, (d) the output image (c) after image enhancement, (e) a computer generated image of a hand, (f) Gaussian noise image, (g) the result of multiplying image (d) and image (e) whose operation adds texture to a computer generated image and (h) image enhanced version of the hand image with texture added by multiplication.

EXAMPLE 3.2.3

We are performing a logic AND on two images. Two corresponding pixel values are 111_{10} in one image and 88_{10} in the second image. The corresponding bit strings are:

$$111_{10} = 01101111_2 \qquad 88_{10} = 01011000_2$$

$$\begin{array}{r} 01101111_2 \\ \text{AND } 01011000_2 \\ \hline 01001000_2 \end{array}$$

The logic operations AND and OR are used to combine the information in two images. This may be done for special effects, but a more useful application for image analysis is to perform a masking operation. AND and OR can be used as a simple method to extract an ROI from an image. For example, a white mask ANDed with an image will allow only the portion of the image coincident with the mask to appear in the output image, with the background turned black; and a black mask ORed with an image will allow only the part of the image corresponding to the black mask to appear in the output image, but will turn the rest of the image white. This process is called *image masking* and Figure 3.2-10 illustrates the results of these operations. The NOT operation creates a negative of the original image, by inverting each bit within each pixel value, and it is shown in Figure 3.2-11. For color images, each individual red, green and blue band is processed separately and then reassembled.

3.2.3 Enhancement with Spatial Filters

Spatial filtering is typically applied for noise mitigation or to perform some type of image enhancement, such as sharpening or smoothing. These operators are called spatial filters since they operate on the raw image data in the (r, c) space, the spatial domain. The spatial filters operate on the image data by considering small neighborhoods in an image, such as 3×3, 5×5 and 7×7, and computing a result based on a linear or nonlinear operation. After computing the result at one pixel location, the filter moves sequentially across and down the entire image, computing a result at each pixel location.

The three types of filters discussed here include (1) mean filters, (2) median filters and (3) enhancement filters. The first two are used primarily to deal with noise in images, although they may also be used for special applications. For instance, a mean filter adds a "softer" look to an image, as in Figure 3.2-12. The enhancement filters highlight edges and details within the image.

Many spatial filters are implemented with convolution masks. Since a convolution mask operation provides a result that is a weighted sum of the values of a pixel and its neighbors, it is called a *linear filter*. One interesting aspect of convolution masks is that the overall effect can be predicted based on their general pattern. For example, if the coefficients of the mask sum to a positive number, the average brightness of the image will be retained. If the coefficients sum to zero, the average brightness will be lost and it will return a dark image. A negative of the image will result if they sum to a negative number. Furthermore, if the coefficients are both positive and negative, the mask is a filter that will sharpen or enhance details in an image; if the coefficients are all positive, it is a filter that will blur the image.

The mean filters are essentially averaging filters. They operate on local groups of pixels called neighborhoods and replace the center pixel with an average of the pixels in this neighborhood. This replacement is done with a convolution mask such as the following 3×3 mask:

$$\frac{1}{9}\begin{bmatrix} 1 & 1 & 1 \\ 1 & 1 & 1 \\ 1 & 1 & 1 \end{bmatrix}$$

The result is normalized by multiplying by 1/9, so overall mask coefficients sum to one. It is more computationally efficient to perform the integer operations and only multiply by 1/9 after the image has been processed. Often, with convolution masks, the normalization factor is implied and may not appear in the mask itself. Since the mask

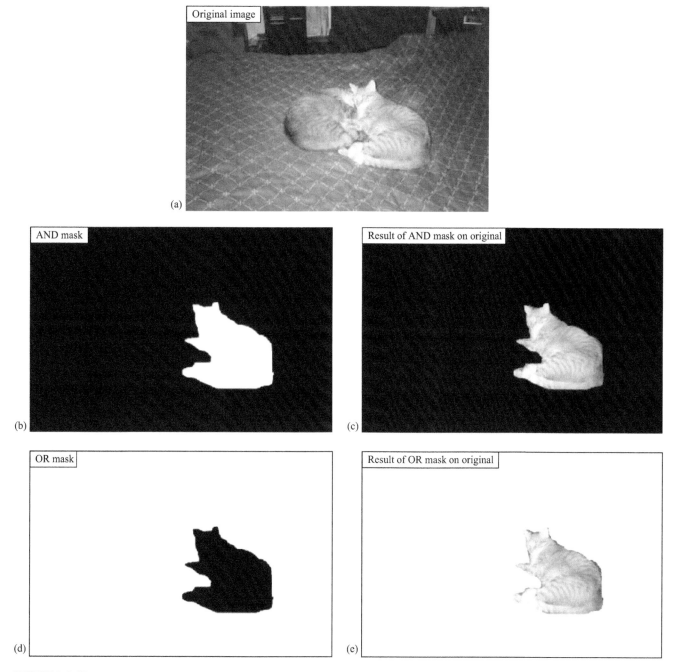

FIGURE 3.2-10
Image masking. (a) Original image of two cats, (b) image mask for AND operation to extract one cat only (c) resulting image from (a) AND (b), resulting in one cat on black background, (d) image mask for OR operation, created by performing a NOT on mask (b), and (e) resulting image from (a) OR (d), resulting in one cat on white background. (e) resulting image from (a) OR (d), resulting in one cat on white background.

coefficients sum to a positive number, the average image brightness will be retained, and since the coefficients are all positive, it will tend to blur the image. Other more complex mean filters are available which are designed to deal with specific types of noise (in CVIPtools, see *Restoration→Spatial Filter*).

The median filter is a nonlinear filter. A *nonlinear filter* has a result that cannot be found by a weighted sum of the neighborhood pixels, such as is done with a convolution mask. However, the median filter does operate on a local neighborhood. After the size of the local neighborhood is defined, the center pixel is replaced with the median or middle value present among its neighbors, rather than by their average.

(a)   (b)

(c)   (d)

FIGURE 3.2-11
Complement image – NOT operation. (a) Monochrome image, (b) NOT operator applied, (c) color image and (d) NOT operator applied.

EXAMPLE 3.2.4

Given the following 3×3 neighborhood:

$$\begin{bmatrix} 5 & 5 & 6 \\ 3 & 4 & 5 \\ 3 & 4 & 7 \end{bmatrix}$$

We first sort the values in order of size: (3, 3, 4, 4, 5, 5, 5, 6, 7), then we select the middle value, in this case, it is 5. This 5 is then placed in the center location.

(a)   (b)

FIGURE 3.2-12
Mean filter. (a) Original image and (b) mean filtered image, 5×5 kernel. Note the softer appearance.

A median filter can use a neighborhood of any size, but 3×3, 5×5 and 7×7 are typical. Note that the output image must be written to a separate image (a buffer), so that the results are not corrupted as this process is performed. Figure 3.2-13 illustrates the use of a median filter for noise removal.

The enhancement filters are linear filters, implemented with convolution masks having alternating positive and negative coefficients, so they will enhance image details. Many enhancement filters can be defined, and here, we include Laplacian-type and difference filters. Three 3×3 convolution masks for the Laplacian-type filters are:

Filter 1   Filter 2   Filter3

$$\begin{bmatrix} 0 & -1 & 0 \\ -1 & 5 & -1 \\ 0 & -1 & 0 \end{bmatrix} \quad \begin{bmatrix} -1 & -1 & -1 \\ -1 & 9 & -1 \\ -1 & -1 & -1 \end{bmatrix} \quad \begin{bmatrix} -2 & 1 & -2 \\ 1 & 5 & 1 \\ -2 & 1 & -2 \end{bmatrix}$$

Theoretically, Laplacian-type filters are rotationally invariant, or isotropic, which means they tend to enhance details in all directions equally. With these examples, only *Filter2* is truly isotropic; *Filter1* is biased for horizontal and vertical edges, and *Filter3* is for diagonal edges.

The difference filters, also called emboss filters, will enhance details in the direction specific to the mask selected. There are four primary difference filter convolution masks, corresponding to edges in the vertical, horizontal and two diagonal directions:

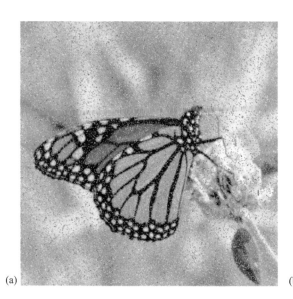

(a)   (b)

FIGURE 3.2-13
Median filter. (a) Original image with added salt-and-pepper noise and (b) median filtered image using a 3×3 mask, where the median filter removes the salt-and-pepper noise. (Original butterfly photo courtesy of Mark Zuke.)

$$
\begin{array}{cccc}
\text{VERTICAL} & \text{HORIZONTAL} & \text{DIAGONAL1} & \text{DIAGONAL2} \\[4pt]
\begin{bmatrix} 0 & 1 & 0 \\ 0 & 1 & 0 \\ 0 & -1 & 0 \end{bmatrix} &
\begin{bmatrix} 0 & 0 & 0 \\ 1 & 1 & -1 \\ 0 & 0 & 0 \end{bmatrix} &
\begin{bmatrix} 1 & 0 & 0 \\ 0 & 1 & 0 \\ 0 & 0 & -1 \end{bmatrix} &
\begin{bmatrix} 0 & 0 & 1 \\ 0 & 1 & 0 \\ -1 & 0 & 0 \end{bmatrix}
\end{array}
$$

Note that these are all simply rotated versions of the first mask. By completing the rotation, we have four more difference filter masks:

$$
\begin{bmatrix} 0 & -1 & 0 \\ 0 & 1 & 0 \\ 0 & 1 & 0 \end{bmatrix} \quad
\begin{bmatrix} 0 & 0 & 0 \\ -1 & 1 & 1 \\ 0 & 0 & 0 \end{bmatrix} \quad
\begin{bmatrix} -1 & 0 & 0 \\ 0 & 1 & 0 \\ 0 & 0 & 1 \end{bmatrix} \quad
\begin{bmatrix} 0 & 0 & -1 \\ 0 & 1 & 0 \\ 1 & 0 & 0 \end{bmatrix}
$$

The results of applying the Laplacian-type and difference filters are shown in Figure 3.2-14. A more detailed discussion of these and related filters is given in Chapter 4, where we see why edges and lines are perpendicular (Figure 4.2-1).

3.2.4 Enhancement with Histogram Operations

Histogram operations are used to improve image contrast. The two methods we will consider here are histogram stretching and histogram equalization. The *gray level histogram* of an image represents the distribution of the gray levels in an image and plots the gray level on the horizontal axis and the count of the number of pixels at that level on the vertical axis. In general, a histogram with a small spread has low contrast and a histogram with a wide spread has high contrast, while an image with its histogram clustered at the low end of the range is dark and a histogram with the values clustered at the high end of the range corresponds to a bright image (see Figure 3.2-15). Observation and manipulation of the histogram provides an intuitive tool when improving or modifying image contrast.

The mapping function for a histogram stretch is defined by the following equation:

$$\text{Stretch}(I(r,c)) = \left[\frac{I(r,c) - I(r,c)_{\text{MIN}}}{I(r,c)_{\text{MAX}} - I(r,c)_{\text{MIN}}} \right] [\text{MAX} - \text{MIN}] + \text{MIN} \tag{3.2-5}$$

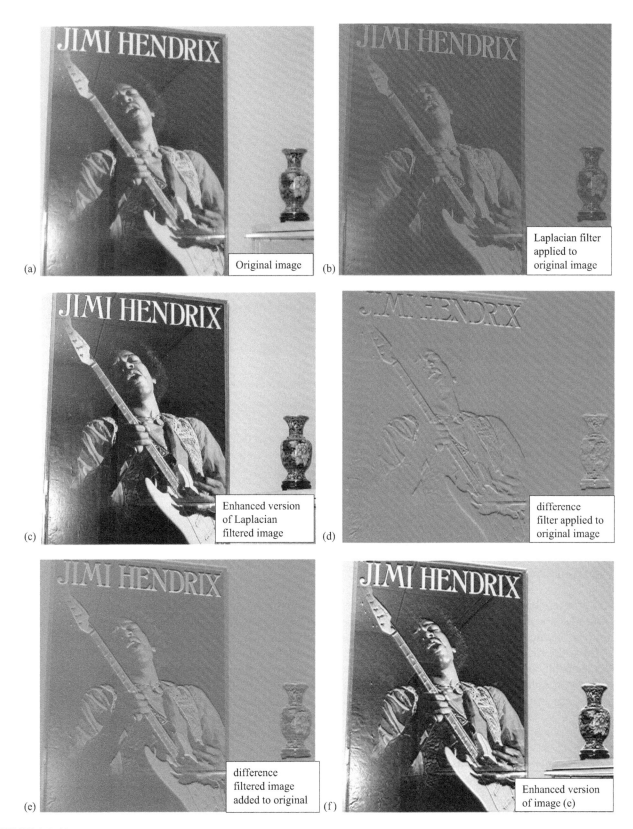

FIGURE 3.2-14
Enhancement filters. (a) Original image; (b) image after Laplacian filter (in CVIPtools be sure to check "Keep DC"); (c) contrast enhanced version of Laplacian filtered image, compare with (a) and note the improvement in fine detail information; (d) result of a difference (emboss) filter applied to image (a); (e) difference filtered image added to the original and (f) contrast enhanced version of image (e).

FIGURE 3.2-15
Contrast and histograms. (a) Low contrast, medium brightness, image and its histogram, (b) low-contrast dark image and its histogram (c) low-contrast light image and its histogram and (d) high-contrast image and its histogram. An image with high contrast will have the gray levels spread across the entire range.

where $I(r, c)_{MAX}$ is the largest gray level value in the image $I(r, c)$ and
  $I(r, c)_{MIN}$ *is the smallest gray level value in* $I(r, c)$.
  MAX and MIN correspond to the maximum and minimum gray level values possible (for an 8-bit image, these are 0 and 255).

This equation will take an image and stretch the histogram across the entire gray level range, which has the effect of increasing the contrast of a low contrast image (see Figure 3.2-16). If a stretch is desired over a smaller range, different MAX and MIN values can be specified. If most of the pixel values in an image fall within a small range, but a few outliers force the histogram to span the entire range, a pure histogram stretch will not improve the image. In this case, it is useful to allow a small percentage of the pixel values to be clipped (truncated) at the low and/or high end of the range (for an 8-bit image, this means truncating at 0 and 255). Figure 3.2-17 shows an example of this where we see a definite improvement with the stretched and clipped histogram compared to the pure histogram stretch.

Histogram equalization is an effective technique for improving the appearance of a poor image. Its function is similar to that of a histogram stretch but often provides more visually pleasing results across a wider range of images. *Histogram equalization* is a technique where the histogram of the resultant image is as flat as possible (with histogram stretching, the overall shape of the histogram remains the same). The theoretical basis for histogram equalization involves probability theory, where the histogram is treated as the probability distribution of the gray levels. This is reasonable since the histogram *is* the distribution of the gray levels for a particular image. Figure 3.2-18 shows that by using histogram equalization, similar results will be obtained regardless of the histogram of the original image.

3.2.5 Image Quantization

Image quantization is the process of reducing the image data by removing some of the detail information by mapping groups of data points to a single point. This can be done to either the pixel values themselves, $I(r, c)$, or the

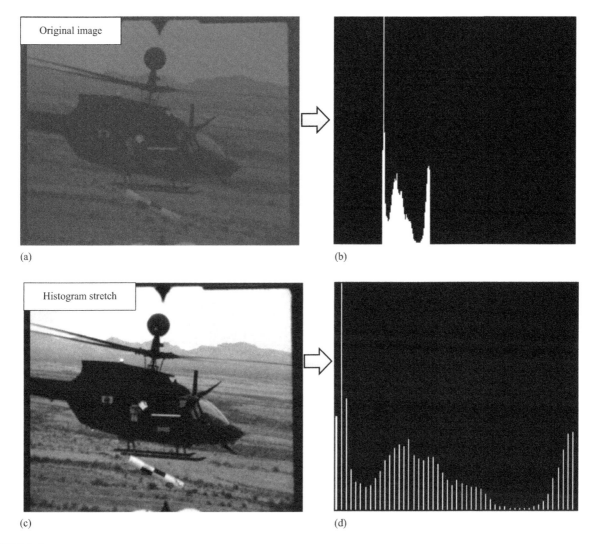

FIGURE 3.2-16
Histogram stretching. (a) Low-contrast image, (b) histogram of image (a), notice the tight cluster, (c) image (a) after histogram stretch and (d) histogram of image after stretch.

spatial coordinates, (r, c). Operating on the pixel values is referred to as *gray level reduction*, while operating on the spatial coordinates is called *spatial reduction*.

The simplest method of gray level reduction is thresholding. A threshold level is selected, and everything above that value is set equal to "1" (255 for 8-bit data) and everything at or below the threshold is equal to "0". This effectively turns a gray level image into a binary, two-level, image and is often used as a preprocessing step in the extraction of object features such as shape, area or perimeter.

A more versatile method of gray level reduction is the process of taking the data and reducing the number of bits per pixel, which allows for a variable number of gray levels. This can be done very efficiently by masking the lower bits via an AND operation. With this method, the number of bits that are masked determines the number of gray levels available.

EXAMPLE 3.2.5

We want to reduce 8-bit information containing 256 possible gray level values down to 32 possible values. This can be done by ANDing each eight-bit value with the bit-string 11111000_2. This is equivalent to dividing by eight (2^3), corresponding to the lower three bits that we are masking, and then shifting the result left three times. Now, gray level values in the range of 0–7 are mapped to 0, gray levels in the range of 8–15 are mapped to 8 and so on.

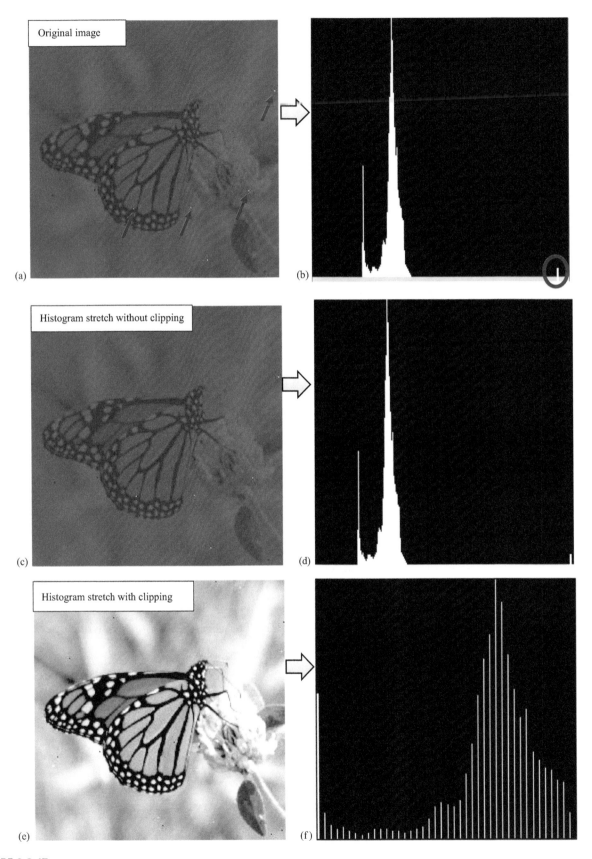

FIGURE 3.2-17

Histogram stretching with clipping. (a) Original image, note a small number of visible high values, shown by arrows on the image and circled in the histogram; (b) histogram of original image; (c) image after histogram stretching without clipping; (d) histogram of image (c); (e) image after histogram stretching with clipping 1% of the values at the high and low.

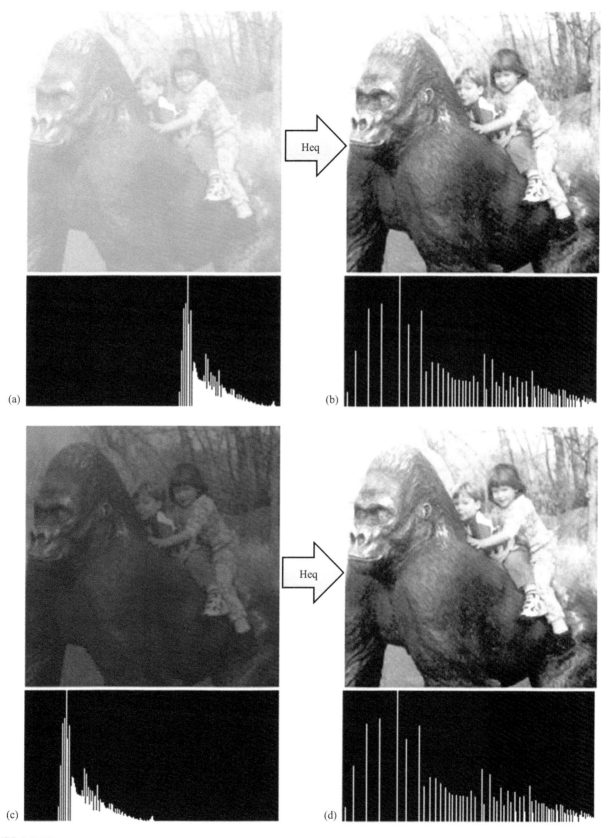

FIGURE 3.2-18
Histogram equalization (Heq) examples. Histograms of the images are directly below them. As can be seen, histogram equalization provides similar results regardless of the input image histogram.

(Continued)

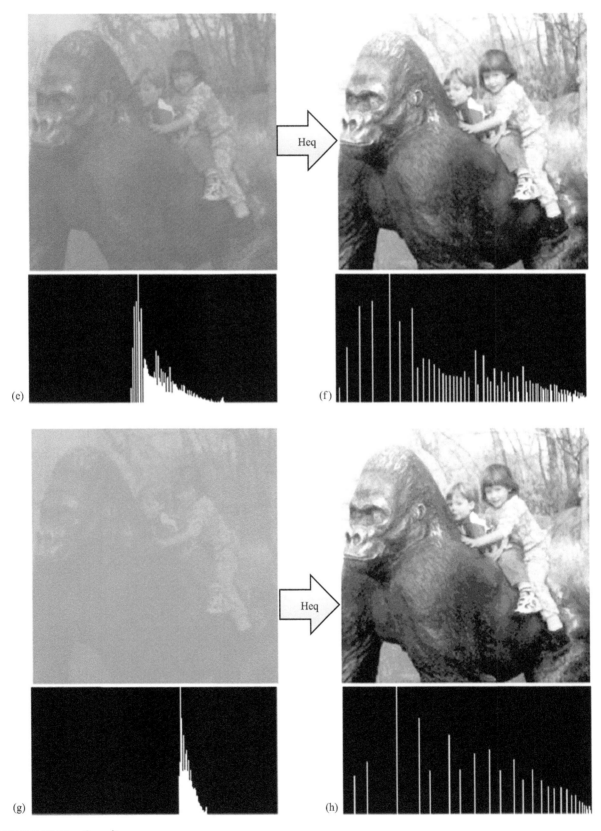

FIGURE 3.2-18 (*Continued*)
Histogram equalization (Heq) examples. Histograms of the images are directly below them. As can be seen, histogram equalization provides similar results regardless of the input image histogram.

We can see that by masking the lower three bits, by setting those bits to 0 in the AND mask, the 256 gray levels are reduced to 32 gray levels: $256 \div 8 = 32$. The general case requires us to mask k bits, where 2^k is divided into the original gray level range to get the quantized range desired. Using this method, the number of gray levels can be reduced to any power of 2.

The AND-based method maps the quantized gray level values to the low end of each range; alternately, if we want to map the quantized gray level values to the high end of each range, we use an OR operation. The number of "1" bits in the OR mask determines how many quantized gray levels are available.

EXAMPLE 3.2.6

To reduce 256 gray levels down to 16, we use a mask of 00001111_2. Now, values in the range of 0–15 are mapped to 15, those ranging from 16 to 31 are mapped to 31 and so on.

To determine the number of "1" bits in our OR mask, we apply a method similar to the AND mask method. We set the lower k bits equal to "1", where 2^k is divided into the original gray level range to get the quantized range desired. Note that the OR mask can also be found by negating (NOT) the AND mask previously described.

Using these AND/OR techniques for gray level quantization, the number of gray levels can be reduced to any power of 2, such as 2, 4, 8, 16, 32, 64 or 128, as illustrated in Figure 3.2-19. As the number of gray levels decreases, we see an increase in a phenomenon called *false contouring*. Contours appear in the images as false edges or lines as a result of the gray level quantization. In the figure, these contour lines do not become very visible until we get down to about 4 bits per pixel and then become very prominent as fewer bits are used.

The false contouring effect can be visually improved upon by using an IGS (improved gray scale) quantization method. The IGS method takes advantage of the human visual system's sensitivity to edges by adding a small random number to each pixel before quantization, which results in a more visually pleasing appearance (see Figure 3.2-20). A close examination of Figure 3.2-20c shows that IGS eliminates the appearance of false contours by breaking the sharp edges into smaller random pieces, so the human visual system does a better job of blending the false contours together.

The way IGS works is similar to *dithering* or *halftoning*, which can be used in printing or in any application where a reduction in the number of gray levels or colors is needed. At one time, newspapers were printed in only two levels, black and white, but photographs still had the illusion of varying shades of gray – this was accomplished through the use of dithering. Many dithering algorithms have been created, and they are based on the idea of diffusing the quantization error across edges, where changes occur in the image. In Figure 3.2-21, we see the results of applying three algorithms which are representative of the types in use. With these techniques, various gray levels are represented by different geometric patterns or various size dots, so the effective spatial resolution is reduced. Looking closely at the examples in Figure 3.2-21, we can see that the closer the black pixels are spaced together, the darker the area appears. As a result, it requires multiple pixels to represent different gray levels and this is what causes the reduction in effective spatial resolution. Figure 3.2-22 shows the same halftoning algorithms applied to a color image.

Gray level quantization using the previously discussed AND/OR method is very efficient for quantization, but it is not flexible since the size of the quantization bins is uniform, which is *uniform bin width quantization* (see Figure 3.2-23a). There are other methods of gray level quantization that allow for variable bin sizes called *variable bin width quantization* (Figure 3.2-23b). These methods are more complicated than, and not as fast as, those used with uniform bins. One such use is in simulating the response of the human visual system by using logarithmically spaced bins. The use of variable bin size is application dependent and requires application-specific information. For example, Figure 3.2-24 shows the result of an application where four specific gray levels provided optimal results. Here, we are applying varying bin sizes and mapping them to specific gray levels. In Figure 3.2-24, the gray levels in the range 0–101 were mapped to 79, 102–188 mapped to 157, 189–234 mapped to 197 and 235–255 mapped to 255. These numbers were determined as the result of application-specific feedback, an important aspect of image analysis as shown in Figure 3.1-3. For this application, the second brightest gray level (197) was used to identify fillings in dental X-rays.

Quantization of the spatial coordinates, *spatial quantization*, results in reducing the actual size of the image. This is accomplished by taking groups of pixels that are spatially adjacent and mapping them to one pixel. This can be done in one of three ways: (1) averaging, (2) median or (3) decimation. For the first method, averaging, the mean value of all the pixels in each group is found by summing the values and dividing by the number of pixels in the

FIGURE 3.2-19
False contouring. (a) Original 8-bit image, 256 gray levels; (b) quantized to 7 bits, 128 gray levels; (c) quantized to 6 bits, 64 gray levels; (d) quantized to 5 bits, 32 gray levels; (e) quantized to 4 bits, 16 gray levels; (f) quantized to 3 bits, 8 gray levels; (g) quantized to 2 bits, 4 gray levels and (h) quantized to 1 bit, 2 gray levels.

FIGURE 3.2-20
IGS quantization. (a) Original image, (b) uniform quantization to 8 gray levels per color band, (c) IGS quantization to 8 gray levels per band, (d) uniform quantization to 4 gray levels per color band and (e) IGS quantization to 4 gray levels per band. (Original butterfly photo courtesy of Mark Zuke.)

FIGURE 3.2-21
Halftoning and dithering. (a) Original image, 8-bit per pixel; (b) Floyd–Steinberg error diffusion, 1-bit per pixel; (c) Bayer's ordered dither, 1-bit per pixel and (d) 45° clustered-dot dither, 1-bit per pixel.

group. With the second method, median, the pixel values are sorted from lowest to highest and then the middle value is selected. The third approach, decimation, also known as sub-sampling, entails simply eliminating some of the data. For example, to reduce the image by a factor of two, every other row and column is removed.

To perform spatial quantization, the desired size of the resulting image is first specified. For example, to reduce a 512×512 image to 1/4 its size, we specify the output image to be 256×256 pixels. We now take every 2×2 pixel block in the original image and apply one of the three methods listed above to create a reduced image. It should be noted that this method of spatial reduction allows for simple forms of geometric distortion, specifically, stretching or shrinking along the horizontal or vertical axis. If a 512×512 image is reduced to a size of 64×128, we will have shrunk the image as well as squeezed it horizontally. This result is shown in Figure 3.2-25, where we can see that the averaging method blurs the image and the median and decimation methods produce some visible artifacts. With the median method, the space in the "s" and the "r" is filled in, and with decimation, the "o" is split and the "s" is filled in.

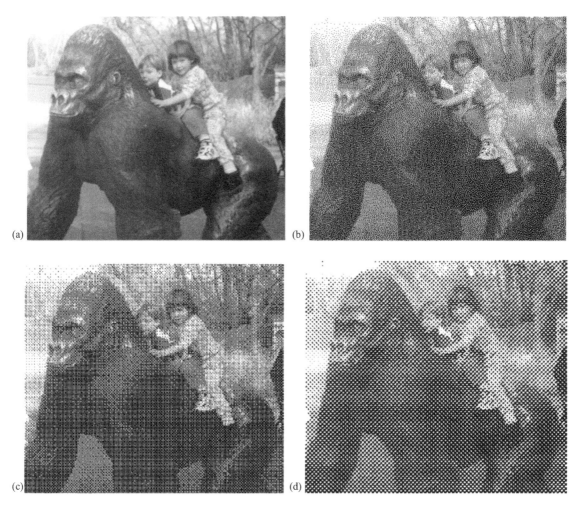

FIGURE 3.2-22
Halftoning and dithering with color image. (a) Color image, 24-bit per pixel; (b) Floyd–Steinberg error diffusion, 3-bit per pixel, 1-bit per color band; (c) Bayer's ordered dither, 3-bit per pixel, 1-bit per color band and (d) 45° clustered-dot dither, 3-bit per pixel, 1-bit per color band.

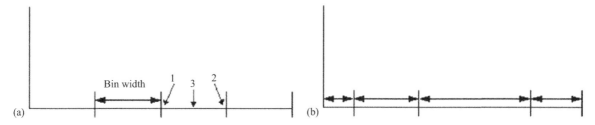

FIGURE 3.2-23
Uniform versus variable bin width quantization. (a) Uniform quantization bins, all bins are of the same width. Values that fall within the same bin can be mapped to the low end (1), high end (2) or middle (3). (b) Variable, or nonuniform, quantization bins are of different widths.

To improve the image quality when applying the decimation technique, we may want to preprocess the image with an averaging, or mean, spatial filter – this type of filtering is called *anti-aliasing filtering*. In Figure 3.2-26, we can compare reduction done with or without an anti-aliasing filter. Here, the decimation technique was applied to a text image with a factor of four reduction; note that without the anti-aliasing filter, the letter "*S*" becomes enclosed. The cost of retaining this information is that the output image is slightly blurred.

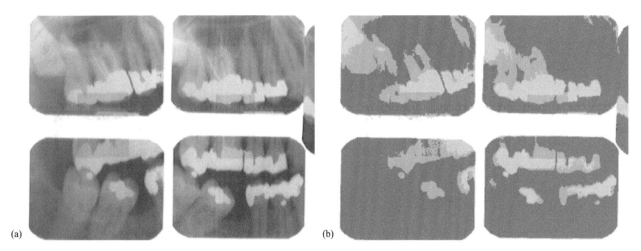

FIGURE 3.2-24
Variable bin width quantization. (a) Original 8-bit image and (b) after variable bin width quantization. For this example, different gray levels were chosen to distinguish gums, teeth and dental work.

FIGURE 3.2-25
Spatial reduction. (a) Original 512×512 image, (b) spatial reduction to 64×128 via averaging, (c) spatial reduction to 64×128 via median method, note the space in the "*s*" and "*r*" is filled in, and (d) spatial reduction to 64×128 via decimation method, note the "*o*" is split and "*s*" is filled in.

FIGURE 3.2-26
Decimation and anti-aliasing filter. (a) Original 512×512 image, (b) result of spatial reduction to 128×128 via decimation and (c) result of spatial reduction to 128×128 via decimation, but the image was first preprocessed by a 5×5 averaging filter, an anti-aliasing filter. Note that the "*s*" is still clear and the "*o*" is not so jagged.

3.3 Binary Image Analysis

To complete this introductory chapter on image analysis, we will look at basic binary object features and examine how they can be applied to the image analysis process shown in Figure 3.1-3. Since most cameras will give us color or gray level images, we will first consider how to create binary images from gray level images, followed by extraction of simple binary features, and finally consider some simple methods to classify binary objects. This will clarify the image analysis process and lay the groundwork for the following chapters.

3.3.1 Thresholding Bimodal Histograms

In order to create a binary image from a gray level image, a threshold operation must be performed. This is done by specifying a *threshold value*, and this will set all values above the specified gray level to "1" and everything below or equal to the specified value to "0". Although the actual values for "0" and "1" can be anything, typically 255 is used for "1" and 0 is used for the "0" value. The "1" value will appear white and the "0" value will appear black.

In many applications, the threshold value will be determined experimentally, and it is highly dependent on lighting conditions and object to background contrast. It will be much easier to find an acceptable threshold value with proper lighting and good contrast between the object and the background. Figure 3.3-1a and b shows an example of

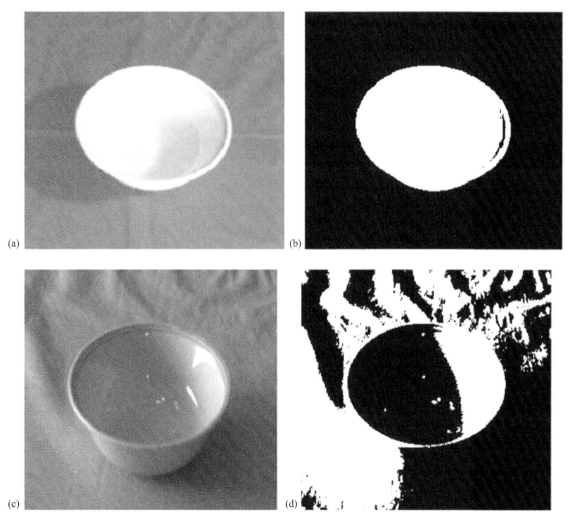

(a) (b) (c) (d)

FIGURE 3.3-1
Effects of lighting and object to background contrast on thresholding. (a) An image of a bowl with high object to background contrast and good lighting; (b) result of thresholding image (a); (c) an image of a bowl with poor object to background contrast and poor lighting; and (d) result of thresholding image (c).

good lighting and high object to background contrast, while Figure 3.3-1c and d illustrates a poor example. Imagine trying to identify the object based on the poor example compared to the good example.

To select the proper threshold value, the histogram is examined. The *histogram* of an image is a plot of gray level versus the number of pixels in the image at each gray level. Figure 3.3-2 shows the two bowl images and their corresponding histograms. The peaks and valleys in the histogram are examined and a threshold is experimentally selected that will best separate the object from the background. Notice the peak in Figure 3.3-2b on the far right; this corresponds to the maximum gray level value and has the highest number of pixels at that value. This peak and the two small peaks to its left represent the bowl. Although many suitable valleys can be seen in the histogram for the poor example (Figure 3.3-2d), none will separate the object from the background successfully, which serves to illustrate the vital importance of proper lighting.

With computer vision applications, the threshold must be found automatically, no person is in the processing loop to examine the image. The basic method of automatically finding a threshold is an iterative process, easily implemented via computer program, and allows the user to specify a parameter to control the process. Presented here is a simplified version of the *isodata* (iterative self-organizing data analysis technique algorithm) method and is basically the *k-means clustering algorithm* used in pattern recognition to separate two clusters. It proceeds as follows:

1. Select an initial value for the threshold, T; typically, the average gray level value for the image.
2. Apply the selected threshold value, T. This will separate the image into two groups of gray levels, those greater than the threshold and those less than or equal to the threshold.
3. Find the average (mean) values for each of these two groups of pixels.

$$\text{Mean for Group 1} = m_1 = \frac{1}{\# \text{ pixels} > T} \sum_{I(r,c)>T} I(r,c) \tag{3.3-1}$$

$$\text{Mean for Group 2} = m_2 = \frac{1}{\# \text{ pixels} \leq T} \sum_{I(r,c)\leq T} I(r,c) \tag{3.3-2}$$

4. Calculate a new threshold by finding the average of the two mean values:

$$T_{new} = (m_1 + m_2)/2 \tag{3.3-3}$$

5. If the change in threshold value from one iteration to the next is smaller than a previously specified limit, we are done:

$$|T_{old} - T_{new}| < \text{Limit ?} \rightarrow \text{Done!} \tag{3.3-4}$$

If the change is still greater than the specified limit, go to step 2 and use T_{new}.

This method will work best for an image with good object to background contrast, with well-separated peaks in the histogram. A good choice for the initial threshold value will help the algorithm to converge faster. Although the image's average gray level is typically used, the weighted average of the two gray levels corresponding to the largest two histogram peaks may also be a good choice for the initial threshold. By weighting this average by the number of pixels at each value, convergence may occur faster. Selection of the value used as a limit in step 5 will not only help determine how long the algorithm will take by limiting the number of iterations but will also affect the resulting image (see Figure 3.3-3).

The *Otsu method* is another thresholding algorithm that works well for computer vision applications with one object against a background of high contrast. It provides a theoretically good solution based on the assumption that each peak has a Gaussian shape and the peaks are fairly well separated. This method is also called *minimizing within-group variance*, and it works as follows:

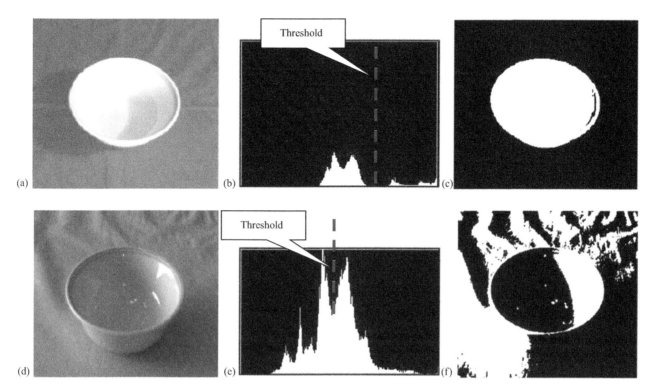

FIGURE 3.3-2
Histograms. (a) An image of a bowl with high object to background contrast and good lighting, (b) the histogram of image (a), showing the threshold that separates object and background, (c) the result after the threshold, (d) an image of a bowl with poor object to background contrast and poor lighting, (e) the histogram of image (d), showing what appears to be a good threshold, but it does not successfully separate object and background, and (f) the result after the threshold.

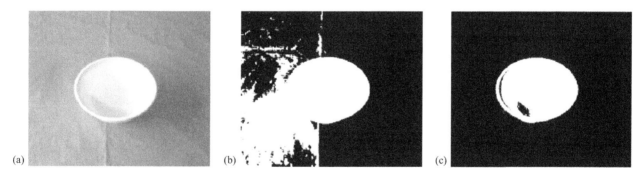

FIGURE 3.3-3
The limit parameter with the automatic thresholding algorithm. (a) An image of a bowl with high object to background contrast and good lighting, (b) result of using the automatic thresholding algorithm with a *limit*=10 and (c) result of using the automatic thresholding algorithm with a *limit*=4. Although using a higher value for the *limit* will require fewer iterations and is faster, the results may be undesirable.

Let $P(g)$ be the histogram probability for gray level g, which is simply the count of the number of pixels at gray level g normalized by the total number of pixels in the image, and is given by:

$$P(g) = \frac{1}{(\#\text{Rows})(\#\text{Columns})} \sum_{I(r,c)=g} \frac{I(r, c)}{g} \qquad (3.3\text{-}5)$$

Let $\sigma^2_w(t)$ be the within-group variance, which is a weighted sum of the variance of the two groups, as a function of the threshold t, defined as follows:

$$\sigma_w^2(t) = P_1(t)\sigma_1^2(t) + P_2(t)\sigma_2^2(t)$$

where

$$P_1(t) = \sum_{g=1}^{t} P(g)$$

$$P_2(t) = \sum_{g=t+1}^{Maxgray} P(g)$$

$$\mu_1(t) = \sum_{g=1}^{t} g \times P(g) / P_1(t) \; ; \qquad\qquad (3.3\text{-}6)$$

$$\mu_2(t) = \sum_{g=t+1}^{Maxgray} g \times P(g) / P_2(t)$$

$$\sigma_1^2(t) = \sum_{g=1}^{t} [g - \mu_1(t)]^2 P(g) / P_1(t) \; ;$$

$$\sigma_2^2(t) = \sum_{g=t+1}^{Maxgray} [g - \mu_2(t)]^2 P(g) / P_2(t)$$

where *Maxgray* is the maximum gray level value.

Now, we simply find the value of the threshold t that will minimize the within-group variance, $\sigma_w^2(t)$. This is done by calculating the values for $\sigma_w^2(t)$ for each possible gray level value and selecting the one that provides the smallest $\sigma_w^2(t)$. We can usually streamline this search by limiting the possible threshold values to those between the modes, the two peaks, in the histogram. Additional algorithms based on the Otsu method to find multiple thresholds and to perform the calculations more efficiently can be explored in the references. Automatically finding methods to separate objects in an image will be examined more thoroughly in Chapters 4 and 5.

3.3.2   Connectivity and Labeling

The images considered in the previous section contained only one object. What will happen if the image contains more than one object? In order to handle images with more than one object, we need to consider exactly how pixels are connected to make an object and then we need a method to label the objects separately. Since we are dealing with digital images, the process of spatial digitization (sampling) can cause problems regarding connectivity of objects. These problems can be resolved with careful connectivity definitions and heuristics applicable to the specific domain. Connectivity refers to the way in which an object is defined; once we performed a threshold operation on an image, which pixels should be connected to form an object? Do we simply let all pixels with value of "1" be the object? What if we have two overlapping objects?

First, we must define which of the surrounding pixels are considered to be neighboring pixels. On a rectangular grid, a pixel has eight possible neighbors: two horizontal neighbors, two vertical neighbors and four diagonal neighbors. We can define connectivity in three different ways: (1) four-connectivity, (2) eight-connectivity and (3) six-connectivity. Figure 3.3-4 illustrates these three definitions. With four-connectivity, the only neighbors considered connected are the horizontal and vertical neighbors; with eight-connectivity, all of the eight possible neighboring pixels are considered connected; and with six-connectivity, the horizontal, vertical and two of the diagonal neighbors are connected. Which definition is chosen depends on the application, but the key to avoiding problems is to be consistent.

If we select four- or eight-connectivity, the *connectivity dilemma* arises. Consider the following binary image segment:

$$
\begin{array}{ccc}
0 & 1 & 0 \\
1 & 0 & 1 \\
0 & 1 & 0
\end{array}
$$

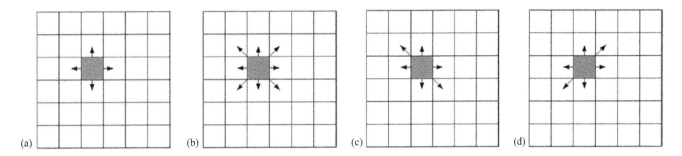

FIGURE 3.3-4
Connectivity. (a) four-connectivity, (b) eight-connectivity, (c) six-connectivity NW/SE and (d) six-connectivity, NE/SW. *Note: six-connectivity NW/SE is used in the book and CVIPtools.*

Assuming four-connectivity, there are four separate objects and five separate background objects. The dilemma is that if the objects are separated, shouldn't the background be connected? Alternately, if we assume eight-connectivity, there is one connected object, a closed curve, but the background is also connected. This creates another dilemma because a closed curve should separate the background into distinct objects. How do we resolve this issue? These are our choices:

1. Use eight-connectivity for background and four-connectivity for the objects.
2. Use four-connectivity for background and eight-connectivity for the objects.
3. Use six-connectivity.

The first two choices are acceptable for binary images, but get complicated when extended to gray level and color images, and we want a standard definition to use throughout this book. The third choice is a good compromise in most situations, as long as we are aware of the bias created by selection of one diagonal direction. That is, connection by a single diagonal pixel will only be defined in one of two possible directions. For most real images, this is not a problem. We will use the definition of six-connectivity as shown in Figure 3.3-4c, with the northwest (NW) and southeast (SE) diagonal neighbors.

After the definition of connectivity is chosen, a labeling algorithm is needed to differentiate between multiple objects within an image. The labeling process requires us to scan the image and label connected objects with the same symbol. With the definition of six-connectivity selected, we can apply the algorithm given in Figure 3.3-5 to label the objects in the image. (Note that, in addition to labeling binary mages, this flowchart will label objects in images with multiple gray levels if we assume that any areas not of interest have been masked out by setting the pixels equal to zero.) The UPDATE block in the flowchart refers to a function that will keep track of objects that have been given multiple labels. This can occur with a sequential scanning of the image if the connecting pixels are not encountered until after different parts of the object have already been labeled (see Figure 3.3-6).

By labeling the objects, an image filled with object numbers is created. With this labeled image, we can extract features specific to each object. These features are used to locate and classify the binary objects. The binary object features defined here include area, center of area, axis of least second moment, projections and Euler number. The first three tell us something about where the object is and the latter two tell us something about the shape of the object. More features are provided in Chapter 6.

3.3.3 Basic Binary Object Features

In order to provide general equations for area, center of area and axis of least second moment, we define a function, $I_i(r, c)$:

$$I_i(r, c) = \begin{cases} 1 & \text{if } I(r, c) = i^{\text{th}} \text{ object number} \\ 0 & \text{otherwise} \end{cases} \tag{3.3-7}$$

Now, we can define the *area* of the ith object as:

$$A_i = \sum_{r=0}^{N-1} \sum_{c=0}^{N-1} I_i(r, c) \tag{3.3-8}$$

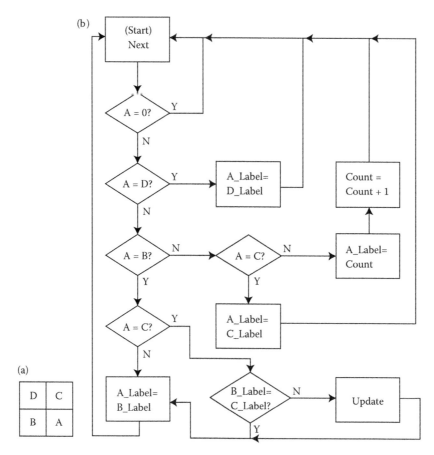

FIGURE 3.3-5
Labeling algorithm flowchart. (a) Definition of pixel neighbors and (b) the flowchart based on six-connectivity with NW/SE diagonal neighbors connected.

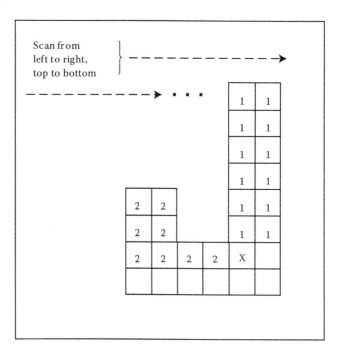

FIGURE 3.3-6
Multiple labels. The labeling algorthm requires an UPDATE function to keep track of objects with more than one label. Multiple labeling can occur during sequential scanning, as shown on the "J" shaped object. We label two different objects until we reach the pixel marked "X", and we discover that objects 1 and 2 are connected.

The area, A_i, is measured in pixels, and it indicates the relative size of the object. We can then define the *center of area* (centroid in the general case), which finds the midpoint along each row and column axis corresponding to the "middle" based on the spatial distribution of pixels within the object. It can be defined by the pair $(\bar{r}_i, \bar{c}_i)$:

$$\bar{r}_i = \frac{1}{A_i} \sum_{r=0}^{N-1} \sum_{c=0}^{N-1} r I_i(r, c); \quad \bar{c}_i = \frac{1}{A_i} \sum_{r=0}^{N-1} \sum_{c=0}^{N-1} c I_i(r, c) \tag{3.3-9}$$

These correspond to the row coordinate of the center of area for the ith object, $\bar{r}_i$, and the column coordinate of the center of area for the ith object, $\bar{c}_i$. This feature will help to locate an object in the two-dimensional image plane. The next feature is the *axis of least second moment*, and it provides information about the object's orientation. This axis corresponds to the line about which it takes the least amount of energy to spin an object of like shape or the axis of least inertia. If we move our origin to the center of area, (r, c), the axis of least second moment is defined as follows:

$$\tan(2\theta_i) = 2 \frac{\displaystyle\sum_{r=0}^{N-1} \sum_{c=0}^{N-1} rc I_i(r, c)}{\displaystyle\sum_{r=0}^{N-1} \sum_{c=0}^{N-1} r^2 I_i(r, c) - \sum_{r=0}^{N-1} \sum_{c=0}^{N-1} c^2 I_i(r, c)} \tag{3.3-10}$$

This is shown in Figure 3.3-7. The origin is moved to the center of area for the object, and the angle is measured from the r-axis counterclockwise.

The *projections* of a binary object, which also provide shape information, are found by summing all the pixels along rows or columns. The sum of the rows is the *horizontal projection*, and the sum of the columns is the *vertical projection*. The horizontal projection, $h_i(r)$, is defined as follows:

$$h_i(r) = \sum_{c=0}^{N-1} I_i(r, c) \tag{3.3-11}$$

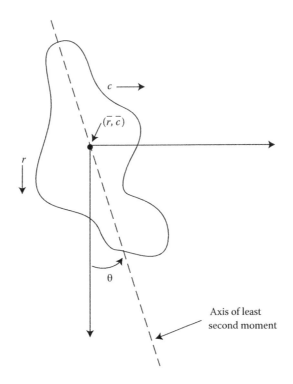

FIGURE 3.3-7
Axis of least second moment. The angle is defined through the centroid and counterclockwise to the vertical axis.

And the vertical projection, $v_i(c)$:

$$v_i(c) = \sum_{r=0}^{N-1} I_i(r, c)$$

(3.3-12)

An example of the horizontal and vertical projection for a binary image is shown in Figure 3.3-8. Projections are useful in applications such as character recognition, where the objects of interest can be normalized with regard to size.

Given the projection equations, the center of area can be defined as follows:

$$\bar{r}_i = \frac{1}{A_i} \sum_{r=0}^{N-1} \sum_{c=0}^{N-1} r I_i(r, c) = \frac{1}{A_i} \sum_{r=0}^{N-1} r h_i(r)$$

(3.3-13)

$$\bar{c}_i = \frac{1}{A_i} \sum_{r=0}^{N-1} \sum_{c=0}^{N-1} r I_i(r, c) = \frac{1}{A_i} \sum_{c=0}^{N-1} c v_i(c)$$

(3.3-14)

With these equations, we can more easily understand their meaning. Referring to Figure 3.3-8 and the above equations, we can see that a larger projection value along a given row or column will weigh that particular row or column value more heavily in the equation. This will tend to move the center of area coordinate toward that particular row or column; note that all values are normalized by the object area.

The *Euler number* of an image is defined as the number of objects minus the number of holes. For a single object, it relates to the number of closed curves the object contains. It is often useful in tasks such as optical character recognition (OCR), as shown by the example in Figure 3.3-9. As shown in Figure 3-3-9(a), we have eight objects (remember the dots on the i's) and one hole; Figure 3.3-9b has three objects and two holes. Note that we can find the Euler number for the entire image or for a single object within the image. For example, the letter "i" has an Euler number of 2 and the letter "o" has an Euler number of 0.

Using the six-connectivity definition previously defined, the Euler can be found by using the number of *convexities* and *concavities*. The Euler number will be equal to the number of convexities minus the number of concavities, which are found by scanning the image for the following patterns (*note: to apply this method, the outer rows and columns of the image must be zeros*):

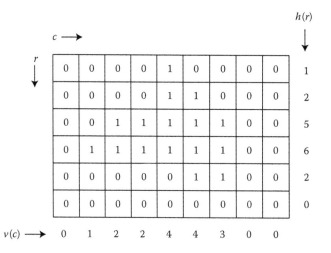

FIGURE 3-3-8
Projections. To find the projections, we sum the number of 1s in the rows and columns. For the horizontal projection, we sum across the columns, and for the vertical projection, we sum down the rows.

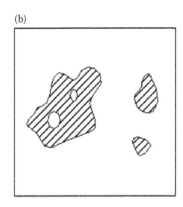

FIGURE 3.3-9
Euler number. (a) This image has eight objects and one hole, so its Euler number is 8 – 1 = 7. The letter "V" has an Euler number of 1, "*i*" = 2, "*s*" = 1, "*o*" = 0 and "*n*" = 1. (b) This image has three objects and two holes, so the Euler number is 3 – 2 = 1.

Each time one of these patterns is found, and the count is increased for the corresponding pattern:

$$Euler\ number = (Count\ of\ CONVEXITIES) - (Count\ of\ CONCAVITIES)$$
$$= (Number\ of\ objects) - (Number\ of\ Holes)$$

(3.3-15)

The number of convexities and concavities can also be useful features for binary objects.

3.3.4 Computer Vision: Binary Object Classification

To complete our introduction to image analysis, we will apply the process (see Figure 3.1-3) to the development of an algorithm for classifying geometric shapes. We will use CVIPtools to create the objects and analyze the images. In this process, we will explore the *Utilities* functions, which include the preprocessing utilities and other utilities, and the *Features* tab of the *Analysis* window. The binary features discussed previously will be used for the classification. For this experiment, we will develop an algorithm to classify the following shapes: (1) circles, (2) ellipses, (3) rectangles and (4) ellipses with holes.

To create the objects, we first invoke CVIPtools and select the *Utilities* functions (Figure 3.3-10, if the MATALB GUI is used it will appear slightly different). Next, we select *Create* and then click on *Circle* (Figure 3.3-11), and select an image size of 512×512 by a mouse click on the arrow next to the *Image width* and *Image height* boxes. Note that these text boxes allow for selection via the mouse and the arrow or allow the user to type in any value. With a mouse click on the *Apply* button in the lower right corner of the window, the circle image is created, as shown in Figure 3.3-12. We want to have two of each type of object, so we create another circle but select a different location and size.

Next, we OR these two images together by using *Arith/Logic→OR* (this is not required, we could use separate images, but it will streamline the processing and help to illustrate some important CVIPtools concepts). This is done by selecting one circle as the current image by clicking on the image or by clicking on the image name in the image queue – the names of the images in the image queue are listed on the left side of the main window. The second image is selected via the mouse and the arrow on the right of the *Second image* box, or it can be selected by holding the *Alt* key on keyboard and a mouse click. The result is shown in Figure 3.3-13. Now, we create four ellipses and two rectangles of various sizes and locations, and OR each new object with the current composite image which contains the previous objects. Note that it is easy to select a location for a new object by moving the mouse pointer on the current composite image and observing the row and column coordinates on the top of the main window.

The next task is to create the ellipses with holes. This is done by creating a small circle in and then performing an XOR operation with the circle and the ellipse. Note that the circles need to be in a location within, and smaller than, the ellipses to create these objects. To do this, select *Arith/Logic→XOR* on the *Utilities* window (Figure 3.3-14). Perform the XOR to create an ellipse with a hole as shown in Figure 3.3-15, followed by repeating the process to make the second example. Next, create the composite image by OR'ing the ellipses with holes with the previous composite image containing all the other objects (Figure 3.3-16).

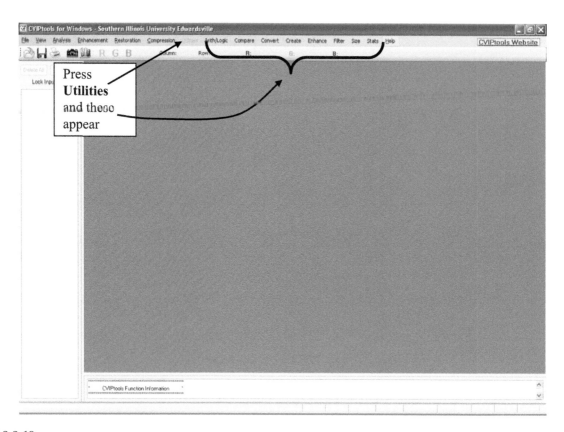

FIGURE 3.3-10
CVIPtools main window and utilities functions.

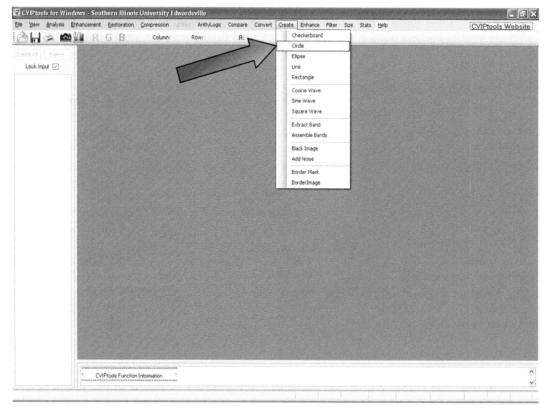

FIGURE 3.3-11
Selection for creating a circle with the utilities.

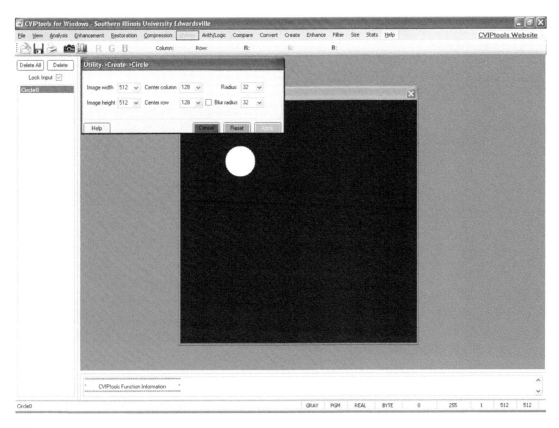

FIGURE 3.3-12
CVIPtools after creating the circle image.

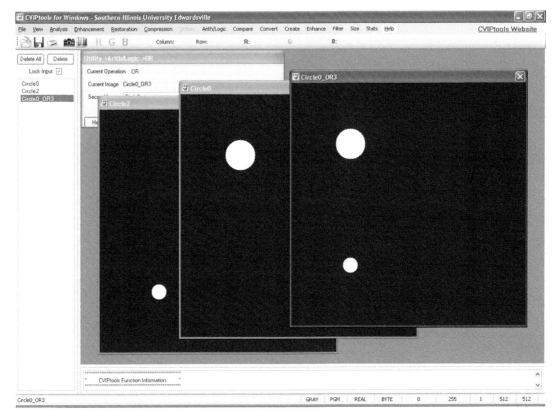

FIGURE 3.3-13
OR'ing two circles together to create a composite image with both objects.

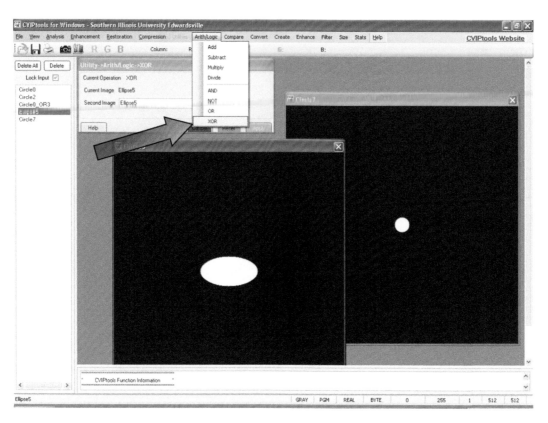

FIGURE 3.3-14
Selection for XOR of two images.

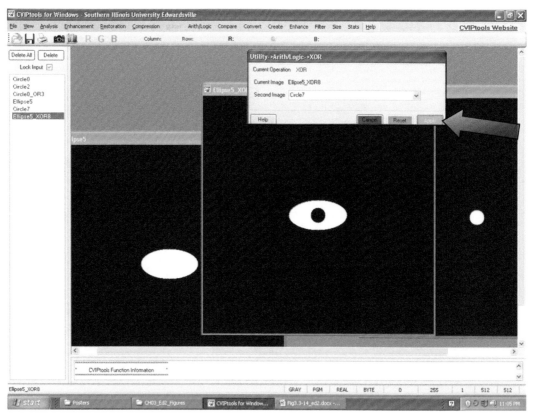

FIGURE 3.3-15
XOR of circle and ellipse to create a new object – ellipse with hole.

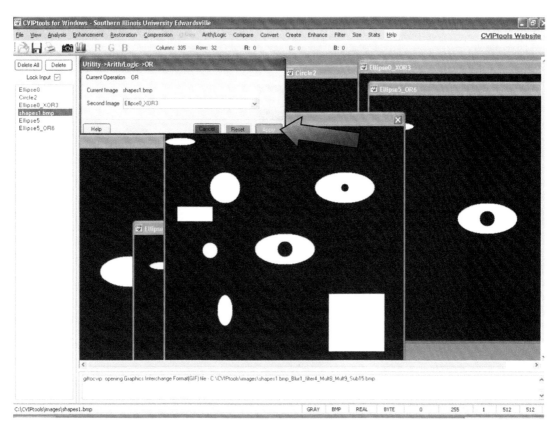

FIGURE 3.3-16
Composite image created by OR'ing individual object images together.

In order to better simulate a real application, we will blur and add noise to the image containing the objects. To blur the image, select *Filter→Specify a Blur*. Use the default parameters and click *Apply*. To add noise, select *Create→Add Noise*. Select *Salt-and-Pepper* noise, and click *Apply*. The result is shown in Figure 3.3-17. We now have an image with two circles, two ellipses, two rectangles and two ellipses with holes; and we have blurred and added noise to better simulate a real application.

Now that our example image database has been created, we are ready to analyze the images and develop our classification algorithm. Referring to Figure 3.1-3, we will try the following steps:

1. **Preprocessing**: noise removal with a median filter.
2. **Segmentation**: thresholding.
3. **Filtering**: none required (we hope!).
4. **Feature extraction**: area, center of area, axis of least second moment, projections and Euler number.
5. **Feature analysis**: we will do this manually by examining the feature file.
6. **Application feedback**: Are we successful in developing an algorithm that will identify the objects? If not, go back to Step (1) and modify the algorithm based on our results.

For step one, select *Filter→Median*. Apply this to our composite image. This is shown in Figure 3.3-18. Here, we see that the noise has been successfully removed. For step two, we want to find a proper threshold so that the blurring is mitigated and the objects are clearly defined. This is done with *Convert→Binary Threshold*. After some experimentation, we determine a threshold of 155 gives us the desired results, as shown in Figure 3.3-19. Now, we are ready to extract the features.

From the main CVIPtools window, select the *Analysis* window and select the *Features* tab. For the original image, we want to use the image after noise removal, and for the segmented image, we will use the image after thresholding. Next, we type in a feature file name, a class name, such as *circle, ellipse, rectangle* or *ellipse_hole*, and any

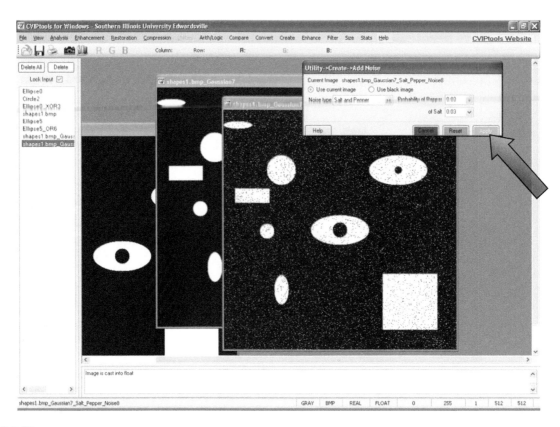

FIGURE 3.3-17
Adding salt-and-pepper noise to the blurred composite image.

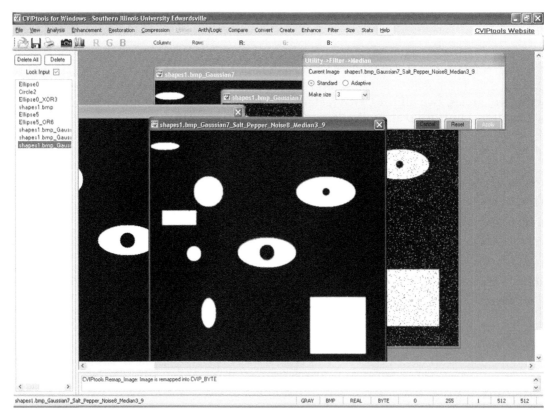

FIGURE 3.3-18
Blurry, noisy composite image after median filtering.

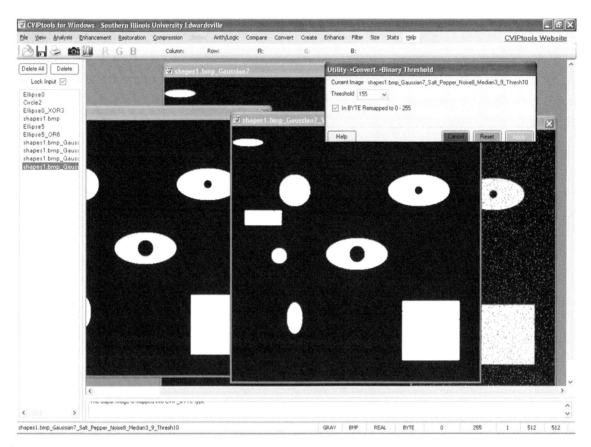

FIGURE 3.3-19
Image after thresholding, note that the output shapes still have some minor distortion.

coordinates within the object of interest. The coordinates can also be selected with a mouse click on the object in the original image. Next, we select the features of interest by clicking on the checkboxes for area, centroid, orientation (axis of least second moment), Euler number and projections (see Figure 3.3-20). Note that for the projections feature, we need to specify the normalizing height and width. The default normalizing size is 10×10, and it will shrink the object into a 10×10 box and then extract the projections. This is done so that the number of projections does not get too large and the values will relate to object shape and not object size.

Now, we are ready to extract the features by clicking on the *Apply* button on the lower right of the *Analysis* window. We do this for each object in our image by selecting the object coordinates and typing in the desired class name. After the features have been extracted for all the objects, we can look at the feature file with the *View Feature File* button. The feature file, shown in Figure 3.3-21, contains the sample number (S. No.), the image file name, the row and column coordinates of a point in the object, followed by the feature values for that object. In the lower right corner of the feature file displayed in CVIPtools is a green button labeled *Save as Excel*, which allows the user to save the file in an Excel spreadsheet. The Excel spreadsheet provides a format that is easy to use, modify and analyze, and it can be imported into MATLAB. The task now is to examine this data and look for features that will differentiate the classes.

First, we deduce that area and centroid may be useful for some applications, but will not help us in classification. The next observation is that the orientation will not be necessary in the classification of these objects, although it, along with the area and centroid, would be useful to control a robot in finding and placing the objects. In Table 3-1, the data from the feature file for the Euler number and projection data is shown.

Next, we observe the Euler number feature will identify the class ellipse_hole, since it is 0 for this class and 1 for all others. Upon close examination of the projections, we can see that they can be used to differentiate the circles, ellipses and rectangle. In general, the ellipses have some zeros and increasing and decreasing projections, the circles have increasing and decreasing projections and the rectangles have constant projections possibly with some zeros. We can develop a simple rule, or classification algorithm, based on this information.

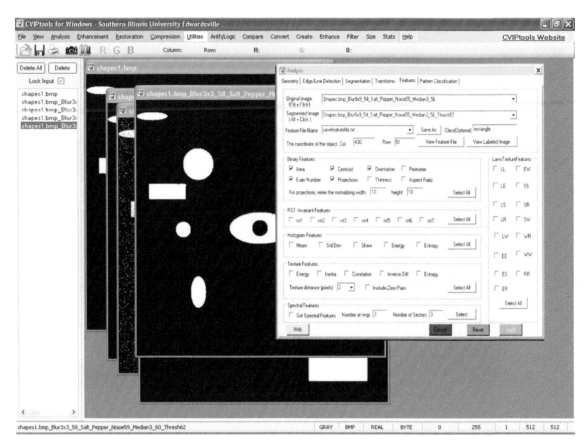

FIGURE 3.3-20
Feature tab with features selected.

In this case, the form of our algorithm is referred as a simple *decision tree*, which can be modeled as an if-then structure:

```
If euler number = 0
      Then Object = ellipse_hole
Else (euler number = 1)
      If projections are increasing and decreasing
            If projections has zeros
                        Then Object = ellipse
                  Else (projections has no zeros)
                        Then Object = circle
            Else (projections not increasing and decreasing)
                  Then Object = rectangle
```

This is shown in flowchart form in Figure 3.3-22. What we have done is develop a classification algorithm by the use of a training set. A *training set* is a set of sample images used to develop an algorithm. To complete step six in the image analysis process, application feedback, we need to generate some test images. This *test set* of images is then used to see how well the algorithm actually works on a different set of images. The idea is that these results will simulate the real application in practice and will not be biased by the training process – it is easy to get 100% success on the training set! Success on the test set increases our confidence that the algorithm will work in practice. Test sets can be created with CVIPtools and it is left as an exercise for the reader to validate the algorithm. Pattern classification will be explored further in Chapter 6.

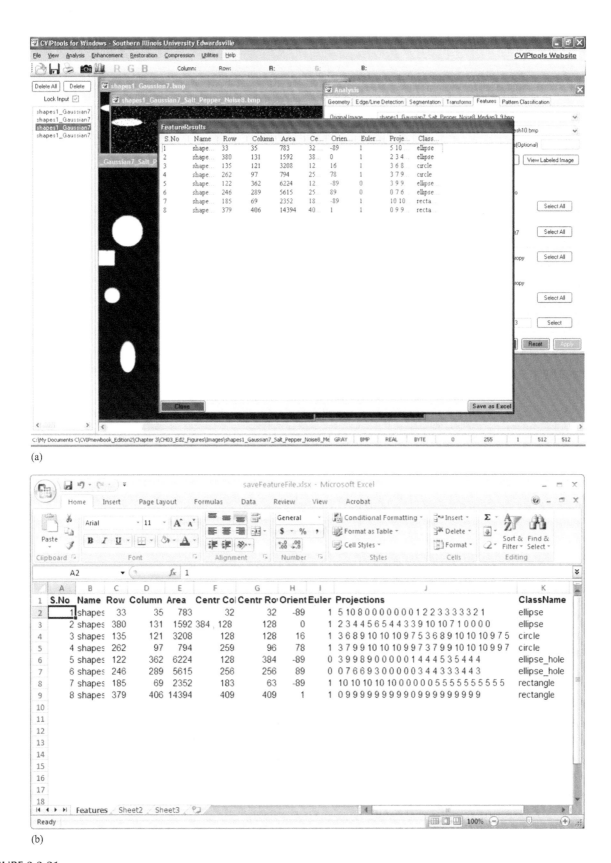

FIGURE 3.3-21
CVIPtools feature file. (a) The feature file displayed in CVIPtools, the green button in the lower right corner can be used to save it as an Excel spreadsheet (b), the feature file after it has been saved as an Excel spreadsheet. Note: In CVIPtools, the feature values for *Projections* are each put in a separate column, and they are displayed this way here for simplicity.

TABLE 3-1

Feature File Data

Object Type	Euler Number	Projections
Ellipse	1	5 10 8 0 0 0 0 0 0 0 1 2 2 3 3 3 3 3 2 1
Ellipse	1	2 3 4 4 5 6 5 4 4 3 3 9 10 10 7 1 0 0 0 0
circle	1	3 6 8 9 10 10 10 9 7 5 3 6 8 9 10 10 10 9 7 5
circle	1	3 7 9 9 10 10 10 9 9 7 3 7 9 9 10 10 10 9 9 7
ellipse_hole	0	3 9 9 8 9 0 0 0 0 0 1 4 4 4 5 3 5 4 4 4
ellipse_hole	0	0 7 6 6 9 3 0 0 0 0 0 3 4 4 3 3 3 4 4 3
rectangle	1	10 10 10 10 10 0 0 0 0 0 5 5 5 5 5 5 5 5 5 5
rectangle	1	0 9 9 9 9 9 9 9 9 0 9 0 9 9 9 9 9 9 9 9

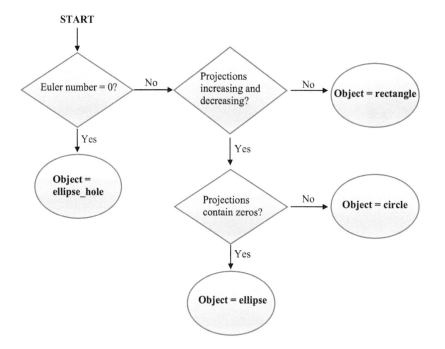

FIGURE 3.3-22

Decision tree as classification algorithm. This is the rule developed based on an analysis of the feature values for four classes of binary object shapes: ellipse_hole, ellipse, circle and rectangle.

3.4   Key Points

Image Analysis Process Model

Image analysis: detailed investigation of the image data to determine exactly the information necessary to help solve a computer imaging problem, primarily a data reduction process.

Image analysis process model (see Figure 3.1-3): consists of three primary stages: (1) preprocessing, (2) data reduction and (3) feature analysis.

Preprocessing: used to remove noise and artifacts, visually irrelevant information; preliminary data reduction.

Noise: unwanted information from the data acquisition process.

Data reduction: reducing data in the spatial domain or transforming into the spectral domain, followed by filtering and feature extraction.

Feature analysis: examining the extracted features to see how well they will solve the application problem.

Application feedback loop: key aspect of the image analysis process that incorporates application-based information in the development process.

Preprocessing

Region of interest geometry: to inspect more closely a specific area of an image.

Crop: process of selecting a portion of an image, a subimage, and cutting it away from the image.

Zoom: enlarging a section of an image. Zero- or first-order hold may be used.

Zero-order hold: repeating pixels.

First-order hold: linear interpolation between adjacent pixels.

Convolution: overlay the mask, multiply coincident values, sum results and move to the next pixel across the entire image (see Figure 3.2-3), Equation (3.2-1):

$$\sum_{x=-\infty}^{\infty}\sum_{y=-\infty}^{\infty}I(r-x,c-y)M(x,y).$$

Vector inner product: multiplying coincident terms of two vectors and summing results.

Translation: moving the image data along the row and/or column axes, Equation (3.2-2):

$$r' = r + r_0$$

$$c' = c + c_0$$

Rotation: clockwise rotation through a fixed angle θ, given by Equation (3.2-3):

$$\hat{r} = r(\cos\theta) + c(\sin\theta)$$

$$\hat{c} = -r(\sin\theta) + c(\cos\theta)$$

Combining rotation and translation: Equation (3.2-4):

$$\hat{r}' = (r + r_0)(\cos\theta) + (c + c_0)(\sin\theta)$$

$$\hat{c}' = -(r + r_0)(\sin\theta) + (c + c_0)(\cos\theta)$$

Arithmetic and logic operations: performed on a pixel by pixel basis; arithmetic operations: add, subtract, multiply and divide; logic operations: AND, OR and NOT.

Addition: used to combine information in two images, applications include creating models for restoration algorithm development, image sharpening algorithms and special effects such as image morphing.

Subtraction: used for motion detection and background subtraction, applications include object tracking and medical imaging.

Multiplication: used to brighten or darken an image or to combine two images.

Division: used to darken or brighten an image.

AND: a logical operation performed on a pixel by pixel basis, using two images, by a logical AND of the corresponding bits in each corresponding pixel, defined for BYTE-type (uint8 or unsigned char) images; used to combine two images or for image masking.

Image masking: extracting a portion of an image with an AND or OR operation using a binary image mask; masking out image artifacts by setting to 0.

OR: a logical operation performed on a pixel by pixel basis, using two images, by a logical OR of the corresponding bits in each corresponding pixel, defined for BYTE-type (uint8 or unsigned char) images; used to combine two images or for image masking.

NOT: creates a negative on an image by performing a logical NOT on each bit.

Spatial filters: operate on the image data by considering small neighborhoods in an image, such as 3×3, 5×5 and 7×7, and returning a result based on a linear or nonlinear operation; moving sequentially across and down the entire image.

Linear filters: can be implemented with a convolution mask, since the output is a linear combination of the (neighborhood) inputs.

Mask coefficients: all positive will blur an image, positive and negative will sharpen an image; if their sum is greater than one, the mask will tend to retain the original image brightness; if they sum to zero, the mask will tend to lose original image brightness.

Mean filters: averaging filters, will blur an image, all mask coefficients are positive.

Median filter: sorts the pixel values in a small neighborhood and replaces the center pixel with the middle value in the sorted list, is a nonlinear filter.

Nonlinear filter: cannot be implemented with a convolution mask since the result cannot be represented as a weighted sum of the neighborhood pixel values.

Enhancement filters: linear filters, the convolution masks have both positive and negative coefficients; will enhance image details via image sharpening and able to enhance details in a specific direction by careful mask selection.

Laplacian filters: enhancement filters with convolution masks of both positive and negative coefficients, rotationally symmetric versions will bring out image details equally in all directions.

Difference (emboss) filters: enhancement filters with convolution masks of both positive and negative coefficients, will bring out image details in a specific direction based on the mask used.

Histogram: A graphical plot of the distribution of the gray levels in an image, with the gray level on the horizontal axis and the count of the number of pixels at that level on the vertical axis.

Histogram modification: Observation and manipulation of the histogram provides an intuitive tool when improving or modifying image contrast.

Histogram stretch: stretching the histogram across the entire range of brightness levels to improve image contrast

$$\text{Stretch}(I(r, c)) = \left[\frac{I(r, c) - I(r, c)_{\text{MIN}}}{I(r, c)_{\text{MAX}} - I(r, c)_{\text{MIN}}} \right] [\text{MAX} - \text{MIN}] + \text{MIN}; \text{Equation (3.2-5)}$$

Histogram equalization: is a technique where the histogram of the resultant image is as flat as possible (Figure 3.2-18).

Image quantization: the process of reducing image data by removing some of the detail information by mapping groups of data points to a single point, performed in the spatial or gray level domain.

Gray level reduction: reducing the number of gray levels, typically from 256 levels for 8-bit per pixel data to fewer than 8 bits, can be performed with AND or OR masks (see Examples 3.2.5 and 3.2.6).

Thresholding: the simplest method of gray level reduction performed by setting a threshold value and setting all pixels above it to "1" (typically 255), and those below it to "0", output is a binary image.

False contouring: artificial lines that appear in images with reduced number of gray levels (Figure 3.2-19).

IGS: improved gray scale, a method to visually improve the results of gray level reduction by adding a random number to each pixel value before the quantization (Figure 3.2-20).

Halftoning/dithering: methods for reducing the number of gray levels by creating dot patterns or dither patterns to represent various gray levels, reduces effective spatial resolution also (Figures 3.2-21 and 3.2-22).

Uniform bin width quantization: the size of the bins for quantization is equal (Figure 3.2-23).

Variable bin width quantization: the size of the bins for quantization is not equal but may be assigned on an application-specific basis (Figures 3.2-23 and 3.2-24).

Spatial quantization: reducing image size by taking groups of spatially adjacent pixels and mapping them to one pixel, can be done by (1) averaging, (2) median or (3) decimation (Figure 3.2-25).

Averaging: performing size reduction by averaging groups of pixels and replacing the group by the average.

Median: sorting the pixel gray values in small neighborhood and replacing the neighborhood with the middle value.

Decimation: also known as sub-sampling, reduces image size by eliminating rows and columns.

Anti-aliasing filtering: a technique to improve image quality by averaging before decimation (Figure 3.2-26).

Binary Image Analysis

Threshold via histogram: examining the histogram to find clusters by looking at peaks and valleys and thresholding the image gray values at one of the valleys in the histogram, effects of lighting and background contrast is important (Figure 3.3-1).

Histogram: a plot of gray values versus numbers of pixels at each gray value (Figure 3.3-2).

Automatic thresholding algorithm: a simplified version of the *isodata* method or *k-means clustering algorithm* for two clusters. (1) Select an initial value for the threshold, T; typically the average gray level value, (2) apply the selected threshold value, T, separating image into two groups, (3) find the average (mean) values for each of these two groups of pixels, (4) calculate a new threshold by finding the average of the two mean values, and (5) if the change in threshold value from one iteration to the next is smaller than a previously specified limit, we are done. If the change is still greater than the specified limit, go to step 2 with the new threshold value.

Otsu method: a thresholding method that minimizes within-group variance, an analytical algorithm that works well for bimodal histograms based on the assumption that each peak is Gaussian shaped and the peaks are well separated.

Connectivity: defining how pixels are connected by selecting which of the eight neighboring pixels, assuming a square gird, are connected to the center pixel (Figure 3.3-4).

Four-connectivity: the connected neighbors are the two horizontal neighbors, to the left and right, and the two vertical neighbors, above and below.

Eight-connectivity: horizontal, vertical and all diagonal neighbors are considered connected.

Six-connectivity: horizontal, vertical and two diagonal neighbors are considered connected, this type of connectivity is used in CVIPtools and the book with NW/SE diagonal neighbors.

Connectivity dilemma: the dilemma that arises when we use four- or eight-connectivity for both objects and background where closed curves do not separate the background (eight-connectivity) or we do not have a closed curve and the background is separated (four-connectivity).

Labeling: the process of assigning labels to connected objects in an image.

Labeling algorithm flowchart: see Figure 3.3-5.

UPDATE: a method needed in a sequential labeling algorithm to deal with the situation when two pixels are found connected, but connected neighbors have different labels.

Binary object features: features that can be extracted from labeled objects in binary images which can be used to classify the objects.

Area: the size in pixels of a binary object, indicating the relative size of the object, found by summing all the pixels in the object, Equation (3.3-8):

$$A_i = \sum_{r=0}^{N-1} \sum_{c=0}^{N-1} I_i(r, c).$$

Center of area (centroid): the midpoint along each row and column axis corresponding to the "middle" based on the spatial distribution of pixels within the object, used to locate the object spatially, defined by Equation (3.3-9):

$$\bar{r}_i = \frac{1}{A_i} \sum_{r=0}^{N-1} \sum_{c=0}^{N-1} r I_i(r, c); \ \bar{c}_i = \frac{1}{A_i} \sum_{r=0}^{N-1} \sum_{c=0}^{N-1} c I_i(r, c)$$

Axis of least second moment: defines the object's orientation, given by Equation (3.3-10):

$$\tan(2\theta_i) = 2 \frac{\displaystyle\sum_{r=0}^{N-1}\sum_{c=0}^{N-1} rc I_i(r, c)}{\displaystyle\sum_{r=0}^{N-1}\sum_{c=0}^{N-1} r^2 I_i(r, c) - \sum_{r=0}^{N-1}\sum_{c=0}^{N-1} c^2 I_i(r, c)}$$

Projections: found by summing pixels along each row or column, provides information about an object's shape and provides simpler equations for center of area.

Horizontal projection: sum of pixels along the rows.

Vertical projection: sum of pixels along the columns.

Euler number: defined as the number of objects minus the number of holes, or the number of convexities minus the number of concavities.

Binary object classification: the process of identifying binary objects through application of the image analysis process given in Figure 3.1-3, consisting of the following steps: (1) preprocessing, (2) thresholding, (3) filtering (optional), (4) feature extraction, (5) feature analysis and (6) application feedback.

Decision tree: a simple form of a classification rule, or classification algorithm, which can be represented as an if-then structure. This is a form of clustering in the feature space developed by finding a rule to separate the classes based on the feature data in the training set.

3.5 References and Further Reading

For related reading on computer vision and image analysis, see Sonka, Hlavac, and Boyle (2014) and Szeliski (2022). The method of zooming via convolution masks is described in Sid-Ahmed (1995). For spatial filtering, Umbaugh (2023), Sonka, Hlavac, and Boyle (2014), Gonzalez and Woods (2018), Pratt (2007), Jain, Kasturi, and Schnuck (1995) and Myler and Weeks (1993) contain additional information. More on connectivity can be found in Jain, Kasturi, and Schnuck (1995), Haralick and Shapiro (1992) and Horn (1986). For more background on Euler number, see Horn (1986). For other Otsu-based algorithms, including multiple thresholds and fast algorithms, see Liao, Chen, and Chung (2001); and for an application to unimodal histograms, see Ng (2006).

More information on halftoning and dithering can be found in Watt and Policarpo (1998), Hill (1990) and Durrett (1987). The definitions for connectivity are described in Horn (1986) and further information can be found in Haralick and Shapiro (1992). More labeling algorithms can be found in Sonka, Hlavac, and Boyle (2014), Shapiro and Stockman (2001) and Jain, Kastuiri, and Schnuck (1995). More on thresholding techniques can be found in Davies (2018) and Shapiro and Stockman (2001). A companion look at improved gray scale (IGS) quantization can be found in Gonzalez and Woods (2018). Additional information on the processing of binary images can be found in Davies (2018), Russ (2015), Shapiro and Stockman (2001) and Jain, Kasturi, and Schunck (1995).

Davies, E.R., *Computer and Machine Vision*, 54th Edition, Waltham, MA: Academic Press, 2018.

Durrett, H.J., Editor, *Color and the Computer*, Boston, MA, Academic Press, 1987.

Gonzalez, R.C., Woods, R.E., *Digital Image Processing*, 4th Edition, New York: Pearson, 2018.

Haralick, R.M., Shapiro, L.G., *Computer and Robot Vision*, Reading, MA: Addison-Wesley, 1992.

Hill, F.S., *Computer Graphics*, New York: Macmillan Publishing Company, 1990.

Horn, B.K.P., *Robot Vision*, Cambridge, MA: The MIT Press, 1986.

Jain, R., Kasturi, R., Schnuck, B.G., *Machine Vision*, New York: McGraw Hill, 1995.

Liao, P.S., Chen, T.S., Chung, P.C., A fast algorithm for multilevel thresholding. *Journal of Information Science and Engineering*, Vol. 17, pp. 713–727, 2001.

Myler, H.R., Weeks, A.R., *Computer Imaging Recipes in C*, Englewood Cliffs, NJ: Prentice Hall, 1993.

Ng, H.-F., Automatic thresholding for defect detection. *Pattern Recognition Letters*, Vol. 27, No. 14, pp. 1644–1649, 2006.

Pratt, W.K., *Digital Image Processing*, New York: Wiley, 2007.
Russ, J.C., *The Image Processing Handbook*, 7th Edition, Boca Raton, FL: CRC Press, 2015.
Shapiro, L., Stockman, G., *Computer Vision*, Upper Saddle River, NJ: Prentice Hall, 2001.
Sid-Ahmed, M.A. *Image Processing: Theory, Algorithms, and Architectures*, New York: McGraw Hill, 1995.
Sonka, M., Hlavac, V., Boyle, R., *Image Processing, Analysis and Machine Vision*, 4th Edition, Boston, MA: Cengage Learning, 2014.
Szeliski, R., *Computer Vision: Algorithms and Applications*, 2nd Edition, Switzerland AG: Springer, 2022.
Umbaugh, S.E, *DIPA: Digital Image Enhancement, Restoration, and Compression*, 4th Edition, Boca Raton, FL: CRC Press, 2023.
Watt, A., Policarpo, F., *The Computer Image*, New York: Addison-Wesley, 1998.

3.6 Exercises

Problems

1. What is image analysis? How is it used in computer vision applications? How is it used in human vision applications? Give examples of each.

2. What are the three primary stages of image analysis? The second stage can be performed in two different domains, what are they?

3. Draw a detailed figure of the image analysis process. Explain each block. Why do we need feedback?

4. List and describe the image geometry operations used in preprocessing for image analysis. Run CVIPtools and experiment with the functions under *Analysis→Geometry* and *Utilties→Size.*

5. Use zero-order hold to increase the size of the following image by a factor of 2:

$$\begin{bmatrix} 6 & 7 & 8 \\ 2 & 6 & 4 \\ 6 & 3 & 8 \end{bmatrix}$$

6. Use first-order hold to increase the image by a factor of about 3. Apply the method which will increase the image size to $K(N-1)+1$. What is the resulting image size? Is this "about a factor of 3"? Why or why not?

$$\begin{bmatrix} 2 & 5 & 9 \\ 5 & 6 & 4 \\ 9 & 3 & 8 \end{bmatrix}$$

7. We want to translate *Image1* by 45 columns to the right and 18 rows up, what are the new coordinates for the point $(r, c) = (120, 22)$? We want to rotate *Image2* $50°$ in the clockwise direction, what are the new coordinates for the point $(r, c) = (42,100)$? We want to rotate and translate *Image3* the same as we did for *Image1* and *Image2*, what are the new coordinates for the point $(r, c) = (100, 66)$?

8. Subtract the following two images. What is an example of an application for image subtraction? How do we display negative numbers?

$$\begin{bmatrix} 2 & 5 & 9 \\ 5 & 6 & 4 \\ 9 & 3 & 8 \end{bmatrix} \begin{bmatrix} 1 & 2 & 7 \\ 3 & 4 & 2 \\ 9 & 3 & 9 \end{bmatrix}$$

In CVIPtools, subtract a dark image from a brighter image. Observe the data range shown in the lower right of the main window. What does CVIPtools do with the negative numbers for display?

9. Perform a logical OR with the following two images. What can this operation be used for?

$$\begin{bmatrix} 2 & 5 & 9 \\ 5 & 6 & 4 \\ 0 & 3 & 8 \end{bmatrix} \begin{bmatrix} 1 & 2 & 7 \\ 3 & 4 & 2 \\ 9 & 3 & 9 \end{bmatrix}$$

Use CVIPtools to OR images together. During this process, consider potential applications.

10. How is image masking performed? What are its uses? Use *Utilities→Create→Border Mask* in CVIPtools to create mask images and then use AND to mask the original image.

11. What does a NOT operation do to the appearance of an image? Perform the NOT operation in CVIPtools on a color image, are the results what you expected? Multiply an image by 1.8 without byte clipping. What is the output image data type? Now, perform a NOT on the image multiplied by 1.8. What is the data type of this output image? Explain.

12. What does a convolution filter do that has all positive coefficients? What does a convolution filter do that has both positive and negative coefficients? How about one where the coefficients sum to zero? What happens if the filter mask coefficients sum to one? Use CVIPtools *Utilities→Filter→Specify a filter* to verify your answers.

13. Are convolution filters linear? Name a nonlinear filter. Given the following 3×3 neighborhood in an image, what is the result of applying a 3×3 median filter to the center pixel?

$$\begin{bmatrix} 1 & 2 & 7 \\ 3 & 4 & 2 \\ 9 & 3 & 9 \end{bmatrix}$$

Use CVIPtools *Utilities→Create→Add Noise* to add salt-and-pepper noise to an image. Now, perform a median filter on the noisy image using *Utilities→Filter→Median*. How does it affect the appearance of the image as you increase mask size of the filter?

14. What are the coefficients for a typical 3×3 mean convolution filter? What are the coefficients for a typical 3×3 enhancement filter? Use CVIPtools to verify your results.

15. Use CVIPtools to subtract Figure 3.2-7a from 3.2-7b. (a) Why does the output appear mostly gray? (hint: *data range* and *remap*). (b) Try and find a method to make the image appear as shown in Figure 3.2-7c. (hint: *histogram stretch*)

16. What are example applications for image multiplication and division? Demonstrate your examples with CVIPtools.

17. What is the bit string we would use for an AND mask to reduce 8-bit image information to 64 gray levels? Does this map the data to the low or high end of the range? Use CVIPtools *Utilities→Convert→Gray Level Quantization* to reduce the number of gray levels of an 8-bit image to 32 gray levels. Look at the histogram of the output image by selecting the bar graph icon just to the left of the RGB icons. Does CVIPtools map the output data to the low or high end of the range?

18. What is false contouring? How can we visually improve this effect? Explain. Use CVIPtools to reduce the number of gray levels on an 8-bit image to 8 gray levels, select standard method. Now, select the IGS method and compare the results.

19. What is halftoning and dithering? Why is it used? Use CVIPtools *Utilities→Convert→Halftone* and compare various methods. Which one do you think works the best? Do you think this is true for all images?

20. Describe variable bin width quantization. Why is it used?

21. Describe the three methods used for spatial reduction. Which method do you think is the fastest? The slowest? When using the decimation technique, how can we improve the results? Use CVIPtools *Utilities→Size→Spatial Quant* to compare the three methods.

22. What is a histogram? How can it be useful?

23. In CVIPtools, you can threshold an image with *Utilties→Convert→Binary Threshold*. Using CVIPtools, try to find a good threshold to separate the object from background in Figure 3.3-1c. Are you successful? Why or why not? Look at the histogram of various images with CVIPtools (the histogram icon looks like a bar graph).

24. Draw a binary image to illustrate the dilemma that arises when using four- or eight-connectivity. Explain three ways to avoid this dilemma. Label all objects and background objects. Remember that a connected line should separate the objects on either side of the line.

25. What is the UPDATE block for in the flowchart in Figure 3.3-5?

26. Given an application where we need to control a robotic gripper to pick and place items on an assembly line, what are the most useful binary features?

27. Find the horizontal and vertical projections for the following binary image:

$$\begin{bmatrix} 0 & 1 & 1 & 1 & 0 \\ 0 & 0 & 1 & 1 & 1 \\ 0 & 0 & 0 & 1 & 1 \end{bmatrix}$$

28. The Euler number for an object is equal to the number of objects minus the number of holes and is equal to the number of convexities minus the number of concavities. Is the number of objects necessarily equal to the number of convexities? Is the number of holes necessarily equal to the number of concavities? Explain.

3.6.1 Programming Exercises

These exercises can be implemented in MATLAB or in C using CVIPlab.

Image Geometry

1. Write a function to implement an image crop. Have the user specify the upper left corner and the size of the cropped area in terms of rows and columns.

2. Write a function to implement an image zoom, have the user specify the starting (r, c) coordinates, the height and width and the zoom factor. Use zero-order hold.

3. Incorporate the CVIPtools *zoom* (in the Geometry library) into your CVIPlab program or experiment with the corresponding MATLAB function (*zoom_cvip*). Experiment with enlarging an image by different factors. The minimum and maximum factors allowed are 1 and 10, respectively. You have the option of choosing the whole of the image, or any particular quadrant, or you can specify the starting row and column, and the width and height for the enlargement of the particular region of the image.

4. Write a function to rotate an image. Experiment with various degrees of rotation. Experiment using CVIPtools with *Analysis→Geometry→Rotate*. Does this differ from how your rotate function works?

Arithmetic/Logic Operations

1. Write functions that perform the following logical operations on two images: AND, OR and NOT. Compare your results to CVIPtools.

2. Write a function to subtract two images. Initially, use BYTE (uint8) data types which will result in clipping at zero for negative results. Next, modify the function to use FLOAT (double) data types (for C programmers, use *cast_Image* in the Image library, or for MATLAB users, use *im2double*) and then remap when the process is completed (in C, use *remap_Image* in the Mapping library, or in MATLAB, use *remap_cvip*). Note that these two methods will result in different output images.

3. Extend the logic operations to work with data types other than BYTE (uint8).

4. Extend the logic operations to include NAND, NOR and more complex Boolean expressions.

5. Extend the subtraction function to perform addition, multiplication and division.

6. Experiment with different methods of handling overflow and underflow with the arithmetic operations.

Spatial Filters

1. Write a program to implement spatial convolution masks. Let the user select from one of the following masks:

   Mean filter masks:

$$\frac{1}{9}\begin{bmatrix} 1 & 1 & 1 \\ 1 & 1 & 1 \\ 1 & 1 & 1 \end{bmatrix} \quad \frac{1}{10}\begin{bmatrix} 1 & 1 & 1 \\ 1 & 2 & 1 \\ 1 & 1 & 1 \end{bmatrix} \quad \frac{1}{16}\begin{bmatrix} 1 & 2 & 1 \\ 2 & 4 & 2 \\ 1 & 2 & 1 \end{bmatrix}$$

   Enhancement filter masks:

$$\begin{bmatrix} -1 & -1 & -1 \\ -1 & 9 & -1 \\ -1 & -1 & -1 \end{bmatrix} \begin{bmatrix} 1 & -2 & 1 \\ -2 & 5 & -2 \\ 1 & -2 & 1 \end{bmatrix} \begin{bmatrix} 0 & -1 & 0 \\ -1 & 5 & -1 \\ 0 & -1 & 0 \end{bmatrix}$$

2. Modify the program to allow the user to input the coefficients for a 3×3 mask.

3. Experiment with using the masks. Try images with and without added noise.

4. Modify the program to handle larger masks.

5. Write a median filtering function. Compare the median filter to the mean filter masks for image smoothing.

6. Incorporate the CVIPtools function *median_filter* (SpatialFilter library for C) or *median_filter_cvip* (for MATLAB) into your CVIPlab program. Is it faster or slower than your median filtering function? Compare your results to CVIPtools *Utilities→Filter→Median*.

Image Quantization

1. Write a function to reduce the number of gray levels in an image by uniform quantization. Allow the user to specify: (1) how many gray levels in the output image and (2) how to map the gray levels to the beginning, middle or end of the range.

2. Write a function to reduce the number of gray levels in an image by non-uniform quantization. Allow the user to specify the input ranges and the output value for up to four output gray levels.

3. Write a function to perform spatial quantization by decimation.

Binary Object Features

1. Write a function to find the area and coordinates of center of area of a binary image. Assume the image only contains one object. Remember that the value that represents "1" for the binary images is actually 255 and "0" is 0.

2. Test this function using images you create with CVIPtools. Use *Utilities* to create test images with the *Create* option (*Utilties→Create*). To create images with multiple objects, use the *AND* and *OR* logic functions available from *Utilties→Arith/Logic*.

3. Write a function to find the number of upstream facing convexities (X), upstream facing concavities (V) and the Euler number for a binary image. Use the method discussed in Section 3.3.3, assuming six-connectivity.
   The function should display the following:
   The number of upstream facing convexities=<X>
   The number of upstream facing concavities=<V>
   The Euler number for the image=<X − V>

4. Test this function using images you create with CVIPtools. Use *Utilities* to create test images with the *Create* option (*Utilities→Create*). To create images with multiple objects, use the *AND* and *OR* logic functions available from *Utilities→Arith/Logic*.

5. Modify the Euler function to find the Euler number for each object in a binary image containing multiple objects.

6. Modify your Euler function to handle other connectivity types (four, eight and four/eight).

7. Modify your functions to handle gray level images.

8. Modify your functions to handle color images.

3.7 Supplementary Exercises

Supplementary Problems

1.

    a. Find the area and the center of area for the following binary image:

$$
\begin{bmatrix}
0 & 0 & 1 & 1 & 1 & 0 & 0 & 0 \\
0 & 1 & 1 & 1 & 1 & 1 & 1 & 0 \\
0 & 0 & 0 & 1 & 1 & 0 & 0 & 0 \\
0 & 1 & 1 & 1 & 1 & 0 & 0 & 0 \\
0 & 0 & 0 & 1 & 0 & 0 & 0 & 0
\end{bmatrix}
$$

    b. find the axis of least second moment,

    c. find the Euler number based on six-connectivity NW/SE,

    d. find the Euler number based on six-connectivity NE/SW.

2. Use CVIPtools to create a test set of images for the algorithm developed in Section 3.3.4. Vary the size of objects, the amount of noise added and the degree of blurring. Extract the features of interest using CVIPtools. Examine the feature file. Does the classification algorithm developed in this section work successfully? How is the success rate affected as the amount of blur and added noise is increased? Develop a more robust algorithm that will work with high levels of blurring and noise.

3. Research and discuss methods for automatic image thresholding. Automatic thresholding refers to algorithmic methods to determine the threshold from the image data itself. Typically, the histogram is used to make this determination.

4. Collect a set of images of various objects that you want to identify. Using CVIPtools, apply the image analysis process. Experiment with preprocessing, segmentation and filtering methods. Extract the features of interest using CVIPtools. Examine the feature file. Develop a classification algorithm. Experiment with blurring and adding noise to the images. Develop a more robust algorithm that will work with high levels of blurring and noise.

5. Apply the basic automatic thresholding algorithm to the following 2-bit per pixel image using a limit of 0.01 and initial value of (a) image mean and (b) weighted average from two histogram peaks. Show your results from each step.

$$
\begin{bmatrix}
1 & 1 & 1 & 1 & 1 & 1 & 1 & 3 \\
1 & 1 & 1 & 1 & 1 & 1 & 1 & 3 \\
3 & 3 & 3 & 3 & 3 & 3 & 3 & 3 \\
3 & 3 & 3 & 3 & 3 & 3 & 3 & 3 \\
3 & 3 & 3 & 3 & 3 & 3 & 3 & 3 \\
3 & 3 & 3 & 3 & 1 & 1 & 1 & 1 \\
1 & 1 & 1 & 1 & 1 & 1 & 1 & 0 \\
2 & 2 & 2 & 2 & 2 & 0 & 0 & 0
\end{bmatrix}
$$

3.7.1 Supplementary Programming Exercises

Connectivity and Labeling

1. Write a function to implement the labeling algorithm described for a 256×256 image. You may assume that the first row and column [(0,0) in C programming and (1,1) in MATLAB] do not contain objects, so start the scan with the second row and column. Follow the flowchart for the labeling algorithm.

2. Test this function using images you create with CVIPtools. Use the *Utilities* to create test images with the *Create* option (*Utilties→Create*). To create images with multiple objects, use the *AND* and *OR* logic functions available from *Utilties→Arith/Logic*.

3. Once you are certain that your function implements the algorithm correctly, modify the label function to allow for the use of any size image.

4. Modify the function so that it will handle objects on the edges of the image.

5. Modify the Update function (see flowchart, Figures 3.3-5 and 3.3-6) so that it does not require multiple image scans, for example, keep a linked list or table of equivalent labels and rescan the image only once (after all the labeling is done).

6. Modify the function to work with gray level images.

7. Modify the function to work with color images.

8. Modify the function to handle any number of objects.

9. Modify the function so that it will output the labeled image (that is, the label array written to disk as an image, with appropriate gray levels to make all the objects visible).

> *Note: If doing this exercise in C, the following will be useful:*

- Define a two-dimensional array for the labels using a fixed size, for example, for a 256×256 image:

```
int label[256][256]; /*declaration*/
```

- Be sure to initialize the array elements (for example, via "for" loops), if needed. When the memory is allocated for the array, it may contain garbage depending on the compiler and the operating system.

- To allow for any size image, use a Matrix structure for the label array. This will allow the use of any size image, without the need to change the size of the array. This is done as follows:

```
Matrix *label_ptr;   /* declaration of pointer to Matrix data structure */
int   **label;       /* declaration of pointer to matrix data */
.....
label_ptr = new_Matrix(no_of_rows, no_of_cols, CVIP_INTEGER, REAL); /*allocating the
memory for the matrix structure*/
label = (int **) getData_Matrix(label_ptr);   /* getting the matrix data into the
label array*/
.....
label[r][c]                                    /*accessing the array elements */
.....
delete_Matrix(label_ptr);        /*freeing the memory space used by the matrix*/
```

Programming Exercise: Image Quantization II

1. Write a function to perform IGS quantization, note that noise functions are available for CVIPlab.

2. Compare your results to those obtained with CVIPtools. Are the results the same? Why or why not?

3. Write a function to quantize images of any image data type. Let the user specify the number of quantization bins.

4. Write a function to allow for variable bin width quantization. Let the user specify the bin ranges and the mapping value(s).

5. Write a function to perform spatial quantization. Allow the user to specify the method: decimation, median and averaging. Incorporate an anti-aliasing filter option for the decimation method.

Programming Exercise: Image Geometry II

1. Write a function to implement an image zoom, have the user specify the starting (r, c) coordinates, the height and width and the zoom factor. Let the user specify zero-order or first-order hold.

2. Write a function to rotate an image. Experiment with various degrees of rotation. Enhance your rotate function to select the center portion of rotated image and enlarge it to the original image size.

3. Write a function to perform spatial quantization. Compare using the three different reduction methods available: average, median and decimation. Compare your results to CVIPtools. Are the same? Why or why not?

Programming Exercise Automatic Thresholding with Otsu Method

1. Write a function to implement the Otsu method for automatic thresholding. Have the function output the image after the thresholding and the threshold value.

2. Write a function to display the histogram of an image with a slider at the bottom so that the user can vary the threshold and see the resultant image.

Programming Exercise Automatic Thresholding with K-means Algorithm

1. Write a function to implement the *k-means clustering algorithm* to separate two clusters for automatic image thresholding. Have the function output the image after the thresholding and the threshold value.

2. Write a function to display the histogram of an image with a slider at the bottom so the user can vary the threshold and see the resultant image.

3. Extend the function to allow for a user-specified number of clusters. You will be required to extend the two cluster method described here and other resources may be used.

Programming Exercise: Image Morphing

1. Write a function to implement image morphing. Allow the user to specify the percentage of the second image to be added to the first after each iteration.

2. Modify the function to allow the user to specify the corresponding (r, c) pairs in image one and image two, and warp the image(s) accordingly as they are morphed together. Hint: linear interpolation is required.

4

Edge, Line and Shape Detection

4.1 Introduction and Overview

The image analysis process requires us to take vast amounts of low-level pixel data and extract useful information. In this chapter, we will explore methods that contribute to the process of dividing the image into meaningful regions by detecting edges, lines, corners and geometric shapes. These shapes represent higher-level information, and these are often precursors to image segmentation, which is explored in the next chapter where we will see that edge and line detection are important steps for one category of image segmentation methods. Edge detection techniques are covered in Section 4.2, as well as metrics to measure edge detector performance. Section 4.3 introduces the Hough transform for line finding and discusses associated postprocessing methods. Section 4.4 will explore corner and shape detection, and this chapter concludes with a discussion of using the extended and generalized Hough transform for shape detection.

4.2 Edge Detection

The edge detection process is based on the idea that if the brightness levels are changing rapidly, there is the potential for an edge to exist at that point. Many different approaches have been explored to facilitate this process. The edge detection operators presented here are representative of the various types that have been developed. Many are implemented with small masks used in a manner similar to the convolution process; by this, we mean they are used to scan the image left to right and top to bottom, and at each pixel, replace the value with the result of a mathematical operation on the pixel's neighborhood. Most edge detectors are based on discrete approximations to differential operators. Differential operations measure the rate of change in a function, in this case, the image brightness function. A large change in image brightness over a short spatial distance indicates the presence of an edge. Some edge detection operators return orientation information – information about the direction of the edge – while others only return information about the magnitude of an edge at each point.

Edge detection methods are used as a first step in the line detection process. Edge detection is also used to find complex object boundaries by marking potential edge points corresponding to places in an image where rapid changes in brightness occur. After these edge points have been marked, they can be merged to form lines and object outlines. Often people are confused about the difference between an edge and a line. This is illustrated in Figure 4.2-1 where we see that an edge occurs at a point, and it is perpendicular to the line. The edge direction is defined as the direction of change; so, on a curve, it will be perpendicular to the tangent line at that point. Note that a line or curve that forms a boundary can be defined as a set of connected edge points.

With many of the edge detection operators, noise in the image can create problems. That is why it is best to preprocess the image to eliminate or at least minimize noise effects. To deal with noise effects, we must make tradeoffs between the sensitivity and the accuracy of an edge detector. For example, if the parameters are adjusted so that the edge detector is very sensitive, it will tend to find many potential edge points that are attributable to noise. If we make it less sensitive, it may miss valid edges. The parameters that we can vary include the size of the edge detection mask and the value of the gray level threshold. A larger mask or a higher gray level threshold will tend to reduce noise effects, but may result in a loss of valid edge points. The tradeoff between sensitivity and accuracy is illustrated in Figure 4.2-2.

Edge detection operators are based on the idea that edge information in an image is found by considering the relationship a pixel has with its neighbors. If a pixel's gray level value is similar to those around it, there is probably not an edge at that point. However, if a pixel has neighbors with widely varying gray levels, it may represent an edge point. In other words, an edge is defined by a discontinuity in gray level values. Ideally, an edge separates two distinct objects. In practice, apparent edges are caused by changes in color, texture or by the specific lighting

DOI: 10.1201/9781003221135-4

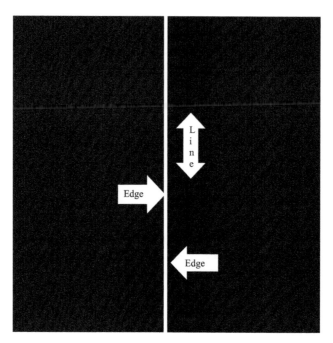

FIGURE 4.2-1
Edges and lines are perpendicular. The line shown here is vertical and the edge direction is horizontal. In this case, the transition from black to white occurs along a row, this is the edge direction, but the line is vertical along a column.

FIGURE 4.2-2
Noise in images requires tradeoffs between sensitivity and accuracy for edge detectors. (a) Noisy image, (b) edge detector too sensitive, many edge points found that are attributable to noise (c) edge detector not sensitive enough, loss of valid edge points and (d) reasonable result obtained by compromise between sensitivity and accuracy.

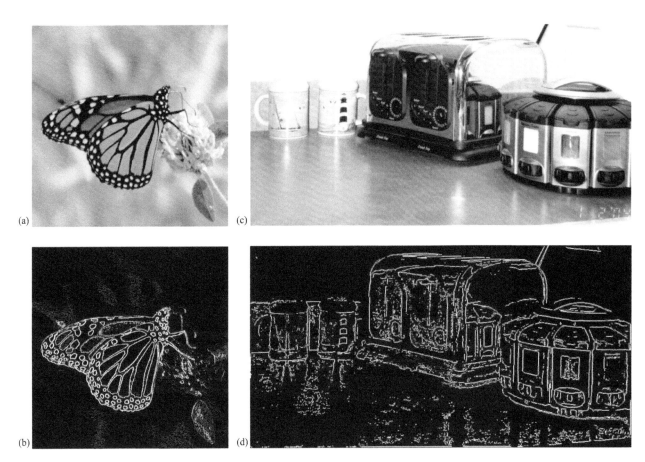

FIGURE 4.2-3
Image objects may be parts of real objects. (a) Butterfly image (original photo courtesy of Mark Zuke), (b) butterfly after edge detection, note that image objects are separated by color and brightness changes, (c) image of objects in kitchen corner, and (d) image after edge detection, note that some image objects are created by reflections in the image due to lighting conditions and object properties.

conditions present during the image acquisition process. This means that what we refer to as image objects may actually be only parts of the objects in the real world; see Figure 4.2-3.

Figure 4.2-4 illustrates the differences between an ideal edge and a real edge. Figure 4.2-4a shows a representation of one row in an image of an ideal edge. The vertical axis represents brightness and the horizontal axis shows the spatial coordinate. The abrupt change in brightness characterizes an ideal edge. In the corresponding image, the edge appears very distinct. In Figure 4.2-4b, we see the representation of a real edge which changes gradually. This gradual change is a minor form of blurring caused by the imaging device, the lenses, and/or the lighting and is typical for real-world (as opposed to computer generated) images. In the figure, where the edge has been exaggerated for illustration purposes, note that from a visual perspective, this image contains the same information as does the ideal image: black on one side and white on the other with a line down the center.

4.2.1 Gradient Operators

Gradient operators are based on the concept of using the first or second derivative of the gray level function as an edge detector. Remember from calculus that the derivative measures the rate of change of a line or the slope of the line. If we model the gray level transition of an edge by a ramp function, which is a reasonable approximation to a real edge, we can see what the first and second derivatives look like in Figure 4.2-5. When the gray level is constant, the first derivative is zero, and when it is linear, it is equal to the slope of the line. With the following operators, we will see that this is approximated with a difference operator, similar to the methods used to derive the definition of the derivative. The second derivative is a positive spike at the change on the dark side of the edge where line brightness is increasing, and it is a negative spike at the change on the light side where the increase stops and zero elsewhere.

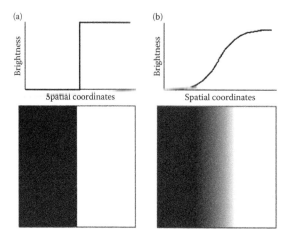

FIGURE 4.2-4
Ideal edge compared to a real edge. (a) Ideal edge and (b) real edge. The ideal edge is an instantaneous change, while a real edge is typically a gradual change. The real edge has been greatly enlarged for illustration purposes, note that from a visual perspective this image contains the same information as does the ideal image: black on one side, white on the other, with a line down the center.

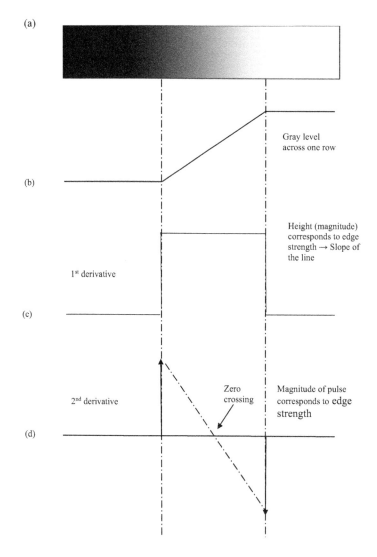

FIGURE 4.2-5
Edge model. (a) A portion of an image with an edge, which has been enlarged to show detail, (b) ramp edge model, (c) first derivative and (d) second derivative with a line drawn between the two pulses which crosses the zero axis at the edge center.

In Figure 4.2-5c, we can see that the magnitude of the first derivative will mark edge points, with steeper gray level changes corresponding to stronger edges and larger magnitudes from the derivative operators. In Figure 4.2-5d, we can see that applying a second derivative operator to an edge returns two impulses, one on either side of the edge. An advantage of this is that if a line is drawn between the two impulses, the position where this line crosses the zero axis is the center of the edge, which theoretically allows us to measure edge location to sub-pixel accuracy. Sub-pixel accuracy refers to the fact that the zero crossing (zc) may be at a fractional pixel distance, for example, halfway between two pixels, so we could say the edge is at, for instance, $zc = 75.5$.

The **Roberts operator** is a simple approximation to the first derivative. It marks edge points only; it does not return any information about the edge orientation. It is the simplest of the edge detection operators, so is the most efficient one for binary images. There are two forms of the Roberts operator. The first consists of the square root of the sum of the differences of the diagonal neighbors squared, as follows:

$$\sqrt{[I(r, c) - I(r-1, c-1)]^2 + [I(r, c-1) - I(r-1, c)]^2} \tag{4.2-1}$$

The second form of the Roberts operator is the sum of the magnitude of the differences of the diagonal neighbors, as follows:

$$|I(r, c) - I(r-1, c-1)| + |I(r, c-1) - I(r-1, c)| \tag{4.2-2}$$

The second form of the equation is often used in practice due to its computational efficiency – it is typically faster for a computer to find an absolute value than to find square roots.

The **Sobel operator** approximates the gradient by using a row and a column mask, which will approximate the first derivative in each direction. The Sobel edge detection masks find edges in both the horizontal and vertical directions, and then combine this information into two metrics – magnitude and direction. The masks are as follows:

VERTICAL EDGE   HORIZONTAL EDGE

$$\begin{bmatrix} -1 & -2 & -1 \\ 0 & 0 & 0 \\ 1 & 2 & 1 \end{bmatrix} \qquad \begin{bmatrix} -1 & 0 & 1 \\ -2 & 0 & 2 \\ -1 & 0 & 1 \end{bmatrix}$$

These masks are each convolved with the image. At each pixel location, we now have two numbers: s_1, corresponding to the result from the vertical edge mask, and s_2, from the horizontal edge mask. We use these numbers to compute two metrics, the edge magnitude and the edge direction, defined as follows:

$$\text{EDGE MAGNITUDE} \sqrt{s_1^2 + s_2^2} \tag{4.2-3}$$

$$\text{EDGE DIRECTION} \tan^{-1}\left[\frac{s_1}{s_2}\right] \tag{4.2-4}$$

As seen in Figure 4.2-1, the edge direction is perpendicular to the line (or curve), because the direction specified is the direction of the gradient, along which the gray levels are changing.

The **Prewitt** is similar to the Sobel, but with different mask coefficients. The masks are defined as follows:

VERTICAL EDGE   HORIZONTAL EDGE

$$\begin{bmatrix} -1 & -1 & -1 \\ 0 & 0 & 0 \\ 1 & 1 & 1 \end{bmatrix} \qquad \begin{bmatrix} -1 & 0 & 1 \\ -1 & 0 & 1 \\ -1 & 0 & 1 \end{bmatrix}$$

These masks are each convolved with the image. At each pixel location, we find two numbers: p_1, corresponding to the result from the vertical edge mask, and p_2, from the horizontal edge mask. We use these results to determine two metrics, the edge magnitude and the edge direction, which are defined as follows:

$$\text{EDGE MAGNITUDE } \sqrt{p_1^{\,2}+p_2^{\,2}} \tag{4.2-5}$$

$$\text{EDGE DIRECTION } \text{Tan}^{-1}\!\left[\frac{p_1}{p_2}\right] \tag{4.2-6}$$

As with the Sobel edge detector, the direction lies 90° from the apparent direction of the line or curve. The Prewitt is easier to calculate than the Sobel, since the only coefficients are 1's, which makes it easier to implement in hardware. However, the Sobel is defined to place emphasis on the pixels closer to the mask center, which may be desirable for some applications.

The **Laplacian operators** described here are similar to the ones used for preprocessing as described in Section 3.2.3. The three Laplacian masks presented below represent various practical approximations of the Laplacian, which is the two-dimensional version of the second derivative (note that these are masks used in practice and true Laplacians will have all the coefficients negated). Unlike the Sobel and Prewitt edge detection masks, the Laplacian masks are approximately rotationally symmetric, which means edges at all orientations contribute to the result. As that is the case, they are applied by selecting *one* mask and convolving it with the image. The sign of the result (positive or negative) tells us which side of the edge is brighter.

LAPLACIAN MASKS

Filter 1   Filter 2   Filter3

$$
\begin{bmatrix} 0 & -1 & 0 \\ -1 & 4 & -1 \\ 0 & -1 & 0 \end{bmatrix}
\qquad
\begin{bmatrix} -1 & -1 & -1 \\ -1 & 8 & -1 \\ -1 & -1 & -1 \end{bmatrix}
\qquad
\begin{bmatrix} -2 & 1 & -2 \\ 1 & 4 & 1 \\ -2 & 1 & -2 \end{bmatrix}
$$

These masks differ from the Laplacian-type previously described in that the center coefficients have been decreased by one. With these masks, we are trying to find edges and are not interested in the image itself – if we increase the center coefficient by one, it is equivalent to adding the original image to the edge detected image.

An easy way to picture the difference is to consider the effect each mask has when applied to an area of constant value. The above convolution masks return a value of zero. If we increase the center coefficients by one, each mask returns the original gray level. Therefore, if we are only interested in edge information, the sum of the coefficients should be zero. If we want to retain most of the information that is in the original image, the coefficients should sum to a number greater than zero. The larger this sum, the less the processed image is changed from the original image. Consider an extreme example in which the center coefficient is very large compared with the other coefficients in the mask. The resulting pixel value will depend most heavily upon the current value, with only minimal contribution from the surrounding pixel values.

4.2.2 Compass Masks

The Kirsch and Robinson edge detection masks are called compass masks since they are defined by taking a single mask and rotating it to the eight major compass orientations: North, Northwest, West, Southwest, South, Southeast, East and Northeast. The **Kirsch compass masks** are defined as follows:

$$
k_0\begin{bmatrix} -3 & -3 & 5 \\ -3 & 0 & 5 \\ -3 & -3 & 5 \end{bmatrix}
\quad
k_1\begin{bmatrix} -3 & 5 & 5 \\ -3 & 0 & 5 \\ -3 & -3 & -3 \end{bmatrix}
\quad
k_2\begin{bmatrix} 5 & 5 & 5 \\ -3 & 0 & -3 \\ -3 & -3 & -3 \end{bmatrix}
\quad
k_3\begin{bmatrix} 5 & 5 & -3 \\ 5 & 0 & -3 \\ -3 & -3 & -3 \end{bmatrix}
$$

$$
k_4\begin{bmatrix} 5 & -3 & -3 \\ 5 & 0 & -3 \\ 5 & -3 & -3 \end{bmatrix}
\quad
k_5\begin{bmatrix} -3 & -3 & -3 \\ 5 & 0 & -3 \\ 5 & 5 & -3 \end{bmatrix}
\quad
k_6\begin{bmatrix} -3 & -3 & -3 \\ -3 & 0 & -3 \\ 5 & 5 & 5 \end{bmatrix}
\quad
k_7\begin{bmatrix} -3 & -3 & -3 \\ -3 & 0 & 5 \\ -3 & 5 & 5 \end{bmatrix}
$$

The edge magnitude is defined as the maximum value found by the convolution of each of the masks with the image. The edge direction is defined by the mask that produces the maximum magnitude; for instance, k_0 corresponds to a horizontal edge, whereas k_5 corresponds to a diagonal edge in the Northeast/Southwest direction (remember edges are perpendicular to the lines). We also see that the last four masks are actually the same as the first four, but flipped about a central axis.

The **Robinson compass masks** are used in a manner similar to the Kirsch masks, but are easier to implement, as they rely only on coefficients of 0, 1, and 2 and are symmetrical about their directional axis – the axis with the zeros which corresponds to the line direction. We only need to compute the results on four of the masks; the results from the other four can be obtained by negating the results from the first four. The masks are as follows:

$$r_0 \begin{bmatrix} -1 & 0 & 1 \\ -2 & 0 & 2 \\ -1 & 0 & 1 \end{bmatrix} \quad r_1 \begin{bmatrix} 0 & 1 & 2 \\ -1 & 0 & 1 \\ -2 & -1 & 0 \end{bmatrix} \quad r_2 \begin{bmatrix} 1 & 2 & 1 \\ 0 & 0 & 0 \\ -1 & -2 & -1 \end{bmatrix} \quad r_3 \begin{bmatrix} 2 & 1 & 0 \\ 1 & 0 & -1 \\ 0 & -1 & -2 \end{bmatrix}$$

$$r_4 \begin{bmatrix} 1 & 0 & -1 \\ 2 & 0 & -2 \\ 1 & 0 & -1 \end{bmatrix} \quad r_5 \begin{bmatrix} 0 & -1 & -2 \\ 1 & 0 & -1 \\ 2 & 1 & 0 \end{bmatrix} \quad r_6 \begin{bmatrix} -1 & -2 & -1 \\ 0 & 0 & 0 \\ 1 & 2 & 1 \end{bmatrix} \quad r_7 \begin{bmatrix} -2 & -1 & 0 \\ -1 & 0 & 1 \\ 0 & 1 & 2 \end{bmatrix}$$

The edge magnitude is defined as the maximum value found by the convolution of each of the masks with the image. The edge direction is defined by the mask that produces the maximum magnitude. It is interesting to note that masks r_0 and r_6 are the same as the Sobel masks. We can see that any of the edge detection masks can be extended by rotating them in a manner like these compass masks, which will allow us to extract explicit information about edges in any direction.

4.2.3 Thresholds, Noise Mitigation and Edge Linking

The gradient and compass mask edge detectors provide measures for magnitude and direction of the brightness gradient at each pixel point. This is only the first step in marking potential edge points which will be used to ultimately find object boundaries. As illustrated in Figure 4.2-2, consideration must be given to the sensitivity versus the accuracy of the edge detector. By considering any points that we do not want or need as "noise" and the valid, typically stronger edge points as the "real" edge points, the primary methods to control sensitivity and accuracy are the following: (1) control of a threshold, so that only the stronger edge points pass, (2) use of large mask sizes to mitigate noise and (3) use of a preprocessing mean filter.

We have discussed two thresholding methods in the previous chapter, the *Otsu Method* and the *Automatic Thresholding* (K-Means) – these algorithms work well with one object and high contrast with the background – a bimodal histogram as shown in Figure 4.2-6. These types of images are obtained in machine vision applications where the lighting can be controlled. This is not typically the case with the magnitude image that results from an edge detector, these images tend to have unimodal (one peak) histograms.

A method that provides reasonable results for unimodal histograms is to use the *average value* for the threshold, as in Figure 4.2-7. With very noisy images and a unimodal histogram, a good rule of thumb is to use 10%–25% of the maximum value as a threshold. An example of this is shown in Figure 4.2-8.

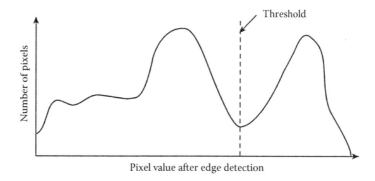

FIGURE 4.2-6
Edge detection thresholding via histogram. The histogram can be examined manually to select a good threshold. This method is easiest with a bimodal (two peaks) histogram. Alternately, the threshold can be found automatically with the Automatic Single Threshold or the Otsu algorithm described in Chapter 3.

FIGURE 4.2-7
Average value thresholding. (a) Original image, (b) image after Sobel edge detector, (c) unimodal histogram of image after Sobel and (d) Sobel image after thresholding with average value.

If the images contain too much noise, most standard edge detectors perform poorly. The edge detector will tend to find more false edges as a result of the noise. We can preprocess the image with mean, or averaging, spatial filters to mitigate the effects from noise, or we can expand the edge detection operators themselves to mitigate noise effects. One way to do this is to extend the size of the edge detection masks. An example of this method is to extend the Prewitt edge mask as follows:

EXTENDED PREWITT EDGE DETECTION MASK

$$
\begin{bmatrix}
1 & 1 & 1 & 0 & -1 & -1 & -1 \\
1 & 1 & 1 & 0 & -1 & -1 & -1 \\
1 & 1 & 1 & 0 & -1 & -1 & -1 \\
1 & 1 & 1 & 0 & -1 & -1 & -1 \\
1 & 1 & 1 & 0 & -1 & -1 & -1 \\
1 & 1 & 1 & 0 & -1 & -1 & -1 \\
1 & 1 & 1 & 0 & -1 & -1 & -1
\end{bmatrix}
$$

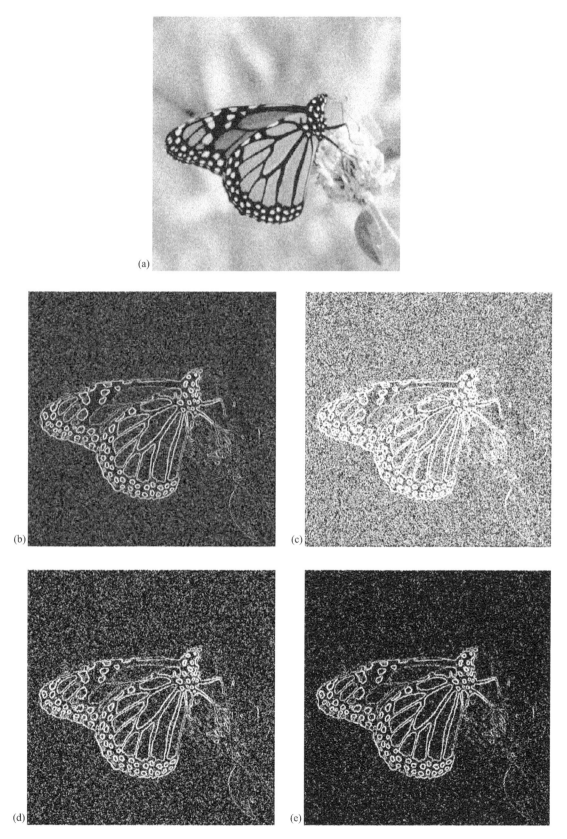

FIGURE 4.2-8
Thresholding noisy images. (a) Original image with Gaussian noise added (zero mean, variance = 800), (b) Sobel edge detector results (remapped), (c) threshold on Sobel at 10% of maximum value, (d) threshold on Sobel at 20% of maximum and (e) threshold on Sobel at 25% of maximum.

We then can rotate this by 90°, and we have both row and column masks which can be used like the Prewitt operators to return the edge magnitude and gradient. These types of operators are called boxcar operators and can be extended to any size, although 7×7, 9×9 and 11×11 are typical. The Sobel operator can be extended in a similar manner:

EXTENDED SOBEL EDGE DETECTION MASK

$$
\begin{bmatrix}
-1 & -1 & -1 & -2 & -1 & -1 & -1 \\
-1 & -1 & -1 & -2 & -1 & -1 & -1 \\
-1 & -1 & -1 & -2 & -1 & -1 & -1 \\
0 & 0 & 0 & 0 & 0 & 0 & 0 \\
1 & 1 & 1 & 2 & 1 & 1 & 1 \\
1 & 1 & 1 & 2 & 1 & 1 & 1 \\
1 & 1 & 1 & 2 & 1 & 1 & 1
\end{bmatrix}
$$

If we approximate a linear distribution, the *truncated pyramid* operator is created as follows:

$$
\begin{bmatrix}
1 & 1 & 1 & 0 & -1 & -1 & -1 \\
1 & 2 & 2 & 0 & -2 & -2 & -1 \\
1 & 2 & 3 & 0 & -3 & -2 & -1 \\
1 & 2 & 3 & 0 & -3 & -2 & -1 \\
1 & 2 & 3 & 0 & -3 & -2 & -1 \\
1 & 2 & 2 & 0 & -2 & -2 & -1 \\
1 & 1 & 1 & 0 & -1 & -1 & -1
\end{bmatrix}
$$

This operator provides weights that decrease from the center pixel outward, which will smooth the result in a more natural manner. These operators are used in the same manner as the Prewitt and Sobel – we define a row and column mask and then find a magnitude and direction at each point. A comparison of applying the extended Prewitt operators with the standard 3×3 operators to an image is shown in Figure 4.2-9. We see that as the mask size increases, the lines thicken and small ones disappear. Figure 4.2-10 shows various edge detectors and the effect of larger masks on an image with Gaussian noise. Comparing Figure 4.2-10c and d and Figure 4.2-10e and f, we see that the extended operators exhibit better performance than the smaller masks. However, they require more computations and will smear the edges, which can be alleviated by postprocessing to thin the smeared edges and remove any leftover noise. Figure 4.2-11 shows results from changing Sobel mask sizes on an image with salt-and-pepper noise.

After a threshold for the edge detected image is determined, we need to merge the selected edge points into boundaries. This is done by *edge linking*. The simplest approach to edge linking involves considering each point that has passed the threshold test and connecting it to all other such points that are within a maximum distance. This method tends to connect many points and is not useful for images where too many points have been marked; it is most applicable to simple images.

Instead of thresholding and then edge linking, we can perform edge linking on the edge detected image before we threshold it. If this approach is used, we look at small neighborhoods (3×3 or 5×5) and link similar points. Similar points are defined as being spatially adjacent and having close values for both magnitude and direction. How close they need to be will be dependent on the application and the types of lines or curves we are wanting to identify. The entire image undergoes this process while keeping a list of the linked points. When the process is complete, the boundaries are determined by the linked points.

4.2.4 Advanced Edge Detectors

The advanced edge detectors are algorithms that use the basic edge detectors and combine them with the noise mitigation concepts and also introduce new ideas such as that of hysteresis thresholding. The edge detectors considered here include the Marr–Hildreth algorithm, the Canny algorithm, the Boie–Cox algorithm, the Shen–Castan

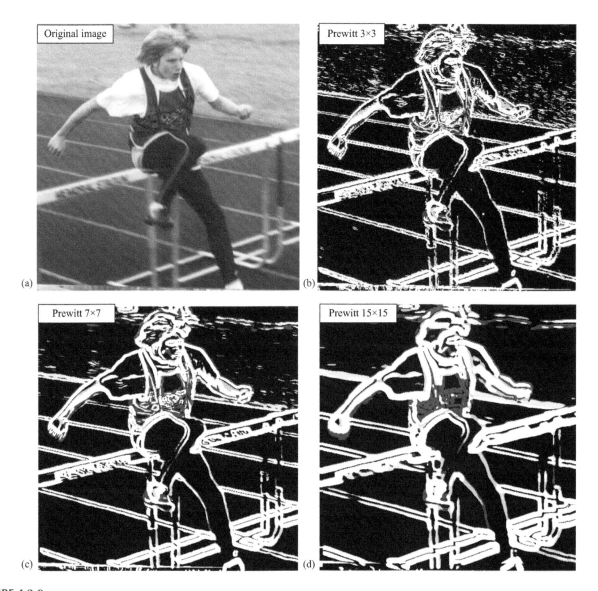

FIGURE 4.2-9
Edge detection example with various mask sizes. (a) Original image, (b) Prewitt magnitude with a 3×3 mask (c) Prewitt magnitude with a 7×7 mask and (d) Prewitt magnitude with a 15×15 mask. The images have undergone a threshold with the average value. Notice that a larger mask thickens the lines and eliminates small ones.

algorithm and the Frei–Chen masks. They are considered to be advanced because they are algorithmic in nature, which basically means they require multiple steps. Except for the Frei–Chen masks, these algorithms begin with the idea that, in general, most edge detectors are too sensitive to noise, and by blurring the image prior to edge detection, we can mitigate these noise effects. The noise considered here includes irrelevant image detail, as well as a combination of blurring from camera optics and signal corruption by camera electronics.

The simplest of these is the **Marr–Hildreth algorithm**, based on a model of the human visual system's response first developed by neuroscientist David Marr in the 1960s. The algorithm requires three steps:

1. Convolve the image with a Gaussian smoothing filter.
2. Convolve the image with a Laplacian mask.
3. Find the zero crossings of the image from Step 2.

By preprocessing with a smoothing filter, we can mitigate noise effects and then use the Laplacian to enhance the edges. By adjusting the spread, or variance, of the Gaussian, we can adjust the filter for different amounts of noise

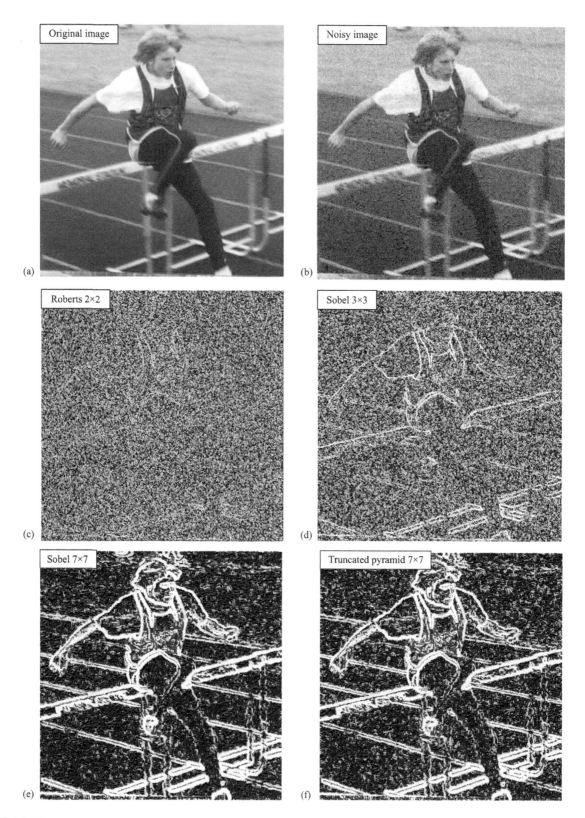

FIGURE 4.2-10
Edge detection examples with Gaussian noise – larger masks mitigate noise effects. (a) Original image, (b) image with added Gaussian noise (c) Robert's edge detection, 2×2, (d) Sobel with a 3×3 mask (e) Sobel with a 7×7 mask and (f) a 7×7 truncated pyramid. The images have undergone a threshold with the average value. In (c), with the 2×2 Roberts, the noise conceals almost all the edges. In (d), with a 3×3 Sobel mask, the edges are visible, but the resultant image is very noisy. With the 7×7 mask, shown in (e) and (f), the edges are much more prominent and the noise is much less noticeable.

FIGURE 4.2-11
Edge detection with salt-and-pepper noise, Sobel example with various mask sizes. (a) Original image, (b) Sobel magnitude with a 3×3 mask (c) Sobel magnitude with a 7×7 mask and (d) Sobel magnitude with a 15×15 mask. The images have undergone a threshold with the average value. Notice that a larger mask helps mitigate the noise substantially, with a 3×3 the image is not even visible.

and various amounts of blurring. The combination of the Gaussian followed by a Laplacian is called a **Laplacian of a Gaussian (*LoG*)** or the *Mexican hat* operator since the function resembles a sombrero (see Figure 4.2-12). Since the process requires the successive convolution of two masks, they can be combined into one *LoG* mask. Commonly used 5×5 and 17×17 masks that approximate the combination of the Gaussian and Laplacian into one convolution mask are as follows:

5×5 Laplacian of a Gaussian mask:

$$
\begin{bmatrix}
0 & 0 & -1 & 0 & 0 \\
0 & -1 & -2 & -1 & 0 \\
-1 & -2 & 16 & -2 & -1 \\
0 & -1 & -2 & -1 & 0 \\
0 & 0 & -1 & 0 & 0
\end{bmatrix}
$$

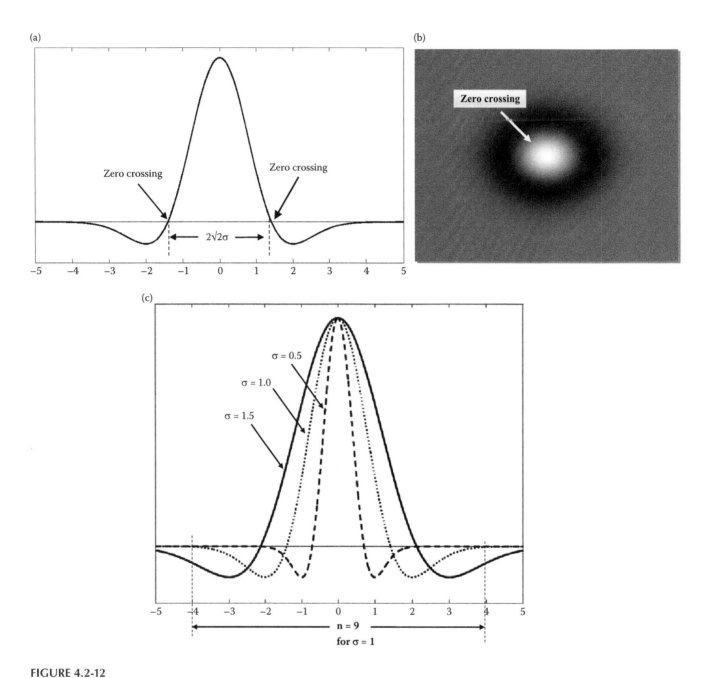

FIGURE 4.2-12
The *inverted* **Laplacian of a Gaussian (*LoG*).** (a) One-dimensional plot of the *LoG* function; (b) the *LoG* as an image with white representing positive numbers, black negative numbers and gray representing zero; and (c) three *LoG* plots with $\sigma = 0.5$, 1.0 and 1.5. Note for $\sigma = 0.5$, the mask size, *n*, should be about 5×5; for $\sigma = 1$, 9×9, and so on. This is done so that the mask covers the entire function as it goes negative and then goes back up to zero. Note this is 4σ to the left, 4σ to the right and the center term corresponding to the term at the 0 point on the graph.

17 × 17 Laplacian of a Gaussian mask:

$$
\begin{bmatrix}
0 & 0 & 0 & 0 & 0 & 0 & -1 & -1 & -1 & -1 & -1 & 0 & 0 & 0 & 0 & 0 & 0 \\
0 & 0 & 0 & 0 & -1 & -1 & -1 & -1 & -1 & -1 & -1 & -1 & -1 & 0 & 0 & 0 & 0 \\
0 & 0 & -1 & -1 & -1 & -2 & -3 & -3 & -3 & -3 & -3 & -2 & -1 & -1 & -1 & 0 & 0 \\
0 & 0 & -1 & -1 & -2 & -3 & -3 & -3 & -3 & -3 & -3 & -3 & -2 & -1 & -1 & 0 & 0 \\
-1 & -1 & -1 & -2 & -3 & -3 & -3 & -2 & -3 & -3 & -3 & -3 & -3 & -2 & -1 & -1 & 0 \\
-1 & -1 & -2 & -3 & -3 & -3 & 0 & 2 & 4 & 2 & 0 & -3 & -3 & -3 & -2 & -1 & 0 \\
-1 & -1 & -3 & -3 & -3 & 0 & 4 & 10 & 12 & 10 & 4 & 0 & -3 & -3 & -3 & -1 & -1 \\
-1 & -1 & -3 & -3 & -3 & 2 & 10 & 18 & 21 & 18 & 10 & 2 & -2 & -3 & -3 & -1 & -1 \\
-1 & -1 & -3 & -3 & -3 & 4 & 12 & 21 & 24 & 21 & 12 & 4 & -3 & -3 & -3 & -1 & -1 \\
0 & -1 & -3 & -3 & -3 & 2 & 10 & 18 & 21 & 18 & 10 & 2 & -2 & -3 & -3 & -1 & -1 \\
0 & -1 & -3 & -3 & -3 & 0 & 4 & 10 & 12 & 10 & 4 & 0 & -3 & -3 & -3 & -1 & -1 \\
0 & -1 & -2 & -3 & -3 & -3 & 0 & 2 & 4 & 2 & 0 & -3 & -3 & -3 & -3 & -1 & 0 \\
0 & -1 & -1 & -2 & -3 & -3 & -3 & -2 & -3 & -2 & -3 & -3 & -3 & -2 & -2 & -1 & 0 \\
0 & 0 & -1 & -1 & -2 & -3 & -3 & -3 & -3 & -3 & -3 & -3 & -2 & -1 & -1 & 0 & 0 \\
0 & 0 & -1 & -1 & -1 & -2 & -3 & -3 & -3 & -3 & -3 & -2 & -1 & -1 & -1 & 0 & 0 \\
0 & 0 & 0 & 0 & -1 & -1 & -1 & -1 & -1 & -1 & -1 & -1 & -1 & 0 & -1 & 0 & 0 \\
0 & 0 & 0 & 0 & 0 & 0 & -1 & -1 & -1 & -1 & -1 & 0 & 0 & 0 & 0 & 0 & 0
\end{bmatrix}
$$

The equation for the LoG filter is:

$$
\text{LoG} = \left[\frac{r^2 + c^2 - 2\sigma^2}{\sigma^4} \right] e^{-\left(\frac{r^2 + c^2}{2\sigma^2} \right)}
\tag{4.2-7}
$$

where (r, c) are the row and column coordinates, and σ^2 is the Gaussian variance and σ is the standard deviation. From the equation, we can see that zero crossings occur at $(r^2 + c^2) = 2\sigma^2$, or $\sqrt{2}\sigma$ from the mean, as shown in Figure 4.2-12a. Note that, in practice, if creating the *LoG* filter mask by convolving a Gaussian and a Laplacian mask, we need to be sure that the Gaussian is normalized to one and that the Laplacian coefficients sum to zero. This is done to avoid biasing the mask with a DC term, which will shift the zero crossings and defeat the filter's purpose.

To determine the size of the mask to use, we consider that 99.7% of the area under a Gaussian curve is within ±3σ of the mean. Keeping in mind that the sampling grid is fixed by the pixel spacing, the variance and the mask size must be related (see Figure 4.2-12c). So, we want to select a value of n for the $n \times n$ convolution mask that is an odd integer greater than or equal to 6σ, or we will get only a portion of the curve with our sampled filter mask. In CVIPtools, we use the following equation to determine n, based on the standard deviation, σ:

$$
n = \left[2 * \text{TRUNCATE}(3.35\sigma + 0.33) + 1 \right]
\tag{4.2-8}
$$

This equation assures us that we have the complete spread of the *LoG* filter and actually provides us with an n that corresponds to about ±4σ. Note that for positive numbers, the *truncate* operation is the same as the *floor* operation.

The third step for the Marr–Hildreth algorithm is to find the zero crossings after the *LoG* is performed. This can be accomplished by considering a pixel and its surrounding pixels, thus a 3 × 3 subimage, and looking for sign changes between two of the opposing neighbors. That is, we check the left/right, up/down and the two diagonal neighboring pairs. Figure 4.2-13 illustrates the results from the standard Marr–Hildreth algorithm. The disadvantage of the Marr–Hildreth algorithm, or any second derivative/zero-crossing method, is that it tends to smooth shapes too much which has the effect of eliminating corners and creating closed loops in the resulting lines/curves. The Marr–Hildreth results are often referred to as a "plate of spaghetti", as seen in Figure 4.2-13b.

In practice, we may want to set a threshold to use before a pixel is classified as an edge. The threshold is tested against the absolute value of the difference between the two pixels that have the sign changes. If this value exceeds the threshold, it is classified as an edge pixel.

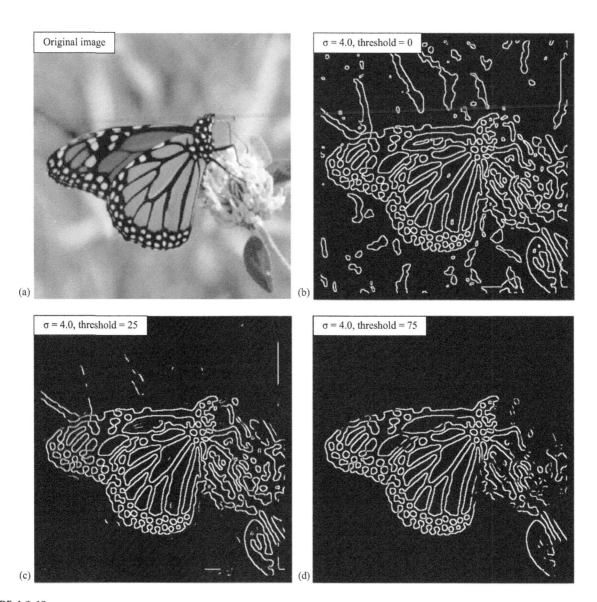

FIGURE 4.2-13
Marr–Hildreth algorithm results. (a) Original image, (b) Sigma (σ) = 4, threshold = 0, note the algorithm creating closed loops Marr–Hildreth algorithm results. (c) Sigma (σ) = 4, threshold = 25 and (d) Sigma (σ) = 4, threshold = 75; these values eliminate most of the background noise, but keep the butterfly.

EXAMPLE 4.2.1: APPLYING A THRESHOLD TO STEP 3 OF THE MARR–HILDRETH ALGORITHM

Suppose, after the *LoG*, we have a 3×3 subimage as follows:

$$\begin{bmatrix} -10 & 11 & 17 \\ 18 & 2 & 15 \\ 21 & 33 & 28 \end{bmatrix}$$

the only pair that has a sign change is the NW/SE diagonal. So, the center pixel may be considered an edge pixel. If we apply a threshold, we calculate the absolute value of the difference of this pair:

$$|-10 - 28| = 38$$

Now, if this value exceeds the threshold we have set, then the center pixel is determined to be an edge pixel.

The Marr–Hildreth as implemented in CVIPtools has a parameter to allow the user to select *single variance* or *dual variance*. If dual variance is selected, the user specifies a *sigma* (σ, standard deviation) value and a *delta* value. CVIPtools then computes the Marr–Hildreth results using two variances – the specified sigma plus the delta value and the specified sigma minus the delta value. These results are then combined into a single image with a logical AND function. For color images, the user can also select to combine the bands, which performs a logical AND of the red, green and blue band results.

The **Canny algorithm**, developed by John Canny in 1986, is an optimal edge detection method based on a specific mathematical model for edges. The edge model is a step edge corrupted by Gaussian noise. The algorithm consists of four primary steps:

1. **Apply a Gaussian filter mask to smooth the image** to mitigate noise effects. This can be performed at different scales by varying the size of the filter mask which corresponds to the variance of the Gaussian function. A larger mask will blur the image more and will find fewer, but more prominent, edges.

2. **Find the magnitude and direction of the gradient** using equations similar to the Sobel or Prewitt edge detectors, for example:

$$\text{VERTICAL} \qquad\qquad \text{HORIZONTAL}$$

$$\frac{1}{2}\begin{bmatrix} -1 & -1 \\ 1 & 1 \end{bmatrix} \qquad\qquad \frac{1}{2}\begin{bmatrix} -1 & 1 \\ -1 & 1 \end{bmatrix}$$

These masks are each convolved with the image. At each pixel location, we find two numbers: c_1, corresponding to the result from the vertical edge mask, and c_2, from the horizontal edge mask. We use these results to determine two metrics, the edge magnitude and the edge direction, which are defined as follows:

$$\text{EDGE MAGNITUDE} \sqrt{c_1^2 + c_2^2} \tag{4.2-9}$$

$$\text{EDGE DIRECTION } \text{Tan}^{-1}\left[\frac{c_1}{c_2}\right] \tag{4.2-10}$$

3. **Apply nonmaxima suppression** which results in thinned edges. This is done by considering small neighborhoods in the magnitude image, for example, 3×3, and comparing the center value to its neighbors in the direction of the gradient. If the center value is not larger than the neighboring pixels along the gradient direction, then set it to zero. Otherwise, it is a local maximum, so we keep it. In Figure 4.2-14, we see an example of a 3×3 neighborhood showing the magnitude at each location and using an arrow to show the gradient direction. The center pixel has a value of 100 and the gradient direction is horizontal (corresponding to a vertical line), so it is compared to the pixels to the right and left which are 40 and 91. Since it is greater than both, it is retained as an edge pixel; if it was less than either one, it would be removed as an edge point. Note that this will have the effect of making thick edges thinner by selecting the "best" point along a gradient direction.

4. **Apply two thresholds** to obtain the final result. This technique, known as *hysteresis thresholding*, helps to avoid false edges caused by too low a threshold value or missing edges caused by too high a value. It is a two-step thresholding method, which first marks edge pixels above a high threshold and then applies a low threshold to pixels connected to the pixels found with the high threshold. This can be performed multiple times, as either a recursive or an iterative process.

$$\begin{bmatrix} \leftarrow 50 & 112 \rightarrow & 20 \rightarrow \\ \leftarrow 40 & 100 \rightarrow & 91 \rightarrow \\ \leftarrow 88 & 95 \rightarrow & 92 \rightarrow \end{bmatrix}$$

FIGURE 4.2-14
Nonmaxima suppression. A 3×3 subimage of the magnitude image, which consists of the magnitude results in an image grid. The arrows show the gradient directions. This particular subimage has a vertical line (a horizontal edge). To apply non-maxima suppression, we compare the center pixel magnitude along the gradient direction. Here, the 100 is compared with the 40 and the 91. Since it is a local maximum, it is retained as an edge pixel.

In CVIPtools, the high threshold is computed from the image by finding the value which is greater than 90% of the pixels after applying nonmaxima suppression to the magnitude images. The high threshold is multiplied with the high threshold factor to obtain the final high threshold for hysteresis. The low threshold is computed from the image by averaging the high threshold and minimum value in the image after applying the nonmaxima suppression to the magnitude images. The low threshold is then multiplied with the low threshold factor to obtain the final low threshold for hysteresis. CVIPtools also allows the variance of the Gaussian filter as an input parameter. Figures 4.2-15 and 4.2-16 show results from varying these parameters.

The **Boie–Cox algorithm**, developed in 1986 and 1987, is a generalization of the Canny algorithm. It consists of similar steps, but uses matched filters and Wiener filters (further explored in the references) to allow for a more generalized edge model. The **Shen–Castan algorithm**, developed in 1992, uses an optimal filter function they derived called an infinite symmetric exponential filter. Shen and Castan claim that their filter does better than the Canny at finding the precise location of the edge pixels. Like the Canny, it uses a smoothing filter followed by a similar multistep algorithm to find edge pixels. The search includes steps similar to the Canny, but with modifications and extensions (for more details, see the references). Figure 4.2-17 shows results from these algorithms.

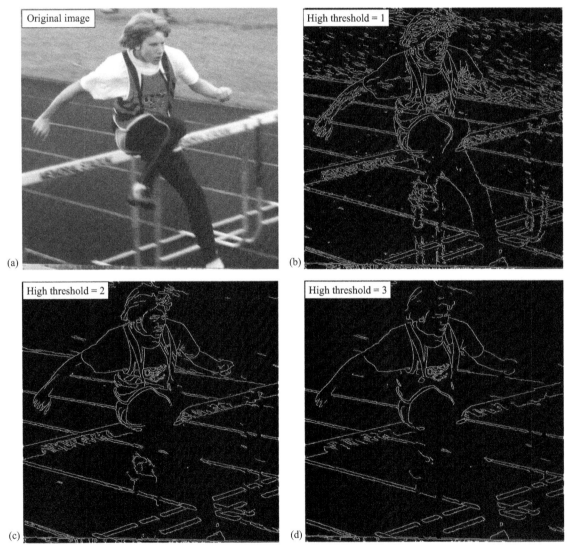

FIGURE 4.2-15
Results from changing high threshold with Canny algorithm. As the high threshold is increased, small details are removed. In the results, the Gaussian = 0.5 and the low threshold = 1. (a) Original image, (b) results high threshold factor = 1 (c) high threshold factor = 2 and (d) high threshold factor = 3.

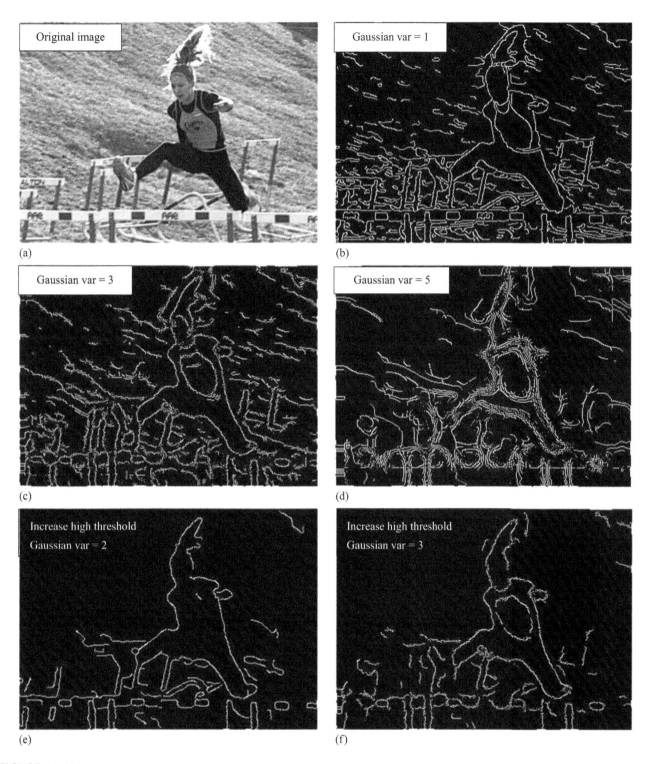

FIGURE 4.2-16

Results from changing Gaussian variance with the Canny algorithm. As the Gaussian variance is increased, the Canny should find fewer, but more prominent edges. In these results, the low and high threshold factors = 1. (a) Original image, (b) Canny results with Gaussian variance = 1, (c) Gaussian variance = 3 and (d) Gaussian variance = 5. Note that if the variance is too large, the image is blurred too much, and instead of finding "fewer, more prominent edges", we find fuzzy and then multiple edges. To avoid this, we need to also increase the high threshold. In the next two images, the low threshold is 1, but the high threshold has been increased to 2. Now we do see fewer, more prominent edges. (e) Gaussian variance = 2 and (f) Gaussian variance = 3. Results with noise in the image. Note that as the variance is increased, the false edges from the salt-and-pepper noise are mitigated.

(Continued)

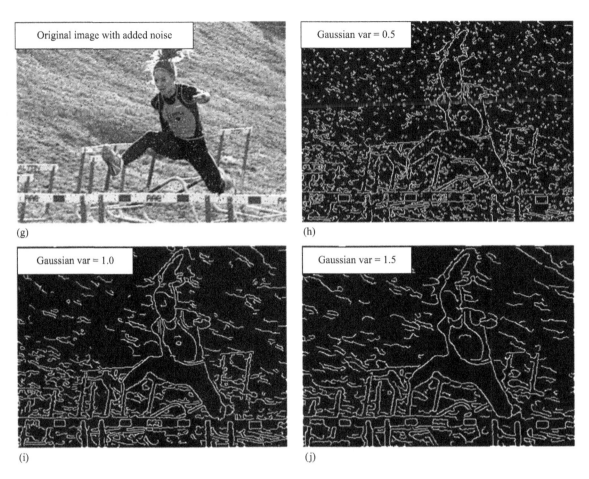

FIGURE 4.2-16 (*Continued*)
(g) original image with salt-and-pepper noise added, 2% each, (h) Canny with variance = 0.5, (i) Canny with variance = 1.0 and
(j) Canny with variance = 1.5.

The **Frei–Chen masks** are unique in that they form a complete set of *basis vectors*. This means we can represent any 3×3 subimage as a weighted sum of the nine Frei–Chen masks (Figure 4.2-18). These weights are found by projecting a 3×3 subimage onto each of these masks. This projection process is similar to the convolution process in that both overlay the mask on the image, multiply coincident terms and sum the results (also called a *vector inner product*). This is best illustrated by example.

EXAMPLE 4.2.2

Suppose we have the following subimage, I_s:

$$I_s = \begin{bmatrix} 1 & 0 & 1 \\ 1 & 0 & 1 \\ 1 & 0 & 1 \end{bmatrix}$$

To project this subimage onto the Frei–Chen masks, start by finding the projection onto f_1. Overlay the subimage on the mask and consider the first row. The 1 in the upper left corner of the subimage coincides with the 1 in the upper left corner of the mask, the 0 is over the $\sqrt{2}$, and the 1 on the upper right corner of the subimage coincides with the 1 in the mask. Note that all these must be summed and then multiplied by the $\dfrac{1}{2\sqrt{2}}$ factor to normalize the masks. The projection of I_s onto f_1 is equal to:

$$\frac{1}{2\sqrt{2}}\left[1(1)+0\left(\sqrt{2}\right)+1(1)+1(0)+0(0)+1(0)+1(-1)+0\left(-\sqrt{2}\right)+1(-1)\right]=0$$

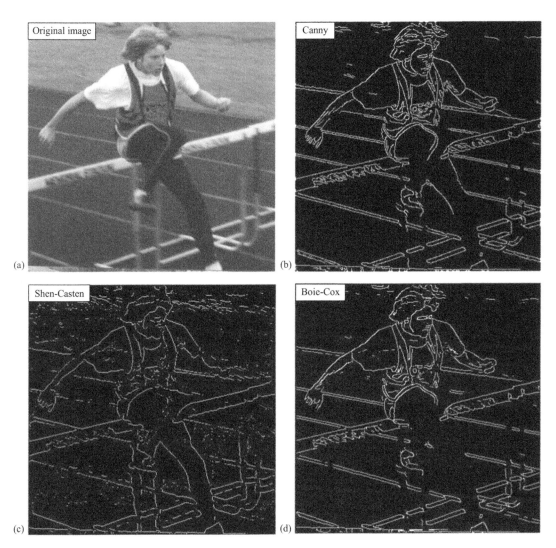

FIGURE 4.2-17
Comparison of the Canny, Shen–Castan and Boie–Cox algorithms. These results used the default parameters in CVIPtools.
(a) Original image, (b) Canny (c) Shen–Castan and (d) Boie–Cox.

If we follow this process and project the subimage, I_s, onto each of the Frei–Chen masks, we get the following:

$$f_1 \to 0,\ f_2 \to 0,\ f_3 \to 0,\ f_4 \to 0,\ f_5 \to -1,\ f_6 \to 0,\ f_7 \to 0,\ f_8 \to -1,\ f_9 \to 2.$$

We can now see what is meant by a complete set of basis vectors allowing us to represent a subimage by a weighted sum. The basis vectors in this case are the Frei–Chen masks, and the weights are the projection values. Take the weights and multiply them by each mask, then sum the corresponding values. For this example, the only nonzero terms correspond to masks f_5, f_8 and f_9, and we find the following:

$$(-1)\left(\frac{1}{2}\right)\begin{bmatrix} 0 & 1 & 0 \\ -1 & 0 & -1 \\ 0 & 1 & 0 \end{bmatrix} + (-1)\left(\frac{1}{6}\right)\begin{bmatrix} -2 & 1 & -2 \\ 1 & 4 & 1 \\ -2 & 1 & -2 \end{bmatrix} + (2)\left(\frac{1}{3}\right)\begin{bmatrix} 1 & 1 & 1 \\ 1 & 1 & 1 \\ 1 & 1 & 1 \end{bmatrix} = \begin{bmatrix} 1 & 0 & 1 \\ 1 & 0 & 1 \\ 1 & 0 & 1 \end{bmatrix} = I_s$$

We have seen how the Frei–Chen masks can be used to represent a subimage as a weighted sum, but how are they used for edge detection? The Frei–Chen masks can be grouped into a set of four masks for an *edge* subspace, four

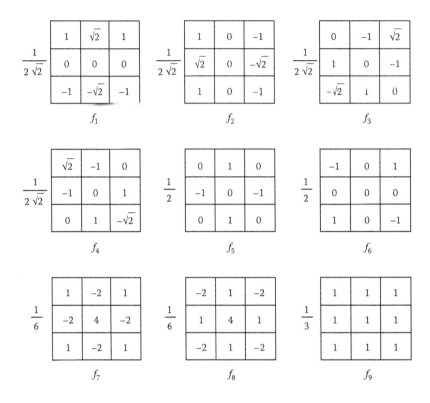

FIGURE 4.2-18
Frei–Chen masks. The first four masks, $f_1 - f_4$, comprise the edge subspace. The next four masks, $f_5 - f_8$, comprise the line subspace. The final mask, f_9, is the average subspace. More specifically, f_1 and f_2 are the *gradient* masks, f_3 and f_4 the *ripple* masks, f_5 and f_6 the *line* masks and f_7 and f_8 the *Laplacian* masks.

masks for a *line* subspace and one mask for an *average* subspace. These subspaces can be further broken down into *gradient, ripple, line* and *Laplacian* subspaces (see Figure 4.2-18). To use them for edge detection, select a particular subspace of interest and find the relative projection of the image onto the particular subspace. This is given by the following equation:

$$\cos(\Theta) = \sqrt{\frac{M}{S}} \tag{4.2-11}$$

where

$$M = \sum_{k \in \{e\}} (I_s, f_k)^2 \tag{4.2-12}$$

$$S = \sum_{k=1}^{9} (I_s, f_k)^2 \tag{4.2-13}$$

The set $\{e\}$ consists of the masks of interest. The (I_s, f_k) notation refers to the process of overlaying the mask on the subimage, multiplying coincident terms and summing the results – a vector inner product. The lengths of the vectors from the origin in the nine-dimensional Frei–Chen space are represented by $\sqrt{M}$ and $\sqrt{S}$, with S corresponding to the entire nine-dimensional subimage vector and M the subspace of interest. An illustration of this is shown in Figure 4.2-19. The advantage of this method is that we can select particular edge or line masks of interest and consider the projection of those masks only. To use for edge detection, we typically set a threshold on the angle to determine if a point will be considered a "hit" for the edge and/or line subspace of interest. Any pixel with a corresponding angle value below the threshold is similar enough to the subspace of interest to be considered a "hit" and is marked accordingly.

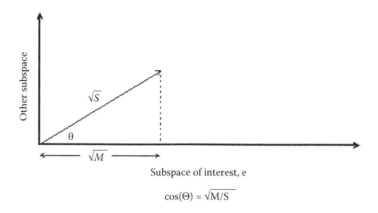

$$\cos(\Theta) = \sqrt{M/S}$$

FIGURE 4.2-19
Frei–Chen projection. A 2-D representation of the Frei–Chen projection concept. The actual Frei–Chen space is nine-dimensional, where each dimension is given by one of the masks, f_k. S is the vector that represents the subimage and M is projection of the subimage vector onto the subspace of interest. The smaller the angle, the larger M is and the more the subimage is similar to the subspace of interest.

In CVIPtools, the user can select one of four different "projection" choices: (1) the edge subspace, (2) the line subspace, (3) the maximum of the edge and line subspace projection and (4) the minimum angle from the edge and line subspace projections. In all cases, CVIPtools will return an image of data type SHORT with the actual projection values. With the first two options, the user selects a threshold for the angle and only the pixel locations where the angle is smaller than the threshold will have the projection value – other pixels are set to zero. In the images shown in Figure 4.2-20, all the results have been postprocessed with a binary threshold operation, using 10% of the

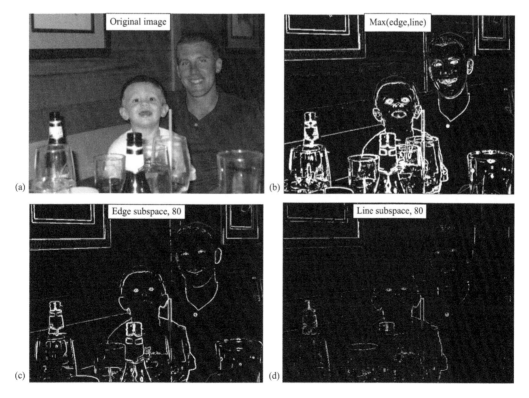

FIGURE 4.2-20
Frei–Chen results using CVIPtools. (a) Original image, (b) results from the maximum of edge and line selection (c) edge subspace angle threshold = 80 and (d) line subspace, angle threshold = 80. Note: for display purposes, the images shown have been postprocessed with a binary threshold operation using 10% of the maximum value of the output image.

maximum value in the Frei–Chen output image as the threshold. Figure 4.2-21 shows the effect of changing the binary threshold value.

The advanced edge detectors can also be used effectively in noisy images. Results from applying the Marr–Hildreth, Canny, Boie–Cox, Shen–Castan and Frei–Chen algorithms to an image with salt-and-pepper noise are shown in Figure 4.2-22. Here, we see that most of these algorithms perform well in the presence of salt-and-pepper noise. However, the Frei–Chen does not do as well as the others and the Marr–Hildreth is plagued by its usual "spaghetti effect". In Figure 4.2-23, we apply the same edge algorithms to an image with Gaussian noise. Here, we see that the Shen–Castan retains numerous spurious edges, and again, the Marr–Hildreth has the spaghetti effect. However, with Gaussian noise, the Frei–Chen, Canny and Boie–Cox appear to perform well.

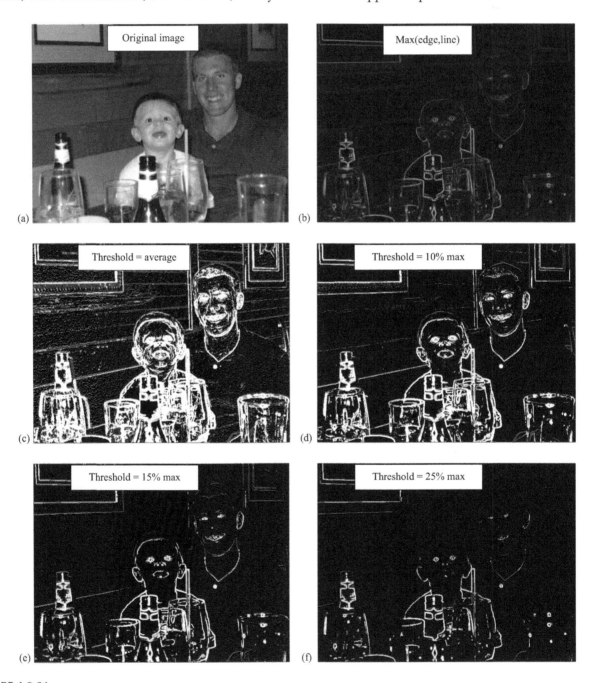

FIGURE 4.2-21
Changing the binary threshold with the Frei–Chen and maximum of edge or line subspace. (a) Original image, (b) output from the maximum value of the edge or line subspace (linearly remapped to BYTE), (c) threshold = average value, (d) threshold = 10% maximum value, (e) threshold = 15% maximum value and (f) threshold = 25% maximum value.

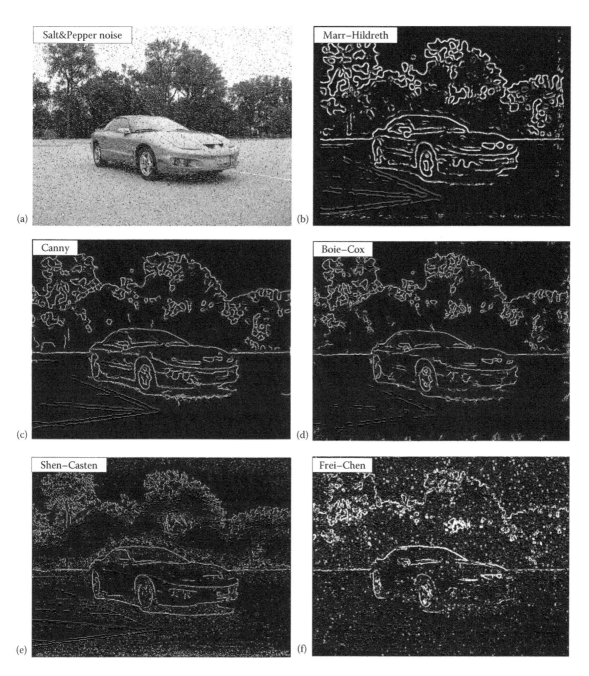

FIGURE 4.2-22

Advanced edge detectors with salt-and-pepper noise. (a) Original image with salt-and-pepper noise added with a probability of 3% each; (b) Marr–Hildreth, single variance, sigma = 4.0, threshold = 65 (c) Canny results, parameters: % Low Threshold = 1, % High Threshold = 1.5, Variance = 2; (d) Boie–Cox results, low threshold factor = 0.3, high threshold factor = 1.0, variance = 2.0 (e) Shen–Castan results, parameters: % Low Threshold = 1, % High Threshold = 2, Smooth factor = 0.9, Window size = 7, Thin Factor = 1; and (f) Frei–Chen results, parameters: Gaussian2 pre-filter, max(edge, line), post-threshold = 190. These results show that the Marr–Hildreth has the "spaghetti effect" as expected and that the Frei–Chen does not work too well with salt-and-pepper noise. The Canny, Boie–Cox and Shen–Castan work the best with salt-and-pepper noise.

4.2.5 Edges in Color Images

We saw in Chapter 1 that color images are described as three bands of monochrome image data and typical images use red, green and blue (RGB) bands. The simplest method to find edges in color images is to operate on each band separately – this is what we did in the previous figures. If color information is not important to the application, we may simply extract the luminance, or brightness, information and use the previously defined methods. Often, the

FIGURE 4.2-23

Advanced edge detectors with Gaussian noise. (a) Original image with Gaussian noise added with zero mean and a variance of 400; (b) Marr–Hildreth, dual variance, = 4.0, delta = 0.8; (c) Canny results, parameters: % Low Threshold = 1, % High Threshold = 1.5, Variance = 1.5; (d) Boie–Cox results, low threshold factor = 0.3, high threshold factor = 1.0, variance = 2.0; (e) Shen–Castan results, parameters: % Low Threshold = 1, % High Threshold = 2, Smooth factor = 0.8, Window size = 7, Thin Factor = 1; and (f) Frei–Chen results, parameters: Gaussian2 pre-filter, max(edge, line), post-threshold = 80. These results show that the Marr–Hildreth has the "spaghetti effect" as expected and that the Shen–Castan retains spurious edges with Gaussian noise. The Canny, Boie–Cox and Frei–Chen work the best with Gaussian noise.

optimal approach for finding edges in color images is application dependent and more than one possible definition of what constitutes a color edge exists.

The color transforms from Chapter 1 can be used to map the RGB images into different color spaces, and edges are found in one of the remapped bands. For example, for a particular application, we may not be interested in changes in brightness, but in changes in what we typically think of as "color"; so, the RGB data can be mapped into the HSV color space and edges are sought in the hue or saturation bands. Figure 4.2-24 illustrates this by showing that the areas of reflection are found in the saturation band, but not in the value (brightness) band.

Alternately, all three bands are used together. We can require an edge to be present in all three bands at the same location. With this scheme, any of the color spaces can be used, depending on the application, and we may want to define a quantum for "location error" and not require the edge to be at *exactly* the same pixel location in all three bands. Also, with this scheme, we can use any of the previously defined edge detection methods on each of the three bands individually. We can then combine the results from all three bands into a three-band image (as is done in CVIPtools, see Figure 4.2-25) or simply retain the maximum value at each pixel location from all three bands and output a monochrome image. With application-specific reasons, a linear combination of all three results can be used to create a monochrome image.

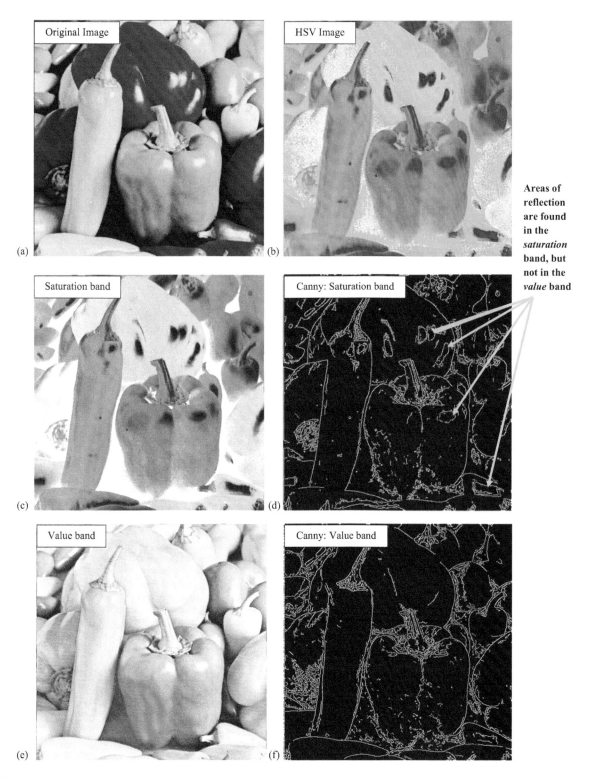

Areas of reflection are found in the *saturation* band, but not in the *value* band

FIGURE 4.2-24
Color edge detection in HSV space. (a) Original image, (b) original image mapped into HSV color space and displayed as an RGB image, (c) the *saturation* band, (d) Canny edge detection applied to the *saturation* band, (e) the *value* band and (f) Canny edge detection applied to the *value* band. Note that the areas of reflection, marked with the yellow arrows on image (d), are found in the *saturation* band, but not in the *value* band, image (f).

FIGURE 4.2-25
Color edge detection in RGB space. (a) Original image in RGB space, (b) Canny edge detector, all three bands displayed and (c) Boie–Cox edge detector, all three bands displayed. The edges that appear white are in all three RGB bands. Note that some edges only appear in one or two color bands.

Another method that uses all three bands simultaneously is to consider the color pixel vectors and search through the image marking edge points only if two neighboring color pixel vectors differ by some minimum distance measure. Here, we can use any vector distance measure, such as Euclidean distance (see Chapter 6 for definitions of other distance measures).

One specific method for finding edges in multispectral images, developed by Cervenka and Charvat in 1987, uses pixel values in all the image bands. This can be applied to three-band color images, as well as multispectral satellite images. It uses equations similar to the Roberts gradient, but is applied to all the image bands with a simple set of equations. The result of this edge detector at pixel (r, c) is the smaller of the two values from these two equations:

$$\frac{\sum_{b=1}^{n}\left[I_b(r,c)-\overline{I}(r,c)\right]\left[I_b(r+1,c+1)-\overline{I}(r+1,c+1)\right]}{\sqrt{\sum_{b=1}^{n}\left[I_b(r,c)-\overline{I}(r,c)\right]^2\sum_{b=1}^{n}\left[I_b(r+1,c+1)-\overline{I}(r+1,c+1)\right]^2}} \tag{4.2-14}$$

$$\frac{\sum_{b=1}^{n}\left[I_b(r+1,c)-\overline{I}(r+1,c)\right]\left[I_b(r,c+1)-\overline{I}(r,c+1)\right]}{\sqrt{\sum_{b=1}^{n}\left[I_b(r+1,c)-\overline{I}(r+1,c)\right]^2\sum_{b=1}^{n}\left[I_b(r,c+1)-\overline{I}(r,c+1)\right]^2}} \tag{4.2-15}$$

where

$\overline{I}(r,c)$ is the arithmetic average of all the pixels in all bands at pixel location (r,c)

$I_b(r,c)$ is the value at location (r,c) in the bth band, with a total of n bands

This edge detector has been used successfully on multispectral satellite images. An example is shown in Figure 4.2-26. Here, we see the Cervenka and Charvat method applied and the results histogram equalized to show detail, and two different thresholds applied to the resultant image.

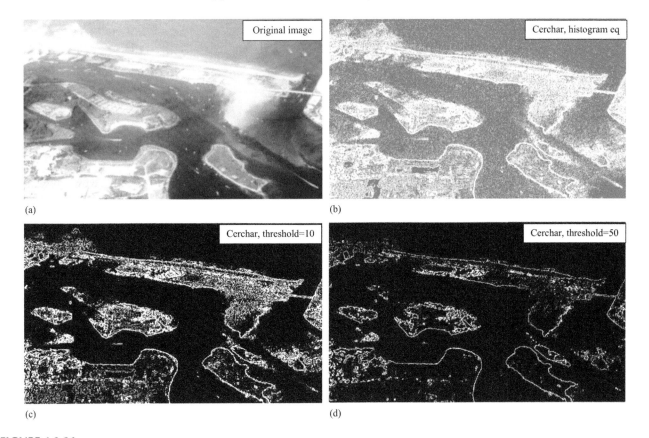

(a) (b) (c) (d)

FIGURE 4.2-26
Cervenka and Charvat multispectral image detector. (a) Original image, (b) result from the *Cerchar* in CVIPtools after histogram equalization to show detail (c) result from thresholding the *Cerchar* image at 10 and (d) thresholding the *Cerchar* results at 50.

4.2.6   Edge Detector Performance

In evaluating the performance of many processes, both objective and subjective evaluation methods can be used. The objective metric allows us to compare different techniques with fixed analytical methods, whereas the subjective methods will include human evaluation as part of the process which may lead to inconsistent results. However, for many image processing applications, the subjective measures tend to be quite useful. Therefore, in the development of an objective metric, it is advantageous to take human visual attributes into consideration. We will examine the types of errors encountered with edge detection, look at an objective measure based on these criteria and review results of the various edge detectors for our own subjective evaluation.

To develop a performance metric for edge detection operators, we need to define what constitutes success. For example, the Canny algorithm was developed considering three important edge detection success criteria:

Detection: the edge detector should find all real edges and not find any false edges.

Localization: the edges should be found in the correct place.

Single response: there should not be multiple edges found for a single edge.

These correlate nicely with *Pratt's Figure of Merit (FOM)* defined in 1978. Pratt first considered the types of errors that can occur with edge detection methods. The types of errors are (1) missing valid edge points, (2) classifying noise pulses as valid edge points and (3) smearing of edges (see Figure 4.2-27). If these errors do not occur, a successful edge detection would have been achieved.

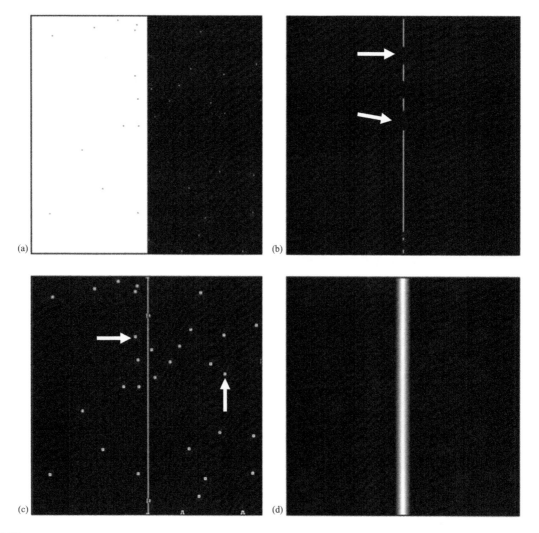

FIGURE 4.2-27
Errors in edge detection. (a) Original image, (b) missed edge points, examples marked with arrows, (c) noise misclassified as edge points, examples marked with arrows and (d) smeared edge.

The **Pratt's FOM** is defined as follows:

$$FOM = \frac{1}{I_N} \sum_{i=1}^{I_F} \frac{1}{1 + \alpha d_i^2} \tag{4.2-16}$$

where
I_N is the maximum of I_I and I_F,
I_I is the number of *ideal* edge points in the image,
I_F is the number of edge points *found* by the edge detector,
α is a scaling constant that can be adjusted to adjust the penalty for offset edges and d_i is the distance of a found edge point to an ideal edge point.

For this metric, FOM will be 1 for a perfect edge. Normalizing to the maximum of the ideal and found edge points guarantees a penalty for smeared edges or missing edge points. In general, this metric assigns a better rating to smeared edges than to offset or missing edges. This is done because techniques exist to thin smeared edges, but it is difficult to determine when an edge is found in the wrong location or is completely missed. The distance, d, can be defined in more than one way and typically depends on the connectivity definition used. The possible definitions for d are as follows:

Let the (r, c) values for two pixels be (r_1, c_1) and (r_2, c_2).

1. **City block distance,** based on four-connectivity:

$$d = |r_1 - r_2| + |c_1 - c_2| \tag{4.2-17}$$

With this distance measure, we can only move horizontally and vertically.

2. **Chessboard distance,** based on eight-connectivity:

$$d = \max(|r_1 - r_2|, |c_1 - c_2|) \tag{4.2-18}$$

With this distance measure, we can move diagonally as well as horizontally or vertically.

3. **Euclidean distance,** based on actual physical distance:

$$d = \left[(r_1 - r_2)^2 + (c_1 - c_2)^2 \right]^{1/2} \tag{4.2-19}$$

EXAMPLE 4.2.3

Given the following image array, find the Pratt FOM for the following found edge points, designated by 1's, in (a), (b) and (c). Let $\alpha = 0.5$, and use the city block distance measure. We assume that actual edge in the locations where the line appears, that is, at the 100's:

Image Array
$$\begin{bmatrix} 0 & 0 & 0 & 0 & 0 \\ 0 & 0 & 0 & 0 & 0 \\ 0 & 100 & 100 & 100 & 0 \\ 0 & 0 & 0 & 0 & 0 \\ 0 & 0 & 0 & 0 & 0 \end{bmatrix}$$

a. $\begin{bmatrix} 0 & 0 & 0 & 0 & 0 \\ 0 & 0 & 0 & 0 & 0 \\ 0 & 1 & 1 & 1 & 0 \\ 0 & 0 & 0 & 0 & 0 \\ 0 & 0 & 0 & 0 & 0 \end{bmatrix}$ b. $\begin{bmatrix} 0 & 0 & 0 & 0 & 0 \\ 0 & 1 & 1 & 1 & 0 \\ 0 & 1 & 1 & 1 & 0 \\ 0 & 0 & 0 & 0 & 0 \\ 0 & 0 & 0 & 0 & 0 \end{bmatrix}$ c. $\begin{bmatrix} 0 & 0 & 0 & 0 & 0 \\ 0 & 0 & 0 & 0 & 0 \\ 0 & 0 & 0 & 0 & 0 \\ 0 & 1 & 1 & 1 & 1 \\ 0 & 0 & 0 & 0 & 0 \end{bmatrix}$

a. $\text{FOM} = \dfrac{1}{I_N} \displaystyle\sum_{i=1}^{I_F} \dfrac{1}{1+\alpha d_i^2} = \dfrac{1}{3}\left[\dfrac{1}{1+0.5(0)^2} + \dfrac{1}{1+0.5(0)^2} + \dfrac{1}{1+0.5(0)^2}\right] = 1$

b. $\text{FOM} = \dfrac{1}{I_N} \displaystyle\sum_{i=1}^{I_F} \dfrac{1}{1+\alpha d_i^2} = \dfrac{1}{6}\left[\dfrac{1}{1+0.5(0)^2} + \dfrac{1}{1+0.5(0)^2} + \dfrac{1}{1+0.5(0)^2} + \dfrac{1}{1+0.5(1)^2} + \dfrac{1}{1+0.5(1)^2} + \dfrac{1}{1+0.5(1)^2}\right] \approx 0.8333$

c. $\text{FOM} = \dfrac{1}{I_N} \displaystyle\sum_{i=1}^{I_F} \dfrac{1}{1+\alpha d_i^2} = \dfrac{1}{4}\left[\dfrac{1}{1+0.5(1)^2} + \dfrac{1}{1+0.5(1)^2} + \dfrac{1}{1+0.5(1)^2} + \dfrac{1}{1+0.5(2)^2}\right] \approx 0.5833$

With result (a), we find a perfect edge. In result (b), we see that a smeared edge provides us with about 83% and an offset edge in (c) gives us about 58%. Note that the α parameter can be adjusted to determine the penalty for offset edges.

Applying the Pratt's FOM to selected edge detectors from each category – gradient operators, compass masks and the advanced edge detectors – results are shown in Figures 4.2-28 and 4.2-29. Figure 4.2-28 shows example test images, and the Pratt FOM results are plotted as the noise variance increases. The original test image has a gray level of 127 on the left and 102 on the right side and then Gaussian noise was added. Figure 4.2-29 shows resulting images with noise variances of 50 and 100 added to the test image. As expected, the advanced algorithms will have the best result as shown here with the Canny.

As previously mentioned, the objective metrics are often of limited use in practical applications, so we will take a subjective look at the results of the edge detectors. The human visual system is still superior, by far, to any computer vision system that has yet been devised and is often used as the final judge in application development. Figure 4.2-30 shows the magnitude images resulting from the basic edge detection operators. The magnitude images have been postprocessed with a threshold operation, using the average value for the threshold. Here, we see similar results from all the operators, but the Laplacian. This results from the Laplacian being based on the second derivative, while the others are based on the first derivative. In Figure 4.2-31, we show the magnitude and direction images from the basic gradient and compass mask edge detection operators. Here, we stretch the histogram of the magnitude images and remap the direction images from 0 to 255 (BYTE data type).

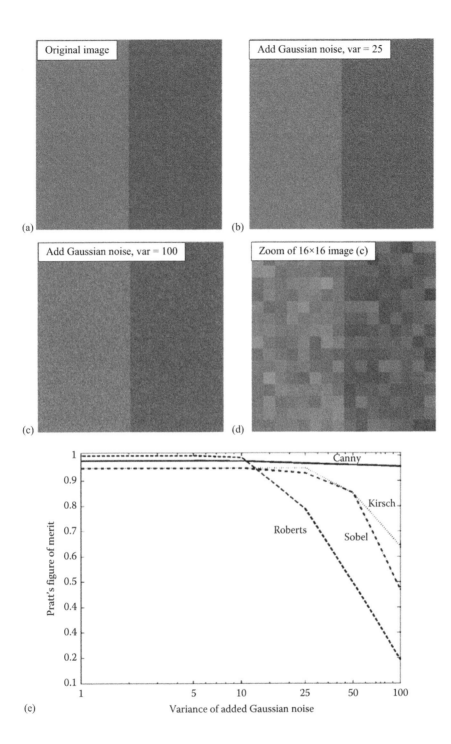

FIGURE 4.2-28

Pratt's figure of merit. (a) The original test image, 256×256 pixels, brightness level of 127 on the left and 102 on the right, (b) test image with added Gaussian noise with a variance of 25, (c) test image with added Gaussian noise with a variance of 100, (d) a 16×16 subimage cropped from image (c), enlarged to show that the edge is not as easy to find at the pixel level, and (e) this graph shows that as the noise variance increases the Canny has the best performance. We also see that the Roberts has the worst performance at high noise levels. The Roberts does poorly due to being based on a 2×2 mask, as opposed to the Sobel and Kirsch which are based on 3×3 masks. As we have seen with noisy images, a larger mask will perform better because it tends to spread the noise out – it is effectively a low-pass filter. The disadvantage of this is that fine details will be missed. This is the tradeoff that occurs with all edge detection – sensitivity versus accuracy. The test image was a step edge with Gaussian noise, so it is expected that the Canny performs the best because its development was based on this model.

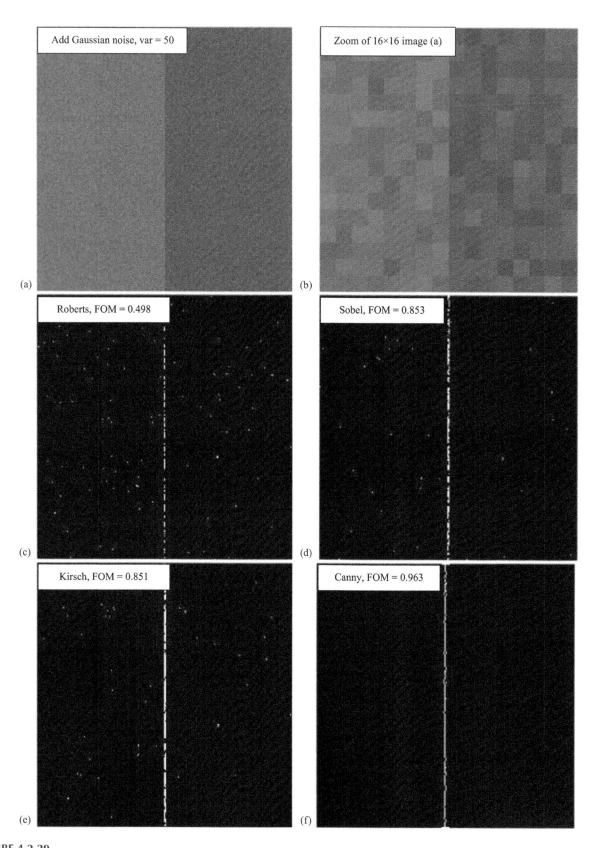

FIGURE 4.2-29

Pratt's figure of Merit images. (a) Test image with added Gaussian noise with a variance of 50, (b) a 16×16 subimage cropped from image (a), enlarged to show that the edge is not as easy to find at the pixel level, (c) Roberts result, FOM = 0.498, (d) Sobel result, FOM = 0.853, (e) Kirsch result, FOM = 0.851, (f) Canny result, FOM = 0.963

(Continued)

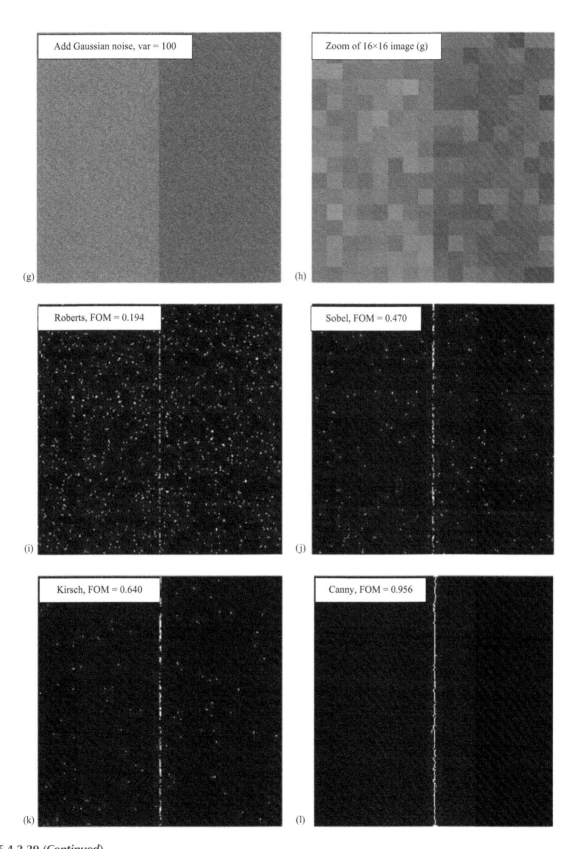

FIGURE 4.2-29 (*Continued*)
(g) test image with added Gaussian noise with a variance of 100, (h) a 16 × 16 subimage cropped from image (g), enlarged to show that the edge is not as easy to find at the pixel level, (i) Roberts, FOM = 0.194, (j) Sobel, FOM = 0.470, (k) Kirsch, FOM = 0.640 and (l) Canny, FOM = 0.956.

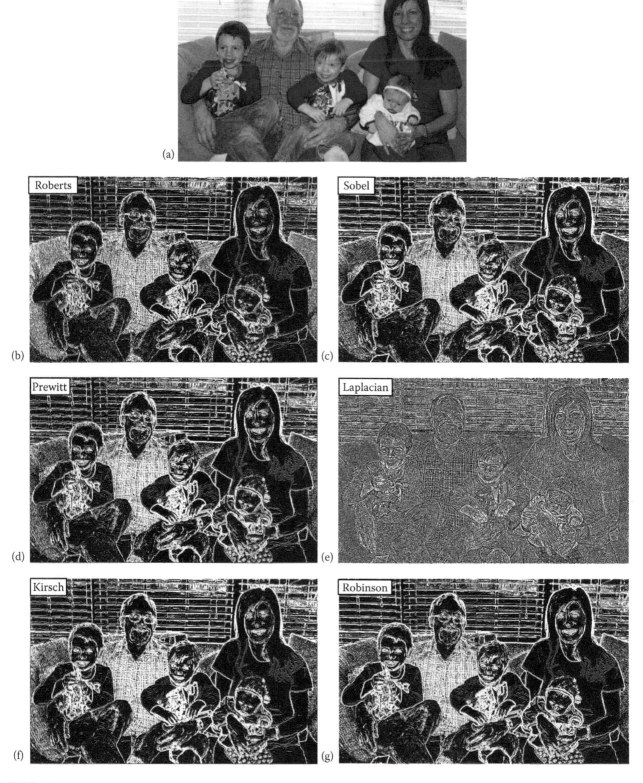

FIGURE 4.2-30
Edge detection examples. After the edge detector operator was performed, a threshold corresponding to the average value was used on the magnitude image. (a) Original image, (b) Roberts operator (c) Sobel operator, (d) Prewitt operator (e) Laplacian operator, (f) Kirsch operator (g) Robinson operator. Note that the resultant images all look similar, except for the Laplacian. The Laplacian is based on the approximation of the second derivative, unlike the others which are based on the first derivative.

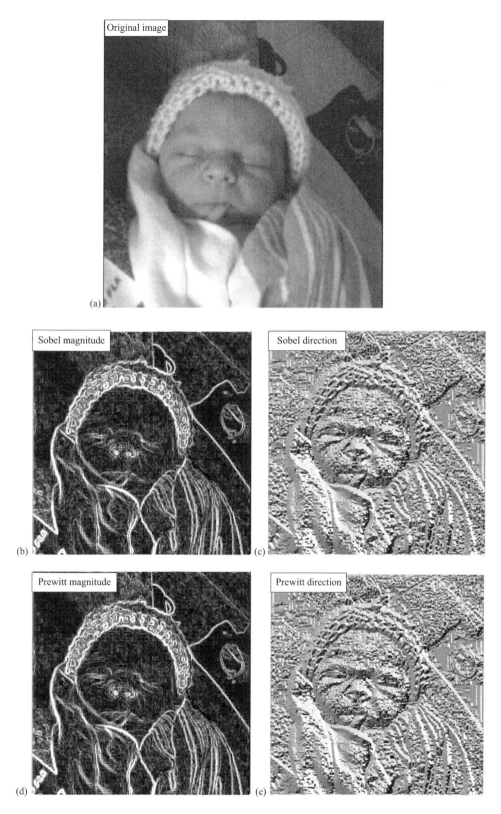

FIGURE 4.2-31
Edge detection examples with direction images. After the edge detector operator is applied, the magnitude image is remapped to BYTE and its histogram is stretched. The direction images are remapped to the BYTE range of 0–255. Note the original range on the direction images is $-\pi$ to $+\pi$. (a) Original image, (b) Sobel magnitude image, (c) Sobel direction image, (d) Prewitt magnitude, (e) Prewitt direction

(Continued)

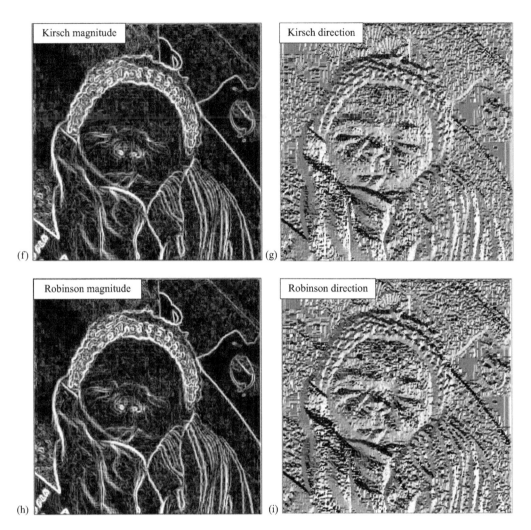

FIGURE 4.2-31 (*Continued*)
(f) Kirsch magnitude, (g) Kirsch direction, (h) Robinson magnitude and (i) Robinson direction. Note that the magnitude images all look similar, but the Sobel/Prewitt direction images differ from the Kirsch/Robinson due to the method in which they are defined.

4.3 Line Detection

4.3.1 Hough Transform

The Hough transform is designed specifically to find lines. A line is a collection of edge points that are adjacent and have the same direction. The Hough transform is an algorithm that will take a collection of n edge points, as found by an edge detector, and efficiently find all the lines on which these edge points lie. Although a brute force search method can be used that will find all the lines associated with each pair of points, by checking every point with every possible line, it involves finding $n(n - 1)/2$ (on the order of n^2) lines and comparing every point to all the lines which is $(n)(n(n - 1))/2$ or about n^3 comparisons. This heavy computational burden is certainly not practical for real-time applications, and this provides much more information than is necessary for most applications. The advantage of the Hough transform is that it provides parameters to reduce the search time for finding lines based on a set of edge points and that these parameters can be adjusted based on application requirements.

To understand the Hough transform, we will first consider the *normal* (perpendicular) representation of a line:

$$\rho = r \cos(\theta) + c \sin(\theta) \tag{4.3-1}$$

Given a line in our row and column, (r, c) based image space, we can define that line by ρ, the distance from the origin to the line along a perpendicular to the line, and θ, the angle between the r-axis and the ρ-line (see Figure 4.3-1). Now, for each pair of values of ρ and θ, we have defined a particular line. The parameter θ ranges from $0°$ to $180°$, and ρ ranges from 0 to $\sqrt{2}\ N$, where $N \times N$ is the image size – for a nonsquare image, it is the diagonal length. Next, we can take this $\rho \cdot \theta$ parameter space and quantize it to reduce our search time. We quantize the $\rho \cdot \theta$ parameter space, as shown in Figure 4.3-2, by dividing the space into a specific number of blocks. Each block corresponds to a line, or group of possible lines, with ρ and θ varying across the increment as defined by the size of the block. The size of these blocks corresponds to the coarseness of the quantization; bigger blocks provide less line resolution.

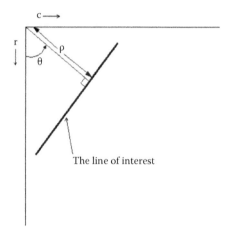

FIGURE 4.3-1
The Hough transform can be defined by using the normal (perpendicular) representation of a line and the parameters ρ and θ.

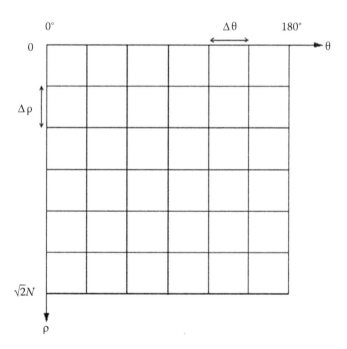

FIGURE 4.3-2
The quantized Hough space. Theta, θ, varies from $0°$ to $180°$, and rho, ρ, varies from 0 to $\sqrt{2}N$ for a square $N \times N$ image. Each block in this quantized space represents a group of lines whose parameters can vary over one increment of ρ and θ, defined by $\Delta\rho$ and $\Delta\theta$.

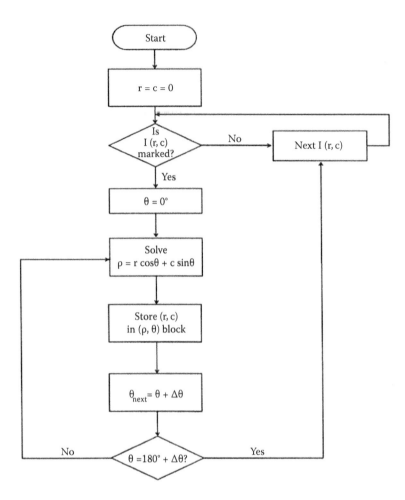

FIGURE 4.3-3
Hough transform flowchart. The flowchart is followed until all $I(r, c)$ have been examined. The entire parameter space, $\rho\theta$, is cycled by using the corresponding quantizations, $\Delta\theta$ and $\Delta\rho$, for each marked point of interest.

The algorithm used for the Hough transform (see Figure 4.3-3 for a flowchart of the process) will help understand what this means. The algorithm consists of three primary steps:

1. Define the desired increments on ρ and θ, $\Delta\rho$ and $\Delta\theta$; quantize the space accordingly.
2. For every point of interest (typically points found by edge detectors that exceed some threshold value), plug the values for r and c into the line equation (4.3-1):

$$\rho = r\ \cos(\theta) + c\ \sin(\theta)$$

   Then, for each value of θ in the quantized space, solve for ρ.
3. For each $\rho \cdot \theta$ pair from step 2, record the r and c pair in the corresponding block in the quantized space. This constitutes a hit for that particular block.

When this process is completed, the number of hits in each block corresponds to the number of pixels on the line as defined by the values of ρ and θ in that block. The advantage of large quantization blocks is that the search time is reduced, but the price paid is less line resolution in the image space. Examining Figure 4.3-4, we can see that this means the line of interest in the image space can vary more. One block in the Hough space corresponds to all the solid lines in this figure – this is what we mean by reduced line resolution.

Next, select a threshold and examine the quantization blocks that contain more points than the threshold. Here, we look for continuity by searching for gaps in the line by looking at the distance between points on the

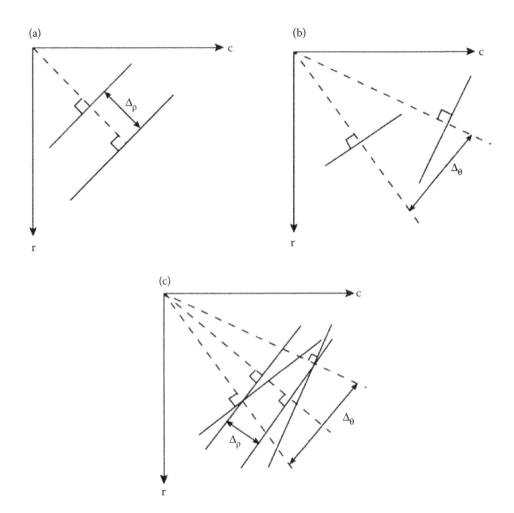

FIGURE 4.3-4
Effects of quantization block size for Hough transform. (a) Range of lines included by choice of $\Delta\rho$. (b) Range of lines included by choice of $\Delta\theta$. (c) Overall range of lines defined by $\Delta\rho$ and $\Delta\theta$, corresponding to a quantization block.

line – remember the points on a line correspond to points recorded in the block. When this process is completed, the lines are marked in the output image. Note that the Hough transform will allow us to look for lines of specific orientation, if desired.

4.3.2 Postprocessing

A more advanced postprocessing algorithm is implemented in CVIPtools with the Hough transform. Images resulting from this algorithm searching for lines at 45° are shown in Figure 4.3-5, and any of these intermediate images is available as output in CVIPtools with the *Output Image* select box for the Hough transform. The algorithm works as follows:

1. Perform the Hough transform on the input image containing marked edge points, which we will call image1. The result, image2, is an image in Hough space quantized by the parameter *delta length* (ρ) and delta angle (fixed at 1° in CVIPtools).

2. Threshold image2 by using the parameter *line pixels*, which is the minimum number of pixels in a line (or in one quantization box in Hough space), and do the inverse Hough transform. This result, image3, is a mask image with lines found in the input image at the specified angle(s), illustrated in Figure 4.3-5c. Note that these lines span the entire image.

3. Perform a logical operation, image1 AND image3. The result is image4, see Figure 4.3-5d.

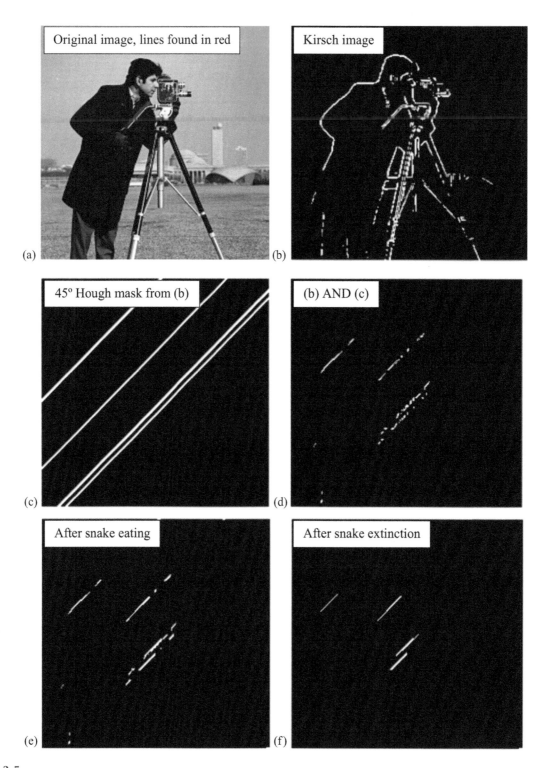

FIGURE 4.3-5

Hough transform postprocessing algorithm details. The Hough parameters used are as follows: *Line Angles*: 45°, *Line Pixels (min)*: 25, *Connect distance (max)*: 5, *Delta Length*: 1 and *Segment Length (min)*: 15. (a) Original image with final lines found in red; (b) image after applying the Kirsch edge operator and a threshold operation; (c) the mask image created from the Hough result for lines at 45°; (d) result of logical AND of the images in (b) and (c); (e) image (d) after snake eating, see that the camera's handle has been connected and (f) the final result after snake extinction, small dashed lines are removed. Note that we have four lines, starting from the upper left: one line corresponding to the lower part of the arm above the elbow, note that the upper part of the arm is missing as it is not quite at 45°; one line for the camera handle; the next line corresponds to the part of his other arm from elbow to wrist and the last line (the lower one) that is not a true line in the image but is created by a combination of the edge detail in that area and using a connect distance of 5.

4. Apply an *edge linking* process to image4 to connect line segments; specifically, we implemented a *snake eating algorithm*. This works as follows:

   a. A line segment is considered to be a snake. It can eat another snake within *connect distance* along *line angles* and becomes longer (see Figure 4.3-5e). This will connect disjoint line segments.

   b. If a snake is too small, less than *segment length*, it will be extinct. This will remove small segments. The output from the snake eating algorithm is the final result, as illustrated in Figure 4.3-5f.

CVIPtools parameters for the Hough transform:

Line angles: The range of angles for which the Hough transform will search.

Line pixels (min): The minimum number of pixels must a line possess to be retained, also referred to as the threshold value in the Hough image.

Connect distance (max): Controls how far apart two line segments can be and still be connected.

Delta length: Quantizes the Hough space ρ parameter. Controls how "thick" a line can be; note that a "thick" line might consist of multiple separate lines if they are in close proximity.

Segment length (min): The minimum number of pixels in a line segment for it to be retained.

Segment length: controls how many pixels a solid line must have, while *line pixels* controls how many pixels a dashed line must have.

The result of applying the Hough transform to an aerial airport image to find the runway is shown in Figure 4.3-6. The Canny edge detection operator was used on the original image to provide input to the Hough transform. The

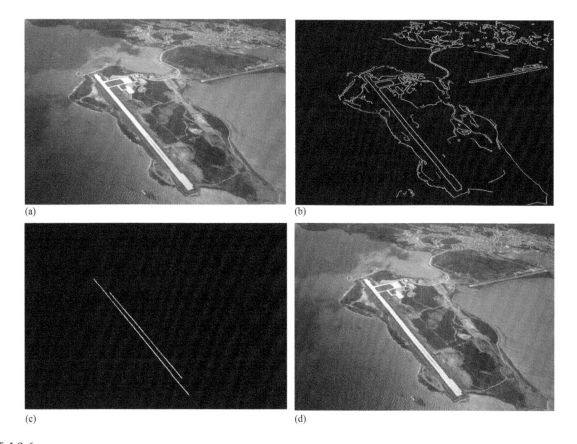

(a) (b)

(c) (d)

FIGURE 4.3-6
Hough transform to find airport runway. (a) Aerial image of an airport; (b) after Canny edge detection, low threshold factor = 1, high threshold factor = 2, variance = 0.5 (c) Hough output with the range of line angles = 130°–170°, delta length (ρ) = 1, minimum number of pixels per line = 35, maximum connect distance = 1, minimum segment size = 35 and (d) Hough output in red superimposed over the original image, showing the airport runway.

Canny parameters were low threshold factor = 1.0, high threshold factor = 2.0 and variance = 0.5. The Hough transform parameter *delta length (rho)* was set at 1, *line pixels* (the number-of-points threshold) was set at a minimum of 35 pixels per line and *segment length* set to 35. We see that the Hough transform provides an efficient line finding algorithm and it can also be used as a boundary detection segmentation method; these are discussed more in Chapter 5.

4.4   Corner and Shape Detection

4.4.1   Corner Detection

We have seen that edges are found by considering the rate of change, or gradient, in image brightness (gray level) in a specific direction. Lines and curves are then a collection of these edge points along a specific path. *Corners* are simply points where there is a high rate of change in more than one direction; using this definition, corners in this sense are also referred to as *points of interest*. Corner detection is useful for many applications. For example, object tracking is facilitated by the ability to delineate an object by its corners and following the movement of the corners through space. In addition to tracking the object in space, the orientation can be followed more easily with corner detection. Corners are also useful features for matching multiple images, for example, to use as match points for creation of three-dimensional models from stereo images.

Corners are used by the human visual system to provide cues about object boundaries and are also important in computer vision applications because they are robust features. We refer to corners as robust features because they can be found accurately in the presence of noise or even if image acquisition conditions, such as lighting or camera angles, vary. Note that even though the corner features themselves are robust, the corner detector may not be.

The **Moravec detector** is the simplest corner detector, but not necessarily robust. It finds points of maximum contrast, which correspond to potential corners and sharp edges. This operator is as follows:

$$\mathrm{MD}\big[I(r,c)\big] = \frac{1}{8} \sum_{i=r-1}^{r+1} \sum_{k=c-1}^{c+1} \big|I(r,c) - I(i,j)\big| \tag{4.4-1}$$

It finds the average of the sum of the absolute values of the differences between a pixel and its neighbors. Or, put more simply, finds the average difference between a pixel and its neighbors in all directions. After this operator is applied, the result can undergo a threshold operation to select only pixels above a certain value. Results of varying the threshold are shown in Figure 4.4-1. Here, we see that as the threshold is increased, we get fewer of the edge pixels and more of the corners only. We can also observe that on a digital, rectangular sampling grid, that curves have "corners".

One drawback to the Moravec corner detector is that it only considers edges oriented on the rectangular grid in 45° increments, using the eight-neighbors, so it may miss some valid corners that are not aligned on the grid. In this sense, the operator is not *isotropic*, which means it does not treat edges in all directions equally. The tradeoff is that it is simple and fast to calculate.

A more robust corner detector is the Harris corner detection algorithm, developed by Harris and Stephens in 1988. The Harris method consists of five steps: (1) Blur the image with a 2-D Gaussian convolution mask; (2) find the approximate brightness gradient in two perpendicular directions, for example, use the two Prewitt or Sobel masks; (3) blur the two brightness results with a 2-D Gaussian; (4) find the corner response function, *CRF(r, c)*; (5) threshold the corner response function and apply nonmaxima suppression, similar to what was done with the Canny.

Now, we need to define the corner response function or *CRF(r, c)*. To do this, we must select a gradient function for step 2; so, for simplicity, we will use the Prewitt edge detector which results in p_1 for the vertical edges (horizontal lines) and p_2 for the horizontal edges (vertical lines). Remember that p_1 and p_2 are both functions of the row and column coordinates, (*r, c*); this is implied in the below equation. Now we can define:

$$\mathrm{CRF}(r,c) = \Big[G\big(p_1^2\big)G\big(p_2^2\big) - \big[G(p_1 p_2)\big]^2\Big] - \alpha\big[G(p_1) + G(p_2)\big]^2 \tag{4.4-2}$$

where $G(\degree)$ represents the result after convolution with a Gaussian.

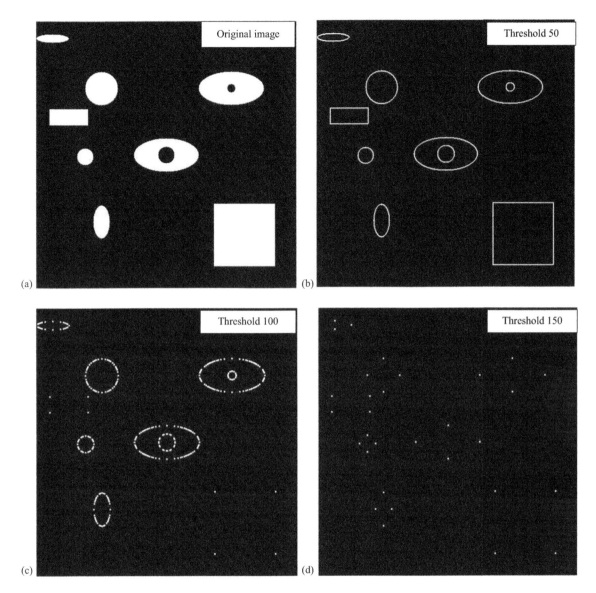

FIGURE 4.4-1
Moravec corner detector. (a) Original image, (b) resultant image from Moravec corner detector with a threshold of 50, (c) threshold of 100 and (d) threshold of 150. Note that the threshold of 150 gets the corners only, whereas lower threshold values get more edge pixels.

The larger the magnitude of CRF(r, c), the more likely a corner is at that point. The parameter α determines the sensitivity of the corner detector – a larger α makes it less sensitive and will result in fewer corners being found. The maximum value for α is 0.25, but typically values vary from 0.04 to 0.15, with 0.06 being the default value.

After the CRF(r, c) is found, it must undergo a threshold process and application of nonmaxima suppression. The threshold is based on image content, and the nonmaxima suppression works by finding the largest value of the CRF within a given spatial area. Figure 4.4-2 shows application of the Harris corner detector with example intermediate images for each step in the process.

The Frei–Chen masks can also be used as a corner detector. Results are shown in Figure 4.4-3. Here, we have simple binary shapes and show the projection onto the edge subspace with a threshold angle of 50° and the projection onto the line subspace with threshold angles of 50° and 40°. Note that the projection onto the edge subspace finds the corners at a 45° angle to the corner and the projection onto the line subspace finds the corners on the corner itself. The edge subspace projection does not find the horizontal and vertical lines at the top and sides of the curves, but the projection onto the lines subspace does. Also, in (d), the line subspace with a lower angle threshold finds the "corners" of the holes only. These results are a function of the Frei–Chen masks (see Figure 4.2-18).

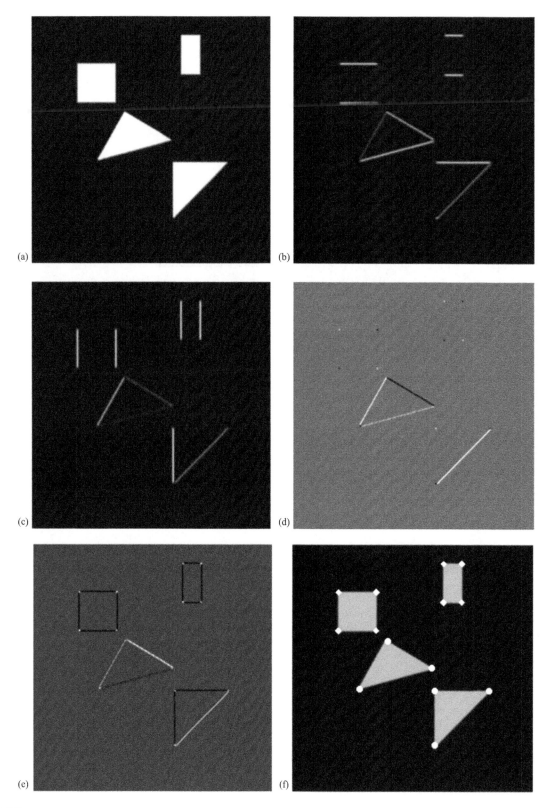

FIGURE 4.4-2
Harris corner detector. (a) Original image after application of 5×5 Gaussian mask, (b) strength of the horizontal lines, from the vertical gradient, by application of Prewitt, p_1, squared followed by a Gaussian, $G\left(p_1^2\right)$, (c) strength of the vertical lines, from the horizontal gradient, by application of Prewitt, p_2, squared followed by a Gaussian, $G\left(p_2^2\right)$, (d) Gaussian of the product of the horizontal and vertical gradient, $G\left(p_1 p_2\right)$, (e) result from the corner response function, $CRF(r, c)$, and (f) the final detected corners after thresholding and nonmaxima suppression of the $CRF(r, c)$, shown overlaid on the original shapes.

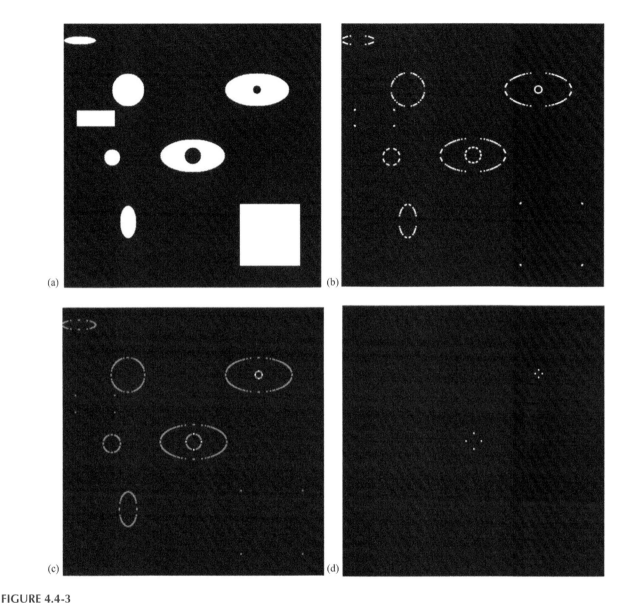

FIGURE 4.4-3
Frei–Chen masks for corner detector. (a) Original image, (b) projection onto edge subspace with a threshold angle of 50°, (c) projection onto line subspace with a threshold angle of 50° and (d) projection onto line subspace with a threshold angle of 40°. Note that the projection onto the edge subspace finds the corners at a 45° angle to the corner and the projection onto the line subspace finds the corners on the corner itself. The edge subspace projection does not find the horizontal and vertical lines at the top and sides of the curves, but the projection onto the lines subspace does. Also, in (d), the line subspace with a lower angle threshold finds the "corners" of the holes only.

4.4.2 Shape Detection with the Hough Transform

If we are searching for specific geometric shapes, we can extend the Hough transform to search for any geometric shape that can be described by mathematical equations, such as circles, ellipses or parabolas. The line finding Hough transform discussed previously was defined by quantizing the parameter space that defined the lines, specifically the mathematical space defined by the parameters ρ and θ. To extend this concept, we simply define a parameter vector and apply the Hough algorithm to this new parameter space. The *extended Hough transform* can be applied to any geometric shape that can described by an equation of the following form:

$$f\left(r,c;\overline{p}\right) = 0 \tag{4.4-3}$$

where $f(\cdot)$ is any function of the row and column coordinates, (r, c), and a parameter vector $\bar{p}$.

In the case of the line finding Hough transform, the function is:

$$\rho = r\cos(\theta) + c\sin(\theta) \tag{4.4-4}$$

and the parameter vector for the line is:

$$\bar{p} = \begin{bmatrix} \rho \\ \theta \end{bmatrix} \tag{4.4-5}$$

In the case of a circle, with the equation of a circle as follows, where a and b are the center coordinates of the circle and d is the diameter:

$$(r-a)^2 + (c-b)^2 = \left(\frac{d}{2}\right)^2 \tag{4.4-6}$$

The parameter vector for the circle is:

$$\bar{p} = \begin{bmatrix} a \\ b \\ d \end{bmatrix} \tag{4.4-7}$$

To apply the Hough transform to find circles, we follow the same procedure as for line finding, but with an increased dimensionality to the search space – it is now a three-dimensional parameter space. This technique can be applied to any geometric shape that can be described by an equation. Another example is the ellipse, where a and b are the center, and the length of the major axis is $2h$ and the minor axis $2k$. For ellipses aligned along the row or column axis:

$$(r-a)^2/h^2 + (c-b)^2/k^2 = 1 \tag{4.4-8}$$

The parameter vector corresponding to the ellipse is:

$$\bar{p} = \begin{bmatrix} a \\ b \\ h \\ k \end{bmatrix} \tag{4.4-9}$$

Now for the ellipse, we apply the same method, but the search space is now a four-dimensional parameter space.

To search for general geometric shapes that are not readily described by parametric equations such as the circle, a *generalized Hough transform* can be used. The generalized Hough works by creating a description of the shape defined by a reference point and a table of lines, called an *R*-table. The reference point, such as the object center of area, is chosen inside the sample shape, and lines are defined from the reference point to a point on the border. This intersection information is recorded in the table. These lines can be defined by the angle they make with the vertical or horizontal axis or any other application-specific method that is useful. The shape is then described by the line intersection information in the *R*-table. The generalized Hough algorithm is then used to search for shapes described by this table. An illustration of how these lines and intersections are defined is shown in Figure 4.4-4.

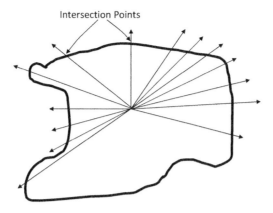

FIGURE 4.4-4
Generalized Hough transform. Arbitrary shape with lines from a given point is shown intersecting with the shape. Often the point selected is the object center of area and the lines can be defined at fixed angles depending on the application. The line parameters and their intersections are kept in an R-table, which is used to describe the shape.

4.5 Key Points

Overview: Edge, Line and Shape Detection

- Image analysis requires extracting useful information from vast amounts of low-level pixel data.
- Dividing the image into meaningful regions by detecting edges, lines, corners and geometric shapes is part of the process.
- The Hough transform is used for line finding.
- The Extended Hough is used to find regular geometric shapes such as circles and ellipses.
- The Generalized Hough is used to find arbitrary shapes.
- Corners represent points of interest, corresponding to places where the gray level is rapidly changing in multiple directions.

Edge Detection

- Edge detection operators are often implemented with convolution masks.
- Edge detection operators are often discrete approximations to differential operators.
- Edge detection operators may return magnitude and direction information, some return magnitude only.
- Edge direction and line direction are perpendicular to each other, because the edge direction is the direction of change in gray level (Figure 4.2-1).
- There is a tradeoff between sensitivity and accuracy in edge detection (Figure 4.2-2).
- Potential edge points are found by examining the relationship a pixel has with its neighbors; an edge implies a change in gray level.
- Edges may exist anywhere and be defined by color, texture, shadow, etc., and may not necessarily separate real-world objects (Figure 4.2-3).
- A real edge in an image tends to change slowly, compared to the ideal edge model which is abrupt (Figures 4.2-4 and 4.2-5).

Gradient Operators

- Gradient operators are based on the idea of using the first or second derivative of the gray level.
- The first derivative will mark edge points, with steeper gray level changes providing stronger edge points (larger magnitudes).
- The second derivative returns two impulses, one on either side of the edge.

Roberts operator: a simple approximation to the first derivative, two forms of the equations:

$$\sqrt{[I(r,c) - I(r-1,c-1)]^2 + [I(r,c-1) - I(r-1,c)]^2} \tag{4.2-1}$$

$$|I(r,c) - I(r-1,c-1)| + |I(r,c-1) - I(r-1,c)| \tag{4.2-2}$$

Sobel operator: approximates the gradient with a row and column mask and returns both magnitude and direction:

$$\begin{bmatrix} -1 & -2 & -1 \\ 0 & 0 & 0 \\ 1 & 2 & 1 \end{bmatrix} \qquad \begin{bmatrix} -1 & 0 & 1 \\ -2 & 0 & 2 \\ -1 & 0 & 1 \end{bmatrix}$$

$$\text{EDGE MAGNITUDE} \sqrt{s_1^2 + s_2^2} \tag{4.2-3}$$

$$\text{EDGE DIRECTION} \operatorname{Tan}^{-1}\left[\frac{s_1}{s_2}\right] \tag{4.2-4}$$

Prewitt operator: approximates the gradient with a row and column mask and returns both magnitude and direction; it is easier to calculate or implement in hardware than the Sobel, as it uses only 1's in the masks:

$$\begin{bmatrix} -1 & -1 & -1 \\ 0 & 0 & 0 \\ 1 & 1 & 1 \end{bmatrix} \qquad \begin{bmatrix} -1 & 0 & 1 \\ -1 & 0 & 1 \\ -1 & 0 & 1 \end{bmatrix}$$

$$\text{EDGE MAGNITUDE} \sqrt{p_1^2 + p_2^2} \tag{4.2-5}$$

$$\text{EDGE DIRECTION} \operatorname{Tan}^{-1}\left[\frac{p_1}{p_2}\right] \tag{4.2-6}$$

Laplacian operators: these are two-dimensional discrete approximations to the second derivative, it is implemented by applying *one* of the following convolution masks:

$$\begin{bmatrix} 0 & -1 & 0 \\ -1 & 4 & -1 \\ 0 & -1 & 0 \end{bmatrix} \qquad \begin{bmatrix} -1 & -1 & -1 \\ -1 & 8 & -1 \\ -1 & -1 & -1 \end{bmatrix} \qquad \begin{bmatrix} -2 & 1 & -2 \\ 1 & 4 & 1 \\ -2 & 1 & -2 \end{bmatrix}$$

Compass Masks

- The compass mask edge detectors are created by taking a single mask and rotating it to the eight major compass orientations.
- The edge magnitude is found by convolving each mask with the image and selecting the largest value at each pixel location.
- The edge direction at each point is defined by the direction of the edge mask that provides the maximum magnitude.

Kirsch Compass Masks

$$
k_0 \begin{bmatrix} -3 & -3 & 5 \\ -3 & 0 & 5 \\ -3 & -3 & 5 \end{bmatrix}
\quad
k_1 \begin{bmatrix} -3 & 5 & 5 \\ -3 & 0 & 5 \\ -3 & -3 & -3 \end{bmatrix}
\quad
k_2 \begin{bmatrix} 5 & 5 & 5 \\ -3 & 0 & -3 \\ -3 & -3 & -3 \end{bmatrix}
\quad
k_3 \begin{bmatrix} 5 & 5 & -3 \\ 5 & 0 & -3 \\ -3 & -3 & -3 \end{bmatrix}
$$

$$
k_4 \begin{bmatrix} 5 & -3 & -3 \\ 5 & 0 & -3 \\ 5 & -3 & -3 \end{bmatrix}
\quad
k_5 \begin{bmatrix} -3 & -3 & -3 \\ 5 & 0 & -3 \\ 5 & 5 & -3 \end{bmatrix}
\quad
k_6 \begin{bmatrix} -3 & -3 & -3 \\ -3 & 0 & -3 \\ 5 & 5 & 5 \end{bmatrix}
\quad
k_7 \begin{bmatrix} -3 & -3 & -3 \\ -3 & 0 & 5 \\ -3 & 5 & 5 \end{bmatrix}
$$

Robinson Compass Masks

$$
r_0 \begin{bmatrix} -1 & 0 & 1 \\ -2 & 0 & 2 \\ -1 & 0 & 1 \end{bmatrix}
\quad
r_1 \begin{bmatrix} 0 & 1 & 2 \\ -1 & 0 & 1 \\ -2 & -1 & 0 \end{bmatrix}
\quad
r_2 \begin{bmatrix} 1 & 2 & 1 \\ 0 & 0 & 0 \\ -1 & -2 & -1 \end{bmatrix}
\quad
r_3 \begin{bmatrix} 2 & 1 & 0 \\ 1 & 0 & -1 \\ 0 & -1 & -2 \end{bmatrix}
$$

$$
r_4 \begin{bmatrix} 1 & 0 & -1 \\ 2 & 0 & -2 \\ 1 & 0 & -1 \end{bmatrix}
\quad
r_5 \begin{bmatrix} 0 & -1 & -2 \\ 1 & 0 & -1 \\ 2 & 1 & 0 \end{bmatrix}
\quad
r_6 \begin{bmatrix} -1 & -2 & -1 \\ 0 & 0 & 0 \\ 1 & 2 & 1 \end{bmatrix}
\quad
r_7 \begin{bmatrix} -2 & -1 & 0 \\ -1 & 0 & 1 \\ 0 & 1 & 2 \end{bmatrix}
$$

Thresholds, Noise Mitigation and Edge Linking

- Noise includes any points not wanted or needed for the application.
- Noise mitigation requires a tradeoff between sensitivity and accuracy.
- Primary methods to mitigate noise: (1) control of a threshold, so that only the stronger edge points pass, (2) use of large mask sizes to mitigate noise and (3) use of a preprocessing mean filter.
- 10%–25% of average value good reference for threshold of unimodal histogram returned by edge detector.
- After edge points are selected, edge linking process combines points into lines and curves.
- Edge linking methods to link the edge points into segments and boundaries, including: (1) consider points that have passed the threshold test and connect them to other marked points within some maximum distance, (2) consider small neighborhoods and link points with similar magnitude and direction, then link points together to form boundaries and (3) the snake eating algorithm described in Section 4.3.2.

Advanced Edge Detectors

Marr–Hildreth algorithm: consists of three steps: (1) convolve the image with a Gaussian smoothing filter, (2) convolve the image with a Laplacian mask and (3) find the zero crossings of the image from step 2. The first two steps can be combined into one convolution filter, referred to as a Laplacian of a Gaussian, or LoG, and is given by this equation:

$$
\text{LoG} = \left[\frac{r^2 + c^2 - 2\sigma^2}{\sigma^4} \right] e^{-\left(\frac{r^2 + c^2}{2\sigma^2} \right)}
\tag{4.2-7}
$$

The LoG is implemented as an approximation with a convolution filter, such as:

$$
\begin{bmatrix}
0 & 0 & -1 & 0 & 0 \\
0 & -1 & -2 & -1 & 0 \\
-1 & -2 & 16 & -2 & -1 \\
0 & -1 & -2 & -1 & 0 \\
0 & 0 & -1 & 0 & 0
\end{bmatrix}
$$

The simplest method to find zero crossings is to examine 3×3 subimages and look for changing signs (positive/negative) in at least two opposing neighbors.

Canny algorithm: an optimal edge detector based on a specific mathematical model; it is a four-step process: (1) apply a Gaussian filter mask to smooth the image to mitigate noise effects, (2) find the magnitude and direction of the gradient, (3) apply nonmaxima suppression which results in thinned edges and (4) apply two thresholds known as hysteresis thresholding.

Hysteresis thresholding: mark pixels above a high threshold and then apply a low threshold to pixels connected to those marked by the high threshold.

Boie–Cox algorithm: a generalization of the Canny algorithm using matched filters and Wiener filters.

Shen–Castan algorithm: developed as an optimal solution to a specific mathematical model, similar to Canny, but with modifications and extensions.

Frei–Chen masks: they form a complete set of basis vectors, which means any 3×3 subimage can be represented as a weighted sum of the basis vectors. The weights are found by projecting the subimage onto each basis vector; that is, perform a vector inner product. Can be used to find edges or lines of specific orientation.

Vector inner product: found by multiplying coincident terms of two vectors and summing the results.

Edges in Color Images

Edge detection in color images is performed on the original RGB data, or after mapping into another color space, with these methods:

1. Extract the luminance or brightness information and apply a monochrome edge detection method. The brightness information can be found by averaging the RGB components: $I = \dfrac{(R+G+B)}{3}$, or by the luminance equation: $Y = 0.299R + 0.587G + 0.114B$, or by the vector length: $L = \sqrt{R^2 + G^2 + B^2}$.

2. Apply a monochrome edge detection method to each of the RGB bands separately and then combine the results into a composite image.

3. Apply a monochrome edge detection method to each of the RGB bands separately and then retain the maximum value at each location.

4. Apply a monochrome edge detection method to each of the RGB bands separately and then use a linear combination of the three results at each location.

5. Apply a monochrome edge detection method to each of the RGB bands separately and then select specific criteria at each pixel location to find an edge point.

6. Equations for multispectral edges, developed by Cervenka and Charvat:

$$\frac{\sum_{b=1}^{n}\left[I_b(r,c)-\bar{I}(r,c)\right]\left[I_b(r+1,c+1)-\bar{I}(r+1,c+1)\right]}{\sqrt{\sum_{b=1}^{n}\left[I_b(r,c)-\bar{I}(r,c)\right]^2 \sum_{b=1}^{n}\left[I_b(r+1,c+1)-\bar{I}(r+1,c+1)\right]^2}} \tag{4.2-14}$$

$$\frac{\sum_{b=1}^{n}\left[I_b(r+1,c)-\bar{I}(r+1,c)\right]\left[I_b(r,c+1)-\bar{I}(r,c+1)\right]}{\sqrt{\sum_{b=1}^{n}\left[I_b(r+1,c)-\bar{I}(r+1,c)\right]^2 \sum_{b=1}^{n}\left[I_b(r,c+1)-\bar{I}(r,c+1)\right]^2}} \tag{4.2-15}$$

where

$\bar{f}(r,c)$ is the arithmetic average of all the pixels in all bands at pixel location (r,c)

$f_b(r,c)$ is the value at location (r,c) in the bth band, with a total of n bands

Edge Detector Performance

- Objective and subjective evaluations can be useful.
- Success criteria must be defined, such as was used to develop the Canny algorithm: (1) Detection – find all real edges and not find any false edges. (2) Localization – the edges are found in the correct place. (3) Single response – no multiple edges found for a single edge.

Pratt's Figure of Merit (FOM): an objective measure developed by Pratt in 1978, which ranges from 0 (0%) for a missing edge to 1 (100%) for a perfectly found edge. It is defined as follows:

$$\text{FOM} = \frac{1}{I_N} \sum_{i=1}^{I_F} \frac{1}{1 + \alpha d^2} \tag{4.2-16}$$

where I_N is the maximum of I_I and I_F; I_I is the number of ideal edge points in the image; I_F is the number of edge points found by the edge detector; α is a scaling constant that can be adjusted to adjust the penalty for offset edges and d is the distance of a found edge point to an ideal edge point.

The distance measure can be defined in one of three ways:

1. **City block distance**, based on four-connectivity:

$$d = |r_1 - r_2| + |c_1 - c_2| \tag{4.2-17}$$

   With this distance measure, we can only move horizontally and vertically.

2. **Chessboard distance**, based on eight-connectivity:

$$d = \max\left(|r_1 - r_2|, |c_1 - c_2| \right) \tag{4.2-18}$$

   With this distance measure, we can move diagonally, as well as horizontally or vertically.

3. **Euclidean distance,** based on actual physical distance:

$$d = \left[(r_1 - r_2)^2 + (c_1 - c_2)^2 \right]^{1/2} \tag{4.2-19}$$

Line Detection
Hough Transform

- The Hough transform is an efficient method for line finding, input is a set of marked edge points. Consists of three primary steps based on using the normal representation of a line, $\rho = r \cos(\theta) + c \sin(\theta)$:
1. Define the desired increments on ρ and θ, Δ_ρ and Δ_θ, and quantize the space accordingly.
2. For every point of interest, typically points found by edge detectors that exceed a threshold value, plug the values for r and c into the line equation:

$$\rho = r \cos(\theta) + c \sin(\theta) \tag{4.3-1}$$

   Then, for each value of θ in the quantized space, solve for ρ.
3. For each $\rho \cdot \theta$ pair from step 2, record the r and c pair in the corresponding block in the quantized space. This constitutes a hit for that particular block.

After performing the Hough transform, postprocessing must be done to extract the line information.

Postprocessing

1. Perform the Hough transform on the input image containing marked edge points.
2. Threshold by using the parameter *line pixels*, the minimum number of pixels in a line, do the inverse Hough transform.
3. Perform a logical AND operation on the original image and output image from (2).
4. Apply an *edge linking* process to connect line segments; specifically, a *snake eating algorithm* (Figure 4.3-5):
   a.   A line segment is a snake. It can eat another snake within *connect distance* along *line angles*.
   b.   If a snake is less than *segment length*, it is removed.

Corner and Shape Detection

Corner Detection

- *Corners* are points with a high rate of change in more than one direction, which are also known as *points of interest*.
- Corners are robust features.
- Corners are useful features in object tracking.
- Corners are useful in matching multiple images, for example, creating 3-D models from stereo images.
- Corners are used by the human visual system to provide cues about object boundaries.

Moravec corner detector: simplest, not necessarily very robust, finds points of maximum contrast (see Figure 4.4-1):

$$\mathrm{MD}\big[I(r,c)\big]=\frac{1}{8}\sum_{i=r-1}^{r+1}\sum_{k=c-1}^{c+1}\big|I(r,c)-I(i,j)\big| \tag{4.4-1}$$

Harris corner detection algorithm: (1) Blur the image with a 2-D Gaussian convolution mask, (2) find the approximate brightness gradient in two perpendicular directions, for example, use the two Prewitt or Sobel masks, (3) blur the two brightness results with a 2-D Gaussian and (4) find the corner response function:

$$\mathrm{CRF}(r,c)=\Big[G\big(p_1^2\big)G\big(p_2^2\big)-\big[G\big(p_1p_2\big)\big]^2\Big]-\propto\big[G\big(p_1\big)+G\big(p_2\big)\big]^2 \tag{4.4-2}$$

(5) Threshold the corner response function and apply nonmaxima suppression, similar to what was done with the Canny (see Figure 4.4-2).

Frei–Chen masks: can be used for corner detection (see Figure 4.4-3).

Shape Detection with the Hough Transform

- **Extended Hough transform** is used to find shapes and mark boundaries that can be defined by analytical equations, such as circles or ellipses. The search space is a parameter space, where the parameters are found in the equation describing the shape of interest.
- **Generalized Hough transform** is used to find any arbitrary shape (Figure 4.4-4). It works by creating a description of the shape defined by a reference point and a table of line parameters and their intersections, which is called the R-table.

4.6 References and Further Reading

Companion reading regarding edge detection includes Nixon and Aguado (2020), Davies (2018), Gonzalez and Woods (2018), Sonka, Hlavac, and Boyle (2014), Pratt (2007), Forsyth and Ponce (2011) and Shapiro and Stockman (2001). More on thresholding algorithms and edge linking can be found in Gonzalez and Woods (2018), Davies (2018), Sonka, Hlavac, and Boyle (2014), Baxes (1994) and Dougherty and Lotufo (2009).

Details on the Marr–Hildreth algorithm can be found in Marr and Hildreth (1980), and for more information on the LoG and its relationship to biological vision systems, see Marr (1982) and Shapiro and Stockman (2001). More details on implementation of the LoG and the Marr–Hildreth algorithm can be found in Parker (1997) and Haralick and Shapiro (1992).

For more details on the Canny algorithm, see Sonka, Hlavac, and Boyle (2014), Jain, Kasturi, and Schunck (1995) and Canny (1986); on the Shen–Castan algorithms, see Shen and Castan (1992) and Parker (1997); and for more on the Boie–Cox algorithm, see Boie and Cox (1987) and Seul, O'Gorman, and Sammon (2000). Shapiro and Stockman (2001) have a different, and potentially useful, approach based on energy for using the Frei–Chen masks (Frei and Chen, 1977).

The multispectral edge detection equations were found in Sonka, Hlavac, and Boyle (2014) from the original paper Cervenka and Charvat (1987). The Hough transform as described here can also be found in Gonzalez and Woods (2018), Davies (2018) and the original patent in Hough (1962). Additional line finding methods can be found in Nixon and Aguado (2020) and Davies (2018), including the RANSAC (RANdom Sampling Consensus) statistical method. Additional resources for the extended Hough transform for finding circles and ellipses include Nixon and Aguado (2020), Davies (2018) and Haidekker (2011). More details on the generalized Hough transform and corner detection can be found in Nixon and Aguado (2020) and Sonka, Hlavac, and Boyle (2014). For algorithm details and code to implement the Harris corner detection algorithm, see Burger and Burge (2008) and Harris and Stephens (1988). Companion sources for the Moravec and Harris corner detectors include Davies (2018) and Sonka, Hlavac, and Boyle (2014).

Baxes, G.A., *Digital Image Processing: Principles and Applications*, New York: Wiley, 1994.

Boie, R.A. and Cox, I., Two dimensional optimum edge recognition using matched and wiener filters for machine vision. *Proceedings of the IEEE First International Conference on Computer Vision*, New York, pp. 450–456, 1987.

Burger, W., Burge, M.J., *Digital Image Processing: An Algorithmic Introduction Using Java*, New York: Springer, 2008.

Canny, J., A computational approach for edge detection. *IEEE Transactions on Pattern Analysis and Machine Intelligence*, Vol. 8, No. 6, pp. 679–698, 1986.

Cervenka, V., and Charvat, K, Survey of Image Processing Research Applicable to the Thematic Mapping Based on Aerocosmic Data (in Czech). Technical Report A 12-346-811, Prague, Czechoslovakia: Geodetic and Cartographic Institute, 1987.

Davies, E.R, *Computer Vision: Principles, Algorithms, Applications and Learning*, 5th Edition, Cambridge, MA: Academic Press, 2018.

Dougherty, G., *Digital Image Processing for Medical Applications*, Cambridge: Cambridge University Press, 2009.

Forsyth, D.A., Ponce, J., *Computer Vision*, Upper Saddle River, NJ: Pearson, 2011.

Frei, W., Chen, C.C., Fast boundary detection: A generalization and a new algorithm. *IEEE Transactions on Computers*, Vol. C-26, No. 10, pp. 988–998, 1977.

Gonzalez, R.C., Woods, R.E., *Digital Image Processing*, 4th Edition, London: Pearson, 2018.

Haidekker, M.A., *Advanced Biomedical Image Analysis*, Hoboken, NJ: Wiley, 2011.

Haralick, R.M., Shapiro, L.G., *Computer and Robot Vision*, Reading, MA: Addison-Wesley, 1992.

Harris, C.G, Stephens, M., A combined corner and edge detector, in Taylor, C.J, editor, *Proceedings of the 4th ALVEY Vision Conference*, pp. 147–151, Manchester: University of Manchester, 1988.

Hough, P.V.C, *Methods and Means for Recognizing Complex Patterns*, Washington, DC: U.S. Patent 3,069,654, 1962.

Jain, R., Kasturi, R., Schnuck, B.G., *Machine Vision*, New York: McGraw Hill, 1995.

Marr, D., *Vision*, New York: Freeman and Company, 1982.

Marr, D., Hildreth, E., Theory of edge detection, *Proceedings of the Royal Society*, B Vol. 207, pp. 187–217, 1980.

Nixon, M.S., Aguado, A.S., *Feature Extraction and Image Processing for Computer Vision*, 4th Edition, Cambridge, MA: Academic Press, 2020.

Parker, J.R., *Algorithms for Image Processing and Computer Vision*, New York: Wiley, 1997.

Pratt, W.K., *Digital Image Processing*, New York: Wiley, 2007.

Seul, M., O'Gorman, L., Sammon, M.J., *Practical Algorithms for Image Analysis*, Cambridge: Cambridge University Press, 2000.

Shapiro, L., Stockman, G., *Computer Vision*, Upper Saddle River, NJ: Prentice Hall, 2001.

Shen, J. and Castan, S., An optimal linear operator for step edge detection, *Computer Vision, Graphics, and Image Processing: Graphical Models and Understanding*, Vol. 54, No. 2, pp. 112–133, 1992.

Sonka, M., Hlavac, V., Boyle, R., *Image Processing, Analysis and Machine Vision*, 4th Edition, Boston, MA: Cengage Learning, 2014.

4.7 Exercises

Problems

1. Many edge detectors operate in a manner similar to convolution. What exactly does this mean?

2. What does a differential operator measure and how does this relate to edge detectors?

3. In dealing with noise in edge detection, there is a tradeoff between sensitivity and accuracy. Explain what this means.

4. Compare and contrast an ideal edge and a real edge in an image. Draw a picture of both.

5. (a) Explain the idea on which gradient edge detection operators are based. (b) How do the results differ if we use a second order compared to a first order derivative operator? (c) Explain what is meant by sub-pixel accuracy and how it relates to gradient-based edge detectors.

6. Find the results of applying Robert's edge detector to the following image. Use the absolute value form of the operator. For the result, don't worry about top row and left column.

$$\begin{bmatrix} 5 & 7 & 4 & 3 \\ 4 & 0 & 0 & 0 \\ 6 & 1 & 2 & 1 \end{bmatrix}$$

7. Find the results, magnitude and direction, of applying the Prewitt edge detector to the following image. For the result, ignore the outer rows and columns.

$$\begin{bmatrix} 0 & 8 & 0 & 0 \\ 0 & 8 & 0 & 0 \\ 0 & 8 & 0 & 0 \\ 0 & 8 & 0 & 0 \end{bmatrix}$$

8. Two of the three Laplacian masks given are based on eight-connectivity, and the other one is based on four-connectivity – which one? Devise a Laplacian-type edge detection mask based on six-connectivity.

9. Find the results of applying the Robinson compass masks to the following image. For the result, ignore the outer rows and columns. Keep track of the maximum magnitude and which mask corresponds to it.

$$\begin{bmatrix} 0 & 0 & 0 & 0 \\ 0 & 0 & 0 & 0 \\ 5 & 5 & 5 & 5 \\ 0 & 0 & 0 & 0 \end{bmatrix}$$

10. Use CVIPtools to explore the basic edge detection operators. (a) Run CVIPtools and load test images of your choice. As one of the test images, create a binary image of a circle with *Utilities→Create→Circle*. (b) Select *Utilities→Create→Add noise*. Add noise to your test images. Use both Gaussian and salt-and-pepper noise. (c) Select *Analysis→Edge/Line Detection*. Compare thresholding the output at different levels with the

Kirsch, Pyramid and Robinson edge detection operators. In CVIPtools, select the desired edge detector, select none for pre-filtering and select the desired threshold with post-threshold option. Alternately, select none for post-threshold and use the green *Threshold at* button in the top section – this allows for the testing of different threshold levels without the need to rerun the edge detection operation. (d) For the images containing noise, compare the resultant images with and without applying a lowpass filter as a preprocessing step (use the pre-filter option in CVIPtools).

11. Use CVIPtools to explore the basic edge detection operators. (a) Run CVIPtools and load test images of your choice. As one of the test images, create a binary image of a circle with *Utilities→Create→Circle.* (b) Select *Utilities→Create→Add noise*. Add noise to your test images. Use both Gaussian and salt-and-pepper noise. (c) Select *Analysis→Edge/Line Detection*. (d) Compare using different size kernels with the Sobel and Prewitt operators. In CVIPtools, select the desired edge detection operator and select the kernel size. (e) For the images containing noise, compare the resultant images with and without applying a lowpass filter as a preprocessing step (use the pre-filter option in CVIPtools). Also, compare the results with different size kernels (masks). Does the 3×3 or 7×7 provide better results in the presence of noise?

12. Use CVIPtools to explore the basic edge detection operators. (a) Run CVIPtools and load test images of your choice. As one of the test images, create a binary image of a circle with *Utilities→Create→Circle.* (b) Select *Utilities→Create→Add noise*. Add noise to your test images. Use both Gaussian and salt-and-pepper noise. (c) Select *Analysis→Edge/Line Detection*. (d) Use the Roberts and Laplacian and compare with and without using the Add to Original checkbox. (e) For the images containing noise, compare the resultant images with and without applying a lowpass filter as a preprocessing step (use the pre-filter option in CVIPtools).

13. The Canny algorithm for edge detection was developed based on a specific edge model, what is it? What are the three criteria used to develop the algorithm? How do the four algorithmic steps relate to these three criteria?

14. Use CVIPtools to explore the Laplacian and Frei–Chen edge detection operators. Use real images and create some simple geometric images with *Utilities→Create*. Additionally, add noise to the images. (a) In *Analysis→Edge/Line Detection*, select the Frei–Chen, compare the line subspace versus the edge subspace, with the projection option in CVIPtools. Experiment with various threshold angles, as well as post-threshold values. Examine the histogram to select good threshold values. Compare the threshold values that work the best to the images with and without noise, are they the same? Why or why not? (b) Using the Laplacian in *Analysis→Edge/Line Detection*, select pre-filtering with a Gaussian – this will perform a LoG filter. Examine the histogram to select good threshold values. (c) Use *Utilities→Filter→Specify a Filter* to input the values for the 5×5 LoG filter given in the text. Do this by selecting the 5×5 and then entering the values in the box (note: the <tab> key, or the mouse, can be used to move around the box), then select OK. Compare these results to the results from (b). Are they similar? Why or why not?

15. Use CVIPtools to explore the Canny, Boie–Cox and Shen–Castan algorithms. Use *Utilities→Create* to create circle with a radius of 32 and a blur radius of 128. (a) Select the Canny algorithm. Use the Low Threshold Factor = 1, High Threshold Factor = 0.5 and compare results with a variance of 0.5, 1.5 and 3. Next, use Low Threshold Factor = 1, High Threshold Factor = 1 and compare results with a variance of 0.5, 1.5 and 3. Now apply the Canny to a complex image of your choice. Experiment with the parameters until you achieve a good result. (b) Select the Boie–Cox algorithm and apply it to your blurred circle image. Experiment with the various parameters. Next, apply it to the complex image you used with the Canny. Which settings work best for your images? (c) Select the Shen–Castan algorithm and apply it to your blurred circle image. Use the Low Threshold Factor = 1, High Threshold Factor = 1, Smoothing Factor = 0.9, Window Size = 5 and compare results with a Thin Factor of 1, 3 and 6. Next, apply it to the complex image you used with the Canny. Which settings work best for your images? (d) Repeat (a)–(c), but add noise to the images.

16. Select a color image of your choice. Use *Utilities→Convert→Color Space* to explore edge detection using various color spaces, and *Utilities→Create→Extract Band* to operate on individual bands and use *Utilities→Create→Assemble Bands* to combine resulting bands into composite images. Devise an algorithm that works best for your particular image.

17. In the following image, find the distance between the points labeled *a* and *b* in the following image:

$$
\begin{bmatrix}
5 & 7 & 8 & b & 12 \\
3 & 6 & 7 & 6 & 6 \\
6 & a & 10 & 10 & 11 \\
7 & 7 & 0 & 0 & 0 \\
0 & 7 & 9 & 1 & 0
\end{bmatrix}
$$

(a) Use city block distance, (b) use chessboard distance and (c) use Euclidean distance

18. Given the following image, apply a Robert's edge detector, absolute value format, to the image (do not worry about the top row and leftmost column). Next, threshold the image with the following values and find Pratt's FOM for the found edge points. Let $\alpha = 0.5$ and use the chessboard distance measure. Threshold values: (a) 5, (b) 12 and (c) 22.

$$
\begin{bmatrix}
0 & 0 & 0 & 0 & 0 \\
0 & 0 & 0 & 0 & 0 \\
0 & 10 & 10 & 10 & 0 \\
0 & 0 & 0 & 0 & 0 \\
0 & 0 & 0 & 0 & 0
\end{bmatrix}
$$

19. List all the steps in the process of using the Hough transform for line finding.

20. Use CVIPtools to explore the Hough transform and the postprocessing edge linking algorithm on an artificial image. (a) Use *Utilities→Create* to create a circle and perform an edge detector of your choice, (b) threshold the resultant image, (c) perform the Hough transform on the thresholded image, input 5 for both *line pixels* and *segment length*, then select line angles 0, (d) 90, (e) 0–20, (f) 0–45, (g) 0–90, (h) 0–150 and (i) 0–180. Do the results make sense? How are the results affected by increasing the connect distance? How are the results affected by increasing the segment length?

21. Use CVIPtools to explore the Hough transform and the postprocessing edge linking algorithm on a real image. (a) select an image of your choice and perform an edge detection, (b) threshold the resultant image, (c) perform the Hough transform on the thresholded image, input 5 for both *line pixels* and *segment length*, then select line angles 0, (d) 90, (e) 0–20, (f) 0–45, (g) 0–90, (h) 0–150 and (i) 0–180. Do the results make sense? How are the results affected by increasing the *connect distance*? Find a *connect distance* that gives you the desired results. How are the results affected by increasing the *segment length*? Find a *segment length* that gives you the desired results.

4.7.1 Programming Exercises

These exercises can be implemented with CVIPlab in MATLAB or in C/C++.

Edge Detection – Roberts and Sobel

1. Write a function to implement the Roberts edge detector. Let the user select either the square root or the absolute value form. Be careful of data type to avoid overflow problems. Compare the results from the two methods by using the *Utilities→Compare* selection in CVIPtools.

   Note: If doing this exercise in C, the following will be useful:

   • The C functions for absolute value and square root are abs() and sqrt().

   • Note that you will need to deal with potential overflow problems, as the results may be greater than 255. This may be dealt with by using a floating point image structure as an intermediate image and then remapping the image when completed. This is done as follows:

```
Image *outputimage; /*declaration of image structure pointer*/
float **image_data; /* declaration of image data pointer*/
.....
outputimage = new_Image(PGM, GRAY_SCALE, no_of_bands, no_of_rows, no_of_cols, CVIP_FLOAT,
REAL); /*creating a new image structure*/
image_data = getData_Image(outputimage, bands); /*getting the data into an array that can be
accessed as: image_data[r][c] */
.....
outputimage = remap_Image(outputimage, CVIP_BYTE, 0, 255); /*remapping a float image to byte
size, this is done before writing the image to disk with the write_Image function*/
```

2. Write a function to implement the Sobel edge detector. The function should output an image that contains the Sobel magnitude, and it is remapped as with the Roberts. Test the function on gray level images of your choice.

3. Modify the functions to handle multiband (color) images.

4. Use the *Analysis→Edge/Line detection→Edge link* selection in CVIPtools to connect the lines in the output images. Note that this requires a binary image, so be sure to apply a threshold operation to the images first. Thresholding can be performed directly in this window by typing the threshold value in the entry box and clicking on the green *Threshold at* button next to the entered value.

Edge Detection – Robinson and Kirsch Compass Masks

1. Write a function to implement the Robinson compass masks edge detector.

2. Have the function return two images: one for the magnitude and one for the direction.

3. Modify the function to handle color images.

4. Modify the function to handle non-byte images.

5. Modify the function to allow the user to choose Robinson or Kirsch masks.

Otsu and K-means Thresholding

1. Write a function to implement the Otsu thresholding method described in Chapter 3.

2. Apply the Otsu function to magnitude images that have undergone Roberts, Sobel, Prewitt and Laplacian edge detection. Compare and contrast the results, especially comparing the first derivative based to the second derivative based models. Compare results to CVIPtools.

3. Write a function to implement the K-means thresholding method described in Chapter 3.

4. Apply the K-means function to magnitude images that have undergone Roberts, Sobel, Prewitt and Laplacian edge detection. Compare and contrast the results, especially comparing the first derivative based to the second derivative based models. Compare results to CVIPtools.

Edge Linking

1. Write a function to implement the simple edge linking process described in Section 4.2.3. Consider each point that has passed the threshold test and connect it to all other such points that are within a maximum distance. Let the user specify a maximum connect distance.

2. Test this function on various edge detected images. Do you think it works very well?

3. Implement a function for edge linking before thresholding using small neighborhoods as described in Section 4.2.3. Let the user specify maximum range for magnitude and direction to consider points as similar.

4. Test this function on various edge detected images. Do you think it works better than the first function?

4.8 Supplementary Exercises

Supplementary Problems

1. (a) Apply the Prewitt to the following image, keep both magnitude and direction. Do not calculate Prewitt for outer rows and columns. (b) Which points are connected if the magnitude can vary by 0.5 and the angle must be an exact match (assume eight-connectivity)?

$$
\begin{bmatrix}
1 & 1 & 1 & 1 & 1 & 1 & 1 \\
1 & 0 & 0 & 1 & 0 & 0 & 1 \\
1 & 1 & 1 & 1 & 1 & 1 & 1 \\
1 & 0 & 0 & 0 & 0 & 0 & 1 \\
1 & 1 & 1 & 1 & 1 & 1 & 1 \\
1 & 1 & 1 & 1 & 1 & 1 & 1 \\
1 & 1 & 0 & 0 & 1 & 1 & 1
\end{bmatrix}
$$

2.

a. Apply nonmaxima suppression to the pixels in the center column:

$$
\begin{bmatrix}
\leftarrow 70 & 116 \rightarrow & 220 \rightarrow \\
\leftarrow 20 & 90 \rightarrow & 51 \rightarrow \\
\leftarrow 88 & 95 \rightarrow & 127 \rightarrow
\end{bmatrix}
$$

b. Apply hysteresis thresholding to the following image with a high threshold of 200 and a low threshold of 150. Assume four-connectivity:

$$
\begin{bmatrix}
22 & 34 & 32 & 44 & 45 & 45 & 43 & 43 \\
27 & 11 & 12 & 11 & 12 & 11 & 12 & 18 \\
22 & 221 & 223 & 226 & 222 & 199 & 10 & 9 \\
2 & 3 & 3 & 178 & 4 & 4 & 5 & 4 \\
7 & 7 & 7 & 216 & 7 & 7 & 7 & 7 \\
18 & 23 & 23 & 166 & 23 & 66 & 65 & 65 \\
188 & 76 & 75 & 198 & 199 & 187 & 184 & 123 \\
222 & 177 & 188 & 222 & 222 & 14 & 14 & 13
\end{bmatrix}
$$

3. (a) Project the following subimage onto the Frei–Chen masks. (b) Find the projection angles onto the line subspace, the edge subspace and the average subspace. (c) Use the Frei–Chen weights to get the subimage back. Did you get it back exactly the same? Why or why not?

$$
\begin{bmatrix}
1 & 1 & 1 \\
0 & 0 & 0 \\
1 & 1 & 1
\end{bmatrix}
$$

4. Given the following image, apply the Otsu method to find the best threshold:

$$
\begin{bmatrix}
23 & 34 & 34 & 45 & 45 & 45 & 45 & 45 \\
23 & 12 & 77 & 12 & 12 & 77 & 12 & 12 \\
23 & 222 & 222 & 222 & 222 & 199 & 77 & 77 \\
3 & 3 & 3 & 199 & 3 & 3 & 3 & 3 \\
77 & 77 & 77 & 222 & 77 & 77 & 77 & 77 \\
23 & 23 & 23 & 199 & 23 & 65 & 65 & 65 \\
199 & 77 & 77 & 199 & 199 & 199 & 199 & 199 \\
222 & 222 & 222 & 222 & 222 & 12 & 12 & 12
\end{bmatrix}
$$

5. (a) Explain how the extended Hough transform could be used to find ellipses that are aligned along the row or column axis. (b) How many dimensions is the search space? What are they? (c) How can this be extended to find ellipses of any orientation?

6. (a) If the Laplacian masks as defined in this chapter are applied to an image, such as in CVIPtools, the sign (positive or negative) on the results seems to be the opposite of what is shown in Figure 4.2-5. Why is that? (b) Is the Type 1 Laplacian mask actually isotropic in all directions?

7. Explain how the Hough transform can be used to find gaps between line segments on a given line. Allow for different connectivity and distance definitions.

4.8.1 Supplementary Programming Exercises

These exercises can be implemented with CVIPlab in MATLAB or in C/C++.

Canny Edge Detection

1. Write a function to implement the Canny edge detection algorithm. Use a fixed 3×3 Gaussian approximation mask for step one and the gradient edge detector given in the chapter for step 2.

2. Modify your function to allow for any size Gaussian up to a 9×9 in step one and a 3×3 Prewitt or Robinson for step two.

3. Compare your results to CVIPtools. Are they the same? Why or why not?

Boie–Cox Edge Detection

1. Use the references to research the Boie–Cox algorithm.

2. Write a function to implement the algorithm.

3. Compare your results to CVIPtools. Are they the same? Why or why not?

Shen–Castan Edge Detection

1. Use the references to research the Shen–Castan algorithm.

2. Write a function to implement the algorithm.

3. Compare your results to CVIPtools. Are they the same? Why or why not?

Hough Transform

1. Write a function to implement a Hough transform. Let the user enter the line angles of interest and the minimum number of pixels per line.

2. Compare your results to those obtained in CVIPtools.

3. Extend your Hough transform function to find circles.

4. Extend your Hough transform function to find ellipses.

Moravec Corner Detection

1. Write a function to implement the Moravec corner detector.
2. Compare your results to CVIPtools. Are they the same? Why or why not?

Harris Corner Detection

1. Write a function to implement the Harris corner detection algorithm. Write a separate function for each step and output the intermediate images.
2. Compare your results to CVIPtools. Are they the same? Why or why not?

Generalized Hough

1. Write a function to implement the generalized Hough transform.
2. Note that it is helpful to define a standard size and orientation. Use a size of 32 × 32, and orientation so that the axis of least second moment is horizontal, and the center of area is used as the reference point.
3. Experiment with random shapes created in CVIPtools with *Utilities→Create→Black Image* and *Utilities→Create→Border Mask*.

5

Segmentation

5.1 Introduction and Overview

Image segmentation is one of the most important processes for many computer vision and image analysis applications. Segmenting the image correctly into real objects of interest is critical for object classification which will determine the success or failure of the algorithm. For example, in a robotic control application that needs to remove "bad" parts from an assembly line, incorrect classification will result in bad parts being shipped to the customer or good parts being removed. In either case, the cost to the manufacturer is increased. In a medical diagnostic application, a poor classification process can be even more costly in terms of both dollars and human life.

In many applications, the illumination system is critical to acquiring an image that has a reasonable chance for a successful segmentation. The lighting system in industrial inspection applications can be controlled and designed to make the segmentation process easier. Special purpose lighting is often used in these types of applications where the designer can control the environment. Other applications may not allow for environmental control, such as satellite, surveillance or automated driving applications, but the imaging system designer can specify the types of sensors to be used. For example, infrared imaging sensors are a natural choice for image acquisition in applications where the objects of interest radiate heat, such as people, engines or factories. Satellites typically acquire data across a wide range of the electromagnetic spectrum, so they require sensors that will respond to all these frequencies and thus allow for the collection of image data that can be used for many different types of applications. These examples all serve to illustrate the importance of the application feedback loop in the image analysis process (see Figure 3.1-3).

5.1.1 Segmentation System Model and Preprocessing

The segmentation system model discussed here is a three-stage process. As shown in Figure 5.1-1, the three stages are (1) preprocessing, (2) segmentation and (3) postprocessing. During the *Preprocessing* stage, the image is simplified to facilitate the segmentation process itself. The simplification is usually done by filtering or grouping small areas or brightness values of pixels together. Typical operations that may be performed during this stage include gray level quantization, spatial quantization, median filtering, Kuwahara filtering, anisotropic diffusion filters and superpixel extraction. The second and primary stage of the process is the *Segmentation* method itself, which will be discussed in the following sections and stage three, *Postprocessing*, will be further explored in the section on morphological filters.

Figure 5.1-2 shows output images from preprocessing operations, and we can see that this simplification of the image itself can aid in the segmentation process. In some cases, it may be difficult to distinguish the change visually, so we have included the labeled number of connected objects with each image. The superpixel algorithm, referred to as the *simple linear iterative clustering* (SLIC) method, is essentially the k-means clustering algorithm but using a 5-dimensional vector containing the red, green, blue components and the row and column coordinates. For some applications, the SLIC algorithm can be used as a segmentation method itself. With k-means clustering, we can specify the value for k, which in this case is the number of superpixels in the output image. In Figure 5.1-3,

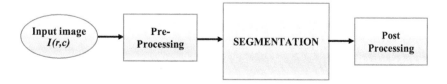

FIGURE 5.1-1

Image segmentation process. Image segmentation can be modeled as a three-stage process: (1) preprocessing to simply the image, (2) the segmentation method itself and (3) postprocessing, usually in the form of morphology filtering, to further refine the segmentation.

DOI: 10.1201/9781003221135-5

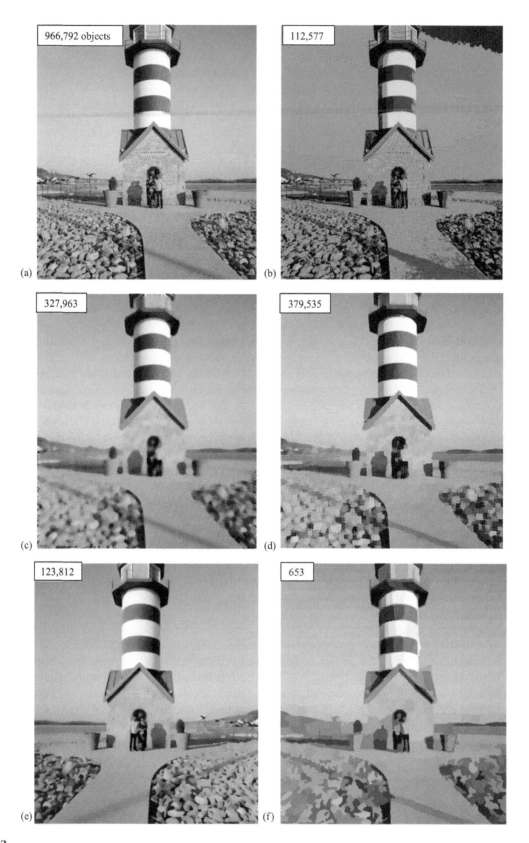

FIGURE 5.1-2
Image segmentation preprocessing. (a) Original image, (b) gray level quantization, (c) median filter, (d) Kuwahara filter, (e) anisotropic diffusion filter and (f) superpixel. We can see the simplification by the number of connected objects in the processed images compared to the orginal. The superpixel approach has the greatest reduction, so for some applications is used as a segmentation method itself.

FIGURE 5.1-3
Superpixel algorithm with different K values. For some applications, the superpixel approach is used as a segmentation method itself. (a) Original image with the found superpixel grid imposed with $K = 300$, (b) the image with 300 superpixels, (c) grid with $K = 50$, (d) the image with 50 superpixels (e) grid with $K = 20$ and (f) the image with 20 superpixels.

we see application of the superpixel algorithm to an image with various values for the number of superpixels. Details of the preprocessing methods can be explored in the references.

5.1.2 Image Segmentation Categories

The goal of image segmentation is to find regions that represent objects or meaningful parts of objects. Image segmentation methods will look for objects that either have some measure of homogeneity within themselves or have some measure of contrast with the objects on their border. The homogeneity and contrast measures can include features such as gray level, color and texture. In Figure 5.1-4 are the four categories of image segmentation methods: (1) region growing/shrinking, (2) clustering, (3) boundary detection and (4) deep learning. The first category, region growing and shrinking, is limited to the (r, c) image space, but the clustering category can be expanded to look for clusters in multi-dimensional feature spaces that may or may not include the (r, c) spatial domain. Boundary detection uses an indirect method of segmenting the image by finding the boundaries that separate objects, as opposed to finding the object themselves. Figure 5.1-4c has a result from a Canny edge detector, and we can see that edge

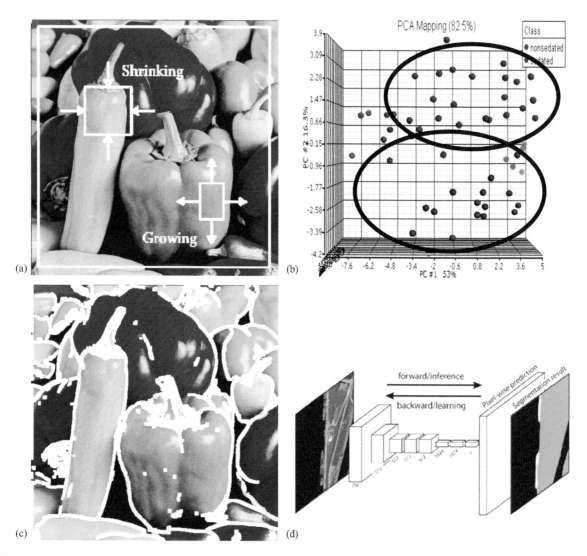

FIGURE 5.1-4

Image segmentation categories. (a) Region growing/shrinking is performed by finding homogeneous regions and changing them until they no longer meet the homogeneity criteria, (b) clustering looks for data that can grouped in domains other than the spatial (r,c) domain, a 3-D mathematical space is shown, in general, the space can be N-dimensional, (c) boundary detection works indirectly by finding places of change to separate objects and (d) deep learning approaches are trained with many thousands of images so that each pixel is classified into one of the assigned classes.

detection alone will not necessarily provide an adequate boundary detection method for segmentation. Deep learning approaches to image segmentation have had great success in a number of application areas; but they "learn" by being indirectly trained with tens of thousands, or even millions, of sample images and will classify each pixel based on the functionality of the trained network. In this chapter, we will discuss algorithms that are representative of each of these categories.

5.2   Region Growing and Shrinking

Region growing and shrinking methods segment the image into regions by operating principally in the row and column, (r, c), based image space. Some of the techniques used are local in which small areas of the image are processed at a time, while others are global with the entire image considered during processing. Methods that can combine local and global techniques, such as **split and merge**, are referred to as state space techniques and use graph structures to represent the regions and their boundaries. The data structure most commonly used for this is the quadtree. A tree is a data structure which has nodes that point to (connect) the elements. The top element is called the parent, and the connected elements are called children. In a *quadtree*, each node can have four children; this is illustrated in Figure 5.2-1. This data structure facilitates the splitting and merging of regions.

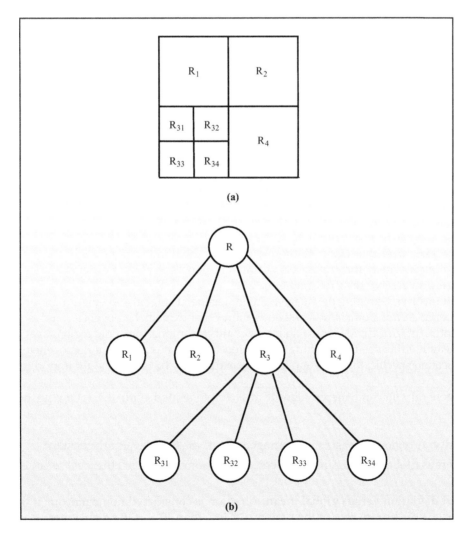

FIGURE 5.2-1
Quadtree data structure. (a) A partitioned image where R_i represents different regions and (b) the corresponding quadtree data structure. R denotes the entire image, and at each level, another subscript is added as shown.

Various split and merge algorithms have been developed, but they all are most effective when heuristics applicable to the domain under consideration can be applied. This gives a starting point for the initial split. In general, the **split and merge** technique proceeds as follows:

1. Define a homogeneity test. This involves defining a homogeneity measure, which may incorporate brightness, color, texture or other application-specific information, and determining a criterion the region must meet to pass the homogeneity test.
2. Split the image into equal-sized regions.
3. Calculate the homogeneity measure for each region.
4. If the homogeneity test is passed for a region, then a merge is attempted with its neighbor(s). If the criterion is not met, the region is split.
5. Continue this process until all regions pass the homogeneity test.

There are many variations of this algorithm. For example, we can start out at the global level, where we consider the entire image as our initial region, and then follow an algorithm similar to the above, but without any region merging. Algorithms based on splitting only are called **multiresolution** algorithms. Alternately, we can start at the smallest level and only merge with no region splitting. This merge-only approach is one example of region growing methods. Often the results from all of these approaches will be quite similar, with the differences apparent only in computation time. Parameter choice, such as the minimum block size allowed for splitting, will heavily influence the computational burden as well as the spatial resolution available in the results.

The user-defined homogeneity test is largely application dependent, but the general idea is to find features that will be similar within an object and different from the surrounding objects. In the simplest case, the gray level is used as the feature of interest. Here, the gray level variance can be used as our homogeneity measure and we can define a homogeneity test that requires the gray level variance within a region to be less than a specified threshold. We can define *gray level variance* as follows:

$$\text{Gray level variance} = \frac{1}{N-1} \sum_{(r,c) \in \text{REGION}} [I(r,c) - \bar{I}]^2$$

$$\text{where} \qquad \bar{I} = \frac{1}{N} \sum_{(r,c) \in \text{REGION}} I(r,c)$$

(5.2-1)

Note that the sum is taken over the region of interest and N is the number of pixels in the region. The variance is basically a measure of how widely the gray levels within a region vary. Higher order statistics can be used for features, such as texture, and are explored in Chapter 6.

A similar approach involves searching the image for a homogeneous region and enlarging it until it no longer meets the homogeneity criteria. At this point, a new region is found that exhibits homogeneity and is grown. This process continues until the entire image is divided into regions. With this technique, the initial regions are called *seed regions* and their selection can heavily influence the resulting segmented image. The choice of a homogeneity metric for the seed regions will be application specific; for some applications, texture may be of paramount importance, and for others, it may be color.

In CVIPtools, a general split and merge algorithm is implemented with the following homogeneity criteria available:

1. **Pure uniformity**: A region is considered homogeneous if the gray levels are constant.
2. **Local mean versus global mean**: A region is considered homogeneous if the local mean is greater than the global mean.
3. **Local standard deviation versus global mean**: A region is considered homogeneous if the local standard deviation, which is the square root of the variance, is less than 10% of the global mean.
4. **Variance**: A region is considered homogeneous if a minimum percentage of the pixels, specified by the CVIPtools parameter *Percentage*, are within two standard deviations of the local mean, unless the standard deviation exceeds a maximum *Threshold* value.

5. **Weighted gray level distance**: A region is considered homogeneous if the weighted gray level value, which is based on the mode and the gray level distance from the mode weighted by the distribution, is less than a specified *Threshold* value.

6. **Texture**: A region is considered homogeneous if the four quadrants of the region have similar texture, based on five of the textural features defined in Chapter 6; specifically, *energy, inertia, correlation, inverse difference* and *entropy*. The parameters specified are *pixel distance* and *similarity*.

Figure 5.2-2 shows the results of applying the split and merge algorithm to an image with various homogeneity criteria. The original image is 512 × 512 pixels, and the *Entry-level* parameter determines the size of the initial regions.

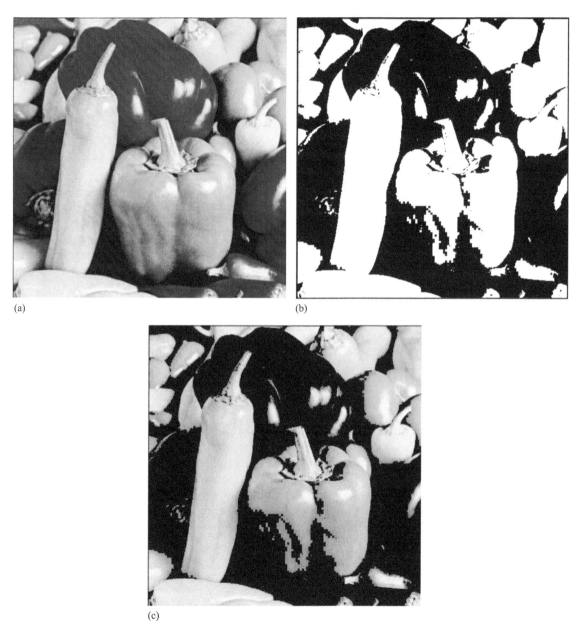

(a)   (b)

(c)

FIGURE 5.2-2
Segmentation with the split and merge algorithm. (a) Original image, (b) split and merge results with *local standard deviation versus global mean* as the homogeneity criterion, and the PCT selected and (c) logical AND of the original and the segmented image. Here, we can see that these parameters separate the green peppers from the red peppers, with the shiny reflections and shadows caused by the lighting being the only potential difficulties.

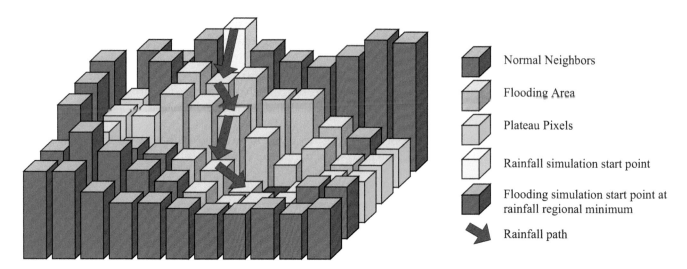

FIGURE 5.2-3
The watershed algorithm. The height of the bar corresponds to the brightness of the pixel. A rainfall simulation starts at a high point and flows down to the lowest level. The flooding procedure starts and floods the area until two pools meet and a dam is built. The resulting pools are the watershed segments.

For example, if the entry level is 1, the image is divided once (see Figure 5.2-1), so the initial region size is 256×256 for a 512×512 image. If the entry level is 2, the initial region is 128×128 for a 512×512 image. In this figure, the entry level was set to 8, which provides an initial region size of $512/2^8 \times 512/2^8$ or 2×2 pixels. Note that this particular image is probably not a good candidate for texture-based segmentation due to the smooth surface of the peppers.

Another segmentation method we include in the region growing and shrinking category is the **watershed segmentation algorithm**. This method is often classified as a morphological technique because it is implemented with morphological methods (see Section 5.7). We include it here since it operates in the row- and column-based image space. The watershed algorithm is a morphological technique based on the idea of modeling a gray level image as a topographic surface, with higher gray levels corresponding to higher elevations (see Figure 5.2-3). The image is then flooded with a rainfall simulation, and pools of water are created corresponding to segments within the image. When rising water reaches a point where two pools will merge, a dam is built to prevent the merging. These dams are the *watershed lines*, which mark the boundaries used to segment the image into its various regions.

Many different variations of the watershed algorithm can be implemented. The watershed segmentation algorithm as implemented in CVIPtools was initially designed to separate a single object from the background in color images. It provides the user with two parameters – merge and threshold. The *merge* parameter has a checkbox, to merge or not to merge. If merge is selected, the *threshold* parameter determines the amount of merging that will occur. The threshold parameter works by creating a histogram using the average gray value within each watershed segment. Next, it finds the maximum value in the histogram and merges this group with adjacent lower and higher gray levels until the threshold is reached. The threshold represents the percent of total area in the image.

In Figure 5.2-4, we show a skin lesion image where the goal is to separate the lesion (tumor) from normal skin. The results of the watershed segmentation are shown along with various values for the threshold. In Figure 5.2-4c, we can tell that the maximum histogram value corresponds to the bright area to the left and right of the lesion. As the threshold is increased in the following three images, we can see this area expand as it is merged with neighboring gray level values.

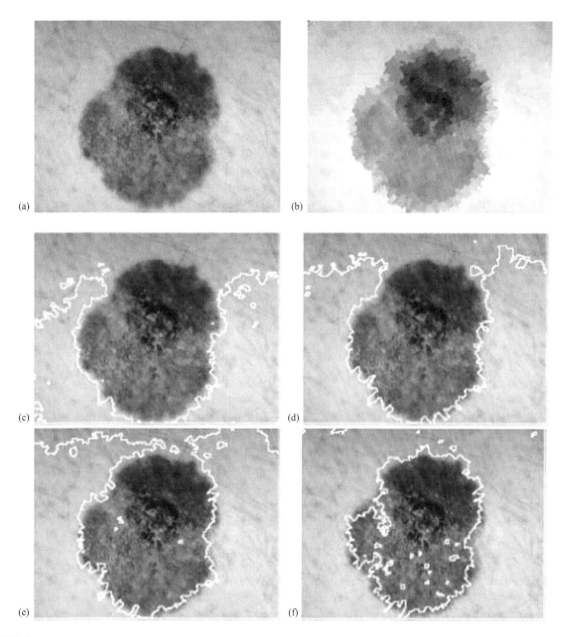

FIGURE 5.2-4
Watershed segmentation. (a) Original image of a skin lesion, (b) result of watershed segmentation without merging, (c) borders shown after merging with a threshold of 0.4, (d) merge with a threshold of 0.5, (e) merge with a threshold of 0.6 and (f) merge with a threshold of 0.7.

5.3 Clustering Techniques

Clustering techniques are image segmentation methods by which individual elements are placed into groups; these groups are based on some measure of similarity within the group. The major difference between these techniques and the region growing techniques is that domains other than the row and column, (r, c), based image space (the spatial domain) may be considered as the primary domain for clustering. Some of these other domains include color spaces, histogram spaces or complex feature spaces. *Note that the terms domain and space are used interchangeably here, these terms both refer to some abstract N-dimensional mathematical space, not to be confused with the spatial domain, which refers to the row and column, (r, c), image space.*

What is done is to look for clusters in the domain, or mathematical space, of interest. The simplest method is to divide the space of interest into regions by selecting the center or median along each dimension and splitting it there; this can be done iteratively until the space is divided into the specific number of regions needed. This method is used in the SCT/Center and PCT/Median segmentation algorithms. This method will be most effective if the algorithm is designed in conjunction with the application and the mathematical space being used. Otherwise, the center or median split alone may not find good clusters.

The next level of complexity uses an adaptive and intelligent method to decide where to divide the space. These methods include histogram thresholding and other, more complex feature-space-based statistical methods. Two histogram thresholding methods for binary segmentation were discussed in Chapter 3, the Otsu method and the K-means for two clusters (*Auto Single Threshold* in CVIPtools). The K-means algorithm can be used for segmentation and is also used in the superpixel preprocessing step with the SLIC algorithm. For the more complex methods, representative algorithms will be discussed conceptually here, and a detailed look will be taken at two application-specific algorithms.

Recursive region splitting is a clustering method that was a technique developed in the early days of image segmentation. This method uses a thresholding of histograms technique to segment the image. A set of histograms is calculated for a specific set of features, and then each of these histograms is searched for distinct peaks (see Figure 5.3-1). The best peak is selected and the image is split into regions based on this thresholding of the histogram. One of the first algorithms based on these concepts proceeds as follows:

1. Consider the entire image as one region and compute histograms for each component of interest (for example, red, green and blue for a color image).
2. Apply a peak finding test to each histogram. Select the best peak and put thresholds on either side of the peak. Segment the image into two regions based on this peak.
3. Smooth the binary thresholded image so that only a single connected subregion is left.
4. Repeat steps 1–3 for each region until no new subregions can be created, that is, no histograms have significant peaks.

Many of the parameters of this algorithm are application specific. For example, what peak finding test do we use and what is a "significant" peak? An example of histogram thresholding-based image segmentation is shown in Figure 5.3-2. In addition to the two basic binary thresholding algorithms in CVIPtools, the Otsu and automatic single threshold method, we have two gray level or color histogram thresholding-based segmentation methods, called **histogram thresholding** and **fuzzy c-means**. These are explored in the exercises at the end of this chapter and details of these particular algorithms can be found in the references.

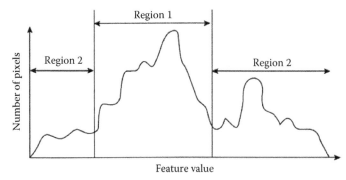

Two thresholds are selected, one on each side of the best peak. The image
is then split into two regions. Region 1 corresponds to those pixels with
feature values between the selected thresholds, known as those in the peak
region. Region 2 consists of those pixels with feature values outside the threshold.

FIGURE 5.3-1
Histogram peak finding.

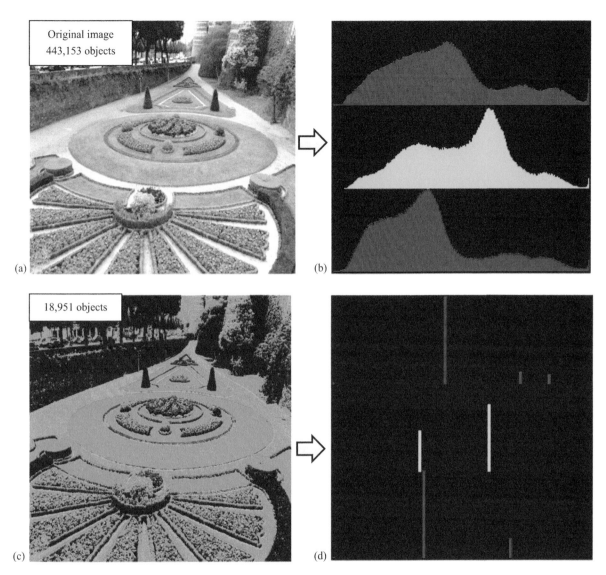

FIGURE 5.3-2
Histogram thresholding segmentation. (a) Original image and (b) its histogram; (c) image after histogram thresholding segmentation and (d) its histogram. The number of connected objects is displayed on each and we can see a reduction in the number of objects by a factor more than 23. This data reduction is an important part of image analysis. By comparing the histograms, we can see the peaks that were selected.

The **SCT/Center** color segmentation algorithm was initially developed for the identification of variegated coloring in skin tumor images. Variegated coloring is a feature believed to be highly predictive in the diagnosis of melanoma, the deadliest form of skin cancer. The spherical coordinate transform (SCT) was chosen for this segmentation method, as it decouples the color information from the brightness information. The brightness levels may vary with changing lighting conditions; so by using the two dimensional color subspace defined by two angles (Figure 5.3-3a), we have a more robust algorithm.

If a plane is sliced through the RGB color space, we can model a color triangle (Figure 5.3-3b). The vertices of the color triangle were chosen to bear some correlation to the human visual system. The placement of blue at the top of the triangle and the way in which the spherical transform was defined relate to the physiological fact that the cones in the human visual system that see blue are more discriminatory than the red or green sensitive cones. We can segment the image by taking the color triangle and dividing it into blocks based on limits on the two angles. Figure 5.3-3c shows the shape of the resulting blocks. We can see that for a region defined by a range of minima and maxima on the two angles, the side of the region that is closest to the blue vertex is shorter than the side that is closest to the line that joins the red and green vertices.

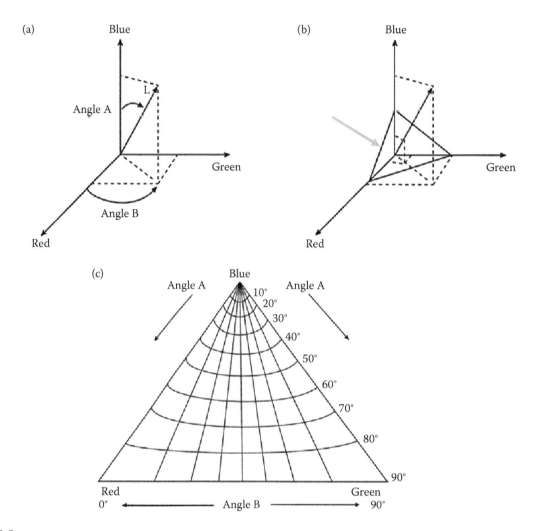

FIGURE 5.3-3
SCT/center color segmentation and color triangle. (a) The spherical coordinate transform separates the red, green and blue information into a 2-D color space defined angles A and B and a 1-D brightness space defined by L. (b) The color triangle in RGB space. (c) The color triangle showing regions defined by 10° increments on angle A and angle B.

Also, the distortion caused by the transform facilitates the perception-based aspect of the image segmentation; the closer the perimeter of the triangle, the larger the region that is defined by a fixed angle range. This is analogous to the observation that as the white point is approached in the color space, a greater number of hues will be observable in a fixed area by the human visual system than on the perimeter of the color triangle. This observation is application specific, since it only applies to colors from white (in the center of the triangle) to the green and red vertices. Skin tumor colors typically range from white out to the red vertex.

The SCT/Center segmentation algorithm is outlined as follows:

1. Convert the (R, G, B) triple into spherical coordinates – (L, angle A, angle B).
2. Find the minima and maxima of angle A and angle B.
3. Divide the subspace, defined by the maxima and minima, into equal-sized blocks.
4. Calculate the RGB means for the pixel values in each block.
5. Replace the original pixel values with the corresponding RGB means.

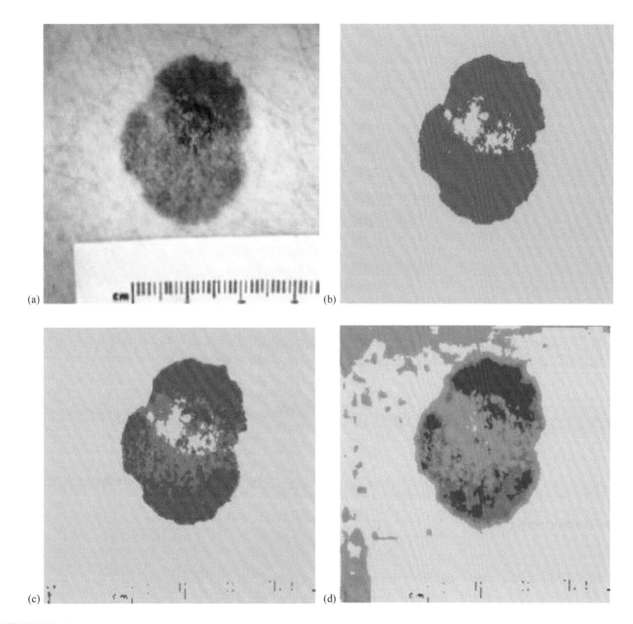

FIGURE 5.3-4
SCT/Center segmentation algorithm applied to a skin lesion image. (a) Original image, (b) SCT/Center segmentation result with two colors, (c) segmentation into four colors and (d) segmentation into six colors.

For the identification of variegated coloring in the skin tumor application, it was determined that segmenting the image into four colors was optimal. An example of this segmentation method is shown in Figure 5.3-4.

The **PCT/Median** color segmentation algorithm was developed because, for certain features other than variegated coloring, the results provided by the previously described algorithm were not totally satisfactory for skin lesion segmentation. This algorithm is based on the principal components transform (PCT). The median split part of the algorithm is based on an algorithm developed for color compression to map 24 bits per pixel color images into images requiring an average of 2-bits per pixel.

The PCT is based on statistical properties of the image, and it can be applied to any K-dimensional mathematical space. In this case, the PCT is applied to the three-dimensional color space. It was believed that the PCT used in conjunction with the median split algorithm would provide a satisfactory color image segmentation,

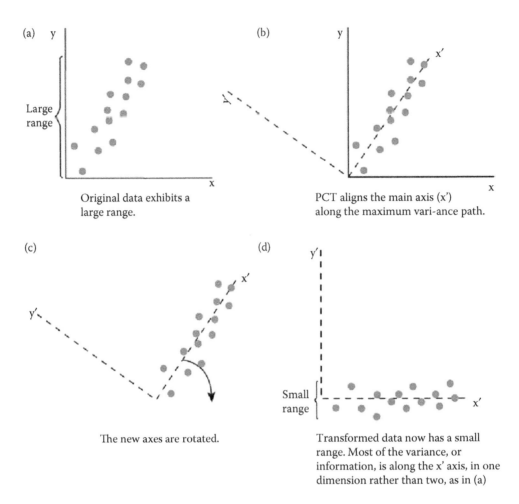

(a) Original data exhibits a large range.

(b) PCT aligns the main axis (x') along the maximum vari-ance path.

(c) The new axes are rotated.

(d) Transformed data now has a small range. Most of the variance, or information, is along the x' axis, in one dimension rather than two, as in (a)

FIGURE 5.3-5
Principal components transform.

since the PCT aligns the main axis along the maximum variance path in the data set (see Figure 5.3-5). In pattern recognition theory, a feature with large variance is said to have large discriminatory power. Once we have transformed the color data so that most of the information (variance) lies along a principal axis, we proceed to divide the image into different colors by using a median split on the transformed data.

The PCT/Median segmentation algorithm proceeds as follows:

1. Find the PCT for the RGB image. Transform the RGB data using the PCT.
2. Perform the median split algorithm: find the axis that has the maximal range (initially it will be the PCT axis). Divide the data along this axis so that there are equal numbers of points on either side of the split – the median point. Continue splitting at the median along the maximum range segment until the desired number of colors is reached.
3. Calculate averages for all the pixels falling within a single parallelepiped (box).
4. Map each pixel to the closest average color values, based on a Euclidean distance measure.

For the skin tumor application, it was determined that the optimum number of colors was dependent upon the feature of interest. Results of this segmentation algorithm are shown in Figure 5.3-6. Here, we observe that if the image is segmented with more colors, then more of the details in the image are retained (as expected), while a smaller number of colors will segment the image on a coarser scale, leaving only relatively large features. Selection of the number of colors for segmentation has a significant impact on the difficulty of the feature identification task – if the proper number of colors is selected for a specific feature, it can make the feature identification process relatively easy.

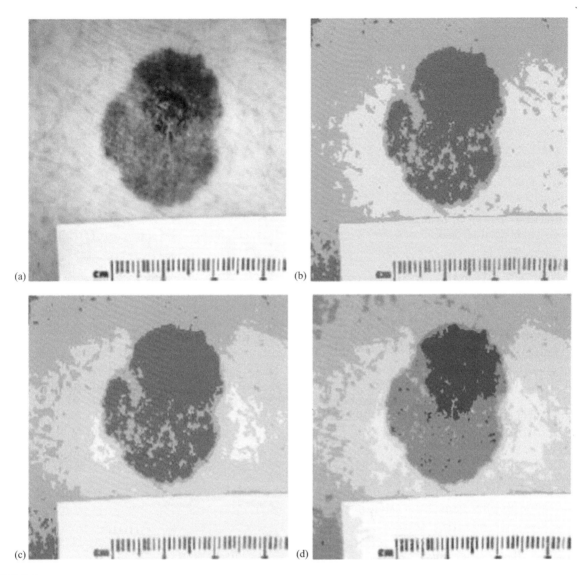

FIGURE 5.3-6
PCT/Median segmentation algorithm, (a) Original image, (b) PCT/Median segmented image with three colors, (c) PCT/Median segmented image with six colors and (d) PCT/Median segmented image with eight colors.

5.4 Boundary Detection

Boundary detection, as a method of image segmentation, is performed by finding the boundaries between objects, thus indirectly defining the objects. This method usually starts by marking points that may be a part of an edge. These points are then merged into connected segments and the segments are then merged into object boundaries. The edge detectors previously described are used to mark points of rapid change, thus indicating the possibility of an edge. These edge points represent local discontinuities in specific features, such as brightness, color or texture.

After the edge detection operation has been performed, the next step is to threshold the results. One method to do this is to consider the histogram of the edge detection results, looking for the best valley manually (Figure 5.4-1). This method works well when we can control the lighting conditions, such as with industrial applications. By controlling the lighting we can create good background to object contrast, resulting in a bimodal histogram. We have already explored two algorithms to do this, the K-means algorithm and the Otsu method. We have also seen that most edge detectors result in unimodal histograms and that 10%–25% of the mean generally provides reasonable results. We can also apply line or shape detectors, if we know the shape of the objects of interest.

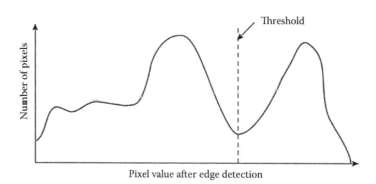

FIGURE 5.4-1
Edge detection thresholding via histogram. The histogram can be examined manually to select a good threshold. This method is easiest with a bimodal (two peaks) histogram. Alternately, the threshold can be found automatically with the Otsu method or the K-means algorithm.

One of the most flexible shape detection methods is the generalized Hough defined in Chapter 4. The implementations for this method can be divided into two primary categories: (1) the table-based methods and (2) the centroidal profile. Details for the *R*-table method are as follows: (1) Find the center of area of the object, (2) find the axis of least second moment for the object, (3) align this axis along the horizontal, (4) define $\Delta\theta$ which determines the shape resolution and (5) create a table called the *R*-table and fill with values corresponding to the ratio of adjacent radii length for each value of θ. These ratios are used so that the shape is size-invariant, without the need to normalize the object size explicitly. The idea is that the *R*-tables for the shape of the objects of interest are stored and the found shape can be compared to the *R*-tables. For segmentation, the one with the closest match can be filled with the same color or gray level. The closest match can be determined by finding the smallest error:

$$\text{Error} = \sum_i \left(R_i/R_{i+1} - U_i/U_{i+1} \right)^2 \tag{5.4-1}$$

where R_i are from a database sample and U_i from the unknown object, and i is for each increment of θ
    Alternately, the absolute value form can be used (Figure 5.4-2):

$$\text{Error} = \sum_i \left| R_i/R_{i+1} - U_i/U_{i+1} \right| \tag{5.4-2}$$

The second method to implement the generalized Hough is called the centroidal profile. Here, instead of using a table, we create a graph of the radii versus the angle, an (R, θ) plot, as shown in Figure 5.4-3. Now, for any particular

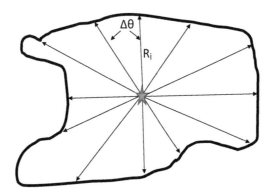

FIGURE 5.4-2
Use of a radius table with the generalized Hough transform. The star is located at the center of area, and the horizontal axis is orientated along the axis of least second moment. The increment $\Delta\theta$ defines the shape resolution; the smaller the increment, the greater the resolution. The radii from the centroid to the shape boundary are represented by R_i. The *R*-table can then be populated with the ratio of adjacent radii. By using ratios, we avoid the need for size normalization.

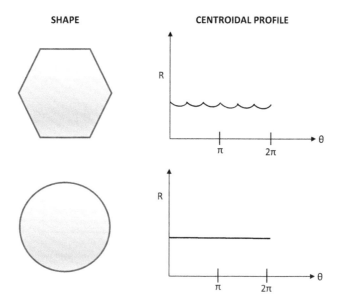

SHAPE CENTROIDAL PROFILE

FIGURE 5.4-3
Centroidal profile and the generalized Hough transform. On the left is the shape and on the right is the centroidal profile.

shape of interest, we can store the centroidal profile and compare the boundary of our found image points to the stored profiles. To make the process rotationally invariant, we can slide the found boundary along the stored boundaries to find the best match, which also allows us to determine the orientation of the object relative to the stored boundary. The closest match can be determined by finding the smallest error:

$$\text{Error} = \sum_i (R_i - U_i)^2 \tag{5.4-3}$$

where R_i are from a database sample and U_i from the unknown object, and i is for each increment of θ. Alternately, the absolute value form can be used in the following equation:

$$\text{Error} = \sum_i |R_i - U_i| \tag{5.4.4}$$

Ratios of adjacent values, as in Equation (5.4-1) or (5.4-2), can also be used to calculate error. Note that the *Generalized Hough* is also a simple pattern classification method.

Another approach to image segmentation via boundary detection is the use of active contours or snakes. For these types of methods, an initial boundary must be estimated or given, and then the active contour or snake is deformed by consideration of application features of interest. Typically, this is done mathematically by minimizing an energy function and is controlled by the features of interest and the application. As the border is deformed, there are vectors, or forces, pushing it in, and vectors, or forces, pushing it out in an attempt to reach equilibrium.

We implemented a *gradient vector flow* (GVF) snake for an application to find skin lesion borders. The algorithm is initialized by a rough approximation to the border, and it is obtained, in this case, by preprocessing the original image and then drawing an approximate border. This initial border, referred to as a snake, is then iteratively processed to converge on the actual border. For this application, the features of interest selected to control the process include the image edge strengths and internal properties such as smoothness (texture).

To use the algorithm, the image must be properly preprocessed to segment the image, and then a line is drawn around the object of interest in the segmented image. For a skin lesion image, typical preprocessing includes a rough image segmentation followed by morphological filtering. In Figure 5.4-4, we see the results from application of the GVF snake to a skin lesion image. The original image is preprocessed by these steps: (1) Otsu thresholding segmentation, (2) a logical NOT operation, (3) a color to gray level conversion using a luminance transform, (4) a binary threshold operation, (5) morphological dilation with a circular element of diameter of 5

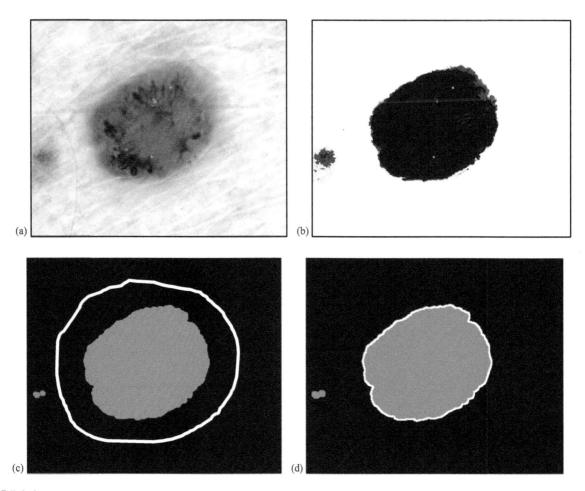

FIGURE 5.4-4
Gradient vector flow snake applied to a skin lesion image. The gradient vector flow (GVF) snake needs preprocessing for use with real images. (a) Original image; (b) image after an Otsu thresholding segmentation; (c) Otsu image after a logical NOT, color to gray conversion, a binary threshold operation, morphological filtering, multiplication by 0.5 so the white border will be visible and the initial border drawn around the object of interest; and (d) image after GVF snake and morphological dilation to thicken the border.

and (6) multiplying by 0.5 so that the white border will be visible. Figure 5.4-4 shows that real images, properly preprocessed, can benefit from using the GVF snake for border delineation.

5.5 Deep Learning Segmentation Methods

Deep learning methods for image segmentation refer to the use of many layered convolution neural networks (CNNs) that are trained to take the original image as an input and output a segmented image. Depending on the application, the segmentation method can be semantic or instance based. Semantic segmentation methods will classify each pixel with a particular class, or object type, by assigning it the class label or color. Instance-based segmentation methods will classify each object with its own individual label, such as when we are trying to identify a specific person's face, for example, "John". With semantic segmentation, specific instances of an object are not individually labeled, but each pixel belonging to a class, such as "sky", "land", "water" or "boat", is assigned the same label, corresponding to a specific color in the segmented image (see Figure 5.5-1). Applications for semantic segmentation include medical imaging, autonomous driving, industrial inspection and satellite image analysis. Instance-based segmentation can be modeled as semantic segmentation followed by an identification process. Here, we will focus on semantic segmentation.

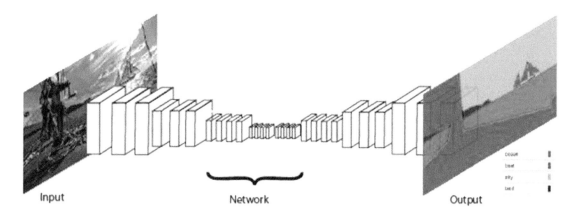

Input   Network   Output

FIGURE 5.5-1
Semantic segmentation process. The goal for the network with semantic segmentation is to label each pixel as belonging to a specific class.

5.5.1 Convolution Neural Networks

A CNN is a specific type of artificial neural network (ANN) that is used for image segmentation because they are adept at recognizing patterns. The general form of an ANN is shown in Figure 5.5-2. With semantic segmentation, the input is the image and the outputs are the classes to which the pixels are assigned. The circles are the processing elements called neurons or nodes, and for a typical neural network will perform a summation process, but for a CNN will perform a convolution (as was shown in Figure 3.2-3). Remember a convolution is the weighted sum of the input subimage, and here, the weights are the convolution mask or filter coefficients.

After the summation, the output of the neuron is controlled by an *activation function*, which for most of the inner layers in a CNN is a rectified linear unit. This activation function operates like a rectifier in electrical circuits – it eliminates the negative parts of the signal and allows the positive to pass through unchanged. Without the rectified linear unit, the deep network will learn very slowly and may not ever reach a point of efficacy. However, the final output layer typically uses a softmax or sigmoid activation function – all these will be explored further in the pattern classification chapter.

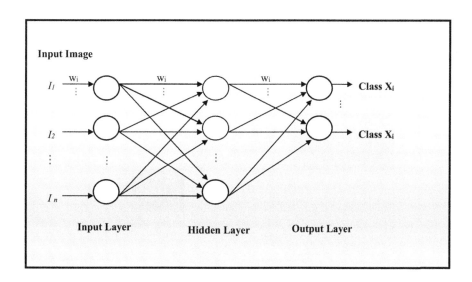

FIGURE 5.5-2
Artificial neural network. Here, we show a neural network architecture with an input layer, where the image is the input, one hidden layer and the output layer. In this case, the output layer corresponds to the classes. The circles are the processing elements, neurons, and the arrows represent the connections. Associated with each connection is a weight (w_i, shown only across the top for clarity) by which the signal is multiplied. These weights are adjusted during the training (learning) phase.

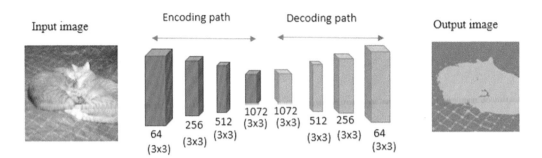

Input image   Encoding path   Decoding path   Output image

1072 1072
(3x3) (3x3)
256   512   512   256
64   64
(3x3) (3x3) (3x3)   (3x3) (3x3)   (3x3)

FIGURE 5.5-3

An encoder/decoder structure is commonly used for image segmentation with a CNN. The image is downsampled during encoding, which reduces image size, and is upsampled during decoding to generate the final image. The numbers under each layer represent the number of filters in each layer, while the numbers in parenthesis represent the filter size.

A standard CNN typically has many hidden layers, and a number of these are convolution layers. A convolution layer in a CNN is specified by the number and size of the filters. The reason that this process is referred to as deep learning is that the convolution layers are numerous, so the network has many layers, and the deeper we get into the network, the more specific and complex the filters are. The learning aspect of the process requires the network to be exposed to many, many sample images along with the desired output images. During the learning, or training, process, the many samples and the correct results are used via various mathematical processes that search in the very high-level feature space to minimize some error function or maximize a success function. During the training process, the weights of the filters are adjusted to achieve optimal results.

The general form of a network used for segmentation uses the encoder/decoder structure shown in Figure 5.5-3. During the encoding phase, the image is downsampled and the lower resolution of the images works to help find features to discriminate between classes. During the decoding phase, the image is upsampled back to its original size which will enable us to recreate the full-size image. The image can be downsampled with a simple averaging technique, but a *max pooling* method is often used for CNNs. An example of max pooling is shown in Figure 5.5-4. The image can later be upsampled with any standard method, but with a CNN a *transposed convolutional layer* is often used. It works by stretching the image and zero-padding, adding rows and columns of zeros and then performing the convolution, as shown in Chapter 3.

In practice, the developer who wants to use a CNN for segmentation can start with one of the standard networks that has already been trained with millions of images, and thousands of classes, and develop an output layer that is specific to the application. If we investigate the filters that have been developed in these networks, we see that

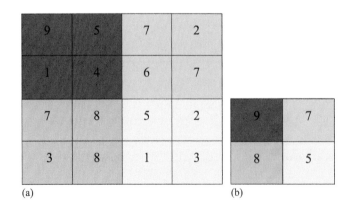

(a)   (b)

FIGURE 5.5-4

Max pooling. This illustrates how max pooling works to downsample an image in a CNN by selecting the maximum value in a small region. (a) The image and (b) the result of max pooling with a filter size = 2 × 2.

the first layers generate filters that extract very primitive features, such as edges, and as we get deeper into the network, we see filters for corners, shapes, textures and so on. The deeper we get into the network, the more complex the filters that are developed and the less likely it will be for us to actually make any sense out of what is going on. This is why neural networks in general are often considered as black boxes, where we can train them, but really do not know the details of how they are working. In general, they have been trained via mathematical models to minimize some error function and/or maximize a success metric. More information about neural networks will be explored in the pattern classification chapter.

5.6 Combined Segmentation Approaches

Image segmentation methods may actually be a combination of region growing methods, clustering methods, boundary detection and deep learning. As previously mentioned, we could consider the region growing methods to be a subset of the clustering methods by allowing the space of interest to include the row and column parameters. Quite often, in boundary detection, heuristics applicable to the specific domain must be employed in order to find the true object boundaries. What is considered noise in one application may be the feature of interest in another application. Finding boundaries of different features, such as texture, brightness or color, and applying deep learning techniques at a higher level to correlate the feature boundaries found to the specific domain may give the best results. Optimal image segmentation is likely to be achieved by focusing on the application and on how the different methods can be used, singly or in combination, to achieve the desired results. See the references for further information.

5.7 Morphological Filtering

Morphology relates to the structure or form of objects. Morphological filtering simplifies a segmented image to facilitate the search for objects of interest. This is done by smoothing out object outlines, filling small holes, eliminating small projections and with other similar techniques. While this section will focus on applications to binary images, the extension of the concepts to gray level images will also be discussed. For color images, each band can be processed separately. We will look at the different types of operations available and at some examples of their use.

5.7.1 Erosion, Dilation, Opening, Closing

The two principal morphological operations are dilation and erosion. *Dilation* allows objects to expand, thus potentially filling in small holes and connecting disjoint objects. *Erosion* shrinks objects by etching away (eroding) their boundaries. These operations can be customized for an application by the proper selection of the *structuring element*, which determines exactly how the objects will be dilated or eroded. Basically, the structuring element is used to probe the image to find how it will fit, or not fit, into the image object(s). For the following discussion, we assume that the images are binary where the objects are "1" and the background is "0".

The dilation process is performed by laying the structuring element on the image and sliding it across the image in a manner similar to convolution. The difference is in the operation performed. It is best described in a sequence of steps:

1. If the origin of the structuring element coincides with a "0" in the image, there is no change; move to the next pixel.
2. If the origin of the structuring element coincides with a "1" in the image, perform the OR logic operation on all pixels within the structuring element.

An example is shown in Figure 5.7-1. Note that with a dilation operation, all the "1" pixels in the original image will be retained, any boundaries will be expanded and small holes will be filled.

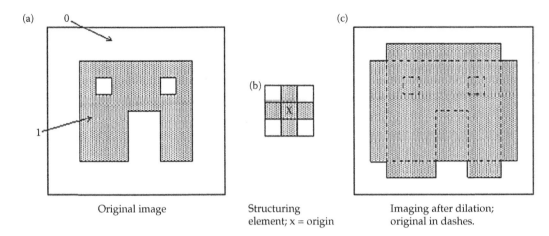

Original image   Structuring   Imaging after dilation;
                               element; x = origin   original in dashes.

FIGURE 5.7-1
Dilation. Dilation retains all the original object pixels and expands the object and fills in small holes, based on the size and shape of the structuring element. Note also that the output image takes on a shape similar to the structuring element.

Given the following image and structuring element, perform a dilation operation. We assume the origin of the structuring element is in the center and ignore cases where the structuring element extends beyond the image. Note that since the holes are all smaller than the structuring element, they are all filled.

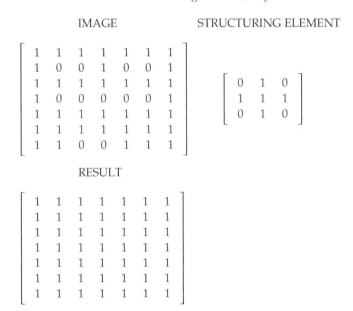

IMAGE   STRUCTURING ELEMENT

$$\begin{bmatrix} 1 & 1 & 1 & 1 & 1 & 1 & 1 \\ 1 & 0 & 0 & 1 & 0 & 0 & 1 \\ 1 & 1 & 1 & 1 & 1 & 1 & 1 \\ 1 & 0 & 0 & 0 & 0 & 0 & 1 \\ 1 & 1 & 1 & 1 & 1 & 1 & 1 \\ 1 & 1 & 1 & 1 & 1 & 1 & 1 \\ 1 & 1 & 0 & 0 & 1 & 1 & 1 \end{bmatrix} \qquad \begin{bmatrix} 0 & 1 & 0 \\ 1 & 1 & 1 \\ 0 & 1 & 0 \end{bmatrix}$$

RESULT

$$\begin{bmatrix} 1 & 1 & 1 & 1 & 1 & 1 & 1 \\ 1 & 1 & 1 & 1 & 1 & 1 & 1 \\ 1 & 1 & 1 & 1 & 1 & 1 & 1 \\ 1 & 1 & 1 & 1 & 1 & 1 & 1 \\ 1 & 1 & 1 & 1 & 1 & 1 & 1 \\ 1 & 1 & 1 & 1 & 1 & 1 & 1 \\ 1 & 1 & 1 & 1 & 1 & 1 & 1 \end{bmatrix}$$

The erosion process is similar to dilation, but pixels are changed to "0", not "1". As before, slide the structuring element across the image, and:

1. If the origin of the structuring element coincides with a "0" in the image, there is no change; move to the next pixel.

2. If the origin of the structuring element coincides with a "1" in the image and any of the "1" pixels in the structuring element extend beyond the object ("1" pixels) in the image, then change the "1" pixel in the image, whose location corresponds to the origin of the structuring element, to a "=0".

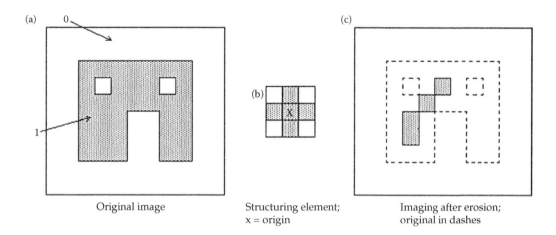

Original image | Structuring element; x = origin | Imaging after erosion; original in dashes

FIGURE 5.7-2
Erosion. Erosion reduces the object size by etching away from the boundary inward. Note that only the center pixels remain in places where the structuring fits entirely into the object.

In Figure 5.7-2, the only remaining pixels are those that coincide to the origin of the structuring element where the entire structuring element was contained in the existing object. Since the structuring element is three pixels wide, the two-pixel-wide right "leg" of the image object was eroded away, but the three-pixel-wide left "leg" retained some of its center pixels.

EXAMPLE 5.7.2: EROSION

Given the following image and structuring element, perform an erosion operation. We assume the origin of the structuring element is in the center and ignore cases where the structuring element extends beyond the image. Note the only 1's left inside the image mark places where the shape of the structuring element exists in the original image.

IMAGE STRUCTURNG ELEMENT

$$
\begin{bmatrix}
1 & 1 & 1 & 1 & 1 & 1 & 1 \\
1 & 0 & 0 & 1 & 0 & 0 & 1 \\
1 & 1 & 1 & 1 & 1 & 1 & 1 \\
1 & 0 & 0 & 1 & 0 & 0 & 1 \\
1 & 1 & 1 & 1 & 1 & 1 & 1 \\
1 & 1 & 1 & 1 & 1 & 1 & 1 \\
1 & 1 & 0 & 0 & 1 & 1 & 1
\end{bmatrix}
\qquad
\begin{bmatrix}
1 & 0 & 0 \\
1 & 1 & 1 \\
1 & 0 & 0
\end{bmatrix}
$$

RESULT

$$
\begin{bmatrix}
1 & 1 & 1 & 1 & 1 & 1 & 1 \\
1 & 0 & 0 & 0 & 0 & 0 & 1 \\
1 & 1 & 0 & 0 & 1 & 0 & 1 \\
1 & 0 & 0 & 0 & 0 & 0 & 1 \\
1 & 1 & 0 & 0 & 1 & 0 & 1 \\
1 & 1 & 1 & 0 & 0 & 1 & 1 \\
1 & 1 & 0 & 0 & 1 & 1 & 1
\end{bmatrix}.
$$

These two basic operations, dilation and erosion, can be combined into more complex sequences. The most useful of these for morphological filtering are called opening and closing. *Opening* consists of an erosion followed by a dilation, and it can be used to eliminate all pixels in regions that are too small to contain the structuring element. In this case, the structuring element is often called a *probe*, as it is probing the image looking for small objects to

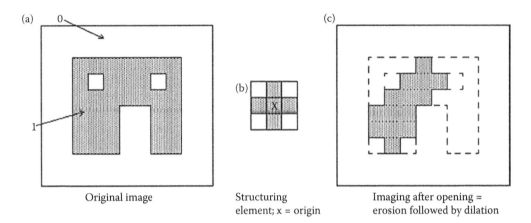

FIGURE 5.7-3

Opening. The opening operation is an erosion followed by a dilation. It retains all pixels where the structuring element fits inside the object and opens holes. Note that the resulting object takes on the general shape of the structuring element.

filter out of the image. In Figure 5.7-3, we can see that opening expands holes ("opens" them up) and may erode edges in a way that depends on the structuring element shape. The output image tends to take a shape similar to the structuring element itself.

Closing consists of a dilation followed by erosion, and it can be used to fill in holes and small gaps as shown in Figure 5.7-4. Here, we see that the two small holes have been closed and the gap has been partially filled; if a different structuring element is used, the results will be similar but different (see some of the following figures). Comparing Figures 5.7-3 and 5.7-4, we see that the order of operation is important. Closing and opening will have different results even though both consist of an erosion and a dilation.

The following two figures show results of dilation from varying the shape and size of the structuring element. The original image is a microscopic image of a cell that has undergone a threshold operation to create a binary image. Figure 5.7-5 illustrates dilation using different shape structuring elements. Here, we see that the small objects, as well as edges on larger objects, will take on the shape of the structuring element itself. In Figure 5.7-6, we see that effect of using the same shape structuring element, but increasing the size of the structuring element – as it gets larger, the size of the holes that get filled increases. Here, we also see that small objects are merged together by

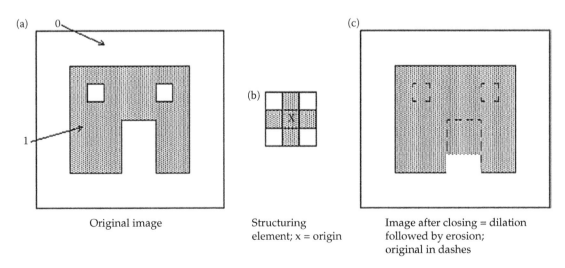

FIGURE 5.7-4

Closing. The closing operation is a dilation followed by an erosion and it will fill in (close) small holes and gaps.

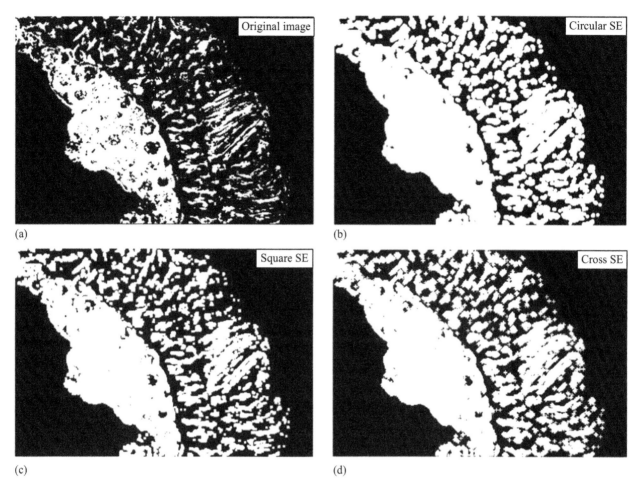

(a)

(b)

(c)

(d)

FIGURE 5.7-5
Binary dilation with various shape structuring elements. (a) Original image, a microscope cell image that has undergone a threshold operation (original image courtesy of Sara Sawyer, SIUE), (b) dilation with a circular structuring element (SE), (c) dilation with a square structuring element (d) dilation with a cross shape structuring element. Note that small objects take on the shape of the structuring element.

dilation and that the degree of the merging depends on the size of the structuring element. Also note that in Figure 5.7-6b, even though a circular structuring element was used, the small objects appear to be rectangular – why is this? (Hint: consider the shape of a binary circle on a 4 × 4 rectangular grid).

Figure 5.7-7 illustrates erosion using different shape structuring elements. Here, we see that the holes, as well as edges on larger objects, will take on the shape of the structuring element itself. Figures 5.7-8 and 5.7-9 show the results of opening and closing using various shape structuring elements. Here, we can see how the shape of the structuring elements affects the results of these operations. In Figure 5.7-10, we see a comparison of opening and closing with different size circular structuring elements.

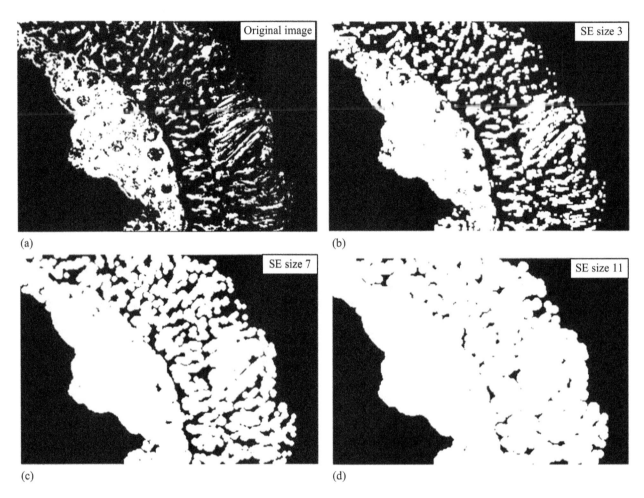

(a)

(b)

(c)

(d)

FIGURE 5.7-6
Dilation with different size structuring elements. (a) Original image, (b) dilation with a circular structuring element (SE) of size 3, (c) dilation with a circular structuring element of size 7 (d) dilation with a circular structuring element of size 11. As the size of the structuring element is increased, the size of the holes that get filled in is larger and the distance between small objects that are merged is greater.

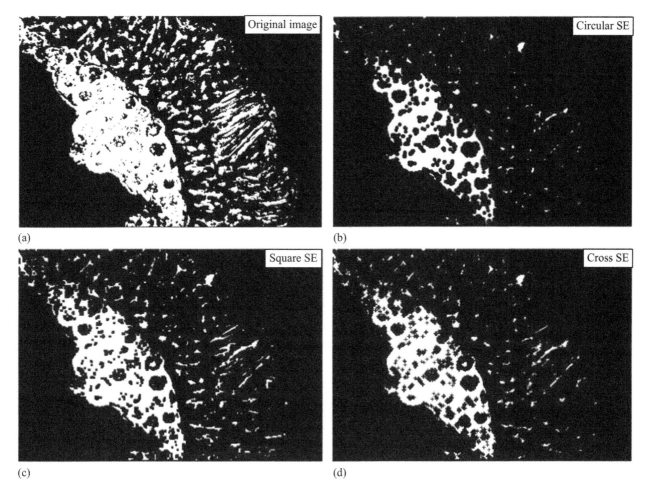

(a)   (b)   (c)   (d)

FIGURE 5.7-7
Binary erosion with various shape structuring elements. (a) Original image, a microscope cell image that has undergone a threshold operation. (Original image courtesy of Sara Sawyer, SIUE.) (b) erosion with a circular structuring element, (c) erosion with a square structuring element and (d) erosion with a cross shape structuring element. Note that holes take on the shape of the structuring element.

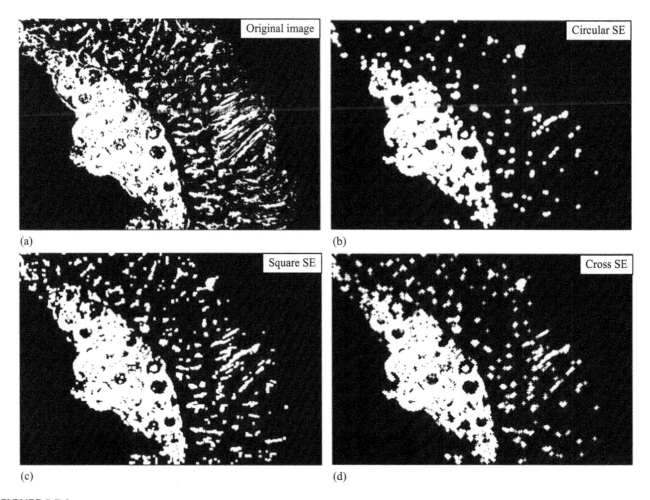

(a)

(b)

(c)

(d)

FIGURE 5.7-8
Binary opening with various shape structuring elements. (a) Original image, a microscope cell image that has undergone a threshold operation. (Original image courtesy of Sara Sawyer, SIUE), (b) opening with a circular structuring element (c) opening with a square structuring element and (d) opening with a cross shape structuring element. Note that small objects take on the shape of the structuring element.

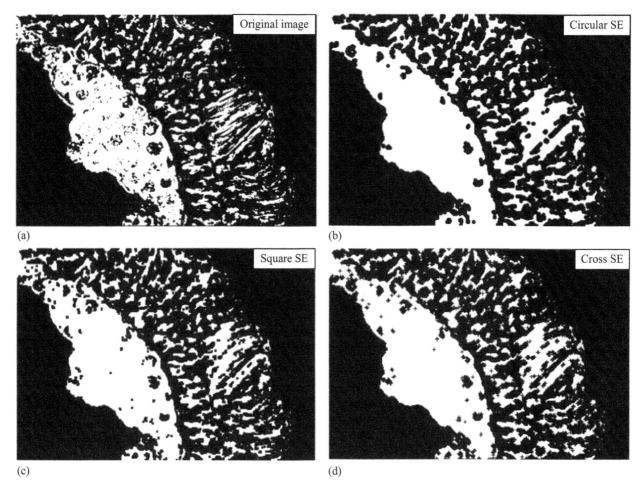

(a) (b) (c) (d)

FIGURE 5.7-9
Binary closing with various shape structuring elements. (a) Original image, a microscope cell image that has undergone a threshold operation (original image courtesy of Sara Sawyer, SIUE), (b) closing with a circular structuring element, (c) closing with a square structuring element (d) closing with a cross shape structuring element. After closing, holes will take on the shape of the structuring element.

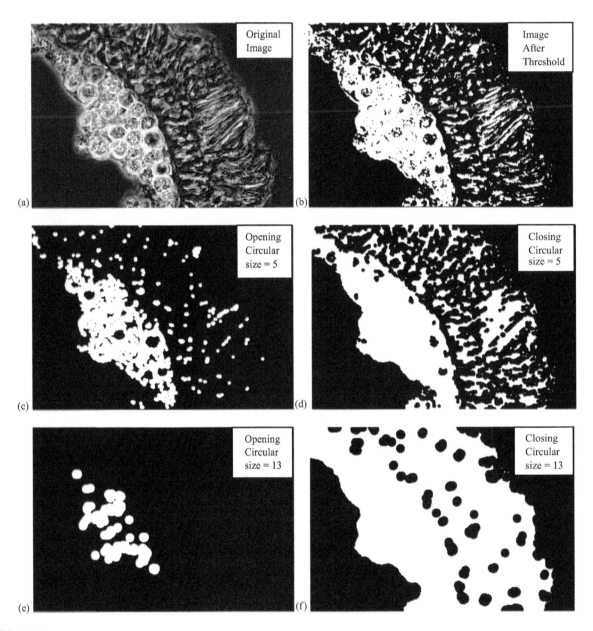

FIGURE 5.7-10
Opening and closing with different size structuring elements. (a) Original microscopic cell image (courtesy of Sara Sawyer, SIUE), (b) image after undergoing color to gray conversion and a threshold operation, (c) opening with a circular structuring element of size 5, (d) closing with a circular structuring element of size 5, (e) opening with a circular structuring element of size 13 and (f) closing with a circular structuring element of size 13.

5.7.2 Hit-or-Miss Transform, Thinning and Skeletonization

The morphological *hit-or-miss transform* is a fundamental method for detection of simple shapes. It is a basic pattern recognition tool that, like the previous morphological methods, uses a structuring element (SE) to determine the patterns or shapes it detects. In addition to the 1's (object) and 0's (background), the structuring element may contain "don't cares", specified with an x. The hit-or-miss transform works by overlaying the structuring element on the image and requires an exact match for a "hit" to occur – a hit is marked with a 1. The following example shows a hit-or-miss transform that finds the upper right corner points of binary objects.

EXAMPLE 5.7.3: HIT-OR-MISS TRANSFORM

Finding upper right corner points with the hit-or-miss transform

IMAGE   SE

$$
\begin{bmatrix}
0 & 0 & 0 & 0 & 0 & 0 & 0 & 0 \\
0 & 0 & 1 & 1 & 1 & 1 & 1 & 0 \\
0 & 1 & 1 & 1 & 0 & 0 & 1 & 0 \\
0 & 1 & 1 & 1 & 0 & 0 & 1 & 0 \\
0 & 1 & 1 & 1 & 1 & 1 & 1 & 0 \\
0 & 1 & 1 & 1 & 1 & 1 & 1 & 0 \\
0 & 1 & 1 & 1 & 0 & 0 & 0 & 0 \\
0 & 0 & 0 & 0 & 0 & 0 & 0 & 0
\end{bmatrix}
\qquad
\begin{bmatrix}
x & 0 & 0 \\
1 & 1 & 0 \\
x & 1 & x
\end{bmatrix}
$$

HIT-OR-MISS RESULT

$$
\begin{bmatrix}
0 & 0 & 0 & 0 & 0 & 0 & 0 & 0 \\
0 & 0 & 0 & 0 & 0 & 0 & 1 & 0 \\
0 & 0 & 0 & 0 & 0 & 0 & 0 & 0 \\
0 & 0 & 0 & 0 & 0 & 0 & 0 & 0 \\
0 & 0 & 0 & 0 & 0 & 0 & 0 & 0 \\
0 & 0 & 0 & 0 & 0 & 0 & 0 & 0 \\
0 & 0 & 0 & 0 & 0 & 0 & 0 & 0 \\
0 & 0 & 0 & 0 & 0 & 0 & 0 & 0
\end{bmatrix}
$$

Note that there is only one upper right corner to this object.

To find all the corners with a hit-or-miss transform, we need to consider the four types of corners – upper right, upper left, lower right and lower left, and their corresponding structuring elements. To detect all the corners, we combine the results from the hit-or-miss transform with each structuring element by using a logical OR operation. The following example illustrates this.

EXAMPLE 5.7.4: FINDING ALL CORNER POINTS WITH THE HIT-OR-MISS TRANSFORM

STRUCTURING ELEMENTS

$$
\begin{bmatrix}
x & 0 & 0 \\
1 & 1 & 0 \\
x & 1 & x
\end{bmatrix},
\begin{bmatrix}
0 & 0 & x \\
0 & 1 & 1 \\
x & 1 & x
\end{bmatrix},
\begin{bmatrix}
x & 1 & x \\
1 & 1 & 0 \\
x & 0 & 0
\end{bmatrix},
\begin{bmatrix}
x & 1 & x \\
0 & 1 & 1 \\
0 & 0 & x
\end{bmatrix}
$$

IMAGE   ORing HIT-OR-MISS FROM EACH SE

$$
\begin{bmatrix}
0 & 0 & 0 & 0 & 0 & 0 & 0 & 0 \\
0 & 0 & 1 & 1 & 1 & 1 & 1 & 0 \\
0 & 1 & 1 & 1 & 0 & 0 & 1 & 0 \\
0 & 1 & 1 & 1 & 0 & 0 & 1 & 0 \\
0 & 1 & 1 & 1 & 1 & 1 & 1 & 0 \\
0 & 1 & 1 & 1 & 1 & 1 & 1 & 0 \\
0 & 1 & 1 & 1 & 0 & 0 & 0 & 0 \\
0 & 0 & 0 & 0 & 0 & 0 & 0 & 0
\end{bmatrix}
\qquad
\begin{bmatrix}
0 & 0 & 0 & 0 & 0 & 0 & 0 & 0 \\
0 & 0 & 1 & 0 & 0 & 0 & 1 & 0 \\
0 & 1 & 0 & 0 & 0 & 0 & 0 & 0 \\
0 & 0 & 0 & 0 & 0 & 0 & 0 & 0 \\
0 & 0 & 0 & 0 & 0 & 0 & 0 & 0 \\
0 & 0 & 0 & 0 & 0 & 0 & 1 & 0 \\
0 & 1 & 0 & 1 & 0 & 0 & 0 & 0 \\
0 & 0 & 0 & 0 & 0 & 0 & 0 & 0
\end{bmatrix}
$$

Note that all corner points have been detected.

One important operation, which is a controlled erosion process, is called skeletonization. It is used in applications with the need to reduce a binary object to its fundamental shape, such as optical character recognition. A *skeleton* is what is left of an object when it has been eroded to the point of being only one pixel wide. To find the skeleton of a binary image, we first define the *thinning* operation, with a given structuring element, SE:

$$\text{Thin}\big[I(r, c), \text{SE}\big] = I(r, c) - \text{hit-or-miss}\big[I(r, c), \text{SE}\big] \tag{5.7-1}$$

In other words, the thinning operation is defined by subtracting the result from the hit-or-miss operation from the original image at each point. Note that this subtraction is the logical subtraction defined by:

$$A - B = (A)\,\text{AND}\,(\text{NOT}\,B), \text{ where the AND and NOT are logical operators} \tag{5.7-2}$$

The typical thinning operation uses the line detection structuring elements shown in the next example. The process of skeletonization gives the result from applying each of the line structuring elements to thin the image and then performing a logical AND of the thinned results. Note that the AND should be performed after each iteration. This process is continued until the lines are one pixel wide and no changes in connectivity have occurred, that is, no change in the Euler number.

EXAMPLE 5.7.5: THINNING THE TOP HORIZONTAL LINE.

$$SE_1 = \begin{bmatrix} 0 & 0 & 0 \\ x & 1 & x \\ 1 & 1 & 1 \end{bmatrix} \qquad \text{image} = I(r,c) = \begin{bmatrix} 0 & 0 & 0 & 0 & 0 & 0 & 0 & 0 \\ 0 & 1 & 1 & 1 & 1 & 1 & 1 & 0 \\ 0 & 1 & 1 & 1 & 1 & 1 & 1 & 0 \\ 0 & 1 & 1 & 1 & 1 & 1 & 1 & 0 \\ 0 & 1 & 1 & 1 & 1 & 1 & 1 & 0 \\ 0 & 1 & 1 & 1 & 1 & 1 & 1 & 0 \\ 0 & 0 & 0 & 0 & 0 & 0 & 0 & 0 \\ 0 & 0 & 0 & 0 & 0 & 0 & 0 & 0 \end{bmatrix}$$

$$\text{hit-or-miss}\big[I(r,c),\,SE_1\big] = \begin{bmatrix} 0 & 0 & 0 & 0 & 0 & 0 & 0 & 0 \\ 0 & 0 & 1 & 1 & 1 & 1 & 0 & 0 \\ 0 & 0 & 0 & 0 & 0 & 0 & 0 & 0 \\ 0 & 0 & 0 & 0 & 0 & 0 & 0 & 0 \\ 0 & 0 & 0 & 0 & 0 & 0 & 0 & 0 \\ 0 & 0 & 0 & 0 & 0 & 0 & 0 & 0 \\ 0 & 0 & 0 & 0 & 0 & 0 & 0 & 0 \\ 0 & 0 & 0 & 0 & 0 & 0 & 0 & 0 \end{bmatrix}$$

then,

$$\text{Thin}\big[I(r,c),SE_1\big] = I(r,c) - \text{hit-or-miss}\big[I(r,c),SE_1\big] = \begin{bmatrix} 0 & 0 & 0 & 0 & 0 & 0 & 0 & 0 \\ 0 & 1 & 0 & 0 & 0 & 0 & 1 & 0 \\ 0 & 1 & 1 & 1 & 1 & 1 & 1 & 0 \\ 0 & 1 & 1 & 1 & 1 & 1 & 1 & 0 \\ 0 & 1 & 1 & 1 & 1 & 1 & 1 & 0 \\ 0 & 1 & 1 & 1 & 1 & 1 & 1 & 0 \\ 0 & 0 & 0 & 0 & 0 & 0 & 0 & 0 \\ 0 & 0 & 0 & 0 & 0 & 0 & 0 & 0 \end{bmatrix}$$

Next, we apply the thinning operation with each of the other structuring elements, then perform a logical AND of all four results for each iteration. This process continues until the skeleton is obtained as shown in the next example.

EXAMPLE 5.7.6: SKELETONIZATION. THINNING WITH THE FOUR LINE STRUCTURING ELEMENTS AND ANDING THE RESULTS.

The other three structuring elements:

$$SE_2 = \begin{bmatrix} 1 & x & 0 \\ 1 & 1 & 0 \\ 1 & x & 0 \end{bmatrix}, SE_3 = \begin{bmatrix} 1 & 1 & 1 \\ x & 1 & x \\ 0 & 0 & 0 \end{bmatrix}, SE_4 = \begin{bmatrix} 0 & x & 1 \\ 0 & 1 & 1 \\ 0 & x & 1 \end{bmatrix}.$$

After thinning with each of the four structuring elements and the logical AND of the results, we obtain:

$$\begin{bmatrix} 0 & 0 & 0 & 0 & 0 & 0 & 0 & 0 \\ 0 & 1 & 0 & 0 & 0 & 0 & 1 & 0 \\ 0 & 0 & 1 & 1 & 1 & 1 & 0 & 0 \\ 0 & 0 & 1 & 1 & 1 & 1 & 0 & 0 \\ 0 & 0 & 1 & 1 & 1 & 1 & 0 & 0 \\ 0 & 1 & 0 & 0 & 0 & 0 & 1 & 0 \\ 0 & 0 & 0 & 0 & 0 & 0 & 0 & 0 \\ 0 & 0 & 0 & 0 & 0 & 0 & 0 & 0 \end{bmatrix}$$

After one more iteration for the skeletonization process, we obtain:

$$\begin{bmatrix} 0 & 0 & 0 & 0 & 0 & 0 & 0 & 0 \\ 0 & 1 & 0 & 0 & 0 & 0 & 1 & 0 \\ 0 & 0 & 1 & 0 & 0 & 1 & 0 & 0 \\ 0 & 0 & 0 & 1 & 1 & 0 & 0 & 0 \\ 0 & 0 & 1 & 0 & 0 & 1 & 0 & 0 \\ 0 & 1 & 0 & 0 & 0 & 0 & 1 & 0 \\ 0 & 0 & 0 & 0 & 0 & 0 & 0 & 0 \\ 0 & 0 & 0 & 0 & 0 & 0 & 0 & 0 \end{bmatrix}$$

At this point, we cannot thin anymore, so the skeletonization process is complete.

Using only the four masks previously defined may not complete the process. We can add four more structuring elements as follows:

$$SE_5 = \begin{bmatrix} x & 0 & 0 \\ 1 & 1 & 0 \\ 1 & 1 & x \end{bmatrix}, SE_6 = \begin{bmatrix} 1 & 1 & x \\ 1 & 1 & 0 \\ x & 0 & 0 \end{bmatrix}, SE_7 = \begin{bmatrix} x & 1 & 1 \\ 0 & 1 & 1 \\ 0 & 0 & x \end{bmatrix}, SE_8 = \begin{bmatrix} 0 & 0 & x \\ 0 & 1 & 1 \\ x & 1 & 1 \end{bmatrix}$$

We call these four masks the *diagonal masks,* as the elements appear in a group of four in each diagonal corner of the square mask.

In Figure 5.7-11, we compare using the original four structuring elements, the horizontal and vertical (called the *4-masks*), the set of four diagonal masks and with both sets combined to create the *8-masks*. Here, we see regularly shaped objects, rectangles, squares, ellipses and ellipses with holes and how the different mask groups affect the resulting images. Note that the mask name refers to the mask shape, not the shape of the skeletonized objects.

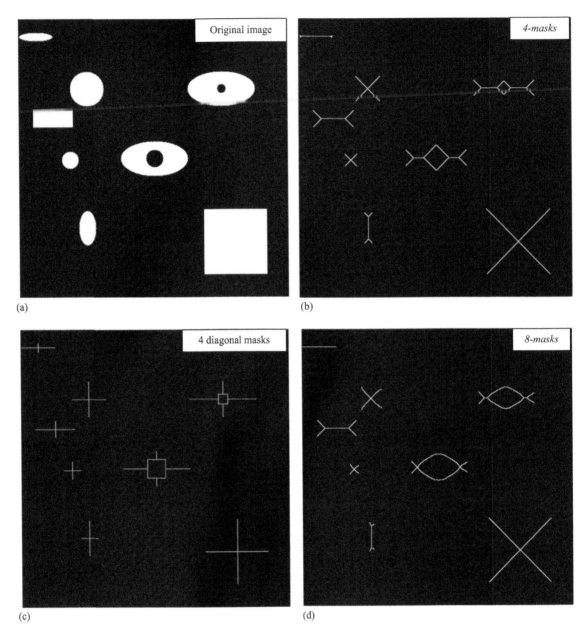

FIGURE 5.7-11
Skeletonization with simple shapes. (a) Original image, (b) resultant image with the *4-masks* (horizontal and vertical), (c) resultant image after using the four diagonal masks and (d) resultant image using the *8-masks*. Note that the mask name refers to the mask shape, not the shape of the skeletonized objects.

With more irregularly shaped objects, the process is more complex. In Figure 5.7-12, we compare results from using the *4-masks* to using the *8-masks*. Here, we see that it requires all eight masks to get the desired results. Even if we continued processing with the *4-masks*, no further changes will occur. Why not?

Using the previously described method, which ANDs the images from all the masks after thinning, can result in loss of connectivity, as shown in Figure 5.7-13b and c. One method to avoid this problem is to use the output image after thinning with one mask as input to the thinning with the next mask. This is done sequentially for all masks, and no AND operation is performed. Thus, we have two methods available in CVIPtools – the AND method and the sequential method. Figure 5.7-13d and e shows results from the sequential method. Here, we see that the sequential method maintains connectivity, but that extra lines appear that may be desired or extraneous, depending on the application.

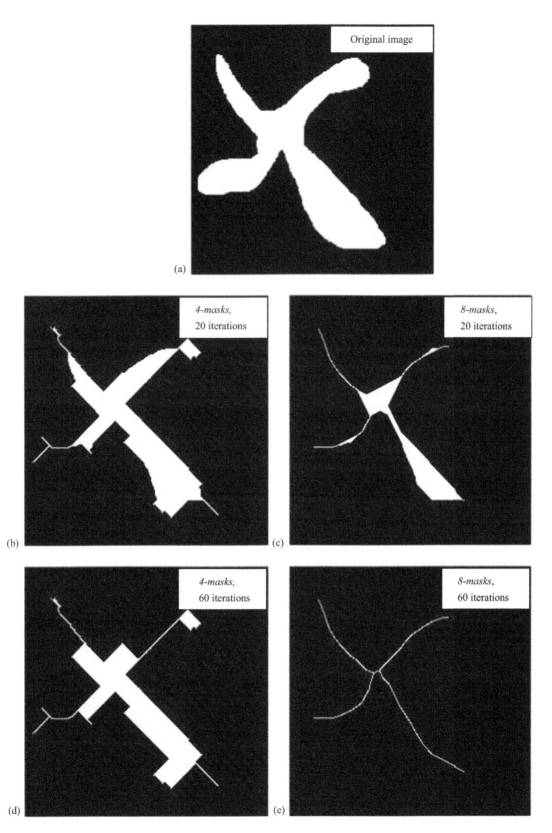

FIGURE 5.7-12
Skeletonization with irregular shapes using four or eight masks, (a) Original image, (b) resultant image after 20 iterations with the four original masks – horizontal and vertical only (*4-masks*), (c) resultant image after 20 iterations with the four original masks and the four diagonal masks (*8-masks*), (d) resultant image after 60 iterations with the *4-masks* and (e) resultant image after 60 iterations with the *8-masks*. Continued skeletonization with the *4-masks* alone will not change image (d).

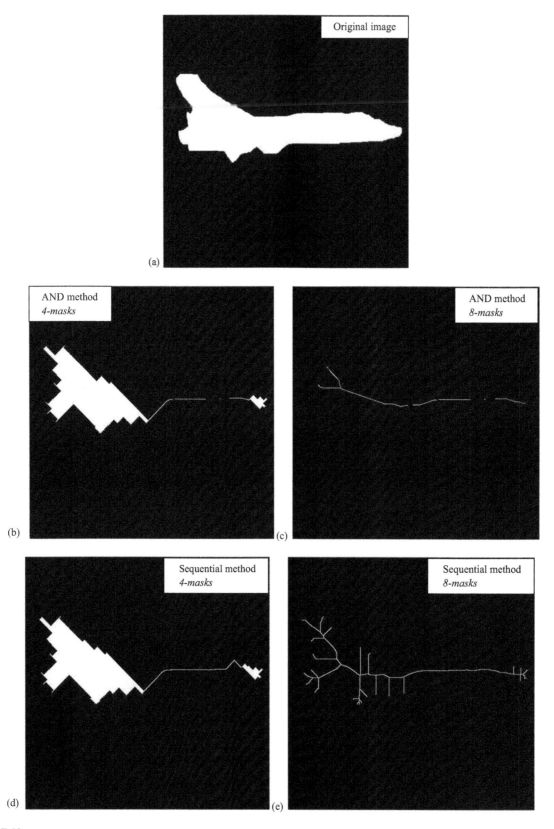

FIGURE 5.7-13
Skeletonization using four or eight masks with AND or sequential method. The number of iterations is until no further changes occur. (a) Original image, (b) results with 4-masks and AND method, (c) results with 8-masks and AND method, (d) results with 4-masks and sequential method and (e) results with 8-masks and sequential method. With the AND method, connectivity may be lost. With the sequential method, connectivity is maintained, but more lines may occur.

The skeletonization process works best with elongated shapes such as is found in applications as hand-written character recognition or in blood vessel recognition. With complex shapes, the skeletonization process often leaves many extra small lines, called *spurs*, which must be dealt with through a pruning process. One method of pruning to remove undesired, small line segments is to use the Hough transform algorithm in CVIPtools, where the minimum segment size is one of the parameters. Examples of this are shown in Figure 5.7-14.

The standard pruning operation is a form of thinning with a single pixel as the structuring element. The structuring element is rotated throughout the eight possible compass directions to prune lines in all directions. Typically pruning is only performed for a small number of iterations to remove small spurs or all lines except for closed loops will be removed.

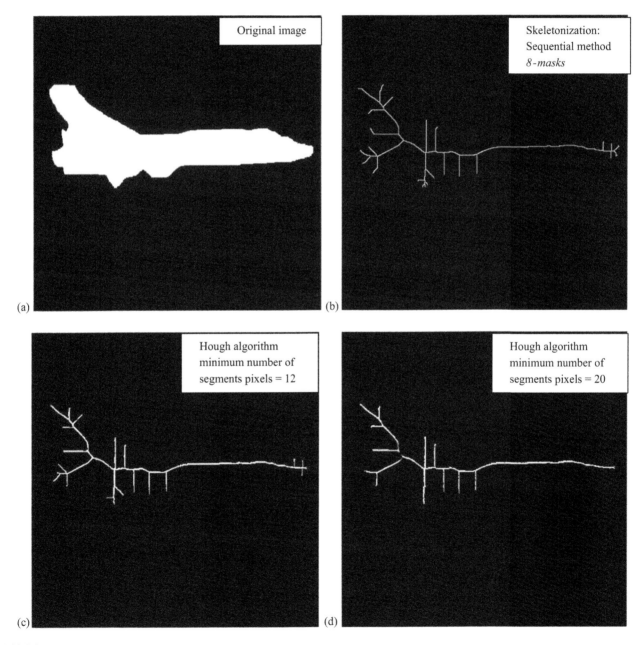

FIGURE 5.7-14
Spur removal by pruning using Hough algorithm. Extra lines, or spurs, may be desired or extraneous depending on the application. (a) Original image, (b) skeletonization results with 8-masks and sequential method, (c) using the Hough algorithm to remove spurs from (b) with minimum number of segment pixels = 12 and (d) using the Hough algorithm to remove spurs from (b) with minimum number of segment pixels = 20.

EXAMPLE 5.7.7: PRUNING

The structuring elements for pruning:

$$SE_1 = \begin{bmatrix} 0 & 0 & 0 \\ 0 & 1 & 0 \\ 0 & x & x \end{bmatrix} SE_2 = \begin{bmatrix} 0 & 0 & 0 \\ 0 & 1 & 0 \\ x & x & 0 \end{bmatrix}, SE_3 = \begin{bmatrix} 0 & 0 & 0 \\ x & 1 & 0 \\ x & 0 & 0 \end{bmatrix}, SE_4 = \begin{bmatrix} x & 0 & 0 \\ x & 1 & 0 \\ 0 & 0 & 0 \end{bmatrix}$$

$$SE_5 = \begin{bmatrix} x & x & 0 \\ 0 & 1 & 0 \\ 0 & 0 & 0 \end{bmatrix} SE_6 = \begin{bmatrix} 0 & x & x \\ 0 & 1 & 0 \\ 0 & 0 & 0 \end{bmatrix}, SE_7 = \begin{bmatrix} 0 & 0 & x \\ 0 & 1 & x \\ 0 & 0 & 0 \end{bmatrix}, SE_8 = \begin{bmatrix} 0 & 0 & 0 \\ 0 & 1 & x \\ 0 & 0 & x \end{bmatrix}$$

Results from the previous skeletonization:

$$\begin{bmatrix} 0 & 0 & 0 & 0 & 0 & 0 & 0 & 0 \\ 0 & 1 & 0 & 0 & 0 & 0 & 1 & 0 \\ 0 & 0 & 1 & 0 & 0 & 1 & 0 & 0 \\ 0 & 0 & 0 & 1 & 1 & 0 & 0 & 0 \\ 0 & 0 & 1 & 0 & 0 & 1 & 0 & 0 \\ 0 & 1 & 0 & 0 & 0 & 0 & 1 & 0 \\ 0 & 0 & 0 & 0 & 0 & 0 & 0 & 0 \\ 0 & 0 & 0 & 0 & 0 & 0 & 0 & 0 \end{bmatrix}$$

Application of one iteration of pruning to the result from the previous example.

$$\begin{bmatrix} 0 & 0 & 0 & 0 & 0 & 0 & 0 & 0 \\ 0 & 0 & 0 & 0 & 0 & 0 & 0 & 0 \\ 0 & 0 & 1 & 0 & 0 & 1 & 0 & 0 \\ 0 & 0 & 0 & 1 & 1 & 0 & 0 & 0 \\ 0 & 0 & 1 & 0 & 0 & 1 & 0 & 0 \\ 0 & 0 & 0 & 0 & 0 & 0 & 0 & 0 \\ 0 & 0 & 0 & 0 & 0 & 0 & 0 & 0 \\ 0 & 0 & 0 & 0 & 0 & 0 & 0 & 0 \end{bmatrix}$$

5.7.3 Iterative Modification

Another approach to binary morphological filtering is based on an iterative approach. The usefulness of this approach lies in its flexibility. It is based on a definition of six-connectivity in which each pixel is considered connected to its horizontal and vertical neighbors, but to only two diagonal neighbors (the two on the same diagonal). This connectivity definition is equivalent to assuming that the pixels are laid out on a hexagonal grid, which can be simulated on a rectangular grid by assuming that each row is shifted by one-half a pixel (see Figure 5.7-15). With this definition, a pixel can be surrounded by 14 possible combinations of 1's and 0's, as seen in Figure 5.7-16; we call these different combinations *surrounds*. For the *iterative modification* approach to morphological filtering, we define:

1. The set of surrounds S, where $a = 1$.
2. A logic function, $L(a, b)$, where b is the current pixel value, and the function specifies the output of the morphological operation
3. The number of iterations, n.

The function $L(a, b)$ and the values of a and b are all functions of the row and column, (r, c), but for concise notation this is implied. Set S can contain any or all of the 14 surrounds defined in Figure 5.7-16. $L(a, b)$ can be any logic function, but it turns out that the most useful are the AND and OR functions. The AND function tends to etch

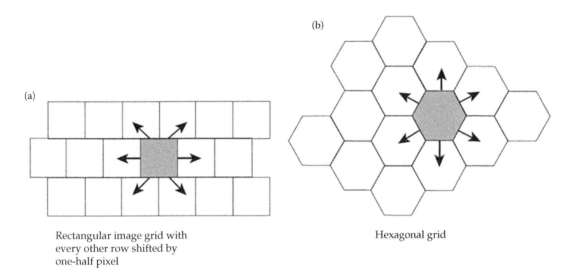

FIGURE 5.7-15
Hexagonal grid. Using a six-connectivity definition is equivalent to assuming that the pixels are laid out on a hexagonal grid, which can be simulated on a rectangular grid by assuming that each row is shifted by one-half a pixel.

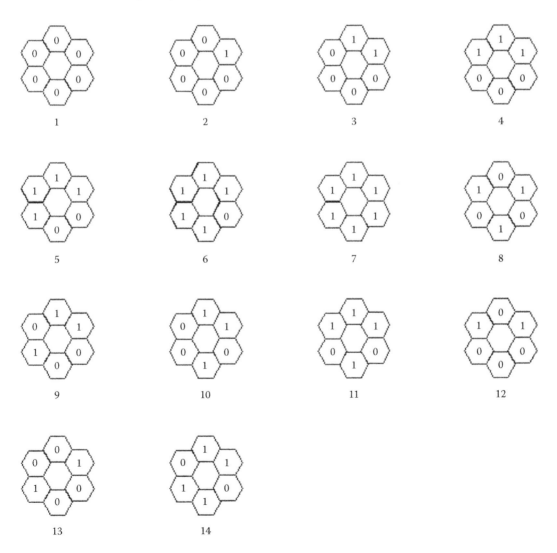

FIGURE 5.7-16
Surrounds for iterative morphological filtering.

away at object boundaries (erosion) and the OR function tends to grow objects (dilation). The following examples illustrate iterative modification for morphological filtering. In these examples, we will not change the outer rows and columns, since the image is undefined beyond the borders and the 3×3 surrounds will not fit within the image in these cases.

EXAMPLE 5.7.8: EROSION

Let $L(a, b) = ab$ (logical AND operation).

$$
\text{IMAGE} \begin{bmatrix}
0 & 0 & 0 & 0 & 0 & 0 & 0 & 0 \\
0 & 1 & 1 & 1 & 1 & 1 & 1 & 0 \\
0 & 1 & 0 & 1 & 1 & 1 & 1 & 0 \\
0 & 0 & 0 & 0 & 1 & 1 & 1 & 0 \\
0 & 1 & 1 & 1 & 1 & 1 & 1 & 0 \\
0 & 0 & 0 & 0 & 0 & 0 & 0 & 0
\end{bmatrix}
$$

$$
S = \{5\} = \begin{bmatrix}
1 & 1 & x \\
1 & x & 1 \\
x & 0 & 0
\end{bmatrix}; \text{ assume the origin is in the center}
$$

Note: this means the set S contains surround number 5 from Figure 5.7-16 and the x's are not neighbors, since we are using six-connectivity.

The window S (a 3×3 window) is scanned across the image. If a match is found, then $a = 1$ and the output is computed by performing the specified $L(a, b)$ function, in this case, by ANDing a with b (b is the center pixel of the subimage under the window). This gives the value of our new image, which will equal $ab = (1)b = b$. If the window S does not match the underlying subimage, then $a = 0$ (false) and $L(a, b) = ab = (0)b = 0$. In either case, the resulting value is written to the new image at the location corresponding to the center of the window.

The window S is scanned across the entire image in this manner and the resultant image is as follows:

$$
\begin{bmatrix}
0 & 0 & 0 & 0 & 0 & 0 & 0 & 0 \\
0 & 0 & 0 & 0 & 0 & 0 & 0 & 0 \\
0 & 0 & 0 & 0 & 0 & 0 & 0 & 0 \\
0 & 0 & 0 & 0 & 0 & 0 & 0 & 0 \\
0 & 0 & 0 & 0 & 0 & 1 & 0 & 0 \\
0 & 0 & 0 & 0 & 0 & 0 & 0 & 0
\end{bmatrix}
$$

Here, we see that the AND operation erodes the object. Also note that the set S can contain more than one surround; if it does, then $a = 1$ when the underlying neighborhood matches *any* of the surrounds in the set S. Another parameter which can be considered is the rotation of the surrounds in S. For example, rotating surround $S = \{5\}$ counterclockwise, we have the following possibilities:

$$
\begin{bmatrix} 1 & 1 & x \\ 1 & x & 1 \\ x & 0 & 0 \end{bmatrix},
\begin{bmatrix} 1 & 1 & x \\ 1 & x & 0 \\ x & 1 & 0 \end{bmatrix},
\begin{bmatrix} 1 & 0 & x \\ 1 & x & 0 \\ x & 1 & 1 \end{bmatrix},
\begin{bmatrix} 0 & 0 & x \\ 1 & x & 1 \\ x & 1 & 1 \end{bmatrix},
\begin{bmatrix} 0 & 1 & x \\ 0 & x & 1 \\ x & 1 & 1 \end{bmatrix},
\begin{bmatrix} 1 & 1 & x \\ 0 & x & 1 \\ x & 0 & 1 \end{bmatrix}
$$

With iterative morphological filtering, normally it is implied that the surrounds in S can be rotated when looking for a match. Additionally, since this is an iterative approach, n is used to define the number of iterations. The following are more examples of this technique.

EXAMPLE 5.7.9: CREATING A NEGATIVE IMAGE

$S = \{\ \}$, $L(a, b) = (!b)$, $n = 1$

In this case, $a = 0$, but this is irrelevant since $L(a, b) = !b$, which implies that the center pixel is negated (complimented).

If $b = 1$, $L(a, b)(!1) = 0$;

Elseif $b = 0$, $L(a, b) = (!0) = 1$;

EXAMPLE 5.7.10: EROSION, APPENDAGE REMOVAL

$$S = \{7\}, L(a,\ b) = ab, n = 1; \qquad S = \{7\} = \begin{bmatrix} 1 & 1 & x \\ 1 & x & 1 \\ x & 1 & 1 \end{bmatrix}$$

Consider the following image:

$$\begin{bmatrix} 0 & 0 & 0 & 0 & 0 & 0 & 0 & 0 & 0 \\ 0 & 1 & 1 & 1 & 1 & 1 & 1 & 0 & 0 \\ 0 & 1 & 1 & 1 & 1 & 1 & 1 & 0 & 0 \\ 0 & 1 & 1 & 1 & 1 & 1 & 1 & 0 & 0 \\ 0 & 1 & 1 & 1 & 1 & 1 & 1 & 0 & 0 \\ 0 & 1 & 1 & 0 & 0 & 0 & 0 & 0 & 0 \\ 0 & 1 & 1 & 0 & 0 & 0 & 0 & 0 & 0 \\ 0 & 1 & 1 & 0 & 0 & 0 & 0 & 0 & 0 \\ 0 & 0 & 0 & 0 & 0 & 0 & 0 & 0 & 0 \end{bmatrix}$$

If the surround is not all 1's, then $L(a, b) = 0(b) = 0$. If the pixel is surrounded by 1's, then $L(a, b) = 1(b) = b$. The resultant image is as follows:

$$\begin{bmatrix} 0 & 0 & 0 & 0 & 0 & 0 & 0 & 0 & 0 \\ 0 & 0 & 0 & 0 & 0 & 0 & 0 & 0 & 0 \\ 0 & 0 & 1 & 1 & 1 & 1 & 0 & 0 & 0 \\ 0 & 0 & 1 & 1 & 1 & 1 & 0 & 0 & 0 \\ 0 & 0 & 0 & 0 & 0 & 0 & 0 & 0 & 0 \\ 0 & 0 & 0 & 0 & 0 & 0 & 0 & 0 & 0 \\ 0 & 0 & 0 & 0 & 0 & 0 & 0 & 0 & 0 \\ 0 & 0 & 0 & 0 & 0 & 0 & 0 & 0 & 0 \\ 0 & 0 & 0 & 0 & 0 & 0 & 0 & 0 & 0 \end{bmatrix}$$

Since the logic function is a logical AND operation, the edges are removed. This operation retains a cluster of "1's" with the edge pixels removed. So, the appendages (thin lines) are removed from the original image – this is an erosion operation. Also, compared to Example 5.7.8, we can see that even though the AND logical operator implies erosion, the selection of the set S is critical to exactly what happens to the image.

EXAMPLE 5.7.11: EDGE DETECTION

$$S = \{1, 7\}, L(a, b) = (!a)b, n = 1$$

Consider the following image with the surrounds $\{S\}$:

$$\begin{bmatrix} 0 & 0 & 0 & 0 & 0 & 0 & 0 & 0 & 0 \\ 0 & 1 & 1 & 1 & 1 & 1 & 1 & 0 & 0 \\ 0 & 1 & 1 & 1 & 1 & 1 & 1 & 0 & 0 \\ 0 & 1 & 1 & 1 & 1 & 1 & 1 & 0 & 0 \\ 0 & 1 & 1 & 1 & 0 & 0 & 0 & 0 & 0 \\ 0 & 1 & 1 & 1 & 0 & 0 & 0 & 0 & 0 \\ 0 & 0 & 0 & 0 & 0 & 0 & 0 & 0 & 0 \\ 0 & 0 & 0 & 0 & 0 & 0 & 0 & 0 & 0 \\ 0 & 0 & 0 & 0 & 0 & 0 & 0 & 0 & 0 \end{bmatrix}$$

Let $S = \{1,7\}$, that is $S = \left\{ \begin{bmatrix} 0 & 0 & x \\ 0 & x & 0 \\ x & 0 & 0 \end{bmatrix}, \begin{bmatrix} 1 & 1 & x \\ 1 & x & 1 \\ x & 1 & 1 \end{bmatrix} \right\}$

If $b = 1$, $L(a, b) = (!a)1 = !a$;
Elseif $b = 0$, $L(a, b) = (!a)0 = 0$;
The new image after the above operation is:

$$\begin{bmatrix} 0 & 0 & 0 & 0 & 0 & 0 & 0 & 0 & 0 \\ 0 & 1 & 1 & 1 & 1 & 1 & 1 & 0 & 0 \\ 0 & 1 & 0 & 0 & 0 & 0 & 1 & 0 & 0 \\ 0 & 1 & 0 & 1 & 1 & 1 & 1 & 0 & 0 \\ 0 & 1 & 0 & 1 & 0 & 0 & 0 & 0 & 0 \\ 0 & 1 & 1 & 1 & 0 & 0 & 0 & 0 & 0 \\ 0 & 0 & 0 & 0 & 0 & 0 & 0 & 0 & 0 \\ 0 & 0 & 0 & 0 & 0 & 0 & 0 & 0 & 0 \end{bmatrix}$$

We can see that this operation removes interior pixels and keeps the edges only. Hence, this is an edge detection operation.

EXAMPLE 5.7.12: DILATION

Let $S = \{2,3,4,5,6,7\}$ and $L = a + b$. $(+ = OR)$

IMAGE

$$\begin{bmatrix} 0 & 0 & 0 & 0 & 0 & 0 & 0 & 0 & 0 \\ 0 & 1 & 1 & 0 & 0 & 0 & 0 & 0 & 0 \\ 0 & 1 & 0 & 0 & 0 & 0 & 0 & 0 & 0 \\ 0 & 1 & 1 & 0 & 0 & 0 & 0 & 0 & 0 \\ 0 & 1 & 1 & 0 & 0 & 0 & 0 & 0 & 0 \\ 0 & 0 & 1 & 0 & 0 & 0 & 0 & 0 & 0 \\ 0 & 0 & 1 & 1 & 1 & 1 & 1 & 1 & 0 \\ 0 & 0 & 0 & 0 & 0 & 0 & 0 & 0 & 0 \\ 0 & 0 & 0 & 0 & 0 & 0 & 0 & 0 & 0 \end{bmatrix}$$

$$S = \left\{ \begin{bmatrix} 0 & 1 & x \\ 0 & x & 0 \\ x & 0 & 0 \end{bmatrix}, \begin{bmatrix} 1 & 1 & x \\ 0 & x & 0 \\ x & 0 & 0 \end{bmatrix}, \begin{bmatrix} 1 & 1 & x \\ 1 & x & 0 \\ x & 0 & 0 \end{bmatrix}, \begin{bmatrix} 1 & 1 & x \\ 1 & x & 0 \\ x & 1 & 0 \end{bmatrix}, \begin{bmatrix} 1 & 1 & x \\ 1 & x & 1 \\ x & 1 & 0 \end{bmatrix}, \begin{bmatrix} 1 & 1 & x \\ 1 & x & 1 \\ x & 1 & 1 \end{bmatrix} \right\}$$

Because $L(a, b)$ is an OR operation, all pixels that are 1 in the original will remain 1. That is:

$$L = a + b = a + 1 = 1$$

The only pixels that will change are those that are 0 in the original image and have a surround that is S (this means that $a = 1$). That is:

$$L = a + b = a + 0 = a$$

If we examine the set S, we see that this set contains all pixels that are surrounded by a connected set of 1's. This operation will expand the object, and it illustrates that the OR operation results in a dilation. The resultant image is:

$$\begin{bmatrix} 0 & 0 & 0 & 0 & 0 & 0 & 0 & 0 & 0 \\ 0 & 1 & 1 & 1 & 0 & 0 & 0 & 0 & 0 \\ 0 & 1 & 1 & 1 & 0 & 0 & 0 & 0 & 0 \\ 0 & 1 & 1 & 1 & 0 & 0 & 0 & 0 & 0 \\ 0 & 1 & 1 & 1 & 0 & 0 & 0 & 0 & 0 \\ 0 & 1 & 1 & 1 & 1 & 1 & 1 & 1 & 0 \\ 0 & 1 & 1 & 1 & 1 & 1 & 1 & 1 & 0 \\ 0 & 1 & 1 & 1 & 1 & 1 & 1 & 1 & 0 \\ 0 & 0 & 0 & 0 & 0 & 0 & 0 & 0 & 0 \end{bmatrix}$$

We can see from these examples that this iterative modification morphological approach is quite versatile. The process can be iterated or repeated to any degree desired. We can use this technique to define methods for dilation, erosion, opening, closing, marking corners, finding edges and other binary morphological operations. For this technique, the selection of the set S is comparable to defining the structuring element in the previously described approaches, and the operation $L(a, b)$ defines the type of filtering that occurs. In general, if $L(a, b)$ is an OR operation, it will tend to grow or dilate objects. When $L(a, b)$ is an AND operation, it will tend to shrink, or erode, objects.

As illustrated in Figure 5.7-17, we can use the iterative modification approach to find the skeleton of a binary image by using the following parameters: $L(a, b) = (a!)b$ and $S = (3,4)$. In this figure, we show results as the number of iterations is increased, and it can be compared to results from using the previously defined skeletonization method. In Figure 5.7-18, we use the same operation, but change the set S and see that it now works as an edge detector. In this case, these are the parameters: $L(a, b) = (a!)b$ and $S = (1,7)$.

The morphological operations described (dilation, erosion, opening and closing) can be extended to gray level images in different ways. The easiest method is to simply threshold the gray level image to create a binary image and then apply the existing operators. For many applications, this is not desired as too much information is lost during the thresholding process. Another method that allows us to retain more information is to treat the image as a sequence of binary images by operating on each gray level as if it were the "1" value and assuming everything else to be "0". The resulting images can then be combined by laying them on top of each other and "promoting" each pixel to the highest gray level value coincident with that location.

An example of results from gray level morphological filtering is shown in Figure 5.7-19. For this application, an opening operation followed by a closing operation was performed. A circular structuring element was used, as the object of interest was the skin tumor border. The opening procedure served to smooth the contours of the object, break narrow isthmuses and eliminate thin protrusions and small objects. Next, the closing was performed to fill in gaps and eliminate small holes. To fully understand gray level morphology, we must remember that with two adjacent gray levels, the brightest one is considered to be the object (the equivalent of "1" in a binary image) and the darker is the background (the "0" equivalent in binary morphology). In this figure, we see the tremendous data reduction achieved, as the original image had 42,216 objects. After segmentation, we had 1,095 objects, and morphological filtering provided a decrease to 189 objects, thus simplifying the process of identifying the tumor features of interest.

(a) Original image
(b) 5 iterations
(c) 10 iterations
(d) Iterate until no change
(e) AND method *4-masks*
(f) Sequential method *8-masks*

FIGURE 5.7-17

Skeletonization. For the iterative approach: $L(a,b) = (!a)b$, and $S = (3,4)$. (a) Original image, (b) after five iterations, (c) after 10 iterations, (d) iterating until no more changes occur, (e) results from the previous skeletonization technique with *4-masks*, AND method and (f) results from the previous skeletonization technique with *8-masks*, sequential method.

FIGURE 5.7-18
Edge detection via iterative modification morphological filtering. In this example: $L(a,b) = (!a)b$, and $S = (1,7)$. (a) Original image, (b) resultant image after one iteration

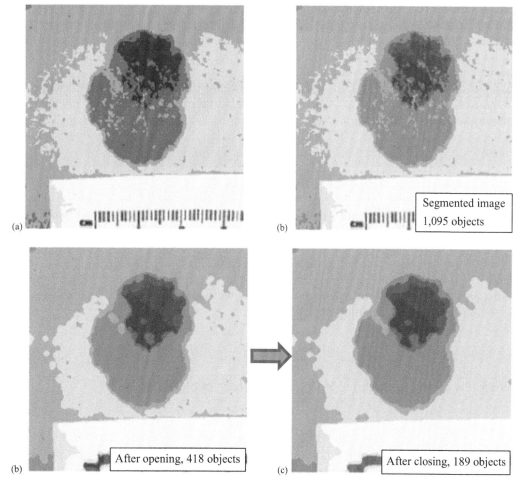

FIGURE 5.7-19
Gray level morphological filtering. Morphological filtering is used to reduce the number of objects after segmentation. (a) Original segmented skin lesion image, segmented with *fuzzy c-mean*, $\sigma = 3$, (b) after color to gray conversion, it contains 1,095 objects, (c) Image (b) after morphological opening using a 7×7 circular structuring element, contains 418 objects and (d) Image (c) after morphological closing using a 7×7 circular element, contains 189 objects.

5.8   Segmentation Evaluation Methods

Evaluating the success for the segmentation of a complex image is a very difficult task. Evaluation methods can operate on the entire segmented image or reduce the image to a smaller number of significant parts and can evaluate the segmentation based on a part by part basis. The evaluation methods can be separated into two categories: (1) objective methods and (2) subjective methods. The objective methods will generate an analytical result, typically with an equation or set of equations, and generate a resultant metric that can be analyzed directly or statistically. Subjective evaluation methods require the use of people-friendly metrics and the design of experiments that require people to evaluate the images. In addition to these two types of evaluation methods, we can further consider (1) supervised methods and (2) unsupervised methods. With the supervised methods, we have what we call *ground truth*, or *gold standard*, segmented images for comparison that are meant to show the correct segmentation result for a set of sample images. Methods are then devised to compare the results from the segmentation algorithm to the "true" result. With unsupervised methods, the "true result" is unknown and the application-specific approaches are developed to use for segmented image evaluation.

5.8.1   Binary Object Shape Comparison Metrics

The simplest type of image to evaluate for a segmentation method is one that consists of two types of elements, referred to as object and background, and it can be represented by a binary image. These types of application are numerous, such as finding the specific areas of necrotic tissue in liver samples (see Figure 5.8-1), separating the blood vessels in eye fundus images (see Figure 5.8-2), finding the region of interest in veterinary thermograms, finding the border of skin lesions in photographic images or finding an object on a surface for a robotic vision application. These metrics are all supervised methods, requiring the creation of ground truth images, which can be labor intensive.

The four metrics discussed here are (1) Dice coefficient, (2) Jaccard index, (3) overlap coefficient and (4) XOR error. To apply these metrics to binary images, A is the count of the white pixels in one image (the area in pixels) and B is the area of the white pixels in the other image. The intersection is the count of the overlap, and the union is the count of both images minus the overlap. The *Dice coefficient* is defined as two times the intersection divided by the sum of both areas:

$$2 \times (A \cap B) / (A + B) \tag{5.8-1}$$

The Dice coefficient has a range of 0–1, with 1 being a perfect match and 0 being the worst possible due to no intersection or overlap. The *Jaccard index* is the intersection over the union, also called the IoU metric:

$$(A \cap B) / (A \cup B) \tag{5.8-2}$$

The Jaccard index also ranges from 0 to 1, with 1 being a perfect match. Note that the union is equal to the sum minus the intersection for the area of binary objects:

$$(A \cup B) = (A + B) - (A \cap B) \tag{5.8-3}$$

The *overlap coefficient* is the intersection divided by the minimum of the two shapes:

$$(A \cap B) / \mathrm{MIN}(A, B) \tag{5.8-4}$$

The overlap coefficient ranges from 0 to 1. It should be interpreted differently than the previous two metrics, because for a value of 1 it means that the smaller of the two objects is fully contained in the larger object, not that it is an exact match. The XOR *error* is defined as the logical exclusive or of the two images, divided by the area of the ground truth image:

$$\mathrm{XOR}(A, B) / A \tag{5.8-5}$$

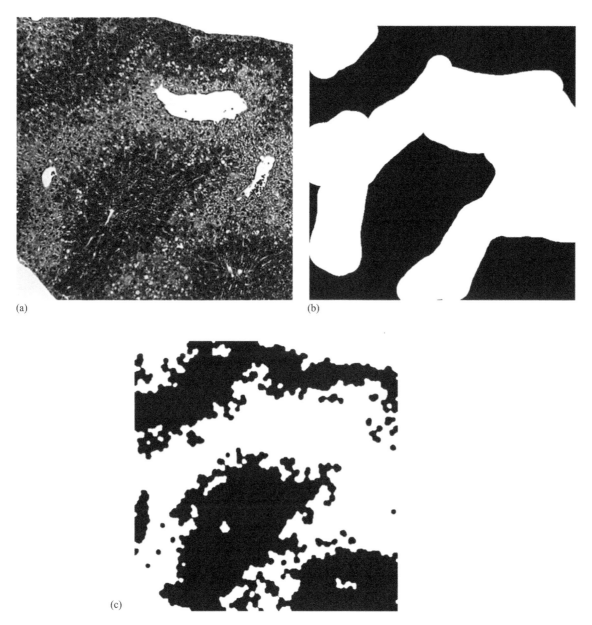

FIGURE 5.8-1
Liver samples for necrotic tissue segmentation. Applications where the output is a binary image allow for the use of the binary object shape error metrics to measure segmentation success. (a) Original liver sample, (b) ground truth image created manually and (c) result from a segmentation algorithm under development.

This metric requires a careful interpretation due to the open-ended range, which is from 0 to X, where X depends on the object(s) and image size. Also, note that a perfect match results in a value of 0 because this metric measures the error. This metric is typically used where we are determining the border of a single object, such as a skin lesion, or finding the region of interest within an image. With this metric, the image A is assumed to be the gold standard image; so, it measures the ratio of the areas where A and B differ (from the XOR) from the area of the true object.

5.8.2 Subjective Methods for Complex Images

The subjective measures provide a result based on human visual perception, because they involve people evaluating the images. The suitability of this approach is application dependent. These methods can be performed in a supervised manner, where ground truth images are provided, or an unsupervised approach can be taken where

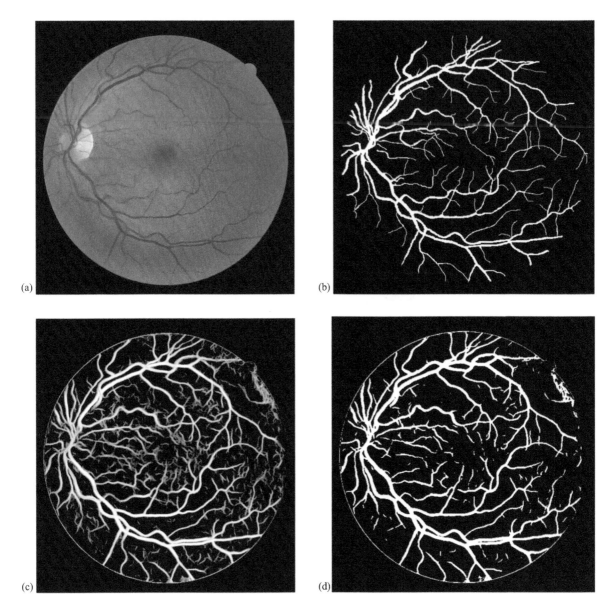

FIGURE 5.8-2
Retinal fundus image for blood vessel segmentation. Applications where the output is a binary image allow for the use of the binary object shape error metrics to measure segmentation success. (a) Original fundus image, (b) ground truth image created manually, (c) result from segmentation using a convolution neural network and (d) segmentation output after threshold.

we rely on the people performing the evaluation to provide their own "ground truth" images based on experience. To generate a subjective score for a segmented image, designing and performing experiments is required in which a group of people evaluate the images. The methodology used for subjective testing includes creating a database of images to be tested, gathering a group of people that are representative of the desired population and then having all the test subjects to evaluate the images according to a predefined scoring criterion. The results are then analyzed statistically, typically using the averages and standard deviations as metrics.

Subjective fidelity measures can be classified into three categories. The first type are referred to as *difference tests*, where the test subjects score the images in terms of how *bad* they are compared to the "correct" (ground truth) segmentation. The second type are *quality tests*, where the test subjects rate the images in terms of how *good* they are compared to the "correct" segmentation. The third type are called *comparison tests*, where parameters in a segmentation method are varied to provide multiple segmented images and the images are evaluated on a side-by-side basis. The comparison tests are considered to provide the most reliable, consistent and useful results, as they provide a relative measure, which is the easiest metric for most people to determine. Difference and quality

TABLE 5-1

Subjective Fidelity Scoring Scales

Difference	Quality	Comparison
5-Imperceptible difference	A-Excellent	+2 much better
4-Perceptible difference	B-Good	+1 better
3-Moderately different	C-Fair	0 the same
2-Severely different	D-Poor	−1 worse
1-Completely different	E-Bad	−2 much worse

tests require an absolute measure, which is more difficult to determine in an unbiased and consistent manner. In Table 5-1 are examples of scoring scales for these three types of subjective measures.

In the design of experiments that perform subjective evaluation, care must be taken so that the experiments are reliable, robust and repeatable. The specific conditions must be carefully defined and controlled. The following exemplify the items that need to be specified: (1) The scoring scale to be used – it is best to have scoring sheets designed so that the test subjects can easily rate the images with a minimum of distraction, (2) the display to be used, and settings such as the brightness and contrast, (3) the resolution setting for the display, (4) the lighting conditions in the room, (5) the distance the test subjects are from the display screen, (6) the amount of time the images are to be displayed, (7) the number of test subjects participating in the experiment, (8) the type of people performing the experiment, that is, are they "average people off the street" or experts in a specific field, and (9) the methods and metrics used for analysis of the results, for example, averages and standard deviations of all the scores. The details for the experiment will be application dependent and additional parameters may be required. After the experiment is complete, the results will be evaluated based on the defined methods and metrics.

5.8.3   Objective Methods for Complex Images

The objective methods use standard equations that are used to compare two signals of any type, where here those signals are segmented images. Consequently, ground truth images are required, so the use of these equations is a supervised approach to evaluating image segmentation methods. Additionally, these methods require careful application to ensure that the comparisons are valid. For example, if the segmentation replaces the pixel values of a segment with the average of all of the segment's pixels, then the ground truth images must be created using the same procedure.

Standard objective measures include the root-mean-square error, e_{RMS}, the root-mean-square signal-to-noise ratio, SNR_{RMS}, and the peak signal-to-noise ratio, SNR_{PEAK}. To understand these measures, we first define the error between a pixel value from the ground truth image and the corresponding segmented pixel value as:

$$\text{error}(r,c) = \hat{I}(r,c) - I(r,c)$$

Where $I(r,c)$ = the ground truth image   (5.8-6)

$\hat{I}(r,c)$ = the segmented image

Next, we can define the total error in an $N \times N$ segmented image as:

$$\text{Total error} = \sum_{r=0}^{N-1}\sum_{c=0}^{N-1}\left[\hat{I}(rc) - I(r,c)\right]$$ (5.8-7)

Typically, we do not want the positive and negative errors to cancel each other out, so we square the individual pixel error. The *root-mean-square error* is found by taking the square root ("root") of the error squared ("square") divided by the total number of pixels in the image ("mean"):

$$e_{RMS} = \sqrt{\frac{1}{N^2}\sum_{r=0}^{N-1}\sum_{c=0}^{N-1}\left[\hat{I}(r,c) - I(r,c)\right]^2}$$ (5.8-8)

If we consider the segmented image, $\hat{I}(r,c)$, to be the "signal" and the error to be "noise", we can define the *root-mean-square signal-to-noise ratio* as follows:

$$\text{SNR}_{\text{RMS}} = \sqrt{\frac{\displaystyle\sum_{r=0}^{N-1}\sum_{c=0}^{N-1}\left[\hat{I}(r,c)\right]^2}{\displaystyle\sum_{r=0}^{N-1}\sum_{c=0}^{N-1}\left[\hat{I}(r,c)-I(r,c)\right]^2}}\tag{5.8-9}$$

Another related metric, the *peak signal-to-noise ratio*, is defined as follows:

$$\text{SNR}_{\text{PEAK}} = 10\log_{10}\frac{(L-1)^2}{\dfrac{1}{N^2}\displaystyle\sum_{r=0}^{N-1}\sum_{c=0}^{N-1}[\hat{I}(r,c)-I(r,c)]^2}$$

Where L = the number of gray levels   (5.8-10)

(e.g., for 8 - bits $L = 256$)

The binary object shape comparison metrics can also be extended to handle multi-level images, such as gray scale or color images. The potentially most useful for this are the Dice coefficient and the Jaccard index. To do this, we need to replace the intersection operator with a bitwise logical AND (&&), the union operator with a bitwise logical OR (||) function, and instead of simply counting the pixels, perform a summation operation. For example, if we want to change the Dice coefficient to operate on multi-level images, the equation is as follows:

$$2\times\sum_{(r,c)}\left[I_1(r,c)\,\&\&\,I_2(r,c)\right]\bigg/\sum_{(r,c)}\left[I_1(r,c)+I_2(r,c)\right]\tag{5.8-11}$$

And the equation for the Jaccard index is as follows:

$$\sum_{(r,c)}\left[I_1(r,c)\,\&\&\,I_2(r,c)\right]\bigg/\sum_{(r,c)}\left[I_1(r,c)\,||\,I_2(r,c)\right]\tag{5.8-12}$$

Although these objective measures are easy to generate and seemingly unbiased due to their analytical nature, as previously noted care must be taken with their use to assure the comparisons are valid. In some cases, it may be more useful to label the image segments and apply these equations to the labeled images. In addition to the methods discussed here for the evaluation of image segmentation algorithms, there are other methods that can be explored in the references.

5.9   Key Points

Segmentation

- The segmentation process has three stages: (1) preprocessing to simplify the image, (2) segmentation, and (3) postprocessing via morphological filters.
- Typical preprocessing operations: gray level quantization, median filtering, Kuwahara filtering, anisotropic diffusion filters and superpixel extraction.
- Superpixel extraction can be most useful preprocessing, as it works by aggregating groups of pixels with similar characteristics using the *simple linear iterative clustering* (SLIC) method.
- The goal of segmentation is to find regions that represent objects or meaningful parts of objects.

- Image segmentation methods look for regions that have some measure of homogeneity within themselves or some measure of contrast with objects on their border.
- Four categories for image segmentation methods: (1) Region growing and shrinking, (2) clustering methods, (3) boundary detection and (4) deep learning, using convolution neural networks.

Region Growing and Shrinking

- Operate principally on the row and column, (r, c), based image space.
- Methods can be local, operating on small neighborhoods, global, operating on the entire image, or a combination of both.

Split and merge: a segmentation method that divides regions that do not pass a homogeneity test and combines regions that pass the homogeneity test. This technique proceeds as follows:

1. Define a homogeneity test. This involves defining a homogeneity measure, which may incorporate brightness, color, texture or other application-specific information, and determining a criterion the region must meet to pass the homogeneity test.
2. Split the image into equal-sized regions.
3. Calculate the homogeneity measure for each region.
4. If the homogeneity test is passed for a region, then a merge is attempted with its neighbor(s). If the criterion is not met, the region is split.
5. Continue this process until all regions pass the homogeneity test.

Quadtree: a data structure used in split and merge in which each node can have four children.

Homogeneity criteria: a measure of similarity within a region in an image. In CVIPtools, these are available: (1) Pure uniformity, (2) local mean versus global mean, (3) local standard deviation versus global, (4) variance, (5) weighted gray level distance and (6) texture.

Watershed algorithm: a morphological technique based on the ideas of modeling a gray level image as a topographic surface, with higher gray levels corresponding to higher elevations. The image is then flooded with a rainfall simulation, and pools of water are created corresponding to segments within the image.

Clustering Techniques

- Segment the image by placing similar elements into groups, or clusters, based on some similarity measure.
- Differ from region growing and shrinking methods in that the mathematical space includes dimensions beyond the row and column image space.
- The mathematical space used for clustering may include, as examples, color spaces, histogram spaces or complex feature spaces.

Recursive region splitting: uses a thresholding of histograms to segment the image. An example of this type of algorithm:

1. Consider the entire image as one region and compute histograms for each component of interest (for example, red, green and blue for a color image).
2. Apply a peak finding test to each histogram. Select the best peak and put thresholds on either side of the peak. Segment the image into two regions based on this peak.
3. Smooth the binary thresholded image so only a single connected subregion is left.
4. Repeat steps 1–3 for each region until no new subregions can be created, that is, no histograms have significant peaks.

SCT/Center algorithm: a color segmentation algorithm initially developed for use in skin tumor identification, defined based on the human visual system response. The algorithm proceeds as follows:

1. Convert the (R, G, B) triple into spherical coordinates – (L, angle A, angle B).
2. Find the minima and maxima of angle A and angle B.

3. Divide the subspace, defined by the maxima and minima, into equal-sized blocks.
4. Calculate the RGB means for the pixel values in each block.
5. Replace the original pixel values with the corresponding RGB means.

PCT/Median algorithm: a color segmentation method initially developed for use in skin tumor identification, based on the principal components transform (PCT). The PCT provides a linear transform that will align the primary axis along the path of maximum variance. The algorithm proceeds as follows:

1. Find the PCT for the RGB image. Transform the RGB data using the PCT.
2. Perform the median split algorithm: find the axis that has the maximal range (initially, it will be the PCT axis). Divide the data along this axis so that there are equal numbers of points on either side of the split – the median point. Continue splitting at the median along the maximum range segment until the desired number of colors is reached.
3. Calculate averages for all the pixels falling within a single parallelepiped (box).
4. Map each pixel to the closest average color values, based on a Euclidean distance measure.

Deep Learning Methods

- Use many layered (deep) convolution neural networks (CNNs).
- A CNN is a specific type of artificial neural network (ANN).
- An ANN has neurons that perform a weighted summation of the inputs with a bias term; in the case of CNN, the weights are the filter coefficients.
- CNNs are used for segmentation because they are good pattern classifiers.
- CNNs are defined by the number of layers, the number and size of the filters in each layer.
- During learning or training, the filter coefficients are adjusted to minimize error or maximize success.
- The first layers of a deep CNN will extract simple features such as edges, and the deeper into the network, the filters will deal with more and more complex image features.
- In practice, generic CNNs that have been trained on millions of images can be used by designing and training the output layer for the specific application.

Combined Segmentation Approaches

- Image segmentation methods may actually be a combination of region growing methods, clustering methods, boundary detection and CNNs.
- Optimal image segmentation is likely to be achieved by focusing on the application.
- Finding boundaries of different features, such as texture, brightness or color, and applying deep learning techniques at a higher level to correlate the feature boundaries found to be the specific domain may give the best results.

Morphological Filtering

- Morphology relates to structure or form of objects.
- Morphological filtering simplifies segmented images by smoothing out object outlines, filling small holes, eliminating small projections or *skeletonizing* a binary object down to lines that are a single pixel wide.
- Primary operations are *dilation* and *erosion*.
- These operations use a structuring element which determines exactly how the object will be dilated or eroded.
- *Opening* and *closing* are useful combinations of dilation and erosion.

Dilation: the process of expanding image objects by changing pixels with value of "0" to "1". It can be done in two steps:

1. If the origin of the structuring element coincides with a "0" in the image, there is no change; move to the next pixel.
2. If the origin of the structuring element coincides with a "1" in the image, perform the OR logic operation on all pixels within the structuring element.

Erosion: the process of shrinking binary objects by changing pixels with a value of "1" to "0". It can be done in two steps:

1. If the origin of the structuring element coincides with a "0" in the image, there is no change; move to the next pixel.

2. If the origin of the structuring element coincides with a "1" in the image and any of the "1" pixels in the structuring element extend beyond the object ("1" pixels) in the image, then change the "1" pixel in the image, whose location corresponds to the origin of the structuring element, to a "0".

Opening: an erosion followed by a dilation. This will eliminate all pixels in regions too small to contain the structuring element. It will expand holes, erode edges and eliminate small objects. It may split objects that are connected by narrow strips and it may eliminate peninsulas.

Closing: a dilation followed by an erosion. It can used to fill holes and small gaps. It will also connect separate objects, if the gap is smaller than the structuring element.

Hit-or-miss transform: The morphological *hit-or-miss transform* is a fundamental method for detection of simple shapes and works by overlaying the structuring element on the image, and it requires an exact match for a "hit" to occur – a hit is marked with a 1. See Examples 5.7.3 and 5.7.4.

Thinning: etching away at an object boundary with a structuring element, *SE,* by this equation (see Example 5.7.5):

$$\text{Thin}\big[I(r, c), \text{SE}\big] = I(r, c) - \text{hit-or-miss}\big[I(r, c), \text{SE}\big] \tag{5.7-1}$$

Skeleton: What is left of a binary object after it has been eroded to the point of being only one pixel wide.

Skeletonization: A controlled erosion process to create a skeleton of a binary object (see Example 5.7.6).

Spur: small, extraneous lines left after the skeletonization process (see Figure 5.7-14).

Pruning: Iteratively removing spurs from a skeleton (see Example 5.7.7, Figure 5.7-14).

Iterative morphological filtering: based on a definition of six-connectivity, so a pixel can be surrounded by 14 possible combinations (allowing for rotation, see Figures 5.7-15 and 5.7-16). Used to dilate, erode, open, close, skeletonize, mark corners, find edges and perform other binary morphological operations. Define: (1) The set of surrounds S, where $a = 1$. (2) A logic function, $L(a, b)$, where b is the current pixel value, the function is output. (3) The number of iterations, n (see Examples 5.7.8–5.7.12).

Gray level morphological filtering: previously defined binary operations extended to gray level images in various ways: (1) threshold the image to create a binary image and apply binary operators, (2) treat the image as sequence of binary images by operating on each gray level as if it were the "1" value and assuming everything else to be "0". Resulting images combined by overlaying and "promoting" to the highest gray level value coincident with that location.

Segmentation Evaluation Methods

- Evaluating the success for the segmentation of a complex image is a very difficult task.
- Evaluation methods can operate on the entire segmented image or a smaller number of significant parts.
- **Two categories**: (1) objective methods generate an analytical result via equation and (2) subjective methods require people to evaluate the images.
- **Two methods**: (1) supervised methods, need *ground truth*, or *gold standard*, segmented images for comparison, and (2) unsupervised methods, the "true result" is unknown and application-specific approaches are developed to use for segmented image evaluation.

Binary Object Shape Comparison Metrics

Dice coefficient: ranges from 0 to 1, 1 is the perfect match

$$2 \times (A \cap B) / (A + B) \tag{5.8-1}$$

Jaccard index: ranges from 0 to 1, 1 is the perfect match

$$(A \cap B)/(A \cup B) \tag{5.8-2}$$

Overlap coefficient: ranges from 0 to 1, a value of 1 it means that the smaller of the two objects is fully contained in the larger object, not that it is an exact match

$$(A \cap B)/\text{MIN}(A,B) \tag{5.8-4}$$

XOR error: ranges from 0 to X; X depends on object size and it needs careful interpretation

$$\text{XOR}(A,B)/A \tag{5.8-5}$$

Subjective Methods for Complex Images

- The subjective measures may more accurately reflect our visual perception than objective measures.
- To generate subjective scores, we must perform experiments with people evaluating according to a predefined scoring criterion.
- Experimental design requires careful definition and controls so that the experiments are reliable, robust and repeatable.
- The results are then analyzed statistically, typically using the averages and standard deviations as metrics.
- Three categories: (1) impairment tests, (2) quality tests and (3) comparison tests.

   Impairment tests: test subjects rate images in terms of how *bad* they are.

   Quality tests: test subjects rate images in terms of how *good* they are.

   Comparison tests: test subjects evaluate images on a side-by-side basis.

- Comparison tests provide the most useful results due to relative measures providing the most consistent results from human test subjects.

Objective Metrics for Complex Images

- Uses equations for comparing two signals and requires ground truth images to compare with the segmentation result.
- Requires careful consideration for format of segmented and ideal images, and they must match.
- The Dice coefficient and Jaccard index can be extended to handle complex images.
- Standard equations for comparisons:

Root-mean-square error:

$$e_{\text{RMS}} = \sqrt{\frac{1}{N^2} \sum_{r=0}^{N-1} \sum_{c=0}^{N-1} \left[\hat{I}(r,c) - I(r,c) \right]^2} \tag{5.8-8}$$

Root-mean-square signal-to-noise ratio:

$$\text{SNR}_{\text{RMS}} = \sqrt{\frac{\sum_{r=0}^{N-1} \sum_{c=0}^{N-1} \left[\hat{I}(r,c) \right]^2}{\sum_{r=0}^{N-1} \sum_{c=0}^{N-1} \left[\hat{I}(r,c) - I(r,c) \right]^2}} \tag{5.8-9}$$

Peak signal-to-noise ratio:

$$\text{SNR}_{\text{PEAK}} = 10 \log_{10} \frac{(L-1)^2}{\dfrac{1}{N^2} \displaystyle\sum_{r=0}^{N-1} \sum_{c=0}^{N-1} [\hat{I}(r,c) - I(r,c)]^2}; \qquad (5.8\text{-}10)$$

Where L = the number of gray levels

Extending Binary Metrics for Complex Images

- Replace the intersection operator with a bitwise logical AND (&&) and union operator with a bitwise logical OR (||)
- Instead of counting the pixels, perform a summation operation

Dice coefficient to operate on multi-level images:

$$2 \times \sum_{(r,c)} \left[I_1(r,c) \,\&\&\, I_2(r,c) \right] \Big/ \sum_{(r,c)} \left[I_1(r,c) + I_2(r,c) \right] \qquad (5.8\text{-}11)$$

Jaccard index for multi-level images:

$$\sum_{(r,c)} \left[I_1(r,c) \,\&\&\, I_2(r,c) \right] \Big/ \sum_{(r,c)} \left[I_1(r,c) \,\|\, I_2(r,c) \right] \qquad (5.8\text{-}12)$$

5.10   References and Further Reading

Additional general information regarding image segmentation can be found in Gonzalez and Woods (2018), Davies (2018), Sonka, Hlavac, and Boyle (2014), Pratt (2007), Shapiro and Stockman (2001), Jain, Kasturi, and Schnuck (1995), Castleman (1996), Haralick and Shapiro (1992) and Schalkoff (1989). Shapiro and Stockman (2001) have detailed examples for using the *K*-means algorithm (superpixel) for image segmentation and Davies (2018) has additional details on the centroidal profile approach to boundary detection. More information on the Kuwahara and anisotropic diffusion filters, which can be used for segmentation preprocessing methods, can be found in Umbaugh (2023). More on active contours or snakes can be found in Nixon and Aguado (2020), Davies (2018), Gonzalez and Woods (2018) and Sonka, Hlavac, and Boyle (2014). Specific details of the GVF snake algorithm and related method(s) can be found in Sonka, Hlavac, and Boyle (2014) and Haidekker (2011).

The PCT/Median and SCT/Center image segmentation methods presented are described in Umbaugh (1990) and applied in Umbaugh, Moss, and Stoecker (1989), Umbaugh, Moss, and Stoecker (1993) and Umbaugh, Moss, and Stoecker (1992). For details on the principal components transform and using it in imaging applications, see Umbaugh (2023). More on thresholding algorithms and the watershed algorithm can be found in Nixon and Aguado (2020), Sonka, Hlavac, and Boyle (2014), Gonzalez and Woods (2018), Baxes (1994) and Dougherty and Lotufo (2003). For other Otsu-based algorithms, including multiple thresholds and fast algorithms, see Liao, Chen, and Chung (2001). The histogram thresholding segmentation algorithms in CVIPtools are based on the Lim and Lee (1990) and Carlotto (1987) papers. For more in-depth information and a survey of state-of-the-art deep learning segmentation methods, see Minaee et al. (2020).

Detailed information on tree data structures can be found in Shapiro and Stockman (2001) and Weiss (1997). More information on image morphology and skeletonization is found in Nixon and Aguado (2020), Sonka, Hlavac, and Boyle (2014), Dougherty (2009), Gonzalez and Woods (2018), Shapiro and Stockman (2001) and Jain, Kasturi, and Schnuck (1995). The definitions for connectivity are described in Horn (1986), and further information can be found in Haralick and Shapiro (1992). For a practical approach with numerous examples of morphological processing, see Dougherty and Lotufo (2003). The iterative method to morphological filtering is described in Horn (1986). For an extensive review of state-of-the-art image segmentation evaluation methods, see Wang, Wang, and Zhu (2020). In addition to CVIPtools, explore Keras, PyTorch and TensorFlow software tools available on the internet for machine learning approaches.

Baxes, G.A., *Digital Image Processing: Principles and Applications*, New York: Wiley, 1994.

Castleman, K.R., *Digital Image Processing*, Upper Saddle River, NJ: Prentice Hall, 1996.

Carlotto, M., Histogram analysis using a scale-state approach, *IEEE Transactions on Pattern Analysis and Machine Intelligence*, Vol. 9, No. 1, pp. 121–129, 1987.

Davies, E.R, *Computer Vision: Principles, Algorithms, Applications and Learning*, 5th Edition, Cambridge, MA: Academic Press, 2018.

Dougherty, G., *Digital Image Processing for Medical Applications*, Cambridge: Cambridge University Press, 2009.

Dougherty, E., Lotufo, *Hands-on Morphological Image Processing*, Bellingham, WA: SPIE Press, 2003.

Gonzalez, R.C., Woods, R.E., *Digital Image Processing*, 4th Edition, London: Pearson, 2018.

Haidekker, M.A., *Advanced Biomedical Image Analysis*, Hoboken, NJ: Wiley, 2011.

Haralick, R.M., Shapiro, L.G., *Computer and Robot Vision*, Reading, MA: Addison-Wesley, 1992.

Horn, B.K.P., *Robot Vision*, Cambridge, MA: The MIT Press, 1986.

Hough, P.V.C, *Methods and Means for Recognizing Complex Patterns*, Washington, DC: U.S. Patent 3,069,654, 1962

Liao, P.S., Chen, T.S., Chung, P.C., A fast algorithm for multilevel thresholding. *Journal of Information Science and Engineering*, Vol. 17, pp. 713–727, 2001.

Jain, R., Kasturi, R., Schnuck, B.G., *Machine Vision*, New York: McGraw Hill, 1995.

Lim, Y., Lee, S., On color segmentation algorithm based on the thresholding and fuzzy c-means techniques, *Pattern Recognition*, Vol. 23, No. 9, pp. 935–952, 1990.

Minaee, S., Boykov, Y., Porikli, F., Plaza, A., Kehtarnavaz, N., Terzopoulos, D., *Image Segmentation Using Deep learning: A Survey*, 2020, https://arxiv.org/abs/2001.05566v5.

Nixon, M., Aguado, A., *Feature Extraction and Image Processing for Computer Vision*, 4th Edition, Cambridge, MA: Academic Press, 2020.

Pratt, W.K., *Digital Image Processing*, New York: Wiley, 2007.

Schalkoff, R.J., *Digital Image Processing and Computer Vision*, New York: Wiley, 1989.

Shapiro, L., Stockman, G., *Computer Vision*, Upper Saddle River, NJ: Prentice Hall, 2001.

Sonka, M., Hlavac, V., Boyle, R., *Image Processing, Analysis and Machine Vision*, 4th Edition, Boston, MA: Cengage Learning, 2014.

Umbaugh, S.E, *DIPA: Digital Image Enhancement, Restoration and Compression*, 4th Edition, Boca Raton, FL: CRC Press, 2023.

Umbaugh, S.E., Moss, R.H., Stoecker, W.V., Automatic color segmentation of images with application to detection of variegated coloring in skin tumors, *IEEE Engineering in Medicine and Biology*, Vol. 8, No. 4, Dec. 1989.

Umbaugh, S.E., *Computer Vision in Medicine: Color Metrics and Image Segmentation Methods for Skin Cancer Diagnosis*, PhD dissertation, Ann Arbor, MI: ProQuest/UMI Dissertation Service, 1990.

Umbaugh, S.E., Moss, R.H., Stoecker, W.V., An automatic color segmentation algorithm with application to identification of skin tumor borders, *Computerized Medical Imaging and Graphics*, Vol. 16, No. 3, 1992.

Umbaugh, S.E., Moss, R.H., Stoecker, W.V., Automatic color segmentation algorithms with application to skin tumors feature identification, *IEEE Engineering in Medicine and Biology*, Vol. 12, No. 3, Sept. 1993.

Wang, Z., Wang, E., Zhu, Y., Image segmentation evaluation: A survey of methods, *Artificial Intelligence Review*, Vol. 53, pp. 5637–5674, 2020, Doi: 10.1007/s10462-020-09830-9.

Weiss, M., *Data Structures and Algorithm Analysis in C*, Reading, MA: Addison-Wesley, 1997.

5.11 Exercises

Problems

1. (a) What is the goal of image segmentation? (b) What type of objects do segmentation methods look for? (c) List the four categories of segmentation methods.

2. What is a quadtree and for which segmentation algorithms is it used? Why is it useful for these algorithms?

3. Compare and contrast region growing and shrinking segmentation methods from clustering methods.

4. Regarding split and merge segmentation algorithms, what is a homogeneity test? Describe three different homogeneity criteria.

5. Briefly describe the watershed algorithm. To which category of segmentation methods does it belong? Explain why or why not it belongs in this category.

6. Use CVIPtools to explore histogram thresholding segmentation methods, including the *histogram thresholding* and *fuzzy c-means* algorithms. Select an image of your choice and (a) examine the histogram,

(b) perform *histogram thresholding* segmentation, and (c) compare the histogram of the image from *histogram thresholding* segmentation to the histogram of the original image. If you had manually selected the peaks, are these the ones you would have selected? Looking at the segmented image, do you think the segmentation was effective? (d) Do parts (a)–(c) using the *fuzzy c-means* algorithm. Note that with this algorithm, we can control the degree of segmentation with the *Gaussian kernel variance*. What happens as we increase this parameter?

7. Use CVIPtools to explore various segmentation methods and their associated parameters. Select an image that allows you to judge when the segmentation has been successful.

8. (a) Most deep learning segmentation methods use a specific type of artificial neural network, what are they? (b) How does a semantic segmentation method work? (c) What type of activation function is typically used in the deep convolution layers of a CNN, and what does it do?

9. (a) In image analysis, what do we call the type of spatial filtering typically performed after segmentation? (b) What are the two principal operations called? Briefly describe each.

10. Given the following image and structuring element, perform an opening operation. Assume the origin of the structuring element is in the center. Ignore cases where the structuring element extends beyond the image.

STRUCTURING ELEMENT

$$\begin{bmatrix} 1 & 0 & 0 \\ 1 & 1 & 1 \\ 1 & 0 & 0 \end{bmatrix}$$

IMAGE

$$\begin{bmatrix} 1 & 1 & 1 & 1 & 1 & 1 & 1 \\ 1 & 0 & 0 & 1 & 0 & 0 & 1 \\ 1 & 1 & 1 & 1 & 1 & 1 & 1 \\ 1 & 0 & 0 & 0 & 0 & 0 & 1 \\ 1 & 1 & 1 & 1 & 1 & 1 & 1 \\ 1 & 1 & 1 & 1 & 1 & 1 & 1 \\ 1 & 1 & 0 & 0 & 1 & 1 & 1 \end{bmatrix}$$

11. Applying the iterative morphological filtering method, what will be the resultant pixel values after operating on the following image? Assume all rotations of the surrounds are included in S.

IMAGE

$$\begin{bmatrix} 1 & 1 & 1 & 1 & 1 & 1 & 1 \\ 1 & 0 & 0 & 1 & 0 & 0 & 1 \\ 1 & 1 & 1 & 1 & 1 & 1 & 1 \\ 1 & 0 & 0 & 0 & 0 & 0 & 1 \\ 1 & 1 & 1 & 1 & 1 & 1 & 1 \\ 1 & 1 & 1 & 1 & 1 & 1 & 1 \\ 1 & 1 & 0 & 0 & 1 & 1 & 1 \end{bmatrix}$$

a. $S = \{2,3,4,5,6\}$, $L(a, b) = a\bar{b}$, $n = 1$. Find the resultant pixel values at $(r, c) = (3,2)$; $(r, c) = (3,3)$; $(r, c) = (4,5)$ and $(r, c) = (3,5)$.

b. $S = \{7\}$, $L(a, b) = a+b$, $n = 1$. Find the resultant pixel values at $(r, c) = (4,5)$; $(r, c) = (2,2)$; $(r, c) = (4,2)$ and $(r, c) = (4,4)$.

5.11.1 Programming Exercises

These exercises can be implemented with CVIPlab in MATLAB or in C/C++.

SCT/Center Segmentation

1. Write a function to implement the SCT/Center segmentation algorithm. Let the user enter the number of colors along the *angle A* and *angle B* axes.
2. Compare your results to those obtained in CVIPtools.

Histogram Thresholding Segmentation

1. Use the CVIP MATLAB Toolbox, or CVIPtools libraries, to experiment with the histogram-based thresholding segmentation functions. In MATLAB, these are the *autothreshold_cvip*, *hist_thresh_cvip* and *fuzzyc_cvip*; and for C programmers, they are *auto_threshold_segment*, *hist_thresh_segment* and *fuzzyc_segment*.
2. Compare your results to those obtained in CVIPtools.

Morphological Filters

1. Write functions to implement dilation, erosion, opening and closing for binary images. Let the user enter the nine 0's and 1's for a 3×3 structuring element.
2. Compare your results to those obtained in CVIPtools.

Iterative Morphological Filters

1. Use the CVIP MATLAB Toolbox or CVIPtools libraries to experiment with iterative morphological functions. In MATLAB, use the *morphitermod_cvip* function; and for C programmers, the *morphIterMod_Image* or *morpho* function can be used.
2. Compare your results to those obtained in CVIPtools.

5.12 Supplementary Exercises

Problems

1. Apply the hit-or-miss transform with the structuring element, SE, to the following image:

$$SE = \begin{bmatrix} 1 & 0 & 0 \\ x & 1 & x \\ 1 & x & 1 \end{bmatrix}$$

$$I(r,c) = \begin{bmatrix} 0 & 0 & 0 & 0 & 0 & 0 & 0 & 0 \\ 0 & 1 & 0 & 0 & 0 & 0 & 1 & 0 \\ 0 & 1 & 1 & 1 & 1 & 1 & 1 & 0 \\ 0 & 1 & 1 & 1 & 1 & 1 & 1 & 0 \\ 0 & 1 & 1 & 1 & 1 & 1 & 1 & 0 \\ 0 & 1 & 1 & 1 & 1 & 1 & 1 & 0 \\ 0 & 0 & 0 & 0 & 0 & 0 & 0 & 0 \\ 0 & 0 & 0 & 0 & 0 & 0 & 0 & 0 \end{bmatrix}$$

2. Apply the skeletonization process to the following image:

$$\begin{bmatrix} 0 & 0 & 0 & 0 & 0 & 0 & 0 & 0 \\ 0 & 1 & 1 & 1 & 1 & 1 & 1 & 0 \\ 0 & 1 & 1 & 1 & 1 & 1 & 1 & 0 \\ 0 & 1 & 1 & 1 & 1 & 1 & 1 & 0 \\ 0 & 1 & 1 & 1 & 1 & 1 & 1 & 0 \\ 0 & 1 & 1 & 1 & 1 & 1 & 1 & 0 \\ 0 & 0 & 0 & 0 & 0 & 0 & 0 & 0 \\ 0 & 0 & 0 & 0 & 0 & 0 & 0 & 0 \end{bmatrix}$$

3. (a) Apply the Moravec corner detector to the following image and show the result. (b) Mark the corner points found using a threshold of 7 (do not check outer rows and columns):

$$\begin{bmatrix} 6 & 3 & 3 & 6 & 12 \\ 3 & 6 & 6 & 6 & 6 \\ 6 & 15 & 14 & 0 & 0 \\ 7 & 15 & 0 & 0 & 0 \\ 0 & 7 & 3 & 1 & 0 \end{bmatrix} \text{Results}: \begin{bmatrix} x & x & x & x & x \\ x & \square & \square & \square & x \\ x & \square & \square & \square & x \\ x & \square & \square & \square & x \\ x & x & x & x & x \end{bmatrix}$$

4. Find the Dice coefficient and the Jaccard index comparing these two binary images.

$$\begin{bmatrix} 0 & 0 & 0 & 0 & 0 & 0 & 0 & 0 \\ 0 & 1 & 0 & 0 & 0 & 0 & 1 & 0 \\ 0 & 1 & 1 & 1 & 1 & 1 & 1 & 0 \\ 0 & 1 & 1 & 1 & 1 & 1 & 1 & 0 \\ 0 & 1 & 1 & 1 & 1 & 1 & 1 & 0 \\ 0 & 1 & 1 & 1 & 1 & 1 & 1 & 0 \\ 0 & 0 & 0 & 0 & 0 & 0 & 0 & 0 \\ 0 & 0 & 0 & 0 & 0 & 0 & 0 & 0 \end{bmatrix} \begin{bmatrix} 0 & 0 & 0 & 0 & 0 & 0 & 0 & 0 \\ 0 & 1 & 1 & 1 & 1 & 1 & 1 & 0 \\ 0 & 1 & 1 & 1 & 1 & 1 & 1 & 0 \\ 0 & 1 & 1 & 1 & 1 & 1 & 1 & 0 \\ 0 & 1 & 1 & 1 & 1 & 1 & 1 & 0 \\ 0 & 1 & 1 & 1 & 1 & 1 & 1 & 0 \\ 0 & 0 & 0 & 0 & 0 & 0 & 0 & 0 \\ 0 & 0 & 0 & 0 & 0 & 0 & 0 & 0 \end{bmatrix}$$

5. Find the Overlap coefficient and the XOR error for the following two images:

$$\text{Image A} \begin{bmatrix} 0 & 0 & 0 & 0 & 0 & 0 & 0 & 0 \\ 0 & 1 & 0 & 0 & 0 & 0 & 1 & 0 \\ 0 & 1 & 1 & 1 & 1 & 1 & 1 & 0 \\ 0 & 1 & 1 & 1 & 1 & 1 & 1 & 0 \\ 0 & 1 & 1 & 1 & 1 & 1 & 1 & 0 \\ 0 & 1 & 1 & 1 & 1 & 1 & 1 & 0 \\ 0 & 0 & 0 & 0 & 0 & 0 & 0 & 0 \\ 0 & 0 & 0 & 0 & 0 & 0 & 0 & 0 \end{bmatrix}$$

$$\text{Image B} \begin{bmatrix} 0 & 0 & 0 & 0 & 0 & 0 & 0 & 0 \\ 0 & 1 & 1 & 1 & 1 & 1 & 1 & 0 \\ 0 & 1 & 1 & 1 & 1 & 1 & 1 & 0 \\ 0 & 1 & 1 & 1 & 1 & 1 & 1 & 0 \\ 0 & 1 & 1 & 1 & 1 & 1 & 1 & 0 \\ 0 & 1 & 1 & 1 & 1 & 1 & 1 & 0 \\ 0 & 0 & 0 & 0 & 0 & 0 & 0 & 0 \\ 0 & 0 & 0 & 0 & 0 & 0 & 0 & 0 \end{bmatrix}$$

6. Find the Dice coefficient and the Jaccard index for the following 3-bit per pixel images:

$$
\begin{bmatrix}
0 & 0 & 0 & 0 & 0 & 0 & 0 & 0 \\
0 & 3 & 0 & 0 & 0 & 0 & 7 & 0 \\
0 & 3 & 2 & 2 & 1 & 6 & 7 & 0 \\
0 & 3 & 2 & 2 & 1 & 6 & 7 & 0 \\
0 & 7 & 2 & 2 & 1 & 6 & 7 & 0 \\
0 & 7 & 2 & 2 & 1 & 6 & 7 & 0 \\
0 & 0 & 0 & 0 & 0 & 0 & 0 & 0 \\
0 & 0 & 0 & 0 & 0 & 0 & 0 & 0
\end{bmatrix}
\begin{bmatrix}
0 & 0 & 0 & 0 & 0 & 0 & 0 & 0 \\
0 & 3 & 3 & 3 & 3 & 3 & 7 & 0 \\
0 & 2 & 2 & 2 & 1 & 6 & 7 & 0 \\
0 & 2 & 1 & 2 & 1 & 5 & 6 & 0 \\
0 & 7 & 2 & 2 & 1 & 5 & 5 & 0 \\
0 & 6 & 2 & 2 & 1 & 4 & 5 & 0 \\
0 & 0 & 0 & 0 & 0 & 0 & 0 & 0 \\
0 & 0 & 0 & 0 & 0 & 0 & 0 & 0
\end{bmatrix}
$$

7. Find the *root-mean-square error* and the *root-mean-square signal-to-noise ratio* for the following two images. For the SNR_{RMS}, use the first image as the signal.

$$
\begin{bmatrix}
0 & 0 & 0 & 0 & 0 & 0 & 0 & 0 \\
0 & 3 & 0 & 0 & 0 & 0 & 7 & 0 \\
0 & 3 & 2 & 2 & 1 & 6 & 7 & 0 \\
0 & 3 & 2 & 2 & 1 & 6 & 7 & 0 \\
0 & 7 & 2 & 2 & 1 & 6 & 7 & 0 \\
0 & 7 & 2 & 2 & 1 & 6 & 7 & 0 \\
0 & 0 & 0 & 0 & 0 & 0 & 0 & 0 \\
0 & 0 & 0 & 0 & 0 & 0 & 0 & 0
\end{bmatrix}
\begin{bmatrix}
0 & 0 & 0 & 0 & 0 & 0 & 0 & 0 \\
0 & 3 & 3 & 3 & 3 & 3 & 7 & 0 \\
0 & 2 & 2 & 2 & 1 & 6 & 7 & 0 \\
0 & 2 & 1 & 2 & 1 & 5 & 6 & 0 \\
0 & 7 & 2 & 2 & 1 & 5 & 5 & 0 \\
0 & 6 & 2 & 2 & 1 & 4 & 5 & 0 \\
0 & 0 & 0 & 0 & 0 & 0 & 0 & 0 \\
0 & 0 & 0 & 0 & 0 & 0 & 0 & 0
\end{bmatrix}
$$

8. For the following descriptions of iterative modification schemes, define the set of surrounds, S, and the logic function, $L(a,b)$, that will perform the function: a) Resets all pixels to zero, b) Performs a logical NOT, c) removes edges and keeps interiors, d) removes interiors, keeps edges, e) only keeps isolated pixels that are one, f) Removes isolated pixels that are one and leaves the rest of the image alone, g) marks endpoints of lines, h) removes all but corners.

5.12.1 Supplementary Programming Exercises

These exercises can be implemented with CVIPlab in MATLAB or in C/C++.

Morphological Filters II

1. Write functions to implement dilation, erosion, opening and closing for multi-level images. Let the user enter the nine 0's and 1's for a 3×3 structuring element.
2. Compare your results to those obtained in CVIPtools. Are they the same? Why or why not?
3. Expand the structuring element size to include 5×5 and 7×7 structuring elements.
4. Compare your results with CVIPtools. Are they the same? Why or why not?

Skeletonization

1. Write a function to implement the skeletonization algorithm. Let the user select the *4-horizontal/vertical masks*, *8-masks* or the *4-diagonal* masks. Also, let the user specify the AND method or the sequential method.
2. Compare your results to CVIPtools. Are they the same? Why or why not?
3. Modify your function to allow the user to select any subset of the eight possible masks. Describe an application where this would be useful.
4. Modify your function to automatically iterate (a) until no further changes occur or (b) until the number of connected components does not change. Allow the user to specify the type of connectivity.

Objective Segmentation Evaluation Metrics

1. Write a function to implement the Dice coefficient and Jaccard index for binary images.
2. Test your functions and compare to CVIPtools results. Are they the same? Why or why not?
3. Enhance your functions to work on gray level and color images.
4. Test your functions and compare to CVIPtools results. Are they the same? Why or why not?
5. Write functions to implement the RMS error and Peak SNR error metrics.
6. Test your functions and compare to CVIPtools results. Are they the same? Why or why not?

Subjective Segmentation Evaluation Metrics

1. Design an experiment to compare two different segmentation methods for an application of your choice using a comparison metric.
2. Apply the two segmentation methods, or one method with two parameter settings, to at least ten images for your application.
3. Perform the experiment with at least five participants.
4. Analyze the results using averages and standard deviations from the participants' ratings.

6

Feature Extraction and Analysis

6.1 Introduction and Overview

Feature analysis and pattern classification are often the final steps in the image analysis process. *Feature analysis* involves examining the features extracted from the images and determining if and how they can be used to solve the imaging problem under consideration. In some cases, the extracted features may not solve the problem and the information gained by analyzing the features can be used to determine further analysis methods that may prove helpful, including additional features that may be needed. *Pattern classification*, also called pattern recognition, involves the classification of objects into categories or classes. For many imaging applications, this classification needs to be done automatically via computer. The patterns to be classified consist of the extracted feature information, which are associated with image objects and the classes or categories will be application dependent. In this chapter, we focus on feature extraction and analysis and in the next chapter on pattern classification.

As discussed in Chapter 3, the goal in image analysis is to extract information useful for solving application-based problems. This is done by intelligently reducing the amount of image data with the tools we have explored, including image segmentation, which will help to separate objects within the image. After these operations are performed, the image has been modified from the lowest level of pixel data into higher-level representations and we are ready to extract features that can be useful for solving the imaging problem. The object features of interest include the geometric properties of binary objects, histogram features, spectral features, texture features and color features. After we have extracted the features of interest, we can analyze the image.

Exactly how we use the features to analyze the image will be application dependent. If we are working on an industrial robotic arm control application, we may need to classify objects to determine where each type of object will be placed. If we are working to develop a medical diagnostic tool, we will need to determine what image data is important for the particular pathology and the best features for the application. For an autonomous driving system, there are numerous tasks to be dealt with. We must integrate the data from various image sources, whether they be sonar, radar, lidar or video data, and then extract the necessary features from each source and determine how they will be used to drive the vehicle.

As shown in Figure 3.1-3, feature extraction is part of the data reduction process and is followed by feature analysis. One of the important aspects of feature analysis is to determine exactly which features are important, so the analysis is not complete until we incorporate application-specific feedback into the system (see Figure 6.1-1). Determining the important features is part of the feature selection process, and there are typically at least two iterations of feature selection: (1) initial selection before feature extraction and before any analysis or pattern classification and (2) selection after analysis to determine which features will work best for pattern classification and to solve the imaging problem under consideration.

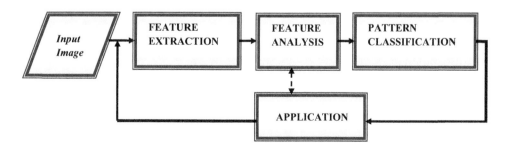

FIGURE 6.1-1
Feature extraction, feature analysis and pattern classification. To be effective, the application-specific feedback loop is of paramount importance.

DOI: 10.1201/9781003221135-6

6.1.1 Feature Extraction

Feature extraction is a process that begins with initial feature selection. The selected features will be the major factor that determines the complexity and success of the analysis and pattern classification process. Initially, the features are selected based on the application requirements and the developer's experience. After the features have been analyzed, with attention to the application, the developer may gain insight into the application's needs which will lead to another iteration of feature selection, extraction and analysis. The overall process shown in Figure 6.1-1 will continue until an acceptable success rate is achieved for the application.

When selecting features for use in a computer imaging application, we want to consider the following desirable attributes. A good feature is:

- **Robust**: it will have similar results under various conditions, such as lighting, cameras and lenses.
- **Discriminating**: it is useful for differentiation of classes (object types) of interest.
- **Reliable**: it provides consistent measurements for similar classes (objects).
- **Independent**: it is not correlated to other features.

For example, if developing a system to work under any lighting conditions, do not use features that are lighting dependent – they will not provide consistent results in the application domain and are not robust. If a feature has similar values for different types of objects, it is not a discriminating feature; we cannot use it to separate the different classes. A feature that has different values for similar objects is not reliable. Features which are correlated have redundant information which may confuse the classifier and waste processing time.

A specific type of robustness, especially applicable to shape features, is called RST-invariance, where the RST means rotation, size and translation. A very robust feature will be RST-invariant, meaning that if the image object is rotated, shrunk or enlarged, or translated (shifted left/right or up/down), the value for the feature will not change. As we explore the binary object features, consider the invariance of each feature to these simple geometric operations.

6.2 Shape Features

Shape features depend on a silhouette of the image object under consideration, so only a binary image is needed. We can think of this binary image as a mask of the image object, as shown in Figure 6.2-1. The basic binary object features are in Section 3.3.3, including area, center of area, axis of least second moment, projections and Euler number. Here, we will add perimeter, thinness ratio, irregularity, aspect ratio, moments and a moment related set of RST-invariant features.

The *perimeter* of the object can help provide us with information about the shape of the object. The perimeter can be found in the original binary image by counting the number of "1" pixels that have "0" pixels as neighbors. Perimeter can also be found by application of an edge detector to the object, followed by counting the "1" pixels. Note that counting the "1" pixels is the same as finding the area, but in this case we are finding the "area" of the border. Since the digital images are typically mapped onto a square grid, curved outlines tend to be jagged, so these methods only give an estimate to the actual perimeter for objects with curved edges. For an irregular shape, an improved estimate to the perimeter can be found by multiplying the results from either of the above methods by $\pi/4$. If better accuracy is required, more complex methods which use chain codes for finding perimeter can be used (see references). An illustration of perimeter is shown in Figure 6.2-2.

In Chapter 3, we found the area of a binary object by counting the number of "1" pixels in the object. Given the area, A, and perimeter, P, we can calculate the *thinness ratio* T:

$$T = 4\pi\left(\frac{A}{P^2}\right) \tag{6.2-1}$$

This measure has a theoretical maximum value of 1, which corresponds to a circle, so this also is used as a measure of roundness. In practice, due to the square grid typically used for digital images which only approximates curves, and dependent upon the method used for calculating perimeter, the maximum may actually be closer to 1.3.

FIGURE 6.2-1
Shape features need a simple binary image. (a) The original image, (b) the image divided into image objects via segmentation, (c) the segmented image with an outline drawn in red on one of the drumhead image objects. (d) the binary mask image for the marked image object which is used for extraction of features related to object shape, in this case, the elliptical shape can help identify it as a drumhead.

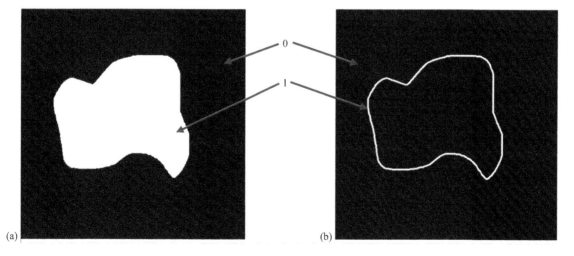

FIGURE 6.2-2
Perimeter. (a) Image with a binary object. We can find the perimeter by counting the number of "1" pixels that have "0" as a neighbor and (b) image after Sobel edge detection. We can find perimeter by counting the "1" pixels.

However, it is still useful as a relative measure. As the value approaches the maximum, the object is more like a circle. As the perimeter becomes larger relative to the area, this ratio decreases and the object is getting thinner. This metric is also used to determine the regularity of an object: regular objects have higher thinness ratios than similar but irregular objects. The inverse of this metric, $1/T$, is the *irregularity* or *compactness* ratio. The area to perimeter ratio, A/P, has properties similar to the thinness ratio, but is easier to calculate.

A related feature is the *aspect ratio* (also called *elongation* or *eccentricity*), defined by the ratio of the bounding box of an object. This can be found by scanning the image and finding the minimum and maximum values on the row and columns where the object lies. This ratio is then defined by:

$$\frac{c_{max} - c_{min} + 1}{r_{max} - r_{min} + 1} \tag{6.2-2}$$

Note that this definition is not rotationally invariant, so to be useful as a comparative measure the objects should be rotated to some standard orientation, such as orientating the axis of least second moment in the horizontal direction.

Moments can be used to generate a set of RST-invariant features. Given a binary image, where $I(r, c)$ can only be "0" or "1", the *moment of order* $(p+q)$ is:

$$m_{pq} = \sum_r \sum_c r^p c^q I(r,c) \tag{6.2-3}$$

In order to be translationally invariant, we use the *central moments* defined by:

$$\mu_{pq} = \sum_r \sum_c (r - \bar{r})^p (c - \bar{c})^q I(r,c) \tag{6.2-4}$$

where

$$\bar{r} = \frac{m_{10}}{m_{00}} \text{ and } \bar{c} = \frac{m_{01}}{m_{00}}$$

Note that these central moments are simply the standard moments shifted to the center of area of the object – compare the equations for $\bar{r}$ and $\bar{c}$ to the center of area as defined in Chapter 3. To create the RST-invariant moment-based features, we need the *normalized central moments*:

$$\eta_{pq} = \frac{\mu_{pq}}{\mu_{00}^\gamma} \tag{6.2-5}$$

where

$$\gamma = \frac{p+q}{2} + 1, \text{ for } (p+q) = 2,3,4\ldots$$

Given these normalized central moments, a set of RST-invariant features, $\varphi_1 - \varphi_7$, can be derived using the second and third moments. These *invariant moment features* are shown in Table 6-1.

An example image with binary objects showing the results of extracting these features is shown in Figure 6.2-3. Here, we see two squares of different sizes (scales), two rotated rectangles and two objects that are scaled and rotated. All the objects are translated since they are all in different locations. We see that these features for the same shaped objects are identical, which makes these features *robust*, *discriminating* and *reliable*. In Figure 6.2-4, we have added noise to the image, performed a simple threshold at 128 to get the segmented image and extracted the RST-invariant features. Here, we see that the objects can still be classified with the first one or two features. Thus, these features are robust to noise as well as being RST invariant.

Fourier descriptors (FDs) represent a group of methods often used in shape analysis which require representing the shape as a one- or two-dimensional signal and then taking the Fourier transform of the signal. For imaging applications, the simplest method is to use the binary image of the object and use the spectral features defined in Section 6.5. Other FD methods include representing the outline of the object in various mathematical forms and finding the one- or two-dimensional Fourier transform of the signal; details of these methods can be explored with the references.

TABLE 6-1

Invariant Moment Features

$$\varphi_1 = \eta_{20} + \eta_{02}$$

$$\varphi_2 = \left(\eta_{20} - \eta_{02}\right)^2 + 4\eta_{11}^2$$

$$\varphi_3 = \left(\eta_{30} - 3\eta_{12}\right)^2 + \left(3\eta_{21} - \eta_{03}\right)^2$$

$$\varphi_4 = \left(\eta_{30} + \eta_{12}\right)^2 + \left(\eta_{21} + \eta_{03}\right)^2$$

$$\varphi_5 = \left(\eta_{30} - 3\eta_{12}\right)\left(\eta_{30} + \eta_{12}\right)\left[\left(\eta_{30} + \eta_{12}\right)^2 - 3\left(\eta_{21} + \eta_{03}\right)^2\right] + \left(3\eta_{21} - \eta_{03}\right)\left(\eta_{21} + \eta_{03}\right)\left[3\left(\eta_{30} + \eta_{12}\right)^2 - \left(\eta_{21} + \eta_{03}\right)^2\right]$$

$$\varphi_6 = \left(\eta_{20} - \eta_{02}\right)\left[\left(\eta_{30} + \eta_{12}\right)^2 - \left(\eta_{21} + \eta_{03}\right)^2\right] + 4\eta_{11}\left(\eta_{30} + \eta_{12}\right)\left(\eta_{21} + \eta_{03}\right)$$

$$\varphi_7 = \left(3\eta_{21} - \eta_{03}\right)\left(\eta_{30} + \eta_{12}\right)\left[\left(\eta_{30} + \eta_{12}\right)^2 - 3\left(\eta_{21} + \eta_{03}\right)^2\right] - \left(\eta_{30} - 3\eta_{12}\right)\left(\eta_{21} + \eta_{03}\right)\left[3\left(\eta_{30} + \eta_{12}\right)^2 - \left(\eta_{21} + \eta_{03}\right)^2\right]$$

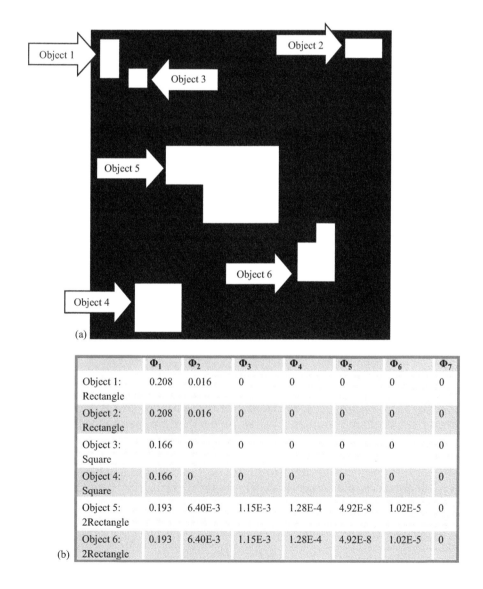

(a)

	Φ_1	Φ_2	Φ_3	Φ_4	Φ_5	Φ_6	Φ_7
Object 1: Rectangle	0.208	0.016	0	0	0	0	0
Object 2: Rectangle	0.208	0.016	0	0	0	0	0
Object 3: Square	0.166	0	0	0	0	0	0
Object 4: Square	0.166	0	0	0	0	0	0
Object 5: 2Rectangle	0.193	6.40E-3	1.15E-3	1.28E-4	4.92E-8	1.02E-5	0
Object 6: 2Rectangle	0.193	6.40E-3	1.15E-3	1.28E-4	4.92E-8	1.02E-5	0

(b)

FIGURE 6.2-3

RST-invariant features. (a) The image with the six objects, (b) the extracted feature data (values less than 1.0E-10 are shown as 0). Here, we see that the same shaped objects have identical feature values, even though they have been rotated, scaled and translated. This makes these features *robust*, *discriminating* and *reliable*.

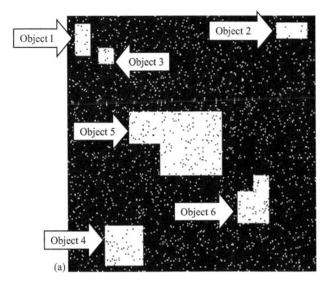

(a)

	Φ_1	Φ_2	Φ_3	Φ_4	Φ_5	Φ_6	Φ_7
Object 1:	0.212	0.016	8.79E-7	8.75E-8	0	-1.19E-9	0
Rectangle	(0.208)	(0.016)	(0)	(0)	(0)	(0)	(0)
Object 2:	0.213	0.017	9.01E-7	2.07E-7	0	2.83E-9	0
Rectangle	(0.208)	(0.016)	(0)	(0)	(0)	(0)	(0)
Object 3:	0.172	2.17E-6	4.84E-6	8.69E-7	0	0	0
Square	(0.166)	(0)	(0)	(0)	(0)	(0)	(0)
Object 4:	0.172	3.19E-6	8.29E-8	1.17E-7	0	0	0
Square	(0.166)	(0)	(0)	(0)	(0)	(0)	(0)
Object 5:	0.199	6.88E-3	1.25E-3	1.39E-4	5.81E-8	1.15E-5	-1.60E-9
2Rectangle	(0.193)	(6.40E-3)	(1.15E-3)	(1.28E-4)	(4.92E-8)	(1.02E-5)	(0)
Object 6:	0.198	6.60E-3	1.22E-3	1.34E-4	5.42E-8	1.08E-5	-3.95E-9
2Rectangle	(0.193)	(6.40E-3)	(1.15E-3)	(1.28E-4)	(4.92E-8)	(1.02E-5)	(0)

(b)

FIGURE 6.2-4
RST-invariant features with noise. (a) The image with the six objects and noise added and (b) the extracted feature data, with the data from the images without noise in parenthesis (values less than 1.0E-10 are shown as 0). Here, we see that the same shaped objects have very similar feature values, even with the added noise. This makes these features *robust* in the presence of noise.

6.3   Histogram Features

The *histogram* of an image is a plot of the gray level values versus the number of pixels at that value. The shape of the histogram provides us with information about the nature of the image or subimage if we are considering an object within the image. For example, a very narrow histogram implies a low contrast image, a histogram heavily weighted toward the high end implies a bright image and a histogram with two major peaks, called bimodal, implies an object that is in contrast with the background. Examples of the different types of histograms are shown in Figure 6.3-1.

The histogram features that we will consider are statistical-based features, where the histogram is used as a model of the probability distribution of the gray levels. These statistical features provide us with information about the characteristics of the gray level distribution for the image or subimage. We define the first-order histogram probability, $P(g)$, as follows:

$$P(g) = \frac{N(g)}{M} \tag{6.3-1}$$

M is the number of pixels in the image or subimage (if the entire image is under consideration, then $M = N^2$ for an $N \times N$ image) and $N(g)$ is the number of pixels at gray level g. As with any probability distribution, all the values for

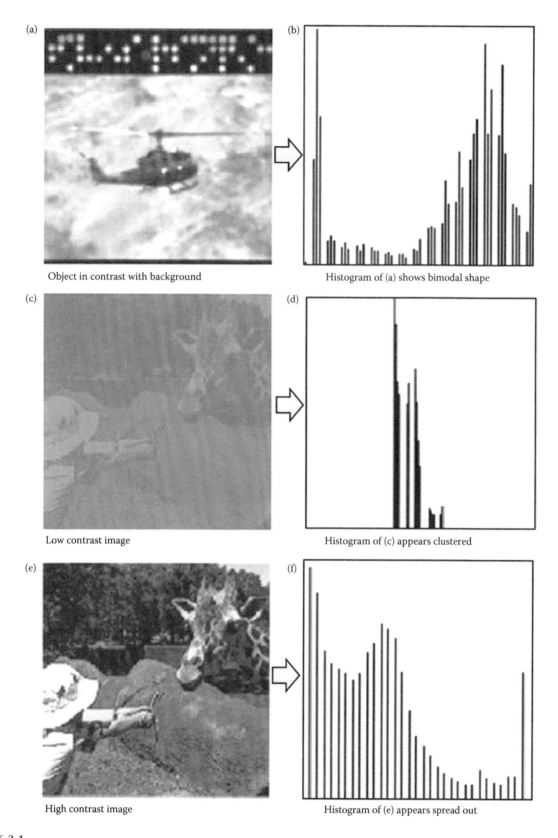

FIGURE 6.3-1

Histograms. The histogram is a plot of the image brightness levels versus the numbers of pixels at each level. The shape and position of the image histogram contains information about the image contrast and brightness.

(Continued)

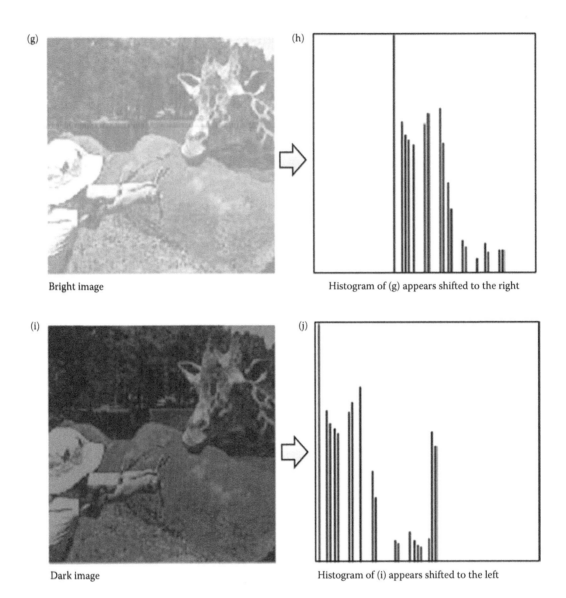

(g) Bright image

(h) Histogram of (g) appears shifted to the right

(i) Dark image

(j) Histogram of (i) appears shifted to the left

FIGURE 6.3-1 (*Continued*)
Histograms. The histogram is a plot of the image brightness levels versus the numbers of pixels at each level. The shape and position of the image histogram contains information about the image contrast and brightness.

$P(g)$ are less than or equal to 1, and the sum of all the $P(g)$ values is equal to 1. The features based on the first-order histogram probability are the mean, standard deviation, skew, energy and entropy.

The *mean* is the average value, so it tells us something about the general brightness of the image. A bright image will have a high mean and a dark image will have a low mean. We will use L as the total number of gray levels available, so the gray levels range from 0 to $L - 1$. For example, for typical 8-bit image data, L is 256 and ranges from 0 to 255. We can define the mean as follows:

$$\bar{g} = \sum_{g=0}^{L-1} g P(g) = \sum_{r}\sum_{c} \frac{I(r,c)}{M} \tag{6.3-2}$$

If we use the second form of the equation, we sum over the rows and columns corresponding to the pixels in the image or subimage under consideration.

Feature Extraction and Analysis 283

The *standard deviation*, which is also known as the square root of the variance, tells us something about the contrast. It describes the spread in the data, so a high contrast image will have a high variance and a low contrast image will have a low variance. It is defined as follows:

$$\sigma_g = \sqrt{\sum_{g=0}^{L-1} (g - \overline{g})^2 P(g)} \qquad (6.3\text{-}3)$$

The *skew* measures the asymmetry about the mean in the gray level distribution. It is defined as follows:

$$\text{SKEW} = \frac{1}{\sigma_g^3} \sum_{g=0}^{L-1} (g - \overline{g})^3 P(g) \qquad (6.3\text{-}4)$$

The skew will be positive if the tail of the histogram spreads to the right (positive) and negative if the tail of the histogram spreads to the left (negative). Another method to measure the skew uses the mean, mode and standard deviation, where the *mode* is defined as the peak, or highest, value:

$$\text{SKEW}' = \frac{\overline{x} - \text{mode}}{\sigma_g} \qquad (6.3\text{-}5)$$

This method of measuring skew is more computationally efficient, especially considering that, typically, the mean and standard deviation have already been calculated.

The *energy* measure tells us something about how the gray levels are distributed:

$$\text{ENERGY} = \sum_{g=0}^{L-1} [P(g)]^2 \qquad (6.3\text{-}6)$$

The energy measure has a maximum value of 1 for an image with a constant value, and it gets increasingly smaller as the pixel values are distributed across more gray level values (remember all the $P(g)$ values are less than or equal to 1). The larger this value is, the easier it is to compress the image data. If the energy is high, it tells us that the number of gray levels in the image are few, that is, the distribution is concentrated in only a small number of different gray levels.

The *entropy* is a measure that tells us how many bits we need to code the image data and is given by:

$$\text{ENTROPY} = -\sum_{g=0}^{L-1} P(g) \log_2 [P(g)] \qquad (6.3\text{-}7)$$

As the pixel values in the image are distributed among more gray levels, the entropy increases. A complex image has higher entropy than a simple image. This measure tends to vary inversely with the energy.

Figure 6.3-2 shows images and the corresponding histogram features. In Figure 6.3-2a–d, we see what occurs when an image is segmented. In the segmented image, the mean, standard deviation and skew remain about the same, but the energy goes up and the entropy goes down. The energy goes up as the image is simplified and the individual probabilities increase, which also causes the entropy to decrease. In Figure 6.3-2e–h, we see what occurs when an image is enhanced with a histogram stretch. In the enhanced image, the energy and the entropy remain about the same, but the mean, standard deviation and skew are changed. The mean increases due to an increase in average brightness, the standard deviation increases from the spread in the histogram increasing. In this case, the skew decreased due to the clipping from the histogram stretch. Note that, in general, the histogram energy is the opposite of what might be expected – a simpler image has more histogram energy than a complex image.

Second-order histogram features, which contain information about the relationship *between pixels*, are used to obtain texture information. These are discussed in Section 6.6.

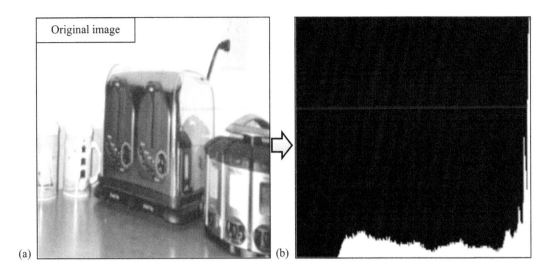

Mean	Standard Dev	Skew	Energy	Entropy
174	73	-0.33	0.014	7.11

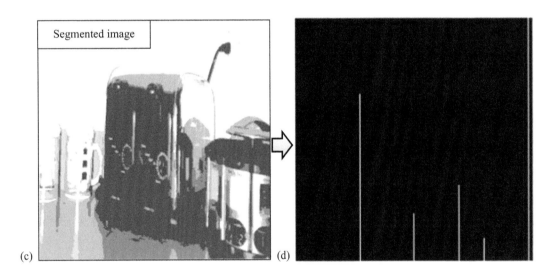

Mean	Standard Dev	Skew	Energy	Entropy
173	78	-0.31	0.309	1.91

FIGURE 6.3-2
Histogram features. Comparing images (a) and (c), we observe that as the image is simplified by segmentation, the energy goes up and the entropy goes down, but the mean, σ and skew remain the same.

(*Continued*)

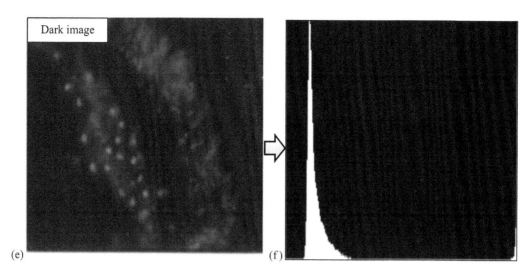

Mean	Standard Dev	Skew	Energy	Entropy
37	35	5.3	0.050	4.94

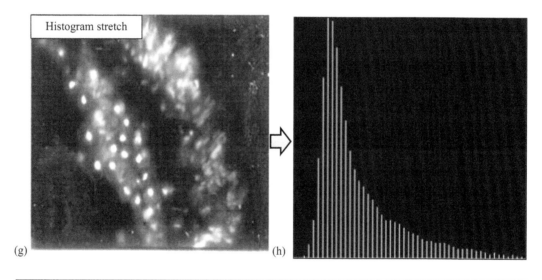

Mean	Standard Dev	Skew	Energy	Entropy
75	56	1.7	0.051	4.76

FIGURE 6.3-2 (*Continued*)

Comparing images (e) and (g), we observe that as we stretch the histogram, the energy and entropy do not change much, but the mean and standard deviation increase. Note with a positive skew, the tail is to the right; while, with a negative skew, the tail is to the left.

6.4   Color Features

Color is useful in many applications. Typical color images consisting of three color planes, red, green and blue, can be treated as three separate gray scale images. This approach allows us to use any of the gray level features, but with three times as many, one for each of the three color bands. By using this approach, we may be able to determine that information useful for the application is contained in one, two or all three of the color bands.

Often, when interested in color features, we want to incorporate information into the feature vector pertaining to the relationship *between* the color bands. These relationships are found by considering normalized color or relative color differences. This is done by using the color transforms defined in Chapter 1 and then applying to this new representation the features previously defined. For example, the chromaticity transform provides a normalized color representation, which will decouple the image brightness from the color itself. Many color transforms, including HSI, HSL, HSV, Spherical, Cylindrical, L*u*v* and L*a*b*, will provide us with two color components and a brightness component. The YIQ and YCrCb provide us with color difference components that signify the relative color. After performing a color transform, depending on the application, we may be interested in a specific aspect of the color information, such as hue or saturation. If this is the case, we can extract features from the band of interest.

The color features chosen will be primarily application specific, but caution must be taken in selecting color features. Typically, some form of relative color is best, because most absolute color measures are not very robust. In many applications, the environment is not carefully controlled, so a system developed under specific color conditions using absolute color may not function properly in a different environment. Remember all the factors that contribute to the color – the lighting, the sensors, optical filtering and any print or photographic process in the system model. If any of these factors change, then absolute color measures, such as red, green or blue, will change. An application-specific relative color measure can be defined or a known color standard, such as the *Macbeth Color Chart*, can be used for comparison. When using a known color standard, the system can be calibrated if the conditions change.

An example of the problem caused by using absolute color arose during the development of a system to automatically diagnose skin lesions. An algorithm was found that seemed to always correctly identify melanoma – a deadly form of skin cancer. At one point in the research, the algorithm ceased to work. What had happened? A big mistake had been made in developing the algorithm – it had relied on some absolute color measures. The initial set of melanoma images had been digitized from Ektachrome slides, and the non-melanoma lesion images had been digitized from Kodachrome slides. Due to the types of film involved, all the melanomas had a blue tint (Ektachrome), while all the other tumor images had a red tint (Kodachrome). Thus, with the first set of tumor images, the use of average color alone provided an easy way to differentiate between the melanomas and non-melanomas. As more images became available, both melanoma and non-melanomas were digitized from Kodachrome (red tint), so the identification algorithm ceased to work. A senior member of the research team had a similar experience while developing a tank recognition algorithm based on Ektachrome images of Soviet tanks and Kodachrome images of U.S. tanks. Avoid absolute color measures for features, except under very carefully controlled conditions.

6.5   Fourier Transform and Spectral Features

To discuss spectral features, we must first introduce the Fourier transform, which is widely used in engineering applications. It was developed by Jean Baptiste Joseph Fourier (1768–1830) to explain the distribution of temperature and heat conduction. Since that time, the Fourier transform has found numerous uses, including vibration analysis in mechanical engineering, circuit analysis in electrical engineering, and here, in computer vision and image processing. The Fourier transform decomposes a complex signal into a weighted sum of a zero frequency term (the DC term which is related to the average value) and sinusoidal terms. These sinusoidal terms are called *basis functions*, because any complex signal can be represented by or deconstructed into a combination of the terms. With the Fourier transform, each sinusoid in the set of basis functions is a positive integer multiple of the fundamental. The *fundamental* is the basic or lowest frequency, and the *harmonics* are frequency multiples of the fundamental – the fundamental is also called the first harmonic. We can recreate the original signal by adding the fundamental and all the harmonics, with each term weighted by its corresponding transform coefficient. This is shown in Figure 6.5-1.

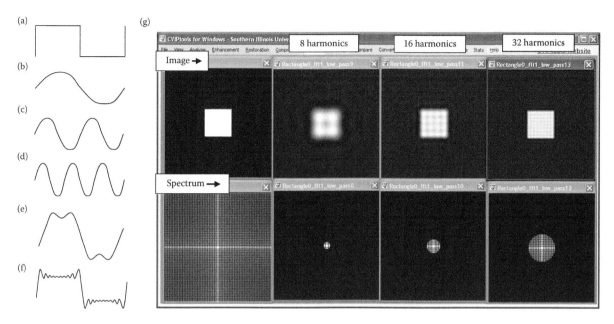

FIGURE 6.5-1
Decomposing a square wave with a Fourier transform. (a) The 1-D square wave, (b) the fundamental, or first harmonic, (c) the second harmonic, (d) the third harmonic, (e) approximation to the sum of the fundamental and the first three harmonics, (f) approximation to sum of the first 20 harmonics and (g) CVIPtools screen capture of a 2-D square and successively adding more harmonics. Across the top are the reconstructed squares with approximately 8, 16 and then 32 harmonics. Across the bottom are the corresponding Fourier transform magnitude images, the Fourier spectrum.

For computer imaging applications, the frequency being considered is referred to as spatial frequency. The concept of spatial frequency may differ from what is typically thought of as frequency. *Spatial frequency* measures how fast a signal is changing in space. In this case, the signal consists of the brightness values in the image. This is illustrated in Figure 6.5-2, where we see that the frequency is defined as being *relative to the size of the image*. Additionally, for the discrete functions discussed here, the continuous functions are sampled as shown in Figure 6.5-3. This corresponds to the pixel grid in a digital image.

The equation for the one-dimensional discrete Fourier transform (DFT) is:

$$F(v) = \frac{1}{N} \sum_{c=0}^{N-1} I(c) e^{-j2\pi vc/N} \tag{6.5-1}$$

The inverse DFT is given by:

$$F^{-1}[F(v)] = I(c) = \sum_{v=0}^{N-1} F(v) e^{j2\pi vc/N} \tag{6.5-2}$$

where v is the frequency and the $F^{-1}[\ ]$ notation represents the inverse transform. These equations correspond to one row of an image; note that as we move across a row, the column coordinate, c, is the one that changes. The base of the natural logarithmic function, e, is about 2.71828; j, the imaginary coordinate for a complex number, equals $\sqrt{-1}$. The basis functions are sinusoidal in nature, as can be seen by Euler's identity:

$$e^{j\theta} = \cos(\theta) + j\sin(\theta) \tag{6.5-3}$$

Putting this equation into the DFT equation by substituting $\theta = -2\pi vc/N$ and remembering that $\cos(\theta)=\cos(-\theta)$ and $\sin(-\theta)=-\sin(\theta)$, the one-dimensional DFT equation can be written as:

$$F(v) = \frac{1}{N} \sum_{c=0}^{N-1} I(c)\left[\cos(2\pi vc / N) - j\sin(2\pi vc / N)\right] = \mathrm{Re}(v) + j\,\mathrm{Im}(v) \tag{6.5-4}$$

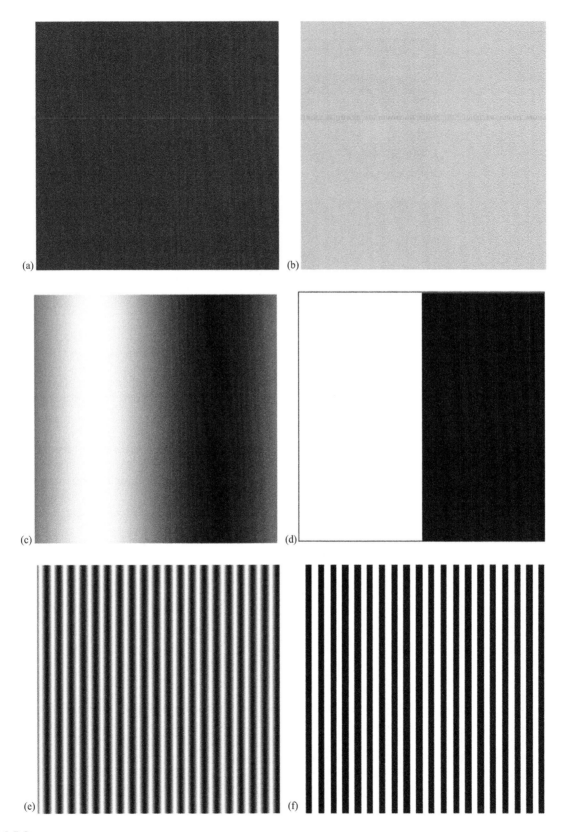

FIGURE 6.5-2
Spatial frequency. (a) Frequency=0, gray level=51, (b) Frequency=0, gray level=204, (c) Frequency=1, horizontal sine wave, (d) Frequency=1, horizontal square wave, (e) Frequency=20, horizontal sine wave and (f) Frequency=20, horizontal square wave.

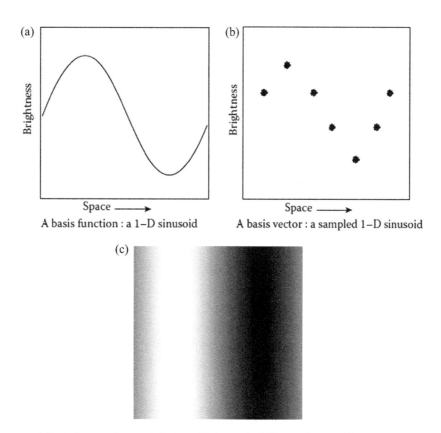

A basis image: A sampled sinusoid shown in 2-D as an image. The pixel brightness in each row corresponds to the sampled values of the 1-D sinusoid, which are repeated along each column. This is a horizontal sine wave of frequency 1.

FIGURE 6.5-3
Sampled continuous functions and digital images.

In this case, *F(v)* is also complex, with the real part corresponding to the cosine terms, and the imaginary part corresponding to the sine terms. If we represent a complex spectral component by $F(v) = \text{Re}(v) + j\,\text{Im}(v)$, where $\text{Re}(v)$ is the real part and $\text{Im}(v)$ is the imaginary part, then we can define the magnitude and phase of a complex spectral component as:

$$\text{MAGNITUDE} = |F(v)| = \sqrt{[\text{Re}(v)]^2 + [\text{Im}(v)]^2} \tag{6.5-5}$$

and

$$\text{PHASE} = \varphi(v) = \text{Tan}^{-1}\left[\frac{\text{Im}(v)}{\text{Re}(v)}\right] \tag{6.5-6}$$

The magnitude of a sinusoid is simply its peak value, and the phase determines where the origin is or where the sinusoid starts (see Figure 6.5-4). Keep in mind that the basis functions are simply sinusoids at varying frequencies, the complex exponential notation, e^{jx}, is simply a mathematical notational tool to make it easier to write and manipulate the equations. In Figure 6.5-5, we see that a complex number can be expressed in rectangular form, described by the real and imaginary part, or in exponential form, by the magnitude and phase. A memory aid for evaluating $e^{j\theta}$ is given in Figure 6.5-6.

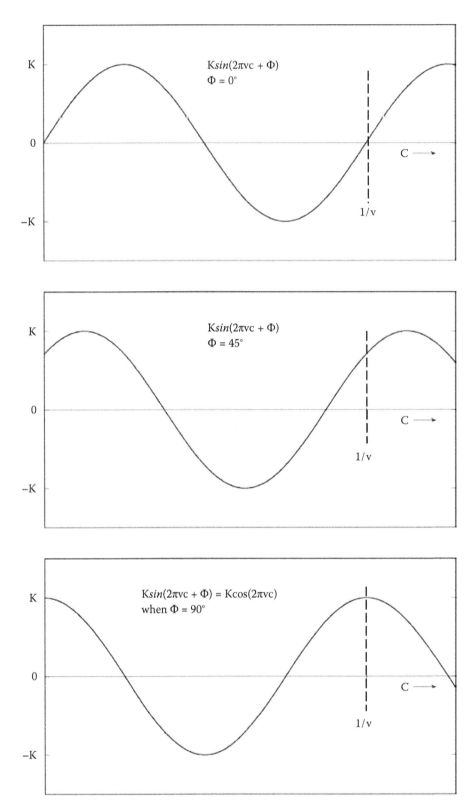

FIGURE 6.5-4
Magnitude and phase of sinusoidal waves.

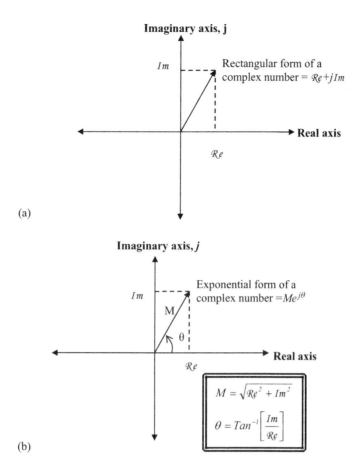

(a)

(b)

FIGURE 6.5-5
Complex numbers. (a) A complex number shown as a vector and expressed in rectangular form, in terms of the real, Re, and imaginary components, Im, (b) a complex number expressed in exponential form in terms of magnitude, M, and angle, θ. Note that θ is measured from the real axis counterclockwise.

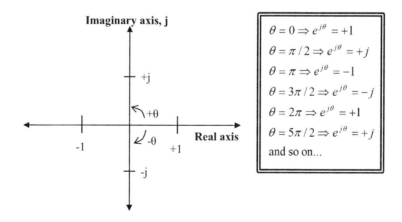

FIGURE 6.5-6
A memory aid for evaluating $e^{j\theta}$. The angle is measured from the real axis counterclockwise.

EXAMPLE 6.5.1: FOURIER TRANSFORM OF ONE ROW

Given $I(c) = [3, 2, 2, 1]$, corresponding to the brightness values of one row of a digital image.
Find $F(v)$ in both rectangular form and exponential form.

$$F(v) = \frac{1}{N} \sum_{c=0}^{N-1} I(c) e^{-j2\pi vc/N}$$

$$F(0) = \frac{1}{4} \sum_{c=0}^{3} I(c) e^{-j2\pi vc/4} = \frac{1}{4} \sum_{c=0}^{3} I(c) e^{0} = \frac{1}{4}\left[I(0) + I(1) + I(2) + I(3)\right]1 = \frac{1}{4}[3 + 2 + 2 + 1] = 2$$

$$F(1) = \frac{1}{4} \sum_{c=0}^{3} I(c) e^{-j2\pi(1)c/4} = \frac{1}{4}\left[3e^{0} + 2e^{-j\pi/2} + 2e^{-j\pi} + 1e^{-j3\pi/2}\right] = \frac{1}{4}[3 + 2(-j) + 2(-1) + 1(j)] = \frac{1}{4}[1-j]$$

$$F(2) = \frac{1}{4} \sum_{c=0}^{3} I(c) e^{-j2\pi(2)c/4} = \frac{1}{4}\left[3e^{0} + 2e^{-j\pi} + 2e^{-j2\pi} + 1e^{-j3\pi}\right] = \frac{1}{4}[3 + (-2) + 2 + (-1)] = \frac{1}{2}$$

$$F(3) = \frac{1}{4} \sum_{c=0}^{3} I(c) e^{-j2\pi(3)c/4} = \frac{1}{4}\left[3e^{0} + 2e^{-j\pi3/2} + 2e^{-j3\pi} + 1e^{-j\pi9/2}\right] = \frac{1}{4}[3 + 2j + 2(-1) + 1(-j)] = \frac{1}{4}[1+j]$$

Therefore, we have:

$$F(v) = \left[2, \frac{1}{4}[1-j], \frac{1}{2}, \frac{1}{4}[1+j]\right]$$

Next, put these into exponential form:

$$F(0) = 2 = 2 + 0j \Rightarrow M = \sqrt{2^2 + 0^2} = 2; \theta = \tan^{-1}\left[\frac{0}{2}\right] = 0$$

$$F(1) = \frac{1}{4}[1-j] = \frac{1}{4} - \frac{1}{4}j \Rightarrow M = \sqrt{\left(\tfrac{1}{4}\right)^2 + \left(-\tfrac{1}{4}\right)^2} \cong 0.35; \theta = \tan^{-1}\left[\frac{-\tfrac{1}{4}}{\tfrac{1}{4}}\right] = -\pi/4$$

$$F(2) = 1/2 = 1/2 + 0j \Rightarrow M = \sqrt{(1/2)^2 + 0^2} = 0.5; \theta = \tan^{-1}\left[\frac{0}{1/2}\right] = 0$$

$$F(3) = \frac{1}{4}[1+j] = \frac{1}{4} + \frac{1}{4}j \Rightarrow M = \sqrt{\left(\tfrac{1}{4}\right)^2 + \left(\tfrac{1}{4}\right)^2} \cong 0.35; \theta = \tan^{-1}\left[\frac{\tfrac{1}{4}}{\tfrac{1}{4}}\right] = \pi/4$$

Therefore, we have:

$$F(v) = \left[2, 0.35e^{-j\pi/4}, 0.5, 0.35e^{j\pi/4}\right]$$

Extending the DFT to the two-dimensional (2-D) case for images, and using u and v for the frequency variables, we can decompose an image into a weighted sum of 2-D sinusoidal terms. The physical interpretation of a 2-D sinusoid is shown in Figure 6.5-7. Here, we see that a sinusoid that is not directly on the u or the v axis can be broken down into separate frequency terms by finding the period along each axis. Assuming a square $N \times N$ image, the equation for the 2-D DFT is:

$$F(u,v) = \frac{1}{N} \sum_{r=0}^{N-1} \sum_{c=0}^{N-1} I(r,c) e^{-j2\pi(ur+vc)/N} \tag{6.5-7}$$

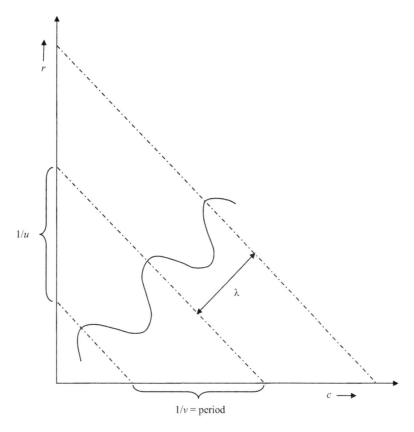

FIGURE 6.5-7
Physical interpretation of a two-dimensional sinusoid. The wavelength of the sinusoid is $\lambda = 1/\sqrt{u^2 + v^2}$, where (u, v) are the frequencies along (r, c), the periods are $1/u$ and $1/v$.

As before, we can also write the Fourier transform equation as:

$$F(u,v) = \frac{1}{N}\sum_{r=0}^{N-1}\sum_{c=0}^{N-1} I(r,c)\left[\cos\left(\frac{2\pi}{N}(ur + vc)\right) - j\sin\left(\frac{2\pi}{N}(ur + vc)\right)\right] \qquad (6.5\text{-}8)$$

Now, $F(u, v)$ is also complex, with the real part corresponding to the cosine terms and the imaginary part corresponding to the sine terms. If we represent a complex spectral component by $F(u,v) = \text{Re}(u,v) + j\text{Im}(u,v)$, where $\text{Re}(u,v)$ is the real part and $\text{Im}(u,v)$ is the imaginary part, then we can define the magnitude and phase of a complex spectral component as:

$$\text{MAGNITUDE} = |F(u,v)| = \sqrt{[\text{Re}(u,v)]^2 + [\text{Im}(u,v)]^2} \qquad (6.5\text{-}9)$$

and

$$\text{PHASE} = \varphi(u,v) = \text{Tan}^{-1}\left[\frac{\text{Im}(u,v)}{\text{Re}(u,v)}\right] \qquad (6.5\text{-}10)$$

Figure 6.5-8 shows images recovered with the phase or magnitude only. With phase only, we lose the relative magnitudes, which results in a loss of contrast (see Figure 6.5-8b), but we retain the relative placement of objects – in other words, the phase data contains information about *where objects are* in an image. With the magnitude-only image, we retain the contrast, but lose all the important details which are essential for image understanding. (Note: to obtain these images in CVIPtools, use *Analysis→Transforms→Extract Phase/Magnitude-Only Image.*)

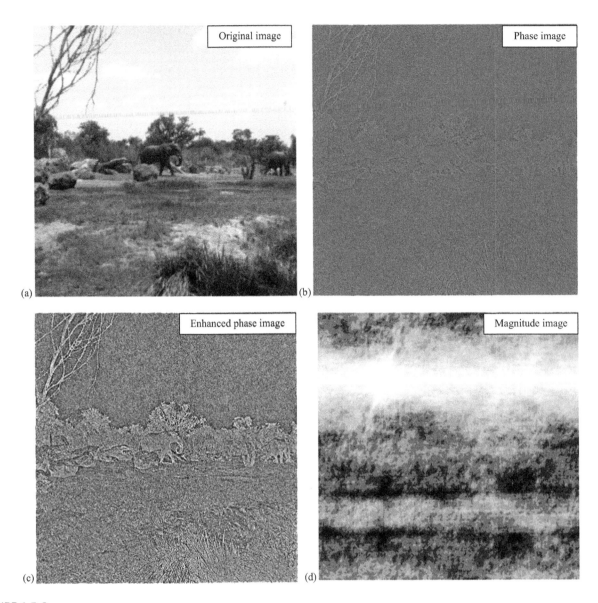

FIGURE 6.5-8
Fourier transform phase and magnitude image information. (a) Original image, (b) phase-only image, (c) contrast enhanced version of image (b) to show detail and (d) magnitude-only image after histogram equalization. The phase-only image is created by taking a Fourier transform, setting all the magnitudes equal to 1 and performing an inverse Fourier transform. The magnitude-only image is created by taking a Fourier transform, setting the phase to a fixed value, such as 0, then performing an inverse Fourier transform. (Note: to obtain these images in CVIPtools, use *Analysis→Transforms→Extract Phase/Magnitude-Only Image*.)

After the transform is performed, to get our original image back, we need to apply the *inverse transform*. The inverse 2-D DFT is given by:

$$F^{-1}[F(u,v)] = I(r,c) = \frac{1}{N}\sum_{u=0}^{N-1}\sum_{v=0}^{N-1}F(u,v)e^{j2\pi(ur+vc)/N} \qquad (6.5\text{-}11)$$

The $F^{-1}[\ ]$ notation represents the inverse transform. This equation illustrates that the function, $I(r,c)$, is represented by a weighted sum of the basis functions, and that the transform coefficients, $F(u,v)$, are the weights. With the inverse Fourier transform, the sign on the basis functions' exponent is changed from –1 to +1. However, this only corresponds to the phase and not the frequency and magnitude of the basis functions (see Figure 6.5-8 and compare Equations 6.5-7 and 6.5-11).

One important property of the Fourier transform is called *separability*, which means that the two-dimensional basis image can be decomposed into two product terms where each term depends only on the rows or columns. Also, if the basis images are *separable*, then the result can be found by successive application of two one-dimensional transforms. This is illustrated by first separating the basis image term (also called the transform kernel) into a product, as follows:

$$e^{-j2\pi(ur+vc)/N} = e^{-j2\pi ur/N} \, e^{-j2\pi vc/N} \qquad (6.5\text{-}12)$$

next, we write the Fourier transform equation in the following form:

$$F(u,v) = \frac{1}{N} \sum_{r=0}^{N-1} \left(e^{-j2\pi ur/N} \right) \sum_{c=0}^{N-1} I(r,c) e^{-j2\pi vc/N} \qquad (6.5\text{-}13)$$

The advantage of the separability property is that $F(u, v)$ or $I(r, c)$ can be obtained in two steps by successive applications of the one-dimensional Fourier transform or its inverse.

Expressing the equation as follows:

$$F(u,v) = \frac{1}{N} \sum_{r=0}^{N-1} F(r,v) e^{-j2\pi ur/N} \qquad (6.5\text{-}14)$$

where

$$F(r,v) = (N)\left(\frac{1}{N} \right) \sum_{c=0}^{N-1} I(r,c) e^{-j2\pi vc/N} \qquad (6.5\text{-}15)$$

For each value of r, the expression inside the brackets is a one-dimensional transform with frequency values $v = 0,1,2,3,\ldots N-1$. Hence, the two-dimensional function $F(r, v)$ is obtained by taking a transform along each row of $I(r, c)$ and multiplying the result by N. The desired result, $F(u, v)$, is obtained by taking a transform along each column of $F(r, v)$.

Often, the DFT is implemented as a Fast Fourier Transform (FFT) and is based on the input data having a number of elements that are a power of two. Images with dimensions of powers of two were common in the early days of imaging, but today images of all sizes are more typical. In general, these algorithms take advantage of the many redundant calculations involved and operate to eliminate this redundancy. The transforms in CVIPtools are implemented with fast algorithms based on powers of two, which means that any image that is not a power of two will be zero padded.

With regard to spectral features or frequency-domain based features, the primary metric is *power*. How much spectral power do we find in various parts of the spectrum? Texture is often measured by looking for peaks in the power spectrum, especially if the texture is periodic or directional. The power spectrum is defined by the magnitude of the spectral components squared:

$$\text{POWER} = \left| F(u,v) \right|^2 \qquad (6.5\text{-}16)$$

The standard approach for spectral features is to find power in various spectral regions, and these regions can be defined as rings, sectors or boxes. In Figure 6.5-9, examples of these types of spectral regions are shown, for both types of symmetry under consideration. The power in a region of interest is then measured by summing the power over the range of frequencies of interest:

$$\text{SPECTRAL REGION POWER} = \sum_{u \in \text{REGION}} \sum_{v \in \text{REGION}} \left| F(u,v) \right|^2 \qquad (6.5\text{-}17)$$

The *box* is the easiest to define by setting limits on u and v.

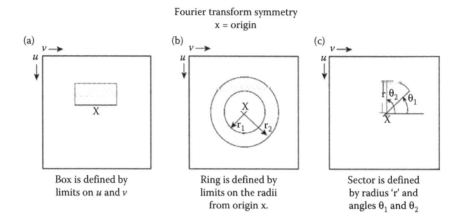

Fourier transform symmetry
x = origin

Box is defined by
limits on u and v

Ring is defined by
limits on the radii
from origin x.

Sector is defined
by radius 'r' and
angles θ_1 and θ_2

FIGURE 6.5-9
Regions for spectral features. Spectral features can be used as texture metrics. Ring measures tend to be rotation invariant, and sector measures tend to be size invariant.

EXAMPLE 6.5.2: BOX SPECTRAL REGION

We may be interested in all spatial frequencies at a specific horizontal frequency, $v=20$. So, we define a spectral region as follows:

$$\text{Region of interest} = \begin{cases} -\dfrac{N}{2} < u < \dfrac{N}{2} \\ 19 < v < 21 \end{cases} \tag{6.5-18}$$

Then, we calculate the power in this region by summing over this range of u and v.

The *ring* is defined by two radii, r_1 and r_2. These are measured from the origin, and the summation limits on u and v, for Fourier symmetry, are as follows:

$$u \Rightarrow -r_2 \leq u < r_2$$
$$v \Rightarrow \pm\sqrt{r_1^2 - u^2} \leq v < \pm\sqrt{r_2^2 - u^2} \tag{6.5-19}$$

The *sector* is defined by a radius, r, and two angles, θ_1 and θ_2. The limits on the summation are defined by:

$$\theta_1 < \tan^{-1}\left(\frac{v}{u}\right) < \theta_2 \tag{6.5–20}$$

$$u^2 + v^2 \leq r^2 \tag{6.5-21}$$

The sector measurement will find spatial frequency power of a specific orientation whatever the frequency (limited only by the radius), while the ring measure will find spatial frequency power at specific frequencies regardless of orientation. In terms of image objects, the sector measure will tend to be size invariant and the ring measure will tend to be rotation invariant.

Due to the redundancy in the Fourier spectral symmetry, we often measure the sector power over one-half the spectrum, and the ring power over the other half of the spectrum (see Figure 6.5-10). In practice, we may want to normalize these numbers, as they get very large, by dividing by the DC (average) value – this is done in CVIPtools spectral feature extraction. (Note: In CVIPtools, if the DC value in the magnitude image of a Fourier transform is examined, it needs to be divided by $N \times N$ to get the true average value, due to the implementation of the Fourier transform.)

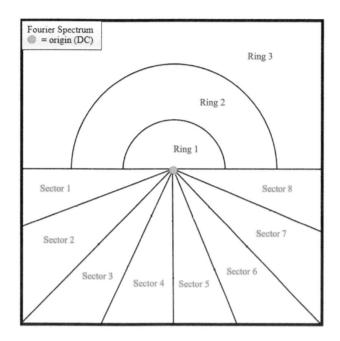

FIGURE 6.5-10
Fourier spectrum power. With Fourier spectral symmetry, which contains redundant information, we often measure ring power over half the spectrum and sector power over the other half. The radius values for the outer ring and the sectors are typically limited by the bounds of the spectrum itself. Shown here is division of the Fourier spectrum into three rings and eight sectors. The spectral power feature values are calculated by summing the square of all the Fourier coefficients in the region of interest: $\sum\limits_{u \in \text{REGION}} \sum\limits_{v \in \text{REGION}} |F(u,v)|^2$.

6.6 Texture Features

Texture is related to properties such as smoothness, coarseness, roughness and regular patterns. Spectral features can be used as texture features; for example, the ring power can be used to find texture. High power in small radii (ring 1) corresponds to low frequency and thus coarse textures – those with large element sizes; as the ring number increases, the frequencies are higher and correspond to finer textures. As the frequency gets very high, for example, in the outer ring, the textures will appear very fine and may actually appear smooth. This is really a function of the human visual system's perception – we see texture as rapidly changing variation in the brightness due to the object scattering the light. At some point, the variation in brightness becomes too fast for us to perceive, so the texture appears smooth.

Texture is also a function of image size relative to the object, as well as magnification of the original image. Remember that the frequency as defined is relative to the image size. Figure 6.6-1 shows a corduroy material at different magnifications, along with the corresponding spectra. Here, we see that a higher magnification corresponds to larger element size and lower frequency energy, and as we "zoom out", the element size decreases and the energy spreads out to higher frequencies.

If the magnification is unknown or variable, but has a known orientation, the spectral sector measures may be useful for providing us with textural information. The power in a sector includes all frequencies, which corresponds to all sizes of elements or magnifications, but has a fixed orientation. In practice, the spectral features can be calculated for 10 or 20 or more rings and sectors, and the magnitudes plotted to look for signature shapes which will correspond to specific textures.

Another approach to measuring texture is to use the second-order histogram of the gray levels based on a joint probability distribution model. The *second-order histogram* provides statistics based on pairs of pixels and their corresponding gray levels. The second-order histogram methods are also referred to as *gray level co-occurrence matrix* or *gray level dependency matrix* methods. These features are based on two parameters: (1) distance and (2) angle.

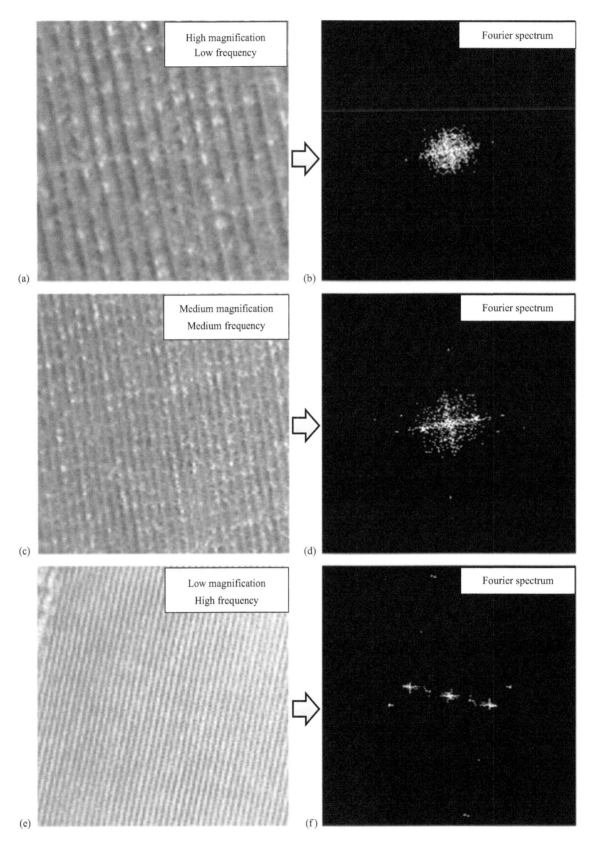

FIGURE 6.6-1
Texture at varying magnification and their spectra. With higher magnification, the texture pattern appears larger corresponding to lower frequencies. As we decrease the magnification, the frequency energy spreads out across higher frequencies. (*Note*: the Fourier spectra were remapped to BYTE and then histogram equalized.)

The distance is the pixel distance between the pairs of pixels used for the second-order statistics, and the angle refers to the angle between the pixel pairs. Typically, four angles are used corresponding to vertical, horizontal and two diagonal directions. The pixel distance chosen depends on the resolution of the image and the coarseness of the texture of interest, although it is typical to use small values, such as 1–6. To make the features rotationally invariant, they can be calculated for all angles and then averaged – in the CVIPtools C functions, the average and the range of these features are returned for the four angles; in the MATLAB CVIP Toolbox, the average, range, and the variance is also available.

Numerous features have been derived via these methods, but these five have been found to be the most useful: energy, inertia, correlation, inverse difference and entropy. The energy measures homogeneity, or smoothness, by calculating the distribution among the gray levels. The inertia is a measure of contrast, while the correlation measures similarity between pixels at the specified distance. The inverse difference provides a measure for the local homogeneity of the texture, and the entropy measures the information content. Note that entropy and energy tend to be inversely related – a smooth area will have higher energy, but smaller entropy. Its smoothness means that most of the pixels are similar so there is not much information content or entropy.

Calculation of these texture features is done as follows. Let c_{ij} be the elements in the co-occurrence matrix *normalized by dividing by the sum of the number of pixel pairs in the matrix*, and assume a given distance and angle (direction). The equations are given by:

$$\text{Energy} = \sum_i \sum_j c_{ij}^2 \tag{6.6-1}$$

$$\text{Inertia} = \sum_i \sum_j (i-j)^2 c_{ij} \tag{6.6-2}$$

$$\text{Correlation} = \frac{1}{\sigma_x \sigma_y} \sum_i \sum_j (i - \mu_x)(j - \mu_y) c_{ij}$$

$$\text{where: } \mu_x = \sum_i i \sum_j c_{ij}$$

$$\text{and: } \mu_y = \sum_j j \sum_i c_{ij} \tag{6.6-3}$$

$$\text{and: } \sigma_x^2 = \sum_i (i - \mu_x)^2 \sum_j c_{ij}$$

$$\text{and: } \sigma_y^2 = \sum_j (j - \mu_y)^2 \sum_i c_{ij;}$$

$$\text{InverseDifference} = \sum_i \sum_j \frac{c_{ij}}{|i-j|}; \text{for}: i \neq j \tag{6.6-4}$$

$$\text{Entropy} = -\sum_i \sum_j c_{ij} \log_2 c_{ij} \tag{6.6-5}$$

An example of the gray level co-occurrence matrices is shown in Figure 6.6-2. Note in the calculation of these matrices that each pixel pair, with coordinates $[(r_1, c_1), (r_2, c_2)]$, actually represents two pixel pairs where the second one is represented by $[(r_2, c_2), (r_1, c_1)]$. In other words, for example, when counting horizontal pixel pairs, first look left to right (0°) and then right to left (180°) across the image. Also remember, before calculating the texture features, normalize by dividing them by the number of pixel pairs in the matrix. The figure illustrates the complexity involved with a small image and a small number of gray levels, so in practice the number of gray levels may be quantized to reduce the number of calculations involved and to reduce effects caused by noise in the images.

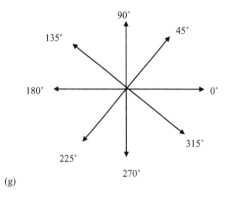

(a) Gray Level 'i'

$$\begin{matrix} & \text{Gray level 'j'} & 0 & 1 & 2 & 3 \\ 0 & \begin{bmatrix} \#(0,0) & \#(0,1) & \#(0,2) & \#(0,3) \\ \#(1,0) & \#(1,1) & \#(1,2) & \#(1,3) \\ \#(2,0) & \#(2,1) & \#(2,2) & \#(2,3) \\ \#(3,0) & \#(3,1) & \#(3,2) & \#(3,3) \end{bmatrix} \end{matrix}$$

(b) $\begin{bmatrix} 1 & 1 & 0 & 0 \\ 2 & 2 & 3 & 3 \\ 1 & 2 & 3 & 0 \\ 3 & 3 & 3 & 3 \end{bmatrix}$

(c) $\begin{pmatrix} 2 & 1 & 0 & 1 \\ 1 & 2 & 1 & 0 \\ 0 & 1 & 2 & 2 \\ 1 & 0 & 2 & 8 \end{pmatrix}$ (d) $\begin{pmatrix} 0 & 0 & 0 & 4 \\ 0 & 0 & 3 & 1 \\ 0 & 3 & 2 & 1 \\ 4 & 1 & 1 & 4 \end{pmatrix}$ (e) $\begin{pmatrix} 0 & 0 & 0 & 2 \\ 0 & 0 & 1 & 2 \\ 0 & 1 & 2 & 2 \\ 2 & 2 & 2 & 2 \end{pmatrix}$ f) $\begin{pmatrix} 0 & 0 & 1 & 2 \\ 0 & 0 & 2 & 0 \\ 1 & 2 & 0 & 2 \\ 2 & 0 & 2 & 4 \end{pmatrix}$

(g)

FIGURE 6.6-2

Example of gray level co-occurrence matrices. Given a 4×4 image with four possible gray levels, 2-bits per pixel and using a distance $d=1$, we have (a) general form of the matrix, where each entry is the number (#) of occurrences of the pair listed, (b) an example 4×4 image, (c) the matrix corresponding to the horizontal direction (0° and 180°), (d) the matrix corresponding to the vertical direction (90° and 270°), (e) the matrix corresponding to the left diagonal direction (135° and 315°), (f) the matrix corresponding to the right diagonal direction (45° and 225°) and (g) angle definitions. Remember it is *important to normalize* the values in the co-occurrence matrix by dividing by the sum of the number of pixel pairs in the matrix before calculating the texture features – for example, with the matrix shown in (c) divided by (2+1+0+1+1+2+1+0+0+1+2+2+1+0+2+8)=24.

Laws texture energy masks are another method for measuring texture. They operate by finding the average gray Level, Edges, Spots, Ripples and Waves in the image. They are based on the following five vectors:

$$L_5 = (1,\ 4,\ 6,\ 4,\ 1)$$

$$E_5 = (-1,-2,\ 0,\ 2,\ 1)$$

$$S_5 = (-1,\ 0,\ 2,\ 0,-1) \qquad (6.5\text{-}6)$$

$$R_5 = (1,-4,\ 6,-4,\ 1)$$

$$W_5 = (-1,\ 2,\ 0,-2,\ 1)$$

These are used to generate the Laws 5×5 filter masks by finding the *vector outer product* of each pair of vectors. For example (see Figure 6.6-3), using L_5 and S_5, we obtain:

$$\begin{bmatrix} -1 & 0 & 2 & 0 & -1 \\ -4 & 0 & 8 & 0 & -4 \\ -6 & 0 & 12 & 0 & -6 \\ -4 & 0 & 8 & 0 & -4 \\ -1 & 0 & 2 & 0 & -1 \end{bmatrix}$$

S_5

	-1	0	2	0	-1
1	-1	0	2	0	-1
4	-4	0	8	0	-4
6	-6	0	12	0	-6
4	-4	0	8	0	-4
1	-1	0	2	0	-1

L_5 (row labels on left)

FIGURE 6.6-3
Vector outer product for Laws masks. The *vector outer product* creates the 2-D Laws filter masks from the corresponding two 1-D Laws vectors. Here, we create the 2-D 5×5 Laws filter mask for *Level*, L_5, and *Spots*, S_5. Each value in the resulting 2-D mask is obtained by multiplying corresponding components of each vector.

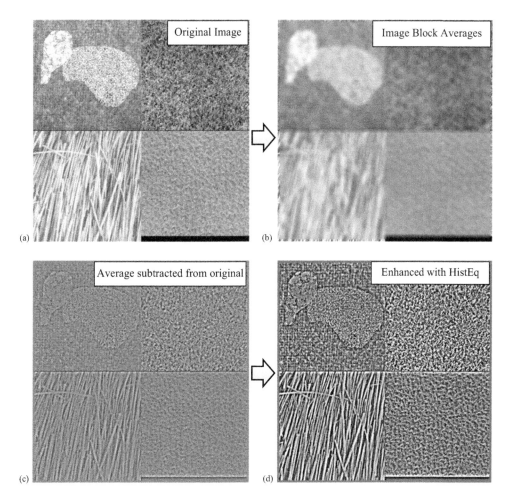

(a) Original Image — (b) Image Block Averages — (c) Average subtracted from original — (d) Enhanced with HistEq

FIGURE 6.6-4
Preprocessing to remove artifacts caused by uneven lighting. (a) Original texture image with six textures, (b) block averages of original, (c) image after subtracting the block averages and (d) histogram equalized version of image (c). Note that the texture remains, but any variation in lighting or brightness has been removed.

The first step to applying these masks is to preprocess the image to remove artifacts caused by uneven lighting – actually this technique is useful as a preprocessing step for all texture measures. The easiest method for this is to subtract the local average from every pixel, using, for example, a 15×15 block size (Figure 6.6-4). To do this, move across the image, such as is done with convolution, find the average gray level value in the block and then subtract this average from the current pixel in the center of the block. Be sure to put the output into another image buffer (structure), so the current image is not overwritten. This will create an image with average local gray levels close to zero.

The next step is to convolve the masks with the image to produce the texture filtered images, $F_k(r, c)$ for the kth filter mask. These texture filtered images are used to produce a *texture energy map*, E_k for the kth filter:

$$E_k(r,c) = \sum_{j=c-7}^{c+7} \sum_{i=r-7}^{r+7} |F_k(i,j)| \tag{6.5-7}$$

For these energy maps, the range on the summations depend on the block size, here we specified a block size of 15×15. These energy maps are then used to generate a texture feature vector for each pixel, which can be used for texture classification and image segmentation. For pattern classification of objects, as implemented in CVIPtools, the energy maps for objects of interest are used and histogram statistics (mean, standard deviation, skew, energy and entropy) are generated from just the part of the energy map corresponding to the object of interest. These are then used as texture features for the object.

Gabor filters represent another approach to texture features which is theoretically similar to the Laws texture feature approach in that they both use combinations of convolution masks of varying parameters to extract texture features. The Gabor filter is a linear filter which is excellent for edge detection and has both frequency- and orientation-selective properties. Therefore, the Gabor filter is particularly appropriate for texture discrimination, texture analysis and feature classification.

The Gabor filter can be viewed as a sinusoidal wave of specified frequency and orientation, convolved by a Gaussian envelope. A 2-D Gabor filter acts as a local bandpass filter with specific frequency and orientation. Mathematically, in the spatial domain, a 2-D Gabor filter is the result of multiplication of a 2-D Gaussian function and a complex exponential function, which can be represented as follows:

$$g(\lambda,\theta,\varphi,\sigma,\gamma) = \exp\left(-\frac{c(\theta)^2 + \gamma^2 r(\theta)^2}{2\sigma^2}\right) \exp\left(j\left(2\pi\frac{c(\theta)}{\lambda} + \varphi\right)\right) \tag{6.5-8}$$

where λ is the wavelength, so $1/\lambda$ is the frequency, θ is the orientation angle, φ is the phase offset, σ represents the standard deviation of the Gaussian factor, γ is the aspect ratio of the Gabor equation, r is the row and c is the column coordinate.

According to Euler's equation $e^{j\theta} = \cos(\theta) + j\sin(\theta)$, the complex form is expressed as a real number plus an imaginary number. Therefore, the complex Gabor filter can be separated with real and imaginary parts:

$$\text{Real}: g(\lambda,\theta,\varphi,\sigma,\gamma) = \exp\left(-\frac{c(\theta)^2 + \gamma^2 r(\theta)^2}{2\sigma^2}\right)\cos\left(2\pi\frac{r(\theta)}{\lambda} + \varphi\right) \tag{6.5-9}$$

$$\text{Imaginary}: g(\lambda,\theta,\varphi,\sigma,\gamma) = \exp\left(-\frac{c(\theta)^2 + \gamma^2 r(\theta)^2}{2\sigma^2}\right)\sin\left(2\pi\frac{c(\theta)}{\lambda} + \varphi\right) \tag{6.5-10}$$

where

$$c(\theta) = c\cos\theta + r\sin\theta, \; r(\theta) = -c\sin\theta + r\cos\theta \tag{6.5-11}$$

Often, in practice, only the real part of the Gabor filter is used. After the Gabor filters are convolved with the image, the texture features can be extracted by using the histogram statistics of the Gabor filtered image(s), as was done with the Laws texture features. Using Gabor filters in an application requires selection of frequencies, orientations, phases, standard deviations of the Gaussian and aspect ratios of interest. These will be image and application dependent. Often, application domain knowledge will guide a process of experiments to determine the factors that will work the best for the application.

6.7 Region-Based Features: SIFT/SURF/GIST

Features have been developed to extract information from generic image regions, which are meant to be robust and applicable to a wide variety of images and applications. These include the scale-invariant feature transform, SIFT, the speeded up robust features, SURF, and GIST. These features are different from those previously discussed in that they are defined at multiple spatial scales and are typically used to search images for objects of interest or to classify the image itself. They are in used in segmentation, object classification, object tracking and scene identification.

The SIFT-based features are invariant to scale (size), orientation, minimal amounts of distortion, occlusion and lighting changes. Different image sizes (scales) are created by application of a Gaussian smoothing filter and then subsampling. Key points are found by searching for local maxima and minima in the difference of Gaussian (DoG) images at different scales. A DoG image is shown in Figure 6.7-1, which is created by subtracting a blurred version of the image from a less blurry version. This will act as a bandpass filter and is used in feature extraction as a method to enhance image detail, or in this case, to enhance spatial frequencies between the two blurred images.

After the key points are determined, the features are extracted and used for classification by comparison to a known database of image regions/scenes SIFT feature vectors. One of the drawbacks is that the SIFT feature vector

(a) (b) (c) (d)

FIGURE 6.7-1
Difference of a Gaussian, DoG. (a) Original image, (b) image blurred by a 3×3 convolution mask, (c) image blurred by a 9×9 convolution mask and (d) the DoG image found by subtracting image (c) from (b), this image was histogram equalized for better visualization.

is typically 128-dimensional, which is quite large for comparison to a large image database. The high computational burden and the corresponding complexity led to the development of more efficient methods.

The SURF features were originally developed to exhibit a similar functionality to the SIFT features, but to execute faster and thus be more successful in a wider variety of applications. They use the Haar wavelet response, and they are only 64 dimensions to speed processing. More details of the SIFT/SURF features and algorithms can be found in the references. Also, note that MATLAB has SIFT/SURF functions available.

The GIST features use Gabor filters at four scales and eight orientations, and use the resulting images as feature maps. Each map is divided into regions and then the values are averaged over each of the regions to produce the feature values. These values are then all used as the GIST feature descriptor. Conceptually, the GIST features are a consolidation of the gradient information for different parts of an image, which provides a coarse description (the gist) of the scene. This is similar to how we used the Gabor filters for texture features, except that we extracted complete statistics, not just the means, from the Gabor filtered images.

6.8 Feature Extraction with CVIPtools

CVIPtools allows the user to extract features from objects within the image. This is done by using the original image and a segmented or mask image to define the location of the object. Figure 6.8-1 shows the CVIPtools main window and the *Analysis→Features* window. To extract features, we need to enter the original image, the segmented image, a feature file name, select the desired features and select the image object coordinates by clicking on any image with the mouse. Note that a name for the object *class* can be entered, this is optional, but necessary for pattern classification. The original image can be selected via the dropdown or with the keyboard *Ctrl*-key and a left mouse click, and the segmented can be selected via the dropdown or with the keyboard *Alt*-key and a left mouse click.

The CVIPtools software can be used for feature extraction in three primary ways: (1) extract features for the entire image, (2) extract features for an image object using a segmented image or (3) extract features for an

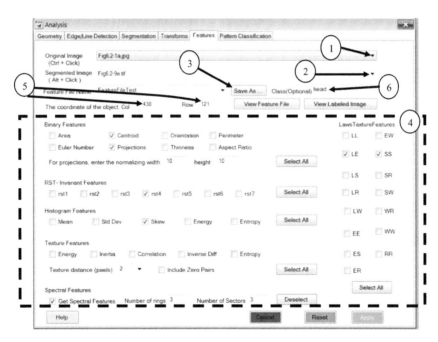

FIGURE 6.8-1

Using CVIPtools *Analysis→Features* window for feature extraction. (1) Select an original image from which you want to extract features. It can be selected via the dropdown arrow as shown or by using the keyboard/mouse with a *<Ctrl>/left mouse* click. (2) Select a segmented image; this can be a rectangle that has been created, an image that has been segmented or a border mask that has been created. It can be selected via the dropdown arrow as shown or by using the keyboard/mouse with a *<Alt>/left mouse* click. (3) Enter a name for the feature file using the *Save As* button. (4) Select the desired features; all features of a specific type can be selected with the *Select All* button or individual features can be selected with the checkboxes. (5) Enter any coordinates within the object by clicking on the object in the *Original* or the *Segmented* image. (6) A *Class* for the object is optional, but is needed for pattern classification and will be included in the feature file.

image object using a mask image. To extract features from the entire image, create an all white image with *Utilities→Create→Rectangle* that is the same size as the original image and use that as the segmented image (*Note: if the binary object features or the RST-invariant features are used with this method, features will be extracted for the object, that is, the rectangle object of the all white image*). To use a segmented image, select the *Segmentation* tab on the *Analysis* window, perform the segmentation method along with any post-segmentation morphological filtering to get the desired objects and use the output image as the segmented image in the *Features* window. If segmentation does not provide the desired results, use *Utilities→Create→Border Mask* to create an image with an outline of the desired object (see Figure 6.8-2).

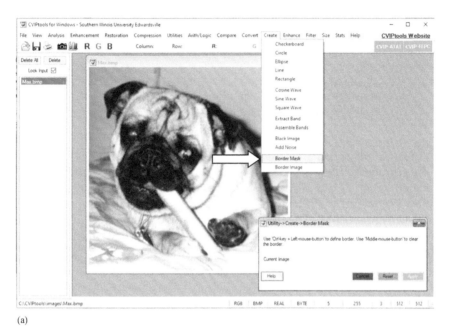

(a)

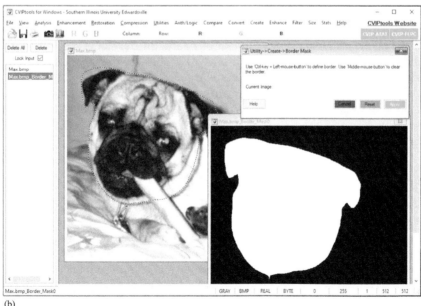

(b)

FIGURE 6.8-2
Creating a border mask image to extract features. (a) selecting *Utilties→Create→Border Mask* function, (b) after using the mouse to draw a border, by holding the *Control* key on the keyboard and using the left mouse button (hold and drag), and then clicking on *Apply*. The border will be shown with a crawling dotted line, and it will automatically complete the closed curve if you release the mouse button before the ends are connected. The border mask image can now be used as the *Segmented image* in the Features window to extract features relating to the outlined object.

TABLE 6-2

Feature Extraction with CVIPtools

Feature Category	How the Features Are Extracted
Binary object	The labeled image is used by selecting the object corresponding to the row and column coordinates and treating the object as a binary image with the object="1" and the background="0"
RST invariant moment-based	The labeled image is used by selecting the object corresponding to the row and column coordinates and treating the object as a binary image with the object="1" and the background="0"
Histogram	The labeled image is used by selecting the object corresponding to the row and column coordinates, and then this binary object is used as a mask on the original image to extract features. This is done by only including in the calculations pixels that are part of the object
Texture	The labeled image is used by selecting the object corresponding to the row and column coordinates, and then this binary object is used as a mask on the original image to extract features. This is done by only including in the calculations pixels that are part of the object
Spectral	The labeled image is used by selecting the object corresponding to the row and column coordinates, and then this binary object is used as a mask on the original image to extract features. This is done by creating a black image (all zeros) with dimensions a power of 2, imbedding the object from the original image within the black image and then calculating the Fourier transform on this image

After the segmented or mask image is created, the selected features are extracted with the *Apply* button. CVIPtools does this by labeling the segmented image, selecting the object corresponding to the row and column coordinates and then using the labeled image as a mask on the original image to extract the features for the selected object (see Table 6-2 for details). The features will be written to a feature file or can be saved as an Excel spreadsheet, as described in Chapter 3 (see Figure 3.3-21). The original feature files can be found in the CVIPtools main directory in the *bin/features* directory. During processing, the feature file can be viewed with the *View Feature File* button, and the labeled image can be viewed with the *View Labeled Image* button.

6.9   Feature Analysis

After the features have been extracted, feature analysis is important to aid in the feature selection process. Initially, the features are selected based on the understanding of the problem and the developer's experience. Now that the features have been extracted, they can be carefully examined to see which ones are the most useful and put back through the application feedback loop (see Figure 6.1-1) in the development process. To understand the feature analysis process, we need to define the mathematical tools to use, including feature vectors, feature spaces, distance and similarity measures to compare feature vectors, and various methods needed to preprocess the data for development of pattern classification algorithms. After these are understood, the feature analysis process begins with selection of the tools and methods that will be used for our specific imaging problem.

6.9.1   Feature Vectors and Feature Spaces

A feature vector is one method to represent an image, or part of an image (an object), by finding measurements on a set of features. The *feature vector* is an n-dimensional vector that contains these measurements, where n is the number of features. The measurements may be symbolic, numeric or both. An example of a symbolic feature is color such a "blue" or "red"; an example of a numeric feature is the area of an object. If we take a symbolic feature and assign a number to it, it becomes a numeric feature. Care must be taken in assigning numbers to symbolic features, so that the numbers are assigned in a meaningful way. For example, with color, we normally think of the hue by its name such as "orange" or "magenta". In this case, we could perform an HSL transform on the RGB data and use the H (hue) value as a numeric color feature. But with the HSL transform, the hue value ranges from $0°$ to $360°$, and 0 is "next to" 360, so it would be invalid to compare two colors by simply subtracting the two hue values.

Symbolic or qualitative features are typically considered to be binary, present or absent, true or false. One method to deal with symbolic features is through the application of fuzzy features and fuzzy measures. A *fuzzy feature* measure takes on a value between 0 and 1, but is essentially considered to be present/true or absent/false. Unlike the numeric features where we have a value that has been measured in the real world, fuzzy feature values represent how likely

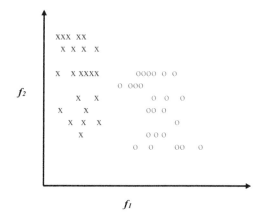

FIGURE 6.9-1

A two-dimensional feature space. This shows a two-dimensional feature space defined by feature vectors, $F = \begin{bmatrix} f_1 \\ f_2 \end{bmatrix}$, and two classes represented by x and o. Each x and o represents one sample in the feature space defined by its values for f_1 and f_2. One of the goals of feature analysis and pattern classification is to find clusters in the feature space which correspond to different classes.

it is that a specific feature is present or true for a given feature vector. The closer the value is to 1, the more likely that the feature is a part of the feature vector in question – it is true for that feature vector. As the fuzzy value approaches ½, we have no information as to if the feature is true or present in, this feature vector. If it is less than ½, most likely it does not belong to the feature vector. If it is greater than ½, it is more likely to belong to the feature vector. A value of 0 means the feature is absent or false. Although we will focus primarily on numeric features and related methods, we will consider the fuzzy similarity metric in the next section.

The feature vector can be used to classify an object or provide us with condensed higher-level image information. Associated with the feature vector is a mathematical abstraction called a *feature space*, which is also *n*-dimensional and is created to allow visualization of feature vectors and relationships between them. With two- and three-dimensional feature vectors, the feature space is modeled as a geometric construct with perpendicular axes and created by plotting each feature measurement along one axis (see Figure 6.9-1). For *n*-dimensional feature vectors, it is an abstract mathematical construction called a *hyperspace*. As we shall see, the creation of the feature space allows us to define distance and similarity measures which are used to compare feature vectors and aid in the classification of unknown samples.

EXAMPLE 6.9.1: FEATURES FOR ROBOT CONTROL APPLICATION

A computer vision system is under development for robotic control. We need to control a robotic gripper which picks parts from an assembly line and puts them into boxes. To do this, we need to determine: (1) Where the object is in the two-dimensional plane in which the objects lie; (2) What type of object it is; one type goes into Box A, another type goes into Box B. First, we define the feature vector that will solve this problem. We determine that knowing the area, and center of area of the object, defined by an (r, c) pair, will locate it in space. Additionally, if the object perimeter is known, we can identify the object. So, our feature vector contains four feature measures, and the feature space is four-dimensional. We can define the feature vector for this application as [area, r, c, perimeter].

6.9.2 Distance and Similarity Measures

The feature vector is meant to represent the object and will be used to classify it. To perform the classification, we need methods to compare two feature vectors. The primary methods are to measure either the *difference (distance)* between the two or the *similarity*. Two vectors that are closely related will have a small difference and a large similarity.

The difference can be measured by a *distance measure* in the *n*-dimensional feature space; the bigger the distance between two vectors, the greater the difference. *Euclidean distance* is the most common metric for measuring the distance between two vectors and is given by the square root of the sum of the squares of the differences between vector components. Given two vectors **A** and **B**, where

$$\mathbf{A} = \begin{bmatrix} a_1 \\ a_2 \\ \vdots \\ a_n \end{bmatrix} \text{and } \mathbf{B} = \begin{bmatrix} b_1 \\ b_2 \\ \vdots \\ b_n \end{bmatrix} \tag{6.9-1}$$

the Euclidean distance is given by:

$$d_E(A,B) = \sqrt{\sum_{i=1}^{n}(a_i - b_i)^2} = \sqrt{(a_1 - b_1)^2 + (a_2 - b_2)^2 + (a_3 - b_3)^2 + \cdots + (a_n - b_n)^2} \tag{6.9-2}$$

Another distance measure, called the *city block, Manhattan,* or *absolute value metric,* is defined as follows (using **A** and **B** as above):

$$d_{CB}(A,B) = \sum_{i=1}^{n}|a_i - b_i| \tag{6.9-3}$$

This metric is computationally faster than the Euclidean distance, but gives similar results. A distance metric that returns the largest difference between feature components is the *maximum value* metric defined by:

$$d_{\mathrm{MAX}}(A,B) = \max\{\,|a_1 - b_1|\,,|a_2 - b_2|\,,\ldots,|a_n - b_n|\,\} \tag{6.9-4}$$

Since it results in only the vector component with the maximum distance, its use is highly application dependent. A generalized distance metric is the *Minkowski distance* defined as follows:

$$d_M(A,B) = \left[\sum_{i=1}^{n}|a_i - b_i|^r\right]^{1/r} \quad \text{where } r \text{ is positive integer} \tag{6.9-5}$$

The Minkowski distance is referred to as generalized because, for instance, if $r = 2$, it is the same as Euclidean distance, and when $r = 1$, it is the city block metric.

The second type of metric used for comparing two feature vectors is the *similarity measure.* Two vectors that are close in the feature space will have a large similarity measure. The most common form of the similarity measure uses one that we have already seen, the *vector inner product.* Using our definitions for the two vectors **A** and **B**, we can use the *normalized vector inner product* as a similarity measure, defined by the following equation:

$$s_{\mathrm{NIP}}(A,B) = \frac{\sum_{i=1}^{n} a_i b_i}{\sqrt{a_1^2 + a_2^2 + \cdots + a_n^2}\ \sqrt{b_1^2 + b_2^2 + \cdots + b_n^2}} \tag{6.9-6}$$

Another commonly used similarity measure is the *Tanimoto metric,* defined as follows:

$$s_T(A,B) = \frac{\sum_{i=1}^{n} a_i b_i}{\sum_{i=1}^{n} a_i^2 + \sum_{i=1}^{n} b_i^2 - \sum_{i=1}^{n} a_i b_i} \tag{6.9-7}$$

This metric takes on values between 0 and 1, which can be thought of as a "percent of similarity" since the value is 1 (100%) for identical vectors and gets smaller as the vectors get farther apart.

The *correlation coefficient* is also frequently used as a similarity metric. Note that this metric assumes that the features have been normalized with standard normal density (see the next section). Also called *Pearson's correlation coefficient* or the *correlation factor*, it is defined as follows:

$$\text{Correlation coefficient} = s_{cc} = \frac{\sum_{i=1}^{n}(a_i - \bar{a})(b_i - \bar{b})}{\sqrt{\sum_{i=1}^{n}(a_i - \bar{a})^2 \sum_{i=1}^{n}(b_i - b)^2}} \tag{6.9-8}$$

where $\bar{a} = \dfrac{1}{n}\sum_{i=1}^{n}a_i$ and $\bar{b} = \dfrac{1}{n}\sum_{i=1}^{n}b_i$, the average or mean values of the vectors.

Note that this metric takes on a value between –1 and +1. Two identical vectors will have a value of +1, and two vectors with identical magnitudes for each feature, but opposite signs will have a correlation coefficient of –1:

EXAMPLE 6.9.2: CORRELATION COEFFICIENT

We have two feature vectors:

$$\mathbf{A} = \begin{bmatrix} 1 \\ 2 \\ 3 \end{bmatrix} \text{ and } \mathbf{B} = \begin{bmatrix} 1 \\ 2 \\ 3 \end{bmatrix}$$

To find the correlation coefficient: $\bar{a} = \dfrac{1}{3}(1+2+3) = \dfrac{6}{3} = 2 = \bar{b}$

And $s_{cc} = \dfrac{(1-2)(1-2)+(2-2)(2-2)+(3-2)(3-2)}{\sqrt{\left[(1-2)^2+(2-2)^2+(3-2)^2\right]\left[(1-2)^2+(2-2)^2+(3-2)^2\right]}} = \dfrac{2}{2} = 1$

Alternately, by negating the above vector **B**, we have:

$$\mathbf{A} = \begin{bmatrix} 1 \\ 2 \\ 3 \end{bmatrix} \text{ and } \mathbf{B} = \begin{bmatrix} -1 \\ -2 \\ -3 \end{bmatrix}$$

To find the correlation coefficient: $\bar{a} = \dfrac{1}{3}(1+2+3) = \dfrac{6}{3} = 2$

In this case, we have a different mean for **B**: $\bar{b} = \dfrac{1}{3}(-1+-2+-3) = \dfrac{-6}{3} = -2$

And $s_{cc} = \dfrac{(1-2)(-1+2)+(2-2)(-2+2)+(3-2)(-3+2)}{\sqrt{\left[(1-2)^2+(2-2)^2+(3-2)^2\right]\left[(-1+2)^2+(-2+2)^2+(-3+2)^2\right]}} = \dfrac{-2}{2} = -1$

If two feature vectors have a correlation coefficient of 1, we say they are maximally positively correlated; this means as one varies the other, one varies in the same manner. In other words, they are very much alike or very similar. If two feature vectors have a correlation coefficient of –1, we say they are maximally negatively correlated, which means as one changes the other one changes in the opposite direction. Therefore, these two feature vectors, with a negative correlation, are not very similar and tend to be opposite, as in the following additional example.

EXAMPLE 6.9.3: CORRELATION COEFFICIENT

$$\mathbf{A} = \begin{bmatrix} 1 \\ 2 \\ 3 \end{bmatrix} \text{ and } \mathbf{B} = \begin{bmatrix} 3 \\ 2 \\ 1 \end{bmatrix}$$

To find the correlation coefficient: $\bar{a} = \frac{1}{3}(1+2+3) = \frac{6}{3} = 2 = \bar{b}$

And $s_{cc} = \dfrac{(1-2)(3-2)+(2-2)(2-2)+(3-2)(1-2)}{\sqrt{\left[(1-2)^2+(2-2)^2+(3-2)^2\right]\left[(3-2)^2+(2-2)^2+(1-2)^2\right]}} = \dfrac{-2}{2} = -1$

Note that this example illustrates that for negative correlation, we do not need a sign change in the feature values, but simply have a case where as one goes up the other goes down. Note that here, for these values, feature one is minimum for vector **A** and maximum for vector **B**. When two vectors are uncorrelated, they will have a correlation coefficient of 0 – these are two vectors that have nothing in common they are orthogonal. As the value of this similarity metric goes from 0 to +1, feature vectors are getting more similar. As the correlation coefficient goes from 0 down to –1, they are becoming more dissimilar.

Fuzzy features must be treated with fuzzy methods. Remember fuzzy features take on values between 0 and 1, and the feature is present or "true" as we get closer to 1. The feature is absent or false as we get closer to 0. We can define the similarity between two fuzzy feature vectors as follows:

$$s_f(\mathbf{A}, \mathbf{B}) = \frac{1}{n}\sum_{i=1}^{n} s(a_i, b_i) \tag{6.9-9}$$

where $s(a_i, b_i) = \max\left[\min(1-a_i, 1-b_i), \min(a_i, b_i)\right]$.

The range of values for this metric is between 0 and 1, with 1 being a perfect match and 0 being no similarity. Note that fuzzy self-similarity, defined as the similarity a fuzzy feature vector has with itself, is from 0.5 to 1. The following example illustrates the varying similarity a fuzzy feature vector can have to itself, the self-similarity.

EXAMPLE 6.9.4: FUZZY SELF-SIMILARITY

Given the following four fuzzy feature vectors:

$$\mathbf{A} = \begin{bmatrix} 1 \\ 1 \\ 1 \end{bmatrix} \quad \mathbf{B} = \begin{bmatrix} 1 \\ 0 \\ 1 \end{bmatrix} \quad \mathbf{C} = \begin{bmatrix} 0.5 \\ 0.5 \\ 0.3 \end{bmatrix} \quad \mathbf{D} = \begin{bmatrix} 0.5 \\ 0.5 \\ 0.5 \end{bmatrix}$$

Find the similarity these have with themselves, the self-similarity:

$$s_f(\mathbf{A}, \mathbf{A}) = \frac{1}{3}\sum_{i=1}^{n} s(a_i, b_i) = 3\left\{\max\left[\min(1-1, 1-1), \min(1,1)\right]\right\} = 3\left\{\max(0,1)\right\} = 1$$

$$s_f(\mathbf{B}, \mathbf{B}) = \frac{1}{3}\sum_{i=1}^{n} s(a_i, b_i) = 2\left\{\max\left[\min(1-1, 1-1), \min(1,1)\right]\right\} + \max\left[\min(1-0, 1-0), \min(0,0)\right] = 1$$

$$s_f(\mathbf{C}, \mathbf{C}) = \frac{1}{3}\sum_{i=1}^{n} s(a_i, b_i) = 2\left\{\max\left[\min(1-0.5, 1-0.5), \min(0.5, 0.5)\right]\right\} + \max\left[\min(1-0.3, 1-0.3), \min(0.3, 0.3)\right] = 1.7/3 \approx 0.57$$

$$s_f(\mathbf{D}, \mathbf{D}) = \sum_{i=1}^{n} s(a_i, b_i) = 3\left\{\max\left[\min(1-0.5, 1-0.5), \min(0.5, 0.5)\right]\right\} = 1.5/3 = 0.5$$

This example shows that as long as the values are all 1 or 0, we will have a maximum self-similarity. That is, for each feature, we know if it is present (true) or not. When all the values are 0.5, we get minimal self-similarity. Because we know nothing about his feature vector or any of its feature components! Each feature might be present (true) or absent (false). For a fuzzy feature to have a value of 0.5 simply means we know nothing about it.

However, we are interested in comparison of two different fuzzy feature vectors. The following example show how fuzzy features and their similarity differ from normal, non-fuzzy feature vectors.

EXAMPLE 6.9.5: FUZZY SIMILARITY

Given the following 4 fuzzy feature vectors:

$$\mathbf{A} = \begin{bmatrix} 1 \\ 1 \\ 1 \end{bmatrix} \mathbf{B} = \begin{bmatrix} 0.75 \\ 0.75 \\ 0.75 \end{bmatrix} \mathbf{C} = \begin{bmatrix} 0.5 \\ 0.5 \\ 0.5 \end{bmatrix} \mathbf{D} = \begin{bmatrix} 0.25 \\ 0.25 \\ 0.25 \end{bmatrix}$$

We note that using standard vector distance metrics, such as Euclidean distance, vectors A&B and C&D are equally far apart. However, comparing the same pairs using fuzzy similarity, we find:

$$s_f(\mathbf{A},\mathbf{B}) = \frac{1}{3}\sum_{i=1}^{n} s(a_i,b_i) = 3\left\{ \max\left[\min(1-1,\ 1-0.75), \min(1,0.75) \right] \right\} = 3\left\{ \max(0.0,0.75) \right\} = 0.75$$

$$s_f(\mathbf{C},\mathbf{D}) = \frac{1}{3}\sum_{i=1}^{n} s(a_i,b_i) = 3\left\{ \max\left[\min(1-0.5,\ 1-0.25), \min(0.5,0.25) \right] \right\} = 3\left\{ \max(0.5,0.25) \right\} = 0.5$$

This example shows that as the vectors get closer to the "center", where the values approach 0.5, the similarity decreases because the actual values are less certain. In other words, the fuzzy similarity depends not only on the distance between the two vectors but also how close they are to the center of the feature space. Remember, in fuzzy feature space, as we approach 1, the feature is certain to exist or is true, and as 0 is approached, we know the feature is absent or false.

EXAMPLE 6.9.6: FUZZY SIMILARITY

Given the following four fuzzy feature vectors, and finding the similarity between **A** and **B,** and between **C** and **D**:

$$\mathbf{A} = \begin{bmatrix} 1 \\ 1 \\ 1 \end{bmatrix} \mathbf{B} = \begin{bmatrix} 0.75 \\ 0.75 \\ 0.75 \end{bmatrix} \mathbf{C} = \begin{bmatrix} 0 \\ 0 \\ 0 \end{bmatrix} \mathbf{D} = \begin{bmatrix} 0.25 \\ 0.25 \\ 0.25 \end{bmatrix}$$

$$s_f(\mathbf{A},\mathbf{B}) = \frac{1}{3}\sum_{i=1}^{n} s(a_i,b_i) = 3\left\{ \max\left[\min(1-1,\ 1-0.75), \min(1,0.75) \right] \right\} = 3\left\{ \max(0,0.75) \right\} = 0.75$$

$$s_f(\mathbf{C},\mathbf{D}) = \frac{1}{3}\sum_{i=1}^{n} s(a_i,b_i) = 3\left\{ \max\left[\min(1-0,\ 1-0.25), \min(0,0.25) \right] \right\} = 3\left\{ \max(0.75,0) \right\} = 0.75$$

Note that these pairs of feature vectors are "equally" similar, but one pair is at the high end and one is at the low end. If we find the similarity between the pairs **A** & **D** and **B** & **C**:

$$s_f(\mathbf{A},\mathbf{D}) = \frac{1}{3}\sum_{i=1}^{n} s(a_i,b_i) = 3\left\{ \max\left[\min(1-1,\ 1-0.25), \min(1,0.25) \right] \right\} = 3\left\{ \max(0,0.25) \right\} = 0.25$$

$$s_f(\mathbf{B},\mathbf{C}) = \frac{1}{3}\sum_{i=1}^{n} s(a_i,b_i) = 3\left\{ \max\left[\min(1-0.75,\ 1-0), \min(0.75,0) \right] \right\} = 3\left\{ \max(0,0.25) \right\} = 0.25$$

Note that these pairs are quite dissimilar, so have a low similarity value. Now comparing **A** & **C**:

$$s_f(\mathbf{A},\mathbf{C}) = \frac{1}{3}\sum_{i=1}^{n} s(a_i,b_i) = 3\left\{\max\left[\min(1-1\ ,\ 1-0),\min(1,0)\right]\right\} = 3\left\{\max(0,0)\right\} = 0$$

We obtain the minimum lower bound of 0 and observe that these two feature vectors have maximum dissimilarity.

6.9.3 Data Preprocessing

Now that we have seen methods to compare two vectors, we need to analyze the set of feature vectors and prepare them for use in developing the classification algorithm. The data preprocessing consists of three potential steps: (1) noise removal, (2) data normalization and/or decorrelation and (3) insertion of missing data. Many of the classification algorithm development methods are based on mathematical theory that assumes specific distributions in the feature data and requires data normalization. One often used standard assumption is zero mean, Gaussian distributed data for each feature vector component. For some methods, it is desirable that the features are uncorrelated. In either case, the first step is noise removal, also called *outlier removal*.

An outlier is a data point that is alone very far from the average value. The assumption in removing it is that it is "bad" or noisy data. Possibly, a mistake was made during its measurement or it does not really represent the underlying structure. In the development of a classification algorithm, a major part of what we are trying to do is to find a model for the underlying structure. The sample feature vectors are used to develop this model, so any "bad" samples will hinder the process. Before any samples are discarded, care must be taken that they do not represent a subgroup for which we simply do not have many samples.

The distance and similarity measures defined before may be biased due to the varying range on different components of the vector. For example, one component may only range from 1 to 5 and another may range from 1 to 5,000, so a difference of five for the first component will be maximum, but a difference of five for the second feature may be insignificant. It may help to *range normalize* the vector components by dividing by the range on each vector component, where the range is simply the maximum value for that component minus the minimum. This is done as follows, given a set of three feature vectors, {$\mathbf{F}_1, \mathbf{F}_2, \mathbf{F}_3$}, with three features in each vector.

EXAMPLE 6.9.7: RANGE NORMALIZATION

Given the three feature vectors

$$F_1 = \begin{bmatrix} 3 \\ 50 \\ 1 \end{bmatrix}, F_2 = \begin{bmatrix} 6 \\ 100 \\ 2 \end{bmatrix}, F_3 = \begin{bmatrix} 1 \\ 10 \\ 1 \end{bmatrix}$$

We find range on each component by subtracting the minimum value for that feature from the maximum value. The first component, or feature, has values of 3, 6 and 1, so the range is:

$$MAX - MIN = 6 - 1 = 5$$

Second component range:

$$MAX - MIN = 100 - 10 = 90$$

Third component range:

$$MAX - MIN = 2 - 1 = 1$$

New range-normalized vectors:

$$
F_1' = \begin{bmatrix} 3/5 \\ 50/90 \\ 1/1 \end{bmatrix} \cong \begin{bmatrix} 0.6 \\ 0.56 \\ 1 \end{bmatrix}, F_2' = \begin{bmatrix} 6/5 \\ 100/90 \\ 2/1 \end{bmatrix} \cong \begin{bmatrix} 1.2 \\ 1.1 \\ 2 \end{bmatrix}, F_3' = \begin{bmatrix} 1/5 \\ 10/90 \\ 1/1 \end{bmatrix} \cong \begin{bmatrix} 0.2 \\ 0.1 \\ 1 \end{bmatrix}
$$

It can be seen that the larger feature vector components (in this case, the second component) will not greatly skew any distance metrics used with these new normalized values. Also, note that relationships between components within a vector are lost.

Another option is to perform *unit vector normalization* which will modify the feature vector components so that the range of each is between 0 and 1. To do this, we normalize the vector components by dividing by the Euclidean distance of a vector consisting of all the values for one feature component.

EXAMPLE 6.9.8: UNIT VECTOR NORMALIZATION

Given the three feature vectors

$$
F_1 = \begin{bmatrix} 3 \\ 5 \\ 1 \end{bmatrix}, F_2 = \begin{bmatrix} 6 \\ 10 \\ 2 \end{bmatrix}, F_3 = \begin{bmatrix} 1 \\ 1 \\ 1 \end{bmatrix}
$$

We find the Euclidean distance (from the origin) for each component.
First component Euclidean distance from the origin:

$$
\sqrt{(3-0)^2 + (6-0)^2 + (1-0)^2} = \sqrt{9+36+1} = \sqrt{46}
$$

Second component:

$$
\sqrt{5^2 + 10^2 + 1^2} = \sqrt{25 + 100 + 1} = \sqrt{126}
$$

Third component:

$$
\sqrt{1^2 + 2^2 + 1^2} = \sqrt{1 + 4 + 1} = \sqrt{6}
$$

Next, we normalize by dividing by the corresponding distances:

$$
F_1' = \begin{bmatrix} \dfrac{3}{\sqrt{46}} \\ \dfrac{5}{\sqrt{126}} \\ \dfrac{1}{\sqrt{6}} \end{bmatrix} \cong \begin{bmatrix} 0.44 \\ 0.45 \\ 0.41 \end{bmatrix}, F_2' = \begin{bmatrix} \dfrac{6}{\sqrt{46}} \\ \dfrac{10}{\sqrt{126}} \\ \dfrac{2}{\sqrt{6}} \end{bmatrix} \cong \begin{bmatrix} 0.88 \\ 0.89 \\ 0.82 \end{bmatrix}, F_3' = \begin{bmatrix} \dfrac{1}{\sqrt{46}} \\ \dfrac{1}{\sqrt{126}} \\ \dfrac{1}{\sqrt{6}} \end{bmatrix} \cong \begin{bmatrix} 0.14 \\ 0.09 \\ 0.41 \end{bmatrix}
$$

We see here that relationships across components are retained. For example, the first component of F_1 is still twice the value of the first component of F_2 – in the original vectors, we have 3 and 6, and after normalization, 0.44 and 0.88. However, as with all normalization methods, the relationship *between* feature values within a feature vector is lost. For example, F_1 originally had values of 3, 5 and 1; after normalization, all the values are almost the same.

A commonly used statistical-based method to normalize these measures is to take each vector component and subtract the mean and divide by the standard deviation. This method can be applied to any of the measures, both distance and similarity, but it requires knowledge of the probability distribution of the feature measurements. In practice, the probability distributions are often estimated by using the existing data. This is done as follows, given a set of k feature vectors, $\mathbf{F}_j = \{\mathbf{F}_1, \mathbf{F}_2, ..., \mathbf{F}_k\}$, with n features in each vector:

$$F_j = \begin{bmatrix} f_{1j} \\ f_{2j} \\ \vdots \\ f_{nj} \end{bmatrix} \text{ for } j = 1, 2, \ldots, k$$

$$\text{means} \Rightarrow m_i = \frac{1}{k}\sum_{j=1}^{k} f_{ij} \quad \text{for } i = 1, 2, \ldots, n \tag{6.9-10}$$

$$\text{standard deviation} \Rightarrow \sigma_i = \sqrt{\frac{1}{k}\sum_{j=1}^{k}(f_{ij} - m_i)^2} = \sqrt{\frac{1}{k}\sum_{ji=1}^{k}(f_{ij})^2 - m_i^2} \quad \text{for } i = 1, 2, \ldots, n$$

Now, for each feature component, we subtract the mean and divide by the standard deviation:

$$f_{ij\text{SND}} = \frac{f_{ij} - m_i}{\sigma_i} \quad \text{for all } i, j \tag{6.9-11}$$

This will give us new feature vectors where the distribution has been normalized so that the means are 0 and the standard deviations are 1; the resulting distribution on each vector component is called the *standard normal density* (SND).

Other linear techniques can be used to limit the feature values to specific ranges, such as between 0 and 1, by scaling or shifting. Note that in above equation, we have simply shifted the data by the mean and scaled it by the standard deviation. To map the data to a specified range, S_{MIN} to S_{MAX}, but still retain the relationship between the values, we use min–max normalization:

$$f_{ij\text{MINMAX}} = \left(\frac{f_{ij} - f_{i\text{MIN}}}{f_{i\text{MAX}} - f_{i\text{MIN}}}\right)(S_{\text{MAX}} - S_{\text{MIN}}) + S_{\text{MIN}} \tag{6.9-12}$$

where
S_{MIN} and S_{MAX} are minimum and maximum values for the specified range
and
$f_{i\text{MIN}}$ and $f_{i\text{MAX}}$ are minimum and maximum values for feature i.

Nonlinear methods may be desired if the data distribution is skewed; that is, not evenly distributed about the mean. One common method, called *softmax scaling*, requires two steps:

$$\text{STEP1} \Rightarrow y = \frac{f_{ij} - m_i}{r\sigma_i}$$

$$\text{STEP2} \Rightarrow f_{ij\text{SMC}} = \frac{1}{1 + e^{-y}} \quad \text{for all } i, j \tag{6.9-13}$$

This is essentially a method that compresses the data in the range of 0–1. The first step is similar to mapping the data to the SND, but with a user-defined factor, r. The process is approximately linear for small values of y with respect to f_{ij}, and then it compresses the data exponentially as it gets farther away from the mean. The factor r determines the range of values for the feature, f_{ij}, that will fall into the linear range. In addition to moving the mean and normalizing the spread of the data, this transform will change the shape of the distribution.

It is important when data normalization techniques are applied to take care that the method selected will serve the application since they will move the mean and change the spread and/or shape of the resulting data distribution. In some cases, this may not be desired. If useful information is contained in the mean, spread or shape of the data distribution, be careful not to lose that information since the choice of the wrong normalization method will effectively filter it out. Additionally, remember that relationships between features within a vector will be lost. For some applications, this may be important. The model for normalization is based on the idea that all the features are of equal importance to the classification problem. Also, be aware that the results will only be useful if the set of sample vectors represent the entire population, including all the classes. In practice, this means that the sample set is large, the more the better. How many? It depends on the application. In general, as many as are practical for the application and as many as the development schedule allows.

Performing a principal components transform (PCT) in the n-dimensional feature space provides new features that are linear transforms of the original features and are uncorrelated. This is desirable for some classification algorithm development methods, such as neural networks. Use of the PCT, also referred to as principal components analysis (PCA), is also useful for data visualization in a high dimensional feature space. With an n-dimensional feature space, it is very difficult to represent the space visually, although investigation into data visualization techniques to address this problem is currently an active research area. However, a useful tool for feature analysis is to perform the PCT and view the first two or three components graphically.

Theoretically, the final step in data preprocessing is to insert missing data. The idea being that the available data is incomplete and we can estimate samples that should be in the development set of feature vectors. The method for creating the artificial data is to analyze the distribution of the sample feature vectors and, based on a desired data distribution, create feature vectors that we think belong to the desired distribution and include them in our feature vector set. This becomes rather tricky and fraught with dangers as it presupposes that we can predict the model that we are trying to find! In practice, this is typically not done, as it may bias the results by the creation of artificial data.

To fully apply the methods discussed here requires a complete understanding of the problem, including how the features relate to the desired output and the underlying structure of each feature's distribution. Typically, this information is unknown, so a trial and error approach is used during development. As shown in Figure 6.1-1, the feature analysis is not complete until pattern classification results are fed back through the application.

6.10 Key Points

Overview: Feature Extraction and Analysis

- Feature extraction is finding values for the initially selected features for objects of interest in the image.
- Feature analysis involves examining the extracted features and determining if and how they can be used to solve the imaging problem.

Feature Extraction

- Feature extraction starts with initial feature selection.
- Feature selection is important for successful pattern classification
- There are typically at least two iterations of feature selection: (1) initial selection before any analysis or pattern classification and (2) selection after analysis to determine which features will work best for pattern classification
- A good feature is:
  - **Robust**: it will have similar results under various conditions, such as lighting, cameras and lenses.
  - **Discriminating**: it is useful for differentiation of classes (object types) of interest.
  - **Reliable**: it provides consistent measurements for similar classes (objects).
  - **Independent**: it is not correlated to other features.
- RST-invariant features do not change under rotation, scale (size) or translation (movement) of the image object.

Shape Features

- Shape features depend on a silhouette of the image object, so they require only a binary image.
- Shape features include area, center of area, axis of least second moment, projections and Euler number from *Section 3.3.3*, and perimeter, thinness ratio, irregularity, aspect ratio, moments, set of seven based RST-invariant features and Fourier descriptors.

Perimeter: is found by (1) counting the number of "1" pixels next to "0" in the binary shape image, or (2) performing an edge detector and counting "1" pixels, or (3) using chain code methods for better accuracy. These approximations can be improved by multiplying the result by $\pi/4$ for arbitrary, curved, shapes. See Figure 6.2-2.

Thinness ratio: has a theoretical maximum value of 1, corresponding to a circle, and decreases as object gets thinner or perimeter gets more convoluted:

$$T = 4\pi\left(\frac{A}{P^2}\right) \tag{6.2-1}$$

Irregularity or compactness ratio: $1/T$, reciprocal of the thinness ratio.

Aspect ratio: also called elongation or eccentricity, ratio of bounding box:

$$\frac{c_{max} - c_{min} + 1}{r_{max} - r_{min} + 1} \tag{6.2-2}$$

To be useful as a comparative measure, the objects should be rotated to some standard orientation, such as orientating the axis of least second moment in the horizontal direction.

Moments: for binary images, they are used to generate moment-based RST-invariant features given in Table 6-1, defined by the *moment order* $(p+q)$:

$$m_{pq} = \sum_r \sum_c r^p c^q I(r,c) \tag{6.2-3}$$

To generate the features we also need the *central moments* (Equation 6.2-4) and the *normalized central moments* (Equation 6.2-5).

Fourier descriptors: use binary image of the object and find spectral features defined in Section 6.5.

Histogram Features

- The histogram is a plot of gray level values versus the number of pixels at that value.
- The histogram tells us something about the brightness and contrast.
- A narrow histogram has low contrast; a histogram with a wide spread has high contrast.
- A bimodal histogram has two peaks, usually object and background.
- A histogram skewed toward the high end is bright and the one skewed toward the low end is dark.
- First-order histogram probability:

$$P(g) = \frac{N(g)}{M} \tag{6.3-1}$$

M is the number of pixels in the image or subimage, and $N(g)$ is the number of pixels at gray level g.

Mean: average value, which tells us something about the general brightness of the image:

$$\bar{g} = \sum_{g=0}^{L-1} gP(g) = \sum_r \sum_c \frac{I(r,c)}{M} \tag{6.3-2}$$

Standard deviation (SD): tells us about the contrast, high SD=high contrast, low SD=low contrast:

$$\sigma_g = \sqrt{\sum_{g=0}^{L-1}(g-\bar{g})^2 P(g)} \tag{6.3-3}$$

Skew: measures asymmetry about the mean, positive for a tail spreading to the right and negative for spreading to the left:

$$\text{SKEW} = \frac{1}{\sigma_g^3} \sum_{g=0}^{L-1} (g - \bar{g})^3 P(g) \qquad (6.3\text{-}4)$$

Energy: relates to gray level distribution, with a maximum value of 1 for an image of constant value and decreases as the gray levels are more widely distributed:

$$\text{ENERGY} = \sum_{g=0}^{L-1} [P(g)]^2 \qquad (6.3\text{-}5)$$

Entropy: varies inversely with energy, as defined measures how many bits are needed to code the data:

$$\text{ENTROPY} = - \sum_{g=0}^{L-1} P(g) \log_2 [P(g)] \qquad (6.3\text{-}6)$$

Color Features
- Color images consist of three bands, one each for red, green and blue or RGB.
- All of the features can be calculated separately in each color band.
- Alternately, we desire information about the relationship *between* color bands.
- To include between band information preprocess with a color transform (defined in Chapter 1).
- Most color transforms will decouple color and brightness information.
- Avoid absolute color measures as they are not robust.
- A relative color measure can be used which is typically application specific, or a known color standard, such as the Macbeth Color Chart, can be used for comparison.
- When using a known color standard, the system can be calibrated if conditions change.

Fourier Transform and Spectral Features
- The Fourier transform decomposes an image into complex sinusoidal terms.
- These terms include a zero frequency term, also called the DC term, related to the average value.
- The higher order terms include the fundamental or lowest frequency term, and harmonics which are multiples of the fundamental.

One-Dimensional DFT
- The one-dimensional (1-D) DFT corresponds to one row (or column) of an image.
- Basis vectors are complex sinusoids, defined by Euler's Identity:

$$e^{j\theta} = \cos(\theta) + j\sin(\theta) \qquad (6.5\text{-}3)$$

- Forward

$$F(v) = \frac{1}{N} \sum_{c=0}^{N-1} I(c) e^{-j2\pi vc/N}$$

$$= \frac{1}{N} \sum_{c=0}^{N-1} I(c)[\cos(2\pi vc/N) - j\sin(2\pi vc/N)] = \text{Re}(v) + j\,\text{Im}(v) \qquad (6.5\text{-}1)$$

- Inverse

$$F^{-1}[F(v)] = I(c) = \sum_{c=0}^{N-1} F(v)e^{j2\pi vc/N} \tag{6.5-2}$$

- The $F(v)$ terms can be broken down into a magnitude and phase component:

$$\text{MAGNITUDE} = |F(v)| = \sqrt{[\text{Re}(v)]^2 + [\text{Im}(v)]^2} \tag{6.5-5}$$

also called the Fourier spectrum or frequency spectrum

$$\text{PHASE} = \varphi(v) = \text{Tan}^{-1}\left[\frac{\text{Im}(v)}{\text{Re}(v)}\right] \tag{6.5-6}$$

Two-dimensional DFT

- Basis images are complex sinusoids:

$$e^{-j2\pi(ur+vc)/N} = \cos\left(\frac{2\pi}{N}(ur+vc)\right) - j\sin\left(\frac{2\pi}{N}(ur+vc)\right)$$

- Forward

$$F(u,v) = \frac{1}{N}\sum_{r=0}^{N-1}\sum_{c=0}^{N-1} I(r,c)e^{-j2\pi(ur+vc)/N}$$

$$= \frac{1}{N}\sum_{r=0}^{N-1}\sum_{c=0}^{N-1} I(r,c)\left[\cos\left(\frac{2\pi}{N}(ur+vc)\right) - j\sin\left(\frac{2\pi}{N}(ur+vc)\right)\right] \tag{6.2-19, 6.2-20}$$

- Inverse:

$$F^{-1}[F(u,v)] = I(r,c) = \frac{1}{N}\sum_{u=0}^{N-1}\sum_{v=0}^{N-1} F(u,v)e^{j2\pi(ur+vc)/N} \tag{6.5-11}$$

- $F(u,v) = \text{Re}(u,v) + j\text{Im}(u,v)$, $\text{Re}(u,v)$ is the real part and $\text{Im}(u,v)$ is the imaginary part, then we can define the magnitude and phase of a complex spectral component as:

$$\text{MAGNITUDE} = |F(u,v)| = \sqrt{[\text{Re}(u,v)]^2 + [\text{Im}(u,v)]^2} \tag{6.5-9}$$

also called the Fourier spectrum or frequency spectrum

$$\text{PHASE} = \varphi(u,v) = \text{Tan}^{-1}\left[\frac{\text{Im}(u,v)}{\text{Re}(u,v)}\right] \tag{6.5-10}$$

- The 2-D DFT is separable, which means the basis image can be broken down into product terms where eachcns:

$$e^{-j2\pi(ur+vc)/N} = e^{-j2\pi ur/N}\,e^{-j2\pi vc/N} \tag{6.5-12}$$

- Separability also implies that the 2-D DFT can be found by successive application of two 1-D DFTs

Spectral Features

- Primary metric is power.

$$POWER = |F(u,v)|^2 \qquad (6.5\text{-}16)$$

- Measure power in specific regions in the spectrum.
- The regions are box, ring or sector (wedge) shaped (see Figure 6.5–9).

$$SPECTRAL\ REGION\ POWER = \sum_{u \in REGION} \sum_{v \in REGION} |F(u,v)|^2 \qquad (6.5\text{-}17)$$

- Due to the redundancy in the Fourier spectral symmetry, we often measure the sector power over one-half the spectrum and the ring power over the other half of the spectrum (see Figure 6.2-10).

Texture Features

- Spectral features can be used as texture features.
- Texture is a function of image size relative to the object, as well as magnification.
- In practice, the spectral features can be calculated for 10 or 20 (or more) rings and sectors and the magnitudes plotted to look for signature shapes which will correspond to specific textures.
- Second-order histogram methods, also called gray level co-occurrence matrix methods, measure texture by considering relationship between pixel pairs and require the parameters *distance* and *angle* between pixel pairs.
- Let c_{ij} be the elements in the co-occurrence matrix normalized by the sum of the number of pixel pairs in the matrix, and assume a given distance and angle (direction), the equations are as follows:

$$Energy = \sum_i \sum_j c_{ij}^2 \qquad (6.6\text{-}1)$$

$$Inertia = \sum_i \sum_j (i-j)^2\, c_{ij} \qquad (6.6\text{-}2)$$

$$Correlation = \frac{1}{\sigma_x \sigma_y} \sum_i \sum_j (i-\mu_x)(j-\mu_y) c_{ij}$$

$$where: \mu_x = \sum_i i \sum_j c_{ij}$$

$$and: \mu_y = \sum_j j \sum_i c_{ij} \qquad (6.6\text{-}3)$$

$$and: \sigma_x^2 = \sum_i (i-\mu_x)^2 \sum_j c_{ij}$$

$$and: \sigma_y^2 = \sum_j (j-\mu_y)^2 \sum_i c_{ij;}$$

$$InverseDifference = \sum_i \sum_j \frac{c_{ij}}{|i-j|}\, ; for: i \neq j \qquad (6.6\text{-}4)$$

$$Entropy = -\sum_i \sum_j c_{ij} \log_2 c_{ij} \qquad (6.6\text{-}5)$$

- Laws energy masks can be used for measuring texture and are generated as the vector outer product of pairs of the following vectors, which correspond to gray level, edges, spots, ripples and waves:

$$L_5 = (1,4,6,4,1)$$

$$E_5 = (-1,-2,0,2,1)$$

$$S_5 = (-1,0,2,0,-1) \tag{6.5-6}$$

$$R_5 = (1,-4,6,-4,1)$$

$$W_5 = (-1,2,0,-2,1)$$

Laws filters are used by first removing the local average (Figure 6.6-4) and then convolving the masks with the image to produce the texture filtered images, $F_k(r, c)$ for the kth filter mask

These texture filtered images are used to produce a *texture energy map*, E_k for the kth filter, using a 15×15 window:

$$E_k(r,c) = \sum_{j=c-7}^{c+7} \sum_{i=r-7}^{r+7} |F_k(i,j)| \tag{6.5-7}$$

For pattern classification of objects, as implemented in CVIPtools, the energy maps for objects of interest are used and histogram statistics (mean, standard deviation, skew, energy and entropy) are generated from just the part of the energy map corresponding to the object of interest. These are then used as texture features for the object.

- *Gabor filters* represent another approach to texture features. The Gabor filter can be viewed as a sinusoidal wave of specified frequency and orientation, convolved by a Gaussian envelope, as shown in Equations (6.5-8)–(6.5-11). In the spatial domain, a 2-D Gabor filter is the result of multiplication of a 2-D Gaussian function and a complex exponential function. After convolving the image with the Gabor filters of interest, histogram statistics are extracted and used as texture features.

Region-Based Features: SIFT/SURF/GIST

- These features are defined at multiple spatial scales and are typically used to search images for objects of interest or to classify the image itself.
- They are used in segmentation, object classification, object tracking and scene identification.
- SIFT, scale-invariant feature transform, uses difference of Gaussian (DoG) images at different scales to find key points.
- SURF, the speeded up robust features, uses the Haar wavelet.
- GIST uses Gabor filters to extract the "gist" or essence of regions in the image.

Feature Extraction with CVIPtools

- Extraction of features with CVIPtools requires the original image and a segmented or mask image.
- A segmented image can be created with *Analysis→Segmentation* followed by any desired morphological filtering.
- A mask image can be created with *Utilities→Create→Border Mask*.
- Methods used for feature extraction by category are in Table 6-2.

Feature Analysis

- Feature analysis is important to aid in final feature selection.
- After feature extraction, the feature analysis process includes consideration of the application.
- The feature analysis process begins by the selection of tools and methods that will be used for the imaging problem.

Feature Vectors and Feature Spaces

Feature vector: an n-dimensional vector containing measurements for an image object, where n is the number of features. Feature vectors are symbolic, numeric or both. Two feature vectors, **A** and **B**, are represented as:

$$\mathbf{A} = \begin{bmatrix} a_1 \\ a_2 \\ \vdots \\ a_n \end{bmatrix} \text{ and } \mathbf{B} = \begin{bmatrix} b_1 \\ b_2 \\ \vdots \\ b_n \end{bmatrix} \tag{6.9-1}$$

Feature space: a mathematical abstraction created to allow visualization of feature vectors and relationships between them. Two- and three-dimensional feature vectors are modeled as a geometric construct with perpendicular axes and created by plotting each feature measurement along one axis. For n-dimensional feature vectors, it is a mathematical construction called a *hyperspace*.

Distance and Similarity Measures

Distance measures: used to compare two vectors in feature space by finding the distance or error between the two; the smaller the metric, the more alike the two are.

Euclidean distance: geometric distance in feature space

$$d_E(A,B) = \sqrt{\sum_{i=1}^{n}(a_i - b_i)^2} = \sqrt{(a_1 - b_1)^2 + (a_2 - b_2)^2 + (a_3 - b_3)^2 + \cdots + (a_n - b_n)^2} \tag{6.9-2}$$

City block, Manhattan or absolute value metric: results similar to Euclidean, but faster to calculate

$$d_{CB}(A,B) = \sum_{i=1}^{n}|a_i - b_i| \tag{6.9-3}$$

Maximum value metric: only counts largest vector component distance

$$d_{MAX}(A,B) = \max\{|a_1 - b_1|, |a_2 - b_2|, \ldots, |a_n - b_n|\} \tag{6.9-4}$$

Minkowski distance: generalized distance metric

$$d_M(A,B) = \left[\sum_{i=1}^{n}|a_i - b_i|^r\right]^{1/r} \text{ where } r \text{ is positive integer} \tag{6.9-5}$$

Similarity measure: used to compare two vectors in feature space by finding the similarity between the two; the larger the metric, the more alike the two are.

Normalized vector inner product:

$$s_{NIP}(A,B) = \frac{\sum_{i=1}^{n} a_i b_i}{\sqrt{a_1^2 + a_2^2 + \cdots + a_n^2}\sqrt{b_1^2 + b_2^2 + \cdots + b_n^2}} \tag{6.9-6}$$

Tanimoto metric: takes on values between 0 and 1; 1 for identical vectors

$$s_T(A,B) = \frac{\sum\limits_{i=1}^{n} a_i b_i}{\sum\limits_{i=1}^{n} a_i^2 + \sum\limits_{i=1}^{n} b_i^2 - \sum\limits_{i=1}^{n} a_i b_i} \tag{6.9-7}$$

Correlation coefficient: takes on a value between –1 and +1; 1 for identical vectors, also called *Pearson's correlation coefficient* or the *correlation factor*:

$$\text{Correlation coefficient} = s_{cc} = \frac{\sum\limits_{i=1}^{n} (a_i - \overline{a})(b_i - \overline{b})}{\sqrt{\sum\limits_{i=1}^{n} (a_i - \overline{a})^2 \sum\limits_{i=1}^{n} (b_i - b)^2}} \tag{6.9-8}$$

where $\overline{a} = \dfrac{1}{n}\sum\limits_{i=1}^{n} a_i$ and $\overline{b} = \dfrac{1}{n}\sum\limits_{i=1}^{n} b_i$, the average or mean values of the vectors.

Fuzzy similarity: Fuzzy features take on values between 0 and 1, and the feature is present or "true" as we get closer to 1. The feature is absent or false as we get closer to 0. The similarity between two fuzzy feature vectors is:

$$s_f(\mathbf{A},\mathbf{B}) = \frac{1}{n}\sum\limits_{i=1}^{n} s(a_i, b_i) \tag{6.9-9}$$

where $s(a_i, b_i) = \max\left[\min(1 - a_i,\ 1 - b_i),\min(a_i, b_i)\right]$

Data Preprocessing

Data preprocessing: to prepare the feature vectors for use in pattern classification algorithm development; consists of up to three steps: (1) noise (outlier) removal, (2) data normalization and/or decorrelation and (3) insertion of missing data.

Noise (outlier) removal: removal of feature vectors that are so far from the average, and/or isolated, as to be considered noise. Possibly due to measurement error.

Data normalization and/or decorrelation: performed to avoid biasing the distance or similarity measures and to prepare the data for pattern classification methods.

Range normalize: divide each vector component by the data range for that component.

Unit vector normalization: divide each vector component by the magnitude of the vector created by using all the values of that particular feature component across all the sample feature vectors.

Standard normal density normalization: creating a distribution with 0 mean and standard deviation of 1:

Given a set of k feature vectors, $\mathbf{F}_j = \{\mathbf{F}_1, \mathbf{F}_2, ..., \mathbf{F}_k\}$, with n features in each vector:

$$\mathbf{F}_j = \begin{bmatrix} f_{1j} \\ f_{2j} \\ \vdots \\ f_{nj} \end{bmatrix} \quad \text{for } j = 1, 2, ..., k$$

$$\text{means} \Rightarrow m_i = \frac{1}{k}\sum\limits_{j=1}^{k} f_{ij} \quad \text{for } i = 1, 2, ..., n \tag{6.9-10}$$

$$\text{standard deviation} \Rightarrow \sigma_i = \sqrt{\frac{1}{k}\sum\limits_{j=1}^{k} (f_{ij} - m_i)^2} = \sqrt{\frac{1}{k}\sum\limits_{ji=1}^{k} (f_{ij})^2 - m_i^2} \quad \text{for } i = 1, 2, ..., n$$

Now, for each feature component, we subtract the mean and divide by the standard deviation:

$$f_{ij\text{SND}} = \frac{f_{ij} - m_i}{\sigma_i} \quad \text{for all } i, j \tag{6.9-11}$$

Min–max normalization: to map the data to a specified range:

$$f_{ij\text{MINMAX}} = \left(\frac{f_{ij} - f_{i\text{MIN}}}{f_{i\text{MAX}} - f_{i\text{MIN}}}\right)(S_{\text{MAX}} - S_{\text{MIN}}) + S_{\text{MIN}} \tag{6.9-12}$$

where S_{MIN} and S_{MAX} are minimum and maximum values for the specified range and $f_{i\text{MIN}}$ and $f_{i\text{MAX}}$ are minimum and maximum for feature i.

Softmax scaling: a nonlinear normalization method for use with skewed data distributions:

$$\text{STEP1} \Rightarrow y = \frac{f_{ij} - m_i}{r\sigma_i}$$

$$\text{STEP2} \Rightarrow f_{ij\text{SMC}} = \frac{1}{1 + e^{-y}} \quad \text{for all } i, j \tag{6.9-13}$$

Principal components transform: performed in the n-dimensional feature space to decorrelate the data; useful preprocessing for neural networks.

Insertion of missing data: analyze the distribution of the sample feature vectors and, based on a desired data distribution, create feature vectors that belong to the desired distribution and include them; used for mathematical modeling, recommendation to avoid use in practice.

6.11 References and Further Reading

For related reading regarding feature extraction and selection, see Gonzalez and Woods (2018), Theodoridis and Koutroumbas (2009), Forsyth and Ponce (2011), Duda, Hart, and Stork (2001) and Ripley (1996). Information regarding chain codes can be found in Gonzalez and Woods (2018), Costa and Cesar (2001), Nadler and Smith (1993), Jain, Kasturi, and Schnuck (1995) and Ballard and Brown (1982). For an excellent book on shape analysis and classification, see Costa and Cesar (2001). More information on shape features can be found in Forsyth and Ponce (2011), Shapiro and Stockman (2001), Castleman (1996), Schalkoff (1989), Horn (1986) and Levine (1985). More details on color features can be found in Forsyth and Ponce (2011) and Shapiro and Stockman (2001). Details regarding Fourier descriptors can be found in Nixon and Aguado (2020), Gonzalez and Woods (2018), Sonka, Hlavac, and Boyle (2014) and Nadler and Smith (1993). For additional information for the Fourier transform, other image transforms and filters in both the spatial and frequency domains, see Umbaugh (2023).

Companion reading for texture-based features includes Gonzalez and Woods (2018), Sonka, Hlavac, and Boyle (2014), Ranagayyan (2005), Shapiro and Stockman (2001), Castleman (1996), Granlund and Knutsson (1995), Haralick and Shapiro (1992), Pratt (1991) and Rosenfeld and Kak (1982). Additional reading for using the co-occurrence matrix for texture can be found in Gonzalez and Woods (2018), Sonka, Hlavac, and Boyle (2014), Shapiro and Stockman (2001), Haralick and Shapiro (1992) and Nadler and Smith (1993), with the original 14 defined in Haralick, Shanmugam, and Dinstein (1973). Details for the new co-occurrence matrix texture features in the MATLAB CVIP Toolbox can be found in Milosevic, Janovic, and Peilic (2014), where they define a total of 20 features. An example of using spectral feature plots for texture identification is found in Nadler and Smith (1993). The information regarding the Laws energy mask is found in Sonka, Hlavac, and Boyle (2014) and Shapiro and Stockman (2001). More on Gabor filters can be found in Prince (2012), Theodoridis and Koutroumbas (2009) and Haidekker (2011). More on the RST-invariant moment features can be found in Gonzalez and Woods (2018), Costa and Cesar (2001), Nadler and Smith (1993) and Schalkoff (1989). Additional general information on the SIFT/SURF/GIST features can be found in Toennies (2012); specifics for SIFT in Lowe (2004), Gonzalez and Woods (2018), Lowe (1999); SURF in Bay, Tuytelaars, and van Gool (2006); and GIST in Torralba (2003).

A more complete mathematical analysis of distance and similarity measures can be found in Theodoridis and Koutroumbas (2009) and Duda, Hart, and Stork (2001). For more on fuzzy set theory and fuzzy feature classification, see Theodoridis and Koutroumbas (2009) and Gonzalez and Woods (2018). For practical books on statistics, see Johnson (2010) or Kennedy and Neville (1986). For an excellent handbook on image processing, quite useful for feature extraction, see Russ (2015). Two excellent texts for feature recognition and classification with medical applications are Dougherty (2009) and Ranagayyan (2005).

Ballard, D.H., Brown, C.M., *Computer Vision*, Upper Saddle River, NJ: Prentice Hall, 1982.
Bay, H., Tuytelaars, T., van Gool, L., SURF: Speeded up robust features. *European Conference on Computer Vision, ECCV, LNCS*, Vol. 3951, pp. 404–417, 2006.
Castleman, K.R., *Digital Image Processing*, Upper Saddle River, NJ: Prentice Hall, 1996.
Costa, L., Cesar, R.M., *Shape Analysis and Classification: Theory and Practice*, Boca Raton, FL: CRC Press, 2001.
Dougherty, G., *Digital Image Processing for Medical Applications*, Cambridge: Cambridge University Press, 2009.
Duda, R.O., Hart, P.E., Stork, D.G, *Pattern Classification*, New York: Wiley 2001.
Forsyth, D.A., Ponce, J., *Computer Vision*, Upper Saddle River, NJ: Prentice Hall, 2011.
Gonzalez, R.C., Woods, R.E., *Digital Image Processing*, 4th Edition, Hoboken, NJ: Pearson Education, 2018.
Granlund, G., Knutsson, H., *Signal Processing for Computer Vision*, Boston, MA: Kluwer Academic Publishers, 1995.
Haidekker, M.A., *Advanced Biomedical Image Analysis*, Hoboken, NJ: Wiley, 2011.
Haralick, R.M., Shapiro, L.G., *Computer and Robot Vision*, Reading, MA: Addison-Wesley, 1992.
Haralick, R.M, Shanmugam, K., Dinstein, I., Textural features for image classification, *IEEE Transaction of Systems, Man and Cybernetics*, Vol SMC-3, No. 6, pp. 610–621, November 1973.
Horn, B.K.P., *Robot Vision*, Cambridge, MA: The MIT Press, 1986.
Jain, R., Kasturi, R., Schnuck, B.G., *Machine Vision*, New York: McGraw Hill, 1995.
Johnson, R.A., *Miller & Freund's Probability and Statistics for Engineers*, 8th Edition, New York: Pearson, 2010.
Kennedy, J.B., Neville, A.M., *Basic Statistical Methods for Engineers and Scientists*, New York: Harper and Row, 1986.
Levine, M.D., *Vision in Man and Machine*, New York: McGraw Hill, 1985.
Lowe, D.G., Distinctive image features from scale-invariant keypoints, *International Journal of Computer Vision*, Vol. 60, No. 2, pp. 91–110, 2004.
Lowe, D.G., Object recognition from local scale-invariant features, *International Journal of Computer Vision*, Vol. 2, pp. 1150–1157, 1999.
Milosevic, M., Jankovic, D., Peulic, A., Thermography based breast cancer detection using texture features and minimum variance quantization, *EXCLI Journal 2014*, Vol. 13, pp. 1204–1215, 2014.
Nadler, M., Smith, E.P., *Pattern Recognition Engineering*, New York: Wiley, 1993.
Nixon, M., Aguado, A., *Feature Extraction and Image Processing for Computer Vision*, 4th Edition, Cambridge, MA: Academic Press, 2020.
Pratt, W.K., *Digital Image Processing*, New York: Wiley, 1991.
Prince, S.J.D., *Computer Vision: Models Learning and Inference*, New York: Cambridge University Press, 2012.
Ranagayyan, R.M., *Biomedical Image Analysis*, New York: CRC Press, 2005.
Ripley, B.D., *Pattern Recognition and Neural Networks*, New York: Cambridge University Press, 1996.
Rosenfeld, A., Kak, A.C., *Digital Picture Processing*, San Diego, CA: Academic Press, 1982.
Russ, J.C., *The Image Processing Handbook*, 7th Edition, Boca Raton, FL: CRC Press, 2015.
Schalkoff, R.J., *Digital Image Processing and Computer Vision*, New York: Wiley, 1989.
Shapiro, L., Stockman, G., *Computer Vision*, Upper Saddle River, NJ: Prentice Hall, 2001.
Sonka, M., Hlavac, V., Boyle, R., *Image Processing, Analysis and Machine Vision*, Florence, KY: Cengage-Engineering, 2014.
Theodoridis, S., Koutroumbas, K., *Pattern Recognition*, 4th Edition, New York: Academic Press, 2009.
Toennies, K.D., *Guide to Medical Image Analysis: Methods and Algorithms*, New York: Springer, 2012.
Torralba, A., Murphy, K.P., Freeman, W.T., Rubin, M.A., Context-based vision system for place and object recognition, *Proceedings Ninth IEEE International Conference on Computer Vision*, pp. 273–280, Vol. 1, 2003, doi: 10.1109/ICCV.2003.1238354.
Umbaugh, S.E, *DIPA: Digital Image Enhancement, Restoration, and Compression*, 4th Edition, Boca Raton, FL: CRC Press, 2023.

6.12 Exercises

Problems

1. (a) In Figure 6.1-1, there is a dotted line between *Feature Analysis* and *Application*. Explain. (b) In the same figure, there is a feedback loop from *Pattern Classification* and *Application*. Explain.

2. Why might image segmentation be performed before feature extraction and analysis?

3. (a) Name the first step in feature extraction. Why is this important? (b) Why is it important for a feature to be robust?

4. (a) Describe a method to find perimeter of a binary object. (b) How can this estimate be improved for objects with curved boundaries and complex shapes?

5. (a) What is the thinness ratio of a circle? (b) What is the thinness ratio of a rectangle that is 20 pixels wide by 80 pixels high? (c) What values do you get in CVIPtools for (a) and (b)? Are these the same as your calculated values? Why or why not? (d) Create an ellipse with CVIPtools. Next, use *Utilities→Create Border Mask* to create a version of the ellipse with a wavy border. Extract the thinness ratio with *Analysis→Features* from both. Which object has a smaller thinness measure? Explain.

6. (a) What is the aspect ratio of circle with a radius of 25? (b) Why rotate an object before finding the aspect ratio?

7. (a) For the moment-based features defined, why do we need the normalized central moments, instead of the regular moments? (b) Of what use are the RST-invariant moment-based features?

8. Use CVIPtools to explore the RST-invariant features. (a) Create binary objects using *Utilities→Create* and *Utilities→Arith/Logic* to OR objects together, (b) use *Analysis→Features* to extract the RST-invariant features from the objects, (c) add noise to your objects with *Utilities→Noise* and extract the features from the noisy objects. Compare the results for the objects with and without noise, can you still classify the objects? Why or why not?

9. (a) What can we say about an image with a narrow histogram? (b) What can we say about an image with a low histogram mean? (c) What is a histogram with two major peaks called? What do the peaks typically correspond to?

10. (a) What does the standard deviation of the histogram tell us about the image? (b) What is maximum value for histogram energy? What image type does this correspond to? (c) What does histogram entropy tell us? (d) What is the relationship between histogram energy and entropy?

11.

   a. Given the following binary checkerboard image, where the image is 256×256 pixels and the squares are 32×32, calculate the histogram features, mean, standard deviation, skew, energy and entropy. Verify your results with CVIPtools using *Utilities→Stats→Image Statistics*. Are they the same? Why or why not?

b. Given the following binary circle image, where the image is 256×256 pixels and the radius of the circle is 32, calculate the histogram features, mean, standard deviation, skew, energy and entropy by using the equation of the area of a circle (πr^2). Verify your results with CVIPtools using *Utilities→Stats→Image Statistics*. Are they the same? Why or why not?

12. a) Describe the easiest method to obtain color features. (b) Why might this method not be what we want? How can we get the information we do want?

13. (a) What is the primary metric for spectral features? (b) Regarding spectral features explain the statement: "The sector measure will tend to be size invariant, and the ring measure will tend to be rotation invariant". Sketch images to illustrate this. (c) Are the sector or ring spectral features translationally invariant? That is, if an object moves in the image, will the values change?

14. (a) As we zoom in on a textured object, how does this affect the spectral features? (b) As we zoom out on a textured object, how does this affect the spectral features?

15. Using a pixel distance, $d = 1$, find the gray level co-occurrence matrices for the horizontal, vertical, right diagonal and left diagonal directions, for the following image:

$$\begin{bmatrix} 0 & 0 & 1 & 1 \\ 0 & 0 & 1 & 1 \\ 0 & 2 & 2 & 2 \\ 2 & 2 & 3 & 3 \end{bmatrix}$$

16. (a) Find the 5×5 Laws texture energy mask for spots and edges, (b) find the 5×5 Laws texture energy mask for gray level and ripples, (c) find the 5×5 Laws texture energy mask for ripples and waves, (d) What, if any, preprocessing is necessary to use the Laws energy masks?

17. Use CVIPtools to explore feature extraction. (a) Select an image(s) of your choice with objects of interest, (b) use *Utilities→Create→Border Mask* to create mask images for your objects of interest, (c) use *Analysis→Features* to extract features that you think will be of interest for these objects. Examine the feature file. Are they results what you expected? Why or why not?

18. (a) Define a feature vector that is useful to classify engineers and non-engineers and (b) define a classification rule for these two classes based on your feature vectors.

19. Given the following two feature vectors, find the following distance and similarity metrics:

$$F_1 = \begin{bmatrix} 5 \\ 8 \\ 2 \end{bmatrix} F_2 = \begin{bmatrix} 6 \\ 10 \\ 1 \end{bmatrix}$$

(a) Euclidean distance, (b) city block distance, (c) maximum value, (d) Minkowski distance, with $r=2$, (e) normalized vector inner product, (f) Tanimoto metric

20. Given the following two feature vectors, find the following distance and similarity metrics:

$$F_1 = \begin{bmatrix} 5 \\ 8 \\ 2 \end{bmatrix} F_2 = \begin{bmatrix} 6 \\ 10 \\ 1 \end{bmatrix}$$

First, perform unit vector normalization using the two vectors to find the component magnitudes.

21. Given the following two feature vectors, find the following distance and similarity metrics:

$$F_1 = \begin{bmatrix} 5 \\ 8 \\ 2 \end{bmatrix} F_2 = \begin{bmatrix} 6 \\ 10 \\ 1 \end{bmatrix}$$

First, range normalize the vectors using the following ranges:

$$f_1 \rightarrow \text{range} = 10, f_2 \rightarrow \text{range} = 20, f_3 \rightarrow \text{range} = 5$$

(a) Euclidean distance, (b) city block distance, (c) maximum value, (d) Minkowski distance, with $r=2$, (e) normalized vector inner product, (f) Tanimoto metric

6.12.1 Programming Exercises

These exercises can be implemented in MATLAB or in C/C++ using CVIPlab.

Perimeter

1. Write a function to find the perimeter of a solid (no holes) binary object. The input parameters to the function are the binary image with the object and a row and column coordinate within the object. The function will label the image and then estimate perimeter by counting the number of "1" pixels next to "0" pixels.

2. Test this function using images you create with CVIPtools. Use *Utilities→Create* to create test images. To create images with multiple objects, use the *AND* and *OR* logic functions available from *Utilities→Arith/Logic*.

3. Modify the function to estimate perimeter by performing a Roberts edge detection followed by counting the number of "1" pixels for the object of interest. Test the function with the images you created.

4. Modify the function to find the perimeter of all objects in the image, if passed (–1, –1) as row and column coordinates. Output the object number along with its perimeter to the user.

Thinness Ratio

1. Write a function to find the thinness ratio of a solid (no holes) binary object. The input parameters to the function are the binary image with the object and a row and column coordinate within the object.

2. Test this function using images you create with CVIPtools. Use *Utilities→Create* to create test images. To create images with multiple objects, use the *AND* and *OR* logic functions available from *Utilities→Arith/Logic*.

3. Modify the function to find the thinness ratio of all objects in the image, if passed (–1, –1) as row and column coordinates. Output the object number along with its perimeter to the user.

Aspect Ratio

1. Write a function to find the aspect ratio of a binary object. The input parameters to the function are the binary image with the object and a row and column coordinate within the object.

2. Test this function using images you create with CVIPtools. Use *Utilities→Create* to create test images. To create images with multiple objects, use the *AND* and *OR* logic functions available from *Utilities→Arith/Logic*.

3. Modify the function to find the aspect ratio after rotating the object so that the axis of least second moment is horizontal. Use the C/C++ function *orientation,* or *orientation_cvip with MATLAB,* to find the axis of least second moment.

Moment-based RST-Invariant Features

1. Incorporate the CVIP function for the RST-invariant features into your CVIPlab. Note that the C function returns an array (vector) of the seven features and the MATLAB function returns only the selected features.

2. Verify that the function is working properly by comparison to results you obtain with CVIPtools.

Histogram Features

1. Write a function to find the histogram features for a gray level image: mean, standard deviation, skew, energy and entropy.

2. Extend the function to work with color images.

3. Modify the function to find these features for individual image objects by passing the input image, a segmented image and row and column coordinates within the object. Note that a labeled image must be generated from the segmented image and used in conjunction with the original image.

Color Features

1. Incorporate the CVIP function(s) for color transforms into CVIPlab,

2. Experiment by performing the HSL and CIE L*u*v* transform and then extracting histogram features on the resulting three bands.

3. Verify that the function is working properly by comparison to results you obtain with CVIPtools using *Utilities→Convert→Color Space* and *Analysis→Features.*

Spectral Features

1. Incorporate the CVIP function for spectral features into your CVIPlab. Note that the C function and the MATLAB function return the data in different ways. See the respective Help page for details.

2. Verify that the function is working properly by comparison to results you obtain with CVIPtools.

Texture Features

1. Incorporate the CVIP function for texture features into your CVIPlab. Note that the C function and the MATLAB function return the data in different ways. See the respective Help page for details.

2. Verify that the function is working properly by comparison to results you obtain with CVIPtools. Note that in CVIPtools, the average and range of five of the texture features are returned.

Distance and Similarity Measures

1. Write a function to calculate the Minkowski distance between two vectors. The input parameters include the *r* value, the two vectors as arrays (vectors). Put it in your CVIPlab.

2. Write a function to find the similarity measure, *normalized vector inner product*, of two vectors. Put it in your CVIPlab.

3. Write a function to normalize the vector parameters to *standard normal density* by passing the function the mean and standard deviation for each vector component, along with a vector. Put it in your CVIPlab.

6.13 Supplementary Exercises

1. Using a pixel distance, $d = 1$, (a) find the gray level co-occurrence matrices for the horizontal, vertical, right diagonal and left diagonal directions, for the following 8×8 image, (b) find the texture features energy, inertia, correlation, inverse difference and entropy.

$$
\begin{bmatrix}
1 & 1 & 5 & 6 & 7 & 7 & 2 & 3 \\
2 & 3 & 5 & 7 & 1 & 5 & 7 & 0 \\
4 & 5 & 7 & 1 & 2 & 2 & 0 & 2 \\
7 & 5 & 1 & 2 & 5 & 3 & 5 & 6 \\
7 & 1 & 1 & 5 & 6 & 7 & 7 & 2 \\
3 & 5 & 7 & 0 & 2 & 0 & 2 & 3 \\
5 & 6 & 7 & 1 & 1 & 5 & 6 & 7 \\
2 & 3 & 5 & 7 & 1 & 4 & 5 & 7
\end{bmatrix}
$$

2. Using a pixel distance, $d = 2$, (a) find the gray level co-occurrence matrices for the horizontal, vertical, right diagonal and left diagonal directions, for the 8×8 image from the previous exercise, (b) find the texture features energy, inertia, correlation, inverse difference and entropy.

3. Find the fuzzy similarity between the following feature vectors: (a) **A** & **B**, (b) **A** & **C**, (c) **A** & **D**, (d) **B** & **C**, (e) **B** & **D**, (f) **C** & **D**, (g) Explain the results

$$
\mathbf{A} = \begin{bmatrix} 1 \\ 1 \\ 0 \end{bmatrix}
\quad
\mathbf{B} = \begin{bmatrix} 0.75 \\ 0.75 \\ 0.5 \end{bmatrix}
\quad
\mathbf{C} = \begin{bmatrix} 0.25 \\ 0.5 \\ 0.5 \end{bmatrix}
\quad
\mathbf{D} = \begin{bmatrix} 0.25 \\ 0.25 \\ 0.25 \end{bmatrix}
$$

4. (a) Find the DFT of the following row of an image: [2 2 2 2], (b) Do the inverse DFT on the result. Did you get your image row back? Why or why not? (c) Find the DFT of the following row of an image: [2 4 4 2], (d) Do the inverse DFT on the result. Did you get your image row back? Why or why not?

5. For the 4×4 image shown below, do the following:

$$
\begin{bmatrix}
2 & 2 & 2 & 2 \\
2 & 4 & 4 & 2 \\
2 & 4 & 4 & 2 \\
2 & 2 & 2 & 2
\end{bmatrix}
$$

a. Perform the 2D DFT. Show the results after transforming each row and after each column. Leave answers in $R + jI$ form.

b. Perform the inverse DFT on result of (a). Did you get the same data back? Why or why not?

c. Multiply each element in the original image by $(1)^{(r+c)}$ and repeat (a). Calculate F(u, v). Is it shifted to the center? Where is the "center" on a 4×4 grid?

6.13.1 Supplementary Programming Exercises

These exercises can be implemented in MATLAB or in C/C++ using CVIPlab.

Similarity Measures

1. Write a function to calculate the correlation coefficient between two feature vectors. Perform an experiment comparing the correlation coefficient and the Euclidean distance metrics. Do they always give related results? Why or why not?

2. Write a function to find the fuzzy similarity measure of two feature vectors. What happens when you use feature values with non-fuzzy values?

3. Write a preprocessing function for the fuzzy similarity function to remap the values to the range of 0–1. Now run this on some feature vectors with non-fuzzy values. Do the results make sense? Why or why not?

Color Features

1. Put the CVIP color transform(s) and histogram feature functions into your CVIPlab.

2. Design a pattern classification experiment using color images and histogram features.

3. Perform experiments using different color spaces. For your application, which color space gives the best results? Why do you think this is the case?

Data Normalization

1. Write a function to implement unit vector normalization on a set of feature vectors. Compare your results to CVIPtools. Note that when you perform pattern classification in CVIPtools, the normalized files can be found in the *CVIPtools/bin/feature* folder.

2. Write a function to implement min–max normalization on a set of feature vectors. Compare your results to CVIPtools.

3. Write a function to implement softmax normalization on a set of feature vectors. Compare your results to CVIPtools.

4. Write a function to implement standard normal density normalization on a set of feature vectors. Compare your results to CVIPtools.

7

Pattern Classification

7.1 Introduction

Pattern classification is a critical process for computer vision applications and is often the final step in algorithm development. With these applications, the goal is to identify objects in order for the computer to perform a vision-related task. We have seen that data reduction is a key aspect to the image analysis process, and finding a single class that will represent many pixel values is the culminating step for this data reduction process. The object class is identified by using the extracted features and the tools from Chapter 6 and then by applying a classification method. The types of computer vision tasks to which these methods are applied are many and varied, ranging from computer diagnosis of medical images to object classification for robotic control. In this chapter, we will define pertinent terms, conceptually discuss the most widely used current methods and look in detail at some of the basic classification algorithms.

7.2 Algorithm Development: Training and Testing Methods

The first step in development of a classification algorithm is to divide our images into a training set and a test set. The selection of the training and test sets should be done before development starts to avoid biasing the test results. The *training set* is used for algorithm development and the *test set* is used to test the algorithm for success. If this is not done, and we test the algorithm with the same set with which it was developed, the success we measure is not a reliable indicator of success on any other set of images such as those encountered when the system is deployed. In addition, to work properly, both the training and test sets should completely represent all types of images that will be seen in the application domain.

The use of two distinct sets of images allows us to have confidence that the success measured with the test set is a good predictor of the success we can expect to achieve in the actual application. Additionally, during development, we may iteratively divide the training set into a training and a *validation set*. The validation set is used during development to see how well the current classifier works on an independent set, and it can guide the developer in defining parameters for the classifier as well as determining the best classifier for the application. Often development is an iterative process and the validation set is effectively a test set used during a particular iteration. The size of the sets depends on many factors, but in practice it is common to use 50%–80% for training, leaving 20%–50% for validation. Theoretically, we want to maximize the size of the training set to develop the best algorithm, but the larger the validation set, the more confidence we have that the results will be similar with the final test set and are indicative of application success. It is often instructive to use increasingly larger training sets (randomly selected) and analyze the results. What we expect to achieve is an increasing success rate as the training set size increases. If this does not happen, we need to verify that our training set(s) actually represents the domain of interest. It may be that there are not enough samples in the training set or it may be that the set of features being used is incomplete. Figure 7.2-1 shows the results from an experiment to classify skin lesions which illustrates this.

Figure 7.2-1a shows the results from using 13 features. The training set size was increased (horizontal axis), with the success plotted on the vertical axis. Here, we see that, at least for the YES class, the success rate was not necessarily increasing, which led us to believe that the features in the training set were incomplete. In Figure 7.2-1b and c are the results of increasing the number of features in the feature vectors. We see that, with 18 features (Figure 7.2-1c), we achieved an essentially increasing success rate as the training set size was increased, which is a good indicator that set of vectors in our training data is complete.

An alternative to randomly separating the samples into training and validation sets is the *leave-one-out-method*, also known as *cross-validation*. This is advantageous if the data set available is small, as it allows all the samples to be used in training and validation. With the technique, all but one of the samples is used for training, and then it

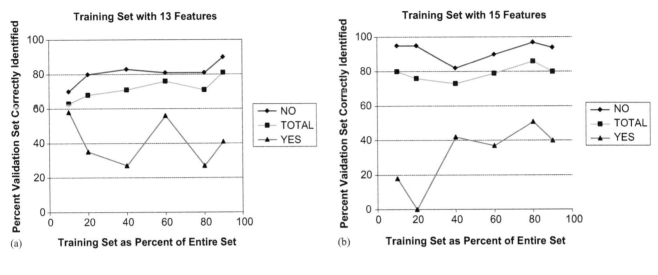

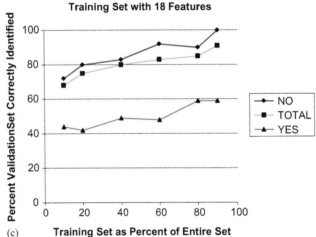

FIGURE 7.2-1

Example of increasing the training set size. These are results from an experiment to classify skin tumor images using a decision tree. (a) Results with 13 features, with the success rate jumping around we are not confident in the feature set being complete, (b) results with 15 features, better results but still not increasing consistently and (c) results with 18 features, the consistently increasing success rate as we increase the training set size gives us confidence in the completeness of the feature set being used.

is validated on the one that was left out. This is done as many times as there are samples, and the number misclassified represents the error rate. If we have a very large data set, it may not be practical to use *leave-one-out*, so the *leave-K-out-method* can be applied, where K is a developer defined constant. Also known as *N-fold cross-validation*, N is defined based on the size of the sample set available, the available resources for validation and development and the time allowed. Note that N = (*total number of samples*)/K. In general, the smaller the value for K and the larger the value for N, the greater the confidence we have in the results. To use this approach, we leave K vectors out and train (develop) the classification algorithm and then test on the K vectors left out. We do this for all N sets and average the results to predict application success. Figure 7.2-2 illustrates an example with N = 4 or 4-fold cross-validation.

There are many methods available for pattern classification and we will first consider basic representative methods. The general approach is to use the information in the training set to develop the best algorithm to finally be tested on classifying the "unknown" examples in the test set. It is assumed that all the samples available have a known classification – in pattern classification, knowing the class is also referred to as *supervised learning*. *Unsupervised learning* looks for clusters in the feature space without necessarily knowing the classes.

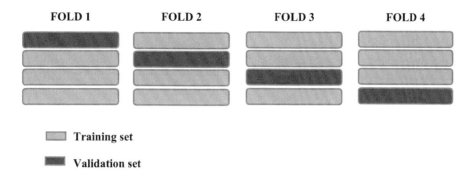

FOLD 1   FOLD 2   FOLD 3   FOLD 4

■ Training set

■ Validation set

FIGURE 7.2-2
Example of *N*-fold cross-validation with *N* = 4. The data is divided into four groups. The model is trained with four different training sets and tested on the corresponding validation set. The overall success metrics are obtained by averaging the success for ten training/testing iterations.

7.3   Nearest Neighbor (NN), K-NN, Nearest Centroid, Template Matching

The simplest algorithm for identifying a sample from the test set is called the *Nearest Neighbor* (NN) method. The object of interest is compared to every sample in the training set, using a distance measure, a similarity measure or a combination of measures. The "unknown" object is then identified as belonging to the same class as the closest sample in the training set. This is indicated by the smallest number if using a distance measure or the largest number if using a similarity measure. This process is computationally intensive and not very robust.

We can make the NN method more robust by selecting not just the closest sample in the training set, but by consideration of a group of close feature vectors. This is called the *K-NN* method, where, for example, $K = 5$. Then, we assign the unknown feature vector to the class that occurs most often in the set of K-Neighbors. This is still very computationally intensive, since each unknown sample is still compared to every sample in the training set, and we want the training set as large as possible to maximize success.

We can reduce this computational burden by using a method called *Nearest Centroid*. Here, we find the centroids for each class from the samples in the training set and then compare the unknown samples to the representative centroids only. The centroids are calculated by finding the average value for each vector component in the training set.

EXAMPLE 7.3.1: NEAREST CENTROID CLASSIFICATION

Suppose we have a training set of four feature vectors and we have two classes:

$$\text{Class } \mathbf{A}: \mathbf{A}_1 = \begin{bmatrix} 3 \\ 4 \\ 7 \end{bmatrix} \text{ and } \mathbf{A}_2 = \begin{bmatrix} 1 \\ 7 \\ 6 \end{bmatrix}$$

$$\text{Class } \mathbf{B}: \mathbf{B}_1 = \begin{bmatrix} 4 \\ 2 \\ 9 \end{bmatrix} \text{ and } \mathbf{B}_2 = \begin{bmatrix} 2 \\ 3 \\ 3 \end{bmatrix}$$

The representative vector, centroid, for class **A** is:

$$\begin{bmatrix} (3+1)/2 \\ (4+7)/2 \\ (7+6)/2 \end{bmatrix} = \begin{bmatrix} 2 \\ 5.5 \\ 6.5 \end{bmatrix}$$

The representative vector, centroid, for class **B** is:

$$\begin{bmatrix} (4+2)/2 \\ (2+3)/2 \\ (9+3)/2 \end{bmatrix} = \begin{bmatrix} 3 \\ 2.5 \\ 6 \end{bmatrix}$$

To identify an unknown sample, we need to only compare it to these two representative vectors, not the entire training set. The comparison is done using any of the previously defined distance or similarity measures. With a distance measure, the distance between the unknown sample vector and each class centroid is calculated and it is classified as the one it is closest to – the one with the *smallest* distance. With a similarity measure, the similarity between the unknown sample vector and each class centroid is calculated and it is classified as the one it is closest to – the one with the *largest* similarity.

This method of using the centroid as a model for each class is one method to find the templates in *template matching*, where templates are used to represent the classes of interest. In template matching, the raw pixel values in small subimages are used directly as the feature vectors. The templates are devised via a training set, which are then compared to subimages by using a distance or similarity measure. Typically, a threshold is set on this measure to determine when we have found a match, that is, a successful classification. This may be useful for applications where the size, orientation and gray level characteristics of the objects are known and the objects' shapes are regular. For example, for the recognition of computer generated text. If the objects are not of standard size, orientation and gray level characteristics, then preprocessing can be performed to standardize image and object parameters.

7.4 Bayesian, Support Vector Machines, Random Forest Classifiers

The previous methods all function by using the training set of feature vectors to classify the test samples directly. This works well when the training set is large and complete (as long as the process can be performed within a time limit suitable for the application). If the training set is not complete, these techniques will not necessarily be very robust. They may, in fact, fail completely if a new sample from a new subclass in the feature space is found. To avoid this, we want to develop a classification method that is generalizable – that is, it finds an underlying model in the feature space and find rules or algorithms to separate the classes. A simple method for this was used in Chapter 3, Section 3.3.4. The classification rule developed was a *decision tree*, and it can be modeled as a nested If-then structure, which divides the feature space into classes based on feature values or relationships between the values (see Figure 3.3-22).

Bayesian theory provides a statistical approach to the development of a classification algorithm. To apply Bayesian analysis, we need a complete statistical model of the features and need to normalize the features so that their distribution is standard normal density (see Section 6.9). If these distribution requirements are met, then the Bayesian approach provides a classifier that has an optimal classification rate. This means that the boundaries that separate the classes provide a minimum average error for the samples in the training set. These boundaries are called *discriminant functions*, and an example is shown in Figure 7.4-1. Here, we have two classes in two-dimensional feature space and show a *linear discriminant function* to separate the two classes. This type of plot is called a *scatterplot* and is a useful visualization technique to find clusters corresponding to classes with the sample feature vectors. With the scatterplot, we can find the desired line to separate the two classes. Note that principal components analysis (PCA or PCT for principal components transform as in CVIPtools) can be used to reduce n-dimensional data into two or three uncorrelated components that contain much of the original information, and these can then be used for visualization.

In practice, the feature space is typically larger than two-dimensional, and since the three-dimensional form of a linear function is a plane, the n-dimensional form of a linear function is called a *hyperplane*. In general, discriminant functions can also be quadratic (curved) or take on arbitrary shapes. Generally, the forms are limited to those that can be defined analytically via equations, such as circles, ellipses, parabolas or hyperbolas. In n-dimensional vector

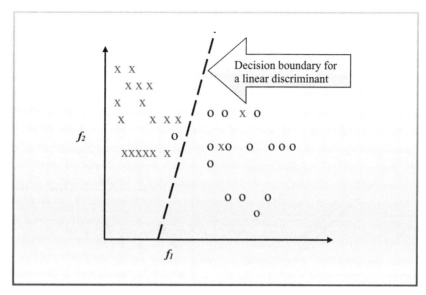

FIGURE 7.4-1
A linear discriminant separating two classes. This shows a two-dimensional feature space defined by feature vectors,
$\mathbf{F} = \begin{bmatrix} f_1 \\ f_2 \end{bmatrix}$, and two classes represented by x and o. Note that this linear discriminant misclassifies two x's and one o.

spaces, these decision boundaries are called *hyperquadrics*; specifically, hyperspheres, hyperellipsoids, hyperparaboloids and hyperhyperboloids.

Another approach that mathematically attempts to find optimal hyperplanes to separate the feature space for classification is *support vector machines* (SVMs). The goal in developing an SVM is to find the hyperplane with the largest margin or the maximum distance from the nearest feature vectors in the training set; these nearest samples are called the *support vectors*. In Figure 7.4-2, we see the optimal hyperplane for separation of the two classes shown. Note that many other hyperplanes could be found to separate the classes. The concept underlying the SVM is that the one with the largest margin will provide the classifier that exhibits the best generalization.

With SVM methods, we can also deal with cases where the classes are not linearly separable in the feature space by attempting to finding a transformation, or mapping, into another mathematical space where the classes are linearly separable. These transforms are referred as *kernel functions*. An example of this type of mapping is shown in Figure 7.4-3. In this figure, we have two classes which are not separable by a single line in the feature space. After using a polar coordinate transform as a kernel mapping function, we put the samples into a new feature space where the classes are separable by a single line. In this case, the transform equations are given by $r^2 = f_1^2 + f_2^2$; $\tan \theta = f_2 / f_1$. Unlike this simple illustrative example, most kernel mappings result in as feature space of a much higher dimension than the original. It can be shown that a nonlinear mapping of sufficient dimensionality can always be found to separate two classes via a hyperplane.

A *random forest classifier* is based on the idea of combining multiple decision trees into a forest and then submitting the classification to each decision tree and using majority vote to determine the class. The key aspect to the random forest concept is that the individual decision trees be relatively uncorrelated. If the individual trees have low correlation, it is unlikely that they will make the same or similar mistakes in classification, so by combining a group or ensemble of these decision trees and taking a majority vote, we can increase our probability of successful classification.

The next question is how do we generate decision trees that have outcomes with a low correlation? – In the development of a decision tree for classification, the specific model that is found is highly dependent on the training data. So, the first step to generate a group of decision trees with a low correlation is to train them with a different set of inputs. Given this method, we can randomly select groups from the training set and use each group as input for the development of an individual decision tree. These decision trees can then be combined into a random forest to be used for classification. Note that we are not dividing the entire training set into separate groups, but randomly selecting sample sets of a given size.

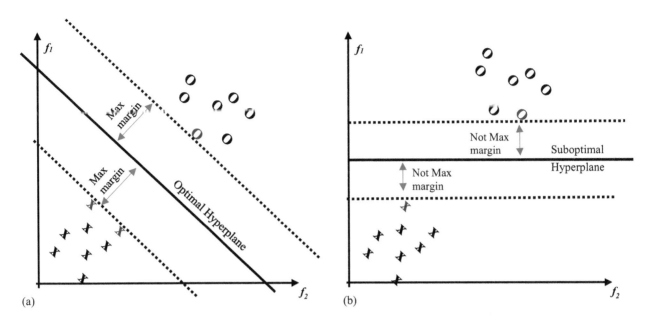

FIGURE 7.4-2
Support vector machine optimal hyperplane. (a) This shows sample training feature vectors from two classes represented by **X** and **O** in the feature space. An SVM is trained by finding the hyperplane that has the maximum distance between it and the closest training feature vectors. These closest feature vectors are called the support vectors and are shown in red. (b) Infinitely many hyperplanes can be found to separate the two classes; here, one example of a suboptimal hyperplane to separate the two classes is shown; it does not have the maximum margin for separation. The concept underlying the SVM is that the one with the largest margin will provide the classifier that exhibits the best generalization.

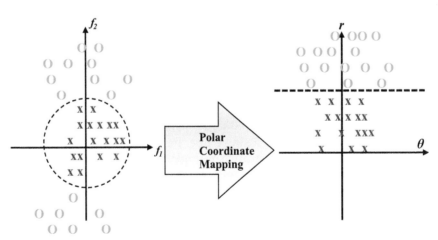

FIGURE 7.4-3
Support vector machine kernel function. This shows a two-dimensional feature space defined by feature vectors,

$F = \begin{bmatrix} f_1 \\ f_2 \end{bmatrix}$, and two classes represented by **X** and **O**. For the kernel function, we use a polar coordinate transform to obtain

$\hat{F} = \begin{bmatrix} r(f_1, f_2) \\ \theta(f_2, f_2) \end{bmatrix}$. In the new transformed feature space, the classes are linearly separable by a single line.

EXAMPLE 7.4.1: SELECTION OF SETS FOR RANDOM FOREST CLASSIFIER

The training set consists of five feature vectors:

$$\left[\, F_1, F_2, F_3, F_4, F_5 \,\right]$$

We decide to use five samples for developing each decision tree. Each member of any set selected is chosen randomly from the original set, so any of these could be possible groups chosen:

$$\left[\, F_1, F_1, F_3, F_4, F_5 \,\right]$$

$$\left[\, F_4, F_2, F_3, F_3, F_5 \,\right]$$

$$\left[\, F_5, F_3, F_3, F_4, F_5 \,\right]$$

Note that the sets can have repeated training feature vectors, because each sample in the set is chosen randomly from the entire original set.

The second step in the development of a random forest classifier is referred to as *feature randomness*. At a given decision node, instead of allowing the selection of the best feature to separate the classes, we only allow a small randomly selected subset of the features to be used. Then, the decision generator will select the best feature from the smaller subset for that decision node. Now, we have a decision tree that is not only trained on a different set of feature vectors but each decision node in the tree also used different random features. This allows us to create a set of decision tress that are not likely to be highly correlated. To complete the random forest, all the decision trees are combined into an ensemble and are used separately on any test samples, and a majority vote is taken for the final classification.

7.5 Neural Networks and Deep Learning

Neural networks represent another category of techniques used for pattern classification. Neural networks are meant to model the nervous system in biological organisms and are thus referred to as *artificial neural networks* (*ANNs*). There is an increasing interest in the use of neural networks to solve a variety of problems in many areas of engineering and medicine. The most recent developments are in an area often referred to as *deep learning* due to the much higher number of network layers compared to the typical ANN. One of the strengths of ANN classifiers is that they are adaptive and work well for many real-world problems. The use of neural networks often reduces the error rates when compared to more conventional statistical approaches. They represent a powerful and flexible method for mapping a fixed number of inputs into a set of discrete classes. Classically, the inputs are the extracted features, but with deep learning approaches the image itself is used as input.

Mathematical models have been developed for these ANNs, based on a simple processing element called a neuron. These neurons function by outputting a weighted sum of the inputs, and these weights are generated during the learning or training phase. The element's output function is called the *activation function*, and the basic types are (1) the identify function, the input equals the output, (2) the rectified linear unit, which removes any negative values but passes through positive values, (3) a threshold function where every input greater than the threshold value outputs a 1 and less than the threshold outputs 0, and (4) a sigmoid function, an S-shaped curve, which is nonlinear and is used most often. The sigmoid function most closely models the biological neurons, and it is given by this equation:

$$S(x) = \frac{1}{1 - e^{-x}} \tag{7.5-1}$$

Single layer networks are limited in their capabilities and nonlinear functions are required to take advantage of the power available in multilayer networks.

A model for the neuron is shown in Figure 7.5-1. Here, we see that each input signal is multiplied by its corresponding weight, summed and then a bias term can be added if required. The bias term can be useful if the network is being trained with unbalanced training sets by injecting the bias value into the output layer for the class that has a smaller number of samples. The output of the neuron is determined by activation function, which takes the neuron sum and any bias as input and generates the output for the neuron.

The neural network consists of the input layer, the output layer and hidden layers, see Figure 7.5-2. The main distinguishing characteristics of the neural network are (1) the *architecture*, which includes the number of inputs, outputs and hidden layers, and how they are all connected, (2) the *activation function*, which is typically used for all processing elements in a layer, but this is not required, and (3) the *learning algorithm*. Many learning algorithms have been developed, but they all work by inputting the training vectors, calculating an error measure and then adjusting the weights to improve the error.

Most learning algorithms are a form of gradient descent which searches the multi-dimensional error space for a local minimum. It can be applied to any differentiable function by moving in the opposite direction of the gradient.

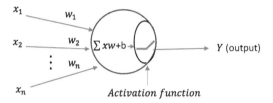

FIGURE 7.5-1
Neuron and activation function. A typical neuron, or processing element, in a neural network. The neuron first calculates the weighted sum and then sends the sum to the activation function that controls the output. The extra term in the summation, b, is called the bias term, and it can be used to deal with bias in unbalanced training sets.

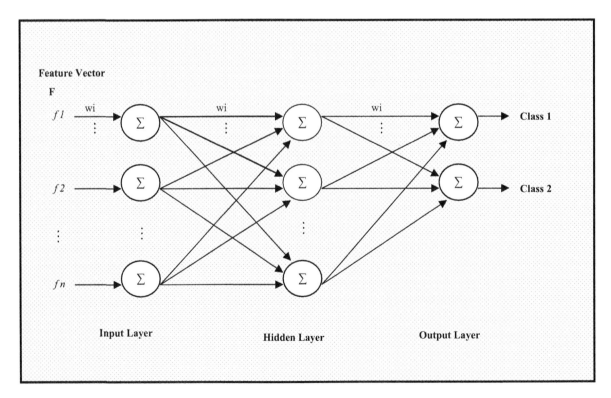

FIGURE 7.5-2
Neural network. Here, we show a neural network architecture with an input layer, where the feature values are input, one hidden layer and the output layer. In this case, the output layer corresponds to two classes. The circles are the processing elements, neurons, and the arrows represent the connections. Associated with each connection is a weight (w_i, shown only across the top for clarity) by which the signal is multiplied. These weights are adjusted during the training (learning) phase.

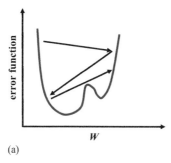
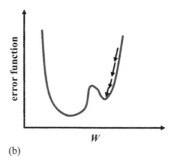

(a)   (b)

FIGURE 7.5-3
Neural network learning with gradient descent. Gradient descent works by following the path toward the minimum derivative, where the slope of the tangent line is minimum. We represent the network weights by W and show a simple two-dimensional function for illustration. (a) With too large of a learning rate, we may miss the minimum and oscillate and (b) with too small a learning rate, it may take many, many iterations and then we may get stuck in a local minimum

The gradient is the direction in which the function is changing the fastest; so, by moving away from it, we can find a minimum. As shown in Figure 7.5-3, with a two-dimensional function for simplicity, the learning takes place by adjusting the weights so that the error moves toward the minimum. Another way to think of this is to follow the path of decreasing slope, the derivative, until it reaches zero. One of the parameters specified when training a neural network is the learning rate. The *learning rate* parameter determines how fast the values are changed when adjusting the weights. With a large learning rate, there will be a larger change per iteration, which may cause overshoot (Figure 7.5-3a) and create undesirable oscillation in the error or success measurements. Using too small of a learning rate will take much longer, and it may get stuck in a local minimum (Figure 7.5-3b).

The training continues for a specific number of iterations, specified by the user, or until a specified error criterion is reached. To achieve optimal results with neural networks, it is important that the feature vectors are preprocessed with a PCT to decorrelate the input data. Training a neural network with features that are highly correlated often results in random success during the training, which provides a classification network that is not robust.

The neural network training process proceeds as follows:

1. Determine the number of iterations, i, for which we will train the neural net. Start with $i = 1$.
2. From the training set, randomly select the iteration training set, train_i, and put the others aside for validation.
3. Train the model using train_i.
4. Test the model on validation_i and record desired success metrics.
5. Increment i and go back to step (2) and continue until the desired number of iterations is achieved or until the minimum error is reached.

Note that one iteration is also called one training *cycle* or one training *epoch*. After the training is complete, the overall training results are analyzed. In general, as the system is trained longer, we should see improved results. However, we also need to avoid *overtraining*, which results when the classifier is trained to the specific data and may not be generalized to the classes as desired. If the network is overtrained, often the variance in the validation results will be large. If this is the case, we will want to change the network architecture and/or training parameters.

As was introduced in Chapter 5 for image segmentation, a special form of neural network called convolutional neural networks (CNNs) are used for "deep" learning. The term deep learning is used as CNNs have many hidden layers. A CNN works differently than the primary feature extraction/pattern classification model we have presented, where first we extract the features and then feed the feature vectors to the neural network for classification. A CNN performs both the functions of feature extraction and pattern classification and takes the image itself as input. It does this by using convolution filters to extract various spatial features, and the convolution filter coefficients are the weights that are adjusted during the learning/training phase.

A convolution layer in a CNN is specified by the number and size of the filters or convolution masks. With many hidden layers, the deeper we get into the network, the more specific and complex the corresponding convolution filters are. A network that consists of only convolution layers, along with up- and downsampling, is referred to as a fully convolutional network (FCN). As introduced in Chapter 5, a typical CNN consists of convolution layers followed by downsampling layers, which can then be upsampled to fully connected layers by "flattening" or vectorizing the data.

One of the key aspects for deep learning approaches is the requirement for very large numbers of input images for training. In many applications under development, the size of the image dataset available for training is limited, so for CNN training we often use data augmentation to enlarge the training set. *Data augmentation* is performed by modifying the existing images to create new images. The techniques applied include geometric operations such as resizing, rotation, flipping, translation, zooming and elastic deformation techniques.

Neural networks have been used successfully in many applications; for example, in the recognition of handwritten characters, for speech recognition, and in vehicle and process control. More recently, deep learning techniques have been developed in conjunction with CNNs for image segmentation (as in Chapter 5), and numerous computer vision recognition tasks such as facial recognition, object classification and scene recognition for autonomous vehicles, and diagnostic assistance with many types of medical images. Other methods for pattern classification are available, including more artificial intelligence approaches, structural approaches, fuzzy logic approaches and genetic algorithms. More information on these methods and those briefly discussed here can be found in the references.

7.6   Cost/Risk Functions and Success Measures

After the samples in the test set have been classified, we need a method to measure the success of the classification algorithm. The simplest method is to consider average success rate and/or average failure rate of each class, or an aggregate average across all classes. In many cases, we may not want to rely on correct classification as the sole criteria in evaluating success of a classification system, because some types of misclassification may be more costly, or have a higher risk, than others. For example, if we are developing a medical system to diagnose cancer, the cost of mistakenly identifying a cancerous tumor as harmless is much higher than the cost of identifying a harmless tumor as cancerous. In the first case, the patient dies; while, in the second case, the patient is subjected to some temporary stress, but survives. Or consider a system to identify land mines – if you are walking through a potential mine field, is it better to misclassify a harmless object or a land mine?

The development of a suitable *cost function,* also referred to as *risk,* is an important concept for the analysis and comparison of pattern classification schemes. The cost function and how it is incorporated into the success measure is highly application dependent. One simple method to quantify cost is to weight the overall success by the relative cost associated with each type of successful classification; these weights should add to 1 or 100%. Note that this method clearly illustrates the concept, but may not be practical in application.

EXAMPLE 7.6.1: A SIMPLE COST FUNCTION

Suppose we have three classes. We determine that successful classification of class A is 80% important, class B 15% and class C 5%. Results from our experiment are as follows:

	% Correctly Classified (%)
Class A	82%
Class B	55%
Class C	22%

Now, we can define our overall success as:

$$\text{Overall success} = 0.8(.82) + 0.15(.55) + 0.05(.22)$$

$$= 0.7495 \text{ or about 75\% success}$$

Care must be taken when using and defining cost metrics. For example, if we weight successful classification of one class at 100%, all we need to do to have a perfect classification algorithm is to classify all objects as members of that one class. In this extreme case, the samples misclassified are not even considered.

Examples of metrics that incorporate the misclassified samples into their measure are *sensitivity* and *specificity*, success measures often used in medical image analysis. As part of the medical diagnostic procedure, two classes can be considered – healthy and diseased classes, also referred to as normal and abnormal classes. If we consider two classes of people, healthy and sick (diseased), and consider finding evidence of disease as the affirmative, we have these definitions:

- **True Positive (TP)**: sick person classified as sick.
- **False Positive (FP)**: healthy person classified as sick.
- **True Negative (TN)**: healthy person classified as healthy.
- **False Negative (FN)**: sick person classified as healthy.

Now, we define *specificity* and *sensitivity* as follows:

$$\text{Sensitivity} = \frac{\text{number of True Positives}}{\text{number of True Positives} + \text{number of False Negatives}} \tag{7.6-1}$$

$$\text{Specificity} = \frac{\text{number of True Negatives}}{\text{number of True Negatives} + \text{number of False Positives}} \tag{7.6-2}$$

Sensitivity tells us how accurate our prediction of the disease is and specificity tells us how accurate our prediction of the absence of the disease is. Note that this idea can be applied to any classification with two values or can be applied to the correctness of any single class. The sensitivity tells us the success rate for a particular class – of all those in the class, the percentage correctly found by the classification algorithm to be in the class. The specificity provides a measure for those not in the class – of those not in the class, it is the percentage found to not be in the class. We can extend these metrics to more than two classes by considering each class versus all other classes.

EXAMPLE 7.6.2: SENSITIVITY AND SPECIFICITY WITH THREE CLASSES

Suppose we have three classes, A, B and C, with 10 samples of each class. The following table lists the results from a particular classification algorithm. The table is in the same format as CVIPtools output files from pattern classification – the actual class is on the left and the classifier results are across the top:

Classification Matrix		Classifier Results			
		A	B	C	Percent Correct (%)
Actual Class	A	8	2	0	80%
	B	1	7	2	70%
	C	0	1	9	90%

Sensitivity of Class A $= \dfrac{8}{8+2} \approx 80\%$; note sensitivity is the percent correct, also called the success rate.

Specificity of Class A $= \dfrac{7+2+1+9}{7+2+1+9+1} \approx 95\%$; note true negatives exclude the row and column corresponding to that particular class.

Here, we see that sensitivity measures the percent of those classified as Class A that are correct. Specificity provides a metric for those not in Class A and measures how many of those are "correctly" classified as not being Class A – note that they still may be incorrectly classified and this will be reflected in the metrics for that class.

$$\text{Sensitivity of Class B } = \frac{7}{7+2+1} \approx 70\%$$

$$\text{Sensitivity of Class B} = \frac{8+9}{8+9+1+2} \approx 85\%$$

$$\text{Sensitivity of Class C} = \frac{9}{9+1} \approx 90\%$$

$$\text{Sensitivity of Class C} = \frac{8+2+1+7}{8+2+1+7+2} \approx 90\%$$

In addition to these metrics, we may be interested in the *positive predictive value* (PPV) also called *precision*, which is the ratio of the true values for a class to all the samples found to be in that class by the classifier:

$$\text{Positive predictive value or Precision} = \frac{\text{True Positives}}{\text{True Positives} + \text{False Positives}} \tag{7.6-3}$$

The *negative predictive value* (NPV) provides us with the ratio of those true negatives to those classified as negative:

$$\text{Negative predictive value} = \frac{\text{True Negatives}}{\text{True Negatives} + \text{False Negatives}} \tag{7.6-4}$$

So, these two metrics provide us with values for the percent correct of those classified with a specific class, the PPV, and the percent correct of those classified as not being in the class, NPV.

EXAMPLE 7.6.3: POSITIVE PREDICTIVE VALUE OR PRECISION

Using the above example with three classes, A, B and C, and classifier results obtained in the following table, we can find the *positive predictive value* or *precision*:

Classification Matrix		Classifier Results			Percent Correct
		A	B	C	
Actual Class	A	8	2	0	80%
	B	1	7	2	70%
	C	0	1	9	90%

$$\text{Precision for Class A} = \frac{\text{True Positives}}{\text{True Positives} + \text{False Positives}} = \frac{8}{8+1} \cong 89\%$$

$$\text{Precision for Class B} = \frac{\text{True Positives}}{\text{True Positives} + \text{False Positives}} = \frac{7}{2+7+1} = 70\%$$

$$\text{Precision for Class C} = \frac{\text{True Positives}}{\text{True Positives} + \text{False Positives}} = \frac{9}{9+2} \cong 82\%$$

Note that in the classification matrix, these values are found along the columns.

One metric that is used in statistics as a single performance measure that combines the precision and the sensitivity (also called *recall*) is the *F-measure*, which is the harmonic mean of precision and sensitivity:

$$F\text{-measure} = 2 \times \left[\frac{\text{precision} \times \text{sensitivity}}{\text{precision} + \text{sensitivity}} \right] \tag{7.6-5}$$

The *F*-measure varies between zero and one, where one corresponds to perfect results – all the images/objects in the class are classified correctly and all the samples outside of the class are found to be not in the class. Another metric that incorporates both sensitivity and specificity is *Youden's index*:

$$Y\text{-index} = \left[\text{Sensitivity} + \text{Specificity} \right] - 1 \tag{7.6-6}$$

Receiver Operating Characteristic

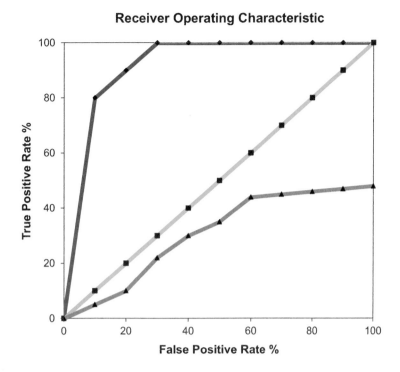

FIGURE 7.6-1
Receiver operating characteristic (ROC) curve. The red curve represents a good ROC, the area under the curve (AUC) is close to 1. The green line represents a marginal ROC, it is the cutoff for where the system has any value – here, the AUC is 0.5, and it represents a system that is equivalent to random guessing. The blue curve has an AUC less than 0.5, so the system has no value, it classifies more samples incorrectly than correctly.

It can also vary between 0 and 1, but it should be noted that this metric weights false positives and false negatives equally.

If we have a binary classifier with a threshold that we can set to separate the classes and if we are determining how well the overall system works, we can consider the *receiver operator characteristic* or ROC curve, often used in medical applications. It is a plot of the sensitivity, or true positive rate, versus the *false positive rate* (FPR):

$$FPR = \left[1 - \text{Specificity} \right] \qquad (7.6\text{-}7)$$

The ROC is characterized by the area under the curve (AUC), which varies between 0 and 1. For a perfect classification, the AUC is 1; if it is 0.5 or less, it indicates that it cannot reliably distinguish between the classes (Figure 7.6-1). The higher the AUC, the better it will separate the classes. The ROC curve can also be examined to determine that best value for the threshold, which is dependent on the specific classification problem. In other words, what are the costs associated with each type of misclassification? – the ROC curve will graphically illustrate the costs.

7.7 Pattern Classification Tools: Python, R, MATLAB and CVIPtools

There are many tools available for those doing research and development in the pattern classification area. Many of these provide a more comprehensive machine learning framework of which pattern classification is a major part. We will briefly discuss the most commonly used tools and consider some of the more useful and popular packages available. The method that the developer uses to access the functionality of the package is through the application programming interface, or API, which provides the user with the necessary functionality to access the included libraries. Another distinction between available languages and software packages is if they are open source or commercial? – If they are open source, this means they are available for use without costs and have minimal, if any, licensing requirements; whereas commercial software requires payment for a license to use the software.

7.7.1 Python

Python is an open source script-based language that is becoming more widely used in machine learning applications. It has an API that allows for rapid prototyping, and a number of useful tools, utilities and libraries are available in the public domain. One of the commonly used platforms to learn more about machine learning is *scikit-learn*. Scikit-learn has a number of useful built-in functions including functions for preprocessing, classification and model selection. It includes pattern classification functions for NN and SVMs, but has its most extensive functionality for random forest algorithms. It also has a number of visualization tools which are very useful in gaining a more complete understanding of the machine learning concepts.

A good tool for using convolutional neural nets in Python is *Keras*, which is also an open source library, often used in conjunction with *TensorFlow*. TensorFlow is also open source, and it provides a higher-level machine learning framework, while Keras can be interfaced with it for the neural network functionality that it provides for deep learning applications. *PyTorch* is another public domain neural network package, but has a lower-level API than Keras, so requires more programming skills but will provide a more efficient implementation and, consequently, a faster run-time.

Caffe provides a deep learning framework that includes a Python interface, although the code was originally written in C++. It is also open source and it allows for graphics processing unit (GPU)-based programming with a simple flag setting. A GPU is hardware designed for parallel processing so can greatly increase the speed of development and training for neural networks. Caffe provides one of the fastest implementations of CNNs, and it is used frequently in academic projects.

7.7.2 R: Bayesian Modeling and Visualization Tools

R has been used historically in the biological and medical sciences, and it was originally developed as a language to allow researchers easy access to statistical-based analysis. R provides an open source scripting language and a software environment which includes linear, nonlinear, statistical modeling and visualization tools. Specifically, for pattern classification, *R* has packages for developing Bayesian models for pattern classification – the BMS (Bayesian Model Sampling) and the BAS (Bayesian Adaptive Sampling) packages. One of the strengths of the *R* scripting language is its data visualization tools, and the many freely available software packages for this task, the most widely used being *ggplot2*. Visualization tools are often an effective aid in feature selection and feature analysis.

Since the *R* programming language is limited to single-thread processing, it cannot take advantage of any parallel processors, such as GPUs and multiprocessor CPUs, so it will be slow with very large data sets. Additionally, *R* keeps data objects in memory so large amounts of memory are required during run-time to efficiently manage large data sets. These are the reasons that *R* is often used as an investigative and exploratory tool to find useful statistical relationships between features and the associated classes, but not to develop pattern classification models for the modern machine learning environment. Its advanced statistical and visualization tools provide a powerful set of tools for this type of preprocessing and offline analysis.

7.7.3 MATLAB: Statistics and Machine Learning

MATLAB is a commercial software environment that was originally developed for engineering applications and is designed for efficient matrix operations. It provides a comprehensive shell for command line processing and a scripting language. The MATLAB environment includes *toolboxes* for specific application areas. MATLAB has a number of commercial toolboxes available for image and pattern classification applications, including their *Computer Vision, Image Processing, Deep Learning* and *Statistics and Machine Learning* toolboxes. One of the advantages of using MATLAB is that there is a large user base and many freely available software packages, but the free packages still require a license to use the MATLAB environment. The MATLAB CVIP Toolbox has already been discussed in Chapter 2, which provides all the functionality as the C/C++ CVIPtools environment. For pattern classification, the MATLAB CVIP Toolbox provides additional support by allowing for batch processing in the pattern classification functions.

7.7.4 CVIPtools

CVIPtools allows the user to perform pattern classification after the feature files have been created. This is done by using training and test set feature files or performing a leave-one-out analysis on a single feature file. In either case, CVIPtools uses a supervised training method, so the examples in the feature file must have the class defined.

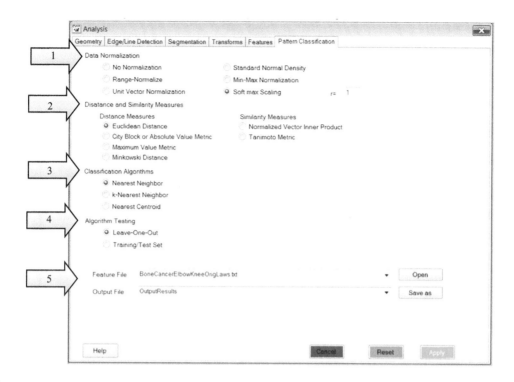

FIGURE 7.7-1

Using the CVIPtools *Analysis→Pattern Classification* window. (1) Select the desired data normalization method, (2) the distance or similarity measure to use, (3) the classification algorithm and (4) the algorithm testing method. (5) Next, enter the feature file name(s). With the *Leave-One-Out* testing method, only one feature file is required. If *Training/Test Set* is selected, the user must enter separate feature files for training and testing. Finally, enter a name for the output file and select the *Apply* button to run the test.

Figure 7.7-1 shows the CVIPtools *Analysis→Pattern Classification* window. To perform pattern classification, we need to select the desired data normalization method, the distance or similarity measure, the classification algorithm and the algorithm testing method along with any associated parameters. Next, we enter the feature file name(s). With the *Leave-One-Out* testing method, only one feature file is required. If *Training/Test Set* is selected, the user must enter separate feature files for training and testing. Finally, enter a name for the output file and select the *Apply* button to run the test.

The output file as displayed in CVIPtools is shown in Figure 7.7-2. At the top of the output file, we see the success rate for all the classes. The success rate for each class is shown on the right, with the class for each example as given in the test set on the left side and the classification results across the top. This information allows us to see how examples are misclassified. In this case, we missed two of the *tex1* class examples and misclassified them as *tex4* (in this example, the classes are different textures). This information, combined with application specific information, may help us to further develop the classification algorithm to improve the results.

The output file also contains all the details relating to the experiment. Following the success rate table are all the pattern classification parameters and file names, followed by the feature file information. First, the names of each column in the feature file are listed (the feature file header) followed by the feature values for each example in the test set. Note that with the *Leave-One-Out* testing method, all the examples are used in the test set, but one at a time. When using the *Training/Test Set* method, the examples from the training set will be listed in the output file.

After a pattern classification test has been performed, the user may want to run more tests by varying the parameters. The initial test results can be used to guide the process. Perhaps, a different data normalization method or distance measure will perform better. In some cases, features may be removed or added to the feature files. It is also imperative to consider the application feedback loop, as shown in the image analysis process, when developing algorithms. Additionally, note that two more extensive development tools are available in the CVIPtools environment and are discussed in the following chapter, along with example applications. Overall, in the development of a pattern classification system, optimal results will be obtained by experimentation, with the developer's tools, skills, knowledge and experience guiding the process.

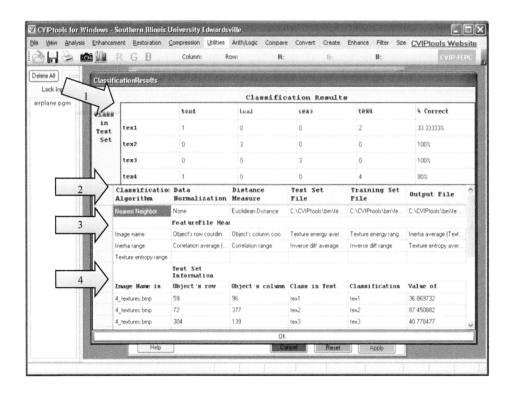

FIGURE 7.7-2
Output from CVIPtools *Analysis→Pattern Classification.* This shows the file as displayed in CVIPtools. The actual file is a text file, but has all the same information. (1) The first block shows the success rate for each class, with the class for each example as given in the test set on the left side and the classification results across the top. This allows us to see how any misclassified examples were misclassified. (2) Next, we see the list of the parameters and files used for the pattern classification test, (3) the feature file header, which lists the features used in the test and (4) details for each example in the test set.

7.8   Key Points

Overview: Pattern Classification

- Pattern classification is a critical process for computer vision applications and is often the final step in algorithm development.
- Pattern classification uses image object features to identify or classify the image object.
- Data reduction is a key aspect to the image analysis process, and finding a single class that will represent many pixel values is the culminating step.
- Computer vision tasks to which these methods are applied are many and varied, ranging from computer diagnosis of medical images to object classification for robotic control.

Algorithm Development: Training and Testing Methods

- Available feature vector samples are divided into a *training set* and a *test set.*
- Each set should represent all types of images in the application domain.
- The *training set* is used for algorithm development.
- The *test set* is used to test the algorithm that was developed with the training set.
- The use of two distinct sets allows us to have confidence that the success measured during development is a good predictor of the success we can expect to achieve in the actual application.
- During development, we may divide the training set into a training and a *validation set.*

- The validation set is used to see how well the current classifier works on an independent set, guides defining parameters and determining best classifier model.
- *Cross-validation* can be performed to use all samples for training and validation, especially if the available image set is small (Figure 7.2-2).

Nearest Neighbor (NN), K-NN, Nearest Centroid, Template Matching

Nearest neighbor: compare an unknown sample to each vector in the training set using a distance or similarity (or both) metric and classify it in the same class as the one it is closest to.

K-nearest neighbor: comparing the unknown feature vector to entire training set and finding the K nearest, where K is an integer such as 5, and classifying it as the class that appears most often in the set of K samples.

Nearest centroid: finding the centroid for each class in the training set and comparing the unknown to the representative centroids, and classifying it in the same class as the class of the closest centroid.

Template matching: Comparing raw image data in small subimages to sample image objects, the templates. Images are first normalized.

Bayesian, Support Vector Machines, Random Forest Classifiers

Bayesian analysis: provides a statistical approach to the development of a classification algorithm which requires a complete statistical model of the features. Preprocess by normalizing the features with standard normal density. The analysis finds boundaries in feature space to separate the classes called *discriminant functions* and provides a theoretically optimal classification rate (see Figure 7.4-1).

Support Vector Machine (SVM): The goal in developing an SVM is to find the hyperplane with the largest margin or the largest distance from the nearest training samples, which will provide the classifier that exhibits the best generalization. If necessary, use a higher dimensional kernel function to map feature data into a space where the classes are linearly separable (see Figure 7.4-2). A nonlinear mapping of sufficient dimensionality can always be found to separate two classes via a hyperplane (see Figure 7.4-3).

Decision tree: can be modeled as a nested If-then structure (see Figure 3.3-22), which divides the feature space into classes based on feature values or relationships between the values.

Random forest classifier: using multiple decision trees that have low correlation and use majority vote. Low correlation of trees ensured by random selection of training data and random selection of features at decision nodes.

Neural Networks and Deep Learning

Neural networks: modeled after the neurological system in biological systems, based on the processing element the *neuron* (see Figure 7.5-1). The main distinguishing characteristics are (1) the *architecture*, which includes the number of inputs, outputs and hidden layers, and how they are all connected (Figure 7.5-2), (2) the *activation function*, typically identity, threshold or sigmoid, and (3) the *learning algorithm*. Learning algorithms work by inputting the training vectors, calculating an error measure and then adjusting the weights to improve the error. To achieve optimal results with neural networks, use a PCT for preprocessing.

Activation function: (1) identify function, input equals output, (2) rectified linear unit, clip negative pass positive values, (3) threshold function, higher than threshold pass 1, else 0, and (4) sigmoid function, nonlinear, models biology (Equation 7.5-1)

Learning algorithm: adjust weights in neural net by using a gradient descent algorithm to search multi-dimensional space to find minimal error (see Figure 7.5-3). Neural nets train or learn for multiple interactions, each cycle also called a learning epoch.

Convolutional neural networks: used for "deep" learning, many hidden layers, use convolution filters to extract features <u>and</u> perform pattern classification by using the image itself as input (not the extracted feature vector as input). Specified by number and size of filters.

Data augmentation: deep learning requires a very large number of input images, so the data set may be increased by applying geometric operations, such as resizing, rotation, flipping, translation, zooming and elastic deformation techniques, to create new images.

Cost Function and Success Measures

- A *cost function*, or *risk*, can be used if different misclassifications have different levels of importance.
- Cost functions can be incorporated by defining multiplying weights for each class success rate into overall success measures, the sum of the weights is 1.

$$\text{Sensitivity} = \frac{\text{number of True Positives}}{\text{number of True Positives + number of False Negatives}} \tag{7.6-1}$$

$$\text{Specificity} = \frac{\text{number of True Negatives}}{\text{number of True Negatives + number of False Positives}} \tag{7.6-2}$$

$$\text{Positive predictive value or Precision} = \frac{\text{True Positives}}{\text{True Positives + False Positives}} \tag{7.6-3}$$

$$\text{Negative predictive value} = \frac{\text{True Negatives}}{\text{True Negatives + False Negatives}} \tag{7.6-4}$$

$$F\text{-measure} = 2 \times \left[\frac{\text{precision} \times \text{sensitivity}}{\text{precision} + \text{sensitivity}} \right] \tag{7.6-5}$$

$$\text{Youden's index} = \text{Y-index} = \left[\text{Sensitivity + Specificity} \right] - 1 \tag{7.6-6}$$

$$\text{False positive ratio (FPR)} = \left[1 - \text{Specificity} \right] \tag{7.6-7}$$

- With a binary classifier and a threshold we can set to classify, the ROC (receiver operator characteristic) provides a plot of sensitivity versus FPR, characterized by area under the curve (AOC). Perfect classification AOC is 1; if less than 0.5, it cannot reliably classify.

Pattern Classification Tools: Python, R, MATLAB, CVIPtools

- Application programming interface, API, defines how user access functions.
- Packages open source, free or commercial, pay for license.
- **Python**: open source, scripting language, API for rapid prototyping. *Scikit-Learn* has NN, SVMs and random forest classifiers.
- **Python**: useful public domain packages, *TensorFlow* – machine learning framework, *Keras* – neural nets, *PyTorch* – neural nets, *Caffe* – fastest deep learning framework written in C++ as it allows GPU use and Python interface.
- **R**: open source scripting language, includes linear, nonlinear, statistical modeling and visualization tools.
- **R**: open source packages for Bayesian analysis – BAS, BMS.
- **R**: limited to single-thread processing and keeps all data in memory so limited use, but powerful set of tools for preprocessing and offline analysis.
- **MATLAB**: commercial software designed for efficient matrix operations, scripting language and shell command line processing.
- **MATLAB**: commercial related toolboxes – *Computer Vision, Image Processing, Deep Learning, Statistics and Machine Learning* and free toolbox – *CVIP* with *CVIPtools GUI*.
- **CVIPtools**: comprehensive software environment in both C/C++ and MATLAB. Separate *Feature Extraction* and *Pattern Classification* windows. Pattern classification includes: six data normalization methods; four distance measures; two similarity metrics; NN, K-NN and nearest centroid classification methods; training/ test set and leave-one-out (cross-validation) testing methods. Batch processing in MATLAB and additional GUI-based development tools are given in in Chapter 8 with example applications.

7.9   References and Further Reading

For more on pattern classification/recognition, see Gonzalez and Woods (2018), Sonka, Hlavac, and Boyle (2014), Theodoridis and Koutroumbas (2009), Ripley (2008), Shapiro and Stockman (2001), Duda, Hart, and Stork (2001), Gose, Johnsonbaugh, and Jost (1996), Nadler and Smith (1993), Banks (1990), Schalkoff (1992), and Tou and Gonzalez (1974). For more on fuzzy set theory and fuzzy feature classification, see Theodoridis and Koutroumbas (2009) and Gonzalez and Woods (2018). More information on template matching is found in Theodoridis and Koutroumbas (2009), Duda, Hart, and Stork (2001), Gose, Johnsonbaugh, and Jost (1996) and Schalkoff (1992). Neural networks are discussed in more depth in Sonka, Hlavac, and Boyle (2014), Forsyth and Ponce (2011), Ripley (2008), Kulkarni (2001) and Gose, Johnsonbaugh, and Jost (1996). More details on the biomedical models and applications for neural nets are in Haidekker (2011), Toennies (2012) and Harvey (1994). Books that relate classical pattern recognition methods and neural nets include Ripley (2008), Kulkarni (2001) and Schalkoff (1992).

For more in-depth practical information regarding machine learning using Python and associated packages, see Geron (2019) and Raschka and Mirjalili (2019), both with excellent and complete practical approaches. For an overview of the use of neural networks in the early days for image processing, see Masters (1994). For details on the experiments used as an example for increasing training set size, see Umbaugh, Moss, and Stoecker (1991). For information on fuzzy logic methods for pattern recognition, see Gonzalez and Woods (2018), Sonka, Hlavac, and Boyle (2014), Kulkarni (2001) and Nadler and Smith (1993). For information on genetic algorithms, see Sonka, Hlavac, and Boyle (2014), Theodoridis and Koutroumbas (2009) and Duda, Hart, and Stork (2001). Two excellent texts for feature recognition and classification with medical applications are Dougherty (2009) and Ranagayyan (2005).

Banks, S., *Signal Processing, Image Processing and Pattern Recognition*, Upper Saddle River, NJ: Prentice Hall, 1990.

Dougherty, G., *Digital Image Processing for Medical Applications*, Cambridge: Cambridge University Press, 2009.

Duda, R.O., Hart, P.E., Stork, D.G, *Pattern Classification*, New York: Wiley 2001.

Forsyth, D.A., Ponce, J., *Computer Vision*, Upper Saddle River, NJ: Prentice Hall, 2011.

Geron, A., *Hands-on Machine Learning with Scikit-Learn, Keras & TensorFlow*, Sebastopol, CA: O-Reilly, 2019.

Gonzalez, R.C., Woods, R.E., *Digital Image Processing*, 4th Edition, Hoboken, NJ: Pearson Education, 2018.

Gose, E., Johnsonbaugh, R., Jost, S., *Pattern Recognition and Image Analysis*, Upper Saddle River, NJ: Prentice Hall, 1996.

Harvey, R.L., *Neural Network Principles*, Upper Saddle River, NJ: Prentice Hall, 1996.

Kulkarni, A., *Computer Vision and Fuzzy-Neural Systems*, Upper Saddle River, NJ: Prentice Hall, 2001.

Masters, T., *Signal and Image Processing with Neural Networks*, New York: Wiley, 1994.

Nadler, M., Smith, E.P., *Pattern Recognition Engineering*, New York: Wiley, 1993.

Ranagayyan, R.M., *Biomedical Image Analysis*, New York: CRC Press, 2005.

Raschka, S., Mirjalili, V., *Python Machine Learning: Machine Learning and Deep Learning with Python, Sscikit-learn, and TensorFlow 2*, 3rd Edition, Birmingham: Packt Publishing, 2019.

Ripley, B.D., *Pattern Recognition and Neural Networks*, Cambridge, UK: Cambridge University Press, 2008.

Schalkoff, R.J., *Pattern Recognition: Statistical, Structural and Neural Approaches*, New York: Wiley, 1992

Shapiro, L., Stockman, G., *Computer Vision*, Upper Saddle River, NJ: Prentice Hall, 2001.

Sonka, M., Hlavac, V., Boyle, R., *Image Processing, Analysis and Machine Vision*, Florence, KY: Cengage-Engineering, 2014.

Theodoridis, S., Koutroumbas, K., *Pattern Recognition*, 4th Edition, New York: Academic Press, 2009.

Toennies, K.D., *Guide to Medical Image Analysis: Methods and Algorithms*, New York: Springer, 2012.

Tou, J.T., Gonzalez, R.C., *Pattern Recognition Principles*, Reading, MA: Addison Wesley, 1974.

Umbaugh, S.E, Moss, R.H., Stoecker, W.V., Applying artificial intelligence to the identification of variegated coloring in skin tumors, *IEEE Engineering in Medicine and Biology*, Vol. 4, pp. 57–62, December 1991.

7.10   Exercises

Problems

1. In the following scatter plot, we have a two-dimensional feature space with all our sample vectors shown for two classes. Discuss any reasons to remove or add any feature vectors to our data set before we begin developing the pattern classification algorithm.

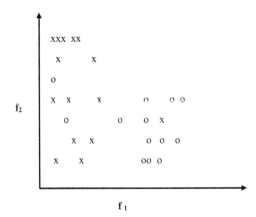

2. (a) When developing a classification algorithm, why do we divide our data into training and test sets? (b) Describe two methods for dividing the data into these two sets. Discuss important factors to consider when selecting the training and test sets. (c) Why do we divide the training set into training and validation sets?

3. Describe the *leave-one-out* and the *leave-K-out* method of developing and testing pattern classification algorithms.

4. Describe an example, other than the ones in the book, which shows why a cost function is important when developing a pattern classification algorithm.

5. Given the following feature vectors, with two classes:

$$\text{Class 1}: \left\{ F_1 = \begin{bmatrix} 5 \\ 8 \\ 6 \end{bmatrix} \quad F_2 = \begin{bmatrix} 7 \\ 6 \\ 1 \end{bmatrix} \quad F_3 = \begin{bmatrix} 6 \\ 7 \\ 2 \end{bmatrix} \right\}$$

$$\text{Class 2}: \left\{ F_1 = \begin{bmatrix} 1 \\ 8 \\ 7 \end{bmatrix} \quad F_2 = \begin{bmatrix} 3 \\ 6 \\ 8 \end{bmatrix} \quad F_3 = \begin{bmatrix} 2 \\ 7 \\ 6 \end{bmatrix} \right\}$$

   a. Using the nearest neighbor classification method, and the absolute value distance metric, classify the following unknown sample vector as Class 1 or Class 2:

$$F = \begin{bmatrix} 4 \\ 6 \\ 9 \end{bmatrix}$$

   b. Use *K*-nearest neighbor, with $K = 3$

6. Given the following feature vectors, with two classes:

$$\text{Class 1}: \left\{ F_1 = \begin{bmatrix} 5 \\ 8 \\ 6 \end{bmatrix} \quad F_2 = \begin{bmatrix} 7 \\ 6 \\ 1 \end{bmatrix} \quad F_3 = \begin{bmatrix} 6 \\ 7 \\ 2 \end{bmatrix} \right\}$$

$$\text{Class 1}: \left\{ F_1 = \begin{bmatrix} 1 \\ 8 \\ 7 \end{bmatrix} \quad F_2 = \begin{bmatrix} 3 \\ 6 \\ 8 \end{bmatrix} \quad F_3 = \begin{bmatrix} 2 \\ 7 \\ 6 \end{bmatrix} \right\}$$

Using the Nearest Centroid classification method and the absolute value distance metric, classify the following unknown sample vector as Class 1 or Class 2:

$$F = \begin{bmatrix} 3 \\ 6 \\ 10 \end{bmatrix}$$

7. Given the following feature vectors, with two classes:

$$\text{Class 1}: \left\{ F_1 = \begin{bmatrix} 5 \\ 8 \\ 6 \end{bmatrix} \quad F_2 = \begin{bmatrix} 7 \\ 6 \\ 1 \end{bmatrix} \quad F_3 = \begin{bmatrix} 6 \\ 7 \\ 2 \end{bmatrix} \right\}$$

$$\text{Class 2}: \left\{ F_1 = \begin{bmatrix} 1 \\ 8 \\ 7 \end{bmatrix} \quad F_2 = \begin{bmatrix} 3 \\ 6 \\ 8 \end{bmatrix} \quad F_3 = \begin{bmatrix} 2 \\ 7 \\ 6 \end{bmatrix} \right\}$$

Using the Nearest Centroid classification method and the normalized vector inner product similarity measure, classify the following unknown sample vectors as Class 1 or Class 2:

a. $F = \begin{bmatrix} 4 \\ 6 \\ 9 \end{bmatrix}$

b. $F = \begin{bmatrix} 8 \\ 6 \\ 4 \end{bmatrix}$

c. $F = \begin{bmatrix} 3 \\ 6 \\ 10 \end{bmatrix}$

8. (a) What type of preprocessing normalization should we do to apply Bayesian analysis? (b) What do we call the n-dimensional form of the linear discriminant function? (c) Given the following scatter plot, draw a linear discriminant function to separate the two classes.

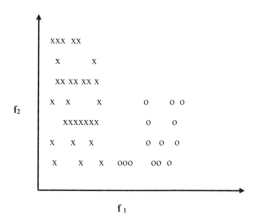

9. (a) What are the main distinguishing characteristics of a neural network? (b) What type of preprocessing should be done to apply a neural network? (c) Describe four types of activation functions. Which one is used most often? (d) In general, how does a learning algorithm work?

10. (a) What is the equation for the *Youden index?* (b) What is the range for this metric? (c) What must we be careful of when using this metric? (d) Provide an example application where this metric alone might be dangerous to use.

11. (a) For what type of classifier is the receiver operator characteristic (ROC) useful? (b) What is the ROC? (c) What does AUC stand for and how is it used with the ROC? (d) What is the range for the AUC, and what do the values mean? (e) What is the value for the AUC below which we cannot consider this classifier to be reliable?

7.10.1 Programming Exercises

Template Matching

1. Write a function to perform template matching and put it in your CVIPlab. The function should take two input images: the image of interest, $I(r, c)$, and the template image, $T(r, c)$. The function will move the template across the image of interest, searching for pattern matches by calculating the error at each point. The distance measure to be used for this exercise is the Euclidean distance measure defined by:

$$D\left(\bar{r}, \bar{c}\right) = \sqrt{\sum_r \sum_c \left[I(r', c') - T(r, c)\right]^2}$$

If we overlay the template on the image, then $\bar{r}, \bar{c}$ are the row and column coordinates of $I(r, c)$ corresponding to the center of the template where a match occurs. The r', c' designation is used to illustrate that as we slide the template across the image, the limits on the row and column coordinates of $I(r, c)$ will vary depending on (1) where we are in the image and (2) the size of the template. You need to only consider parts of the image that fully contain the template image. Your function should handle any size image and template, but you may assume that the template is smaller than the image. A match will occur when the error measure is less than a specified threshold. In your function, the threshold should be specified by user input. Where a match occurs, the program should display the error and the (r, c) coordinates.

2. Test this function with images you create using CVIPtools. For example, create a small image for the template with a single object and then create a larger image with multiple objects for the test image.

3. Expand the function by allowing for the rotation of the template. Consider the error to be the minimum error from all rotations.

4. Modify the function for efficiency by comparing the template only to image objects, not every subimage.

5. Make your function more useful by adding size invariance to the template matching. This is done by growing, or shrinking, the object to the size of the template before calculating the error.

6. Experiment with using different error and similarity measures described in Chapter 6.

Nearest Neighbor (NN) Classification

1. Write a function that will read a CVIP feature file and classify any unknown vectors, those without classes listed, by comparison to all other feature vectors in the file by using NN method and the Euclidean distance metric.

2. Modify your function to perform data normalization before the classification using unit vector normalization.

3. Test your function by comparison to CVIPtools results on the same image sets.

4. Using a feature file with all the samples being classified, apply leave-one-out cross-validation with the NN classification method.

K-NN Classification

1. Modify your NN function to perform K-NN classification on a set of feature vectors, using the leave-one-out method.

2. Modify your function to perform data normalization before the classification using standard normal density (SND) normalization.

3. Test your function on a set of feature vectors you have extracted with CVIPtools.

7.11 Supplementary Exercises

Supplementary Problems

1. Given the following feature vectors for a training set, with two classes:

$$\text{Class 1}: \left\{ F_1 = \begin{bmatrix} 5 \\ 8 \\ 4 \end{bmatrix} \quad F_2 = \begin{bmatrix} 7 \\ 6 \\ 1 \end{bmatrix} \quad F_3 = \begin{bmatrix} 6 \\ 7 \\ 2 \end{bmatrix} \right\}$$

$$\text{Class 2}: \left\{ F_1 = \begin{bmatrix} 1 \\ 8 \\ 7 \end{bmatrix} \quad F_2 = \begin{bmatrix} 3 \\ 6 \\ 8 \end{bmatrix} \quad F_3 = \begin{bmatrix} 2 \\ 7 \\ 6 \end{bmatrix} \right\}$$

 a. Perform SND normalization on the feature vectors.

 b. Using the Nearest Centroid classification method and the normalized vector inner product similarity measure, classify the following unknown sample vectors as Class 1 or Class 2:

 i. $F = \begin{bmatrix} 4 \\ 6 \\ 9 \end{bmatrix}$

 ii. $F = \begin{bmatrix} 8 \\ 6 \\ 4 \end{bmatrix}$

 iii. $F = \begin{bmatrix} 3 \\ 6 \\ 10 \end{bmatrix}$

2. Using a pixel distance, $d = 1$, (a) find the gray level co-occurrence matrices for the horizontal, vertical, right diagonal and left diagonal directions, for the following 4×4 image, (b) find the texture features energy, inertia, correlation, inverse difference and entropy.

$$\begin{bmatrix} 0 & 0 & 1 & 1 \\ 0 & 0 & 1 & 1 \\ 0 & 2 & 2 & 2 \\ 2 & 2 & 3 & 3 \end{bmatrix}$$

3. Given the following feature vectors for a training set, with two classes:

$$\text{Class 1}: \left\{ F_1 = \begin{bmatrix} 5 \\ 8 \\ 4 \end{bmatrix} \quad F_2 = \begin{bmatrix} 7 \\ 6 \\ 1 \end{bmatrix} \quad F_3 = \begin{bmatrix} 6 \\ 7 \\ 2 \end{bmatrix} \right\}$$

$$\text{Class 2}: \left\{ F_1 = \begin{bmatrix} 1 \\ 8 \\ 7 \end{bmatrix} \quad F_2 = \begin{bmatrix} 3 \\ 6 \\ 8 \end{bmatrix} \quad F_3 = \begin{bmatrix} 2 \\ 7 \\ 6 \end{bmatrix} \right\}$$

a. Perform min–max normalization on the feature vectors, using 0 for the minimum and 1 for the maximum.

b. Using the NN classification method and the Minkowski distance measure, with $r = 3$, classify the following unknown sample vectors as Class 1 or Class 2:

i. $F = \begin{bmatrix} 4 \\ 6 \\ 8 \end{bmatrix}$

ii. $F = \begin{bmatrix} 8 \\ 3 \\ 1 \end{bmatrix}$

iii. $F = \begin{bmatrix} 3 \\ 6 \\ 8 \end{bmatrix}$

4. (a) Using CVIPtools, create images of circles, ellipses, rectangles, squares and each of the object types with holes – this gives eight object classes. Create ten objects for each class of various sizes and orientations. Divide the image set into five of each class for training and five for testing. Use CVIPtools to achieve 100% correct classification. What parameters were used to achieve these results? (b) Repeat (a), but blur the image with a 7×7 mean filter. Note that preprocessing steps may improve results. (c) Repeat (a), but add zero mean Gaussian noise with a variance of 400. Note that preprocessing steps may improve results. (d) Repeat (a), but blur the image with a 7×7 mean filter and add zero mean Gaussian noise with a variance of 400. Note that preprocessing steps may improve results.

5. Consider a system to identify land mines where we are classifying found objects. (a) What are the classes? (b) What are the relevant cost functions? In other words, what are the risks? (c) How can we incorporate the cost functions into our analysis of classification algorithms? How can we apply *specificity* and *sensitivity* metrics?

6. Given the following results from an experiment testing a classification algorithm with four classes, A, B, C and D, and results shown in the classification matrix, find for each class, the (a) sensitivity, (b) specificity, (c) precision, (d) the F-measure and (e) Do you think these are good results? Why?

Classification Matrix		Classifier Results			
		A	B	C	D
Actual Class	A	8	1	0	1
	B	1	7	2	0
	C	0	0	9	1
	D	0	2	2	6

7. Find the correlation coefficient for the following feature vectors:

   a. $\mathbf{A} = \begin{bmatrix} 2 \\ 4 \end{bmatrix}$ and $\mathbf{B} = \begin{bmatrix} 4 \\ 2 \end{bmatrix}$

   b. $\mathbf{A} = \begin{bmatrix} 2 \\ 4 \end{bmatrix}$ and $\mathbf{B} = \begin{bmatrix} -2 \\ -4 \end{bmatrix}$

   c. Compare your answers for (a) and (b). Explain.

   d. Graph the two vectors for (a) and (b). After thinking about the results and examining these graphs, do you think the correlation coefficient is an effective similarity measure? Why or why not?

8. (a) Given the following samples in a transformed two-dimensional feature space, with "x" being one class and "O" being a second class, if we are designing a SVM, which separating line would be selected, the red or green one? (b) Explain your answer.

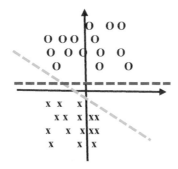

9. (a) What is a random forest classifier? (b) Why do we want decision trees with low correlation? (c) How do we obtain decision trees with low correlation?

10. (a) What type of neural network is associated with deep learning? (b) Why is it referred to as *deep* learning? (c) How does a CNN function differently than a standard neural net? And how does the typical input differ? (d) What is one practical difficulty with training CNNs and how do we handle this problem?

7.11.1 Supplementary Programming Exercises

These exercises can be implemented in MATLAB or in C/C++ using CVIPlab.

Nearest Centroid Classification

1. Write a function that will read a CVIP feature file and calculate the centroid vector for each class contained in the feature file, and write an output file with the class names and the corresponding centroid vectors.

2. Write a function that will read a CVIP feature file and a "centroid file" from the previous function, and classify the feature vectors using Nearest Centroid method.

3. Test your function by comparison to CVIPtools results on the same image sets.

Data Normalization

1. Write functions for data normalization, including range normalization, SND or min–max normalization.

2. Modify your pattern classification functions to allow the user to specify the type of normalization desired, including range normalization, SND or min–max normalization.

3. Test your function by comparison to CVIPtools results on the same image sets.

Distance and Similarity Metrics

1. Write functions to implement the Minkowski distance, normalized vector inner product and Tanimoto metrics.

2. Modify your pattern classification functions to allow the user to specify the type of distance or similarity metric desired.

3. Test your function by comparison to CVIPtools results on the same image sets.

8

Application Development Tools

8.1 Introduction and Overview

Application development is one of the primary motivations to study computer vision and image analysis. As first discussed in Chapter 3 and further developed throughout the book, the application-specific nature of the subject is intrinsic to its study. As shown in Figure 3.1-3, the application feedback loop in the image analysis process is of paramount importance. The application itself drives the algorithm development, whether it is a computer- or human-based application. The method of image acquisition determines the characteristics of the images, which can greatly affect algorithm development. The specific nature of the application will determine the necessary methods best suited for solving the particular imaging problem.

In this chapter, we describe application development tools that are adjuncts to CVIPtools, and we have sample applications where these tools are used to solve computer vision problems. The GUI-based CVIPtools is designed to process one image at a time and allow the user to immediately view results, while adjusting parameters and trying different functions. This paradigm is perfectly suitable for education and initial algorithm exploration, but is rather unwieldy for developing algorithms involving hundreds or thousands of images. The first tool, CVIP Algorithm Test and Analysis Tool (CVIP-ATAT), allows for batch processing and automates front-end algorithm development. This is done by selecting sequences of processes, specifying parameters, and then it will perform algorithms corresponding to all permutations of user-selected processes and parameters.

To illustrate this, we discuss specific applications and provide a step-by-step process for the development of solutions to the particular imaging problems: (1) using CVIP-ATAT in conjunction with MATLAB and the GUI-based CVIPtools to perform preliminary research for the identification of necrotic tissue in liver slide samples, (2) using CVIP-ATAT for the analysis of retinal fundus images by developing automatic segmentation algorithms to identify blood vessels for diagnosing diabetic retinopathy and (3) using CVIP-ATAT to find an algorithm to automate the creation of mask images for gait analysis in canine thermograms.

The second tool, CVIP Feature Extraction and Pattern Classification Tool (CVIP-FEPC), is used to explore features and pattern classification methods after the images have been properly processed to the point where the objects of interest have been identified. After the introduction to the tool and its usage, we discuss applications: (1) preliminary work using CVIP-FEPC toward classification of veterinary thermograms and (2) use of CVIP-FEPC to develop algorithms for the identification of bone cancer in canine thermograms.

The final application discusses the development of the MATLAB CVIPtools GUI and how it was used for the detection of syrinx in canines with Chiari malformation, a brain disease that also occurs in humans. These applications typify research and development projects that have utilized our image analysis process and the CVIPtools development environment.

8.2 CVIP Algorithm Test and Analysis Tool

8.2.1 Overview and Capabilities

The Computer Vision and Image Processing Algorithm Test and Analysis Tool, CVIP-ATAT, was created to facilitate the development of both human and computer vision applications. The primary function of this tool is to allow the user to explore many more algorithmic possibilities than can be considered by processing one image at a time with the GUI-based CVIPtools. It allows for the automatic processing of large image sets with many different algorithmic and parameter variations. We call this the "front-end" tool because its primary purpose is to find the best algorithm to preprocess, segment and postprocess a set of images for a particular application in order to best separate the most important regions of interest (ROIs) within the image.

DOI: 10.1201/9781003221135-8

It has a GUI which allows the user to enter multi-stage algorithms for testing and analysis. At each stage, the user can specify a number of different processes to test and a range for the processes' parameters. The user also specifies a set of images to process and a set of "ideal" output images which will be used to determine the success for each algorithm. Note that *one algorithm is defined as a specific set of processes and a specific set of parameter values.*

The tool will then automatically perform algorithms which consist of all the permutations of the values for each of the parameters for each process and all the processes for each stage. Next, the user can compare the various algorithm results to determine the best set of processes and parameters for the particular application. The tool is useful for application development where the ideal image results are available or can be created. Additionally, it can serve as a front-end development tool for image analysis to find the optimal set of processes and parameters for extracting ROIs for further processing.

8.2.2 How to Use CVIP-ATAT

8.2.2.1 Running CVIP-ATAT

The easiest way to invoke CVIP-ATAT is by clicking on the icon on the CVIPtools toolbar (see Figure 8.2-1). CVIP-ATAT requires two files: CVIP-ATAT.exe and CVIPtools.dll. The GUI is implemented in file CVIP-ATAT.exe. All C functions for image processing and analysis are implemented in file CVIPtools.dll, which is invoked by CVIP-ATAT.exe. Alternately, the user can run the executable directly, if desired.

8.2.2.2 Creating a New Project

A new project should be created for the images that will be tested and analyzed. Different projects can be created for different types of images; however, just one project can be opened at one time. In order to create a new project, the following steps should be followed:

1. Select *File* from the menu toolbar and then select *New Project* to open the New Project dialog box. See Figures 8.2-2a (first step) and 8.2-2b (second step).

FIGURE 8.2-1
Invoking CVIP-ATAT. Select the CVIP-ATAT button on the top right of the CVIPtools toolbar.

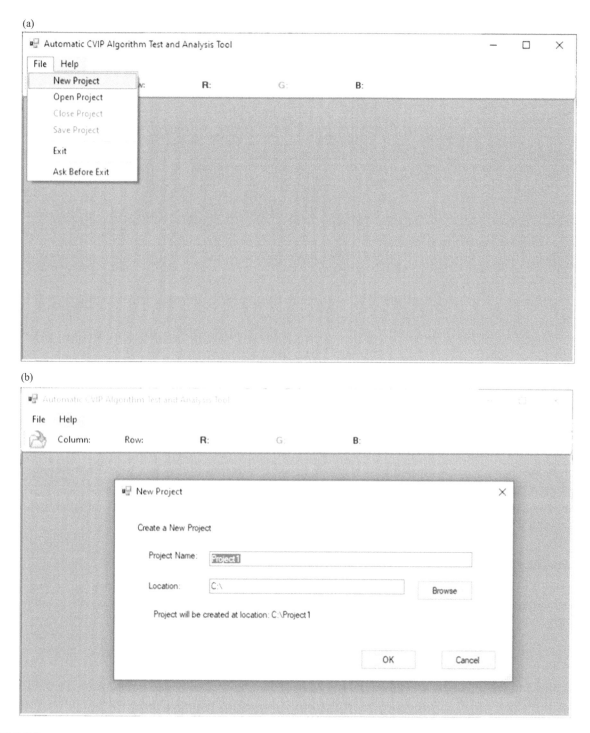

FIGURE 8.2-2
Creating a new project: (a) step 1, select *File-> New Project* and (b) step 2, enter a name for your project and a file folder will be created with that name which will hold all the files related to the project.

2. In the New Project dialog box, type in a directory for the new project or use the *Browse* button to select a directory for the project.

3. In the New Project dialog box, provide a name for the new project. Note that the tool will create a new folder whose name will be identical with the project name and which will contain all of the files related to the new project.

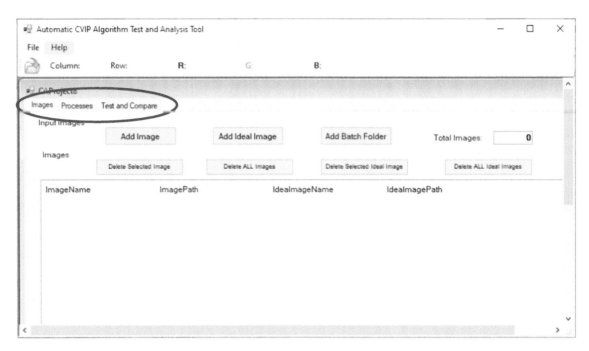

FIGURE 8.2-3
The project interface. With this window, the user has tabs for entering *Images*, *Processes*, and *Test and Compare* functions to be used in the project.

4. Press the *OK* button in the New Project dialog box to complete the creation of the new project. The creation can be stopped simply by pressing the *Cancel* button.

5. The interface of your newly created project will look just like the one in Figure 8.2-3. With this window, the user has tabs for entering images, processes and test functions to be used in the project.

6. Note: after a project has been created, it is opened by selecting *Open Project* from the main menu and open its configuration file, *.cfg.

8.2.2.3 Inserting Images

After creating a new project, the user can import images in the image interface. After opening an existing project, the user can add more images or delete some images for retesting. In order to add or delete images, the user should apply the following steps:

1. The image input interface is one of the three tab pages shown in Figure 8.2-3. If the image interface has not been selected, click on the *Images* tab to open it by clicking on the mouse left key.

2. Click the *Add Image* button to add original images. After clicking the *Add Image* button, an Add Image dialog will appear as shown in Figure 8.2-4. The user can add a single original image or multiple original images at one time. If the user wants to add multiple original images, the *Ctrl* key should be held down, while using the mouse to select several images.

3. After original images have been added, ideal images can be added by clicking the *Add Ideal Image* button. The user then selects the directory where the ideal images are located and the program matches them to the test images by name. *Important note: The file names of the original images and ideal images should be the same, but the file extensions can be different.*

4. The *Add Batch Folder* button can be used to add both test and ideal images using a single folder. Pressing this button will open a file explorer where a folder can be selected. This folder must contain, on the top level, the test images and also a folder titled *Masks* that holds the ideal images. Each test image is analyzed and is added to the table if an ideal match is found. *Important note: The file names of the original images and ideal images should be the same, but the file extensions can be different.*

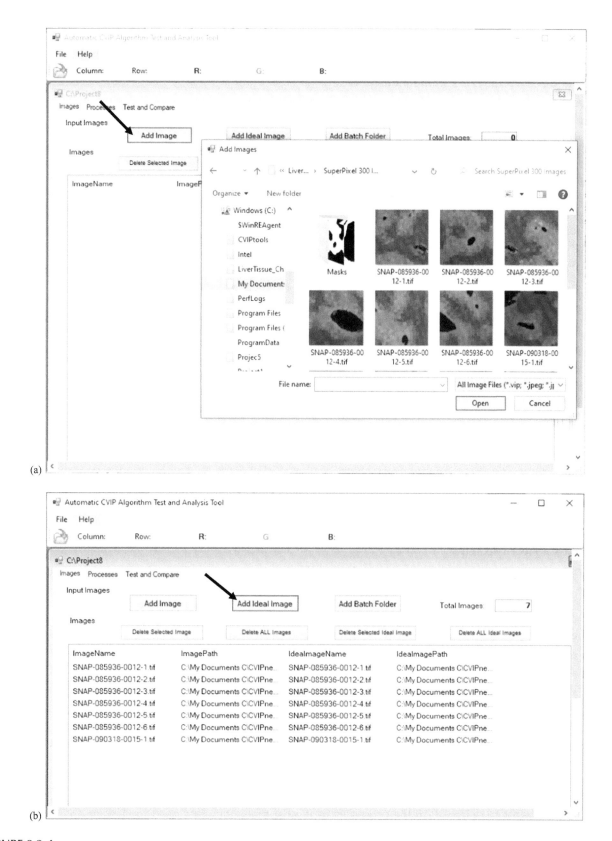

FIGURE 8.2-4
Adding images. (a) After selecting the *Add Image* button, a file selection window will appear. (b) The screen after original images and the corresponding ideal images are added. Ideal images are loaded by selection of the folder that contains them and CVIP-ATAT matches the image to its corresponding ideal image by use of the same file name, but with different file extensions.

5. The user can delete all of the original images (including the ideal images) by clicking the *Delete ALL Images* button or delete some of the original images by clicking the *Delete Selected Image* button. When the user wants to delete some of the original images, the original images that will be deleted should be selected first by holding down the *Ctrl* key and mouse left key.

6. If the user wants to delete the ideal images only, the *Delete Selected Ideal Image* and the *Delete ALL Ideal Images* buttons can be used to do so.

Figure 8.2-4b illustrates how the image interface should look like after the insertion of the images is complete.

NOTES: The original images are used for testing the algorithms(s) and the output images from the algorithm(s) being tested are compared with the ideal images. Note that the ideal image format must match the output image format. Specifically, the ideal images and the corresponding output images must have the same number of bands and size for the seven comparison metrics: (1) Root-Mean-Square (RMS) error, (2) Signal-to-Noise Ratio (SNR), (3) subtraction energy, (4) Dice coefficient, (5) Jaccard index, (6) overlap coefficient and (7) logical XOR. If not, any necessary postprocessing steps can be added to the algorithms to make it so.

8.2.2.4 Inputting an Algorithm

The user can input algorithms that will be tested on the images using the algorithm input interface. The algorithm input interface is shown in Figure 8.2-5.

In order to input an algorithm, the user should apply the following steps:

1. The algorithm input interface is one of the three tab pages shown in Figure 8.2-5. If the algorithm input interface has not been selected, click on the *Processes* tab shown in the figure to open it clicking on the mouse left key.

2. The user can select an algorithm with the dropdown arrow on the *Select Processes* box. After an algorithm is selected, the user can adjust the parameters for that algorithm.

3. The user has to specify a stage for every algorithm with *Select Stage*. Notice that the image testing process can be broken down into several stages and more than one process (function) can be applied for each stage. Each stage can have multiple processes and the tool will test all algorithmic possibilities. Note that for one algorithmic iteration, *only one process, with one set of parameter values, will be tested in each stage*. However, the user is able to test all possible processes and parameter combinations in one run of CVIP-ATAT. See Figure 8.2-6 for an example.

4. After the stage is specified, the user selects the possible parameter values for each parameter of the process. This is done by selecting the *lower, increment* and *upper* values for each parameter. For example, if a parameter's lower value is 1, the increment value is 2 and the upper value is 5, then the possible values for this parameter are 1, 3 or 5. Each process has default values that can be used, or the user can enter the desired values (see Figure 8.2-5b) to limit the number of algorithms tested.

5. After selecting the process and its stage, the user needs to click on the *Add Process* button to add the selected process and its stage into the *Processes* list table. Though when inserting a process into a stage, the user must be careful to put the stages into order without skipping any stage. For example, without stage 3, the user cannot insert a process into stage 4.

6. The user can repeat steps 3, 4 and 5 until all of the required processes have been selected.

7. Note that in some cases, the user may want to test algorithms with different numbers of stages. This is done by selecting the Skip/Null process shown in Figure 8.2-7.

8. The user can delete one or multiple processes listed in the list table easily by checking them using the mouse left key, then by clicking on the *Delete Checked Process* button (see Figure 8.2-5b).

9. If the user wants to delete all of the processes in the list table, they just need to click on the *Delete ALL Process* button.

10. The user can also adjust the order of the processes in the list table by selecting one of the processes and then moving it by clicking on the *Up* button or the *Down* button.

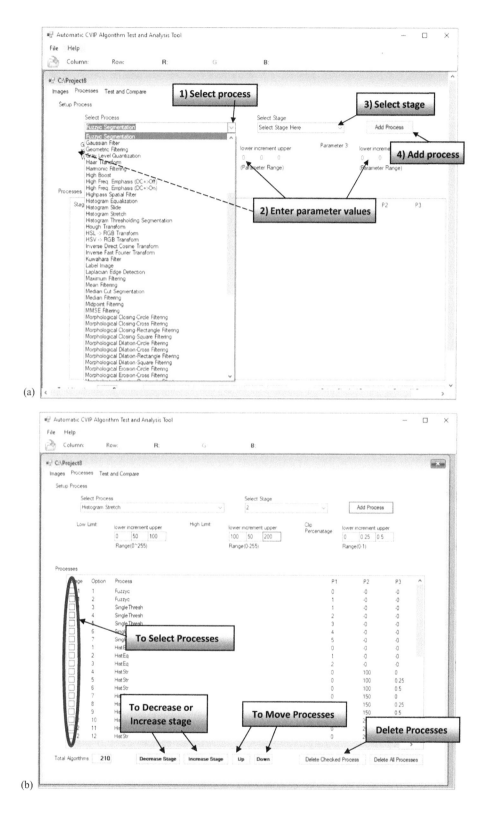

FIGURE 8.2-5

The project interface with the processes tab selected. Here, the user can enter the desired processes for algorithm testing and analysis. (a) Select a process from the list. For each process, the user selects each parameter's range and increment values, and selects the process stage, and then clicks *Add Process*. (b) Here is the window after addition of a few processes. Each stage can have multiple processes and the tool will test all algorithmic possibilities. Note that for one algorithmic run, *only one process, with one set of parameter values, will be tested in each stage*. Note that any processes can be moved or deleted by checkbox for selection and then use of appropriate button. Additionally, the stage for the processes can be changed, if desired.

(a)

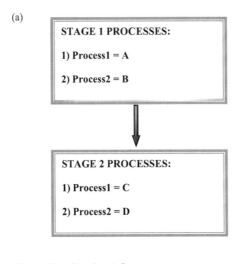

STAGE 1 PROCESSES:

1) Process1 = A

2) Process2 = B

STAGE 2 PROCESSES:

1) Process1 = C

2) Process2 = D

(b)   Algorithm1: A,C

         Algorithm2: A,D

         Algorith m3: B,C

         Algorithm4 : B,D

FIGURE 8.2-6
A two-stage run of CVIP-ATAT. (a) For this algorithm test and analysis, we select two stages and two processes for each stage. (b) The algorithms tested are shown here. Note that for simplicity and clarity, the parameters are not included, but all permutations of all parameters will be tested.

11. The user can also adjust the stage of a specific process using the *Decrease Stage* and *Increase Stage* buttons after selecting the process. Note: Caution should be taken when changing stages so that stages are not skipped.

12. The number of algorithms for one image is displayed at the bottom of the algorithm input interface.

8.2.2.5 Executing an Experiment

The experiment interface (see Figure 8.2-8) is used to test algorithms on images, display the test results and/or compare the result images to the ideal images. The following steps should be followed:

1. The experiment interface is one of the three tab pages shown in Figure 8.2-8. If the experiment interface is not selected, click the *Test and Compare* tab to open it clicking on the mouse left key.

2. The first step in identifying an experiment is to select the type of experiment using three options: Full Test, Only Test or Only Compare. A full test will both test algorithms on each original image and then compare the results to the ideal images, whereas the "Only" options will only execute one. In order to begin the experiment, the user needs to click on the *Run* button. This process may take hours or even days depending on the number of options selected and the resources of the computer being used.

3. If a full test or only compare experiment is selected, the user will need to select comparison parameters. Each error metric can be chosen by checking the box to its left and success threshold values, for each band, can be specified in the three boxes to its right. The average and/or standard deviation of each algorithm can be calculated by checking the boxes next to the Average and/or Standard Deviation text. The only compare option also requires the user to specify a folder containing test images and a folder containing ideal images. An algorithm sheet can be added if desired, but is not required.

4. During the test, a progress bar is used to display the progress, and below it, the percentage of the progress is displayed.

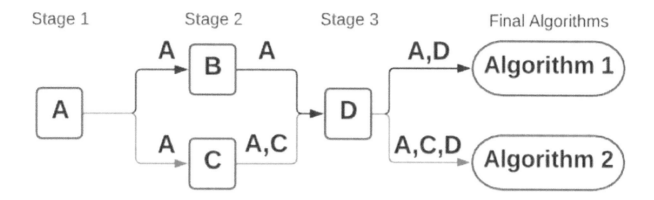

(a)

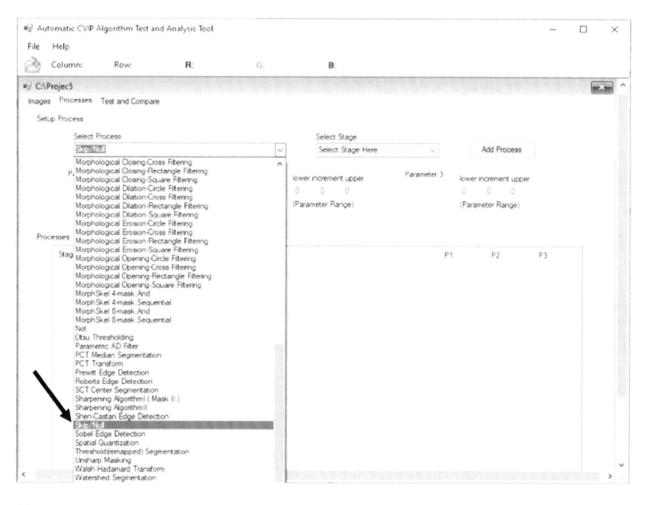

(b)

FIGURE 8.2-7

Using *skip* process for algorithms with different number of stages with CVIP-ATAT. (a) This may be needed for the example shown, where we want one algorithm to consist of processes A, C, D and the other to be simply A, D. In this case, process B is selected to be a *Skip* process. (b) Select the *Skip/Null* process as needed, as shown here.

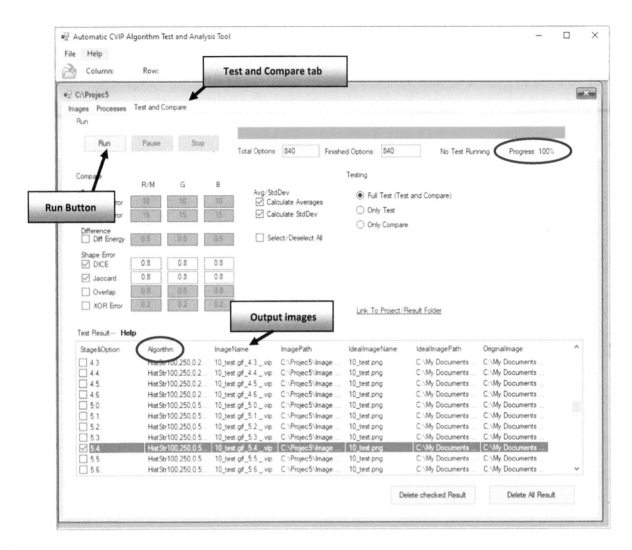

FIGURE 8.2-8

The test interface. The screen after selecting the *Test and Compare Tab*, clicking the *Run* button and test completion. During the test, the green bar and the percent in red below track testing progress. After test completion, all the output images and the corresponding algorithm are shown in the window. The algorithm parameters are shown on the left.

5. Because of the multi-thread technique, the user can pause or stop the test process at any time by clicking on the *Stop* or *Pause* button. After the *Pause* button is clicked on the test, it can be resumed by clicking on the *Run* button again.

6. The test results are displayed in the result list table as shown in Figure 8.2-8. The resultant images can be viewed by double clicking on the image file in the list. This will also open the ideal image with the same list index. If the only compare option is chosen, the user can choose to add the specified images to the table.

7. The user can delete any of the test result images by checking the items in the list table and then by clicking on the *Delete Checked Result* button.

8. The user can also delete all of the test results by clicking on the *Delete All Results* button.

9. If running a full test or only test, an algorithm text file will be created that holds the identification numbers of the algorithms performed during the experiment.

10. Comparison results are found within the project folder via comma-separated-values files. The *Project/Result* folder can be accessed by clicking on the link in the middle of the *Test and Compare* tab. Individual image performance for each algorithm is in the *Images Results* file, while the *Algorithm Results* file contains average and standard deviations across the entire image set for the selected error metrics for each algorithm.

8.3 CVIP-ATAT: Application Development Necrotic Liver Tissue

8.3.1 Introduction and Overview

Here, we will show a preliminary investigation for a biomedical research and development project that is in its initial stages. This is provided because it shows how the CVIP-ATAT can be used in conjunction with other tools to speed the development process. First, by performing preliminary investigation and analysis with CVIPtools, we can find the potential functions and processes that will have a good probability of leading to an efficacious solution to our imaging problem. Additionally, we can find the appropriate ranges for the parameters associated with each process and use that information for designing experiments for the ATAT.

Research in biomedical science often requires the manual examination of large numbers tissue samples. The process of measuring and/or counting of various tissue features is a tedious process which lends itself to automation by computer vision methods. The eventual goal for this research is to assist with the identification of novel therapeutic strategies to treat acute liver injury. For this application, the computer vision task is to (1) first remove the primarily white areas that are veins or arteries and (2) separate the necrotic (dead) tissue from the healthy tissue. In Figure 8.3-1, we see images of slices from a mouse liver that is being used to investigate drug-induced liver toxicity. The goal for the computer vision algorithm is to extract only the necrotic tissue, so that we can measure the percentage of tissue that has died as a result of an acute acetaminophen overdose.

The first step in the algorithm development process is to create masks manually, as shown in Figure 8.3-1b. These can then be used as correct or ideal images for the desired results. Next, to investigate algorithm development, the general procedure is as follows:

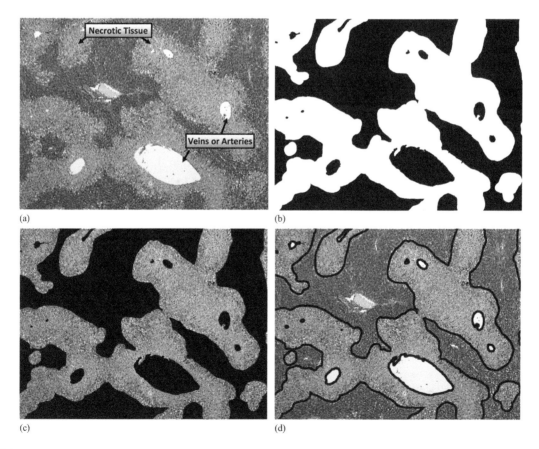

FIGURE 8.3-1
A slice of mouse liver tissue. (a) Here, the white areas that are veins or arteries need to be removed by the computer vision algorithm, and the necrotic tissue is extracted. (b) A manually created mask of the desired area to be extracted. (c) The original image ANDed with the mask and (d) the original image with the areas of interest outlined in black.

1. Determine proper preprocessing needed to obtain images most amenable to the task. This often requires some form of contrast enhancement and noise removal, and this is most easily done with CVIPtools and/ or MATLAB.

2. Determine segmentation options most likely to extract the areas of interest, along with any potential post-processing morphological filtering. This is also done with CVIPtools, both the C# GUI and the MATLAB version.

3. Apply CVIP-ATAT using knowledge gained from (1) and (2) to design and run experiments to find a good algorithm for this application.

8.3.2 The Algorithm

The first step was to find a method to remove the veins and arteries in the images. By using CVIPtools, it was readily determined that this could be done by eliminating areas in the image with average values greater than 200 in the red band. We manually verified this with a small set of ten images and then performed this preprocessing offline – before we started our experiments with ATAT. Next, we found that by preprocessing with the superpixel SLIC algorithm in MATLAB, it was much easier to visually separate the tissue and that a setting of 300 worked the best. Using CVIPtools, we determined that best options for preprocessing contrast enhancement were either a histogram equalization or a histogram stretch. Next, we used CVIPtools to find that the likely best options for segmentation were the K-means or the fuzzy c-means. At this point, we are ready to setup and run our ATAT experiments.

We designed the ATAT experiment to have three stages:

Stage 1:
    Process 1: Histogram equalization, using band 2.

    Process 2: Histogram stretch, with clipping of 0%, 5% or 10%.
Stage 2:
    Process 1: Fuzzy c-means segmentation, Gaussian kernel 1 or 5.

    Process 2: Auto Single Threshold (K-means) segmentation, limit of 1 or 5.
Stage 3: Extract band 2 or 3 (Stage 3 has only one process)

Note that before the ATAT experiment, we performed the following offline preprocessing steps to all the images:

1. Set to zero any pixels in the image that had values greater than 200 in the red band.
2. Apply SLIC superpixel algorithm in MATLAB with parameter set to 300 superpixels.

Figure 8.3-2 shows the images used for this experiment and the ATAT GUI after the images are loaded. Here, we see that the images were organized so that the *Masks* folder is in the folder where the images reside, so this makes it easy to load the image set by simply using the *Add Batch Folder* button in the Images tab.

In Figure 8.3-3, we see that ATAT GUI after the processes have been selected for the algorithm experiment, and the GUI after the test has been completed. The results can be found with the link on the *Test and Compare* tab, as shown in Figure 8.3-3b. Here, the *Algorithm Results* spreadsheet is found, which is explained in Figure 8.3-4. We also have the option of displaying any output image and its corresponding ideal image – this can be instructive to examine how specific algorithms work with specific images. By doing this with difficult images, we may develop insight into how to improve the algorithm.

8.3.3 Conclusion

We used MATLAB, CVIPtools and CVIP-ATAT to develop a preliminary algorithm for separating necrotic tissue from healthy tissue in microscopic images of liver slices. We found a five-step algorithm: (1) set to zero all pixels with value greater than 200 in the red band, to remove veins and arteries, (2) SLIC superpixel algorithm with 300 superpixels, (3) histogram stretch with 10% clipping, (4) K-means segmentation with a limit of 1 and (5) extract band 2, the green band. For application of this algorithm to the training image set, we obtained a Dice coefficient average of 88.5%. Future work will include more development and refinement of the algorithm and eventual application to a test set of images to obtain unbiased results.

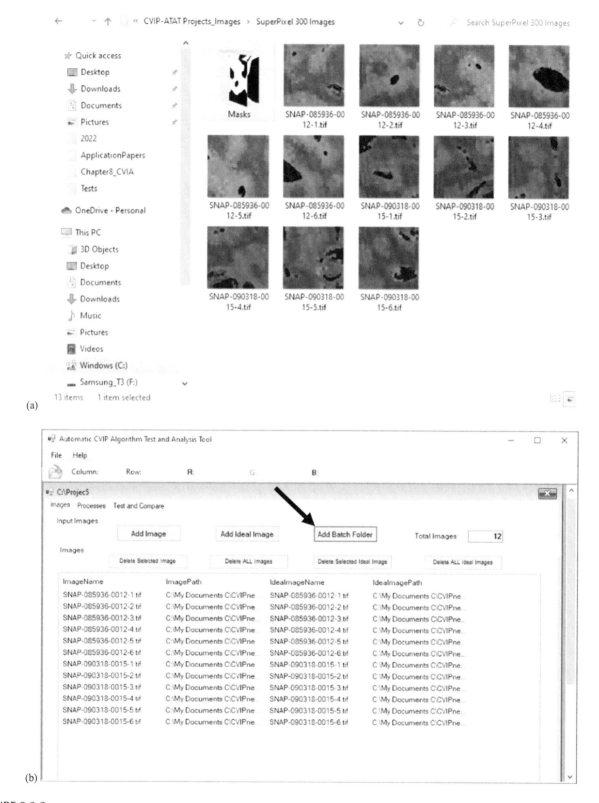

FIGURE 8.3-2
CVIP-ATAT after loading images. (a) Here, we see that the images are organized so that the entire set of original images and ideal images can be loaded with one click by creating a *Masks* folder in the folder where the images reside. (b) In this case, by selection of the *SuperPixel 300 Image* folder, all the images will be loaded at once by selection of the *Add Batch Folder* button.

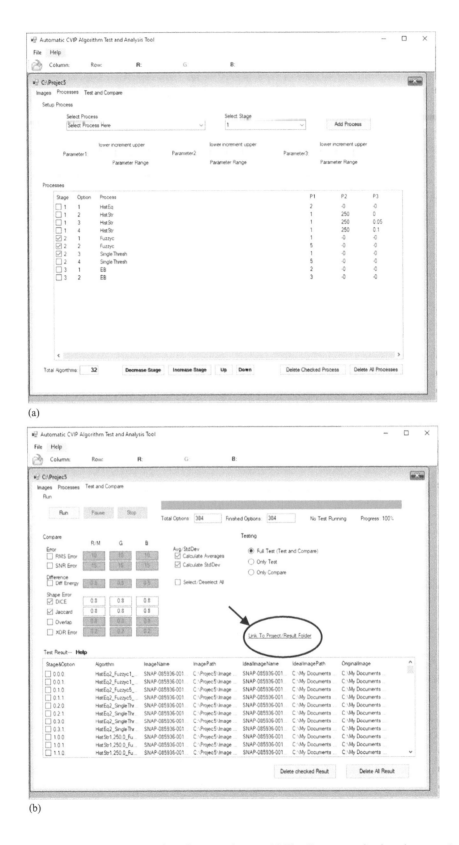

FIGURE 8.3-3
CVIP-ATAT processes after setting up and starting the experiment. (a) The *Processes* tab after the experiment has been set up to run with the processes and stages as described. (b) The *Test and Compare* tab after the experiment has been completed. The link to the Results folder is marked, which is where the *Algorithm Results* and the *Image Results* spreadsheets are found.

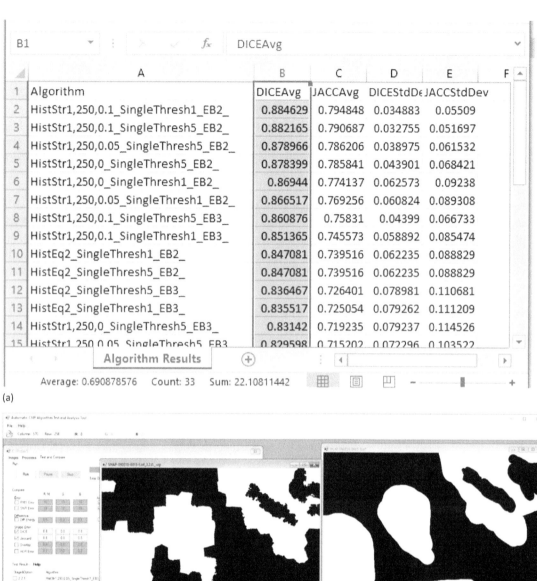

FIGURE 8.3-4

CVIP-ATAT results. (a) The *Algorithm Results* spreadsheet has been sorted with the Dice coefficient largest average at the top. Here, we can see the top algorithm used a histogram stretch with 10% clipping, single threshold (K-means) segmentation with a limit of 1, and then extracted band 2, the green band. This corresponds to Stage 1: Option 4, Stage 2: Option 3 and Stage3: Option 1 (see Figure 8.3-3a). (b) In the *Test and Compare* tab, we can display a particular output image and its corresponding ideal image by clicking on it. In this case, we selected one from the optimal algorithm which uses the option numbers for naming (4.3.1), but since these are zero based that corresponds to 3.2.0.

8.4   CVIP-ATAT: Application Development with Fundus Images

8.4.1   Introduction and Overview

For this application, the goal is to automatically locate the blood vessels in images of the retina of the human eye. The input images are called retinal fundus images. The blood vessel information can be used in diagnosis of various retinal pathologies, such as diabetic retinopathy, where early diagnosis can lead to prevention of blindness.

Ideal images hand drawn by experts (ophthalmologists) were available for comparison. Figure 8.4-1 shows example images, where we can observe that the algorithm developed with the aid of CVIP-ATAT provides encouraging visual results. Here, we see that all the primary vessels are found, but to find the smaller vessels effectively more work is required.

In a previous study, described in the paper *Comparison of Two Algorithms in the Automatic Segmentation of Blood Vessels in Fundus Images*, two algorithms were developed to perform this task. Here, we used CVIP-ATAT to see if a better algorithm could be developed. We describe the new algorithm and compare its results with those from the two algorithms previously developed. Overall, the results obtained from the new algorithm were much better. These comparisons were made using the RMS error, SNR and Pratt's Figure of Merit (FOM) as success metrics.

8.4.2   The New Algorithm

The new algorithm uses a similar structure which was used in the previous study. Through the use of CVIP-ATAT, we determined that by using different filters and repeating some algorithmic steps, better results can be obtained. We also found that removing the outer ring in the fundus images improved the results. The outer ring image masks were

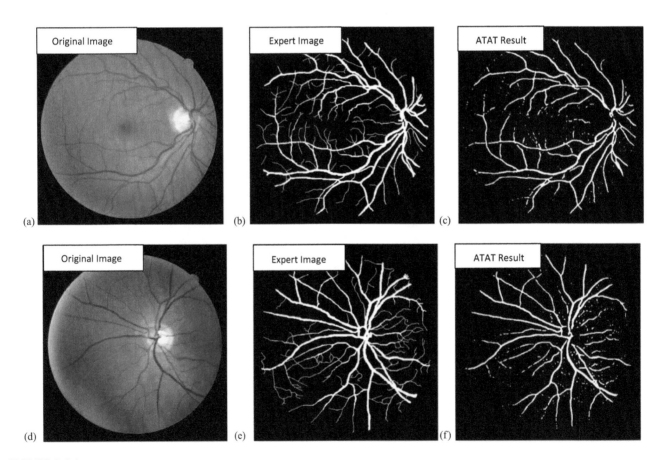

FIGURE 8.4-1
Fundus images application development example. The goal of the project is to automatically locate the blood vessels in the original images. The *Expert Image* is the ideal output image, hand drawn by the expert – an ophthalmologist; The *ATAT Result* is output image generated from the algorithm developed with CVIP-ATAT.

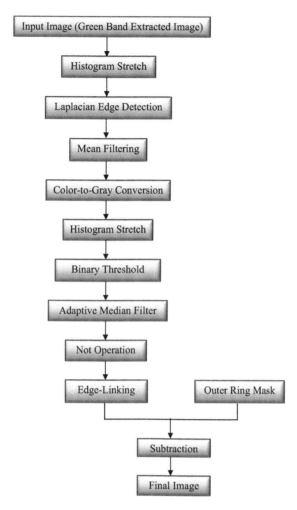

FIGURE 8.4-2
The new algorithm flowchart as developed by CVIP-ATAT.

created by thresholding the original images to create masks of the entire eyeball and then extracting the outer ring only from the resulting sphere. The flow chart of the algorithm developed with CVIP-ATAT is given in Figure 8.4-2.

The number of initial algorithmic and parameter variations was approximately 600,000. After initial studies were performed with CVIP-ATAT, the final algorithm was run on the retinal fundus images. All possible parameter values were tested for every function. The parameter values which gave optimal results were determined. These parameter values are as follows:

- **Histogram stretch**:
  Low Limit: 0
  High Limit: 255
  Low Clip: 0.025
  High Clip: 0.025
- **Laplacian edge detection**:
  Mask Choice: 3
  Mask Size: 1 or 2
  Choice of keeping it DC: 0 (No)
- **Mean filtering**: (was applied three times)
  Mask Size: 3

- **Color-to-gray conversion**: conversion type was selected as *luminance*.
- **Histogram stretch**:

  Low Limit: 0

  High Limit: 255

  Low Clip Percentage: 0.05

  High Clip Percentage: 0.05
- **Binary threshold**: threshold value was selected as 73 (on original image)
- **Adaptive median filter**:

  Mask Size: 3
- Not Operation.
- **Edge-linking**: (was applied twice)

  Max. Connect Distance: 3

Figure 8.4-3 shows examples of the output images obtained from the algorithm.

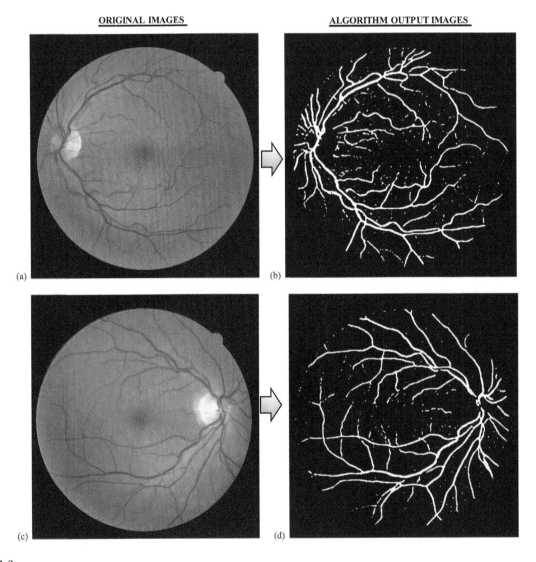

FIGURE 8.4-3

The new algorithm resulting images. The goal of the project is to extract the blood vessels from the original images.

(Continued)

ORIGINAL IMAGES **ALGORITHM OUTPUT IMAGES**

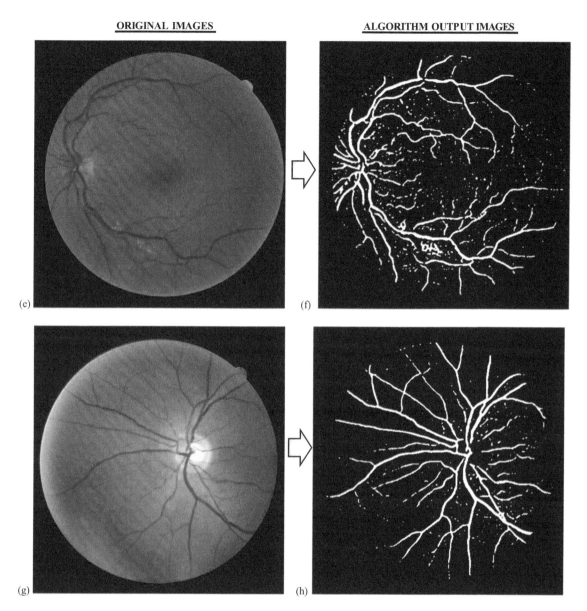

FIGURE 8.4-3 (*Continued*)
The new algorithm resulting images. The goal of the project is to extract the blood vessels from the original images.

After obtaining the resultant images, the success of the algorithm was measured by comparing the resultant images with the ideal images which were hand drawn by ophthalmologists. The comparison metrics used were SNR, RMS error and Pratt's FOM.

The following tables show the SNR, RMS and FOM results, respectively, of the previous two algorithms (Algorithms 1 and 2) and the newly developed algorithm (NEW) along with their average results and the improvement in the results by using the CVIP-ATAT. The original study used 15 fundus images, so the same 15 images were used here for comparison. It should be noted that in the previous algorithms, the outer ring was not removed, so this factor contributed to the improvement.

As seen in Table 8-1, for every output image of the new algorithm, the SNR value is better when compared to both Algorithms 1 and 2.

As seen in Table 8-2, for every output image of the new algorithm, the RMS value is smaller when compared to both Algorithms 1 and 2.

As seen in Table 8-3, for every output image of the new algorithm, the Pratt FOM value is better when compared to both Algorithms 1 and 2.

TABLE 8-1

Results of Comparing the Three Algorithms Using the Signal-to-Noise Ratio (SNR) Comparison Metric

Images	SNR for Algorithm 1	SNR for Algorithm 2	SNR for New CVIP-ATAT Developed Algorithm
Image 1	12.14	10.536	13.667
Image 2	11.11	10.136	13.588
Image 3	11.669	10.859	12.523
Image 4	10.774	9.859	13.627
Image 5	12.952	9.055	13.31
Image 6	11.915	9.749	12.89
Image 7	12.296	10.419	13.038
Image 8	11.961	9.981	12.436
Image 9	10.595	9.736	13.019
Image 10	10.948	9.95	13.495
Image 11	10.166	9.016	12.779
Image 12	10.698	9.744	12.712
Image 13	11.747	10.124	12.96
Image 14	11.3	10.873	13.49
Image 15	10.794	9.356	12.197
AVG:	11.404	9.959	13.109

On average, the new algorithm has an SNR value that is 14.95% higher than Algorithm 1. Again, on average, the new algorithm has an SNR value that is 31.63% higher than Algorithm 2.

Percentage Increase (Alg.1 vs. NEW)	Percentage Increase (Alg.2 vs. NEW)
14.95%	31.63%

TABLE 8-2

Results of Comparing the Three Algorithms Using the Root-Mean-Square (RMS) Error Comparison Metric

Images	RMS for Algorithm 1	RMS for Algorithm 2	RMS for New Algorithm
Image 1	63.027	65.81	52.866
Image 2	70.967	69.389	53.354
Image 3	66.545	63.044	60.31
Image 4	73.76	71.773	53.109
Image 5	57.407	70.435	55.084
Image 6	64.684	73	57.812
Image 7	61.91	66.837	56.838
Image 8	64.339	70.814	60.919
Image 9	75.295	73.122	56.962
Image 10	72.303	71.105	53.495
Image 11	79.108	80.307	58.556
Image 12	79.73	73.048	59.01
Image 13	65.994	69.492	57.35
Image 14	69.429	62.924	53.958
Image 15	73.595	69.823	62.615
AVG:	69.206	70.061	56.815

On average, the new algorithm has an RMS value that is 17.90% lower than Algorithm 1. Again, on average, the new algorithm has an RMS value that is 18.91% lower than Algorithm 2.

Percentage Decrease (Alg.1 vs. NEW)	Percentage Decrease (Alg.2 vs. NEW)
−17.90%	−18.91%

TABLE 8-3

Results of Comparing the Three Algorithms Using the Pratt's Figure of Merit (FOM) Comparison Metric

Images	Pratt's FOM for Algorithm 1 (Scale Factor:1/9)	Pratt's FOM for Algorithm 2 (Scale Factor:1/9)	Pratt's FOM for New Algorithm (Scale Factor: 1/9)
Image 1	0.6506	0.6685	0.9115
Image 2	0.5361	0.5577	0.7301
Image 3	0.6418	0.5825	0.8812
Image 4	0.4877	0.5164	0.7267
Image 5	0.5972	0.5429	0.7219
Image 6	0.6197	0.5734	0.8005
Image 7	0.4996	0.58	0.7625
Image 8	0.5102	0.561	0.8653
Image 9	0.382	0.4453	0.8323
Image 10	0.3421	0.4513	0.8745
Image 11	0.4885	0.4961	0.8108
Image 12	0.4414	0.5158	0.8571
Image 13	0.3592	0.5245	0.7063
Image 14	0.3503	0.593	0.9135
Image 15	0.4205	0.5328	0.7627
AVG:	0.488	0.542	0.810

On average, the new algorithm has an FOM value that is 65.92% higher than Algorithm 1. Again, on average, the new algorithm has an FOM value that is 49.33% higher than Algorithm 2.

Percentage Increase (Alg.1 vs. NEW)	Percentage Increase (Alg.2 vs. NEW)
65.92%	49.33%

8.4.3 Conclusion

The results obtained from the new algorithm developed with CVIP-ATAT were better compared to the previous manually developed algorithms. The results illustrate the efficacy of the CVIP algorithm test and analysis tool (CVIP-ATAT) which enabled us to test many more functions and parameter values than could have been done manually. This task would have been impractical to do manually, one image at a time, one function at a time and one set of parameter values at a time. This is of particular importance in CVIP applications development as the best algorithm is often experimentally determined. This example shows that the CVIP-ATAT is very useful in processing numerous permutations of processes and function parameter values and is a valuable aid in algorithm development for CVIP applications.

8.5 CVIP-ATAT: Automatic Mask Creation of Gait Images

Portions of this section, reprinted with permission, are from "Automatic mask creation of thermographic gait images using CVIPtools ATAT", CB Stacey, SE Umbaugh, DJ Marino, J Sackman, Proceedings of SPIE, Vol. 11743, Thermosense: Thermal Infrared Applications XLII, April 11–15, 2021, https://doi.org/10.1117/12.2585646

8.5.1 Introduction

Using the CVIPtools development environment (Umbaugh, 2018), canine thermographic image analysis has been an active area of research at Southern Illinois University Edwardsville for many years (Gorre et al., 2020; Mishra et al., 2016; Afruz et al., 2010; McGowan et al., 2015; Lama et al., 2016; Alvandipour et al., 2017). This application was developed to automate the task of mask creation for thermographic veterinary images to be used in the study of a canine's gait. Gait can be defined as how an animal moves, whether it is walking, trotting or pacing. Understanding how the animal moves can assist the diagnosis of various pathologies that are common in certain breeds of dogs. The masks are used by the feature extraction software to find the ROI, and find features for the areas within the ROI. The masks are typically created manually (Afruz et al., 2010), a tedious task that leads to nonuniform masks when created by different individuals, so developing an algorithm to automate the process will save time and standardize the masks.

Using CVIP-ATAT, an optimal algorithm for the mask creation of 168 thermographic gait images is obtained. The best algorithm was created by converting the color images to monochrome by the luminance equation followed by the histogram thresholding segmentation method. After binary thresholding, an opening and closing morphological filter were applied to the images. This algorithm can be used to automate thermographic gait mask creation in an efficient manner.

8.5.2 Gait Analysis Images

The image set was provided by the Long Island Veterinary Specialists. The leg images were taken from three different positions giving different subsets including anterior (front), posterior (back) and lateral (side). The three subsets were combined when executing the experiment for a total of 168 images. These images are three band RGB images with datatype of byte. Another 168 ideal images were used as the "goal" of the experiment. These images are one band binary images. They use the byte datatype but are limited to values of only 0 or 255. The purpose of this experiment is to find the best algorithm that will take the original images and create images as close to the ideal images as possible. A thermographic image to be used in gait analysis and its ideal mask is shown in Figure 8.5-1.

8.5.3 Preprocessing

At the top of each image, a Meditherm tag was added during image creation. This tag is located at the top left corner of the image and is made up of white pixels and can interfere with mask creation and further image analysis. To remove the tag from processing, it was assigned to the background by making all of the pixels within zero. Figure 8.5-2 illustrates this process.

8.5.4 Algorithm Combinations

The flowchart for the algorithms being tested by the ATAT is shown in Figure 8.5-3. Here, we see five stages with each stage having between one and four different processes/parameters. The first stage involves simplifying the image from a three band RGB to a one band monochrome image. The purpose of this stage is to allow for faster processing for the remaining stages, particularly the segmentation stage. The color to monochrome change is implemented in two ways: (1) Averaging all three bands into one band or (2) calculating the luminance value as a ratio

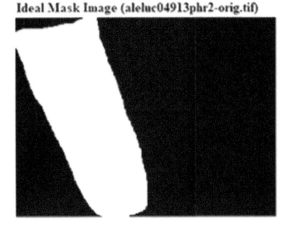

FIGURE 8.5-1
Thermographic gait image and mask example.

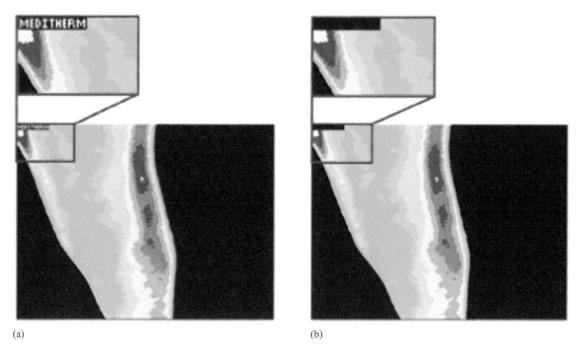

(a)   (b)

FIGURE 8.5-2
Preprocessing: removal of "MEDITHERM". (a) All the images had this word in the upper left, which will interfere with the analysis, (b) after removal of the word by replacing the box with zeros.

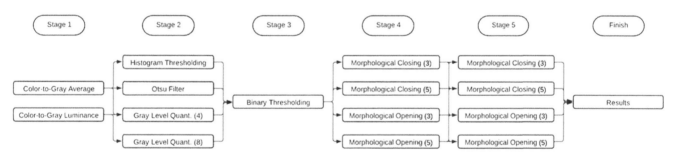

FIGURE 8.5-3
Algorithmic combination flowchart. Here, we see the five stage algorithm testing performed using the CVIP-ATAT.

of the three RGB bands. These methods have the same effect of maintaining the shape while losing thermographic information. These images are then sent into stage two.

The second stage involves further simplification of the image using segmentation (Gorre et al., 2020; Mishra et al., 2016; Afruz et al., 2010). Histogram thresholding and gray level quantization results in gray level images with reduced unique pixel values. The Otsu method will result in a black and white binary image. Examples for each of these segmentation methods are shown in Figure 8.5-4. The Otsu and gray level quantization methods are discussed in Chapter 3. The histogram thresholding function (Umbaugh, 2018; Lim and Lee, 1990) takes a Gaussian mask with a specified variance and works by convolving it with the histogram. This will group similar pixels together into one value by finding peaks during convolution. Peaks are areas in the pixel histogram where many pixels had the same or similar values. If there are no obvious peaks, the thresholding may also group gray levels together with constant values. Essentially, the process uses peaks in the histogram to group likewise gray levels into a single value. This can, for example, result in 255 unique pixel values being mapped into less than ten values, resulting in a simplified image.

The third stage is implemented to create a binary image for comparison to the ideal images; although the Otsu method outputs a binary image in stage 2, the other two segmentation methods do not. Binary thresholding is used to create a black and white image where the only allowed pixel values are 0 or 255. This thresholding method,

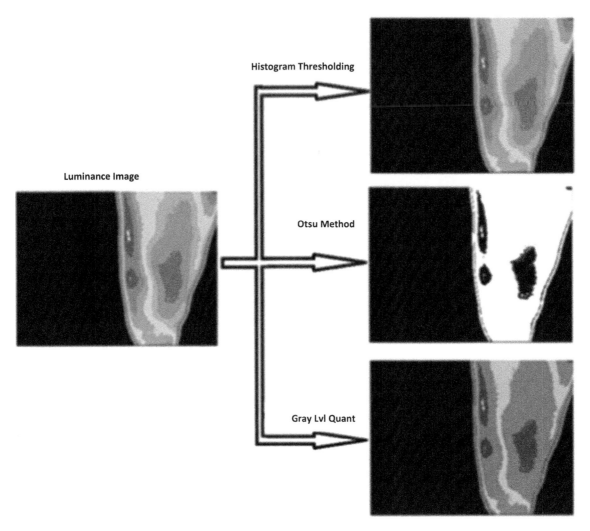

Histogram Thresholding

Luminance Image

Otsu Method

Gray Lvl Quant

FIGURE 8.5-4
Stage 2: segmentation methods.

depending on the chosen gray level, does a good job of maintaining the entire area of importance and simplifies the image for stage 4. For the ATAT experiments, values of 5–40 were used in increments of 5. It was determined that the value of 25 was optimal.

The final two stages use morphological filters to fill in holes and smooth out the mask outlines. In image morphology, opening is defined as an erosion followed by a dilation and closing is a dilation followed by an erosion. To investigate the best option(s), we decided to use opening and closing filters with a circular structuring element and vary the order of execution by using both in the two stages. This experiment will feature 16 combinations, with block sizes of 3 and 5 in stages 4 and 5.

8.5.5   Results Analysis

The final step for ATAT algorithm development is analysis of the results. The shape analysis will be accomplished using the DICE coefficient (Dice, 1945) and the Jaccard index (Jaccard, 1912; Tanimoto, 1958). To facilitate the analysis, the comparison measurements are formatted using an Excel sheet to display the results for each image separately. ATAT also gives the option to include a threshold value for each comparison metric. This threshold value will be compared to the measured value to determine success. The thresholds chosen for the DICE and Jaccard are 0.9 and 0.8, respectively. This means that any image that resulted in a value greater than the threshold was evaluated as successful and marked as TRUE. These results are stored in the *Image Results* file. This file can be referenced to investigate issues with individual images which can help to modify the algorithm if acceptable results are not found.

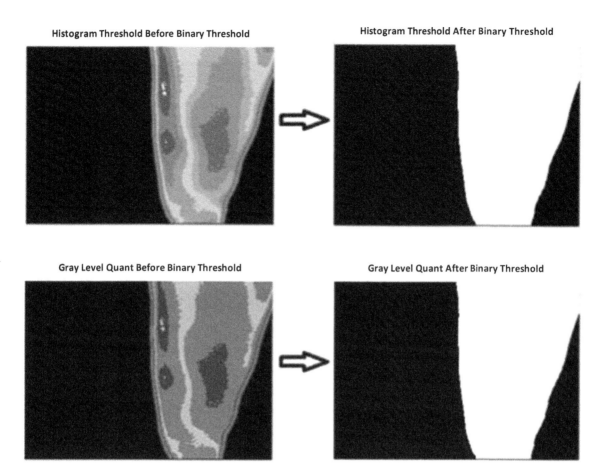

FIGURE 8.5-5
Stage 3: binary thresholding. The ATAT experiments used a range of 5–40 in increments of 5. It was found that the value of 25 was optimal, which was used for these images.

To examine the success of each algorithm, we use the *Algorithm Results* file where we have chosen the average and standard deviation options in the ATAT. This option will take all of the images from a specific algorithm and average its comparison measurements, and it finds the standard deviation for each algorithm. This provides a method to compare each algorithm's success across the entire image set. The algorithm names are combined with the abbreviations from each function in the specific algorithm that created it. Figure 8.5-6 shows the first few lines in the *Algorithm Results* spreadsheet and describes how the algorithms are named.

The combination of functions, parameters and stages in the experiment results in 128 algorithms. With 128 algorithms and 168 images, the number of resultant images is 21,504. Looking through 21 thousand images creates a tedious task, and it can be reduced by creating subsets based on each segmentation process, resulting in 8 algorithms.

	A	B	C	D	E
1	Algorithm	DICE Average	Jacc Average	DICE StdDev	Jacc StdDev
2	C2GL_HistThresh_BT25_MorphOCir5_MorphCCir5	0.946782883	0.902263386	0.04592056	0.076316818
3	_C2GL_HistThresh_BT25_MorphCCir5_MorphOCir5	0.946732684	0.902173979	0.045933537	0.076325642
4	_C2GL_HistThresh_BT25_MorphOCir5_MorphCCir3	0.946654549	0.902041832	0.04599502	0.07642706
5	_C2GL_HistThresh_BT25_MorphOCir3_MorphCCir5	0.94664103	0.902032491	0.046104087	0.076590936
6	_C2GL_HistThresh_BT25_MorphCCir5_MorphOCir3	0.946608185	0.901974383	0.046116374	0.076599139
7	_C2GL_HistThresh_BT25_MorphCCir3_MorphOCir5	0.946578746	0.901907751	0.046018609	0.076452574

FIGURE 8.5-6
Sample algorithm results spreadsheet. The first algorithm has a combination of color-to-gray luminance (C2GL), Histogram Thresholding (HistThresh), binary thresholding (BT25) and two stages of morphological closing (MorphCCir5).

TABLE 8-4

Combined Stage One to Three Algorithm Results

Algorithm	DICE Avg	Jacc Avg	DICE Std	Jacc Std
Avg_GLQ4	0.9423388	0.89458175	0.0481321	0.0796231
Avg_GLQ8	0.9310307	0.87693218	0.064709	0.0991779
Avg_Hist	0.9310307	0.87693218	0.064709	0.0991779
Avg_Otsu	0.9350457	0.88330294	0.0605008	0.0936758
Light_GLQ4	0.9442881	0.89765731	0.0448053	0.0755134
Light_GLQ8	0.9442881	0.89765731	0.0448053	0.0755134
Light_Hist	0.9463643	0.90152504	0.046056	0.0764817
Light_Otsu	0.8638146	0.77173823	0.095536	0.1362051

TABLE 8-5

Success Rate of Best Algorithm

Comparison Algorithm	# Images Successful	# Images Unsuccessful	Percentage of Success (%)
Dice coefficient (0.9)	146	22	86.9
Jaccard index (0.8)	151	17	89.9

The average and standard deviation of the error metrics for the images in each subset are shown in Table 8-4. These values were then analyzed to determine the most efficient segmentation method.

Using Table 8-4, some information about the different algorithms can be determined. First, the luminance versus average measurements seem to depend on the segmentation involved. For instance, the luminance method created better results with the gray level quantization and histogram thresholding methods, but performed much worse with Otsu segmentation. In fact, the luminance–Otsu combination performed the worst out of all algorithms. The best algorithm, highlighted in yellow, is the luminance and histogram thresholding combination with higher averages using both the Dice and Jaccard measurements. The relatively small standard deviations of these two measurements indicate that the mean is a fair representation of the values for most of the images. It is the only algorithm to have both average measurements above 0.9. Further analysis showed that the best performing individual algorithm, with the highest Dice and Jaccard averages, used a morphological opening block size of 5 and the closing block size of 5.

The acceptable threshold was then determined experimentally by surveying the images. It was found that the Dice coefficient values were always larger than the Jaccard index by approximately 0.1 leading to their respective thresholds also being separated by 0.1. The threshold for the Dice measurements is 0.9 and the threshold for the Jaccard index was 0.8. At these thresholds, the resultant images retain an appropriate amount of important object information while not adding an unacceptable number of pixels outside of the object.

Table 8-5 identifies the success rates of the two error methods with the best algorithm. It can be seen that the Dice coefficient with a success threshold of 0.9 had an 86.9% success rate. The Jaccard scored a success rate of 89.9% with a success threshold of 0.8. These measurements determine how close the result image is to the ideal image. Each image that passed the Jaccard test also passed the Dice test.

8.5.6 Conclusion

Using CVIPtools ATAT, an experiment was created using 168 thermographic gait images with 128 unique algorithms resulting in 21,504 resultant images. These algorithms were further categorized into 8 subsets, and statistics were calculated for each subset. Based on this analysis, the optimal algorithm is as follows: (1) color-to-gray luminance, (2) histogram thresholding segmentation, (3) binary thresholding at 25, (4) morphological opening, circular structuring element, 5×5 mask, and (5) morphological closing, circular structuring element, 5×5 mask. The success rate of the optimal algorithm for the DICE coefficient was 87.5% and for the Jaccard index was 89.9%.

References

Afruz, J., Phelps, J., Umbaugh, S.E., Marino, D.J., Loughin, C.A., Automatic mask creation and feature analysis for detection of IVDD in canines. *Proceedings of 5th International Conference on Computer Sciences and Convergence Information Technology*, Nov 30–Dec 2, 2010, Seoul, Korea.

Alvandipour, M., Umbaugh, S.E., Mishra, D., Dahal, R., Lama, N., Marino, D.J., Sackman, J. Thermographic image analysis for classification of ACL rupture disease, bone cancer, and feline hyperthyroid, with Gabor filters. *Proceedings of SPIE Commercial + Scientific Sensing and Imaging, Thermosense: Thermal Infrared Applications XXXIX*, Anaheim, CA, Vol. 10214, April 2017, Doi: 10.1117/12.2261753.

Dice, L.R., Measures of the amount of ecologic association between species. *Ecology*, Vol. 26, No. 3, pp. 297–302. JSTOR, 1945.

Gorre, N., Umbaugh, S.E. Marino, D.J., Sackman, J., Identification of bone cancer in canine thermograms. *SPIE Defense + Commercial Sensing 2020, Proceedings of SPIE, Thermosense: Thermal Infrared Applications XLII*, Conference Online, Vol. 11409, April 28–30 2020.

Jaccard, P., The distribution of the flora in the alpine zone 1. *New Phytologist*, Vol. 11, pp. 37–50, 1912.

McGowan, L., Loughin, C., Marino, D., Umbaugh, S.E., Liu, P., Amini, M. Medical infrared imaging of normal and dysplastic elbows in dogs. *Veterinary Surgery*, September 2015, Doi: 10.1111/vsu.12372.

Mishra, D. Umbaugh, S.E., Lama, N., Dahal, R., Marino, D., Sackman, J., Image processing and pattern recognition with CVIPtools MATLAB toolbox: automatic creation of masks for veterinary thermographic images. *Proceedings of SPIE Optical Engineering + Applications Conference: Applications of Digital Image Processing XXXIX*, San Diego, CA, August, Vol. 9971, 2016.

Lama, N., Umbaugh, S.E., Mishra, D., Dahal, R., Marino, D., Sackman, J. Thermography based diagnosis of ruptured anterior cruciate ligament (ACL) in canines. *Proceedings of SPIE Optical Engineering + Applications Conference: Applications of Digital Image Processing XXXIX*, San Diego, CA, Vol. 9971, August, 2016.

Lim, Y., Lee, S., On color segmentation algorithm based on the thresholding and fuzzy c-means techniques. *Pattern Recognition*, Vol. 23, No. 9, pp, 935–952, 1990.

Umbaugh, S.E., *Digital Image Processing and Analysis: Applications with MATLAB and CVIPtools*, 3rd Edition, Boca Raton, FL: CRC Press, 2018.

Tanimoto, T. T. *An Elementary Mathematical Theory of Classification and Prediction*, New York: International Business Machines Corporation, 1958.

8.6   CVIP Feature Extraction and Pattern Classification Tool

8.6.1   Overview and Capabilities

The Computer Vision and Image Processing Feature Extraction and Pattern Classification Tool, CVIP-FEPC, was created to facilitate the development of both human and computer vision applications. The primary application area is computer vision, but it can be used, for example, as an aid in the development of image compression schemes for human vision applications. This can be done by helping to determine salient image features that must be retained for a given compression scheme. Conversely, computer vision applications are essentially deployed image analysis systems for a specific application, so the feature extraction and pattern classification is an integral part of all computer vision systems.

The primary function of this tool is to explore feature extraction and pattern classification and allow the user to perform batch processing with large image sets and is thus much more efficient than processing one image at a time with CVIPtools. It allows the user to select the features and pattern classification parameters for the automatic processing of these large image sets. CVIP-FEPC enables the user to easily specify the training and test sets and run multiple experiments in an efficient manner. The current implementation includes the capability of performing leave-one-out experiments, and it will run combinations of all features and parameter ranges selected. Its primary purpose is to find the best parameters for a particular application in order to best classify the image objects of interest.

This tool is designed to work with a set of images that have binary masks that have been created for the objects of interest – one object per image. These masks can be created manually with CVIPtools, automatically via an algorithm developed with ATAT, or many image database applications will have the masks available. In general, the user will load the images, specify the classes, select the features, select the test set, choose the pattern classification parameters and then let the program process the entire image set. An output file will be created with the results for the experiment.

8.6.2 How to Use CVIP-FEPC

8.6.2.1 Running CVIP-FEPC

The easiest way to invoke CVIP-FEPC is by clicking on the icon on the CVIPtools toolbar (see Figure 8.6-1a). After this, the main window will appear as shown in Figure 8.6-1b. CVIP-FEPC requires two files: CVIP-FEPC.exe and

(a)

(b)

FIGURE 8.6-1
Invoking CVIP-FEPC. (a) To invoke CVIP-FEPC, select the CVIP-FEPC button on the top right of the CVIPtools toolbar. (b) The main widow for CVIP-FEPC will appear as shown here. The Test type selection buttons are in the lower right corner.

CVIPtools.dll. The GUI is implemented in file CVIP-FEPC.exe. All C functions for image analysis and processing are implemented in file CVIPtools.dll, which is invoked by CVIP-FEPC.exe. Alternately, CVIP-FEPC can be invoked by running the executable directly.

The user determines the type of test to be performed by selection of the buttons in the lower right of the main window (Figure 8.6-1b). The test can be performed with separate training and test sets by selecting *Test/Training Set* or by performing cross-validation and using the entire set with the *Leave-One-Out* selection. Additionally, a *Single Test* can be performed using only the selected set of features or the user can select *Combinatoric* which will run multiple experiments using all possible combinations of features.

8.6.2.2 Creating a New Project

The first step in starting a new project is to organize the images. The images are put in separate folders (directories) based on their class, as shown in Figure 8.6-2. Here, we see 22 separate folders, corresponding to 22 different classes. Each folder should contain all the images in one class and also a subfolder called *Masks*, where all the binary masks for the object of interest in the corresponding class images will be stored. The binary masks will

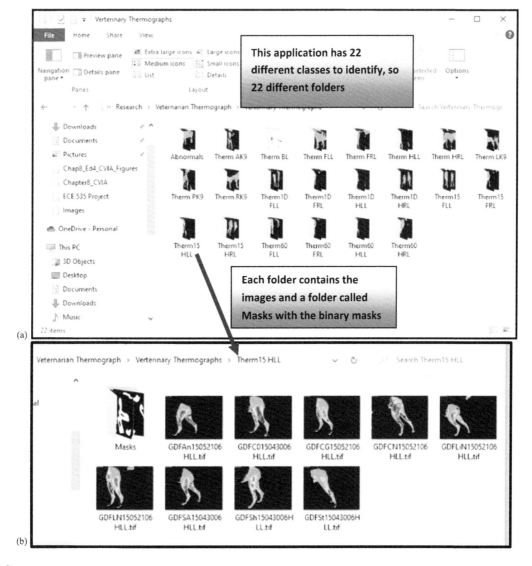

FIGURE 8.6-2
Organization of the image folder. (a) Arrange folders (directories) so that each class has its own folder. All the images for that class will be in the corresponding folder. (b) Each class folder will also contain a subfolder called *Masks*, which contains the binary masks for the object of interest in the original images. The name of the original image and the corresponding mask image should be the same, although the file name extensions may differ.

contain a "1" (typically 255 for 8-bit image data) for the object, and a binary "0" for the background. All the images and their corresponding masks should have same name, but the file extensions may differ. Note that these mask images can be created with CVIPtools using *Utilities->Create->Border Mask*. Be sure to save the border mask images as *bmp* or another uncompressed file format. If they are saved as compressed files, for example, *jpg*, the resulting image may contain more than two gray level values and will not be proper masks.

8.6.2.3   Entering Classes in CVIP-FEPC

The classes are declared in CVIP-FEPC by clicking on *Settings->Class List* in the tool, which brings up the *Class List* window as shown in Figure 8.6-3. Next, the new class name is entered in the *New Class* box, and clicking on the *Add* button adds the class name, as shown in Figure 8.6-3b. Additional class names can be added in a similar manner. After all the desired classes have been entered, click on *OK* button to go back to the main window. All the classes added to the CVIP-FEPC tool can be seen by clicking on the arrow next to the *Class* box.

8.6.2.4   Adding Images and Associated Classes

Images can be added to application by clicking on the *Add files* button from the selection window which allows you to browse for the location of images, as shown in Figure 8.6-4a. Images added to the application can be viewed clicking on the names of the images or by using the arrow buttons beside the image. We can see the original image, mask and the masked image by selecting corresponding radio buttons, as shown in Figure 8.6-4b. All the images in a folder, corresponding to one class, can be added to the application concurrently by selecting them all and clicking *Open*. Now, the class can be assigned by selecting all the images and selecting the class name from the *Class* dropdown box. The class names will be displayed in the *Class* column on the right side, by the image name, as shown in Figure 8.6-4c. This process continues until all the images have been loaded and the classes assigned.

8.6.2.5   Applying Feature Extraction and Pattern Classification

After assigning classes to every image, desired features for the experiment(s) are chosen using the *Feature Selection* window of CVIP-FEPC. The *Features* button in the main window opens the *Feature Selection* window, as shown in Figure 8.6-5a. The user can select the features of interest with the checkboxes and then enter the desired parameter values. After the features have been selected, the user clicks the *OK* button and is now ready to define the pattern classification method(s) to be used. Clicking on the *Classification* button opens the *Pattern Classification* window shown in Figure 8.6-5.b. Here, the user selects the *Data Normalization Method(s)*, the *Distance and Similarity Measure(s)* and the *Classification Algorithm(s)* to be used. Note that if the *Combinatoric* test type has been selected, the buttons that only allow one choice at a time will switch to checkboxes, which allow for multiple selections.

8.6.2.6   Running a Single Test with Training and Test Sets

To run a single test with training and test sets, the user must select the *Test Type* with the *Train/Test Set* and *Single Test* options (Figure 8.6-6). The next step is to determine the training and test sets. The user can select the test set by clicking on the check boxes by the image names, and the unchecked images will automatically be used for the training set. Alternately, the *Random* button can be used to randomly select the test, as shown in Figure 8.6-6a. Next, the test is run by clicking the *Test* button shown in Figure 8.6-6b. After the pattern classification test is complete, a popup window will open showing where the Results file is stored. By default, the results are stored in the *FEPC_Results* folder on user's desktop. After an experimental run, the user may desire to verify or cross-validate success results by swapping the training and test sets. This is easily accomplished by clicking the *Invert* button, as shown in Figure 8.6-6c, which will swap these sets. Following this, the user selects the *Run Test* button and the test will be performed with the previous training and test sets interchanged. If similar results are obtained, this will increase our confidence in the validity of the success results previously obtained.

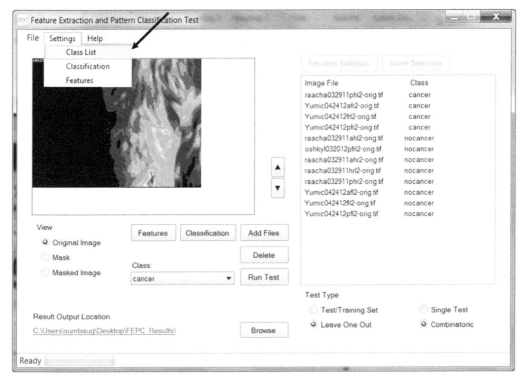

(a)

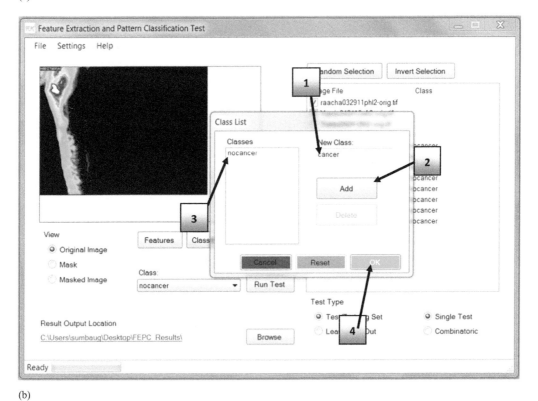

(b)

FIGURE 8.6-3
Entering the classes. (a) Select *Settings->Class List*, this will bring up the *Class List* window. (b) In the *Class List* window, enter the class name, then click *Add* and the class name shows up in the *Classes* box. When the user is done entering all the classes, click the *OK* button. Here, we see the user adding a class name *cancer* after a class *nocancer* has already been put on the list.

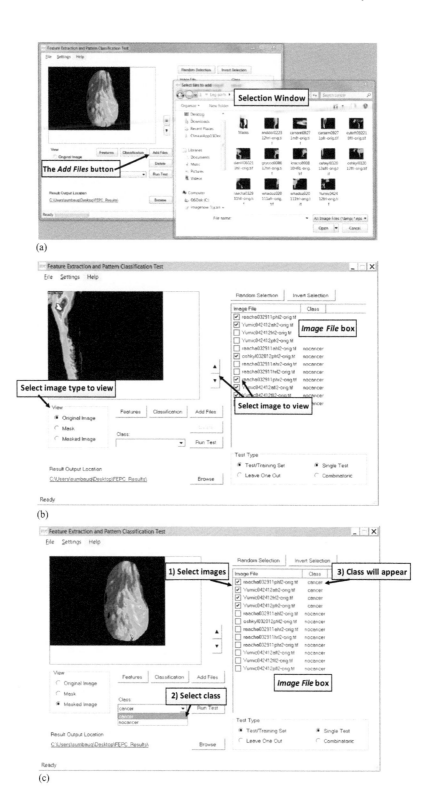

FIGURE 8.6-4

Adding image files and associated classes. (a) Click the *Add Files* button, and the selection window will appear, here the user can select the images to be used. Image names will then appear in the *Image File* box of the main window. (b) An image, its mask image or the corresponding masked image can be viewed by selecting one in the *View* section. The user can scroll through the images with the arrows next to the *Image File* box. (c) The user can associate the class with the images by selecting the image(s) in the *Image File* box and then the class in the *Class* dropdown box.

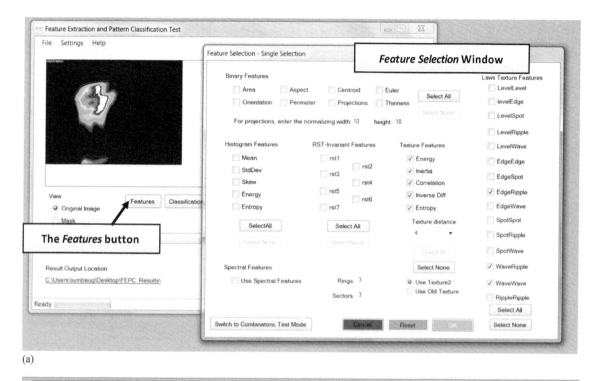

(a)

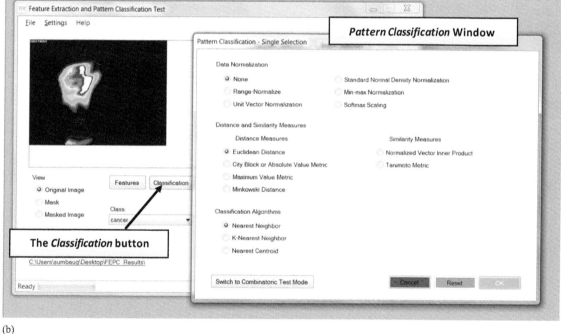

(b)

FIGURE 8.6-5

Feature selection and pattern classification parameters. (a) The *Features* button opens the *Feature Selection* window. Here, the user selects the features of interest for the experiment(s), by checking the corresponding checkboxes and entering desired parameters values. (b) The *Classification* button opens the *Pattern Classification* window. Here, the user selects the *Data Normalization Method(s)*, the *Distance and Similarity Measure(s)* and the *Classification Algorithm(s)* to be used.

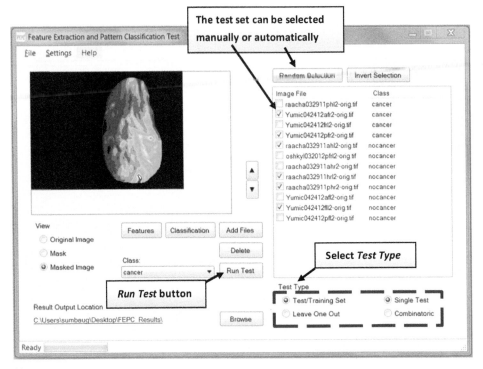

(a)

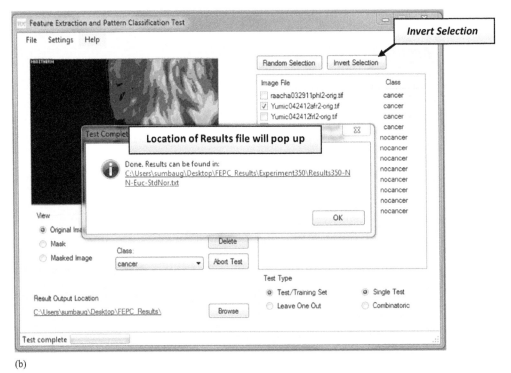

(b)

FIGURE 8.6-6

Single test with training and test sets. (a) The *Test Type* is selected as *Test/Training* and *Single Test*. The user can select the test set manually with the checkboxes or automatically via the *Random Selection* button. Unchecked images will be used for the training set. The *Run Test* button will perform the selected test and (b) output a results file which contains information regarding the classification success rates. The location and name of the results file will appear; the default location is the *FEPC_Results* folder on the desktop, but can be changed with the *Browse* button. A validation experiment can be performed by swapping the training and test sets with the *Invert* button.

8.6.2.7 The Result File

The results file from the pattern classification test contain (1) the selected features, (2) the classification algorithm, (3) the data normalization method, (4) the distance/similarity metric, (5) the name of each image in the test set and its class along with how it was classified in the test and (6) the classification success rates. The success rate table, at the bottom of the file, contains the number of images identified correctly, the number of images misclassified, also the percentage correct for each class. A sample result file is shown in Figure 8.6-7. In addition to the *Result* file, a *Test* set feature file and a *Train* set feature file will be stored in the *FEPC_Results* folder.

8.6.2.8 Running a Leave-One-Out Test in Combinatoric Mode

In addition to the training and test set paradigm, the user can perform *leave-one-out* experiments, which will provide basic cross-validation when only a limited number of images are available. In this case, each image is the test set for one iteration and all the others are used as the training set, and the process automatically continues throughout the entire set. Additionally, the CVIP-FEPC allows the user to operate experiments in combinatoric mode, which will perform separate experiments for each combination of features and pattern classification parameters selected. Operating the FEPC in this mode provides the most powerful experimental method, and

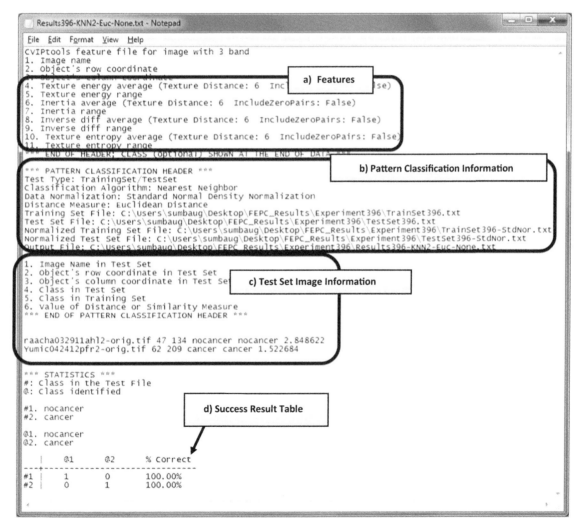

FIGURE 8.6-7
The result file. (a) It contains a list of the features used, (b) The pattern classification parameters, (c) Individual test set images, the correct class, the class found in this test, and the distance measure, (d) Success results. Here, we have the number of images incorrectly classified, correctly classified and the classification success rate for each class.

depending on the features and pattern classification parameters selected and the number of images included, it may take hours or days to complete all the experiments.

Figure 8.6-8 shows using the FEPC in this mode and the corresponding output file. The output file is a spreadsheet where each row contains the parameters and the results for one entire leave one-out experiment.

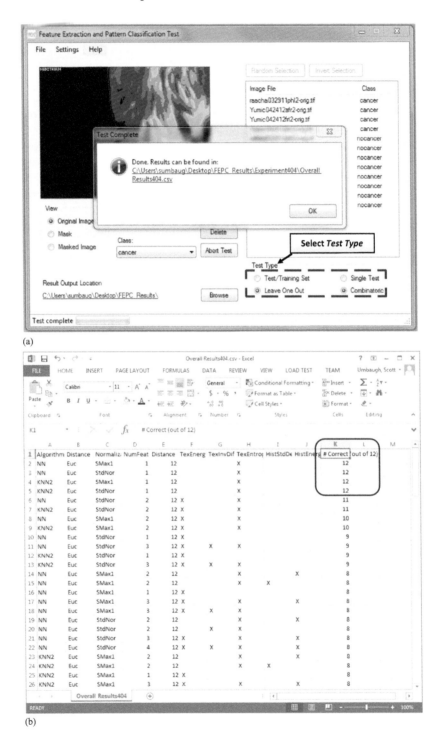

(a)

(b)

FIGURE 8.6-8
***Leave-one-out* testing in *combinatoric* mode.** (a) After selecting *Leave-One-Out* and *Combinatoric* for test type and running the test, the FEPC will pop up the output file location. By clicking on the output file name. (b) an Excel spreadsheet will open which contains a summary of results from all the experiments. Each row contains all the parameters for each experiment. If they are sorted by the *number correct* in the last column, the experiments with the best success will be at the top. Here, we see that for 4 of the experiments, all 12 were classified correctly.

These can be sorted by the last column to determine which experiments, and the corresponding features and pattern classification parameters, provided the best results. This file is called the *Overall Results* file and files for each individual experiment, such as shown in Figure 8.6-7, are in the same file folder and contain all the details for each experiment.

8.7 CVIP-FEPC: Application Development with Thermograms

8.7.1 Introduction and Overview

The application involves preliminary investigation into the efficacy of thermographic images for diagnosis of bone cancer in canines. Pattern classification algorithms were investigated for *cancer* and *nocancer* classes of the pathology. The eventual goal for the research is to be able to differentiate normal and abnormal thermographic patterns in canines as a diagnostic and research tool. In this example, we used thermographic images of canines taken from various views with the two classes. We used the leave-one-out and combinatoric options as experimental methods, as shown in Figure 8.6-8. The features and classification methods were selected based on preliminary experimentation with CVIPtools and a few sample images.

8.7.2 Setting Up Experiments

The first step is to setup the image file organization. Here, we have two classes so we create a *Cancer* and *Nocancer* file folder and subfolders in each one called *Masks*. The images are added to the FEPC using the *Add Files* button, as shown in Figure 8.7-1. Here, we see the *Cancer* folder images and masks being added. A class name is assigned to the added images, *cancer*, and another set of images are added and the *nocancer* class name is assigned for second folder of images.

The *Feature Selection* window is opened by clicking on the *Features* button. As shown in Figure 8.7-2, we next select two histogram features: standard deviation and energy; three texture features: energy, inverse difference and entropy. We set the texture distance parameter to range from 6 to 12 in increments of 2. After the features are selected, we click *OK* and return to the main window.

The next step is to select the pattern classification methods for this experiment. This is done by clicking the *Classification* button on the main window to bring up the *Pattern Classification* window, as shown in Figure 8.7-3.

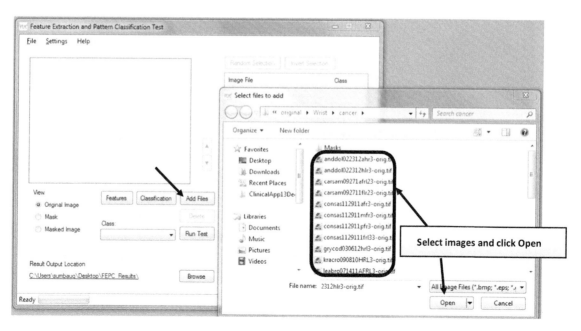

FIGURE 8.7-1
Adding images. Here, we see the cancer class of images being added to CVIP-FEPC.

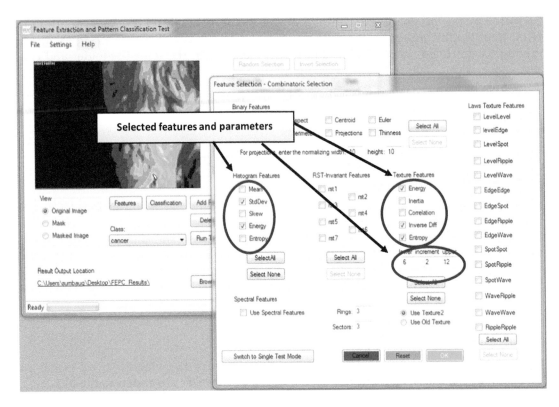

FIGURE 8.7-2
Feature selection. In this case, we select two histogram features: standard deviation and energy; three texture features: energy, inverse difference and entropy. We set the texture distance parameter to range from 6 to 12 in increments of 2. After the features are selected, we click *OK* and return to the main window.

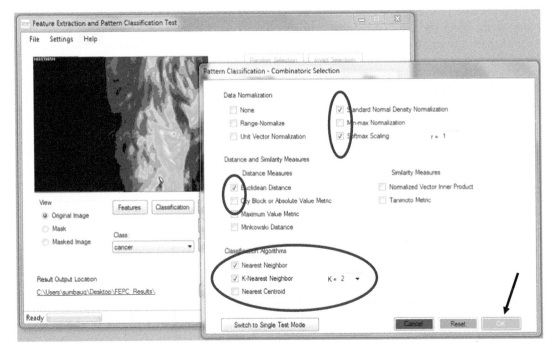

FIGURE 8.7-3
Selecting the pattern classification methods. First, we select the data normalization methods, selecting *SND* and *Softmax Scaling*. Next, we select the *Euclidean distance* as our error metric. Finally, we select *Nearest Neighbor* and *K-Nearest Neighbor* with $K = 2$ for our classification algorithms. Clicking the OK button returns to the main window.

Here, we see that we have selected standard normal density (SND) and softmax scaling for data normalization methods, Euclidean distance only and nearest neighbor and nearest neighbor K-nearest neighbor with $K=2$ for the classification algorithms.

8.7.3 Running the Experiments and Analyzing Results

The experiments, or test, are performed by clicking on the *Run Test* button, and the results are stored on the desktop in the *FEPC_Results* folder (see Figure 8.7-4). Figure 8.7-5 shows that when multiple distance values are selected for the texture features, the CVIP-FEPC creates a separate folder for each value. Figure 8.7-5b has the experimental results in the Overall Results spreadsheet corresponding to a texture distance of 10. Here, we see that 4 of the experiments had a 100% success in classification by classifying 12 out of 12 correct.

Figure 8.7-6 shows an individual result file, which corresponds to one algorithm defined by (1) a specific set of features and parameters, (2) a data normalization method, (3) a distance or similarity metric and (4) a classification method. The success rate is 100% for both classes, *cancer* and *nocancer*. We can see in these files the distance parameter values for each image in the test set, as well as all the other information applicable to each particular test run. With this information, the test can be repeated at a later date, which is often necessary in application development for verification and to test repeatability. Additionally, the details may be used for further application-specific analysis and investigation. Table 8-6 shows the first two test sample results from the result file in Figure 8.7-6. This illustrates how the pattern classification header and the results are related.

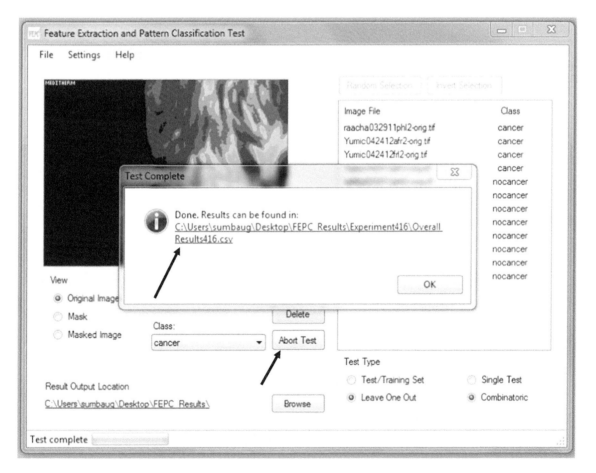

FIGURE 8.7-4
Running the test. The *Run Test* button initiates the process and changes to *Abort Test* during the experimental run. When the test run is completed, the path and file name for the resultant information is shown in a popup window.

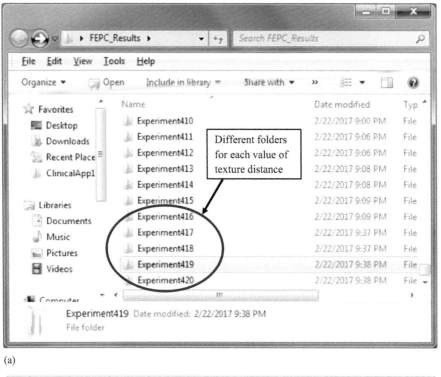

(a)

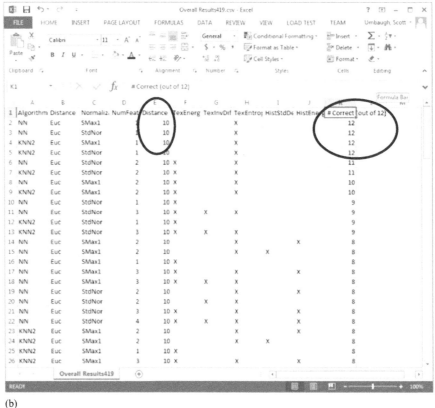

(b)

FIGURE 8.7-5

Overall results. (a) When the user selects multiple distance values for the texture features, the CVIP-FEPC creates a separate folder for each distance value, as shown here. (b) Here, we opened the *Overall Result* file for Experiment419, which had a texture distance of 10. If we sort these by the "# Correct" column, we see that four of the algorithms had 100% success.

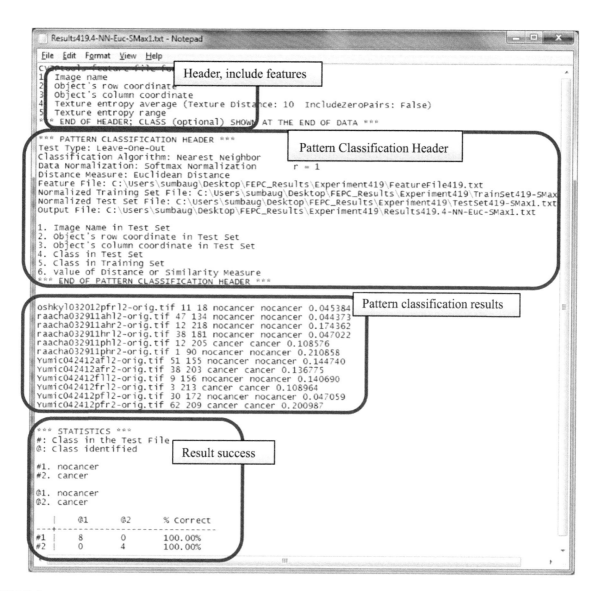

FIGURE 8.7-6

Individual result files. Here is one result file from the folder Experiment419 from Figure 8.7-5 that had a 100% success rate. The header, numbered 1–5, lists the values stored in the individual feature files, which are also in the main folder, in this case Experiment419. The Pattern Classification header contains all the information for the pattern classification parameters; and the numbered items, 1–6, list the order of appearance in the pattern classification results.

TABLE 8-6

First two test sample results from the result file in Figure 8.7-6.

Image Name in Test Set	Object's Row Coordinate in Test Set	Object's Column Coordinate in Test Set	Class in TEST SET	Class in Training Set (of Closest Match)	Value of Distance or Similarity Measure
oshkyl032012pfrl2-orig.tif	11	18	nocancer	nocancer	0.045384
raacha032911ahl2-orig.tif	47	134	nocancer	nocancer	0.044373

8.7.4 Conclusion

The investigation into the efficacy of thermographic images for diagnosis of bone cancer in canines was explored. Pattern classification algorithms were developed for the *cancer* and *nocancer* classes of the pathology. Success rates of 100% were achieved for the two classes. These results are preliminary, only 12 images were used, and the experiment was performed primarily to illustrate the use of CVIP FEPC for algorithm development.

One major advantage of the CVIP-FEPC tool is that any number of images can be processed with no additional effort other than computer processing time. The capability to process and analyze many images is typically necessary for application development, since in most real applications hundreds or thousands of images are needed to create a robust algorithm or system. The CVIP-FEPC is an invaluable tool for algorithm development involving feature extraction and selection followed by pattern classification. The following section explores a more complete investigation into the identification of canine bone cancer using thermographic imaging.

8.8 CVIP-FEPC: Identification of Bone Cancer in Canine Thermograms

Portions of this section, reprinted with permission, are from "Identification of Bone Cancer in Canine Thermograms", N Gorre, SE Umbaugh, DJ Marino, J Sackman, SPIE Defense + Commercial Sensing 2020, Proceedings of SPIE, Vol. 11409, Thermosense: Thermal Infrared Applications XLII, April 28–30 2020.

8.8.1 Introduction

Veterinary medical practice uses a variety of imaging techniques such as radiology, computed tomography (CT) and magnetic resonance imaging (MRI) for diagnosis. But harmful radiation during imaging, expensive equipment setup and excessive time consumption are major drawbacks of these techniques (Ng, 2009). Medical science considers temperature as one of the major health indicators. As per medical thermography, the presence of disease may alter the thermal patterns of the skin surface, and here, we investigate the potential correlation between skin temperature patterns and certain pathological conditions (Marino and Loughin 2010). We have found that these thermal patterns can differentiate between normal and abnormal in the thermographic images by application of computer vision methods.

Thermographic imaging captures infrared radiation to produce images whose pixel values are mapped into appropriate colors that represent the temperature distribution. It will capture the thermal patterns on the body surface which can indicate various underlying pathologies. If there is a pathological symptom in the one part of the body, the pattern of thermal activity in that part can be changed comparatively and detected using thermal imaging (Loughin and Marino 2007). In veterinary practices, the scanning time is critical as the animals may be uncooperative and even aggressive due to increased pain and fear, which makes it difficult for animals to remain still for the time periods necessary for standard imaging without resorting to sedation. With thermography, the imaging process is similar to taking a photograph with a standard camera, which alleviates the time and sedation issue. Also, it addresses the shortcomings of the existing imaging systems as it is a non-invasive technique that avoids harmful radiation and is less expensive in terms of cost and time (Redaelli et al., 2014).

The algorithm being investigated here is for the detection of canine bone cancer in various body parts such as elbow/knee and wrist. Specifically, we investigate the use of the Laws texture features to determine whether results can be improved compared to the previous studies (Umbaugh et al., 2016; Umbaugh and Amini, 2012; Subedi et al., 2014). In the previous study, only the histogram and standard co-occurrence matrix-based texture features were investigated. For these experiments, the Laws features were divided into four different sets to find the best set of features for classification. Due to the extensive processing time required, initial experiments were performed with the optimal pattern classification parameters from the previous study (Subedi et al., 2014) to select the most likely optimal Laws texture features. Next, comprehensive experiments were performed with the FEPC by combining the best Laws features with the histogram and co-occurrence texture features to determine if the Laws features improve the results.

8.8.2 Clinical Application Development

8.8.2.1 Image Database

Images were provided by the Long Island Veterinary Specialists (LIVS), one of the largest research veterinary hospitals and clinics in New York. The database includes different body locations and views: elbow/knee with anterior and lateral views and wrist with lateral view. Images are linearly remapped to 8-bit, 256 gray level data, using a temperature range of 19°C–40°C. This temperature range covers the entire range of interest for the canine images. Figure 8.8-1 shows a sample thermographic image, remapped temperature data in gray scale and the corresponding pseudocolor image. Table 8-7 shows the size of the image sets and corresponding classes used for algorithm development.

8.8.2.2 Feature Extraction and Pattern Classification

The CVIP-FEPC software was used for feature extraction and pattern classification. This software was specifically designed for running combinatoric tests which performs experiments with all the different combinations of selected features, data normalizations and pattern classification methods. The output from the FEPC consists of three different files: (1) a feature file, (2) individual experiment results files with corresponding training and test sets of images and (3) an *Overall Results* file which contains a summary of all the individual results. The summary file has information for the classification success rate and experimental parameters for each particular experiment. The feature file contains feature vectors extracted from all the images that are used as input for pattern classification. The individual experiment result file contains all the details for each experiment along with their respective sensitivity and specificity. These results were then analyzed to determine the most useful features, error metrics, normalization and classification methods to provide a robust and optimal classification algorithm. Note that, in the results section of this paper, the experiment with the highest overall success rate was selected as the best algorithm.

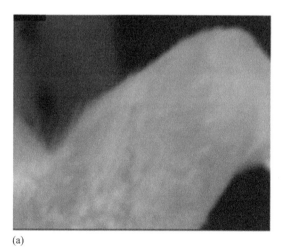 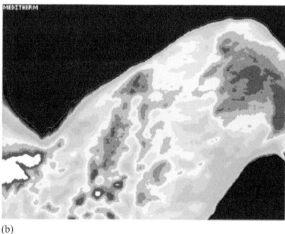

(a) (b)

FIGURE 8.8-1
Canine thermogram. (a) Temperature remapped to 256 gray levels and (b) temperature mapped to 18 colors. Note: this particular limb is positive for bone cancer.

TABLE 8-7

Size of Image Sets Used for Bone Cancer Classification

Pathology	Camera View	Numbers of Images for Each Class in the Database
Bone cancer (Elbow/Knee)	Anterior	20 Cancer & 21 No Cancer
Bone cancer (Elbow/Knee)	Lateral	29 Cancer & 31 No Cancer
Bone cancer (Wrist)	Lateral	15 Cancer & 14 No Cancer

8.8.2.3 *Experimental Setup*

The single band 8-bit temperature remapped thermographic images were used in these experiments. The images are loaded into the FEPC software by clicking the *Add Files* button and the class is assigned using the *Class* button. The ROI images are automatically taken as input from the *Masks* folder. The masks were created manually by members of the SIUE CVIP research team, with training from the veterinary experts. The area defined by the masks determines the ROI from which the features are extracted (see Figure 8.8-2). The specific experimental parameters, including features, normalization methods, error metrics and pattern classification algorithms, were determined by the previous studies (Subedi et al., 2014). For feature extraction, the *Histogram, Texture* and *Laws* features were selected. Data normalization methods used were *Standard Normal* and *Softmax*; distance measures of *Euclidean, Tanimoto* and *Minkowski*; and classification methods explored were *Nearest Neighbor, K-Nearest Neighbor* and *Nearest Centroid*. The *Leave-One-Out* cross-validation test method was used since we had small data sets for development, and this approach allows all samples to be used for training and testing. Additionally, the FEPC allows for testing with all possible combinations selecting the *Combinatoric* test type. After all the experimental parameters have been set, the *Run Test* button is clicked to run the experiment.

(a)   (b)

(c)   (d)

FIGURE 8.8-2
Image masks. (a) Gray level thermogram, (b) its mask image, (c) gray thermogram after mask application and (d) pseudocolor image after mask application.

TABLE 8-8

Features and Classification Parameters Which Worked Best for the Three Different Datasets

Image Data Set	Features	Normalization	Classification Algorithm	Distance Measure	Sensitivity (%)	Specificity (%)
Wrist lateral	Hskew, Llevel-level, Lspot-spot	SND	Nearest centroid	Euclidean (Texture Distance: 9)	87	86
E/K-lateral	Tcor, Hmean, Hstd, Hskew, Henergy, Tcor, Llevel-spot, Llevel-wave, Lspot-spot	SND	Nearest centroid	Euclidean (Texture Distance: 7)	90	81
E/K-anterior	Hmean, Hskew, Tentropy; Laws: level-ripple, edge- ripple	SND	Nearest centroid	Euclidean (Texture Distance: 11)	85	90

H, *Histogram* features; T, standard *texture* features; L, *Laws* features.

8.8.3 Results and Discussion

In addition to determining the efficacy of using the Laws texture features for the classification of bone cancer in canines, in this study we investigated which Laws features are the most useful. Table 8-8 shows the algorithmic parameters which resulted in the best sensitivity and specificity for each dataset, since in medical applications the cost of mis-classification is critical. In this table, we see that Laws features were included in the best result experiment with each data set. This indicates that the Laws features will be useful, as these are the best results out of over 70,000 algorithms from all the possible experimental combinations.

Figure 8.8-3 summarizes the results from the experiments with and without the Laws texture features. In these charts, we plot the overall success rate for classification, as well as the sensitivity and specificity. Sensitivity is the accuracy of the system for predicting the presence of disease and specificity is the accuracy for predicting the absence of disease. In these charts, we can see the results are mixed – in some cases, we see improvements, and in others, a decline in success. Table 8-9 shows the increase or decrease in success rate with addition of the Laws features for each data set and success metric.

The elbow/knee anterior view image set showed a definite improvement with the addition of the Laws texture features, as all metrics either improved or stayed the same. The elbow/knee lateral view results were mixed, but the critical metric for medical applications is sensitivity and here we see an increase of 4%. The wrist lateral view showed a decline in the sensitivity, so the Laws features were not helpful in accurately classifying the animals that do have the disease.

8.8.4 Conclusion

The primary goal of this study was to explore the potential of the Laws features for improving the classification success rate of canine bone cancer as compared to a previous study (Subedi et al., 2014). The overall classification success increased for two sets, but decreased for one set. However, the set that showed a decrease in the overall success rate did show an increase in sensitivity – a critical factor in medical diagnosis. We also determined that the Laws features most useful for this application were level-level, spot-spot, level-spot, level-wave, level-ripple and edge-ripple. Our results indicate that the Laws texture features show promise in the identification of canine bone cancer in thermographic images, but further research is needed.

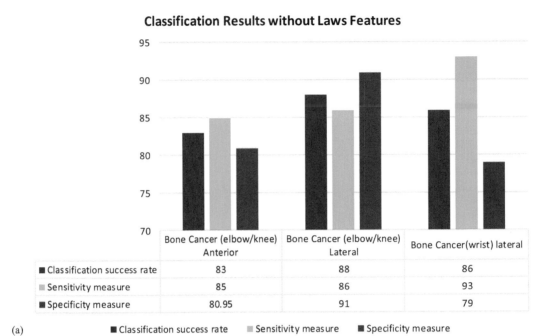

(a)

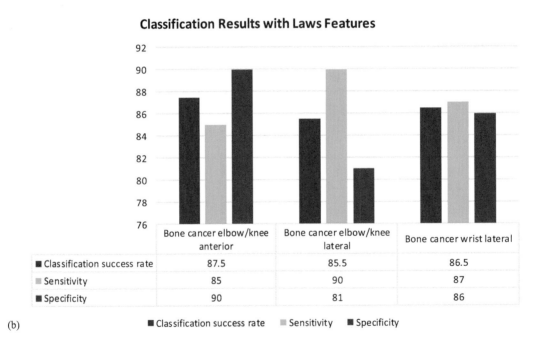

(b)

FIGURE 8.8-3
Success comparison for Laws texture features. (a) Best results without Laws features, (b) best results with the Laws features.

TABLE 8-9

Change in Success Metrics by Adding Laws Features

	Elbow/Knee Anterior (%)	Elbow/Knee Lateral (%)	Wrist Lateral (%)
Success	+4.5	−2.5	+0.5
Sensitivity	+0.0	+4.0	−6.0
Specificity	+9.1	−10	+7.0

References

Loughin, C.A., Marino, D.J., Evaluation of thermographic imaging of the limbs of healthy dogs. *American Journal of Veterinary Research*, Vol. 68, No. 10, pp. 1064–1069, 2007.

Marino, D.J., Loughin, C.A., Diagnostic imaging of the canine stifle: A review. *Veterinary Surgery*, Vol. 39, No. 3, pp. 284–295, 2010.

Ng, E., A review of thermography as promising non-invasive detection modality for breast tumor. *International Journal of Thermal Sciences*, Vol. 48, No. 5, pp. 849–859, 2009.

Redaelli, V., Tanzi, B., Luzi, F., Stefanello, D., Proverbio, D., Crosta, L., Di Giancamillo, M., Use of thermographic imaging in clinical diagnosis of small animal: Preliminary notes. *Annali dell'Istituto Superiore di Sanità*, Vol. 50, No. 2, pp. 140–146, 2014.

Subedi, S., Umbaugh, S.E., Fu, J., Marino, D.J., Loughin, C.A., Sackman, J., Thermographic image analysis as a pre-screening tool for the detection of canine bone cancer. *SPIE Optical Engineering Applications*, San Diego, CA, Vol. 9217, 92171D-92171D-8, 2014.

Umbaugh, S.E., Amini, M., *Veterinary Thermographic Image Analysis: Bone Cancer Application.* SIUE CVIP Lab, Edwardsville, IL, Project Number 7-64878, Report Number 4878-16, May 2012.

Umbaugh, S.E., Lama, N., Dahal, R., *Veterinary Thermographic Image Analysis: LIVS Thermographic Image Clinical Application.* SIUE CVIP Lab, Edwardsville, IL, Project Number 7-064878, Report Number 4878-26, May 2016.

8.9 MATLAB CVIP Toolbox GUI: Detection of Syrinx in Canines with Chiari Malformation via Thermograms

Portions of this section, reprinted with permission, are from "Detection of syrinx in thermographic images of canines with Chiari malformation using MATLAB CVIP Toolbox GUI", JC Buritica, A Karlapalem, SE Umbaugh, DJ Marino, J Sackman, SPIE Commercial + Scientific Sensing and Imaging, 2019, Baltimore Convention Center, April 14–18, 2019, Proceedings of SPIE, Vol. 11004, Thermosense: Thermal Infrared Applications XLI, 1100405 (2 May 2019), DOI: 10.1117/12.2519112; https://doi.org/10.1117/12.2519112

Note to readers: the GUI version of the MATLAB CVIP Toolbox described here, version 3.x, is now available at https:// cviptools.siue.edu

8.9.1 Introduction

Thermographic imaging, also known as infrared thermography or thermal imaging, has seen a recent increase in usage in a variety of applications. The camera detects temperature information by capturing radiation in the infrared range. Any object with a temperature above absolute zero emits infrared radiation. The amount of infrared radiation is proportional to the temperature of the object. Hence, warm-blooded bodies such as human beings and animals can be distinctly distinguished using a thermographic camera. This imaging technique has its roots in many applications ranging from the construction industry to archeological imaging to security and medical diagnostic procedures. Use of thermographic imaging for clinical purposes has reduced the time taken for diagnostic procedures and the cost when compared to other medical modalities such as MRI and CT (Dahal et al., 2017).

Veterinary diagnostic procedures may involve the use of the thermographic imaging technique. It is believed that the presence of a disease changes the surface temperature patterns on the skin. Using the thermographic cameras to capture these patterns assists in the diagnosis of a variety of diseases. The Chiari malformation is a medical condition where structural defects in the skull cause a downward displacement of the cerebellum obstructing the flow of cerebrospinal fluid resulting in neurological disorders. The blockage of the flow of the cerebrospinal fluid causes syrinx, a fluid-filled cavity in the spinal cord or brain stem. Some of the symptoms of this condition are headaches, nausea, poor limb coordination, difficulty swallowing and speech problems. It is believed that the Chiari malformation medical condition is similar in human beings and in canines. Hence, it is easier to study the condition in canines to help understand the effects of this condition better in the case of human beings (Chiari & Syringomelia Foundation, 2017). This condition has been identified specifically in the Cavalier King Charles Spaniel (CKCS) canine breed. This condition is hereditary in the case of the CKCS canine breed due to the natural formation of their skull.

In this study, the primary aim was to develop a custom Graphical User Interface (GUI) using MATLAB and the CVIPtools MATLAB Toolbox that can apply and investigate different pattern classification algorithms as potential classifiers to detect the Chiari malformation condition in the CKCS canine breed. The thermographic images used in this study were photographed in temperature-controlled room in the Long Island Veterinary Hospital, New York.

8.9.2 Material and Methods

The general methodology to be applied in this research is the software design for the MATLAB GUI, and the image processing, feature extraction and pattern classification for syrinx detection. The GUI was modeled on the existing C# GUI for CVIPtools that has been used for many years.

8.9.2.1 Image Data Acquisition

The image data set used in this study was obtained from the Long Island Veterinary Specialists (LIVS). The original images are 18-color temperature remapped images. The thermographic camera used for image capture remaps the variations in the temperature pattern on the skin of the canine into 18 different colors. The range of the temperature remapped is from 19°C to 40°C. The lowest temperature is remapped to blue, whereas the highest temperature is remapped to red (Pant et al., 2017). The temperature information is extracted from the 18-color TIFF image files and are remapped into 256-gray levels on a single-band image using the Compix WINTES2 software. All the images are the top of head view of the canines, see an example in Figure 8.9-1.

8.9.2.2 ROI Extraction

For feature extraction and pattern classification, ROIs were extracted from the gray level images using binary masks. These masks were created using the CVIPtools software, in conjunction with the veterinary staff. The binary masks are drawn to extract only the top of the head portion of canines as the information in the background is not of interest. These regions do not include the ears, nose or eyes of the canine as they are believed to be unnecessary, and these may cause confusion during classification (Pant, 2018). Using these masks, features were extracted for classification.

8.9.2.3 MATLAB

MATLAB is a script based programming platform designed specifically for engineers and scientists. Using a syntax similar to C/C++, MATLAB and its matrix-based language resembles the natural expression of computational mathematics. MATLAB enables the user to analyze data, develop algorithms and create models and applications

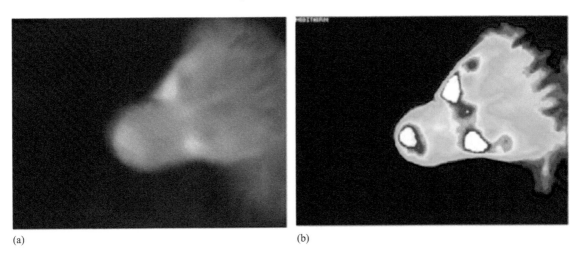

(a)   (b)

FIGURE 8.9-1
Canine thermogram of head for Chiari malformation. (a) Temperature remapped to 256 gray levels and (b) temperature mapped to 18 colors.

(The MathWorks Inc, 2018). For this project, we use the basic features of MATLAB, the functions in the CVIP Toolbox and the GUIDE tool to edit and create GUIs in MATLAB.

8.9.2.4 CVIPtools

CVIPtools is the tool for Computer Vision and Image Processing with programming capabilities that make it a software environment for computer image education, practice and research (Umbaugh, 2018). One of its primary objectives is to provide for the exploration of the power of computer vision and image processing methods (Umbaugh, 2019a). CVIPtools allows the user to apply computer imaging operations from simple image editing to complex analysis, enhancement, restoration or compression algorithms.

8.9.3 MATLAB CVIP Toolbox

As discussed in Chapter 2, this is an installable software environment developed at the SIUE CVIP Lab. The toolbox allows users to experiment and practice with computer vision and image processing operations in MATLAB. Once installed, the toolbox appears as an Add-On in the MATLAB desk and the user can explore and manage it and its functions. The toolbox includes a collection of functions for arithmetic, logic and color operations, geometry and edge detection, conversion of image files, filters, transforms, feature extraction and pattern classification (Umbaugh, 2019b).

8.9.3.1 Feature Extraction and Pattern Classification

Feature extraction for pattern classification in this project uses an image set with the classes *Syrinx* and *No Syrinx*. For each class, 35 images with the corresponding image masks were used. The classification was performed by doing several experiments using the following parameters (Fu, 2018):

8.9.3.2 Features

- CVIP Toolbox GUI histogram features: *Average, Standard Deviation, Skew, Energy* and *Entropy.*
- CVIP Toolbox GUI texture features: *Angular Second Moment (Energy), Variance (Inertia), Correlation, Inverse difference* and *Entropy.* Texture distances of 4–8 were used.

8.9.3.3 Data Normalization Methods

- *Softmax* with $r=1$, *Standard Normal Density.*

8.9.3.4 Distance Metrics

- *Euclidean distance.*
- *Normalized Vector Inner Product* similarity metric.
- *Tanimoto* similarity metric.

8.9.3.5 Classification Methods

- *K*-Nearest Neighbor with $K=3$, $K=5$, $K=10$, Nearest Centroid.

Due to the small image set, the testing and validation method used was *Leave-One-Out.*

8.9.4 CVIPtools MATLAB Toolbox GUI

The version of the CVIP MATLAB Toolbox which includes the GUI is 3.X.; the Toolbox functions without the GUI are 2.5. The GUI for the CVIP MATLAB Toolbox is a set of MATLAB figures (.fig files) and MATLAB code files (.m files) that resembles the appearance and behavior of the C# CVIPtools GUI. To perform the image operations, the GUI uses events called "callbacks" to invoke the .m functions available in the Toolbox. Figure 8.9-2 shows the

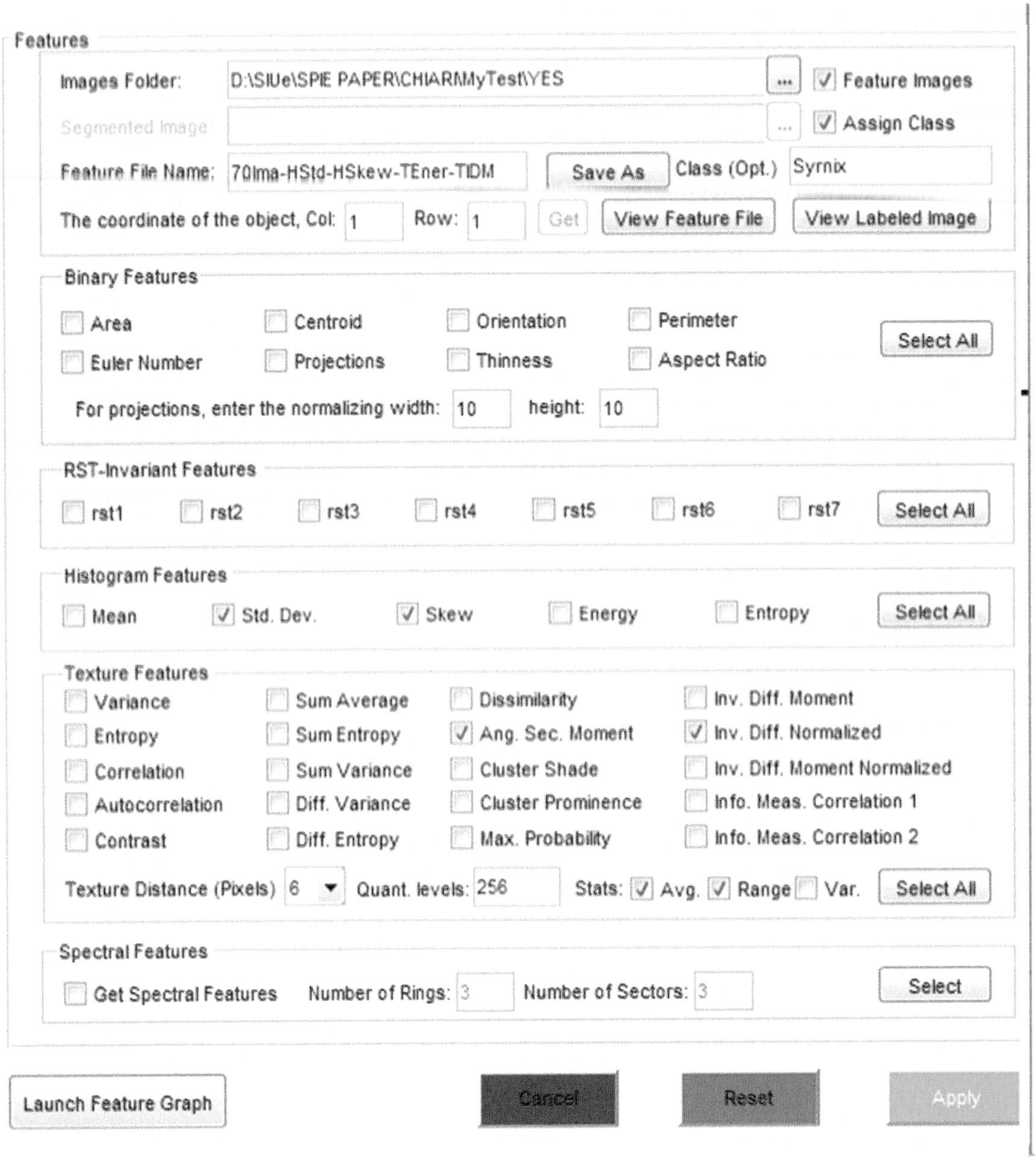

FIGURE 8.9-2
CVIP Toolbox MATLAB GUI for feature extraction.

initial Features GUI (Laws features were added later). In the next sections, a brief description of the figures and functions to perform the feature extraction, data normalization and pattern classification operations is shown.

8.9.4.1 Feature Extraction Using the MATLAB GUI

The GUI for feature extraction has five sections with features to select; these are the Binary, RST-Invariant, Histogram, Texture and Spectral features. Additional parameters that the user can set appear in the Texture features section. *Texture Distance* specifies the number of pixels to be taken in each orientation in computing the features, the *Quantization Level* allows the user to reduce the number of gray levels to be analyzed; by default, if the parameter value is not specified, the default quantization level is equal to the number of gray levels in the input image, and the Statistics (Stats) specifies if the results will include the average, range and/or variance across all orientations into the co-occurrence matrix created to extract the features. By default, the average and range of the

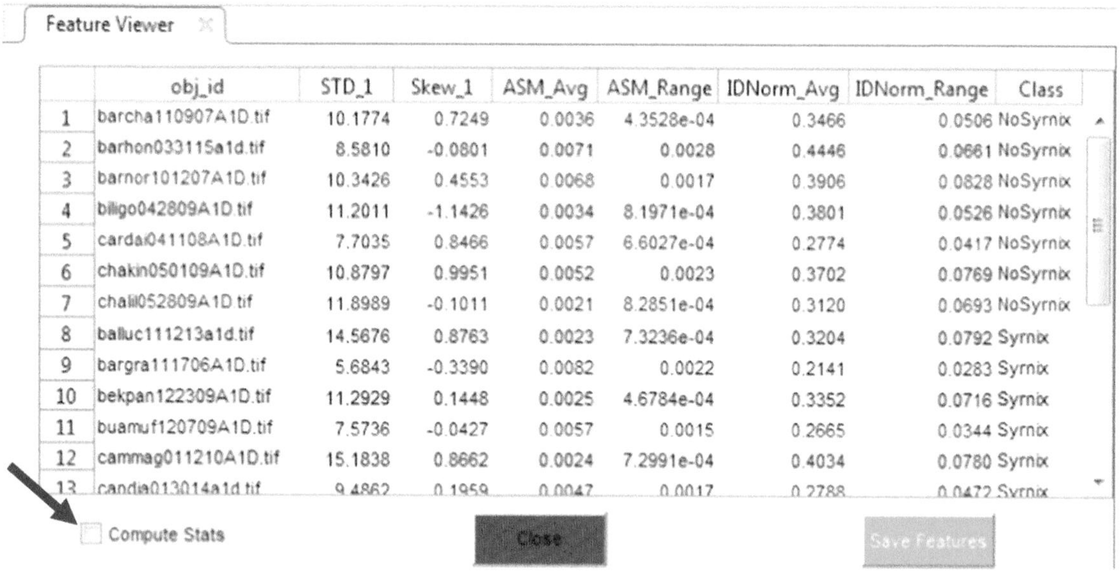

FIGURE 8.9-3

CVIP Toolbox MATLAB feature viewer. The viewer will display one image per row along with the associated feature values that have been extracted. The *Compute Stats* check box allows the user to see the mean and the standard deviation of the features across all the processed images.

results are computed. In addition, to check the general behavior of the selected features, in the *Feature Viewer* (see Figure 8.9-3) and *Compute Stats*, check box is included and the user can observe the mean and the standard deviation of the features across all the processed images.

The GUI has three different alternatives for feature extraction methods: (1) To select features from one object within a single image. To use this function, the user must select the original image, the segmented image mask, select the desired features, check the *Assign Class* option, then click on the object in the image mask and finally get the object coordinates. Next, the user clicks the *Apply* button and the *Feature Viewer* will appear with the features extracted from the selected object. (2) To extract features from *all the objects* within a single image. This method requires the original image and the segmented image that delineates the separate objects. The function will label the segmented image, and the results are shown based on the assigned labels. This is the default option for feature extraction (with the *Assign Class* option not selected). (3) To select features from a single object in each image across a group of images, with a separate mask for each image. With the *Feature Images* checkbox selected, the program will extract the selected features from a set of images into a directory, the segmented images (masks) must be in the image directory within a folder with the name "MASKS" and each corresponding mask file must have the same name as the original image file – they can have different file extensions (e.g. *.mask). The *Feature Image* function was used in this project due to the number of images to be processed and the features to be extracted. Note that the user can assign the class to a set of images with this method by selecting the *Assign Class* checkbox.

8.9.4.2 Pattern Classification Using MATLAB GUI

The Pattern Classification GUI is shown in Figure 8.9-4. At the top are the data normalization choices, which is a preprocessing step before the application of the classification algorithm. The next section shows the distance and similarity measures that can be selected and then the classification algorithms. When using *Training/Test Set* as the method for *Algorithm Testing*, the classes defined in the training set are used to classify the objects in the test set according to the *Data Normalization, Distance and Similarity Measure* and *Classification Algorithm* choices selected. If the user selects the *Leave-One-Out* for *Algorithm Testing*, a test set is created by selecting the first feature vector in the feature file and using the remaining features vectors as the training set and performing the classification according to the defined parameters. With *Leave-One-Out* validation, this process continues until each feature vector has been tested against all the others.

After setting the classification parameters, the *Classification Viewer* appears showing the results of the classification process. In this viewer, the first part shows the percentage of correct images classified for each class,

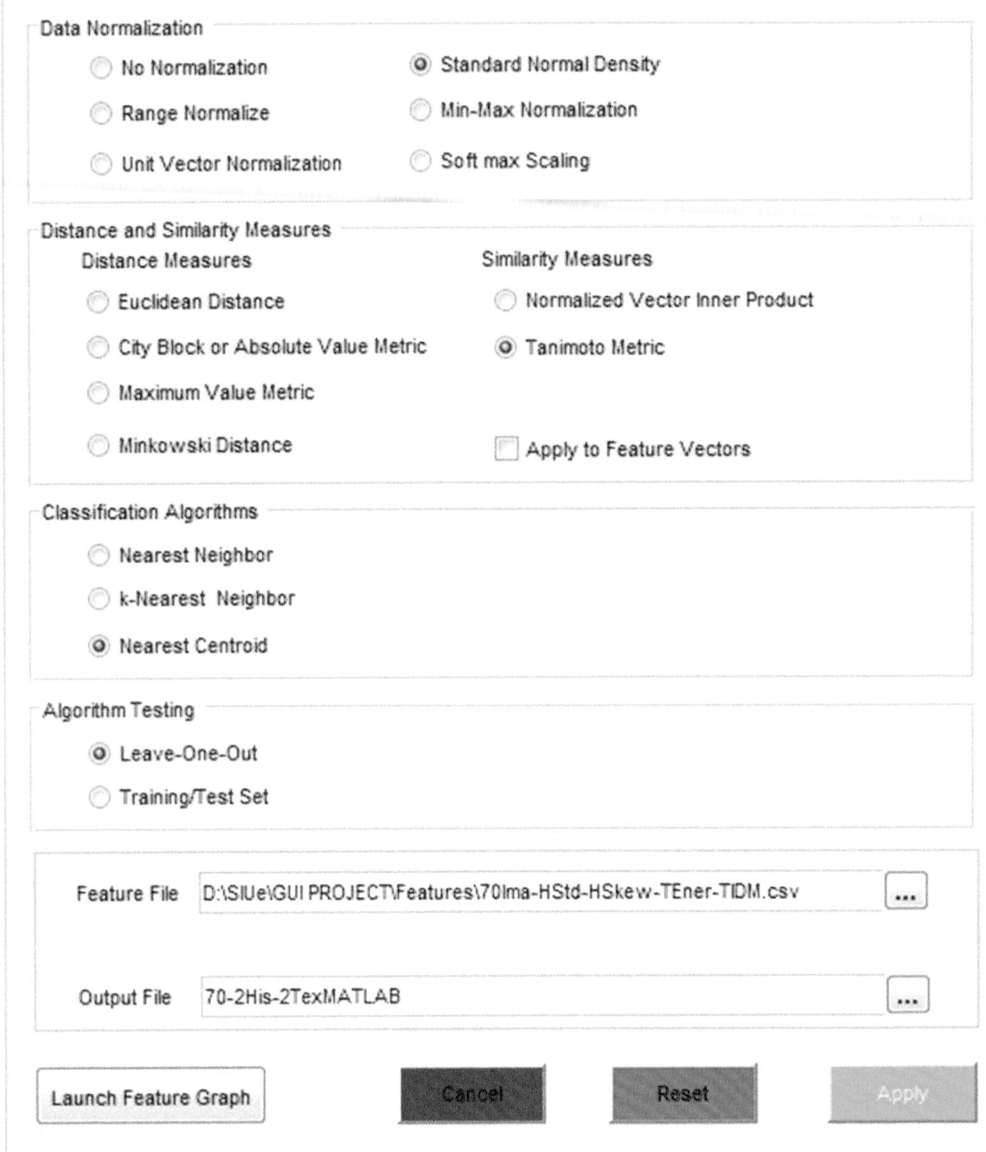

FIGURE 8.9-4
Pattern classification GUI.

followed by the parameters used in the classification, the feature specific information and the list of features included in the feature file. The next part shows the *Test Set Information* with the list of the images or objects, the "True" or "Original" class in the test set, the new class assigned according to the classification process and the value of the distance or similarity metric calculated in the classification. Figure 8.9-5 shows the *Classification Viewer* once a classification was performed by using the Leave-One-Out method for *Algorithm Testing*, Nearest Centroid for *Classification Algorithm*, Tanimoto Metric as *Distance and Similarity Measure*, and Standard Normal Density in *Data Normalization*. Additional information is also available in this viewer such as the features information with the texture distance, quantization levels and statistics used.

8.9.5   Results and Discussion

LIVS provided a total set of 148 images. Of the original set of 148, we determined that 70 of the images were of sufficient quality for these experiments; the others were blurry or had too much size or distance variability. The subset of 70 images of consistent quality have been used in this study to differentiate between normal, *No Syrinx*, and

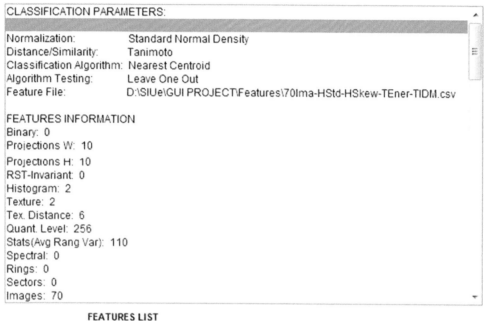

CLASSIFICATION RESULTS

		NoSyrnix	Syrnix	% Correct
Class in Test Set	NoSyrnix	28	7	80
	Syrnix	11	24	68.5714

CLASSIFICATION PARAMETERS:

Normalization: Standard Normal Density
Distance/Similarity: Tanimoto
Classification Algorithm: Nearest Centroid
Algorithm Testing: Leave One Out
Feature File: D:\SIUe\GUI PROJECT\Features\70Ima-HStd-HSkew-TEner-TIDM.csv

FEATURES INFORMATION
Binary: 0
Projections W: 10
Projections H: 10
RST-Invariant: 0
Histogram: 2
Texture: 2
Tex. Distance: 6
Quant. Level: 256
Stats(Avg Rang Var): 110
Spectral: 0
Rings: 0
Sectors: 0
Images: 70

FEATURES LIST

	1	2	3	4	5	6
1	STD_1	ASM_Avg	IDNorm_Avg			
2	Skew_1	ASM_Range	IDNorm_Range			

TEST SET INFORMATION

	Image/Object	True Class from Test Set	Classification Result	Distance/Similarity
1	barcha110907A1D.tif	NoSyrnix	Syrnix	0.1280
2	barhon033115a1d.tif	NoSyrnix	NoSyrnix	0.0787
3	barnor101207A1D.tif	NoSyrnix	NoSyrnix	0.0991
4	biligo042809A1D.tif	NoSyrnix	NoSyrnix	0.0167
5	cardai041108A1D.tif	NoSyrnix	NoSyrnix	0.0018
6	chakin050109A1D.tif	NoSyrnix	NoSyrnix	0.0550
7	chalil052809A1D.tif	NoSyrnix	Syrnix	0.0844
8	chapet052709A1D.tif	NoSyrnix	NoSyrnix	0.0451
9	colmol080610a1d.tif	NoSyrnix	NoSyrnix	0.0229
10	copcha011413a1d.tif	NoSyrnix	Syrnix	0.0300
11	deejim020909A1D.tif	NoSyrnix	Syrnix	0.1210

FIGURE 8.9-5
Classification viewer. At the top is the classification results for the images that were tested. Below that is a list of the classification and feature parameters. The *Test Set Information* section at the bottom has an entry for each image tested, the actual (true) class and how the classifier classified this image. The last entry is the distance or similarity measure for the sample in the training set for which this image is closest to and thus how it is classified.

abnormal, *Syrinx* classes. Experiments with many different classification parameter combinations were performed in this study. Accuracy, Sensitivity and Specificity from the experiments were calculated as measure of performance for the classifiers. The features that achieved these best results were histogram standard deviation and skew, the texture features energy and inverse difference (using average and range as its statistics). The classification

TABLE 8-10

Classification Parameters for Best Four Experiments

	Distance/Similarity Metric	Normalization Method	Classification Method
Experiment 1	Tanimoto	Standard normal density	Nearest centroid
Experiment 2	Euclidean	Standard normal density	Nearest centroid
Experiment 3	Euclidean	Softmax, $r=1$	Nearest centroid
Experiment 4	Tanimoto	Softmax, $r=1$	Nearest centroid

TABLE 8-11

Classification Results of Test Data

Texture distance	Accuracy (%)				Sensitivity (%)				Specificity (%)			
	Exp1	Exp2	Exp3	Exp4	Exp1	Exp2	Exp3	Exp4	Exp1	Exp2	Exp3	Exp4
4	71.4	71.4	60.0	60.0	71.4	71.4	60.0	60.0	71.4	71.4	60.0	60.0
5	74.3	74.3	61.4	61.4	71.4	71.4	60.0	60.0	77.1	77.1	62.9	62.9
6	81.4	80.0	60.0	58.6	74.3	74.3	60.0	60.0	85.7	85.7	60.0	57.1
7	48.6	50.0	47.2	48.6	48.6	48.6	54.3	54.3	48.6	51.4	40.0	42.9
8	44.3	42.9	40.0	40.0	51.4	45.7	57.1	54.3	37.1	40.0	22.9	25.7

Highest values are shown in blue and red.

parameters for the four experiments that brought the highest measures of performance are shown in Table 8-10. The success metrics for these four experiments are tabulated in Table 8-11.

The results show that the best texture distance to be used for classification is six and that Experiments 1 and 2 show the most promise. From examining the results of all the sets, we believe that further investigation is needed in finding the subsets of features that can distinctly separate the classes with greater than 80% sensitivity and specificity. The data set is small to keep the good quality images (not blurry) and homogeneous (same area of dogs in picture and same distance from the camera), so it will be expanded for future research.

8.9.6 Conclusion

The GUI tool is a new and potentially useful software tool for use in research and development of medical diagnostics. Also, as CVIPtools does, this GUI and the MATLAB toolbox it belongs to is a powerful and practical tool for computer vision and image processing education. By including functions to perform image operations for image analysis from geometry operations to pattern classification and by including utilities for image arithmetic and logic operations, comparison, conversion, creation, enhance, filtering, size and statistics extraction, the Toolbox and GUI cover all the subjects related to computer vision and image processing and provides the programming flexibility and power of MATLAB.

The primary aim in this study was to develop a software tool integrating the MATLAB CVIP Toolbox to perform feature extraction and pattern classification. As an application of the developed software tool, experiments were performed with the GUI using pattern classification algorithms on thermographic images of the CKCS canine breed with Chiari malformation to classify the presence or absence of syrinx. Many different experiments were performed on the thermographic images using the GUI, and the top four were selected to present here. The results differentiate the classes with an accuracy around 80%, examining the feature file suggests using different subsets of features will improve the results. Further investigation to effectively classify Chiari malformation is currently underway. One of the primary aims is to improve classification results by implementing an additional tool that performs classification by combining the available features to identify the best feature set(s) for classification.

References

Chiari & Syringomelia Foundation, *Chiari-Like Malformation & Syringomyelia in Animals*, https://csfinfo.org/education/canine-information, 2017.

Dahal, R., Umbaugh, S.E., Mishra, D., Lama, N., Alvandipour, M., Umbaugh, D., Marino, D.J., Sackman, J., Thermography based prescreening software tool for veterinary clinics. *Proceedings of SPIE 10214, Thermosense: Thermal Infrared Applications XXXIX*, Anaheim, CA, 102141A, 5 May 2017.

Fu, J., *Using Thermographic Image Analysis in Detection of Canine Anterior Cruciate Ligament Rupture Disease*, Master's degree thesis, Southern Illinois University Edwardsville, Edwardsville, IL, December 2014.

Pant, G., *Comparison of Features and Mask Size in Thermographic Images of Chiari (CLMS/COMS) Dogs for Syrinx Identification*, Master's degree thesis, Southern Illinois University Edwardsville, Edwardsville, IL, December 2018.

Pant, G., Umbaugh, S.E., Dahal, R., Lama, N., Marino, D.J., Sackman, J., Veterinary software application for comparison of thermograms for pathology evaluation. *Proceedings of SPIE 10396, Applications of Digital Image Processing XL*, Vol. 10396, p. 103962B, 19 September 2017.

Umbaugh, S., *Digital Processing and Analysis*, 3rd Edition, CRC Press, 2018.

Umbaugh, S., *CVIPtools Home Page*, https://CVIPtools.siue.edu/, SIUE, Edwardsville, IL, 2019a.

Umbaugh, S., *MATLAB Toolbox Function List*, https://cviptools.siue.edu/MATLABToolboxFunctionList.html, 2019b.

The MathWorks Inc, *MATLAB® What is MATLAB?* https://www.mathworks.com/discovery/what-is-matlab.html?s_tid=srchtitle, 2018.

Additional Material

Test your knowledge with these true and false quizzes (add the quizzes here). This is for ebook+ The students can choose either true or false and then they will know the answer once they have done so.

For supplementary material, refer to www.routledge.com/9781032071299.

Index

Note: **Bold** page numbers refer to tables, *italic* page numbers refer to figures.